THE FRENCH STUDENT UPRISING
NOVEMBER 1967–JUNE 1968

The French Student Uprising
November 1967–June 1968

An Analytical Record

by <u>Alain Schnapp</u> and
Pierre Vidal-Naquet

Translated by Maria Jolas

Beacon Press   Boston

With grateful acknowledgment to Pierre Vidal-Naquet for his
careful reading of the English-language manuscript. *Translator's note*

First published in France in 1969 by Éditions du Seuil, under the title, *Journal de la Commune Étudiante: Textes et Documents Novembre 1967–Juin 1968*
Copyright © 1969 by Éditions du Seuil
This edition has been abridged and updated by Pierre Vidal-Naquet.
English translation © 1971 by Beacon Press
Library of Congress catalog card number: 74–156452
International Standard Book Number: 0–8070–4388–5
Beacon Press books are published under the
auspices of the Unitarian Universalist Association
Simultaneous publication in Canada by Saunders of Toronto, Ltd.
Printed in the United States of America

Contents

From the People's *atelier,* Montpellier, in early June. "Beauty is in the streets." *Photograph by J. C. Vaysse.*

From *Ecole des Beaux-Arts,* at the end of May. "A generation of young people that is too frequently disturbed about the future" (quotation from General de Gaulle's speech of May 24, 1968). *Photograph by J. C. Vaysse.*

Situationist wall writing in the Sorbonne rectorate, in May. The fresco represents the reception of the *Ecole Normale Supérieure* into the University, in 1905. The balloon, which says: "Humanity will not be happy until the day when the last bureaucrat has been hung with the guts of the last capitalist," parodies the formula used by the Curé Meslier (18th century priest and the author of a radical manifesto made use of by Voltaire): "Humanity will not be happy until the day when the last aristocrat has been hung with the guts of the last priest." *Photograph by Jo. Schnapp.*

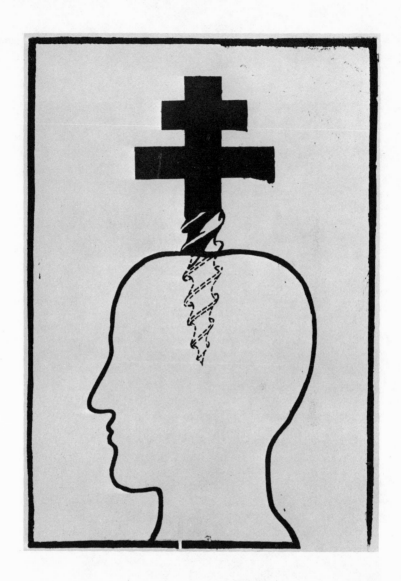

From the *atelier* of the *Ecole nationale des Arts Décoratifs,* in early June.
(Refers to a nationally known advertisement for a health powder which
recommended that its virtues should be "hammered into your head." *Translator's note.*) *Photograph by J. C. Vaysee.*

Situationist writing on a Latin Quarter wall. *Photograph by Jo. Schnapp.*

Entrance to the big amphitheatre of the Sorbonne, in May. "I take my desires for reality because I believe in the reality of my desires." *Photograph by Jo. Schnapp.*

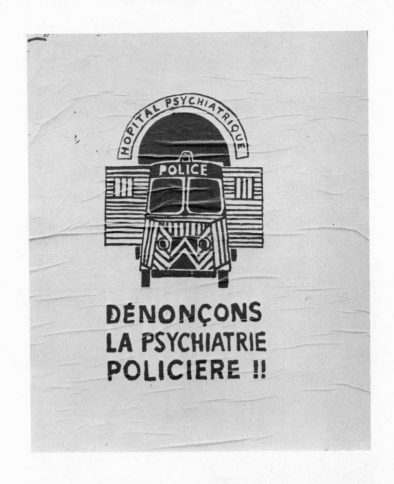

From a *Faculté de Médecine* wall, about June 20. Poster printed by *Ecole des Beaux-Arts*. "We must denounce police psychiatry." *Photograph by J. C. Vaysse.*

From *Ecole des Beaux-Arts,* in early June, 1968. Roger Frey was Minister of the Interior at the time of the Charonne subway massacre (February 8, 1962). In the Pompidou government he was given an assignment called "civic action." *Photograph by J. C. Vaysse.*

From *Ecole des Beaux-Arts,* June 13. "Under 21, here's your ballot." *Photograph by J. C. Vaysse.*

Outline of a Revolution

This book is not a history of the "May movement." Being centered on the student revolution, and hardly touching upon the other great event of those weeks, i.e., the revival of the worker movement and the wave of strikes, which was far more extensive than in June 1936, it will try to let the texts speak for themselves and bring out the interplay of all their different facets; hence its bulk. Years of research and study will be needed to understand all the aspects of an episode which, while it belongs in the international context of student revolution, is nevertheless unique for its breadth and florescence in postwar industrial society.

Before May 1968 a certain number of apparently undisputed dogmas had invaded sociological teaching. These were: the relative stability of industrial societies as opposed to the upheavals in the Third World, in China, in the "tempest zone" (this dogma was implicitly accepted both in Peking and in the writings of Raymond Aron); the all but complete integration of the working classes into modern society, achieved through trade-union and revolutionary party channels; easy assessment of public opinion through opinion "polls"; massive depolitization of young people, particularly of students, whose only concern was supposed to be the rights of boys to visit girls in university dormitories (totally ignoring the political significance of the problem); the need to "rationalize" all protest movements (as for instance, Black protest in the United States,[1] even Vietnamese protest in Southeast Asia), to give the opponent an equal chance, hence renunciation of "blind" violence as a counter-weapon. Then there were the various metaphysical concepts that asserted the death of man as a thinking, doing being, individually or collectively (Cartesian or Marxist); of "superdetermined" man, who did not speak, but through whom "they" spoke, "they" thought, the "they" that seemed to be a mythical transposition of the rational machine, of the technocratic system; the "they" that may be identified, of course, with the American war machine inflicting "democracy" on Vietnam with personnel bombs, or with the overwhelming economic apparatus that forces continually lower prices for raw materials on Third World countries, "continually worsening trade conditions." But also, dialectically, it could be identified with "Him" who was "the living brain of the proletariat," and with His successors, who did not hesitate, after May, to engage in "fraternal" talks with their "comrades" in Czechoslovakia, while surrounding them with tanks, before invading them on the night of August 20–21; or with Mao Tse-tung's hypostatic "thought," generator of ping-pong victories as well as of atom bombs.

An American philosophy student, Mario Savio, who took a leading part in the Berkeley revolt of September 14 to December 8, 1964, has written as follows: "Here is the real contradiction: the bureaucrats hold history as ended. As a result significant parts of the population, both on campus and off, are dispossessed and these dispossessed are not about to accept this ahistorical point of view."[2] In 1968, in France, one man only, General de Gaulle, assumed the right to be an agent of history, even to present himself as being "in the direction of history." France condemned the American aggression in Vietnam, but the "Russell Tribunal" was not allowed to convene in Paris. University reform was carried out by a commission of ten "wise men," chosen on the basis of mysterious criteria, without the professors—let alone the students—being consulted.

In February 1968, Henri Langlois was driven from the *Cinémathèque* that he himself had created, by André Malraux. Sociologists specializing in labor disputes, modestly call this state of affairs a "break in communications." Actually the break was complete. The May revolution restored first to the students and then to all the other victims of this "state of affairs," the right to speak out. This led to a challenging not only of the government but also of all those who on every level of the social hierarchy, university "mandarins," labor and party leaders, had monopolized this right. "They" were the real victims of the May revolution, which does not mean, of course, that they were absent from it. "They," that is to say, "the organization men," to quote W. H. Whyte, were present in May, against the movement, but were also a part of it, despite acute fears of "co-option." The dream of a society that would be pure speech[3] characterized the movement, but it was just that: a dream, since in reality "pure speech" can only lead to "pure action," another dream of the movement. Actually, this dream could only develop because "regulative centers," revolutionary *groupuscules* and labor unions, functioned apart from activism, and dialectically opposed those who sought and triumphantly found a place where speech could be free.

Once the explosion had occurred, people looked for the causes and precursory signs: the authoritarian nature and "absolutely aberrant administrative centralization" (Raymond Aron) of University institutions, the fragility of social stability. "Once more, the crisis has shed light on the tragic precariousness of the country's social structures," wrote this theoretician of the "integrated"[4] industrial society. As a matter of fact, precursory signs—or those which were to become such —had not been lacking, both in Nanterre and elsewhere. During the months that preceded May 1968, workers' demonstrations had taken a "wildcat" turn, in Caen, Lyons, and Redon, due, above all, to the action of young workers, to their resistance to "inurement" (Georges Friedmann), and to co-option. Henri Langlois's eviction had given rise to a whole series of demonstrations that went well beyond cinema circles and used such terms as "self-management" and even "insurrection."[5]

In May 1966, students from the "Situationist International" had "seized power" in the Strasburg Students' Association and had immediately set out to liquidate the institutions of the student world.[6] The main themes that were to triumph in May already had a long history. Without going back as far as Bakunin and anarchistic criticism, denunciation of "bureaucratization" of the labor movement is as old as Trotskyism—which, moreover, has continued to give rise to microbureaucracies—but seems not really to have taken hold.[7] From 1945 to 1965 the radical review, Socialisme ou Barbarie, had shown that in modern industrial societies there had been added to the classic opposition, since Marx, between the beneficiaries of the plus-value (the exploiters) and those who furnish the plus-value (the exploited), an opposition that is actually not so much economic as social between those who are vested with the right to give orders (officials of all kinds, managers) and the mass who execute them, without whose participation no society can function, but whose lives are crushed under the parallel, competitive hierarchies of business, government, unions, and political parties. In 1956 workers' councils had reappeared in Hungary and in Poland. They furnished a model. But the review died in 1965.[8]

Finally, the situationists had developed the critical thesis outlined by Henri Lefebvre[9] of daily life as alienation in the face of "merchandise" or "spectacle," the latter identified indifferently with modern art as a consumer product, the "personality cult," or the "thought" of infallible leaders.[10] The Hegelian-Marxist idea of "alienation," which had been declared equivocal and pre-scientific by Jean-Marie Domenach, a Roman Catholic, as well as by Louis Althusser, a Marxist, proved applicable to the study of daily life and brought on violent discussion in which at times certain of the May quarrels may be foreseen.[11] But beyond the confines of Strasburg, Nanterre, and Nantes, the Strasburg affair had made people laugh when it had not made them cry, and conceptual discussion was limited to a tiny minority of students and faculty.

There remains the fact that a precedent did exist: the Algerian war, a precedent that in one sense is microscopic, but the evident anticipatory nature of which furnishes a point of departure for an approach to May 1968.[12] In fact, it was during the Algerian war that criticism of the party machines on the one hand, and a young, "extra-parliamentary" opposition on the other, seem to have appeared. One of the essential causes of this was the behavior of the French Communist Party. For very complex reasons: distrust of the Algerian Nationalist Movement, which it did not control, and which quite justifiably seemed to be foreign to the traditions of the revolutionary workers' movement; the feeling, at first legitimate, that the war in Algeria was not unpopular and that the French proletariat had a racist attitude toward the Algerian subproletariat; an obsession with the 1956 parliamentary possibilities at the time of the "Republican Front" (the vote in favor of "emergency powers" on March 12); the isolation it had been subjected to after its approval of Budapest. The French Communist Party, while remaining the classical political force most firmly opposed to colonial wars, did not exert the same amount of energy that it had succeeded in marshaling against the war in Indochina. Especially, it had given no support other than verbal to the spontaneous movement of recalled reservists who in 1955 and above all in 1956 had momentarily upset military discipline.[13] At the end of 1956 this movement had died, just as, after Budapest, the first committees of intellectuals founded to work against the war, coalition committees that had in fact lived in a state of permanent tension, had also died.[14] Then, in 1957, the resistance reappeared in the form of denunciation of torture.[15] The Maurice Audin Committee, founded in November, functioned until just after the war on the triple basis of refusal of coalitions between representatives of the party machines, autonomous action, and unconditional denunciation of the use of torture, whoever the victims (even if, as in 1961–62, they were oas members). This brought it several times into conflict with the Communist Party machine which, at certain moments, was not sure whether Robert Lacoste, the Socialist Minister for Algeria, was (or would again become) a "comrade,"[16] and was reluctant to see denunciation of the methods used by Massu's soldiers become widespread. Another field for action was liberty of information. *Témoignages et Documents* (from January 1958), and *Vérité-Liberté* (from May 1960) set an example of a press that refused self-censorship and took seizure in its stride; a semilegal press, distributed independently of party machines by militants from all sides (Communist Party members, Catholics, Protestants, anarchistically inclined school teachers). Beginning May 7, 1968, *Action* set an example of a similar unauthorized press, but with far greater breadth and far greater success.[17] Unlicensed films, made and distributed by the same organizations, followed: *J'ai huit ans, Octobre à Paris*. Meanwhile, inside the Communist Party itself numerous opposition currents, represented by *L'Etincelle, La Voix Communiste, Voies Nouvelles, Unir,* were building up their activities and their press in semiclandestinity.

In 1960 a different type of movement appeared to accompany and relay the preceding one. Although there were never more than a few hundred resistants and as many militants giving practical support to the NLF, the repercussions of their action, publicized by the *Manifesto of the 121* (September 5, 1960), and the suit brought against the "Jeanson network," excited all the more interest by the fact that it was in direct opposition to the government and aroused the hostility of all organized political groups.[18] The principal rebel organization, *Jeune Résistance,* also wanted to stand for resistance of young people in general to the generation that, from the post-Liberation years until May 13, 1958, had known nothing but defeat.[19]

It was then that the UNEF (*l'Union Nationale des Etudiants de France*) which, in 1956, had been taken over by the so-called "minos," moderately antiwar Catholics or other minority sympathizers with the "New Left," from the supposedly apolitical "majos" (majority groups), had the force and the courage to assume the leadership of public opposition to the war. After a collision with the Gaullist government, which withdrew its annual subsidy, it renewed contact with the Algerian student organization in June,[20] and in September, waving the red flag of *resistance to conscription,* without ever making a slogan of it,[21] the UNEF took the initiative—against the French Communist Party—in organizing the first big demonstration against the war. This was the October 27th meeting at *La Mutualité* and the violent demonstration that followed. The UNEF then received the support, half sincere, half self-interested, of all the trade-union and political forces of the nonCommunist Left (including the SFIO (Socialist Party). The *Mutualité* meeting, which was chaired by P. Gaudez, President of the UNEF, surrounded by representatives of the CFTC, FO, FEN, and a few dissidents of the CGT (iron construction workers' union), was in a way a prefiguration of the *Stade Charléty* demonstration of May 27, 1968. But the UNEF had set the tone by demanding that "young people should be able to live without shame in the national community," and a group of intellectuals and union leaders had responded: "Whatever concerns our youth concerns the nation, and therefore, all of us." A philosopher who was to reappear in May 1968, wrote at that time:

> What we call the Left is as divided as it was before May 13 [1958] (date of the Algiers putsch, after which de Gaulle returned to power). The political parties and the big trade unions, who are prisoners of their past policies, more concerned with watching one another than with action, busy justifying the totality of their theories, conserving or strengthening their party machines, have lost the freedom to confront events or to confer unity upon the opposition these events provoke. There is no use in expecting from them what they cannot give, or in expecting nothing at all from them, in the vain hope of a movement which would be so spontaneous and so uncompromising that, in one day, it would give rise to new institutions and new men. The opposition will not win otherwise than by virtue of a continual dialectics between individuals and organizations, between those who are political and those who are not. Realism exists no longer in the ruse of a monarch, or of this or that party leader, but in a new mode of thought and conduct, which has become that of an increasing number of persons.[22]

The "opposition" did not win. Still less did we see, as some had hoped we would,[23] the birth of a revolutionary movement emanating from the advance guard that encouraged resistance to conscription and helped the NLF, and which Gilles Martinet, PSU leader, condemned as being the coalition of "Worker Priests and St. Germain des Prés." One year after the *Manifesto of the 121* a leader of *Jeune Résistance* wrote quite clearsightedly from prison: "If we except impostors and informers, if we make allowances for exaggeration and excitement, we are obliged to acknowledge that we're a very fragile advance-guard. I have occasionally suggested, in joking, that a little more, and we would have novels about support for the NLF but no support, a manifesto on the right to resist conscription, but no resisters."[24]

What was the explanation of this total, foreseeable failure? The reasons for it seem quite clear. Gaullist policy could not afford to leave the monopoly of Algerian demands to the parliamentary Left, and even less so, to the extra-parliamentary Left. The President of the Republic, speaking on November 4th, roundly condemned the "two packs" confronting each other on the subject of Algeria, but he already referred to the "Algerian Republic." After the December 1960 demonstrations in Algerian cities, and the January 8, 1961 Referendum on self-determination, Gaullist France slowly but surely took the road that was to lead to confrontation with the oas and the Evian Agreements (March 18, 1962).[25] During the last year of this crisis, the danger of real fascism appeared sufficiently serious for all "revolutionary" plans to give way to the needs of an antifascist front.[26]

For the "disrespectful" Left, as opposed to Marcel Péju's "Respectful Left" (*Les Temps Modernes,* April–May, 1960) the nlf had seemed to offer a model of a revolutionary organization that had set itself up outside and in opposition to the classical political parties; of an adventure which, having started with the nine "historical leaders" of November 1, 1954, had ended in general subversion and agrarian revolution. But aside from the fact that the idea of "historical leaders" should have led to second thoughts, the nlf split up on the eve of independence, exposing its deep disunion, its advanced stage of "bureaucratization," and its complete lack of social content[27] (the movement for self-determination did not start in the nlf). A microstalinism based on the nlf as a fighting force had undoubtedly appeared among extreme-leftist intellectuals with a nostalgia for a revolutionary fatherland; it became frankly ridiculous, however, when the question arose of identifying oneself, as many tried to do, with Ben Bella's "political committee," "Boudiafist opposition," or with the anl (in which some saw the "spearhead" of the revolution), or even with "Wilaya IV."

Finally and above all, for young Frenchmen, including part of the student body, prolonged military service and the war itself, in spite of all it involved and gave rise to, were unusually powerful factors in favor of social integration. For revolutionary defeatism to acquire meaning, the 1917 defeats of the Czarist armies were necessary. The French army was not defeated, and many conscripts who had been with the demonstrators in 1956, ended by being "good soldiers." One of them has the following to say of this period:

> When the reservists who had been called up re-embarked
> seven months later, not very proud of themselves, not very
> satisfied with the others, either, the officials did not succeed,
> in spite of zealous 'officering,' in recording tapes of *C'est nous
> les Africains qui revenons de loin.* (We're the men from
> Africa, back from far away.) But the 'Africans' did not complain
> either, or hardly, and a certain proportion of them, which varied
> according to the unit, were wearing 'Pacification' medals.[28] In

the Algerian branch of the army, one single episode took on
a revolutionary aspect, and that was the uprising of conscript
troops, who set up soldiers' committees at the time of the
Generals' putsch (on April 21st to 24th, 1961). However, this
uprising remained profoundly legalistic, the putsch
only lasted four days, and very quickly everything was back in
order.[29] But inversely, who can say to what extent the end of
colonial wars and the considerable reduction of military
service influenced the young people's revolt in May 1968? And
there's no doubt that, however bitter the experience of the
'Algerian generation' may have seemed to some, through the
anti-war struggle, through demonstrations, resistance to
conscription, clandestinity, help for the Algerians and discussions
about the revolution, a minority of students had also become
aware of what opposed them to their *own society*. Without
always being able to formulate it clearly to themselves, they
sensed that only revolution could change a society, and bring
about a new human order.[30]

It is striking to note that the same phenomenon of crystallization
that had been visible with regard to Algeria, was reproduced, on a
much broader scale, from 1966 on, especially with regard to Vietnam.
The organizations that took the lead: the *"Collectif intersyndical"* (associated faculty and student unions) which grouped, among others, the
UNEF and the SNESup., and which included a number of Communist opponents—the "Russell Tribunal," *"Comités Vietnam de base"*
(autonomous, Maoist-oriented), the *"Comité Vietnam National,"* the
"Mouvement du Milliard" (a fundraising group)—were set up outside
the traditional Left and frequently in opposition to it. When the CVN
was founded, at a meeting that took place November 28, 1966, and
which had been called, with the support of the UNEF, by five university
professors and other intellectuals, nearly 10,000 young revolutionaries
followed one another at *La Mutualité*. But however exemplary the NLF
struggle (or the struggle of Che Guevara), neither could offer a model
for revolutionary action in an industrial society. On March 22, 1968,
after the arrest of six CVN militants, a group of Nanterre students decided to begin the struggle in France, by occupying the *faculté* council
room. This conversion is one of the origins of the May revolution.

The UNEF of 1968 was not the same as that of 1960; profound
changes in the student movement had taken place in the meantime.
The student union, which even when it tries to copy the labor unions,

is very different, because of the rapid renewal of its officers[31] (the president is reelected every year) had become greatly weakened as regards its role of representative organization: from some 100,000 members in 1960, which constituted a good third of the total number, there were in 1968, 50,000, representing less than one-tenth of the student body. The visible signs of this crisis are well known. Since 1965 no national board has been able to serve the full year for which it was elected, and the local general associations seem to be the special preserves of political groups and factions (the PSU in Lyons and Grenoble, the UEC in Lille, and the CLER in Clermont-Ferrand).[32]

Although the different "groupuscules" that developed, especially after 1966, with mutually opposed revolutionary ideologies, did play an effective role of "diastasis" (Edgar Morin) in politization of the student population, the terrorism practiced by all sides in their mutual confrontations (and in which the CLER particularly distinguished itself, to the point of obliging the national board to hold its general assembly in a Communist town hall with the protection of a detachment of CGT marshals), in reality prevented all activity in common on the national level. In May 1968, the president of the UNEF having resigned, one of the vice presidents, Jacques Sauvageot, who headed a PSU board, represented the student union. Since 1963, attempts had nevertheless been made, particularly in the FGEL,[33] by a group of militants (M. Kravetz, J.-L. Péninou, B. Besnier, A. Griset) who reappeared in 1968 in the *Mouvement d'Action Universitaire* (MAU), to give student unionism a doctrine and a "University" oriented form of action.[34] Recalling the successes of the UNEF during the Algerian war, they were contemplating autonomous action, on the labor union model, with the University as their terrain (in the same way that the factory is the worker's terrain). The student population was defined as a specific one having its own interests, faced with the government's University policy, and also with the professors as transmitters of the liberal University heritage, but concerning whom experience had shown that they refuse all action in common with the students on matters concerning the University.

At the Sorbonne, although the *faculté* Assembly of March 28, 1963 had decided to set up mixed commissions to consider student demands, the dean, with the unanimous support of the Assembly, informed the FGEL, on November 23, that "the *faculté* did not have and had never had any intention of creating *mixed commissions* which, with or without equal representation, would be obliged to examine problems *that touched upon organization of academic courses.*" The FGEL leaders had also suggested forms of grass roots democracy such as lecture hall committees which would combat the inherent corporatism of both *faculté* and local associations. This "University" line dominated the UNEF discussions until the election, in April 1966, of a board which in the course of the year showed the influence of Marxist-Leninists (among them the president, Jean Terrel), and which in the autumn tried to campaign against a class University.[35] The campaign was marked by a confrontation of two currents: the "universityites," who attached prime importance to the question of student salaries, and the "structuralists," who insisted on the necessity of presenting "counter-plans" to all official projects.

These disputes did not take hold among the students generally, because of the fact that they did not involve action by the rank and file,[36] and certain activists in the FGEL ended by asking themselves, in 1965, if the student milieu which, unlike the worker milieu, has "no memory," "will ever be able to advance beyond the level of understanding in which it is now marking time, without an incursion from the outside that will force it to see itself as it is." They concluded that it would be militant revolutionaries, "a detachment of the advance-guard of the proletariat who, by their *praxis,* would make student protest outgrow its circular nature."[37] The failure appeared all the more evident in that the Union of Communist Students, which was in a state of rapid decomposition, divided as it was between "orthodox," "Italian," and both Trotskyist and pro-Chinese leftists, was reduced by the party to an essentially administrative type of activity plus defense of the demands of both "the student masses" and the "underprivileged students"; in addition, the revolutionary groups that were set up on its ruins in 1966, could hardly claim to be "detachments of the advance-guard of the proletariat."

But however great the UNEF's destitution in 1968, no other student organization had developed either to the Right or to the Left of it, that could compete with it. It still had an address, an office, and a telephone (when the service was not discontinued). The very fact that as a union machine it had broken down allowed it in May to participate more flexibly in the choice of meeting places and directives that would be acceptable to everybody.

Furthermore, it was during this period of ebb tide that the essential problems were discussed, particularly by the leaders of the FGEL: problems concerning the pedagogical relationship experienced as being authoritarian, and the possibility of a "non-directive" pedagogy that would resemble the methods used in "progressive schools" and be in the libertarian tradition of C. Freinet.[38] All very real problems even though, in passing, there emerged a rather caricatural portrait of the typical professor, who was described as "a petty, threatened god who battens on the passivity and dependence of students."[39] Problems of national education, of secondary or higher education, as implements of social selection, immediately led to considerable discussion of *Les Héritiers,* by P. Bourdieu and J. C. Passeron.[40] In order to realize how normal this situation could seem to a large section of the teaching body, it will suffice to quote the following reply, reminiscent of Paul Bourget, to an *enquête* published by a left-wing review which, in 1964, devoted a special issue to an essential "dossier for higher educational reform":

> I am aware that 'sensitive souls' are shocked by the fact that although they are the same age, a school teacher's or an engineer's offspring can handle syntax and conceptual thinking better than the son of a practically untutored manual worker. This inequality is almost unavoidable, of course, unless children are forcibly removed from their family environment. . . .
> Nor has it been demonstrated that there are only advantages in the son of a laborer becoming, after a few years of study, a diplomat, a finance inspector, or even a professor. Except in cases of very superior intelligence, I believe in the virtues of one *stage* at a time.[41]

More fundamentally still, perhaps, student unionism, or what was left of it, posed the key problems that were to arise in 1968: the problem of value as an instrument of world transformation; of the cultural heritage, especially as it is handed down by the *Facultés des Lettres;* of the University's social function beyond that of its own self-perpetuation, that is, of providing training for professors. Finally, the problem of the irresistible transformation of the liberal University into a technocratic University, which the former Minister Fouchet would like to "adapt" to industry by industrializing the University itself. Here we see already the types of relationships that characterize modern bureaucratic-capitalist society.[42]

Partly influenced by the student movement, and also by that of the lecturers and assistant professors, the minority union of higher education faculty members (snesup.) had also posed these problems, although its members frequently conducted themselves quite differently, according to whether they were meeting in a union or in a faculty assembly. Immediately after the Algerian war, under the influence of a fraction of the Communist faculty members, the union had seemed to be closed to all but essentially quantitative and categorial demands, in an attempt to obtain unanimity of the teaching body, and leaving the posing of political problems—to begin with, the question of "democratic" University reform[43]—to representatives of the political Left, particularly to the French Communist Party. The tendency that won out, after sharp discussion, at the 1967 Convention (the Geismar group) agreed, in addition to the material demands that remained posed, "to really change University practice, in order to obtain reforms that, in their essential features, depend entirely on the members of the University themselves, and should permit wide commitment among them." The accent is placed, therefore, on the pedagogical relationship, on the struggle between categories inside the University, but also on the University as being the center of the contradictions of society itself, due to the fact, among others, of the constantly increasing cost of training technically skilled workers, which the University must turn out in ever greater numbers, without society assuming the students' upkeep during the training period.[44]

This tendency was contradictory in that it brought together at the same time (a) those who accepted as an established fact the University's recent evolution, and wanted to transform from within faculty-student relationships and the structure of the University by means of reforms that only depended on the University itself; (b) those who wanted to "bring pressure to bear on the contradictions," "if need be, through strikes and street demonstrations,"[45] and (c) those who, in the wake of the Nanterre movement, were seeking new forms of liaison with the revolutionary workers,[46] but who denied the existence of an essentially University-centered crisis.

But perhaps, just here, it may be well to say something about what French education was like, just before the events of May 1968.

French education, which is essentially secular, state organized, and "free" in the sense that school fees are very small or nonexistent, is run by a huge Ministry of National Education which, employing as it does more than 700,000 persons in a variety of posts, is far and away the biggest business in the country.

Three words: *centralization, authoritarianism,* and *elimination,* suffice to characterize it briefly.

Centralization, which existed before Napoleon, was enforced to a ludicrous degree. Technically it offered both advantages and disadvantages, and the French school system is indebted to it, in part, for its extraordinary capacity of assimilation. But from one end of the country to the other, the study curricula of the primary classes and the *lycées* were exactly the same, and all decisions concerning them were made in the offices of the Ministry. Even the University curricula had to be countersigned in Paris, and uniformity was guaranteed in the *Facultés des Lettres et des Sciences Humaines,* and also, partially, in the *Facultés des Sciences,* by obliging professors to prepare their students for competitive national examinations (*concours*) aimed at recruiting teachers for the second degree (*agrégation* and CAPES). One of these competitions, the *agrégation,* had in fact become the royal road of access to a University professorship (the vast majority of instructors in the *Facultés des Lettres* being holders of the *agrégation* diploma). The government-sponsored Doctoral Dissertation (*Doctorat d'Etat*), which was practically always "defended" at the Sorbonne, and a "masterpiece" requiring, in Letters, from ten to twenty years of often sterilizing research, gave uniformity to recruitment of titular faculty members (*maîtres de conférences* and Professors). Recruitment of professors who had not followed the traditional channels was difficult, not to say impossible (Albert Einstein, who had been expelled from Nazi Germany, was not able to obtain a professorship in France), although certain institutions (the *Collège de France* and especially the *Ecole Pratique des Hautes Etudes*) can play the role of safety valve.

Authoritarianism did not only define the relationship between teacher and pupil, professor and student (there has been no influence in France that could be compared to that of John Dewey in the United States), but also the type of teaching that consists of a prepared lecture delivered before a class taking notes, was dominant in all three "degrees," primary, secondary, and university, of public instruction. In the primary grades,[47] the progressive education movement had not really affected any but the kindergarten classes and certain private school sectors. Authoritarianism, then, also characterized the relationship between the various teaching categories: no less than eight in second degree instruction and no less than twelve in the higher degree. Each one of these categories tended to block off the next lower category and to protect its own meager privileges. The teaching unions only weakly opposed this state of affairs, and the expression used by Cournot to describe society under the *ancien régime*—"a cascade of contempt"—gives an excellent definition of the mutual relationships that obtained between the different teaching categories.

The function of *elimination,* which maintained French instruction within the class system, had long been guaranteed by the hierarchy of the teaching degrees. Until the 1939–1945 war, primary instruction formed a whole which was intended for the lower rural or working classes, and it even offered an ersatz secondary instruction in the form of *Cours Complémentaires* and *Ecoles primaires supérieures.* The children of bourgeois families and holders of scholarships were enrolled, on the contrary, in the lower classes of the *lycée* (the second degree had its own primary teachers). The *baccalauréat* diploma, which alone gave access to the University, or to classes that prepared pupils for the *Grandes Ecoles,* was the equivalent of a diploma guaranteeing a good bourgeois background. The *Facultés des Lettres* and *Sciences* led essentially to the teaching profession, while the *Faculté de Droit* led to judiciary and administrative positions. Doctors and pharmacists had their own *Facultés.* The network of *Grandes Ecoles:* Army, Navy, *Beaux-Arts, Ecole Normale Supérieure,* Polytechnic, Mining, etc., with their almost caricaturally bourgeois student bodies, gave a type of scientific and technical training that was often of a very high order (*Ecole Polytechnique*), but in the long run furnished more administrators and engineers than it did scholars.

The powers of resistance of this system should not be underestimated, and in many respects, it was still intact during the 1960's. The *Cours Complémentaires* had survived under the name *Collèges d'Enseignement général* (CEG) and statistically, children from the country and workers' suburbs, not to mention the huge immigrant subproletariat, continued for the most part to be oriented toward the lower levels of instruction. In spite of a few half-hearted concessions, the *baccalauréat* had lost none of its importance; nor had the relationships between the University and the *Grandes Ecoles* evolved appreciably. There remained, however, the fact that the school "explosion"—that is, the annually increasing number of children and adolescents from the middle classes and, to a lesser degree, from the lower classes, enrolled in both secondary and higher education, added to the demographic explosion (the post-Liberation "baby boom")—had created entirely new problems: the total number of students eliminated continued to increase. The terminology used in secondary instruction, like that of the higher degree, both of which were intended for an "élite" (many of the secondary school exercises have hardly varied since the Eighteenth Century Jesuit schools), had no meaning for the pupils who did not receive in their families a "complementary" education, the essential nature of which has been analyzed in the work of the sociologists P. Bourdieu and J. C. Passeron. The *baccalauréat,* which even though it eliminated a good half of those who had passed through secondary school, appeared nevertheless as a mere sieve in the eyes of the professors of the higher degree, who stated that they favored a policy of *selection* for entrance to the University. Actually a first-year student in the *Faculté des Lettres* had hardly one chance in ten of obtaining the title of *licencié,* and only the minutest chance of becoming an *agrégé de l'université.*

The Fouchet reform (called after the Minister of National Education Christian Fouchet, 1964–67), which continued to be applied by his successor, Alain Peyrefitte—who resigned during the May crisis—did not affect any of these fundamental problems, nor did it even try to correct certain obvious absurdities that had long been exposed by the technocrats (as, for instance, the separation between Political Economy, which is taught in the law schools, and Economic History, which is reserved for the *Facultés des Lettres*). What it did try to do, however, by applying methods that were at once half-hearted and harsh, was to rationalize the system with a view to avoiding over-staffing.

It tended to create inside University instruction (Letters and Sciences) two separate University channels: one based on the former teaching *licence,* and which was to furnish middle echelon cadres for the teaching profession, as well as for the labor market (two or three years of required study); and the other based on the former "diploma of graduate studies,"[48] rebaptized "Master's" in imitation of the Anglo-American M.A., and which, after at least four years of study, would furnish the advanced cadres needed for the country's economy, and open the way to competitive recruiting examinations. The barrier separating the two types of study courses was made legally insuperable by means of a series of pedagogical and administrative measures.

In practice, this reform abolished the former *licence* which had covered one year of general culture (*propédeutique*) and two of specialization, divided into four certificates in Letters and six in Science, and replaced it by a two-year period of general culture (University diploma of literary or scientific studies) and a specialized course limited to one year for the "short" way (*licence*), or two for the "long" way (Master's).

The distinction between *licence* and Master's was very real in Science, because the curricula for both were, from the beginning, clearly differentiated. In Letters it was made practically inoperative through the introduction of an obligation for all students working toward a teaching career to possess the new-style *licence.* Meanwhile, a large majority of these students were working for a Master's, contrary to the wishes of the Ministry. So actually, this famous reform boiled down, when all was said and done, to replacing a cursus of 1 + 2 + 1 years by a cursus of 2 + 1 + 1 years. It therefore satisfied neither the conservatives, whose habits were upset, nor the technocrats, who had succeeded in obtaining neither selection before entrance into the University nor creation of universities with different study levels, as in America (the few "University Institutes of Technology" created at the time, and which were not accessible to those who had not passed the *baccalauréat,* could not fill the role of lower grade universities); nor the students, who were suddenly faced with it at the beginning of the 1967 term with no provision having been made for a transitional period, in the midst of the most enormous administrative confusion. It should perhaps be added that the government had not furnished the means—in spite of constant increases in the budget of the Ministry of National Education—to provide a sufficient number of professors, assistants, and other faculty to meet the needs of the students. As for the way the *Facultés* were run, it will suffice to point out that the credits for running the *Faculté des Lettres* (Sorbonne), which has an enrollment of over 40,000 students, were the equivalent of one million dollars.

The succession of student demonstrations that took place in opposition to the "Fouchet Plan," from 1966 to 1968, are therefore imputable to something else besides the "Fouchet Plan." In order to understand them, they must be examined in an international context.

Student revolts, which have been frequent during recent years,[49] seem to obey a certain number of common rules. The premonitory signs appeared after the end of the cold war, Stalinism and McCarthyism, when a generation that had not had direct knowledge either of war or of its immediate aftermath, reached maturity. It might be added that it was a generation which, at least in Western cities, had passed through liberalized primary classes and enjoyed an uninhibited family life.[50] It was in 1956 that the Left won the majority in the UNEF; it was also about the same time that it re-formed in American universities; and everybody knows the role played by students and intellectuals in Warsaw and Budapest, not to mention the "hundred flowers" in Peking. But no serious differences appeared at that time, for instance, between students and professors. What happened during the sixties had a very different aspect.[51]

Things begin more than often with a stupid blunder on the part of the University or governmental authorities, a blunder that is sometimes spontaneous and sometimes deliberately provoked by the student movement, which wants to show up the implicitly repressive nature of academic authority; to wit, the refusal on September 14, 1964 to allow Berkeley students to engage in political propaganda on the borderline between the campus and the city;[52] the decision on January 16, 1968 in Warsaw[53] to halt performances of a play by Mickiewicz; the refusal on April 8, 1965 by the rector of the Berlin Free University to receive the journalist Erich Kuby, of *der Spiegel,*[54] who had criticized the University; the refusal by the ecclesiastical censor to allow a student newspaper at the Milan Catholic University to publish an article on divorce (May 1967);[55] the decision by Columbia University to build a gymnasium that involved expropriation of park land in Harlem (resulting in a demonstration on April 23, 1968);[56] closing of the Nanterre *Faculté* on May 2, 1968. In Czechoslovakia the incident that led the students in University City to decide to demonstrate, armed with candles, on October 31, 1967, was an electric power cut that had been preceded by many others.[57]

After a rather long period of waiting, the revolt takes place in a form of its own, sometimes non-violent—sit-ins, teach-ins, love-ins, sleep-ins (occupations)—and sometimes violent—broken gates at Columbia, occasional barricades in Paris (as early as May 3). The forms are taken either from the traditions of the Nineteenth Century revolutionary movement, or from different types of non-violent action. In almost every case it was not the "classical" protest groups who led the fight. In Berkeley the Free Speech Movement stretched well beyond the boundaries of the older left wing organizations, and it even contained, at least at first, Republican followers of Barry Goldwater. In Nanterre the *Mouvement du 22 mars* broke through the narrow limits of the "groupuscules";[58] and in Italy, although the Communist Party refrained from making the harsh condemnations of its French counterpart,[59] the *Movimento studentesco,* which included students belonging to every imaginable shade of the extreme Left, among them workers' parties, proclaimed its defiance both of the student associations and of the classical far-leftist parties (PCI and even the PSIUP).[60] In Germany the *Sozialistischer Deutscher Studentenbund* (SDS), which was excluded in 1961 from the Social-Democratic Party, is very far removed from the classical Communist attitude (Rudi Dutschke was writing a dissertation on workers' councils in the Hungary of 1919),[61] and it is also far from having led the revolt alone. At Columbia, two organizations headed the movement: one white, the Students for a Democratic Society (SDSA), and one black, the recently formed Student Afro-American Society. Of course this schema is not intended to conceal the considerable differences that separate the various movements. In France and in Italy the very fact that there exist large workers' parties which are revolutionary in speech if not in practice, in addition to encouraging profound social movements,[62] supported in France by a particularly powerful tradition, gives the student movement extraordinary confidence in the capacity for action of a working class "betrayed" by the unions and political parties, and allows it to present itself as the University detachment of a revolutionary workers' party that does not exist.[63] At times—this was patent in France—the "groupuscules" reason as though they actually were this revolutionary party. In Germany, where the extreme-leftist workers' movement was once very powerful but was destroyed by Nazism, Stalinism, and the postwar West German "miracle," the sds, which has hardly more than two thousand members, oscillates between an advance-guard conception, inherited from Lenin, and the keen awareness, stimulated by the writings of Marcuse, that in a modern industrial country, students are the only confrontation force, the only isolated individuals in the present stage of advanced capitalism,[64] and that it is their function to act with the Third World movements as example. They also oscillate between the Leninist conception of a highly organized party made up of professional revolutionaries, and spontaneity.[65]

In the United States, the most clear thinking among the radicals marvel that, in the midst of a manipulated, *kitsch* society, a student movement of such proportions could exist.[66] Here, however, it is the minority movement of the blacks, not the workers' movement either past or present, that can serve as reference. Yet whatever the differences, one finds everywhere, at least in the Western world, a common determination, which is, to discover forms of organization that will allow people to act and at the same time leave them total *freedom of speech*. Another characteristic feature of the movement is the festive, joyous atmosphere in which it functions: there were jazz, a piano, and singing at the Sorbonne on the *"Nuit de la liberté"* (May 13–14), the barricades had been a huge street fair, and there were guitars and singing at Columbia. Michael Rossman, one of the leaders of the Berkeley revolt, wrote that "the Free Speech Movement was distinguished throughout by a fierce joy,"[67] the joy of action in common, in a universalist outlook, the joy of free speech and verbal invention, the joy of doing away with social barriers, including sex barriers.[68] The joy at Columbia somewhat diminished, however, by the demand of the black students, on April 24, to pursue their action separately. "The Blacks ought to be able to do their thing," said one white leader.[69] With this festive attitude, the student movement ties back to the tradition of the worker movement. Raymond Aron, whose estimation of events in France was as pitiless as it was unjust, did at least understand that.

> Once again, both students and workers will retain a radical memory of these days of strikes, parades, endless discussions and riots, in the atmosphere of a street fair, as though the boredom of everyday life, the stifling sensation produced by technical and bureaucratic rationalization, demanded, from

time to time, sudden emotional release; as though the French only escaped from their solitude by means of a revolutionary (or pseudo-revolutionary) psychodrama. Participation, though a vague word, is a powerful concept, which expresses the aspiration toward community living that our hierarchically organized, partitioned society, itself a juxtaposition of privileges, only offers the French during brief moments of lyrical illusion.[70]

Community life has always been more intensely lived in Anglo Saxon or Germanic countries, but what the students in Berlin and Berkeley felt they had set up was a new kind of community.

Inevitably, from Warsaw to Mexico, in Belgrade as well as in Rio de Janeiro, the police intervened, leaving wounded and sometimes dead: a student, Benno Ohnesorg, murdered by K. N. Kurras, a policeman, on June 2, 1967, in Berlin; mass interventions in Rome on February 28 and March 16, 1968; in Paris, on May 3, May 6, May 11, etc.; more than thirty students killed on October 2, 1968, in Mexico City; 814 students arrested in Berkeley, December 3, 1964; 1000 police called in at Columbia by the university authorities, on April 30, 1968, wounding one hundred. Rightist and extreme-rightist (even "leftist") forces also demonstrated publicly; counter demonstrations in Berlin by unions and political parties, on February 21, 1968, in an atmosphere of an anti-student pogrom, followed by an attempt to assassinate Rudi Dutschke on April 11; demonstrations on May 13 in Paris, and the following days, by the neofascist group, *Occident.*

Among the students a certain anguish began to mingle with the festiveness without, however, making it disappear entirely: violent demonstrations in Germany after April 11, the tragic nights in Paris and Lyons of May 24 and 25. During the first stage, at least, police intervention greatly increased the influence of the more radical groups: this was profusely evident in Paris; in Berlin the Left got a large majority in the "student parliament," and in Berkeley a poll showed that one-third of the students approved of the aims and methods of the Free Speech Movement, and two-thirds of its aims only.[71] The episodes of the different demonstrations selected—not to say deformed—by immediate collective memory, rapidly assumed epic coloring: the Paris barricades soon had their veterans, while at Berkeley, humor mingled with the epic saga,[72] and each participant recalled, in a few words, the principal episodes: the police car (on which Mario Savio had perched to speak to 2000 students, on October 1, 1964), the big sit-in (occupation of administrative buildings, on December 2), the strike (that followed the big sit-in), the Greek Theatre, to which the University summoned the students on December 7), the Faculty vote (which gave in on December 8 to the demands of the Free Speech Movement).[73]

The "demands" were of very different types according to country and date. If the expression "participatory democracy" conveys the general aspiration, more than often, the student movement was wary of a type of democracy that would be confined to the university. A student from Trente, Mauro Rostagno, quoted Stokely Carmichael as saying, "We don't want to eat at your table, we want to knock it over." And he proposed the following division of labor: "Let the bureaucrats (professors, administrators, etc.) manage the University, and the students will manage the movement."[74]

Actually things were much more complicated, because to the extent that the former University establishment abandoned its functions, or, as in France, broke down, the students were immediately faced with the problem of management, a problem they were obliged to assume, if the results were not to be apocalyptic. So, dialectically, there existed a confrontation of two attitudes: one which consisted in making a separate society of the University,[75] a sort of shadow society (this was the logic that guided many American radicals and, until rather recently, since the Cordoba manifesto in 1918, the students in Latin America), and another which considered the first attitude as an ostrich policy and tried at all costs to make the University movement overflow into the outside world.[76] In the French documents to follow will be seen expressions of the constant fear of "co-option," and of isolation of the student movement inside the University. The type of free speech demanded at Berkeley is not merely the legal right to have political discussions, or to carry on propaganda on the edge of campus—this freedom was very quickly granted (or rather restored) by the academic authorities—but militant speech freedom (advocacy), which establishes its own laws.[77] They demand participation and refuse integration. Tom Hayden, who founded Students for a Democratic Society, and participated in the revolt at Columbia, writes:

> The students do not want to be included in the decision-making bodies of the military-industrial complex that governs Columbia;[78] *they want to be included only if this inclusion is a step towards transforming the university.* They want a new and independent university standing against the mainstream of American society, or they want no university at all. They are, in Fidel Castro's words, guerillas in the field of culture.[79]

In the same way, the revolutionary students in Rome wanted to make the University "a point at which the system ceases to function."[80] Less exigent, the Czechoslovakian students, on the whole, wanted to protect their autonomy from the system in power. The list of demands that was drawn up after repression of the October 31, 1967 demonstration asked, among other things, for restoration of University extraterritoriality, identification of individual members of the police through numbers that would be clearly visible, interdiction of chemical means of repression, and radical revision of the role of the police in a socialist society.[81] These demands were to contribute largely to the crackup of Stalinism, and on March 13, 1968, *Rude Pravo* announced that autonomy had been granted to the departments, the School councils, and to the student organization.

Free speech demanded and won has usually led to an extraordinary outcropping of various propagandas, as for instance, Trotsky facing Mao Tse-tung in the courtyard of the Sorbonne,[82] a "libertarian republic" as remote from the tyranny of the "little red book" as possible, but which can sometimes be quite brittle.

For that matter, the student revolts are all part of a general anti-imperialist struggle. The June 2, 1967 Berlin demonstration was against the Shah's visit, and the German, French, and Italian movements were profoundly marked by the struggle against the war in Vietnam.[83] In the United States this same struggle took hold at Berkeley and on many other campuses, after the success of the 1964 revolt, and even went so far as refusal to serve in the army. In fact, the university became an all the more favorable terrain for this struggle because of the "uneasy alliance," in the form of secret contracts, that bound the university laboratories and research institutes (as for instance, the Institute for Defense Analysis at Princeton) to the Pentagon. Radical students and professors worked indefatigably, at times successfully, as at the University of Pennsylvania and at Cornell, to have these contracts canceled.[84] At Columbia where as early as 1960 the School of International Affairs was making propaganda for the cia, a group of students, the "radical caucus," took over President Kirk's office on April 25, and found and published documents showing the university's attitude in the affair of expropriation of the black community, as well as its ties with the government military organizations. In France, too, questions were posed[85] concerning the ties linking certain laboratories with the army and manufacture of the atomic bomb.

In Germany, Italy, and in France, the student movement wanted to graft itself onto the workers' movement. In France the slogan "student-worker solidarity" first appeared at Nanterre and was being used early in May. Although France is the only country in which a vast workers' movement was set in motion, in Germany, in April 1968, a very small workers' minority joined the Berlin student demonstrations, and in Italy contact was made with small radical groups of the working class[86] and they were able to organize a few demonstrations together. In Germany, and also in Poland, the authorities tried, with some success, to set the workers against the students. The same thing happened in France as regards the Communist Party. In the United States, where it was confronted with the most integrated and best manipulated society in the world (in the sense that Herbert Marcuse gives to these terms) the student movement tried to achieve (not to speak of such sidelines as L.S.D. or marijuana) what was also called, in Italy, a front composed of "outs,"[87] of people who were excluded from society, that is to say, they tried to join with the black movement. Rap Brown and Stokely Carmichael did, in fact, go to Columbia on April 26.[88] The worker reference existed too in the extent to which the CIO (Congress of Industrial Organizations), dating from the thirties, was often cited as a model at Berkeley.

This determination to break the ties between the university and the surrounding hierarchical society, gave rise to all sorts of centers for reflection and action: the Free University in Berkeley, the Counter university in Berlin, "shadow courses" in Italy, and countless French commissions questioned traditional teaching methods, the language they were presented in, even the cultural heritage itself. Decisions were made and resolutions voted by spontaneous action committees, or by informal assemblies that had broken away from the old student organizations, and in which there reigned (or tried to reign) the principle of direct democracy. Everywhere too, the mass media, which are the principal modern means of manipulation, were at the heart of both the discussion and the action: the demonstration against the Springer Press trust in Germany, and distribution of "counter-papers" to purchasers of Springer newspapers, the appearance or reappearance of a specifically "movement" press in the United States and in France.[89] In Poland, Kuron and Modzelewski's "left wing" manifesto was distributed clandestinely, while in Soviet Russia, distribution of typed (not printed) literature had become one of the main activities of rebellious intellectuals and students. Poetry and religion assumed subversive value.

What was the reaction of the society that was under attack, and, to begin with, of the University authorities? The rectors or University presidents found themselves under direct attack, whether or not they had been named by the government (as in France), elected (as in Germany),[90] or named by trustees (as in the United States). Fundamentally their attitudes were the same, consisting either in calling for discussion or in calling on the police; most often in the use of both methods. For example, rector D'Avack, in Rome, going into the occupied *faculté* of Letters on February 12, 1968 to engage in a dialogue with the students, then calling the police on February 22; or rector Roche, in Paris, calling the police on May 3, and dialoguing during the night of May 10–11, before launching the attack against the barricades; Presidents Kerr and Kirk of Berkeley and Columbia, who did the same; rector Lieber in Berlin on April 22, 1967, threatening suspension of the university constitution and an appeal to a State Commissary.[91]

The strictly professorial reactions were more varied. Very few, however, took the side of the revolting students *before* the outbreak, and we shall see that a majority in the Nanterre *Faculté* council approved of a proposal to organize a police detachment under the authority of the dean.[92] Things change *afterwards,* especially when there has been police intervention. On December 8, 1964, the Berkeley University senate finally passed a law, by a vote of 824 to 115, in favor of the Free Speech Movement.

In reality, however, the situation is a complex one, and everywhere one sees three tendencies emerge. There were few who wholeheartedly backed the student movement (they were a tiny minority in Italy, and very much in the minority in France, Germany, and the United States). In Poland some professors were dismissed for having manifested sympathy that in all probability was not without reservations. Nearly everywhere it was a matter of young professors, or more often of assistants (certain of whom, once they were in the movement, were nevertheless concerned about "saving the professors"). The opposite attitude, however, was frequent. Sydney Hook, a philosophy professor in New York, explained that academic freedoms were reserved for faculty members, and that students had to be satisfied with freedom to learn.[93] The majority in the French *syndicat autonome* (independent teachers' union) were an illustration of this same attitude.[94] Often, however, both in France and in the United States, a third current appeared which accepted the idea of dialogue but was anxious for it to remain within the confines of the university. Certain Columbia professors intervened between the students and the police. In order to reach a solution an ad hoc committee was immediately set up which included a few "radical" professors. The *Columbia Daily Spectator* which, although it is a student paper, seems to express on this point an opinion that is widely shared by liberal professors, wrote on April 24 that "President Grayson Kirk chose to ignore the voice of the students at the university he administers. He is an administrator, and not a king

. . . ," at the same time condemning the fact that students had locked a dean in his office (which the workers at Sud-Aviation did to their director, on May 14, and which the General Secretary of the CGT disavowed) and deploring the fact that "leadership and control of the protest should have fallen into the hands of persons who are not members of the university community, but outside agitators whose interests and aims have only slight connection with those of the demonstrators. . . ." The next day they admitted that rumors of a march on Columbia by the black community were "entirely unsubstantiated," and on April 29, demanded severance of all contact with the Institute for Defense Analysis, asked for an amnesty, and applauded abandonment of the much-disputed gymnasium project.

When the first occupation took place in Rome in 1966, as a result of the murder of a student, Paolo Rossi, by neofascists, a professor who had participated in the start of the occupation declared on April 29:

> My friends . . . I was a guerilla fighter in the mountains, but when we chose resistance we knew perfectly what we were doing, we had estimated our own strength and that of the enemy, as well as the risks we were running. Today, we cannot hold the University; I say this regretfully, at the risk of being unpopular, but after having made a conscientious count of our forces. Let's give up the University tomorrow, at the time of Paolo Rossi's funeral.[95]

These same reactions could be found in all sections of society, only in inverse proportion. The "conspiracy" theory appeared everywhere in caricatured forms. In Poland responsibility for the disturbance was attributed to a "Zionist plot against Poland" and many Jews were dropped from the university, from public office and from the party, and later obliged to leave Poland;[96] while in Germany the Springer press fired volley after volley at the "communist students" who were guilty of subversion. There was the same reaction in the United States, in the rightist and extreme-rightist press, which continued its accusations of Communist, Castroist, Chinese conspiracy.[97] In France also there were various versions, aberrant or official,[98] of the conspiracy theory.

Almost everywhere, too, professors and their teaching came in for criticism, both in France and in the United States. The May 2, 1968, issue of the *Columbia Daily Spectator,* for instance, published an advertisement written by an economist, in the name of the "Committee for Defense of Property Rights," which questioned teaching that declares all cultures to be of equal value, "Afro-Asiatic" as well as American, comfort as well as squalor.

It was a Democratic Governor, Edmund Brown of California, who on December 3, 1964 sent the police to Berkeley; and it was a broad coalition government (Christian Democrats and Social Democrats) that repressed the student movement in Germany; the case of the Socialist Minister of the Interior, Heinemann, asking "how we had contributed to making anti-communism reach a point of attempted murder" remains exceptional. It took a serious political crisis for the Czechoslovak police to ask the students to excuse them for having beaten them on October 31, 1967. In some cases, as in Yugoslavia in June 1968, the government made concessions;[99] and in Rumania, after the events in France, the university authorities decided as a measure of prevention to ease the examination system.

It can be stated that in every case, wherever polls were possible (and particularly election polls), the majority of public opinion was, or became, hostile. The election results illustrated this fact in Germany and in France[100] (where the size of the workers' movement increased a feeling of panic). "We didn't need elections," said one young *lycée* student, "to know that we were in the minority." The French case is a good example of the alternate use of repression and "repressive tolerance," without even approaching the use of police force that was made against the Algerians, for instance, at the time of the pogrom of October 17, 1961, or against the striking workers in 1947–1948. The problem was complicated by the variations of public opinion: a part of the bourgeoisie, at first, refused to allow their children to be beaten, and the inhabitants of the Latin Quarter stood up for the students during the night of May 10–11; as well as by the hazards attached to antiGaullism, which was shared as much by the Left as by a large fraction of the Right.

A curious evolution became evident after the "long march" of the Paris students, on May 7: from having been hostile, *Le Figaro, France-Soir,* and *L'Humanité* became briefly favorable. However, the current in the bourgeois press progressively changed direction very rapidly after the strikes started, and in *L'Humanité* after the CGT, followed by the CFDT, had taken the decision to negotiate (May 22). *Le Monde* made a sharp turn on June 11. After the elections, part of the leading moderate newspapers returned to the fantastic assumptions of a conspiracy to prevent reopening of the university in the fall.[101] At times cleverly, at others clumsily, the government applied repression from May 3 until May 11, capitulated on the evening of the 11th, leaving the student insurrection complete freedom, then progressively returned to repression, beginning on May 15.

The text of an orientation law for higher education, and the speech made by Edgar Faure, the Minister of National Education, on July 24, comparing the situation of the students to that of a colonized people, opening University premises to political discussion, while several revolutionary group leaders were in prison for some time to come, and mass dismissals were taking place at the ORTF (Government Radio-Television), shows how far "repressive tolerance" can go, provided one key problem, the problem of control of the mass media, is not brought up for discussion. General de Gaulle is supposed to have said, "The country has just elected a PSF[102] majority; this majority will carry out PSU policies."[103] The political parties and unions did not support the student movement, except (with occasional eclipses) for the CFDT and the PSU, although the latter was reproached for its election-oriented attitude. The same reproach was aimed in Italy at the PSIUP.

If we eliminate such childish explanations as that of an organized conspiracy, it remains necessary, nevertheless, to comment briefly on the different kinds of explanations that were given for this widespread phenomenon.

There has been much talk everywhere of the "generation conflict," and ad nauseam, especially in the United States, of the Freudian father-son conflict,[104] the university standing in loco parentis. On the contrary, others—among them the CGT, with plain common sense—have pointed out that the generations are self-renewing and that youth is not a social class.[105] Faced with the evident fact that in France the young workers, with the students (and even before them), were the leading actors in the crisis, Edgar Morin, in a short analysis that will remain one of the best, used the expression "juvenile revolution."[106]

But what are we to understand by "juvenile revolution" and "generation conflict"? Do these terms also describe the so-called yé-yé (roughly, "teeny bopper") phenomenon that has existed in France since 1963, or the introduction of "modernity," including yé-yé records,[107] by the young people of Plodémet, in Brittany? For a long time students have had their "initiation rites": French or Italian goliardism, the "corporations" of German students (which were often hotbeds of Nazism), the fraternities in American universities, with their classification according to age group. None of that is entirely dead. Young people in the working class also had similar rites until the Nineteenth Century, in their compagnonnage groups.[108] But was it that? The German movement was in direct opposition to the attitude of the earlier associations, the American movement to that of the fraternities, as well as to the panty raids of a few years back, and the French movement was equally opposed to both the yé-yé attitude and the gay student pranks of the past.[109] Until quite recently, generally accepted bourgeois wisdom declared that "youth will have its fling," and it tolerated many "excesses," in consequence.[110]

The students would readily have said that youth need not have its fling.[111] Shortly before the May revolution an observer who is well acquainted with the problems of youth gangs in contemporary France, compared the internationalism of rock 'n' roll, then of yé-yé, "entirely supported by the mass media," to that of the beatniks (or of the hippies), correlative of an evolution of the ideology itself, diverted from the search for inner, personal achievement or from personal dissolution in what American sociologists call "retreatism," to a commitment, under the sign of nonviolence, to fundamental political causes. Being an international movement, the beatniks have chosen to live in the principal American cities and in all the European capitals, where the police and sometimes commandos (fascist or Communist, according to country) persecute them. With them there's no age limit, and you can remain a beatnik your entire life.[112] Michael Rossman also shows very well how in the American movement there had been cases of hippie attitudes moving on to activism, and vice versa.[113]

In fact, there is no paradox in asserting that a student in revolt is the violent version of a beatnik or a hippie.[114] The film *Loin du Vietnam* showed this, as did the distribution of flowers to the police on June 16, when the Sorbonne was retaken. This was done by members of the Sorbonne Revolutionary Committee for Cultural Agitation (CRAC), in imitation of American "flower power," and before the incidents that suddenly took place in the late afternoon.

As a matter of fact, the attitude toward the mass media furnishes a good criterion. Whereas yé-yé is in reality passive, with a purely consumer attitude, participating only on order, or unleashing its gratuitous violence only when its consumer interests are frustrated,[115] the Paris students, during the night of the first barricades (May 10–11), followed the programs of the nongovernmental radios with an unflagging sense of criticism; and because Jacques Paoli, editor-in-chief of *Europe I*, continually urged his reporters to be more "moderate" in their accounts, he became for a few hours the man the revolting students hated most.[116]

Another cause usually cited to explain student revolts is what is referred to as the "archaism" of the universities in which they took place. This word generally applies to two quite distinct problems. First, the undoubtedly outdated manner of recruiting faculty (the *agrégation* and Doctoral dissertation in France, non-rational criteria almost everywhere else); the relationship between professors and students ("feudal" professors in Germany, "chair barons" in Italy, sovereign rights in France);[117] relationships that remain anonymous during the greater part of the academic period; the obvious lack of material means (libraries, study halls for the students, etc.). And, second, the University's lack of adaptation to modern society and the modern economy—that is, absolute insufficiency of professional training, even for future teachers; insufficiency of institutions to train the middle echelon employees needed in industry and in government service; lack of relationship between the number of students in certain branches, especially the liberal arts branches (psychology, sociology) and the possibilities open to graduates—not to mention non-graduates; liberal, even aristocratic prejudices in France and in Italy against economic careers, prejudices that are particularly prevalent in the *Facultés des Lettres*.

For instance, the dean of the Paris *Faculté des Lettres* noted in 1963 that a letter sent to 6,500 *licenciés* suggesting that they enroll in a section of applied social sciences that would lead to a trial period in an industrial establishment and a well paid official position had only brought 52 replies, and that only 43 of these candidates could be recommended.[118] To all of which is usually added, in France: the absurd centralization inherited from Napoleon (and from before Napoleon); the fact that the *licence* is identically organized everywhere, that the same basic instruction exists everywhere; that the universities are controlled by bureaucrats with authority, the rectors; and that the rules governing the Nanterre university compound had to be signed by the Minister—all these were explosive factors.

And in May, as a point of fact, the demand for autonomy of the different *Facultés,* even of their branches, was fundamental.[119] Finally, the technocrats pointed out quite rightly that the percentage of students who held University diplomas was deplorably low. The "Fouchet Plan" in its first version had tried to correct this by creating examinations (*licence,* Master's) of very different levels, leading to a great variety of careers. In Italy the "Gui Plan" had attacked both the pluralism of the professors who, in addition to their "chair" occupied a quantity of diverse lucrative functions (one rightist deputy objected that Archimedes was not employed full time when he shouted *Eureka!*) and the uniformity of the diplomas, by creating, along with the *licence* (*laurea*) a diploma that was supposed to satisfy two-thirds of the students.[120]

Of course this kind of explanation points up quite real problems and suggests solutions: we can conceive of an autonomous *Faculté des Sciences* in Reims, for instance, in which the biochemical branch—also autonomous—would train students by modern pedagogical methods in sufficient numbers for the Taittinger champagne makers to guarantee them jobs. Big industry in France is aware of these problems and certain firms have considered creating their own institutions of higher education.[121] The discussions that took place in Caen in 1966 were in fact principally concerned with this question. But these arguments encounter one absolutely decisive objection: in the United States the Berkeley revolt, which is the supreme model of revolt, did not take place in an archaic university, but on a campus and in a section of a university which, although run by the state, is autonomous. It is a university admirably equipped, highly selective, perfectly adapted to meeting the needs of a large number of specialized institutes; a university whose regents are among the most important businessmen in California, which is the most modern, most prosperous state in the country; a university that, after the McCarthy years, and in spite of the notorious blunder committed there on September 14, 1964,[122] was the one in which traditional political freedoms were generally more carefully respected than anywhere else (President Clark Kerr had been awarded a prize for his contribution to the cause of academic freedom; Communist speakers had expressed themselves quite freely before the 1964 revolt).[123]

The Free—and autonomous—Berlin University had undoubtedly maintained the earlier Prussian privileges due a professor "ordinarius," but formal democracy was more respected there than anywhere else in Germany, the students had a representative parliament possessing a certain number of powers of control, and the SDS itself was a legally admitted organization. To be sure, certain meetings were prohibited, but although Erich Kuby was unable to speak in the main amphitheatre, he did express himself quite freely on May 7, 1965, in the Student House of the Technical University.

In France, while the equipment at the *Faculté des Lettres* at Nanterre was scandalously insufficient (there was no main library), the teaching body was one of the youngest and most "modern" in France. Political activity could develop there much more freely than at the Sorbonne, and important concessions were granted the students[124] during the year 1967–1968. Finally, the system of examinations by means of periodic tests (partial examinations) to which were added verifications of regularity of attendance reduced considerably the risks of chance. The "Fouchet Plan," which was badly conceived and badly executed by *Facultés* that did not dispose of the funds required, aimed in principle at increasing the output and efficiency of the University mechanism—that is, at industrializing it. So far from admitting that the archaism[125] of the University was an essential factor, it is suggested, rather, that as in the France of 1789, today in France, in Germany and in Italy, it is the mixture of archaic and modern that is a revolutionary factor.

Another way of posing the same problem is to insist on the difficult conditions under which—especially in France and Italy—the changeover from an elitist to a mass type of higher education was carried out. The number of French students has doubled in less than ten years and is now over 500,000. This phenomenon is increased by centralization in Paris, and instruction at the Sorbonne is dispensed in all but "teratological" conditions, all the more so in that the professors are unwilling to give up the privilege of directing the *Thèses d'Etat* for the whole of France.[126] The situation at Nanterre or at the Sorbonne, is like that of the Poutilov factories in Petrograd, in 1917: too rapid growth is an obstacle to social integration and constitutes a revolutionary factor.[127] The "democratization" of higher education, although it has in no way increased, proportionately, the possibilities for lower class young people to obtain access to higher education (contrary to what has happened in Soviet Russia, in China, and in the Eastern bloc countries) has considerably increased, in absolute figures, the number of students who have no inherited culture.[128]

As it happens, this "democratization" has encountered a dual problem: (a) the difficulty that exists for those who enter higher education with no family tradition, to adapt themselves to a type of teaching intended for an "élite," and which has been left untouched;[129] and (b) the incapacity of the French (or Italian) system to assume what is called in America a "cooling-out function," which is a function for gently[130] eliminating people by giving everybody diplomas, even though in a great many cases these may be of no value at all.

At the risk of seeming cynical, it will be recalled that in England, where entry into a university is much more sharply selective than in France—to such an extent that there are half as many British as French students for a population that is higher—the percentage of failure is very much lower (10% as opposed to 50%), which results in the same number of diplomas as in the French universities.[131] With the help of the individual tutoring system, in which a professor follows a small group of students, there has been no student revolution in England.[132]

There remains the fact that in both Italy and France, although there were a number of "perpetual students" (the kind that hang around the classes without passing examinations) taking part in the revolution, generally speaking it was not the most underprivileged students who were in the front line of the movement.[133] Revolution, like any other political activity, presupposes a minimum of availability. Chateaubriand wrote: "Patricians began the revolution, plebeians finished it."

Also proposed was a Marxist type of explanation, which was heard even in Nanterre. Taking as point of departure the indisputable fact that the universities are being industrialized, students then become a proletariat which is exploited economically, either directly by their professors (identified all in one lot with certain *Faculté* heads who actually do use work done by their "slaves" and sign books they didn't write), or indirectly, as was frequently stated in Italy, by society itself, incarnated by academic "authoritarianism." In the United States, the first to offer this type of "explanation" was Paul Goodman, who wrote:

> I am using the word 'exploitation' strictly. It is hard for people in the labor movement to understand this term as applied to students. . . . We would do well to recall Marx's description of the nine-year-olds picking straw, not because this was economically valuable but as training in work habits. Besides, we must notice that nearly fifty percent of the young are now kept in schools till twenty-one and twenty-two years of age; previously most of them would have been in factories, etc., for four or five years by that age.[134]

Somewhat more subtly, a student conference from Pisa, meeting in Rimini in May 1967, took pains to define precisely the idea of proletarization of students, whom they described economically as a "work force in the course of becoming skilled," a terminology that was later tempered by showing that the division between manual and intellectual labor is replaced today by a division between "technico-executive social functions" and the functions of authority and political leadership.[135] It is of course possible to argue at length on the subject of examinations as a means of recruiting a "reserve army" of the intellectual unemployed,[136] although English capitalism—as also in the socialist systems—through preliminary selection, appears to avoid formation of too numerous "reserves." It is hard to see what advantage the capitalist French government would derive from spending vast sums, even during periods other than those of organized unemployment, to hold up entrance into the production ranks of large numbers of young people (it is true, however, that on this point, projects for rationalization exist); although, as a rule, students in the Western world belong in the privileged social categories . . . but above all, in France, this attempt has met with one decisive objection: "contestation" took in all social categories, including the most privileged, all professions, cadres, even priests.[137] The doctor-in-charge of a hospital service who declared that, because of his chief, he had "lived in terror for fifteen years,"[138] was not economically exploited. He was socially and politically humiliated.

It is true that a student's life often has something sinister about it: poor housing, poor food, difficulty in making ends meet, moral and social (even more than economic) distress. "Wandering through a wasteland that is delimited by a few barriers called *curriculum, culture* and *position in society,* a student—and this was written five years ago—feels more tossed about than concerned."[139]

And indeed the student speeches were more apt to be about alienation than about exploitation. From the "specialized robots"[140] in Rome, to the "gorged geese" in Nanterre, denouncing "programmation,"[141] to the Berkeley students[142] transformed into IBM cards, not forgetting Rudi Dutschke's denunciation of a "bureaucratic university" which has as its aim "complete, adapted submission of every detail to the ends of general policy, that is, to the *status quo* of the balance established in domination,"[143] everywhere student language has avoided an exclusively economic terminology in order to restore their dignity to political and social factors.[144]

Naturally, the fact that the student world made ready use of the word alienation, although it has considerable psychological significance, does not in itself prove the "scientific" value of this concept. It is however striking to note that those who refuse to recognize any scientific value in it (as, for instance, the Stalinized Marxists or, on another level, Louis Althusser and his disciples) are the same ones who refuse to concede any intrinsic existence to social and political factors, and would like to reduce Marx to the role of "scientist," or an economist concerning whom they see no reason, moreover, why he should not have become outdated.

The students who revolted wanted to go in for politics in the most active sense of this expression, and even in its "irrational" sense: "Strike now, analyze later,"[145] was said at Berkeley; and a girl student added, "We're asking for what we should have, not for what we can get."[146]

In Eastern Europe, where politics is the absolute monopoly of a few professionals (study hard, if need be make love, but above all no politics, is what Polish students were told) a student may be oriented toward demands of a "formally democratic" type. The same thing is true, for very different reasons, in Madrid or in Barcelona, while in countries where traditional political freedoms are guaranteed, the student movement has tried to restore meaning to these freedoms by leaving institutions in which speech was captive. We can explain in this way—and not by a phenomenon of economic exploitation—their adoption of fighting methods taken over in part from the struggles of the Third World.

As for the social dimension of the struggle, this is explained by the profound transformation of the social structure, and not exclusively by that of the economic role of the University. What has happened is the mutation of the liberal University, closed in upon itself, into an industrial University, playing a leading role in the economy and the social life of the industrialized countries to which it furnishes management personnel and—even more—constant innovations in the scientific and technical domains, innovations that find daily expression in the transformation of production and consumption. The changeover from university to what is now called "multiversity" had its prophet in Clark Kerr, who happened to be president of the University of California at the time of the Berkeley revolt.[147] Basing himself on three fundamental ideas: (a) concentration of knowledge and technique in enormous university complexes; (b) scholastic explosion; and (c) integration of the university into the economic and social life of the country to a point where it could be calculated that at the time Kerr published his book, production, distribution, and consumption of knowledge represented 29% of the Gross National Product of the United States,[148] Kerr described, from an essentially administrative viewpoint, this huge body, with at its head a "mediator-initiator" whose essential functions are peace making[149] and progress, which he alone, acting as a liberal despot in view of his position, can instigate. The fact is that the university is no longer made up of students and professors only, but also of researchers, who have no contact with the students, and of all-powerful administrators. Clark Kerr himself admitted that "the multiversity is a confusing place for the student. He has problems of establishing his identity and sense of security within it." He added that, in spite of the countless possibilities that are open to the students, "the casualty rate is high."[150]

Although in relation to a provincial French university this description may seem to come under the head of science fiction, the fact is that in the great European universities profound changes have taken place which make comparison with the American phenomenon legitimate. These changes concern both the universities themselves and their relationships to the students. One of the most striking phenomena is

the increase in the number of intermediary bodies (functioning between the professors and the students), of the veritable middle social
strata that the assistant professors and simple assistants have become.
Although in the smaller universities the ties between professor and assistant are those of one man to another (which can mean, in certain
cases, ties of confident and almost feudal collaboration), the more a
university develops, the more hierarchic its organization becomes, opposing those who direct (the professors) to those who execute (the assistants). The assistants may, in some cases, be scientifically more
competent, but they have more hours of class and therefore more contact with the students, less room, and fewer research or library credits
than the professors. The role of the instructors and assistant professors
in the May revolution has no other explanation.[151]

Another fundamental feature of the "multiversity" is the increasing difficulty with which it succeeds in integrating first year students,
in spite of the development of these intermediary teaching strata. In
France, on the institutional level, this resulted in the Fouchet Reform,
which replaced the different versions of the *année propédeutique,* or
preparatory year, by a literary or scientific "university studies diploma"
that required two years. The difficulties that accompany democratization could be mentioned, but Berkeley is one of the most "selective"
universities in the world, and Kerr himself noted, in 1963, that there
was "an incipient revolt of undergraduate students against the faculty;
the revolt that used to be against the faculty in loco parentis, is now
against the faculty in absentia."[152] Two of their political science professors noted that a student could become a Bachelor of Arts (B.A.)
without ever having spoken with a single professor.[153] The examinations consisted of a checkup, by means of abstract tests, of the huge
bibliographies that had been distributed. The students identified the
instruction they received with the "organization," with the "machine,"
with the computers that they were tempted to smash, in a reflex of
play, but which they finally learned to use.[154]
Mario Savio said:

> There is a time when the operation of the machine becomes
> so odious, makes you so sick at heart that you can't take part;
> you can't even tacitly take part, and you've got to put your
> bodies on the gears and upon the wheels, upon the levers, upon
> all the apparatus, and you've got to make it stop. And you've
> got to indicate to the people who run it, to the people who own
> it, that unless you're free, the machine will be prevented from
> working at all.[155]

Revolutionary students are therefore aware of the fact that the University is an apparatus, that this apparatus is a power implement which, seen from the outside, functions no doubt as a production apparatus, but the internal function of which is political and social oppression, and the final aim, their implantation in society. If we accept this analysis is something else besides mythology, it is easy to understand the "juvenile" nature of the student revolt, and at the same time the response it met with, particularly among young workers. Analysts of the "bureaucratic phenomenon" as a global social form (in the factory as well as in the office, oppression is not only economic: would we say that a high school pupil is exploited, or that he provides a plus value?) have demonstrated that "accustoming" a young man or a young girl to "rationalized" organization of production and work was an affair of several years.[156] Revolt may come before they get "accustomed" to it.

The fact that Berkeley students use computers is nevertheless symbolic of another fundamental contradiction in the "multiversity," which does not only ask the students to be passive, but also asks them to be intelligent, to show initiative, and if need be, contributes to making them all these things.[157] This phenomenon is not an isolated one; we find it in the most modern forms of factory life, in the post-Taylor forms of work organization, which Alain Touraine was among the first in France to analyze.[158] In the French University the transition from passivity to initiative took place suddenly, between the *licence* and the diploma of *études supérieures* when for the first time a student who had come that far came in contact with research. (Today it occurs between the *licence* and the Master's degree which, however, is accompanied by a certificate.) It is characteristic that all reform proposals—all the texts contesting the former university regime—stress refusal of this separation, which is also symbolized by the opposition between public lecture (*cours magistral*) and study group (*travaux pratiques*).[159]

But the revolutionary role of certain students is also comprehensible. They are no longer in contact, as they once were, with isolated cultural centers of the society that surrounds them, but with highly developed aggregates that play a focal role in the economic and social life of the nation. It is true, of course, that in a country like France this evolution has hardly started, but this is compensated by the ultracentralized nature of the system. In addition to their focal role these aggregates create simultaneously the conditions of passivity and, for those familiar with political action, the intellectual possibilities of revolution. Needless to add, the universally acknowledged role of students of the social sciences, and particularly of psychology and sociology, in contemporary revolts, cannot be explained merely by the problem of possible job openings. We shall leave aside the psychological implications that often underlie the very choice of these careers. Sociology and psychology are, by nature, ambivalent; tools of integration, undoubtedly, but also weapons of fundamental criticism.

Most of the features outlined thus far are to be found in the May revolution. But the unprecedented extent of the phenomenon is worth dwelling upon, to begin with, in order to describe it chronologically. In the following chapters[160] a simple classification has been adopted, which takes into consideration both the interaction of the student and worker movements, and the general political situation. May 14 and 15, with the first factory occupations in Bouguenais (near Nantes) and in Cléon; May 30, with General de Gaulle's speech and the Champs-Elysées demonstration; June 16, with the re-taking of the Sorbonne and the victory of the Gaullist terminology, which an electoral majority then adopted for its own, on June 23 and 30, quite evidently punctuate the movement that began on May 3 with the closing of the Sorbonne. But the history we experienced is not quite that simple, and we shall see, for instance, that well after May 30, the action committees were still talking in terms of revolution, not to say of seizing power, and that, moreover, what has been experienced is not always what is significant.

In appearance the student revolutionary movement, with the support of the working class, reached its climax on May 27: the big demonstration organized by the UNEF at the Charléty stadium brought together fifty thousand people, among them representatives of several CFDT and FO Federations, militants of the CGT, one of its former leaders, André Barjonet, the PSU, and Pierre Mendès-France (who did not speak, however). That same morning the metal workers had refused to accept the Grenelle terms, the CGT had appeared to be outflanked and, following an old tradition, that day it organized only neighborhood meetings. Nothing that took place later was to give such an impression of power, even though the group that had started the entire action— that is, the *Mouvement du 22 mars*—was officially absent from Charléty and also organized neighborhood demonstrations. *France-Soir* announced that the new revolutionary party had been formed.[161] The following day François Mitterrand pointed to the absence of governmental authority and proposed formation of a provisional caretaker government, direction of which would be assumed by Mendès-France.

The day of May 29 was a two-fold day for suckers. Faced with the endeavors of the Federation, faced with Pierre Mendès-France, who declared that he was ready to assume power if it was delegated to him by a "united Left," faced with the very different hopes of the student movement,[162] the CGT, by means of the huge demonstration it organized alone from the Place de la Bastille to the Gare St. Lazare showed that it was still far and away the most powerful organized force among the workers, and that the new order, if it came to pass, would be an order under control of the CGT and of the Communist Party.

The same day General de Gaulle suddenly left the Elysée Palace. The fact that he had left by a side entrance (*la grille du Coq*), the same one through which he had entered it ten years earlier, inspired P. Viansson-Ponté (*Le Monde*), who was well acquainted with Gaullist symbolics, to write that the General had chosen to return to "his village and his heartbreak" and that this, in fact, was "the only solution."[163] The day of May 30 swept all that away. And however dynamic, the June 1 UNEF demonstration could not stand comparison with either the Gaullist demonstration or with Charléty.

The very general impression that the politically decisive days were those from the 27th to the 30th, and that they were successively marked by the defeat of the student-worker revolutionary movement by the Communists and the defeat of the traditional working class by the Gaullists, is nevertheless deceptive. For although the Grenelle agreements did mark a "comeback," as did also, in June, the Flins affair with its sudden new flareup of student-worker fraternity, which ended in the all but desperate demonstration on the night of June 11–12, in reality the die was already cast.

Although the militants of the *Mouvement du 22 mars* had understood before May that the university was a sensitive sector, they had not expected any serious action before October,[164] and it was the decision to close the Sorbonne on May 3 that triggered the unforeseeable events that followed. In spite of the slogans of "Student-Worker Solidarity," the demonstrations that took place from May 6 to 8 were revolutionary in form only, especially the one on May 6. And even then the form was largely determined by police repression.

The three preliminary demands made on May 9 by the UNEF and the SNESup., which are expressed in the slogans: "Liberate our comrades" (Some professors, a bit more paternalistically, changed it to "Liberate our students."); "Mad-dog Fouchet, liberate the Sorbonne"; "Leave the Latin Quarter to the Students," spell out perfectly the demands of the constantly growing number of demonstrators. These slogans were, moreover, picked up by the left-wing and centrist press for their own use. *L'Humanité,* which on May 3 had attacked the "German anarchist, Cohn-Bendit," and used severe language again on the 7th, became suddenly favorably disposed on the 8th, while the *Figaro* showed comprehension. On the 9th, Aragon made an appearance in the Latin Quarter, at the cost of being booed, and his paper (*Les Lettres Françaises*) actually did publish statements by the *"enragés."*

If the Sorbonne had been opened the following day, as the Minister had promised it would be, no doubt everything would have settled down, for the price of an agreement to set up student-teacher commissions in the various *facultés.* During the night of May 10–11, while the barricades were being built in an atmosphere of mixed joy and anguish, the students were listening with passionate interest to the dialogue between the General Secretary of the SNESup., Alain Geismar, and the vice-rector, Chalin, at the same time that they were eagerly awaiting some human sign from the Minister, Peyrefitte, and the results of the talks taking place between a student-professor group and the rector, Jean Roche.

The reply was a brief homily in the best Marshal Pétain style, and an attack by the police. The new factor during the "night of the barricades" was, without question, the appearance on the Place Edmond Rostand of a few groups of young workers and unemployed. With unerring strategic sense, Daniel Cohn-Bendit stressed this fact as he left the rector's office. *L'Humanité,* which completed its about-face on the morning of May 11 with the banner line: "Stop Repression," did not, however, breathe a word on this subject. But from then on, liaison between the worker and student movements existed. In advance of the negotiations that were going on between the UNEF and the labor organizations, and with a view to organizing a joint demonstration to take place on May 14 at 5:30 A.M., on the 11th Cohn-Bendit called on the central committees to declare a general strike on the 13th.

This decision was taken and Georges Pompidou's capitulation on the evening of the 11th, after his return from Afghanistan, did not change matters[165] in spite of some hesitations, especially at the CFDT headquarters. In speaking of his "deep understanding" of the students, Pompidou expressed a general opinion that is borne out by the polls taken at the time. But suddenly the student movement assumed the role of a detector. An order had sufficed for hasty condemnation of the demonstrators (students and non-students) who had been arrested on Sunday, May 5; an order was also to suffice for their hasty release on Monday the 13th. This exploded the myth of magisterial "independence." "I have freed the arrested demonstrators," said Pompidou, quite frankly, on the 16th. The protest against this formula that was made by the Federal Union of Magistrates appeared to be merely a comical feature of the general situation.

Occupation of the Sorbonne annex, *Censier,* by the students on the evening of May 11 was, however, still revolutionary only from the standpoint of university institutions. All the students wanted was to prove, with disarming sincerity, that they were quite at home in the university buildings, and that they knew how to organize and think through their problems.

The strike on May 13 was far from general, but the Paris demonstration was undoubtedly the largest that had taken place there since the funeral on February 13, 1962, of the victims of the Charonne massacre, and this time it was not a funeral. (On February 8, 1962, during an anti-OAS demonstration, nine workers were killed by the police). There were, however, very few revolutionary slogans. Some talked of a march to the Elysée, but the *"enragés"* students, who had succeeded with a certain difficulty in heading the procession, were content to lead a few thousand followers to the Champs-de-Mars. Again during the night of May 13–14 at the Sorbonne, Jacques Monod was warmly applauded at about 3 o'clock in the morning when he suggested that the students organize a "revolution in the University rather than a general revolution with the University as point of departure."[166] Two days later he would have been booed.

It was, however, the occupation of the Sorbonne and of certain provincial *facultés* that had immediately opened their doors to workers and that eventually gave the movement its full dimensions. The idea of "student power" asserted itself with a suddenness that amazed the teaching staff, as for instance at Besançon on May 16 (with allowances for the provinces), according to the account of a Communist faculty member who wrote:

> The day . . . has marked a decisive turning point. First of all, the 'majority' students took the initiative. They set up a certain number of committees in which some faculty members participated without its being clear whether they were doing so on their own or as union members. The relationships between students and teachers were therefore reversed, which had certain consequences. From then on, the students were convinced that they could get whatever they wanted from the teachers, that they no longer had to negotiate reforms but to impose them, that what was refused them one day would be granted the next.[167]

However, while the Communist Party warned on the 16th against "adventurous slogans" at the same time that it proclaimed the need for a change of government; and while Cohn-Bendit on the evening of the 13th had expressed his joy 'at having marched ahead of the "Stalinist scoundrels" (adding that, at best, François Mitterrand could only be made use of), the student movement was unaware of the sum of innovation and "anticipation"[168] that it bore within itself. Being profoundly marked by the revolutionary "tradition," it did not relate to the revolts in Berkeley, Germany, and Italy, but in a mood of inextricably mingled play and seriousness that harked back to 1789, 1848, the Commune,[169] and June 1936, it reenacted, like mummers, the Petrograd Soviet.[170] In the first twenty-four hours, cultural excitement had reinvented the literary and artistic forms discovered by the victorious revolution, from futurism to *Proletkult*.

In fact, even before the news broke, during the night of May 14–15, that the workers at *Sud-Aviation* in Bouguenais had occupied their factory the preceding day, the transition from protest to revolution had been made in Paris, just as it had in Strasburg. The first strikes were like an incarnation of this fact: not really a surprise, but the sense of victory, the impetus they gave to the student movement, should not be underestimated. This was the meaning of the streamer carried at the May 16 demonstration that went to the Renault factory, which read: "The workers will take from the students' frail hands the battle flag of combat against the anti-people's regime."

The politically decisive days, the ones on which workers and students gave the impression of marching in step toward a self-governing society, are the days that went from May 15 to 21 (the latter being the date of the last big strike order, the one issued by the unions of primary and secondary school teachers). The strike started in a "wildcat" atmosphere, without union instructions, and many thought that it had spread the same day, which quite evidently was not the case. In spite of warnings—particularly the fact that on May 16 Renault was closed to the students—the influence of the unions on the workers was enormously underestimated, just as the importance of their material demands for millions of workers was underestimated. Rarely did anyone ask, with the clear-sightedness maintained during those days by the *Figaro*, which, on May 17, hailed the "sense of responsibility" shown by Georges Séguy, comparing him to a "PDG" (President-Director-General), whether the general strike and the movement of quantitative demands launched by the CGT did not aim to "drown" the revolutionary nature of the young worker-student movement.[171] Few remained as coolheaded as Daniel Cohn-Bendit, who declared before

May 20: "I don't believe that a revolution is possible, like that, from one day to the next."[172]

While FO refused to depart from the American tactic of straight union demands, and the CFDT spelled out a series of structural reforms (union rights and the first steps toward self-management), the CGT, between May 15 and May 30, seemed to be hesitating between two courses: whether to stick to union demands, or to force a political change.[173] On Monday May 20 Georges Séguy, speaking at the Renault factory, stressed the essentially economic nature of the movement, and André Barjonet's account shows that, on the 21st, the Confederation board had reached a decision.[174] The CGT did not emphasize political change until after the Grenelle agreements were concluded and had failed (May 27)—that is, not during the period when the movement was gaining momentum, but when it had become stationary and could no longer count on great reserve forces.

On May 21, Georges Séguy proposed a meeting between the unions and the leftist parties. "Public opinion," he said, "is very upset by the disturbances and the violence. It is also dismayed by the complete absence of governmental authority. It has seen in the CGT the great peaceful force that has restored order in the interests of the workers." Continuing, he explained that the movement "was too powerful for there to be any question of its being slowed down by such empty formulas as self-management, structural reforms, plans for social and University reforms, and other inventions that all end by relegating immediate union demands into the background." He added that he was ready to discuss matters with the employers and the government "uninterruptedly, until agreement is reached or disagreement is acknowledged."[175]

That very morning, however, the CGT and the CFDT had called for replacement of the Social Security's board of directors, which was authoritatively named by government decree, by temporary caretaker committees composed of union representatives. The following day Cohn-Bendit's expulsion order coincided with acceptance of immediate negotiations on the part of the CGT and the CFDT, and charges of "incredible pretension" were made by the CGT against the UNEF's vice-president, Jacques Sauvageot. That night violence flared up again in the Latin Quarter. By then, in reality, it looked as though the die were cast.

This break-off did not weaken the student movement which, on the contrary, began to be conscious of its own originality. At the demonstrations that took place on May 22, 23, and 24 the students, plus a number of young workers and members of "youth gangs" (which led people to believe in the existence of numerous armed and well-organized intervention groups) were alone for the first time since May 13.[176] However, it was during the night of May 24–25 that the demonstrations reached their climax of insurrectional tension. The Boulevard St. Michel demonstrators did not wait for the arrival or even the approach of the police to build their barricades. But the festive atmosphere was gone, and the contrast with the night of May 10–11 was a sharp one.

Nor did this change mean that the general protest movement was weakening in the rest of the country. *France-Inter* (a government controlled radio station) was liberated on May 17, and on the evening of May 25, the television (also government owned) went on strike. In spite of jubilant declarations made by *l'Humanité* on the "victorious return to work" (June 6), the worker movement itself showed an incredible capacity for resistance, though mostly on the part of a minority, and certain sectors were still on strike when the elections took place. But what was certain was the general attitude of public opinion, which had undoubtedly changed after May 29. People's main concern now was with the question of the authority of the government, which the movement, in spite of a few texts to the contrary,[177] had never seriously considered "taking over," but which it believed would fall, without the slightest doubt.

The student movement felt that it had been betrayed, but it was wrong; it was what Claude Lefort described as "the new disorder." And apart from the fact that betrayal has never explained much more than surrender of defenses, the Communist Party and the CGT had never ceased to represent a possibility of order—and even, at the climactic moment, of plain "law and order." Conservative academics in the universities and *lycées* made no mistake when they turned desperately to both for help,[178] but it is true that, without resorting to the vocabulary of "subversion," their appeal was couched in double-talk.

It is probable, when all was said and done, that the Communist Party would have preferred to guarantee the continuity of General de Gaulle's foreign policy, rather than attempt the adventurous undertaking that its action committees had been asking for since May 21. This undertaking was to form a "people's union" government with the Federation at the risk of either being rejected by a centrist operation, which was also shaping up, or seeing an authentic opposition appear on its left for the first time since 1920. However this reasoning, which is perfectly coherent in the context of party machine politics, was never formulated publicly, perhaps for the very reason that the May revolution was preeminently a rejection of both calculations and party machines.

As the cultural heir of past revolutions, both bourgeois and proletarian, the May movement was a repetition, if not of their violence and bloodshed (which in the end, in spite of the brutality that marked certain days beginning with the matraque beatings of May 3d, was infinitely less than in any former experience)—at least of their structural schemas. A *lycée* in the Paris area experienced successively, in less than a week, the liberal explosion of 1789, the rarefied atmosphere of 1793, and the reaction of Thermidor. In a Sorbonne lecture hall you could watch in action the process that led from the slogan "soviets everywhere" to a developing bureaucracy.[179] This schematism was perhaps further accentuated by the mimetic awareness that was characteristic of a number of those who participated in the movement. The fact is not new, from the men of '89 reliving a Roman revolution to Lenin reenacting the Commune, or Trotsky denouncing Thermidor and discovering in Spain both the Mencheviks and General Kornilov.

Today we have Raymond Aron, identifying himself with Alexis de Tocqueville in 1848,[180] not to mention the numerous "Versaillais," who were a revelation to themselves and to others after May 30, 1968. The revolutionary vocabulary is sensed as new only when the revolutions are over! From now on, May '68 will serve as a model; but for the historian seeking to bring out the absolute originality of the event, sociologists would rightly show that there is more to be learned from comparing revolutions than from mere linguistic analysis. And to start with, the following, which Tocqueville showed once for all in *l'Ancien Régime et la Révolution,* namely that all revolutionary movements, at the same time that they bring charges against a society, both reflect and show up certain of its features. Thus the laws of '93 apply and consolidate the terrorist methods of the absolute monarchy; and thus Lenin's professional revolutionary is at once the opponent and the opposite number of a Czarist bureaucrat or police officer.

The May movement undoubtedly had its own contradictions, which the following pages will clearly show; contradictions between the political and social groups that took part in the movement and the different strategies they had to propose. To the extent that it was, in a sense, the entire society that was in movement, it was evident that there would be a confrontation of opposing interests: a cadre, even one who protests, has not the same interests as a worker. Besides, due to the mere fact that all social groups were involved, that the field of possibilities seemed open, and that by definition no higher power of arbitration had been constituted by and in the movement, there was nothing to interfere with the demands of the different categories. Otherwise, it is not possible to explain how the hierarchization of salary increases could finally, in spite of certain oppositions (particularly on the part of the CFDT), have been so easily accepted.

In the University too there was the same outbreak of individual considerations.[181] For many assistants or assistant professors the demand for abolishing hierarchies inside the universities supposed their own promotion to the rank of professor. Provincial professors figured that this was a unique opportunity to have themselves appointed in Paris, while others, who were under forty, declared ingenuously that the University should be run by professors who were under forty. Research workers on temporary contract with the CNRS thought that their duty and the interests of research demanded that their contracts should become permanent. The higher one went in the social hierarchy the more self-determination was dictated by selfishness rather than by generosity.

But it would be a mistake to believe that the student movement escaped this inevitable display of appetite—not to mention those who, having suddenly evolved into veterans, were looking for some sort of "modest compensation," in this case a diploma without exams. Among certain of those who demanded abolition of the difference between the study and the practice of a profession, could be felt a desire to avoid the necessities of entry into professional life, to remain eternal students.

These latter inner contradictions are really only one aspect of the fundamental relationship that united the movement to the society it was contesting and combating. The movement attacked the "consumer society" but it respected and adopted for its own certain of its traditions and means of action. The "weekend" remained sacrosanct during almost the entire movement, if not inside the various *facultés* (which at first were lively on Sundays), at least on the outside. One single demonstration, in Paris, was organized on Saturday, and that was on June 1, after the gas stations had reopened and a large part of the population had left the city for the joys of the highways. Not one was organized on Sunday,[182] and quite evidently it was not accidentally that, when the tide began to ebb, the government should have chosen Sunday, June 16 for retaking the Sorbonne. The authorities knew that counteraction would be relatively weak.

All the efforts of the *Mouvement du 22 mars* to combat the "star system" with the statement that they were "all Cohn-Bendits" did not keep the television and the press from making a star of him, even inside the student movement,[183] which made use of all the mass media from loudspeakers to the nonofficial broadcasting stations. But this "counter-information," in its fight against the misinformation and inadequate information that are characteristic of modern society, was it-self not entirely above manipulation. Evelyne Sullerot has pointed out the role that rumor spreading[184] played in the rise of the student move-ment, and it was not easy to make out from the way certain false news spread (from the march of 10,000 workers to the barricades on the night of May 10–11, to the inflated mortality figures that followed the first days of the repression) what was actually just "talk," which is nonetheless characteristic, and what was the result of conscious ma-nipulation. The loudspeakers, which never let up at Nanterre, had ended by seeming to be in the throes of an obsession.

The movement demanded the highest level of culture for every-body (certain plans for reform of higher education drawn up at the *Ecole Normale Supérieure* had been based on the supposition that a first-year student had the capacities and the acquired knowledge of an unusually brilliant "normalien"), but certain facts in themselves were also indicative of today's low cultural level and obscurantism. A mathe-matician was accused of being a bourgeois agent because the mathe-matics he taught was difficult!

The movement wanted to give everyone the right to speak under conditions that would make real self-expression possible. In any case, that was the basic aim of the *Mouvement du 22 mars,* confronted with certain exclusive rights arrogated to themselves by the "groupuscules." This was the way, for instance, that the Strasburg student council functioned. Observers have noted that the person who presided at a meeting was "the only one who never spoke on the actual content of the discussions," and that "the only person who had the right to act (that is, to organize the discussions and give people the floor) was, by common consent, also the person who could not talk about anything. . . ." They remarked, too, that "if everything is to be manifested in the single register of verbalization, this verbalization of everything takes so much time that one would need to have lots to spare."[185] The facts did not always correspond to this ideal schema (which undoubtedly does require unlimited time to be fully realized) and it was obvious that the temptation was great, when a meeting did not react the way two or three activist militants wanted, to consider that it did not take place under conditions that allowed those present to really say what they had to say.

Here we approach the problem of student "terrorism."[186] Appar-ently, in the large majority of cases, there really was free speech in the commissions and assemblies—it being understood that those who did not accept the basic principles of the movement were not very tempted to come and might well have been booed—but not everything is wrong in the following remark of Michel Crozier who, after emphasizing that "the most serious fault with our teaching is to make discussion and dialogue almost impossible," notes that certain procedures that combat this state of affairs "are merely the reflection of the worst authoritarian and intolerant tradition,"[187] to which they assert they will put an end —except, of course, that the "reflection" is subsequent to the tradition itself and is probably its inevitable consequence.

It is a fact, however, that the "direct democracy" of the student assemblies frequently encouraged occult manipulation and maneuvers. The "Rousseauism" of the student world was a strange one. Starting from the principle that the will of the majority was the only right one, it developed plans for reorganizing the University and the whole of society that conformed to the Lenin schema in *State and Revolution,* which would have inevitably been accompanied by an expanding bureaucracy. There was little concern for curbs, which are nevertheless necessary for a University that it was desired should not be a reflection of present-day society. In a project for reorganization of the 6th section of the *Ecole Pratique des Hautes Etudes* someone proposed creation of an "anticouncil," to be the instrument of imagination and verification which, having been named by drawing lots, would confront the council that had been democratically elected. This Athenian suggestion was not followed. The spontaneousness of the movement made it suspicious of any form of organization, with the result that organization took place just the same, but by little groups or little feudal systems—about which, as was evident at the Sorbonne, there was nothing "spontaneous."[188]

Other contradictions had to do with the specific nature of French society. The movement was absolutely opposed to the centralism and authoritarian tradition inherited from Napoleon and there were indubitably "regionalistic" aspects.[189] It would even be interesting to know whether the originality of a movement like the one in Strasburg was not the structural analogue of the originality of Alsace itself as part of the French community—which does not mean, of course, that the "autonomy" proclaimed as early as May 9 in Strasburg had anything to do with the former Alsatian "autonomism," as certain people in Germany thought.

There remains the fact that at a signal from Paris, just as in 1830 and again in 1848, the entire province followed suit, and then the students were faced with problems they had never foreseen.

The movement was internationalist, which was actually its most visible characteristic: revival of singing the *Internationale;* excellent slogans such as "We are all German Jews," which burst forth on May

22; actual participation on the part of many foreigners; the activities of such committees as the Sorbonne "Tricontinental"; effective appeals launched in the direction of foreign immigrant workers. But as long as it lasted, although there were a few public meetings on the international problems that were the easiest to integrate with traditional internationalist schemas[190] (a tragedy such as Biafra was ignored), there was only one attempt—an abortive one—at a demonstration on the problem of Vietnam, and none at all directed at the Greek or the United States embassies. All proposals of this kind met with the classic reply: let's first settle our own problems.

These replies were understandable and even legitimate (it had been such a long time since anything had been done about the problems of France) but in them occasionally could be glimpsed the chauvinism of "la grande nation." Along the same lines, and despite the fact that women played an important part in it, the movement did not avoid the male chauvinism that is characteristic of French society. At the Sorbonne the girls did practically all the cooking, and the movement never really posed the problem of the lack of equality that exists between girls and boys as regards the right to receive an education.[191]

These contradictions may perhaps be summarized by another more fundamental one that would appear to be related to the "apocalyptic," "millenarian" nature of the revolutionary movement, which started partly, both in Paris and in Berkeley, by refusal of the ahistorical, reifying domination of technocracy. But once the revolution had been achieved (or gave appearance of being so), it too, for many, seemed to bring history to a close.

There were those who took pleasure in the idea that revolution consisted simply in "taking this society and turning it inside out like a glove."[192] On this point, historians, who were less aware than sociologists and psychologists of the specifically "social" nature of the oppression to be combated, were more clearsighted. But how many so-called general assemblies, when they represented only a tiny minority, have proclaimed their sovereignty; how many have argued as though they really did have authority, when all they had was an imitation of it!

Such contradictions symbolize the extremely brief period into which the movement was compressed. But obviously it is historical process itself that will allow us to pose them more effectively—perhaps even to solve them. There remains, in spite of everything, even of failure, the "transgression," the "breach," the conscious search for a new political vocabulary; the "sort of alertness crystallized on things that suddenly lost their institutional nature,"[193] the discovery of other people's existence that is expressed in the now famous line written on a

Censier wall: "You, my comrade, you of whom I was unaware beneath the tumult, you who are throttled, afraid, suffocated, come, talk to us."

Before closing I should like to say a few words on the way this book was conceived. It was put together by two historians,[194] both of whom took part in the movement and do not pretend to judge it from the outside, the essential aim being to allow the students to speak.[195] Our reason for including a certain number of documents that are exterior to the student world (as, for instance, the minutes of the Nanterre *Faculté des Lettres* assemblies and council meetings) is to shed light on that world, and show in what political and social context it was placed. The notes and headings are simply to recreate this context and describe it, at times critically. Rather than a purely chronological account, we have chosen to present a survey of interrelated descriptions and successions of documents which clarify the rise of the movement. A first version was ready by mid-August of 1968 and the book was revised and completed during September and October.

We consulted several thousand texts, and many persons—students, professors, and militants from all sides—generously furnished us documents and information. Yet even this basis did not suffice, since certain provincial universities are either badly or not at all represented. The *Facultés des Sciences* are much less well represented than the *Facultés des Lettres,* and the *Facultés de Pharmacie* are not represented at all. Above all, to the extent that with one exception the book only reproduces written texts, it betrays the movement with regard to its use of the spoken word. When all the tapes that were recorded are transcribed, a different picture will emerge.

Certain dates that follow the documents (in brackets) may be only approximate. There must surely be some mistakes, and indeed, we shall be grateful to all those who are kind enough to point them out, which will allow us to correct them. The spelling has been given uniformity, misprints and unintentional linguistic errors have been corrected.

Professors, certain of whom are close colleagues and friends of mine, will probably be shocked by this or that statement. Let me say that I have no intention of judging, and that I am absolutely incapable of saying what my personal reactions would have been at the *Faculté des Lettres* in Nanterre, in 1967–1968. May we be permitted to dedicate this book to those who initiated, and to all those who participated in, the student movement.

PIERRE VIDAL-NAQUET

ACKNOWLEDGMENT

The texts were chosen by mutual consent, as also the book's general plan. Alain Schnapp assembled chapters II, III, V, and VI, and Pierre Vidal-Naquet, in addition to the Introduction, organized the rest of the volume, revised the entire book, and made the Bibliography. We want to thank Jacques Julliard and Jean-Marie Domenach, who were our first readers. For typographical reasons, dates of the texts are placed at the end of the documents, no matter how they may have appeared on the originals.

* * *

The present edition is a somewhat abridged version of the *Journal de la Commune Etudiante*. A little over one third of the documents in the original edition have been omitted, while, on the contrary, the Introduction has been expanded a little in order to furnish certain background information which the English speaking reader may not possess. In some cases new documents have been introduced, and the Bibliography has been greatly enlarged. A brief Postface summarizes the situation as it existed in the autumn of 1970, two years after the events.

The authors want to thank all those who have made the present edition possible, especially Gabriel Kolko, Arno J. Mayer, and, of course, Maria Jolas, on whom the translation has made exceptional demands of scrupulous competence.

P.V.-N.

Notes

1. Cf. Michel Crozier, *Esprit,* January, 1968.
2. "An End to History" in *Revolution at Berkeley* by M. V. Miller and S. Gilmore, New York, 1965, p. 240, and Hal Draper, *Berkeley: The New Student Revolt,* New York, 1965, p. 180. On the movement at Nanterre as a revolt of the historical conscience against a certain type of structuralism, cf. Epistémon, *Ces idées qui ont ébranlé la France,* Fayard, 1968, pp. 27–32. Much earlier, C. Wright Mills vigorously urged that its historical dimension be restored to sociology. Cf. *The Sociological Imagination,* Oxford University Press, New York, 1959.
3. The prestige accorded speech is revealed in the very details of the demands: *oral,* not written, examinations. On the various levels of student speech,

'untamed" or "civilized," cf. R. Barthes, "L'écriture de l'événement"; J. Dubois and J. Sumpf, "Linguistique et révolution"; and especially the excellent article by G. Lanteri-Laura and M. Tardy, "La révolution étudiante comme discours," in *Communications*, 12, 1968; see also M. de Certeau, *La prise de parole*, Desclée, 1968.

4. Raymond Aron, *Le Figaro* of June 5, 1968, article from which the preceding quotation is also taken.

5. A leaflet calling for a demonstration on March 18, 1968, in front of the main office of the French Cinémathèque ends as follows: "La liberté ne se reçoit pas, elle se prend." (Freedom is not granted, it is taken.) As a result of these demonstrations the government had to give up the management and financing of the *Cinémathèque*. Concerning this affair, see, in English, the account given by the cinéast François Truffaut in *Students and Workers*, by John Gretton, London, 1969, p. 101; Paul Thibaud, in *Esprit*, June–July 1968, p. 1032; a collection of protests entitled *L'Affaire Langlois, Dossier no. 1*, Eric Losfeld, Paris, 1968. In passing, it is interesting to recall that Daniel Cohn-Bendit took part in these demonstrations.

6. Cf. below, Chapter I, pp. 65 and 67–69.

7. This negative criticism also has a positive aspect, the defense of spontaneity. For instance, because it has influenced certain prime movers of the movement, one might quote Y. Bourdet's little book, *Communisme et Marxisme*, Michel Brient, 1963, several chapters of which had appeared in *Noir et Rouge* and in *Socialisme ou Barbarie*: see especially the first chapter, a brilliant analysis of *History of the Russian Revolution*, by Trotsky, *"Le Parti révolutionnaire et la spontanéité des masses,"* pp. 13–38.

8. A dissident group, *Pouvoir ouvrier*, continued to publish an information bulletin.

9. *Critique de la vie quotidienne*, Paris, 1946, and *la Vie quotidienne dans le Monde moderne*, Paris, 1967.

10. See, for instance, in *l'Internationale situationniste*, No. 11, October 1967, the caption for a photograph showing a Chinese crowd juxtaposed so as to depict a portrait of Mao. On all of these themes, cf. this volume, Chapters I and VII.

11. Cf. the discussion published by *Raison Présente*, No. 3, May–July 1967. P. Ricoeur, article *"Aliénation,"* in *Encyclopaedia Universalis*; J. F. Lyotard, "l'Aliénation dans le retournement marxiste," *Les Temps Modernes*, August–September 1969, pp. 92–160; Pierre Rolle, "La notion d'aliénation et ses critiques," *Epistémologie sociologique 8*, 2nd semester, 1969, pp. 61–68.

12. This precedent is rather rarely referred to in analyses of the May revolution; see, however, J. Joussellin, *les Révoltes des jeunes*, 1968, pp. 20–22 and *passim*; P. Seale and M. McConville, *The New French Revolution*, Penguin, 1969; L. Rioux and R. Backmann, *L'Explosion de mai*, pp. 180–184.

13. On these events, cf. the bibliography at the end of this volume.

14. Cf. the account by Edgar Morin, *Autocritique*, Paris 1959, pp. 191–197.

15. The first testimony signed by a living victim was that of R. Bonnaud in *Esprit*, April 1957. R. Bonnaud and other witnesses met again in *Jeune résistance*.

16. Michel Crouzet, *la Nef*, October 1962–January 1963, p. 53.

17. Cf. this volume, Chapter V, pp. 364–368. In 1970 the review *Coupure*, Editions Terrain Vague, Paris, also undertook publication of forbidden texts.

18. Due to the stir aroused by the affair at the time, there was talk of the appearance of an international "intellectual party." Cf. the special number of *Lettres Nouvelles*: "Vers un parti intellectuel," February 1961.

19. A theme that was in fact nostalgically developed by J. P. Sartre in his preface to the new edition of *Aden Arabie* (Maspero, 1960) and which he took up again in 1968.

20. On June 2, 1960 appeared the manifesto against the war in Algeria put out by the "Groupe d'études et de rencontres des organisations de jeunesse et d'éducation populaire" (GEROJEP), to which the UNEF belonged.

21. Lucio Magri was wrong when he wrote that, at the time of the Algerian war, "the UNEF organized sabotage and desertion." (*Les Temps Modernes*, August–September 1969, p. 12.) It is true, however, that the conflict between the UNEF and the PCF dates from this period.

22. Claude Lefort, "Le réalisme des professeurs," *le Monde*, November 3, 1960.

23. Including this writer.

24. Robert Bonnaud, letter to *Vérité-Liberté* (October 3, 1961) in *Itinéraire*, Editions de Minuit, 1962, p. 121.

25. This feeling that everything could be "co-opted" by Gaullism was put to a sharp test in May.

26. In the same way, the principal student combat organization was called, in 1962, *le Front universitaire antifasciste* (FUA).

27. For a leftist criticism of the NLF after independence, cf. J.-P. Lyotard, "L'Algérie évacuée," in *Socialisme ou Barbarie*, March–May 1963.

28. Robert Bonnaud, *Itinéraire*, pp. 85–86.

29. For General Challe, the fear of "Communist" agitation among the troops played a determining role in his April 24 decision to abandon the plan.

30. Claude Martin, *Socialisme ou Barbarie*, March–May 1963, p. 55.

31. "Every year, the board of the UNEF, who were elected during their Easter congress, spent a part of the vacation period rereading the documents that date from two to four years previously and realized that certain ideas, which seemed new, had already been expressed by their predecessors." (Dominique Wallon, preface to P. Gaudez, *les Etudiants*, Julliard, 1961, p. 8.)

32. Regarding the "groupuscules," cf. Chapter IV, this volume.

33. Federation of study groups at the *Faculté des Lettres* (the Sorbonne UNEF section).

34. See the references in the bibliography, and especially, Marc Kravetz, "Naissance du syndicalisme étudiant," *les Temps Modernes*, February 1964.

35. This board resigned during the General Assembly of the UNEF; J. Terrel's activity report was published in *Esprit*, April 1967.

36. Attempts at political action had also failed. Thus, on February 21, 1964, the FGEL had tried to mobilize the students against a visit to the Sorbonne by Minister Fouchet and President Segni; the Minister was at that time planning his reforms. The Latin Quarter had been occupied by the police, and the planned demonstration brought out hardly 1,500 students. The preceding day the leaders of the FGEL for the first time had launched the idea of occupation of the Sorbonne, but the order could not be given since there were too few students to carry it out.

37. A. Griset and M. Kravetz, *les Temps Modernes*, May 1965, pp. 2082–2083.

38. See F. Oury and A. Vasquez, *Vers une pédagogie institutionnelle?*, Maspero, 1967, and documentation published since 1966 by the review, *Recherches*, put out by the "Fédération des groupes d'études et de recherches institutionnelles"; naturally, too, all the work of the group of sociologists around P. Bourdieu.

39. J.-C. Passeron, in C. Antoine and J.-C. Passeron, *la Réforme de l'uni-*

versité, Paris, 1966, p. 224. The author does not accept the responsibility for this portrayal.

40. Editions de Minuit, 1964.

41. J.-M. Chevalier, professor at the *Faculté des Lettres* in Besançon, *Esprit*, May–June 1964, p. 717. *L'Etape* is the title of a book by Paul Bourget.

42. See pp. 33 ff. of this book.

43. The very elaborate plan for university reforms presented by the PCF was published in *l'Ecole et la Nation*, September 1966.

44. These ideas, which appear in numerous SNESup. documents dated 1967–1968, owe much to the analysis by A. Gorz, "Etudiants et ouvriers," *le Socialisme difficile*, le Seuil, 1967, pp. 47–67.

45. Cf. Chapter I, p. 115 of this book.

46. See the article by J.-P. Deléage and M. Chalaye, in the *Bulletin du* SNESup., May 1968, in which is also set forth the orthodox Communist point of view.

47. See, for instance, the very characteristic reaction of an American sociologist, faced with French primary education, in L. Wylie's *Village in the Vaucluse*, 2nd edition, Harvard University Press, 1964. Chapter IV.

48. This name was used to designate a long dissertation (at least 100 pages) written after the *licence*, the successful presentation of which was a prerequisite for the *agrégation*.

49. A view of the whole can be had from several volumes: *Daedalus, Journal of the American Academy of Arts and Sciences*, Winter 1968, "Students and Politics," viewpoint of American political science; J. Joussellin, *les Révoltes des jeunes*, Editions ouvrières, 1968 (a very useful compilation of facts); *Kursbuch*, No. 13, 1968, *"Die Studenten und die Macht"* (viewpoint of the revolutionary students). The collection, *Student Power, Problems, Diagnosis, Action*, edited by A. Cockburn and R. Blackburn, Penguin Books, 1969, concerns especially England and the United States. It is of course tempting to take a worldwide view, as does, for example, B. Nirumand in *Die Avantgarde der Studenten im internationalen Klassenkampf*, *Kursbuch*, No. 13, pp. 1–17; at the same time, the student struggle in the large capitalist cities against the monopolies, that of the students of the Third World against the oligarchies, that of the students of the Eastern countries against the bureaucracies—not to mention that of the students in Madrid, Barcelona, or Lisbon against fascism, or of the "Red Guard" against the apparatus of the Chinese Communist Party. On the levels of ideology, politics, and real facts these comparisons are legitimate. On the level of historical and structural analysis they encounter unsurmountable contradictions. It is absolutely true that development of the student movement in Western countries is politically incomprehensible if no reference is made to the constant example of the Third World. The date of February 21, which commemorates a revolt of Indian students (1946) and a revolt of Egyptian students (1947), has been for the last twenty years one of the dates of the student year. And what of the influence of Castroism, of Guevarism, of the Chinese revolution, at least as it is imagined in Western countries?

But even a movement like that of May 4, 1919, in China, which has been compared with the May revolution (J. Chesneaux, *Les Lettres Nouvelles*, September–October 1968, p. 131) because it was spontaneous and entirely outside the control of political parties and their machines, follows in the wake of the European movement of nationalities (cf. Chow Tse-tsung, *The May Fourth Movement*, Cambridge, Mass., 1960, and Marie-Claude Bergère "le Mouvement du 4 mai 1919 en Chine: la conjoncture économique et le rôle de la bourgeoisie nationale," *Revue*

Historique, April–June 1969, pp. 309–326). In the Third World the students appear to be the bearers of the nationalist idea and of modernization (in the 19th Century sense of the word) of archaic societies, although they expect to contravene it by skipping the liberal bourgeois stage. Even a comparison, as outlined here, between the Western movements and those of Eastern Europe runs into very serious difficulties.

I have limited myself here to several examples taken from the United States, Italy, Germany, Czechoslovakia, and Poland. Since writing this, three new books, containing above all, facts, have been published in Paris: J. L. Brau, *Cours, camarade, le vieux monde est derrière toi!*, Albin Michel; J. J. Brochier and B. Oelgart, *l'Internationale étudiante*, Julliard; *Combats étudiants dans le monde*, le Seuil; see also No. 44, Oct.–Nov. 1968 of *Partisans*, and *Esprit*, May 1969.

50. Cf. J.-M. Domenach, *Esprit*, June–July 1968, p. 1029.

51. Seymour Lipset committed, in my opinion, a radical error of evaluation in considering that modern student revolts are *survivals* ("Students and Politics in Comparative Perspective," *Daedalus*, Winter 1968, p. 2). According to him, students have temporarily escaped the "integration" that has divested unions and workers' parties of any revolutionary character. But how can we explain, then, that in the United States, as is underlined in the same review (p. 293) by Richard E. Peterson, the political militancy of students may be a fact of the '60's which cannot depend on any specific example in the past?

52. See the chronology of facts in M. V. Miller and S. Gilmore, *Revolution at Berkeley*, p. XXIV ff. To my mind it is this very radically new nature of the French movement that disqualifies such historical parallels as those drawn by André Coutin in *Huit siècles de violence au Quartier Latin*, Stock, Paris, 1969.

53. On Poland, four well-informed chronicles: A. Martin, "La révolte des jeunes en Pologne," *Etudes*, June–July 1968, pp. 60–79, "Warshauer Bilanz," anonymous, in *Kursbuch*, 13, pp. 91–105, *Combats étudiants . . .*, pp. 207–234, *Esprit*, May 1969, pp. 859–870.

54. Chronology of the facts in S. Bosc and J.-M. Bouguereau, *les Temps Modernes*, July 1968, p. 55 ff.

55. *Università; l'ipotesi rivoluzionaria, documenti delle lotte studentesche, Trento, Torino, Napoli, Pisa, Milano, Roma*, Libri contro No. 1, Marsilio, Padua, 1968, p. 207. From now on I shall refer to *l'Ipotesi rivoluzionaria*. Chronology of the facts in Rome in *Libro bianco sul movimento studentesco, a cura di Massimo Barone*, Edizioni Galileo, 1968. I shall refer to *Libro bianco*. See also the excellent volume by Rossanna Rossanda, *L'Anno degli Studenti*, De Donato, Bari, 1968, the last part of which was translated in *les Temps Modernes*, August–September 1968.

56. Chronology of events at Columbia in *Columbia Daily Spectator* of April 24 to May 8, 1968. See also *Ramparts*, June 11, 1968, and especially, *Crisis at Columbia . . .*, Vintage Books, New York, 1968, pp. 63–142. A brochure was published by the SDS strike committee: *Columbia Liberated*.

57. On Czechoslovakia there is an anonymous document in *Kursbuch*, 13, pp. 67–90. Many facts can be gleaned from P. Tigrid's *le Printemps de Prague*, le Seuil, 1968; *Combats étudiants . . .*, pp. 237–252.

58. Cf. below, Chapter I, pp. 127–132 and 316–320.

59. After a rather long period of occasionally reproachful hesitation, the Italian Communist Party decided to recognize the importance, and respect the autonomy, of the student movement; cf. R. Rossanda, *l'Anno degli Studenti*, pp. 35–36.

60. Cf. *l'Ipotesi rivoluzionaria*, pp. 18, 95, 142, and *passim*.

61. G. Sandoz, preface to R. Dutschke, *Ecrits politiques*, p. 10, wrote erroneously that this theme was based on the 1956 Hungarian revolution.

62. This was clearly perceived by R. Aron, *la Révolution introuvable*, p. 39.

63. Cf. A. A. Ross, "Etudiants et ouvriers," *Revue internationale du socialisme*, June 26–27, 1968, p. 198.

64. R. Dutschke, *Ecrits politiques*, p. 151.

65. Cf. U. Bergmann, R. Dutschke, W. Lefevre, B. Rabehl, *Rebellion der Studenten oder die neue Opposition*, Rowohlt, Reinbeck-bei-Hamburg, 1968, *passim*. R. Reiche and P. Gäng, "L'opposition de gauche," *Partisans*, No. 41, March–April 1968, pp. 15–37, and the documents that appear on pp. 38–56.

66. Arno J. Mayer, Speech at Princeton, May 2, 1968.

67. "Breakthrough at Berkeley," *Center Magazine*, Santa Barbara (California), May 1968, p. 42.

68. At Columbia, April 25th, a male leader asked the girls to volunteer for kitchen duty. He was greeted with laughter and the following retort: "Liberated women are not cooks," and the cooking was done by both men and women (it was not the same at the Sorbonne!). A sign hung in front of the toilets to indicate "desegregated John" read: Men *and* Women; cf. *Ramparts*, June 11, 1968, p. 36.

69. *Ibidem*, p. 35. The police tried to prove to the blacks that they had been "maneuvered" by the whites; in fact, when on April 30 at 2:30 A.M. the police intervened, the sector occupied by the black students, Hamilton Hall, was evacuated without the least resistance; cf. *Crisis at Columbia* . . . , p. 163. SDS literature does not make the slightest allusion to this aspect.

70. *Le Figaro*, June 5, 1968. On May 18 a *Figaro* columnist explained quite seriously that "boredom has always existed." Later, there appeared on the walls at Censier: "Boredom alone is counter-revolutionary."

71. C. Trillin in N. V. Miller and S. Gilmore, *op. cit.*, p. 272. That does not mean, of course, that the majority of the American students have gone over to the side of the "radicals"; in fact, the latter include scarcely 2 percent of the "college students," but they come especially from the "upper middle class," have a very high intellectual level, go to the best universities, are concentrated particularly in the classic and social science departments, and they constitute, in reality, the only effective group; cf. R. E. Peterson, *Daedalus*, Winter 1968, pp. 308–314. In Germany it is impossible to understand the publicity given the SDS unless we recall that the orthodox socialist students and even the Christian Democrats were swept along by the movement; cf. for example, F. Mager and U. Spinnarke, *Was Wollen die Studenten?* pp. 37–40.

72. A parody of Milton's *Paradise Lost* was written on this occasion: *Multiversity Lost*, extracts in M. V. Miller and S. Gilmore, *op. cit.*, pp. 305–312.

73. C. Trillin, *ibidem*, p. 259.

74. *L'Ipotesi rivoluzionaria*, pp. 14–23.

75. Cf. for France, below, Chapter VIII, pp. 500–509.

76. The opposition between the two tendencies was very clear in Venice; cf. R. Rossanda, *l'Anno degli Studenti*, pp. 61–63.

77. The clearest text is reproduced in H. Draper, *The New Student Revolt*, pp. 242–246.

78. On the organization of power at Columbia, cf. the document published by the "North American Congress on Latin America": *Who Rules Columbia?* New York, 1968.

79. *Ramparts*, June 11, 1968.

80. *Libro bianco*, p. 63.

81. Cf. *Kursbuch* 13, pp. 71–75, in which there is a translation of an article by J. Kavan in *Student*.

82. For Berkeley, cf. the graphic report by C. Trillin, *op. cit.*, pp. 253–284.

83. It is not the same in the Eastern countries, where the immediate, imperial reality is the USSR. It seems unjust to me to speak the way H. M. Enzensberger does in *Kursbuch* 13, 1968, p. 106, with respect to the Czech and Polish documents, of a "particularly shrunken horizon." He states, p. 107: "In fact, Stalinism has not only left traces of its crimes in Eastern Europe, it has also engendered an unbelievable political apathy. The profoundly depoliticized masses look upon each slogan that does not concern their immediate material interests—freedom of movement and of speech or legal guarantees—with deep suspicion." It remains to be seen if one can truly speak of "depolitization" with regard to Czechoslovakia (As a matter of fact, the only poll I know of was made in 1965, and the results were published by A. Matejovsky, in *l'Homme et la Société*, April–May–June 1970, pp. 291–295, and prove exactly the contrary.), and if there do not exist for these countries political problems more urgent than Vietnam. Even in France, the war in Vietnam, which played an important role at the beginning of the movement, was relegated to the background during and after the movement. Cf. p. 47 of this book.

84. Cf. Gabriel Kolko, "Uneasy Alliances: Universities and the Pentagon," *The Nation*, October 9, 1967; "The War on Campus," *The Nation*, December 18, 1967; "The Colleges Are Pulling Out," *The Nation*, September 9, 1968.

85. Cf. below, pp. 512–514.

86. Cf. leaflets reproduced in *l'Ipotesi rivoluzionaria*, pp. 78–80.

87. *L'ipotesi revoluzionaria*, p. 70.

88. *Columbia Daily Spectator*, April 27, 1968.

89. Cf. below, Chapter V, pp. 364–368, the case of the publication *Action*.

90. Hans Lieber, elected rector of Berlin University, on June 20, 1965, was a commentator of Marx and a man of the Left.

91. In Italy, only one rector, G. Devoto, in Florence, resigned when the police entered University premises (R. Rossanda, *op. cit.*, p. 26). The rector of the University of Mexico handed in his resignation in September 1968.

92. Cf. below, Chapter I, pp. 132–133.

93. "Academic Freedom and the Rights of Students" in M. V. Miller and S. Gilmore, *op. cit.*, pp. 32–41, and S. M. Lipset and S. S. Wolin, *The Berkeley Student Revolt*, pp. 432–442. These two volumes contain very interesting controversial exchanges between professors "for" and professors "against," especially between Nathan Glazer and Philip Selznick, both professors of sociology at Berkeley.

94. Cf. below, pp. 398–399.

95. G. Morpurgo, "Cronaca dell'occupazione dell'Università di Roma," *Quaderni Piacentini*, September 28, 1966, p. 144. The occupation, begun the 28th of April, lasted until May 3.

96. Cf. the anonymous document published in *les Temps Modernes*, July 1968; the most characteristic document is probably the article that appeared under the title "About the Events at the University of Warsaw," in *Trybuna ludu*, March 11, 1968. Each time the author cites names, he specifies: "Jewish student," or "also Jewish," or "both are Jews," or "wife of a Jewish student," or "daughter of a Jew," or simply "Jew." In the same way, during the trial of the students in Tunis in September 1968, the fact that certain of those indicted were Jews was profusely emphasized by the press, whereas, for Western readers, other persons indicted were wrongly accused of having been involved in the burning of the Great Synagogue in Tunis on June 5, 1967.

97. Cf. the press file (in which California Republican Senator Knowland's *Tribune* is particularly conspicuous), in N. V. Miller and S. Gilmore, *op. cit.*, pp. 313–348. After the Columbia events, the extreme right review USA published a special number (undated) devoted to the "plans of the radical left for the destruction of America," with lists of names and an index for easy reference.

98. Although Raymond Aron brushes aside the hypothesis of an "orchestra leader" (*la Révolution introuvable*, p. 99), the obsession of a plot was one of the features of the French movement. On May 19, veterans of the 2nd Armored Division circulated throughout France a text entitled "La Machine infernale," in which the mechanism of the crisis was presented as having been carefully tried out in advance. Cf. this text in J. R. Tournoux's *Le Mai du Général*, Paris, 1969, pp. 163–181.

But the most aberrant account was that published by a "history professor," F. Duprat, in his book entitled *les Journées de mai '68, les dessous d'une révolution*, 1968. Everything is in it, from good spy stories to invention of imaginary characters (among others, a certain "Goldberg," leader of the JCR, who never existed), to the most blatant mistakes about persons and organizations. It is a very good illustration of a technique for lying and exploitation of a certain type of reader, which N. Cohn has studied thoroughly in his book *Histoire d'un mythe, la conspiration juive et les protocoles des Sages de Sion*, Gallimard, 1967 (English title, *Warrant for Genocide*, Harper and Row, New York, 1967).

To a lesser degree, fear of provocation existed on all levels of the movement, and even the larger organizations were not above facile explanations. The "international organizations" (from Zionism to the CIA) for which D. Cohn-Bendit was supposed to have been an "agent," are too numerous to count. Retrospectively, in reporting the Charléty demonstration, *le Peuple*, a CGT publication, wrote that "several days previously, Barjonet had suddenly fled from all responsibility in the midst of battle, as though he had received an imperative order" (No. 799-800-801, May 16–June 30, 1968, p. 64). Concerning the "conspiracy phantasm," especially among Communists, cf. A. Geismar, S. July, E. Morane, *Vers la guerre civile*, Paris, 1969, pp. 230–251.

99. Concessions accompanied by the usual lies on the part of the government. Tito's speech on June 9, 1968 (excerpts in *Démocratie nouvelle*, June–July 1968, pp. 73–75) was self-critical, granted the students self-government, and congratulated them as a whole for not having allowed "those who support the ideas of Djilas, Rankovic, and Mao Tse-tung to try to pursue their own ends while pretending to be concerned with the students." This mixture of the theoretician for the "new class," the former police chief of the regime, and the Chinese leader is a strange one. On the revolt in Belgrade, cf. D. Plamenic, *New Left Review*, No. 54 (April–May 1969).

100. But not in Italy, where in spite of the fears of the party's right wing the Communist Party won 800,000 votes, notwithstanding the only relative support it had given the students.

101. Cf. for example S. Bromberger in *le Figaro*, August 9, 1968.

102. The French Social Party, a group emanating from the "Croix de feu," founded in 1936 by Colonel de la Roque.

103. Jean Daniel, *le Nouvel Observateur*, August 5, 1968.

104. Cf. for example, H. Draper and R. M. Abrams, in S. M. Lipset and S. S. Wolin, *op. cit.*, pp. 332 and 390, in which this explanation is rejected. Here is a characteristic French text: "The *dominus* and the *magister* are found to converge into a super-determination of the *pater-familias* image. [Why Latin?] This

image which it is not exaggerated to restore in an Oedipus type of totem-tabu polarity, is indeed to be found at the origin of these two sacralizing patterns of conduct . . . the sacred element in transgression and in instatement." J. M. Benoist, *Sciences,* No. 54–55, 1968, p. 5.

A serious study by a group of American "young radicals," organizers of the 1967 Vietnam Summer, demonstrated the contrary of what certain people expected. The "father conflict" among them is on an average less accentuated than among most of their contemporaries, and they appear to be particularly well integrated psychically; cf. K. Kenniston, *Young Radicals, Notes on Committed Youth,* New York, 1968, especially pp. 232 ff. and 316 ff.

Needless to say, the socio-psychoanalytical investigations have almost invariably been made among young people and not among adults. In this connection we recall the remarks of the British anthropologist Edmund Leach, which are valid for many other countries besides Great Britain:

> "Tension between the generations is normal for any society; every son is a potential usurper of his father's throne; every parent feels under threat; but the present anxiety of British parents seems altogether out of proportion. Young people are being treated as an alien category—'wild hearts with whom we cannot communicate'—they are not just rebels but outright revolutionaries intent on the destruction of everything which the senior generation holds to be sacred. Let us be clear about this. What is odd is not the behaviour of the young but the reaction of the old." (*A Runaway World?*, Reith Lectures 1967, BBC, London, 1968, p. 37.)

105. Cf. A. Barjonet, *la Révolution trahie de 1968,* Paris, Didier, 1968, pp. 20–21.

106. "La Commune étudiante" in E. Morin, C. Lefort, J.-M. Coudray, *Mai 1968: la Brèche,* pp. 26–32. E. Morin has since published a more detailed, subtler interpretation: "Culture adolescente et révolte étudiante," *Annales,* ESC Paris, 1969, pp. 765–776. For a serious attempt to explain the "revolutionary" phenomenon historically as a consequence of exceptional demographic pressures of younger age groups, cf. H. Moller, "Youth as a Force in the Modern World," *Comparative Studies in Society and History,* X, 3, April 1968, pp. 237–260. Nevertheless, the author does not take into consideration that the notion of youth has varied a great deal throughout history (Calvin at 26, and, even less, Zwingli at 32, were not, as suggested on p. 239, young men), and especially his positivist method, which combines 1789 and Naziism, does not account for or explain either the social aspects or the ideological aspects of the various "revolutions."

107. Cf. E. Morin, "Salut les copains" (title of a popular radio program), *le Monde,* July 6 and 7, 1963, and in *Commune en France, la métamorphose de Plodémet,* Paris, Fayard, 1967, Chapter 7, "jeunes et vieux," pp. 132–163.

108. May I observe that I do not at all underestimate the importance of "initiation rites." Cf. my article "Le chasseur noir et l'origine de l'éphébie athénienne," in *Annales. Economies, Sociétés, Civilisations,* No. 5, 1968, pp. 947–964, and in English, in *Proceedings of the Cambridge Philological Society,* 1968, pp. 49–64.

109. Cf. earlier, P. Gaudez, *les Etudiants,* pp. 26 ff., for the struggle of the leftist students in Berlin against the "corporations," cf. U. Bergmann in *Rebellion der Studenten,* pp. 10–11.

110. Today this same wisdom is scandalized by the occasional love scenes that took place at the Sorbonne.

111. Or else, which comes to the same, it would have repeated Nizan's famous phrase: "I was twenty years old. I will not permit anyone to say that it is the best time of one's life." Here I agree with A. Touraine, *le Mouvement de mai ou le communisme utopique*, pp. 220–221.

112. J. Monod, *les Barjots, Essai d'ethnologie des bandes de jeunes*, pp. 267–270.

113. *Center Magazine*, Santa Barbara, Calif., May 1968, p. 46. On the "hippy phenomenon" as a moment of the discovery of self-exclusion from society, cf. M. Rostagno (sociology student in Trento) in *l'Ipotesi rivoluzionaria*, p. 69.

114. See especially R. E. Peterson, *Daedalus*, Winter 1968, pp. 299–303, which contains a typological classification of American students according to the degree of their acceptance or rejection of American institutions. Hippies are classed with leftist activists. At the other extremity are placed fully adapted students, working exclusively to acquire a definite occupation (*vocationalist and professionalist*) then, successively, the "collegians" the "folkloric" students (*ritualists*), the future teachers (*academics*), and the "intellectuals."

115. As witness the night on the *Place de la Nation* (June 23, 1963) during which 150,000 "pals" unleashed their violence. The "revolutionary" interpretations of the yé-yé phenomenon (cf. S. Mareuil, "Les jeunes et le yé-yé, *Socialisme ou Barbarie*, April–June 1964) is to say the least incomplete. It is characteristic that almost all the yé-yé stars demonstrated their hostility toward the May movement. The movement accepted jazz; it rejected yé-yé.

116. Cf. W. Lewino, *l'Imagination au pouvoir*, p. 17, and especially the essay by Evelyne Sullerot in Ph. Labro, *Ce n'est qu'un début*, pp. 128–142.

117. In this connection, rector Antoine recalled on television on May 16 that in the United States the professors danced with their girl students. O. Burgelin gave a good summary of the social relationships between professors and students in France before May when he wrote that the university in France constitutes "a social system which the expression 'student power' describes by antiphrasis" (*Communications*, 12, 1968, p. 18).

118. *La Vie française*, November 21, 1963, quoted by Marc Kravetz, *les Temps Modernes*, February 1964, p. 1458.

119. Cf. below, Chapter VIII, pp. 480 ff.

120. Cf. R. Rossanda, *l'Anno degli studenti*, pp. 13–22.

121. There can be no question of discussing here the problem of economic returns on higher education. We shall simply note: (a) along with J.-C. Passeron, *op. cit.*, pp. 189–196, that in any case economic finality is only one of the social functions of higher education and that one would need to take into consideration other factors, beginning with the desire of a given fraction of the population to go on to higher education; and (b) that the calculations of returns can be radically wrong if based on a period of several years and even on one generation.

The mere fact that, through an increase of social mobility such as took place in the United States during the 19th century as a result of immigration, and during the 20th century in the USSR as a result of the revolution, this permitted "children of unskilled laborers" to go on to higher education, and also made it possible, even if they could not "profit" directly from their studies, for them to "become Einsteins."

122. Cf. above, p. 16.

123. Cf. for example, M. Heirich and S. Kaplan, "Yesterday's Discord" in S. M. Lipset and S. S. Wolin, *op. cit.*, pp. 10–35.

124. Cf. below, Chapter I, p. 140 (French edition only).

125. In the smaller French *facultés* full professors enjoyed a monopoly and an unshared authority, all the more so since the students had no possibility of choosing among several specialists on the same subject. The revolt took place in these universities *after* the events in Nanterre and in Paris, and it often assumed less radical forms. In the United States, generally speaking, the less interesting universities escaped the movement of revolt.

126. Cf. G. Antoine and J.-C. Passeron, *op. cit.*, p. 61 and p. 249.

127. The Berkeley campus had an enrollment in 1964 of 27,000 students, more than twice the number at Nanterre in 1967–1968.

128. With regard to the growth of the University population in France, we refer the English-language reader to the book by John Gretton, *Students and Workers*, London 1969, p. 41. Was May '68 "the revolt of the new social strata for whom the development of the 'affluent society' has meant access to university culture"? This interpretation, outlined by Michel Crozier (*Communications*, 12, 1968, p. 43), has been very closely analyzed and developed by Raymond Boudon in "La crise universitaire française. Essai de diagnostic sociologique," *Annales*, ESC, 1969, pp. 736–764.

Since 1965 especially, according to this analysis, French students are a "marginal group living in a state of postponed social integration and of inorganization." University entrance is no longer, as it was once, in correlation with an "anticipatory socialization." The question of outlets is primordial for the students from the middle and lower classes, while the students from well-to-do families feel that they are threatened with social regression.

If this interpretation is accepted, the student revolt would be no different, really, from the revolt of the small shopkeepers who are threatened by "rationalization of distribution." The phenomena M. Crozier and R. Boudon point out were certainly in the background of the French revolt. But can such an explanation account for the revolt at Berkeley?

129. The assertions made by P. Bourdieu and J.-C. Passeron on the determinant nature of the cultural heritage for success or failure in school, would need, however, some qualifications: cf. N. Bisseret, "L'enseignement inégalitaire et la contestation étudiante," *Communications*, 12, 1968, pp. 54–65. "La naissance et le diplôme. Les processus de sélection au cours des études universitaires," *Revue française de sociologie*, 1968, pp. 185–207. The immediate economic factor, and particularly remunerated work or, on the contrary, student availability, are at least as important: "When students of the lower classes are not doing remunerated work, they show . . . a higher rate of success than the students of the bourgeoisie." It is true, however, that they constitute only a very small group.

130. Cf. J.-C. Passeron in C. Antoine and J.-C. Passeron, *op. cit.*, p. 185.

131. Cf. J.-C. Passeron, *op. cit.*, p. 277.

132. There were rather serious incidents, however, in one of the most modern of the British institutions, the "London School of Economics"; cf. A. H. Halsey and S. Marks, "British Student Politics," *Daedalus*, Winter 1968, particularly pp. 126–132, and D. Adelstein, "Roots of the British Crisis," *Student Power*, pp. 59–81.

133. Cf. for example, *Libro bianco*, pp. 67–68. For Berkeley, statistics show a large participation of well-to-do graduate students in the revolt. Cf. G. Lyonns, in S. M. Lipset and S. S. Wolin, *op. cit.*, pp. 520–527.

134. "Berkeley in February" in M. V. Miller and S. Gilmore, *op. cit.*, p. 286. The author does not seem to have realized that in admitting the validity of this comparison, the lesson that can be drawn is social, not economic. A similar theme is

developed with an alarming luxury of arguments by John and Margaret Rowntree, in "Youth as a Class," *International Socialist Journal*, XXV, 1968.

135. *L'Ipotesi rivoluzionaria*, p. 179.

136. In France the FER has voluntarily used this langauge; cf. below, Chapter IV, p. 334 (French edition only).

137. Cf. below, Chapter IX, pp. 535 ff.

138. Cf. below, Chapter VIII, pp. 470–471.

139. D. Gautier, *Socialisme ou Barbarie*, March–May 1964, p. 61.

140. *Libro bianco*, p. 23.

141. Cf. below, Chapter I, pp. 108–110.

142. M. V. Miller and S. Gilmore, S. M. Lipset and S. S. Wolin, *op. cit.*, *passim*.

143. *Ecrits politiques*, p. 57.

144. The students in Naples replied to the students in Pisa: "The type of contradiction that the university student sees, need not be looked for in motives of an economic nature, but in his university life itself and in his general existence in society." (R. Rossanda, *l'Anno degli Studenti*, p. 71).

145. Quoted by M. Peterson, professor of sociology in Berkeley, in S. N. Lipset and S. S. Wolin, *op. cit.*, p. 369. This attitude likens the contesting students to Leninist volunteerism: "strike now, analyze later," and to the political behavior of the Third World.

146. M. V. Miller and S. Gilmore, *op. cit.*, p. 275.

147. *The Uses of the University*, Harvard, 1963; extracts and summaries followed by discussion, in S. M. Lipset and S. S. Wolin, *op. cit.*, pp. 5–26. H. Draper's pamphlet, "The Mind of Clark Kerr," which played an important role during the Berkeley revolt, appears in his book *The New Student Revolt*, and in the work of Lipset and Wolin.

148. C. Kerr, in M. V. Miller and S. Gilmore, *op. cit.*, p. 13.

149. Clark Kerr was a specialist in labor mediation.

150. C. Kerr in S. M. Lipset and S. S. Wolin, *op. cit.*, p. 45.

151. This was clearly understood by R. Aron, *la Révolution introuvable*, pp. 58–59, 63, 93, and is as true of *lycées* as of universities: "To distinguish, in each lycée, between four or five categories separated until the end of their days by diplomas obtained before they are thirty years old, means multiplying the tensions and injustices that are the sources of virulent conflict," p. 63.

152. *The Uses of the University*, p. 103.

153. S. S. Wolin and J. H. Schaar, in S. M. Lipset and S. S. Wolin, *op. cit.*, p. 361.

154. C. Trillin in M. V. Miller and S. Gilmore, *op. cit.*, pp. 257–258. For a similar viewpoint see R. Stith, "Contre la connaissance calculatrice," *Esprit*, August–September 1968.

155. Quoted by S. Stern, in M. V. Miller and S. Gilmore, *op. cit.*, pp. 232–233.

156. Cf. Michel Crozier, *le Phénomène bureaucratique*, Paris, 1963, pp. 94–100. The example studied is particularly characteristic of French bureaucratic absurdity since it concerns habituation to the principle of seniority. In an article that is in many ways prophetic (*Socialisme ou Barbarie*, December 1961–February 1962, pp. 17–42), D. Mothé showed the reactions of the "young working class generation," often just out of technical schools, whose entry into the factories meant sudden humiliation when they were faced with adults and the total uselessness of

their acquired knowledge. During the meeting between workers of the Renault auto plant and students on the night of May 16, the lower echelon jobs given to young workers was one of the major subjects discussed.

157. "At the same time that the University must become bureaucratized, implement mass production of cadres intended for specialized, fragmented work, comply with the imperatives of the demand for human material to man the offices and laboratories of modern enterprise, as well as the enterprises of the government, it must continue to train real scientists, real research workers, real thinkers" (Claude Martin, *Socialisme ou Barbarie*, March–May 1963, p. 48).

158. *L'évolution du travail ouvrier aux usines Renault*, Paris, CNRS, 1955.

159. See below, Chapter VIII.

160. Chapters II, III, VI, this volume.

161. More discerning, at least in retrospect, C. Arnavon wrote: "It was the last festive event: it had something of the sadness of a commemoration. Ever since the night of the 22nd when it was learned that the CGT was negotiating, when, in the crowd of demonstrators, I saw an adolescent in tears, writhing on the ground in hysterical pain, the Revolution was in fact lost; some said, betrayed." *Précis et Procès des humanités*, p. 45.

162. That day, at the *Faculté des Sciences*, Halle aux Vins, someone asked me by what technical means the apparatus of bourgeois government could be destroyed.

163. *Le Monde*, May 30th, 3d edition. G. Martinet devoted a long strategic analysis to the day of May 29th, *La Conquête des pouvoirs*, le Seuil, 1968, pp. 15–29, but he did not set it in the dynamics of the preceding days, and it is permissible to doubt that the meeting that took place "at the home of a Paris doctor" between J. Sauvageot, P. Mendès-France, leaders of the PSU, several union leaders, and himself, had the importance that he attached to it.

164. This is what D. Cohn-Bendit declared on television, for instance, on the evening of May 16.

165. This is the operation that Olivier Burgelin aptly termed "the Pompidou devaluation" (*Communications*, 12, 1968, p. 33).

166. Jean Daniel, *le Nouvel Observateur*, May 15 (published the 22nd). It is not certain, however, that this scene took place in a large amphitheatre.

167. A. Guedj, "La crise de mai à la *Faculté des Lettres* de Besançon," *La Pensée*, August–October 1968, p. 12. This account may be compared to the comment of a Turin student, "How nice it is in the University without the professors!" (R. Rossanda, *op. cit.*, p. 88).

168. The three authors of *La Brèche* understood this very well.

169. The night of the barricades was immediately compared to the Commune.

170. In the main amphitheatre, it was decided during the night that the Sorbonne would constitute a "revolutionary headquarters." Someone shouted "Smolny!" Cf. the very vivid account of an English militant: *Paris, May 1968*, Solidarity Pamphlet, No. 30, Bromley, 1968, pp. 15–21.

171. See the article of the Paris correspondent of *The Observer*, May 19th; see also, similarly oriented, A. Kriegel, *les Communistes français*, le Seuil, 1968, pp. 243–244.

172. Interview in *le Nouvel Observateur* May 20th and *la Révolte étudiante*, p. 88.

173. Of a political, not of a qualitative, change. On the political line fol-

lowed by the leaders of the CGT, see M. Johan, "La CGT et le Mouvement de mai," *les Temps Modernes*, August–September, 1968. One can also glean a certain amount from the book by Ph. Bauchard and M. Bruzek, *le Syndicalisme à l'épreuve*, and still more from the book by L. Rioux and N. Backmann. But a complete study will only be possible after much detailed investigation in working class surroundings. This work has now begun, two years after the strike. See the bibliography at the end of this volume. The official viewpoint of the Confederation is presented in the special number (799-800-801, May 16–June 30, 1968) of *le Peuple*.

174. *La révolution trahie de 1968*, p. 35.

175. *Le Peuple*, special issue, p. 41.

176. The CGT organized its own demonstrations on May 24.

177. Cf. below, p. 427.

178. Jacques Perret, for instance, whose book gives the sincere account of a conservative witness, reproaches the students for not having listened to R. Garaudy's insistence on the need for caution. . . . Garaudy was one of the rare Communist leaders who was "comprehensive" with regard to the student movement (*Inquiète Sorbonne*, 1968, p. 8).

179. Even the *22 mars* movement, however fundamentally antibureaucratic it would have liked to be, did not escape this danger. The *Tribune du 22 mars*, in its June 18th issue, denounced a "dangerous militant clique," composed especially of members of "the naturally repressive faculty," "Machiavellian Leninists," who are accused of confiscating the news media; cf. *Ce n'est qu'un début, continuons le combat*, pp. 54–57.

180. Cf. *le Figaro*, May 29 and June 10, and *la Révolution introuvable*, p. 29.

181. We may doubt, for instance, that C. Arnavon, professor at Nanterre, greatly impressed the CGT representative when he explained to him that his pay was "certainly less than the earnings of a young doctor without hospital degrees who had just started to practice in the Paris suburbs." *Précis et procès des humanités*, p. 50.

182. The only important event (except for the retaking of the Sorbonne) that took place on a Sunday was the skirmish between Jews and Arabs in the Belleville quarter of Paris on June 2, 1968. It would be a mistake to believe that this respect for Sunday is a very old institution. One of the largest post-World War I demonstrations, the one that followed the acquittal of Jaurès' assassin, took place on Sunday, April 6, 1919. The same was true, in a politically different context, of the day of the "barricades" in Algiers, January 24, 1960.

183. Daniel Cohn-Bendit was very clever at exploiting the yellow press for the uses of the movement; cf. Michèle Manceaux's account, in Ph. Labro, *Ce n'est qu'un début*, pp. 24–37.

184. Cf. the above-mentioned analysis, Note 116.

185. G. Lanteri-Laura and M. Tardy, *art. cit. Communications*, 12, 1968, pp. 124 and 125.

186. The physical terrorism with regard to students who opposed the movement was unbelievably limited, and certainly less prevalent during May than before and after May. At the date of this writing the repression that followed the movement had amounted, all in all, to condemnation of three Sorbonne "Katangans" who had brutally interrogated a Gaullist medical student: *le Monde*, October 8, 1968.

187. Letter to *Le Nouvel Observateur*, May 15–21.

188. Cf. below, Chapter V, pp. 343 ff.

189. One night at the Sorbonne I heard the following melancholy remark during a discussion of student security problems: "You must understand that there is no such thing as a popular police."

190. For instance, a meeting on the Palestinian problem on May 15 at the *Mutualité*.

191. After examination of a certain number of leaflets, this was also the conclusion reached by the sociologist Noëlle Bisseret, in *Communications* 12, 1968, pp. 57–58. There appears in Chapter VII of this volume, p. 435, a feminist leaflet, to which there is little to be added except the themes of the "We're on our way" Committee (*Quelle université, quelle société?*), pp. 147–149, which seek to transcend classical feminism.

As regards the movement itself, the facts are complex—so complex in fact that two vary close observers have written respectively: "The May revolt was essentially a masculine affair" (John Gretton, *Students and Workers,* p. 269); the other, "The student movement was extraordinarily feminine" (Paul Rozenberg, *Vivere in Maggio,* Turin, 1969, p. 135). It is not enough to say that the first statement is in general more true of women workers or employees than of students. An amazing example of the way the mass media co-opted, in their fashion, the sensibilities of bourgeois women appeared in the June 17 issue of ELLE (a women's weekly for the middle and upper bourgeoisie). The editorial, by Hélène Gordon-Lazareff, wife of the most powerful press magnate in France, explained that the editors too had looked deep into their hearts and had decided to set up a dialogue with their readers that would be "more intimate and more fruitful"; that they could no longer be content to publish cooking recipes and fashions; and that "nothing would ever be quite the same as before."

There is a feature story, told sympathetically, on the Sorbonne day-nursery. Another story begins "Beneath the balcony where Albertine, aged 5 months, lay sleeping, a revolution broke out." The author continues, "The day of the barricades, I'll admit I thought to myself 'why don't I give them my baby carriage?' It's a bourgeois English landau, if there ever was one, which was what I had wanted. . . . A perfect symbol, then, of renunciation of the famous consumer society everybody talks about. Later, I would have said to Albertine-Colombe, 'Your carriage? I gave it to the students for their barricades.' "

Another woman editor was quoted in the editorial as having "followed the Latin Quarter nightmare from her window with her children and her terrified cat." One article speaks of the movement in the hospitals. Finally, everything is set straight again by an interview with the only woman in the Pompidou government, Mlle Dienesh. The lead article, before the editorial, is in fact devoted not to the crisis but to Ethel Kennedy's dramatic situation. One should perhaps add that this issue was put on sale *after* the end of the crisis, and that neither the preceding issue (dated May 20) nor the following one (dated June 24) made the slightest allusion to it.

192. Cf. below, Chapter VII, p. 425. The presence of millenarian thinking in the movement would be a subject for considerable research. The theme of the radical overthrow of the world social order has an entire history which has been studied, for example, by Norman Cohn, in *The Pursuit of the Millennium,* Martin Secker and Warburg, London, 1957. The idea of an "upside down" world is a commonplace of certain Third World religious movements, and a comparison of the May movement with these "religions of salvation" might be suggestive. Another comparison was outlined by Paul Rozenberg, with 17th Century English Puritanism, *Vivere in Maggio,* pp. 134–135.

193. I quote one of the participants in the discussion published in *Communications* 12, 1968, pp. 161–162.

194. A teacher and a student, working in a "coequal commission"!

195. Except when indicated, the texts presented are uncut. Only outdated or useless material indications have been omitted (addresses, postal-order numbers, etc.).

I

Premonitory Symptoms

Ideological Prelude

Nothing is more equivocal than the idea of premonitory symptoms, especially in ideological matters. As we pointed out in the introduction, the events that preceded the May movement were postulated in the universities of the entire world: in Turin and in Warsaw, in Berlin and in Berkeley, in Dublin as well as in Peking (the Peking of the "hundred flowers," 1956, or the Peking of the "cultural revolution," as understood—very imperfectly—in Paris).

We shall limit ourselves to two documents by way of introduction to this volume. The first is the manifesto that the review *Socialisme ou Barbarie* carried on its cover from 1962 until the end. This manifesto summarizes the radical critical action undertaken in 1949 by a group of Trotskyist dissidents who impartially analyzed the bureaucratic society of Eastern Europe or China, as well as Western, capitalist society, with as much emphasis on the opposition between leaders and executants as between exploiters and exploited. At Nanterre many of the sociology students were well grounded in the articles that appeared in this review.[1] In addition, in Strasburg, during the 1966–1967 academic year, a first "scandal" had already broken out. A small group of militants close to the "situationists"[2] had seized control of the *"Association fédérative générale des étudiants de Strasbourg"* (AFGES) and had taken advantage of their strong position to "destroy" the student movement, which they considered to be participating in bourgeois-bureaucratic society. They reemerged in May as organizers of the student council, modeled on the workers' councils. In the pamphlet they published in November 1966, we note the same derisive tone with regard to the student movement that was to be heard again in May 1968.

They too started with radical criticism of the party's Bolshevik model:

"Theoretical and practical denunciation of every form of
Stalinism should be the basic commonplace of all future

revolutionary organizations. It is evident that in France, for instance, where economic backwardness keeps people from being conscious of the general slump, rebirth of the revolutionary movement cannot take place otherwise than on the ruins of Stalinism. Destruction of Stalinism must become the *Delenda Carthago* of the last[3] prehistoric revolution."

Prehistory itself will have to break for all time with its own pre-history and derive its poetic impulse from the future. The "resurrected Bolsheviks" who are taking part in the farce of "militancy" in the vari-ous leftist[4] "groupuscules" are relics of the past, and in no way do they offer a preview of what the future will hold.

Document 1

One hundred and fifty years of "progress" and "democracy" have proved that no matter what reforms are applied to the capitalist sys-tem they will not change the real situation of the worker. Improvement of his purchasing power, which has been achieved through unceasing struggle, is compensated by continually increasing needs, and above all it is dearly paid for by constantly accelerated and intensified work, by transformation of workers and office personnel into automata. The political and other rights obtained by the workers have not altered the fact that society continues to be dominated by a privileged class of capitalists and upper-echelon bureaucrats, who run it in their own in-terests.

The irremovable bureaucracies that head the reformist parties and labor unions are part of the establishment, and they make use of the workers' struggle to carve out for themselves a place in its man-agement. The "Communist" bureaucracy wants to use the workers' struggle to set up a Russian-type regime, misleadingly called "so-cialist," in which the men who run the government and the economy replace the heads of private enterprise, while the real situation of the worker remains unchanged.

The workers will not be free of oppression and exploitation until their struggles have resulted in setting up a *really socialistic* society, in which *workers' councils* will have all the power, and both production and economic planning will be under *worker management.* The only road that will lead to a socialist society, is the *conscious, autonomous action of the working masses,* not a coup d'état by a bureaucratic, mili-tarized political party which sets up its own dictatorship.

To defend these ideas and give them wide circulation among the workers, a new revolutionary organization based on proletarian democracy is necessary. Its militants will no longer be mere executants in the service of an executive bureaucracy, but will themselves make decisions concerning the orientation and activity of the organization, in all its aspects. The organization will not aim to lead the working class, or force it to accept such leadership, but will be an implement of the workers' struggle.

These ideas, which have been expressed in *Socialisme ou Barbarie* since 1949, form the basis of the group *Socialisme ou Barbarie* in France. Groups basing their action on the same concepts exist in England (Solidarity), and in Italy (Unità Proletaria).

—Manifesto of *Socialisme ou Barbarie*, December 1961—February 1962.

Document 2

French Students Come to Everything Too Late

In their ideological existence French students come to everything too late. All the values and illusions that are the pride of their cloistered world are already doomed as untenable illusions which history has long ago made ridiculous.

Because they share a little of the University's crumbling prestige, students are still pleased to be students. Too late. The mechanical, specialized teaching they receive has fallen as abysmally low (in comparison with the former level of bourgeois general culture)* as their own intellectual level at the time they enter it, due to the single fact that the reality that dominates it all, the economic system, calls for mass production of untutored students incapable of thinking. Being unaware that the University has become institutionalized organization of ignorance, that "higher education" itself is disintegrating at the same tempo that mass production of professors progresses, and that *all* of these professors are morons, most of whom would set any high school student body into an uproar, students continue, therefore, to listen respectfully to their teachers, with the conscious determination to rid themselves of all spirit of criticism, the better to commune in the mystic illusion of having become "students," i.e., persons who are seriously occupied with acquiring *serious* knowledge in the hope that they will

* We do not mean the culture of the *Ecole normale supérieure* or of the "Sorboniqueurs," but that of the Encyclopaedists, or of Hegel.

be entrusted with ultimate truths. This is a menopause of the mind. Everything that is taking place today in school and faculty amphitheatres will be condemned in the future revolutionary society as just so much socially harmful *noise*. From now on, students make people laugh.

Students don't even realize that history is also changing their absurd, "cloistered" world. The famous "crisis of the University," which is a detail of the more general crisis of modern capitalism, remains the subject of a deaf men's dialogue between different specialists. It expresses quite simply the difficulties of belated adjustment by this special production sector to overall transformation of the production apparatus. The leftovers of the old ideology of the liberal bourgeois University become commonplaces as its social basis disappears. The University could consider that it was an autonomous power at the time of free-trade capitalism and liberal government, which left it a certain marginal freedom.

It was in fact closely dependent on the needs of this type of society which were: to give a privileged minority who were pursuing studies an adequate general culture before they joined the ranks of the ruling class, which they had hardly left. Hence the ridiculous position of certain nostalgic* professors, embittered at having lost their former function of watchdogs of future leaders for the much less honorable one of sheep dogs leading flocks of "white collar" workers, according to the planified needs of the economic system, along the path to their respective factories and offices. They are the ones who oppose their archaic ideas to technocratization of the University and continue imperturbedly to impart scraps of the culture called "general" to future specialists who won't know what to do with it.

More serious, and therefore more dangerous, are the modernists on the left and those in the UNEF led by the "ultras" of the FGEL, who demand "structural reform of the University," "re-introduction of the University into social and economic life," that is to say, its adaptation to the needs of modern capitalism. From having been the dispensers of "general culture" for the use of the ruling classes, the various *facultés* and schools, still draped in anachronistic prestige, have been turned into quick-breeding factories for lower and medium cadres. So far from protesting against this historical process that directly subordinates one of the last relatively autonomous sectors of social life to the demands of the mercantile system, our progressives protest against the

---

* Not daring to claim kinship with philistine liberalism, they invent references for themselves to the academic freedoms of the Middle Ages, which was the time of "non-freedom democracy."

delays and lapses that beset its realization. They are the champions of the future cybernetically run University, which is already apparent here and there. The mercantile system and its modern hirelings are the real enemy.[5]

> —Extract from the pamphlet *On student wretchedness considered in its economic, political, psychological, sexual, and particularly its intellectual aspects, and several means for remedying it*, Strasburg, AFGES, 1966, second edition, Situationist International, 1967.

International Models

Events taking place in other countries in 1967–1968 were undoubtedly an incitement to action: Régis Debray's trial during the summer of 1967, the capture (October 8, 1967) and assassination of Che Guevara, the Vietnamese offensive against Saigon obliging the American government to accept talks in Paris, which started on May 13, 1968!, Polish, German, Italian demonstrations, an attempt on the life of Rudi Dutschke (April 11, 1968), radical de-Stalinization in Prague, demonstrations by black Americans and the assassination of Martin Luther King, El Fatah activity on Israeli-occupied territory—there was not one of these events that did not have repercussions in France. But these repercussions were far from unanimous. Only the pro-Chinese and the group that published *Le Communiste* accepted the slogan in favor of destruction of Israel.[6] These same pro-Chinese indiscriminately condemned the Polish students and Gomulka and Moczar, whom they called "revisionist." Their interpretation of the German phenomenon was not the same as that of the JCR militants.[7] Castroism and Guevarism, for them, were "petty bourgeois" ideologies. Vietnam itself did not meet with unanimous approval. Three leading organizations were working among the students, using the slogan "N.L.F. will win": the *Comité Vietnam National,* the *Comités Vietnam de base* (pro-Chinese), the *Collectif intersyndical* (to which the UNEF belonged), and to these could be added the "Russell Tribunal" and the *"Milliard pour le Vietnam."* The relationships of these groups with the Communist Party (which had somewhat hardened its activity and created a "National Action Committee for the support and victory of the Vietnamese people"), went from mere tension to virulent hostility. Nor were relations between the CVN and the CVB (founded in 1966) any better. In short, "groupuscule" ideology and practice enjoyed a free rein on the subject of Vietnam,[8] and Vietnamese representatives were several times obliged to arbitrate between French groups. Vietnam and Guevara's call for "two, three Vietnams" designated the enemy as imperialism, applied an effectively daring moral code, and proposed a method for fighting— that is, guerilla warfare. But how is it possible to fight imperialism in an industrial society? This problem was posed during the Christmas holidays at the Cultural Congress·in Havana, but the subsequent seminar that was held in Rouen on April 26, 27, and 28, 1968, witnessed the confrontation between a majority which, since the Indochinese and Algerian wars, had acquired the habit of transposing its hopes onto the struggles of the Third World (the Arab defeats in June 1967 were, however, a terrible blow for these ideologies) and a minority, among whom were representatives of the Nanterre movement, which considered that henceforth the struggle should be carried on, by priority, in the developed countries.

Here, to start with, is the interpretation that the JCR gave of the February 21 demonstrations (this day being traditionally set aside by the students for anticolonialist activity) in honor of Vietnamese heroism. The criticism aimed at the *Comités Vietnam de base,* which were rivals of the *Comité Vietnam National,* to which the JCR belonged, is an unusually biting one.

Document 3

February 21—A Tribute to Vietnamese Heroism

Wednesday February 21, 1968. At 11:50 A.M. six CVN militants were nimbly maneuvering on the roofs of the Sorbonne. At precisely noon, the flags of the NLF and the DRV were waving in the breeze on the end of two lightning rods. But the action of the fire department, called in by the Rector, proved to be ineffectual; after the firemen had left, new flags replaced the old ones, and remained there all afternoon.

This was the opening volley of anti-imperialist day, on February 21, 1968.

The CVN had been making plans for this day for nearly a month. On this occasion, it decided to inaugurate a new kind of political demonstration, which no doubt would break with the routine of nonchalant processions to which the "great democratic worker organizations" had accustomed us. On their own initiative, the UNEF and the SNESup. called for a demonstration about 6:30 P.M. on the Boulevard St. Michel. This was not a matter of organizing one slipshod demonstration. The idea was to occupy the heart of the Latin Quarter for a good two hours in order to turn it into "Heroic Vietnam Quarter."

HEROIC VIETNAM QUARTER

All afternoon groups of militants walked up and down the Quarter distributing thousands of leaflets, the *Vietnam Courier,* and various pamphlets.

About 5 P.M., certain of these groups had a violent confrontation with an "Occident" commando.

At 6:15, the police held up traffic on the Place St. Michel, to allow the demonstration to start. To turn the Latin Quarter into "Heroic Vietnam Quarter" is not a simple operation, and requires thorough preparation. In addition to the 150 militants acting as marshals, who were particularly "well seasoned" since Berlin, the poster brigades fell into line here and there in the procession. Finally came the "special intervention groups," who were carrying "literature" and other display material, including two magnificent papier-mâché figures representing Lyndon Johnson.

By 6:30 P.M. there were several thousand demonstrators on the Place St. Michel. Some militants from the "intervention groups" climbed on the statue of St. Michael slaying the Dragon, on which they hung a figure of the United States President, one avenging finger pointing heavenward. Numerous NLF flags were held up in front of the fountain, while Johnson was being soaked with gasoline. At 6:35 P.M. the President of the United States burst into magnificent flames to the approval of all the onlookers. When he had been reduced to ashes the demonstration started up again to cries of "N.L.F. will win," "N.L.F. in Saigon. . . ." The procession marched back up the Boulevard St. Michel, while perfect order was maintained by its marshals. When it reached the Boulevard St. Germain, the demo stopped, holding up the traffic.

A militant speaker announced that the Boulevard St. Michel would henceforth be called "Heroic Vietnam Boulevard." While he was shouting his explanations into a loudspeaker, an immense banner started to unfurl above the heads of the marchers. Members of the "intervention groups," perched in trees, let the huge streamer slowly fall down until it reached the middle of the boulevard, while the demonstrators cheered. Written on it in red letters was: "Heroic Vietnam Boulevard." The crowd then sang the *Internationale* and started marching again while the poster-pasters covered the street signs, which would henceforth bear the name of "Heroic Vietnam Boulevard." The demonstration stopped when it reached the *Lycée St. Louis,* against the façade of which an "intervention group" set a ladder in order to hang an NLF flag from the principal's window. The *Lycée St. Louis* would henceforth be called the *"Lycée Nguyen Van-Troi,"* which was the name that now appeared over the entrance. The procession started up once more, then stopped in front of the Luxembourg where the slogan "N.L.F. will win" appeared in letters of fire. Finally it branched off towards the Senate, under the protection of a heavy police force. In order to cut short any tendencies to obstruct the street, the marshals quickened the pace to the rhythm of "Ho-Ho-Ho-Chi-Minh" and "Che-Che-Guevara," both imported from Berlin. We next turned into the Rue de Tournon headed for the Boulevard St. Germain. All along the way the poster-pasters had been covering the street signs with our imitation signs marked "Heroic Vietnam." They also pasted CVN posters proclaiming the recent Front victories on all the walls and billboards. When the demonstration reached the Place Maubert it was met by Comrade Boulte from the national board of the CVN, who said that the Paris American Embassy would follow (which did not necessarily mean that it would be the next target).

The dynamic, militant nature of this occupation of the Latin Quarter presented a contrast with the apathy of traditional demonstrations. The CVN, which had given proof of its influence on the masses on February 3 and 13, showed on the 21st that it knew how to adjust its political actions to the new demands of the present situation in Vietnam, which was marked by the general offensive of the Front and increased risks of escalation. Let us bet that it will be able to carry on and progress in this direction.

SECTARIANISM DOESN'T PAY

Today the pro-Chinese who head the *Comités Vietnam de base* are caught up in a process of sectarian degeneration that has unfavorable consequences for the CVB. For the leaders of the UJC(m-l) they are the only ones in Paris who are not "false friends of the Vietnamese people." This description is used for the CVN as well as for the Vietnam Intervention Center, headed by militants of the *"Parti communiste marxiste-léniniste,"* which is, however, the only pro-Chinese tendency that is "recognized" by Peking.

Needless to say, there was no question of organizing anything whatsoever with these "false friends." The result was that all attempts on the part of the CVN to carry out certain activities together met with stony dismissal by the leaders of the UJC(m-l). They refused to organize a single, central working group for February 21, preferring to let their own mad call for a demonstration on the Champs-Elysées stand until the last moment. But you don't have to be an experienced militant to know that the Champs-Elysées cannot be "held" with 1500 demonstrators. The Champs-Elysées is characterized by pavements that are as wide as avenues and an avenue that is as wide as a public square. The police there are particularly numerous and well equipped (the Elysée Palace, the National Assembly and the American Embassy all being nearby) and there is space for them to move about freely. A demonstration that has been forbidden can not take place on the Champs-Elysées unless there are tens of thousands of persons taking part. The NJC(m-l) leaders attributed all these arguments to the political cowardice of the "false friends of the Vietnamese people." For them there was no such thing as an insuperable "material" obstacle. It was not until February 18 that they began to get panicky and suddenly changed their course. After having announced for a month that, come hell or high water, they would demonstrate on the Champs-Elysées, they summoned their militants to numerous neighborhood meeting places, in order finally to converge in front of the South Vietnamese Embassy.

This change of target was an acknowledgment of the ever-adventurous, irresponsible nature of the first directive, which we had consistently opposed. If the seriousness of political leaders is judged by their capacity to set goals that correspond to the actual relationship between the forces confronting each other, then the UJC(m-l) leaders are completely cockeyed. The more sectarian they become, the more they overdo things, and they ended by being taken in by their own demagogy.

Adventurism and clandestinity were taking hold among their members, and a certain disappointment was felt by numerous pro-Chinese *comités de base* since the failure of the February 21 project. Because even though an NLF flag was actually flown from the balcony of the South Vietnamese Embassy, the subsequent attempt to demonstrate was especially pitiful. Being few in numbers, badly led and badly defended, the CVB militants were violently and rapidly dispersed by the police. Let us hope that they will have learned a lesson from previous activities and that they will express increasingly active opposition to the adventurist sectarianism of their ultra-leftist leadership.

FOR AN NLF VICTORY
AGAINST POLICE REPRESSION OF DEMONSTRATIONS
A UNITED FRONT OF ANTI-IMPERIALIST MILITANTS

—From *Avant-Garde Jeunesse,* Special No. 10-11, February–March 1968.

Both JCR and the "Marxist-Leninists" supported the Berlin demonstrations, but they interpreted them differently. For the former, they

had been carried out by a protest movement which at the same time
that it supported the struggle of the Vietnamese people was in itself
important, whereas for the latter, the student movement as such did
not exist, could only exist to the extent that it placed itself "at the service of the workers." This is evident on the one hand from the account
that appeared in the JCR paper, and on the other from the UJC(m-l)
leaflet calling for a demonstration in Paris on April 19, after the attempt on Rudi Dutschke's life.[9] "Create two, three Berlins, is the slogan" was what JCR wrote.[10]

Document 4

Berlin

30,000 With Red Flags

ROAD LOG

Friday, February 16, 9 p.m.

For more than an hour now our five packed Mercedes-Benz buses have
been traveling in a long convoy towards the Vosges mountains. Inside,
people are wondering and bets are being taken: will we or will we not
pass the frontier? That is the question. The latest news is that the
West Berlin Senate has forbidden the international demonstration. . . .
The Mayor, Klaus Schutz, has called for disbanding of SDS (Union of
Socialist Students). There are 3000 cops headed for Berlin as rein-
forcements. . . . The Chief of Police has reserved 4000 vacancies in
the central prison, located in the English Sector.

The risk of being held up at the frontier is serious, because the
West German government is much opposed to an international demonstration organized by the political groups that participated in the
Brussels Conference. Imagine! Thousands of "Communist agitators"
pouring in from every country towards West Berlin, the "showcase
city" in the heart of the Soviet Zone, the "frontline city" that is the
advance-guard of the Christian Occident; what a scandalous provocation! Thousands of Vietcong supporters mocking the American flag
just a few feet from the "wall," how shameful, what a dishonor for the
authorities! This must be stopped at all cost, was the leitmotiv of the
important West German papers during these first weeks of February.

So the future is uncertain. There will be a showdown. The demonstration looks as though it will be tough. But will we get to Berlin?

Saturday, February 17, 7:30 p.m.

Thank heaven, we got through! We have now crossed the three frontiers that barred our way to West Berlin, without much trouble. When we entered the GDR the *Vopos** held us up a bit, of course, long enough to register the new generation of leftists.

To make them go faster we gave them the complete concert of all our subversive songs, from the *Komintern Call* to the *Boudienny March*. This can be recommended; the effect was immediate. When we left, the Soviet non-coms felt obliged to give us the clenched fist salute! At 7 P.M. we drove into Berlin. In the streets militant groups, walking with an NLF flag, were distributing leaflets and making speeches to the bystanders. The Technical University, which is huge, was covered with flags; there were masses of people, signs, and streamers. The international meeting would take place here. On the stairs, in the halls wired for sound, hundreds of young people were milling about among the literature tables and the luggage. A group of SDS militants kept strict watch at the door of the big amphitheatre into which 3000 students had crowded, in an atmosphere that was like a Turkish bath. The meeting had been going on without interruption since 11 A.M. It was to last until 2 o'clock Sunday morning!

Special halls were set aside for the foreign delegations and the loudspeakers were giving simultaneous translations of what the speakers in the big amphitheatre were saying. In the hall reserved for the French-language delegations we found our fellow students from Strasburg, Metz, Colmar, and Besançon. . . . It was from this hall that the JCR delegation, with its 310 members, took part in the discussions.

The International Meeting

A few representatives of our organization were invited to go to the big hall to deliver the greetings of the JCR. In back of the platform there was a huge Vietnamese flag on which was written "Victory for the Vietnamese revolution; the duty of every revolutionary is to participate in the revolution." Speakers from every country took the floor. At the heart of the discussion were the struggle against U.S. imperialism and our own imperialisms in Western Europe. Discussion was lively—at times violent—punctuated by interruptions, disputes, and impassioned argument. But it was all intensely interesting for the reason that, with few exceptions, these young people represented the very life force of Europe's far-left-wing youth, the ones who in Italy, in Germany, in Belgium, Holland, Denmark, Austria, Spain, and France are actually

* *Volks-polizei:* people's police.

organizing the anti-imperialist and anti-capitalist struggle among large sections of their contemporaries; the ones who speak out and sometimes force a showdown!

There was thunderous applause when the president, Rudi Dutschke, leader of the Berlin sds, invited the jcr speaker to take the floor. Our comrade Alain Krivine described our experiences and made concrete proposals for coordinated action. He was interrupted several times by enthusiastic applause.

From the principal speeches we recall the following points: the commitment to develop mass opposition to renewal in 1969 of the Atlantic Pact, described as a treaty of aggression against the worker countries and the revolutionary movements of national and social liberation; the need to connect anti-imperialist action with action that questions the social policies of our own bourgeois groups *especially as regards professional training and jobs;* a demand for pan-European coordination of the planned anti-imperialist and anti-capitalist struggle; more or less accepted understanding of the limitations of the student and high school movements; and the consequent necessity for putting down roots among the young workers, whose advance-guard today is proving to be more and more recalcitrant to the influence of reformist leadership.

All of these points were amply and systematically treated in a long speech by our comrade Ernest Mandel,[11] who analyzed the process of radicalization that part of our young people are undergoing today, and stressed the decisive importance of this phenomenon for the successful outcome of the essential task of Marxist revolutionaries: which is to construct advance-guard worker parties, without which the proletarian struggle would not lead to a revolutionary showdown with the bourgeois system.

This speech was greeted with a real ovation during which the entire audience stood for several minutes shouting their slogans in rhythm.

Police Withdrawal

During the evening, an astonishing news item received enthusiastic applause: the Berlin administration had set aside the decision of the Senate and of the Burgomeister. The demonstration was legal! In spite of the hysterical campaign against the sds that had been launched by the Springer press; in spite of the categorical attitude of the authorities; in spite of threats of legal action and disbandment, the Berlin dignitaries had been obliged to back down at the last moment and retract when faced with a showdown. The fact is that with each passing day such a showdown proved to be less propitious for the police. When banning was threatened, the sds and the foreign organizations responded with increased efforts for mobilization. The actual organizing of the demonstration was done quite openly: thousands of young people, in different meetings, discussed in detail the best routes to follow, the objectives that should not be missed, and the attitude to be adopted when the police attacked. The success of these preparatory meetings disturbed the police, of course. On the other hand, the continual agitation against the ban kept up by the Berlin sds made it possible to score some points among the unions, the social-democratic party, and the "liberal" youth organizations. The I. G. Metal works, the I. G. Chemical works, and the wood workers' union publicly opposed the ban. In view of this precedent the left wing of the spd manifested considerable bad humor, and the Berlin Evangelical Church let it be known that it would open its places of worship to demonstrators pursued by the police! Then, on February 17, when the West Berlin authorities saw the endless convoy of demonstrators (36 buses and 70 private cars) waiting at the "check point," it became evident that if the ban was not lifted, by Sunday afternoon Berlin would be the scene of unusually violent riots. The city's bourgeois population preferred to circumscribe the damage. After disavowing both Mayor and Senate, it capitulated all down the line, and for consolation planned a huge counter-demonstration to take place the coming week.

Sunday, February 18

At 10 A.M. two comrades, Rudi Dutschke, leader of the Berlin sds, and Salvatore, from the national board, came to welcome the jcr delegation. Rudi Dutschke spoke at length on the need to coordinate our offensive campaigns internationally, on the importance in the present political and social situation of direct mass action, and on the role that could be played by a part of the more radicalized young intellectuals in making the masses consciously anti-capitalistic. As he spoke, the people who worked in the Youth Hostel came into the hall and were listening to "Rudi the Pest," as the German bourgeoisie called him. When our comrades left for the demonstration an old cleaning woman came to ask for his autograph! Without a moment's hesitation Dutschke wrote a veritable pamphlet on the conditions that surround domestic service, to the astonishment of the old woman, whom he had called "comrade"!

At 12:30 P.M. our procession, red flags in front, arrived in perfect order at the monument that commemorates the victims of Nazism. We were joined by other delegations and an sds leader made a short speech. After that the demonstration got under way, with Salvatore and Dutschke leading it. As we advanced the processions began to fall into line with thousands of young people arriving from all sides. Soon there were 25- or 30,000 of us. Hundreds of Vietnamese flags, together with dozens of red ones, were waving above the huge procession. SDS groups were carrying gigantic pictures of Guevara and Ho Chi Minh, but there were also—this was a pleasant surprise—pictures of Rosa Luxembourg, Karl Liebknecht, Lenin! We took up the German slogans ("zwei, drei Vietnam," "Johnson Mörder," "AMI's raus aus Vietnam,"* while the SDS marchers were shouting "FNL vaincra," "FNL à Saigon"!

From time to time the processions broke into a run to the rhythm of "Ho-Ho-Ho-Chi-Minh" or "Che-Che-Guevara." Our delegation walked in perfect order (one SDS leader asked if we had rehearsed!). Far behind us, the Italians of *Folce Martello* and the PSIUP[12] were singing *Bandiera Rossa*. We also noticed the young Socialist Guards' delegation from Belgium, many well-organized Danes, Austrians, Greeks, Dutch, Spanish, English, and even Turkish students!

In spite of the radio and press appeals urging the population to keep away from the "extremists," there were many Berliners massed on the sidewalks. One came up to us and said, "Since 1933, this is the first time you could see so many red flags on a Berlin street!"

Counter-demonstrators

Along the procession route, groups of NPD counter-demonstrators† were carrying anti-Communist posters. They soon regrouped and, when there were between two and three hundred of them, tried to break up our processions by grabbing our streamers and flags and burning them. The SDS gave orders not to respond to the provocateurs, since the cops were ready to seize upon the slightest incident to intervene. However, in passing, we could not resist snatching a magnificent American flag which was being insolently brandished by some young fascists whom we roughed up a bit. "Quickly done, well done": the procession was already far from the scene when the police arrived. To taunt them, the German crowd began to hammer out: "We-are-a-small-radical-minority,"[13] ("small radical minority" being the term used by the reactionary press to designate the SDS). Today, with 30,000, they could afford to use it themselves!

At 4:30 P.M., we arrived at the Opera, now called the "June 2, 1967 Platz," "because it is on this spot, on this date, that the Berlin

---

* "2, 3 Vietnam"; "Johnson assassin"; "U.S. out of Vietnam."
† Neo-Nazi party.

cops shot in cold blood an sds student." The demonstration ended in a big meeting. After a while the npd counter-demonstrators reappeared. They took down our banners, portraits and flags and waving their own, shouted: "The Commies are pigs" and "Get Dutschke out of West Berlin." Headed by an sds leader, we rushed at them, took away their signs and set up a double line of our marchers to isolate them from the meeting. A little while later the sds marshals took our places and we fell back into rank.

At 6 P.M. we were in our buses headed for France, half-dead but happy. The demonstration was a complete success, both because of its militant nature and because of its size. It is undoubtedly going to traumatize the bourgeois of this country, who thought it had got rid of the revolutionary virus for good and all. From the international standpoint it proved the dynamism of an entire series of youth organizations which are developing in spite of the actively hostile attitude of the official workers' movement that has refused to accept them.

It showed too that from now on these organizations constitute a force to be reckoned with. For if they pool their experiences, if they show that they are capable of learning from one another, if they succeed in coordinating their activities, they will be able to play a decisive role in mobilizing young people against the existing order, and make an important contribution, both inside and outside the traditional workers' movement, to the regrouping of a new revolutionary avant-garde.

The movement set up in Liège and in Brussels in 1967, is growing and bearing fruit.

The two days of February 17–18, 1968, in Berlin represent an important stage in its development. The member organizations of the Brussels Conference will have time, next summer in Cuba, once more to confront their different viewpoints and settle upon new objectives.

—Anne-Marie Lespinasse.
—From *Avant-Garde Jeunesse*, Special No. 10-11, February–March 1968.

Document 5

Germany, Italy, France

Students Support the People's Fight

IN WEST GERMANY

Thousands of students are in revolt against the dictatorship of the bourgeoisie, and against the collusion of the German bourgeoisie with

American imperialism. The bourgeois government is repressing this movement and will use any means at its disposal to do so. In view of the attempt on Rudi Dutschke's life, German students will not be intimidated, and in spite of the government's repressive machinery and Kiesinger's threats, they are retaliating in Berlin, Frankfurt, Hamburg, Cologne, and Munich. . . .

IN ITALY

Thousands of students are fighting against the machinery of bourgeois government. On April 13 tens of thousands of workers went on strike at the Fiat factory. Hundreds of students have come from all over Italy to support their struggle and take their places in the picket lines. They are confronting the repression aimed at the strikers, on the side of the workers.

IN FRANCE

The number of students taking part in the revolt is constantly increasing. At Nanterre there are more than 1200 students who refuse to accept the reactionary University system, which they also reject in the name of the workers by refusing to become the ideologists and agents of capitalist exploitation. They understand more and more clearly (a) that the principal victim of University oppression is the working class, and (b) that the consistent way to combat this is to begin today, not tomorrow, to participate in the struggles of the proletariat, which is the main, the dominant force for social transformation.

In fact, workers everywhere are opposing employer repression by justifiable violence. After the magnificent achievements of the Rhodiaceta workers in Lyons, the poor workers and peasants of Redon led a victorious and exemplary fight against their employers, who were forcing them to accept unemployment and starvation wages. Every time there was a strike they visited all the Redon factories to explain why they were fighting, and show their comrades the strength to be gained from unity. In this way they got them to join the fight.

Because they were united and determined, their demands were satisfied.[14]

The Redon workers explained to the students that it would be useful to their struggle if the workers in the region and also the entire population knew about and supported it, for this would strengthen their resolve. The students in Rennes did therefore publicize their struggle everywhere they went. They also (together with students from Creil, Beauvais, and Paris) joined with the workers when they clashed with bourgeois repression. These methods are identical with those used against convinced anti-imperialist militants.

The students revolt, the workers fight.

What the bourgeoisie fears is that the students might join the working class struggle. For nothing on earth does it want the students to give concrete support to the workers' cause, whether in the factory, in the unemployment offices, or in the streets . . . , it does not want them to give effective support to the workers' struggle.

LET'S SUPPORT THE REVOLT OF THE GERMAN STUDENTS
LET'S SUPPORT THE ITALIAN STUDENTS
BACK THE WORKERS!
LET'S DEVELOP IN FRANCE A WIDE MOVEMENT
OF SUPPORT FOR THE WORKERS' FIGHT!

Back the progressist German students who are
combating the special anti-worker laws.
Demonstration Friday at 6:30 P.M.
in the Latin Quarter
Nanterre Movement for Support
of the Workers' Struggle.
April 18, 1968

Generally speaking, the press gave a liberal-bourgeois interpretation of the Polish student demonstrations that took place in March 1968. The J CR made a determinedly leftist analysis of them, which was inspired by the pamphlet published in 1966 by Kuron and Modzelewski entitled *Open Letter to the Polish Communist Party*. On this point the CLER is in agreement with the JCR.

Document 6

The Struggle of the Polish Students

The October '56 Traditions

The October '56 traditions have remained very alive among young intellectuals. For twelve years they have been circulated and analyzed by semi-clandestine groups working among *lycée* and University students.

After 1956 the Polish organization of "red pioneers," copied from the Soviet model, was disbanded. Then Jacek Kuron founded a new organization of Socialist youth which undertook to educate the members politically; in fact, he was awarded an important decoration for this activity. The new pioneer organization was particularly dynamic in the *lycées*. At the same time—but having no connection—there existed the Michnik Club, called by the name of its principal instigator. This was a club composed of *lycée* students, which was tolerated during the period of liberalism when it was referred to as the "diaper" revisionists club. . . . The students who gathered about Kuron and Michnik were known for their open-mindedness and their nonconformist attitude. The tenor of their discussions, however, scandalized the permanent members of the official youth organizations. As members of both organizations, when the *lycée* students reached the University they quite naturally joined together to carry on their critical action.

They organized underground study groups in political economy, history, mathematics, physics, and psychology. Simultaneously they militated in the zms (Young Socialists' Union) in which Modzelewski and Kuron led a political discussion circle. The Modzelewski-Kuron group of young revolutionary intellectuals soon acquired considerable notoriety, and its members were known among the academic bureaucrats as the "paras," or "shock trouble makers." As the régime began to harden, it looked upon the activities of these discussion groups with increasing disquiet.

In 1964 the pioneers were disbanded, as were also the Michnik Club and the zms circle, led by Modzelewski. By the end of the year both Kuron and Modzelewski were expelled from the unified Polish workers' party for being the authors of a manuscript (seized by the police) in which is exposed for the first time their synthesized analysis of Polish society. This manuscript has the same title, *On Renewal of the Republic,* as a work that was published in the Sixteenth Century by a little known Polish author. The famous "open letter" that we are now circulating summarizes the principal analyses contained in this pamphlet.

After their arrest for anti-government activities, Kuron and Modzelewski were condemned to 3 years and 3½ years, respectively, in prison, at a trial which took place *in camera* while three hundred students and other intellectuals staged a demonstration in front of the Court House.

In view of the repressive measures applied, the activity of the discussion groups diminished. However, through a process of selection, their internal cohesion was consolidated, with the result that the political level and maturity of the groups were heightened.

In October 1966 a public meeting was organized in the History

Faculty to mark the anniversary of the 1956 revolution. Professor Kolakovski gave a bitter report on Gomulskyism, followed by several students who spoke in the same vein. Kolakovski was dropped from the Communist Party and seven students were expelled. Out of these seven, however, six were soon reinstated. The seventh, a history student named Michnik, was called before the disciplinary council.

Immediately after, a petition to the authorities was circulated in the form of a round-robin letter demanding, particularly, political freedom of speech and the lifting of disciplinary punishment for offenses of opinion. This petition was signed in April 1967 by more than a thousand students and professors of the Warsaw University.

This successful action was the first precursory sign of student ferment.

Kuron was freed in May 1967 and Modzelewski the following August. In the fall, student unrest broke out in Czechoslovakia and because the Prague events had a great impact on the Polish universities, the government closed the Czech cultural center.

THE MARCH '68 MOVEMENT

It was in this context that the incredible banning of a play by Mickiewicz occurred. The audience, among whom were many students, demonstrated after the last performance. Michnik and Szlafer were arrested and dropped from the University.

The first big demonstration, which took place on March 8th, was organized in protest against these new measures. As in 1956, the spearhead of the student movement was the Polytechnical school, which has the largest number of working class students. Already, before the first demonstrations, a wave of preventive arrests had sent the best known militants to prison. Six months after having been freed, Kuron and Modzelewski were once more back in their cells.

But the movement had spread well beyond anything its instigators had dreamed of and the students were magnificently well organized. At the Polytechnical school the strike accompanied by occupation, took place in excellent order, and the student marshals foiled all provocations. They prevented distribution of anti-socialist propaganda material and their leaflets and streamers proclaimed loudly the revolutionary solidarity of the striking students with the Polish working class and revolutionaries of all countries, beginning with the fighters in Vietnam.

An amusing incident, but one that was revealing of the extreme diversity of the provocations the students had to face, was the following: a small truck filled with cases of vodka of unknown origin was negligently abandoned in the Polytechnic courtyard. But the militia were not called in to carry off drunken students, the marshals having taken it upon themselves to destroy the bottles before their contents could destroy the movement!

In a few days the protest spread to the principal university cities throughout the country. The extreme brutality of the repression did not succeed in making the students give in. New leaders appeared and gained in authority as they fought. After each wave of arrests there were others ready to replace those who were arrested. Today the demands have been clearly stated. In every faculty the students have set up revolutionary committees and are preparing for further action.

ISOLATE THE STUDENT MOVEMENT?

On the very first days of the demonstration the bureaucracy tried to isolate the students. They did all in their power to set the entire working population against them. The press unloaded its usual cartloads of the type of slander that Stalinist newspapermen fabricate whenever there's a question of exciting the workers against the intellectuals. Those who were responsible for the campaign did not hesitate to make ample use of antisemitic arguments.

In the end however, to a large extent, the operation turned out to be a failure, for part of the population participated in the student demonstrations. Among the 1208 demonstrators indicted, only 367 were students. The other 841 persons were referred to as "hooligans"! Everything leads us to believe that many young workers and unemployed joined the students. It is known, moreover, that the population furnished supplies to the Polytechnic strikers, and that 30,000 zlotys were collected for them in the factories (particularly in Zeran).

The all-out action launched by the party machine should fool no one. In Poland, presence at big political meetings is obligatory. An order to stop work is decreed by the management, and the party activists "conduct" the staff to the meeting place.

Although the bureaucrats did not succeed in fomenting hostility among the workers against the students, and although in certain places the workers were even frankly favorable to their struggle, it remains nevertheless true that the student movement is isolated, insofar as, for the moment, it cannot count on the active support of a single social stratum.

Polish workers have lived through the experience of 1956 and its bitter aftermath. The result has been a certain scepticism. They are not prepared to take part in another battle at the end of which they would find themselves just where they were before.

Unless they have serious guarantees, they will not move. What kind of guarantees? In their *Open Letter* Modzelewski and Kuron answer this question: unlike what happened in 1956, the future revolutionary Left must prove itself capable of organizing an autonomous force and adopting a consistent plan of action.

The students realize that they must break out of their isolation. There are among them many sons of workers and white collar employees. They know from experience the situation of the workers and are in a position to make the demands that interest them. The extent of the repression has forced the student avant-garde to organize systematically. Their determination to break out of this isolation will prompt them to give first place to demands that concern the mass of the population. In Poland, as elsewhere, a new generation of militants is being formed as it fights. A new avant-garde is in the making, one that has rid itself of the illusions of 1956 and is resolved to see things through.

—From *Avant-Garde Jeunesse,* No. 12, May, 1968.[15]

French Models

In December at the Rhodiaceta factory (Lyons and Besançon), in January in Caen, in March in Redon, in April in Mulhouse, a type of "wildcat strikes" implicating the union leadership as well as the employers made its reappearance in the French worker movement. The most violent demonstrations, particularly the ones that took place in Caen and Redon, were organized by young workers, and the traditional Left was disconcerted by them. The effect on the student movement was, however, evident.[16] The "leftist 'groupuscules' " seized this additional opportunity to point out the deficiencies of the unions, as witness the account that appeared in the official JCR publication. The conclusion of the "Marxist-Leninists" is even more radical: *Students, mass uprising.* But did their vindication of Stalin, described as "a great proletarian revolutionary" (*Servir le peuple,* April–May 1968) give them the right to call for this mass uprising?

Document 7

Events in Caen

The SAVIEM is a branch of the *Régie Renault,* specialized in the manufacture of industrial vehicles. It employs 11,000 workers, who are divided among eight factories located in Blainville (trucks), Limoges (motors) and Annonay (buses). The Blainville factory (Caen) is the largest. It has 4800 employees, 70 percent of whom are skilled workmen. 15 percent are $P1$ and $P2$ professionals, and another 15 percent are employed on a monthly basis (cadres, master craftsmen, technicians). Skilled workers earn between 600 and 650 francs a month and professional workers (holders of a CAP degree) earn 720 francs a month.

Since June 1967 the working week has been reduced from 47.5 to 45 hours. This reduction was followed by a wage reduction of 6.5 percent. In 1967 the hourly wage increased 8 percent. So that the actual increase in real wages comes to 1.5 percent. But the cost of living has gone up 3 percent. In reality, therefore, the purchasing power of the workers has decreased by 1.5 percent. The management acknowledges this decrease but it refuses any general increase on the pretext that there would be no profits.

The SAVIEM produces today in 45 hours as many vehicles as it did in 1967 in 47.5 hours. The lowered wages that followed the reduction of working hours were accompanied by an increase in the required rate of work per hour. As usual, the management trims all the edges!

The SAVIEM-Blainville factory was opened recently and most of the workers have been hired recently, so they do not yet form a homogeneous group. This is all the more true since new employees are not recruited through reconversion of closed factories, but through an influx of peasant labor, which has been created by the flight from the farms. The SAVIEM workers have not got the political and organizational awareness that is characteristic of workers from the traditional working centers, and the rate of unionization is very low in this factory (6 percent). The CFDT is the dominant union represented.

THE SITUATION OF THE WORKERS AT THE SAVIEM

The management of SAVIEM has carefully set up a complex system with a view to perpetuating the spirit of resigned submission of this new class of workers; it has introduced a perfected hierarchic system in which the functions of a team leader, a shop steward, or a foreman begin by being repressive and disciplinary, not technical. A proof of this, for instance, is that the foreman who is responsible for body-building services, in charge of workers who hold CAP degrees, is a former confectioner! The system of advancement is based more on "loyalty to the firm" than on technical ability, with the result that an OS2 who is smart and who licks a few boots can soon become a foreman, without passing through the normal stages of $P1$, $P2$, and $P3$ (highly skilled worker).

A worker whose name is not suggested by his chief has no chance of promotion. The same is true of salary increases. If recommended by his team head or his foreman, for no reason but that they like his looks, certain workers get as much as two and three increases per year. Others, especially the union militants, are practically never raised individually. This can make a difference of 0.5 francs per hour—that is to say, 100 francs per month. "Divide and rule" is the motto of the bourgeoisie, inside as well as outside business.

Union freedoms are flouted at the SAVIEM where 17 employees' delegates (for 4800 workers) no more, are tolerated by the management. These delegates are allowed fifteen hours per month in which to discharge their functions, and their substitutes are not allowed any time at all for delegation activities. It is also forbidden to distribute leaflets inside the factory, and all posters or notices are subject to management censorship (which is illegal). Consequently, a poster against social security regulations was suppressed. Any sign that openly attacks the management or that calls for action is censored.

To top this structure, the managers of SAVIEM have set up a constant rotation of labor: simultaneously, men are being let off while the newspapers are publishing help wanted ads. This offers economic advantages: persons above a certain echelon are let off in order to take on new ones for lower pay. But above all, a climate of job insecurity is created, which encourages individuals to curry managerial favor.

UNPREPAREDNESS OF THE UNION LEADERS

The managers of SAVIEM thought that they had a long period of peaceful labor relations ahead of them. And yet there has been deep-rooted discontent. Since the first of the year tension has broken out in more or less wildcat forms, either by team or by shop. The ineffectiveness of these scattered movements and the need to broaden the fight were soon understood. An unlimited general strike was therefore decided upon, with the approval of the departmental union leaders. The latter saw in an unlimited strike an opportunity to regain control over disturbances that thus far had remained relatively spontaneous. There was no question of opposing the genuine desire to fight it out. They would therefore have to let things come to a head, then take over the leadership and profit by its quick and inevitable failure to explain the "adventurism" of such actions and the necessity for advancing by stages and increased pressures.

The union wiseacres have been saying for so long now that "the masses aren't ripe" that they have let themselves be convinced by the sound of their own complaints. When they launch into action simply for the sake of action, without knowing very well for what precise objectives or toward what goal, they become indignant and upset because these actions do not bring out many people. The valid tests, from their point of view, are the big nationwide movements. It is true that these have not succeeded in mobilizing many people: we could cite the CGT-CFDT action week, the CGT-CFDT postal strike in October, the CGT railway strike, the day of December 13, 1967—all of which were far from achieving the same results as on May 17.

Being sure of their line of argument, they are unable to take in the fact that these activities with no immediate prospects or plan for carrying them further, only wear out people's patience. And it is not because working class combativeness is no longer given full expression through these actions that we are to conclude that this combativeness does not exist. The union leaders have never even thought about this. They mistake their nets for the bottom of the sea, and when they pull them out practically empty they lament that "all the fish are dead!"

But the fish may have passed them by! Because you'd have to be blind not to see, notwithstanding the urgent calls left unanswered, all the local sporadic violent movements in different sectors that flare up everywhere. Le Mans, Mulhouse, and Nantes were not accidents, but very clear symptoms of a deep national movement which is diffuse and seeking its way.

In Caen the departmental unions had retained the impression made by December 13, when worker participation was particularly weak and the SAVIEM workers had not even come out. But the departmental leaders, blinded by this failure, thought the workers were incurably subnormal except for occasional displays of temper. However, the masses rose up ready for the fight, whereas the organizations were not ready.

THE STRIKE AT THE SAVIEM

On Tuesday, January 23, the SAVIEM strike was all-out, and the Jaeger and Sonormel factories declared an unlimited strike, based on their own demands.

On Wednesday, January 24 an impressive number of police were sent to Caen. The *gardes-mobiles* were stationed at the SAVIEM entrance in order to protect the "freedom to work." At 9 A.M. the strikers left in a procession for Caen. At the city limits the CRS charged, in reply to which the demonstrators armed themselves with sticks and stones. There was some violent fighting, with wounded on both sides, and the strikers broke through the cordon of CRS.

On Friday, at 6 P.M., 10,000 workers from all the factories in the Caen area held a mass meeting.

The union leaders were puzzled. On Tuesday they had believed they were heading some 1500 discontented workers, without either plans or prospects. Now they were confronted with a powerful, overall movement which they had neither foreseen nor prepared. What were they going to do with all those strikers? What action should they propose? This question was all the more difficult to solve since there was another surprise: not only had the union not foreseen the combative spirit of the workers, they had also failed to anticipate the repressive spirit of the government. In fact, most of them were still living back in the Fourth Republic. At that time it was enough to make a few noises in the street and the vibrations would overthrow the ministry. But since 1958 the Gaullist "strong government" has reorganized and added to all its services of repression: whether official or officious, parallel or convergent, the police mechanism is all set and ready, and the authorities do not hesitate to make use of it. One day the lessons this fact holds will have to be learned. But thus far the federation leaders, who are caught up in their reformist illusions, have not known how to adapt their methods of combat. Large mobilizations are only good for pressing negotiations that have floundered, and their goal should be resumption of negotiations.

Very quickly the meeting took on the aspect of decks being cleared for action and the workers booed the FEN representative when he called for a dignified, quiet march. Many young workers made public display of a wide variety of weapons: blackjacks, pea-shooters, lots of real arms! When the procession route was read out, with mention that it would pass in front of police headquarters, this gave reactions of satisfaction. Quite evidently the workers meant to show their animosity even to mere symbols of authority, and they were in no mood to let themselves be blackjacked.

As it happened, when they approached the headquarters building the union marshals were soon overrun. Replying to the tear gas bombs and hand grenades of the *gardes-mobiles* the demonstrators began to throw bolts, blocks of cement and marble, then paving stones. When the fighting was at its height, Molotov cocktails (on the Detroit model) began to explode. The "riot" lasted until midnight, and when it broke up the workers had not left a single window pane in any of the buildings that symbolized their exploitation (chamber of commerce, banks, police headquarters . .. .).

ISOLATION OF THE SAVIEM

On Monday January 29, the entrance to the factory was occupied by *gardes-mobiles,* and picketing was forbidden. As a result, contact between the great majority of the strikers and their delegates was broken off. No information system having been planned, many had to depend for news on the press and the radio, which announced that work had been resumed. Why this negligence? Because it was not until March 31, eight days after the strike began and eleven days after a decision was taken, that a strike committee was set up. The same was true with regard to organization of worker solidarity, which was undertaken much too late. The UD-CFDT, which was in the majority at the factory, refused to take up collections in order to be able to play an important role, when the time came, with their union strike fund.

But it was the refusal of all the unions together to generalize the movement that was most typical of the classical, old fashioned tradeunion strategy, the same that had given such lamentable results at the Dassault factory, at Rhôdia, etc. in St. Nazaire. The departmental and federal leaders considered the SAVIEM an abscess. On those levels it was felt that the strike should either fail or achieve its ends, but in any case it should be limited to the factory itself. A permanent representative of the CFDT explained to the workers at Sonormel that because of the strike at SAVIEM they should not expect any financial support from elsewhere. This was to avoid an unlimited strike—but one broke out nevertheless. At SAVIEM, when the strikers organized collecting teams, they were given precise instructions not to go outside the neighborhood and nearby villages. For collections outside the factory the departmental unions would take care of them—in order, of course, to prevent any practical jokers from sowing the seed of unlimited strike in factories that were still working. The workers' solidarity organization limited its action to belated collections and 24-hour strikes.

And yet it was clear that the movement would have to be taken outside SAVIEM where there was a concentration of several thousand *gardes-mobiles* and CRS troops. The only way to get rid of these, to extend the climate of tension, and in this way save the strike, was therefore to broaden the movement. Work stoppages of 24 hours were perfectly ineffectual. And of course long strikes can not be organized out of solidarity. Movements that started for reasons of solidarity would have to be based on demands that concerned their own sectors. But the union leaders, who were both surprised and disturbed by the rapid evolution of the struggle, had no intention of assuming responsibility for its generalization. Nothing was done, therefore, to really relieve the

SAVIEM's isolation either regionally or nationally (that is, among the other Renault-SAVIEM branches).

WAS THIS FAILURE?

So the SAVIEM workers returned to their jobs without having won anything and their failure underlined the seriousness of the social crisis of our time, which is becoming more and more acute.

There are two sorts of workers' victories. When a capitalist economy is expanding, when production is increasing and sales are good, employers can let the crumbs fall from their tables that will prevent labor agitation without in any way threatening the system. An example of this was the fourth week of annual leave, which was an old workers' demand and was "granted" without contest.

The events in Caen show that this is no longer possible today. French capitalism is in a state of crisis. Production is stagnating and competition is increasing. These are difficult times, and it is very hard to make any profit. So there is no longer any question of "bounty"! On the contrary, the capitalists started the anti-worker offensive we see today, which is an offensive on every front: unemployment, work rhythms, rising prices, curtailment of trade-union privileges, curtailment of worker gains (social security), etc. Not only is the bourgeoisie unable to grant partial advantages, it is even obliged to take back certain earlier concessions. Its margin of maneuver is now considerably reduced and the "carrot" of "prosperous capitalism" has now been openly replaced by the blackjack of "strong government." If working class agitation can no longer be subdued by a few vague gestures of generosity, it will have to be broken by repression commandos. In Caen there were 7000 *gardes-mobiles* and CRS, who had been sent from Rennes and Valenciennes to make a bloody demonstration of this principle. Today, the bourgeoisie is not going to satisfy worker demands unless it is threatened with total loss.

But although it was a failure, the SAVIEM strike did not constitute defeat for the Caen workers. A large section of the SAVIEM workers had lived through the agrarian crisis, had left the land for the factory, and this fact had placed them in the center of a new vise. French capitalism has not satisfied even the least demanding among the workers. Obliged to leave the farm, overexploited in the factory, these workers have finally become angry.

The backward sectors of the proletariat, who are characterized by their individualism, nonunionism, lack of fighting tradition and of class consciousness, do not feel concerned by the day-to-day union struggle. They only join the fight in periods of serious crisis.

Then, however, they recognize the role of the government. They know how to distinguish between the moderate police responses to a peasant demonstration and the relentless repression of a demonstration organized by workers. They come to realize that they belong to a class —the working class—which is a source of disquiet for both the authorities and the bourgeoisie. They have understood the necessity and the advantages of organization.

What a surprise at the SAVIEM when the transmission belt workers found themselves in the picket line with the "chronos" (time keepers) who ordinarily acted as their supervisors. When the police attacked, they were together, which put an end to divisions and hierarchy. Suddenly they all felt a sense of solidarity with one another, and they saw what can be accomplished collectively. Before the confrontation of Friday the 26th, many of them had retained the impression made by the peasant demonstration. Afterwards they knew the difference. Their entire viewpoint changed. "We hadn't had the experience of St. Nazaire," they said. "We've still got much to learn."

And this fact of understanding that there were things to be learned from the experience of St. Nazaire, was more than mere group consciousness, it was class consciousness. To the same degree there occurred an extension of unionization. But this was often precarious, because of the frequent shortcomings of the leadership. It became evident that 24-hour strikes have no effect, that today marshals must be prepared to accept confrontation in order to protect their demonstration from police attacks, and that they should not be afraid to generalize the conflict.

Herein lay the importance of the "events in Caen." This was said, thought, and took place in Caen, and not in St. Nazaire. For the first time, entirely new strata of workers came to take their places alongside the traditionally advanced sectors of the working class, partially assimilating their experiences, but also offering them new prospects. And when the class struggle recruits these new troops, the new blood of revolutions begins to circulate.

—Yves Lenormand, *Avant-Garde Jeunesse,* Special No. 10-11, February–March 1968.

Document 8

Students, Mass Uprising!

To serve the cause of the people is our platform. There are two paths open to students: (a) to become the faithful lackeys of capitalism, or

(b) to place oneself at the service of the workers, laborers, and poor peasants. We have chosen to take our place on the side of the people.

The employers and the government that serves them oppress the people, force them to live in misery. All their pretenses are useless, the facts are there: there are over a million unemployed; all the ones who've been laid off, unemployed young people, women obliged to stay at home even though money is short, peasants driven from the land by sharks. And protesting that they too "have difficulties," the employers say, "It's up to you, the people who have jobs; you should pay them. Look at your comrades who are out of work, you should accept sacrifices, lay-offs, shorter hours, starvation wages, faster work rhythms." To which the workers reply, "That's your business, not ours."

All exploiters are afraid of the people's wrath, they know what it costs, they remember the great battles of the past. This wrath is something they hear daily in the factories, in unemployment offices, they heard it in Le Mans, in Caen, in Lyons, in Redon, a few days ago in La Rochelle; their "brutal but stupid" CRS know how harsh it can be: as they say in Redon, they seek to suppress these struggles by every possible means; they will never succeed!

When workers are united in the fight, when the men who have jobs and those who haven't unite in the fight, when workers and poor peasants unite in the fight against a common enemy, employer pretenses can do nothing. The CRS can do nothing.

UNION IN COMBAT IS THE PEOPLE'S
FORCE AGAINST THEIR EXPLOITERS

This irresistible force is increasing, but there are great difficulties. Division is well organized; by specialists, in fact.

The University will furnish (a) engineers to "organize" the work, which means dictatorship in the factory; (b) psychologists specialized in "human relations"—that is, in factory spying (ask Citroën how it's done); (c) mathematicians to make correct, secret calculations and camouflage public statistics. Prefects, ministers, generals, thousands of bourgeois writers and journalists, will all come out of the University. It's a fine education that's used to oppress the people!

Of course exploitation is not the only thing you learn at the University. People make long speeches about science, culture, art, progress, but what they carefully forget to say to the students is that the employers are the ones who benefit from this famous progress and the workers the ones who pay for it.

Unfortunately for the bourgeoisie, the students realize this. All over France revolt is developing, and the Nanterre movement is the largest. Of course, things are not yet entirely clear; but the motivation of the large mass of the students is their refusal of bourgeois dictatorship and of the role it would like to make them play. This is why Nanterre is being attacked and slandered by all the bourgeois press. The students are called "anarchists," "leftists," and "good-for-nothings," but the academic authorities are congratulated when they eliminate workers' sons from the University by selection, and organize the élite to be at the service of the exploiters. And these are the authorities with whom the students are asked to establish a "dialogue"!

A University at the service of the people will be achieved by the workers, and it will be by working with them and with the peasants that the student revolt will evolve, that it will be able to assist in the transformation of society, that it will equip itself to criticize the class University. Those who think that they can break the spirit of the movement through smears and police repression are mistaken. All they are doing is to cement its unity.

The movement for support of the people's struggle is made up of all who are seeking concrete forms of support for the working class struggle; committees exist in the *facultés* and *lycées,* both in Paris and in the provinces.

There are countless forms. Just now the employers' offensive is unemployment. Isolating the workers is, however, particularly dangerous, which is why we want to help to achieve unity, the unity of a factory as a region, by publicizing the working conditions and the struggles of the different groups. We also want to give concrete help in bringing about a union of the jobless and those with jobs, help materially towards the success of worker action, through propaganda, collections, taking part in demonstrations. . . .

Our paper should serve to publicize the model struggles, to explain our work. Its pages are open to all workers who want to share their experiences or their difficulties with others. It is also open to all progressives who want to offer their services to the cause of the people.

Our principal objectives must be (a) to break the silence which favors the employers, and (b) to give practical assistance to the struggle of the workers.

Can we do this by ourselves? We can not. Only by accepting to serve under the leadership of the great working masses can we know the needs of their combat and try to respond to them; we must learn from them, they are our teachers.

A broad mass movement of students is developing which will analyze the practical aspects of the question of service to the workers.

This is what we want to say to the workers, this is what they ought to know.

They should tell us what is useful to their struggle, they should correct our mistakes, at the very gates of the factories.

It will not be easy, but we are certain that we are on the right road.

—Excerpt from *La Cause du Peuple,* No. 1, May 1, 1968.

Nanterre or the Incarnation

In October 1967 the school year started under all but disastrous conditions. This was the second year of application of the "Fouchet Reform" and some urgent technical problems had arisen, such as "equivalents" between the old and the new University systems (at times students risked losing an entire year for an oral exam), shortage of space, and teaching personnel: already the *faculté des Lettres* at Nanterre, which was built for under 10,000 students, at the beginning of its fourth year had nearly 12,000. One word and one fact dominated the school opening: the word was "selection," but the fact was not always what is meant by that word. The government had not yet decided to limit *faculté* entrance through an examination, and it had abandoned a plan of abrupt separation between the work required for the *licence* (which would have led to the first cycle of secondary school teaching) and that required for the *maitrise,* or Master's degree (which is directed towards the second cycle, higher education and research). As Bourdieu and Passeron showed,[17] the Ministry of National Education itself functioned as a huge machine for selecting and eliminating. In both "classic" and "modern" secondary education, selection took place at the end of the *5e* (at the age of 11 or 12), and often, for lack of a technical instruction equal in quality and in means to secondary school teaching, and accessible otherwise than through what amounted to competitive examinations, orientation boards were obliged to turn children of 14[18] out into the streets.

Generally speaking, the students did not see that far, but they were rightly aware of the fact that more than 70 percent of them were being eliminated through examinations.

Nanterre, which is a concrete nightmare in a nightmarish landscape (that of the shanty town) was where "everything" started, in *C* Building, where the philosophy, psychology, and sociology *facultés* are located. Why Nanterre, why psychologists, and why sociologists? This question has been raised countless times.[19] The problem of future employment, which is frequently mentioned, is only too real: there is no place in secondary instruction, for instance, for psychologists or sociologists. Psychology and sociology offer the students a model (often through the professors themselves) of an integrated society and (often, too, through a group of professors and assistants, occasionally the same ones) the weapons necessary for combatting both psychological repression (segregation by sex in the University dormitories, for instance) and social integration; the techniques of "group dynamics" and "nondirectivity," created by Moreno, Lewin, and Rogers, and made known at the Sorbonne by G. Lapassade, an essential critic of social oppression —the oppression of the hierarchies as distinct from economic oppression.

The *faculté des Lettres* in Nanterre, however, was not the most oppressive or the most tradition-bound *faculté* in France—rather the contrary. Its Dean, Pierre Grappin, a former resistant who escaped from a deportation train and who militated actively against the Algerian war, was a "liberal," but he was also a man who believed in "order" and showed himself as such, with a tendency to reserve the exercise of "academic freedoms" for the faculty. The teaching staff itself contained no more (rather, fewer) fools and conservatives than the average French *faculté*. Little by little, however, it was to be inevitably and dramatically taken to task because what the *"enragés"* demanded was to place the students "beyond the range of application of the laws of a society they were contesting" (Epistémon). Next to the *facultés* there are the University dormitories where, as in Antony, demonstrations broke out and continued to break out against sexual repression: the student houses were not under *faculté* supervision, although the Dean did have authority over them; the *faculté* was "liberal" and the student houses "Napoleonic." One day the student houses tried—in vain—to get the *faculté* to deprive especially over-excited students of certain privileges. The result was an explosive myth, concerning a "blacklist," which certain sociologists (e.g., Henri Lefebvre) helped to propagate.[20]

For the most part the Nanterre students, who were largely from the west end of Paris and generally came from private (Catholic) schools, were neither more nor less to the left than in the other *facultés*. But the action of the group of *"enragés,"* because it posed real problems in a utopian form and with methods that were often ambiguous and occasionally dangerous (one of which was the problem of the relationship between teacher and pupil, and of the finality of the social sciences), little by little was joined by a considerable[21] fraction of the

other students. Because of this, they created among their opponents a
professorial "bloc," consisting principally of titular professors in somewhat the same way that the action of the NLF made good liberals,
(who had been disciples of Camus) into "Algérie Française" desper-
adoes. The May revolution was just what was needed to restore a sense
of equality to relationships between students and professors, even if,
later, this atmosphere was to be spoiled by demagogy on both sides,
though particularly on the part of the professors.

In reply to the fundamental question: "Why sociologists?" here
is the rudiment of an answer which although it is in retrospect and
comes from a "veteran," is nonetheless significant.

Document 9

There Are Stupid Jobs

> "Important group specialized in execution of installation
> operations seeks for its Cultural Equipment Department
> sociologist-urbanist, either sex. Background: Sociology *licence,*
> *Hautes Etudes Commerciales,* or equivalent.
>
> "We can offer this young cadre an opportunity to become
> a specialist in cultural implantation matters and a career with
> a group whose activities are constantly expanding. We want a
> co-worker (man or woman) who is very dynamic, sensitive, and
> interested in human relations and teamwork, and having
> knowledge of and complete familiarity with investigation
> techniques."

I answered this advertisement in the *Figaro.* I am known as a
sociologist-urbanist. If I worked eight hours a day five days a week I
would earn 3000 F. a month. Actually, I earn more. I work ten hours
a day and more than five days a week, which is madness. I studied for
five years; first, two years of specialized tutoring, then, a philosophy
licence. For one year I worked towards the *agrégation,* but I gave that
up in order to preserve the little sanity I had left.

Finally I was hired as a sociologist by an architect who headed
an urban planning office. For one year I went there punctually every
morning. Or, to be exact, I studied, since I was given nothing to do.
Then I began to read all the magazines I came across. I ended by being
called a documentalist, for which, of course, the study of philosophy is

excellent preparation. In the end, seven years at the university, plus two as a documentalist, makes nine years of study.

When I left the architect I went to work for an engineer. There I began to do what is called sociology, social science. That is to say, investigations. I made up my own questionnaires, and got them filled in myself. House to house. Today, in France, the work of a sociologist is just that, house to house canvassing. You visit people, the way commercial travelers and preachers do. Unless, of course, you try for a job as head of personnel in a small factory. You'll have less work and some social cases to settle.

Get an employee whose salary hasn't been raised to be patient, give advice to another about his troubles with his wife, see that the Christmas tree party goes off well.

There are 200 sociologist-urbanists in France. No less. When revolutionary students say they don't want to be sociologist-urbanists because national planning is the worst kind of repression, they're right. The only thing is, that 99 percent of them haven't the slightest chance of reaching the upper echelons in the hierarchy of the defenders of the faith.

I forgot one possible opening, which is industrial sociology. For instance, you study the actual communications value of such and such advertising, 1600 francs a month at *Prouvost's** [22] to analyze the contents of an ad for a certain make of socks. If that interests you. . . . A sociologist's work is never used for what it is. Just now I'm doing investigations for an industrial group which wants to create cultural equipment for its workers and other employees. Obviously, such work as that, by virtue of its very finality, is participating in repression. Shut culture up between four walls, etc. But that's not the worst. In this instance, the sociological investigation consists in listing the cultural activities of a working class town. You have to note down those that exist and those that do not exist. My employers have already stated that those that do not exist correspond to what is needed. So they are already planning on giving operatic performances. Just anything at all. Or, rather, no: cultural activities that the bourgeois like. Sociologists are not even cops. They've got horns.

I don't say that my job interests me. I say that a sociologist-urbanist can fight inside his profession, on condition that he can use the same weapons as his employers. For instance, by choosing the questions and answers that are dangerous for the existing order. Exactly the way those who represent it do.

You know of course that the Sorbonne will soon be moved out to the Vallée de Chevreuse. In order to decide what to put in its place, there has been the semblance of a poll among the people involved. I heard with my own ears a high official and the director of a well-known public opinion institute agree to the following formulation of a question: "Would you like to see an administration building take the place of the Sorbonne?" The building in question is already designated. It will be a home for aging members of the CRS.

—Excerpt from *Action*, No. 2, May 13, 1968.

Although at Nanterre the UNEF is very slightly represented (about five hundred members out of eleven thousand students), it nevertheless succeeded in organizing a strike which, having started on November 17 in the sociology department, was almost total from Monday the 20th to Saturday the 25th of November. The strike made precise technical demands, which were given partial satisfaction. Student delegates were present at the faculty assembly on November 25 and certain adjustments were made in the matter of equivalents. However, this movement was violently criticized in terms of a utopian radicalism, which was very characteristic of the students, who were later called the *"enragés"* by a "group of student phantoms."

Document 10

The Model Nanterre Strike

Last week's strike was very characteristic of the students' preference for cinema and green cheese in place of the moon: it was very democratic, very effective, very new, intelligently carried out, and a real victory!

Abolition of Assiduity Checks

Let's not mention those who, not content with being good students want to oblige others to be like them, and are demanding assiduity checks, either right now or "when there'll be TP's at 25." In reality, this demand was *the only one for which we could get immediate satisfaction,* because it depended on the *fac* heads. But someone (who?) led us to believe that it concerned the departments, that it had some pedagogical importance (banish all frightful recollections of the *lycée*), whereas actually, it was a matter of a police administrative check: these checks are made to keep those who do not come to TP from passing exams, and frequently to influence decisions with regard to cancellation of scholarships. "Fight the phantom students?" They're certainly not the ones who disturb the work of the others, but they may be the ones who have the most fun.

Once the problem had been evaded, and disguised (by whom?), the strike ended without any guarantees on this point having been obtained! The same ones who struck in protest against the assiduity checks will answer "present" when the call comes, if it comes!

Justified Equivalents

The idea of justice or fairness would seem to be out of place. School justice for people who are already privileged is a joke. What was really interesting was to have to pass fewer examinations. Saturday's *fac* assembly ended in nothing but a few well-intentioned resolutions, transformed (by whom?) into a victory. And for very good reasons: (a) it had no power of decision, but was merely consultative and for information, (b) the equivalences were decided by ministerial decree, which leaves the *facs* practically no margin of freedom in their application.[23]

No More T.P., No More Books, a Full Swimming Pool

TP's at 25 is just what the government wants for training "the nation's elite," while the incompetents, the workers, the Jews, the Blacks, and the Asiatics will undergo super-specialized training in businesses to which they are bound by contract. These are, of course, matters that concern the society's global budget and do not come under the dean's or even the minister's authority. The entire question of domination by the ruling classes was up for re-examination! Fortunately the students, who are always in the advance-guard, carried off a great victory Saturday over the *fac* assembly. Baloney.

Against the Administration Blacklist, and Cops in the Fac[24]

Here again, we could do nothing about it directly except one thing: make it known. It is more and more evident that the *fac* administration and the *Cité-U.* administration work hand in hand with the police in order to retain moral and political control over the students. The latest example to date (27/11/67): the head of the *Cité* got the cleaning women to report the names of students who had had girls in their rooms at night. As for cops in the *fac* and on the campus, everybody has seen them, in spite of their legendary inconspicuousness.

A "Democratic" Strike

Apparently, because the TP delegates included UNEF militants and some who were "nonunion," that was considered democratic. But they were given very precise instructions: to get in touch with each other in order to circulate information, to print leaflets calling on all the students to strike, to make contact with the profs, the assistants and the administration to learn "the lay of the land," and to report to their constituents. Actually, even if we admit that the clowning that took place on Tuesday and Saturday entered into these instructions, they overstepped them at least three times:

1. By holding a second-degree election of a "coordinating committee" concerning which there had been no question in the TP. If such a committee had seemed useful or necessary, it should have been elected directly by the base and not on a secondary level. Note that this particular committee had not even been given any instructions whatsoever.[25]

2. By contacting Estier, an EGDS Deputy, whether this was making political use of the strike or not.[26]

3. By holding a press conference on Saturday. What shall we do about it?

This strike has been practically useless except that people "cut classes" for a week.

We should (but nobody will do it) refuse to answer when called on in TP.

We should (but nobody will do it) drive the cops off the campus.

We should (but nobody will do it), if the motion adopted Saturday is to be implemented (combat committees, information and discussion bulletins, youth demonstration),[27] see to it that the committees are not prematurely "coordinated" by one or several political organizations, and above all that the bulletins are open to all points of view.

Finally *we should* (but nobody will do this either) in case of a broad-based youth demonstration, if the demonstration is to be of any use, all learn karaté, and wear helmets and boots, so we won't look ridiculous in front of the police, or in comparison with Japanese students.

P.S. Don't turn the page, you have already read what's on the other side.

P.P.S. Had you noticed that the typing on this side is better than on the other?

Thank you for your attention.

—PSG (Phantom Student Group), late November, 1967.

Leaving Nanterre for the first time, we return to the Sorbonne where, shortly after the November strike, a few copies of a leaflet were distributed which, because of the color of the paper, is known as the "salmon leaflet." The committee that signed it, "the Sorbonne for students," was composed of militants who later, in March 1968, founded the *Mouvement d'action Universitaire*. Criticism of the titular professors was precisely the same that had been heard in Berlin, and which later triumphed in Nanterre. However, this theme met with little interest at the Sorbonne, and the MAU, which was unusually rich in ideas, did not take hold with the students. The passage on the "joy of learning" should be noted, as also the bit that appears to have been added *in extremis* on revolution as a prerequisite to the aforementioned joy.

Document 11

Why Professors?

The assistant ministers, Vedel and Zamansky,[28] the dear old Sorbonne professors, the diggers for odorless profits, all these spuriously renowned and actually commonplace persons who are continually wailing about one another, speak in unison when they utter the following cry of fake anguish:

WHAT'S TO BE DONE WITH THE STUDENTS?
WHAT'S TO BE DONE WITH THIS HORDE?

To hear them, one single creature is making the machine jump the track and that is the student, male or female. When multiplied, this person becomes a "social problem" for professors, one that is foreign to the habits and customs of the Institution.

Faced with point-blank refusal on the part of the student crowds, the "planners" prefer strict supervision over a mass of intellectual apprentices required for the capitalist economy, whose numbers are set by royal prerogative, and whose docility and degree of nonculture is also of their making.

But between the former and the latter the final attitude is the same. With or without the student masses, the hierarchy of knowledge, of administration, of University life is their common social justification, which is consistent with the role that the University plays in an authoritarian society.

There remains the fact that right away the *Alma Mater is desecrated*.

And how did you expect these worthy professors to break with their old mistress? To see her being ill treated like that fills them with the resentful anger of a castoff lover who assumes the role of legal mate, frustrated of his rights. From there to appealing to Government and Justice for protection against these trouble makers, is but a step. The old argument in favor of authority is already being brandished by the learned doctors who believe that they are all-powerful, the same ones who, not so long ago, under the lay Republic, wanted to make their University into a refuge for liberalism and tolerance. But it so happens that, today, students are neither at liberty nor tolerable.

The events of November 9 furnish absolute proof of this, if any more were needed. While in the streets the students were formally inaugurating the new academic year, staid professors and second-rate technocrats were vainly trying to parody goodness-knows-what ceremony of order and merit, under the protection of the very persons who a short while previously they had prided themselves on not allowing to enter the sacred enclosure.[29]

This situation requires measures that are both unequivocal and decisive.

The student union demands that we be properly taught and, to begin with, by young, freshly qualified teachers, who know how to look at our female counterparts. This demand is acceptable if its exact application is explained. Yes, we certainly do want researchers with whom we can talk; yes, we want faculty members whose own unfinished training is a guarantee of controversial, critical analysis. In short, we want thousands of assistants who will have the formidable task of, themselves, being assisted by their students.

BUT WE SOLEMNLY DECLARE THAT THE FEWER PROFESSORS THERE ARE THE GREATER WILL BE THE FREEDOM OF MUTUAL EDUCATION FOR THE ONLY HEALTHY MEMBERS OF THE UNIVERSITY.

No more dusty lectures, no more Bergsonesque mumblings, no more exams for trained monkeys, no more professorial repression. *This is the only prospect that can guarantee us the slightest joy in learning.**

* *Realization of these goals will obviously not be possible without a revolution.*

—*"La Sorbonne aux Etudiants"* Committee, Leaflet No. 1, November 20, 1967.

January 8 was marked by the explosion of the Cohn-Bendit-Missoffe incident.[30] The *"enragés"* had prepared for the minister's visit by announcing that the swimming pool he was to inaugurate would be the scene of "orgies." Actually, Cohn-Bendit challenged him with: "Your *White Book on Young People* doesn't say a word about the problem of sex!" For reply the minister pointed to the pool, which in fact is not open to residents of Nanterre if they are enrolled elsewhere, and which, he said, was intended to solve problems of this type.

Hitlerian rhetoric, came the answer. Its author, threatened with expulsion, was temporarily spared. On January 26 photographs of plainclothesmen walking about the *Faculté* buildings were posted for all to see; administrative personnel were roughly handled; Dean Grappin, who felt insulted and under threat, called the police, but the latter were thrown out by a group of students. In the wake of all these incidents the faculty agreed to set up a "professor-student liaison committee" (the first meeting took place on February 16), whose role was merely one of mutual information. Although the UNEF publication *Nanterre-Information* denounced the myth of coequality, the UNEF and the SNESup. ended by accepting the principle of mixed committees.

Document 12

The Myth of Coequality

One of the demands of the strike committee during the November strike in Nanterre was that coequal committees should be set up on a departmental basis. This proposal emanated above all from nonunionists or from members of recent date, and it made the mistake of ignoring both the ideological and political contexts of coequality, as well as the demobilizing intentions of the faculty administration. Since then, this same administration has practically forbidden several meetings planned by the AFGEN by refusing to permit use of the amphitheatres that had been requested by the federation. The sum total of these facts appears to us to justify the present position taken by the AFGEN—withdrawal from all coequal commissions, whether they involve the entire faculty or simply one department—to begin with, all the experience of both worker and student unionism accumulated during these last years in matters of coequality.

THE IDEOLOGICAL AND POLITICAL CONTEXT OF COEQUALITY
Coequality is an integral part of the neo-capitalist ideology
The fact is that the concept of coequality was first developed in the United States. Coequality applied to industrial relations would mean "transcending traditional contradictions and antagonisms between capital and labor," or at least it would be a "means of maintaining them within an institutional framework in order to domesticate them, to see that there is always a settlement, and that nothing ever explodes" (Bloch-Laîné in *l'Economie concertée*). The coequality ideology cor-

responds to the organizational phase of capitalism, during which the ruling class makes a bid for working class cooperation by integrating to a maximum degree into its own constitutional system types of organization that are suited to the workers. On the union side, this coequal concept was reflected in the ideas of the International Confederation of Free Labor Unions, which in the fifties insisted on the urgent need "to look for necessary and possible points of convergence with employers." As a matter of fact, this concept of the union role ends by both weakening it and depriving it of all combativity, as is shown by the way coequal management usually works.

Outline of the way coequal management works
To work well, coequality assumes mutual respect for the basic data that are supposed to be the rules of the game. Generally this results in accepting as basic data, the original fundaments of the system (as, for instance, a certain concept of the University, defined in terms of legislation) and within this framework, a period of close discussion during which each side tries to obtain the best possible compromise. Generally the incumbent authority uses technical and financial arguments to justify its point of view and the community comes back either with changes that are unimportant, since they must remain within a fixed budget, or a previously set up financial or material technique, or with a moral ideology that lacks technical support and, when all is said and done, is a concession to the technical demonstration of the authorities.

IN ANY CASE COEQUALITY IMPLIES ACCEPTANCE
OF A POLICY OF MERE IMPROVEMENTS ON THE
PART OF THE UNION ORGANIZATION
So, when it works, the coequal structure means domination of one of the partners, the incumbent authority, over the other. Or if, because they are momentarily in a position of strength (as, for instance, during a mass action) the union delegates stubbornly refuse to accept the conditions of the incumbent authority, then we have paralysis of the structure, which becomes ineffectual. Coequal functioning offers the union organization the alternatives of either being defeated or paralyzed.

MOREOVER, A COEQUAL STRUCTURE
IS A CO-OPTED STRUCTURE SINCE
THERE EXISTS AN EXPLICIT CONTRACT
In the long run, coequality assumes that, on a more or less long-term basis, the fundamental interests of the two contracting parties are

reconcilable. However, this is not the case, either with the working class and the employers, or with the present authorities and the student population, in the present context of higher educational reform, which aims at elimination through failure, at social selection, and at subordination of the number of students passed in accordance with the levels of qualification to the immediate needs for skilled technicians (IUT) and middle cadres (DUES, DUEL, *licence*) of the neo-capitalist economy. Government-student coequality is not viable, but constitutes an illusion and a danger for the union organization.

THE PRESENT GOVERNMENT POLICY
WITH REGARD TO COEQUALITY—
AND ITS INCIDENCE IN NANTERRE

At certain periods the authorities, rather than accept coequality and the concessions it implies, have preferred to make decisions alone, confident that they were strong enough to risk a showdown with the working class. The Gaullist régime is one of these periods. For the last ten years it has liquidated the existing coequal organizations—in education, the *Conseil supérieur,* the CNOOSSU,[31] etc.—and tried to keep the upper hand in all important decisions, as, for instance, government seizure of the Social Security Administration. Being a technocratic government serving capitalist construction, the Gaullist government cannot share the power with union organizations and, consequently, it rejects coequality. Better still, it makes its decisions in secret, legislates by enactment, and makes it a rule to place union and political organizations before accomplished facts.

Considering these conditions, two remarks that are important for the union and especially for the AFGEN in Nanterre must be made:

1. Any offer of coequality made by a representative of the authorities is in point of fact, at the present juncture of events, an attempt at ideological co-option, at transforming the union into a corporative body in order to insure the failure of a broadly based membership drive. The tenor of the proposals made by the dean to the federal office confirms this point. The fact is, that in the minds of the Nanterre authorities, the departmental commissions were to be merely "liaison commissions" with no consultative vote and no real power of decision. The coordinating committee that was supposed to be over them, in the overall faculty plan, would not have any real power, either; and neither the assistant teachers nor the assistants would be represented on it. The AFGEN delegates, being in the minority, would therefore be

obliged, through their participation, to sponsor decisions, demands, and resolutions which they in no way approved of.

2. As for the departmental commissions, the principal argument of the University administration consists in dangling before our eyes the possibility of their settling certain matters concerning the department. But we do not think that in order to change the time of a study group, or decide on the syllabus of a partial examination, it should be necessary to call a coequal commission meeting. We believe that the students are sufficiently responsible to send a delegate to the department head, or to the professor concerned, and that the professors are sufficiently enlightened to give positive replies to the student proposals.

CONSEQUENTLY, THE AFGEN HAS REFUSED
TO TAKE PART IN THE COMMISSIONS THAT THE
UNIVERSITY ADMINISTRATION WANTED TO SET UP

On the other hand, it suggests the setting up of student-professor working commissions to be convened by the student union, and that in correlation with these commissions consultations be held on each branch of study. In this way pro-forma charters can be drawn up covering the demands of each department, and lecture hall committees that include both union and nonunion members can be organized to defend their mutual interests as students.

TAKE PART IN THE BRANCH CONSULTATIONS.
CONTACT THE LECTURE HALL COMMITTEES.
UNION OR NONUNION MEMBERS, DEFEND
YOUR INTERESTS.

—Excerpt from *Nanterre-Information,* March 1968.

On February 1, at the faculty assembly, the myth of the "black-list," which had been spread by Henri Lefebvre, among others, collapsed when Henri Raymond, lecturer in Sociology, told how it had originated. A telephone call from the student residence had made the suggestion—which was refused—that the students who had demonstrated at the time of the previous incidents that had taken place on campus in March 1967 should be deprived of certain advantages with regard to examinations that were granted to more assiduous students.

On March 14 further incidents broke out during a psychology lecture given by Professor R. Francès. Sociology students questioned the results of the last partial examination, which they attributed—mistakenly, no doubt—to administrative pressure. They demanded examinations that "called less on memory than on qualities of initiative and individual research."[32] The professor replied that during the first year the work should consist above all in "forming a habit of precise formulation of ideas, and exact understanding of fundamental laws and research. . . . Serious, thorough use of a bibliography did not seem possible to him until such an apprenticeship had taken place. . . ."[33] A leaflet distributed on this occasion entitled *Stuffed Geese* is remarkable from every standpoint, however utopian its demands and unjust certain of its personal attacks.

Document 13

Nanterre, or How to Train Stuffed Geese

Lethargy, disappointment, and disgust compose the daily atmosphere of all lecture halls, nor is this peculiar to the first year. Collapse of any real vocation, dearth of professional openings and esteem, a specialty that boils down to making children count red balls and blue balls, these are the ultimate results for psychologists and sociologists of years of "study," during which all real value, all intellectual dynamism has been nibbled away little by little by the requirements of a type of teaching which is more or less brilliant on the surface, but illusory and rigid in its substratum. Actually, what the *faculté* offers us, when what we are looking for are possibilities of extending our mental horizons, is a crude paternalism which, by promoting the breeding of "stuffed geese" (an expression used by Professor Leprince-Ringuet), maintains us in a state of intellectual sterility.

The problem appears to us to be clearly rooted, on the one hand, in the structure of the kind of instruction given us and, on the other, in the way examinations are held and marked.

TEACHING METHODS
Existing
To begin with, this type of teaching bores us even before we become disgusted by its mechanical, deadly aspects, as also by the banality and extremely insipid way it is presented. The student, being unconcerned by its insipidness, and maintained in a state of mental passivity, becomes a mere scribe who copies the teacher's lifeless words; later, these copies will be useful to him, since he will reproduce them, without

omitting a comma, on his examination paper, as he is required to do by the teacher.

Demanded

We demand an end to illusory, rigid teaching methods, an end to the *faculté* for "stuffed geese." We demand the introduction of genuine dialogue, of real student-professor cooperation. We demand that the insipidness and lethargy of the lecture halls be replaced by an atmosphere of life, enthusiasm, research, and real work in common. We demand that the courses be multicopied well before the lectures take place—in this way they will be better presented—and lastly, that they contain an incitement to original thought and research in the form of bibliographical information that corresponds to precise problems. Then the students will be able to work intelligently on real problems, analyze bibliographic relationships, and discuss among themselves, during their "work group" meetings, all the results of their individual research. In this way they will be glad to attend classes, since these classes will finally be discussion meetings in which a dialogue will be set up between the professor and the students that will permit the latter, who is already familiar with his course, to ask for elucidation of certain delicate questions. (This method has been successfully inaugurated by M. Ricoeur, to whom, in passing, we should like to ask that there be a choice of three subjects for examinations, and also not to give us such subjects as "Judgement, error, will," which can only be treated in class, or as so much sterile talk.)

EXAMINATIONS

Existing

Copying: obviously, any eighth grader would exult in such tests as these, which would recall his easiest written interrogations. He would excel in these exams because he would lend himself perfectly to these checkups merely of the student's faculty of memory. He would be delighted to reply flawlessly, in the form of conditioned reflexes, to a request for the definition of industrial society by Raymond Aron,[34] for Hume's laws on the attraction of ideas, for the date when a certain test was invented, for the way a test is used, or definitions of genetic psychology. Indeed, he would write out in its entirety on the examination paper, with not a comma missing, the exact passage in Aron's book (or in whatever of M. M. Francès's and Anzieu's[35] lectures these questions were treated). He would act in this way just as lots of us have acted because they had understood how to meet the requirements of an examination and how to get the approval of the teaching body, or at least of the assistants. Because quite evidently, for the latter, who give the validity of correction as alibi, the "value" of an answer is proportionate to the degree of perfection with which the lecture is copied, harking back to methods formerly used by primary school teachers for correcting their famous *"copy books."*

Demanded

Open books, justice: we demand that examinations be held with our books open, and should take into consideration, above all, the student's capacity for intellectual initiative and his powers of analysis and in-depth reflection and not, as now, merely the sterile feat of memory.

Doubtless this genuine examination by its very nature would challenge the competence of certain assistants today who, in their hasty, superficial correcting, are too accustomed not to see this capacity for intellectual initiative, and only understand the premise through the exactness of the copy.

As regards marking, we demand the same scale of rating used for all TP groups, that is to say, obligatory, double-checked marking, honestly complied with (we should cease to be the scapegoats for assistants frustrated because they're underpaid).

Lastly, we demand that after each examination our papers be returned to us for a day in order for us to be able to discuss their value in the "study groups" that are now being organized.

These basic demands are vital for us, and must be presented immediately to the faculty members.

—Taken from Epistémon, *Ces idées* . . . , pp. 44–47.

However, once more, let us leave Nanterre. In Amiens, from March 15 to 17, there took place, in the presence of M. Alain Peyrefitte, the third seminar of the *Study Association for Expanding Scientific Research* (which succeeded the Caen discussions of November 11–14, 1966). More than five hundred persons took part in this conference, which included reformers such as A. Lichnerowicz, a professor at the *Collège de France* and President of the Association, as well as SNESUP. militants. The former wanted to adapt the University and the educational system, which they accused of "extreme centralization, rigidity and inertia," to the economy and to the industrial society. A whole series of proposals, some of them interesting, in fact, were made. Alain Geismar, General Secretary of SNESUP., spoke at the last meeting. Later, what he said appeared to have been prophetic.

Document 14

From the Power of the Word to the Strike, or Action in the Streets

The situation of Western European universities has become glaringly manifest even to those who believed that University "values" were indestructible and universal, and today we are witnessing a change of attitude in hitherto conservative circles, which are now calling for renewal and modernization. At the same time, it is also becoming each day clearer that this impulsion is rooted in two fundamental sources:

(a) *the inadequacy of the structures inherited from the Middle Ages, and which the Nineteenth Century transformed at the time of the first industrial revolution;*

(b) *if this adaptation to the Nineteenth Century succeeded in prolonging the life span by one hundred years, it was because Western Europe, at that time, was the headquarters of the industrial revolution, since it was the most highly developed world sector. Today the center of development has moved elsewhere, and we are in the midst of nations who are by way of becoming relatively underdeveloped.*

The fact is that in this age of scientific revolution, which more and more weighs upon economic and social development because of the sharp decrease in the periods of inertia between discoveries and applications that could radically alter the process of production, our societies have shown themselves incapable of assuming integration of the processes of basic research, development research, applied research, and production.

The policies of our government have recognized the importance of research and education, conceived strictly as a means of satisfying the needs of this alteration of the production process. At the same time their determination to use the educational system as the most powerful agent for integrating the individual into the economic and social systems, gives the measure of their limitations. Underneath the finest alloy of traditional freedoms, "liberalism" and humanism, the University, taken in the broadest sense of the term, from kindergarten to higher education, is the greatest of all integration mechanisms, through the mere fact that it steeps in the dominant ideology, to the extent that the political system agrees to certain concessions and maintains these freedoms which threaten it only under exceptional circumstances.

The present response of the political authorities to this contradiction is specialization and fragmentation of knowledge. Curiously enough, the problem of molding the entire human being (which was at the very heart of the discussions, for instance, at the Havana Cultural Congress[36]), has not been among our concerns during these three days. Must we then produce a "happy" humanity, as some have suggested? I don't think so. We want to educate people to be capable of knowing why they are not happy, capable too of bringing influence to bear on this situation. To use a word which risks provoking derision, because it has been rather besmirched, we want revolutionaries.

For this, the only possibility is undoubtedly to see that structural reforms are carried out, but without the illusion that in themselves these reforms, in isolated sectors, can bring us to points beyond which there is no return. To overthrow existing structures is a vital necessity if we are to avoid complete collapse of the social-educative system. The examples of Rome, Berlin, Warsaw, Madrid . . . allow us to think that here the problem will be met in time. But in our opinion any institutional structure, however new or modern, must be accompanied by a structure for contestation, because we challenge paternalism and the mythology of participation. Today contestation will certainly not take the form of demanding to take part in any assembly whatsoever for discussion of technical terms and conditions, however important, and the Madrid students have replied to J. J. Servan-Schreiber on this point.[37]

Unionism can now demonstrate that it is capable of proposing solutions in due form or, at the most, motions for decrees, but it will not agree to act as unpaid technical adviser. If, after hesitating, we accepted to confront the debate in the technical commissions; if we have demonstrated our seriousness in these instances, our capacity to pose problems and to contribute to finding solutions, then we have never lost sight of the guiding thread; and the reason we are so interested in these technical problems is that they are revealing of the policy that has been adopted.

We saw these techniques being applied all through what has been generally called the Fouchet plan.

This whole system is devised to serve as a selective orientation machine in various stages: the first years in primary school, which fulfill their role so well that they've not been touched; entrance into first year *lycée* which, through the expedient of applied termination classes has resulted in flooding the labor market with future unemployed; and, above all, the innovation at the end of the fourth year *lycée* of parking pupils in corridors, leading to various types of baccalauréats. This system has had, in addition, the unbelievable effect of making the teachers themselves responsible for achieving this centrifugation. Because not the least among the contradictions are, (a) the impossibility on the part of the authorities to do without teachers to implement and define their university policy, and (b) the incapacity on the part of the teachers to organically resist this *de facto* integration.

It is important to note that administrative decentralization, through increased institutional and financial autonomy of the various establishments, will accentuate this integration process to such a point that the central authority may take the minimum risk of a skid, and accept this proposal of talks. The teachers themselves, on the local level, will perhaps better understand that the central administration depersonalizes the goals assigned them.

The most striking example exists at the level of the national science policy, where the share of power accorded the scientists in the framework of the National Research Committee has never questioned the program but, on the contrary, has perfected it technically.

It is surprising to note that no amount of constraint has succeeded in bringing the teaching body to revolt. The deterioration in working conditions, the apportionment of shortages have been submitted to in the name of what was considered to be the interest of the pupils, who would be the only victims of a long strike. And yet there are grounds for battle. In the higher echelons the so-called Fouchet Plan tried to adapt our establishments of learning to the single end of research and training of élite teams, while neglecting other types of training, particularly of teachers; but the mere existence of the IPES threatened to upset the difference between a license and a Master's degree:[38] To solve this, sanitary cordons are now set up in the form of IUT's intended to absorb what risked forcing reconsideration of the ultimate goals attributed to higher education; and official resistance to all attempts at real departitioning, through abolition of interdisciplinary scholarships or through assignment to higher education for instance, of professional technological training, will give an idea of the political level of the present crisis.

The question has been raised as to the object of this seminar.
Was the intention, as some think, to "amuse" members of the teaching profession by making them reflect upon projects that are still in preparation in order to divert them from the difficulties of the present?

Is the intention to make them forget the problems of the financial means needed for developing our National Education? Because these budgeting problems and these problems of working conditions are too ubiquitous for it to be possible to escape them, and the finest speeches on what has been accomplished, the finest array of figures, will not bring us one step further than the actual situation.

Moreover, the myth of gratuitous pedagogical renewal, of pedagogy as a substitute for expansion, died in the sphere of higher education when the reforms were put in practice.

Pedagogical research will cost money or there will be none.
Either the functioning of our educational system will cost money or we are on the road to accelerated underdevelopment.

The investments of both capital and men in this bottomless pit that education represents will be enormous, and no arguments can silence this truth.

Teachers have had too many blows; they are now apprehensive, and if they often react as though they were defenders of the besieged Bastille, this is a natural reflex, for they are always the ones who pay. And one day it will have to be understood that new equipment is not the answer, if the working budget—that is, the manpower budget— makes it impossible to make full use of the equipment.

In reality, therefore, things are more subtle.
Suppose it is desired to create an illusion of long term, qualitative planning that will be both a witness and a reference. We had an example of this in the Langevin-Wallon plan.[39]

1. Because it was revolutionary in 1947, it served as an alibi for twenty years; it was a plan of reference presented as long term, but it did not escape short term policies that were in contradiction with its objectives and were adopted in the name of realism.

2. Will the Amiens plan remain in a desk drawer, to be used to dazzle the innocent, or as an alibi for a short term policy that is radically oriented in the opposite direction?

We reject this short term–long term opposition. The long term is *now* or never, and the elements of this policy should be implemented right away, with no stages, no solution for continuing. The intermediate objectives will be outstripped by the dynamics of construction, for every halt leads to inaction and sclerosis. This decision to act will be judged by results, and to begin with, by the amount of capital involved.

There will be no repetition of the Caen seminar operation, which consisted in saturating the innovators and, since they are good technicians, making them set up projects for structural reform as though the University were an isolated whole, having no interaction with society.

It further consisted in setting them in opposition to the unions (presented as restraining elements) and then doing nothing, content in the power of the "word."

A proposal made in Caen by the Director of Higher Education, the former Minister of Research, and present Minister of National Education may abolish the function of research in the first cycle—that is, in an integral part of the University.[40] The teachers are keen for innovation, but they have been subjected so long to winds that blow first hot then cold that they have become hypersensitive. We will not be content merely to judge what will be done with regard to our proposals, but are prepared to move on to a phase of action where, furthermore, we shall not be alone but in liaison with those who are not present at this seminar: the "educatees," the students; even the budding organizations of *lycée* students, who did not join us because they are weary, each time they present their demands, of talking only to administrators who when confronted with the facts have been unable to give them an answer.

Willingness to institute real, progressive innovation is gauged by the laws that govern orientation, curricula, and budgets—or else by strikes and street demonstrations.

—Excerpt from 21-27, *L'Etudiant de France* (UNEF publication), supplement to No. 19, late March 1968.

About the same time a group of sociology students, the same that were to lead the March 22 action, began to distribute a pamphlet demanding reexamination of the evolution of a type of sociology that had placed itself at the service of employers. They also demanded reexamination of the special role of the teaching methods being used in this branch at Nanterre. American readers will observe to what extent the very summary criticism of Touraine recalls the criticism of Clark Kerr's theories that was made in Berkeley in 1964. The influence of the review *Socialisme ou Barbarie,* which had published numerous critical articles on the work of the sociologist Elton Mayo, is very evident.

Document 15

Why Sociologists?

We will consider here only the dominant tendencies in contemporary sociology. This must be followed by more detailed studies: *all boycotting of courses to help us in this is welcome.*

Sociology must be looked at from a historical angle. The crucial date from this point of view is 1930, the date of Mayo's experiment in the Hawthorne factory.

By showing the importance of affective phenomena in small groups and suggesting that human relations should be regulated in order to improve the productivity of workers, Mayo did much more than open a new field of sociology. He closed the epoch of social philosophy and speculative systems concerning society as a whole, and opened the glorious era of empiricism and of "scientific" data collecting. At the same time, in selling his services to the management of a business enterprise, Mayo initiated the age of large scale collaboration by sociologists with all of the powers of the bourgeois world—which was then hard put to rationalize a capitalist system deeply shaken by the crisis of 1929.

The transition from an academic sociology, which had been the vassal of philosophy, to an independent sociology with scientific pretensions corresponds to the transition from competitive capitalism to organized capitalism.

Henceforth, the rise of sociology is increasingly tied to the social demand for rationalized practice in the service of bourgeois aims: money, profit, maintenance of law and order.

There is abundant proof that industrial sociology seeks above all the adaptation of the worker to his work: the inverse perspective is very rare because the sociologist, paid by the management, must respect the goals of the economic system: to produce as much as possible in order to make as much money as possible. Political sociology plans vast studies —usually mystifying—which presuppose that electoral choice is, today, the locus of politics—never asking whether that locus might be elsewhere. Stouffer studies the optimal conditions of the American soldier's morale without posing the structural problems of the role of the army in the society in which he lives.

Sociologists are found in advertising, in the countless forms of consumer conditioning, in the experimental study of media—there too without attempting to criticize the social function of these media.

On the other hand, how do U.S. sociologists conceive the focal problem of social classes? The concepts of class and of "discontinuity" (class struggle) are eliminated and replaced by notions of classes and of strata which have status, power, and prestige. In this conception there exists a continuous scale in which a definite quantity of power and prestige corresponds to each step, in increasing stages as one approaches the summit. And of course each individual is presumed to have, from the outset, the same opportunity to climb the pyramid since we are (here, as everywhere) in a democracy. Besides the theoretical refutations of Mills and D. Riesman, the practical refutation of the subproletariat (the ethnic minorities) in the U.S.A., and those of certain workers' groups against their union apparatus are enough to dispel the dream of an achieved integration.

Only recently, riots by Black Americans created such fear that supplementary credits were voted for sociologists to study the movements of mobs and furnish recipes for repression.

Finally—bitter irony!—when the U.S. Secretary of Defense, Mr. McNamara, launched an anti-subversion project in Latin America (the infamous "Project Camelot"), he could imagine no better way to disguise it than to call it a "sociological" study project. . . .

And in France?

Rationalization of capitalism began, certainly, after World War II (with the creation of planning), but only became effective with Gaullism and its authoritarian structures. It is not by chance that the "degree" in sociology was created in 1958. The unequal development of French capitalism as compared with U.S. capitalism is seen too on the level of ideas: all current sociology in France is imported from the U.S., with a few years' delay. Everyone knows that the most esteemed sociologists are those who follow most attentively American publications.

Sociological "Theory"

We have seen sociology's close tie with social demand. The practice of organizing capitalism creates a mass of contradictions; and for each particular case a sociologist is put to work. One studies juvenile delinquency, another racism, a third slums. Each seeks an explanation of his partial problem and elaborates a "theory" proposing solutions to the limited conflict that he is studying. Thus while serving as a "watchdog," our sociologist will at the same time make his contribution to the mosaic of sociological "theories."

The confusion of the social sciences, which has its source here, can be seen in the interdisciplinary approach that is so fashionable today (cf. the critique by Louis Althusser). The uncertainty of each specialist when confronted with the uncertainties of other specialists can only give rise to immense platitudes.

Behind this confusion lies the absence, never stressed, of a theoretical status for sociology and the social sciences. Their only point in common is finally that they constitute "for the most part methodological techniques of social adaptation and readaptation," not to mention the reintegration of all forms of contestation: the majority of all our sociologists are "Marxists." We can mention, in support of our argument, the conservative character of concepts currently in use: hierarchy, ritual, integration, social function, social control, equilibrium, and so on. The "theoreticians" must explain localized conflicts without reference to the social totality that provoked them.

This supposedly objective procedure implies *partial* perspectives (in both senses of the word) in which phenomena are not connected (but racism, unemployment, delinquency, and the slums constitute a unity), and in which the rationality of the economic system is taken for granted. The word profit having become shocking, one now speaks of "growth," or of adaptation to a "changed reality." But where does this change lead? Whence does it come? Who organized it? Who profits from it? Are such questions too speculative to be of interest to science?

These considerations lead us to conclude, simply, that the unrest of sociology students cannot be understood unless one questions the social function of sociology. It appears that, in the present conflicts, sociologists have chosen their camp: the camp of business executives and of the government that assists them. Under these conditions, what does the "defense of sociology" recommended by some really mean?

The Case of Nanterre
The preceding general analysis throws light on the particular case of Nanterre. There too: crisis in sociology, uneasiness about careers, confusion in the teaching, and importations of "theories" made in U.S.A. Those who remain outside the positivist-empiricist current are led to retreat into a verbal critique which has the merit of avoiding total "one-dimensionalization," but which confirms isolation and impotence.

Among the "hopefuls" of French sociology, Parsonian jargon and the cult of statistics (at last! a scientific field) are the key to all problems. The study of society has managed the *tour de force* of depoliticizing all teaching—that is to say, in legitimizing the existing politics. And all of this is joined to a fruitful collaboration with the ministers and technocrats seeking to form their cadres. Our professors, it is true, are considered "Leftists," compared with those flourishing in other departments who yearn nostalgically for the old days. The reason is that these latter give up with regret the mandarinate of the University established by liberal capitalism, whereas the sociologists know where the "change" is leading: organization, rationalization, production of human commodities made to order for the economic needs of organized capitalism.

Here it is necessary to refute the conceptions defended by Professor M. Crozier (*Esprit,* January 1968) and Professor A. Touraine (*Le Monde,* 7 and 8 March, 1968) with regard to the discussions that we are now concerned with. For Crozier, American unrest does not reside—as some naïve persons might think—in the violence of the Negroes, exacerbated by the conditions of their lives, or in the horror of the imperialist war in Vietnam—that "accident," that "folly," as Crozier puts it (he had been thought to be more attached to scientific explanation than to magic words). Neither is it found in the dissolution of all values as they give way to exchange value, to money. No; this exists, but it is only an appearance. Violence has always existed in the U.S.A. What is new, Crozier tells us, is the invasion of rationalism. It is the change of mentality necessary to familiarize oneself with the "world of abstract reasoning." Present history is not a real struggle between social groups fighting for material interests and different socioeconomic priorities. It is the field in which two phantasmagoric entities confront each other: rationalism in the service of growth, versus the irresponsible anarchy of those who are frightened by change. This "sociological" version is not worth the trouble of refutation, save for the probable ideological importance it contains. For Crozier counsels the blacks not to demand power, but to undergo "an intellectual mutation" (sic!), all of which leads to the Grand Celebration of the American Way of Life, which today produces new, creative, and dynamic individuals.

In his recent articles, Touraine has presented the following conception: there exists a University system whose function is to produce knowledge in the service of growth (again!). Changing this system depends on the fruitful contradiction between students and professors that it contains. The University in its conflicts and its essential social function is analogous to nineteenth century business enterprise.

But it is false to oppose the nineteenth and twentieth centuries. It is not true "that knowledge and technical progress are the motors of the new society." Knowledge and technical progress are subordinated to the struggles between firms for profit (or, which is the same, for monopolistic hegemony), and to the military and economic confrontation between East and West. Scientists are not the innocent entrepreneurs that they are made out to be; nor is science that glorious autonomous activity which seeks only its own development.

The unit of reference, the University, is not viable. The contradictions occur on the level of society as a whole, and the University is implicated in them. The majority of professors and students are committed to the maintenance of order, and only a minority have taken part in the struggle that is developing in the imperialist countries and in the exploited countries. The recent motion made by student groups here at Nanterre (not at all upset by their own servility) in support of the administration and the majority of the teaching corps is the latest evidence.

Possibilities and Limits of Student Struggle
Within the University, the perspectives are limited: the essential thing to do is to enlighten the rest of the students on the social function of the University. Especially in sociology is it necessary to unmask false arguments, throw light on the generally repressive meaning of a career in sociology, and dispel illusions on this subject.

The hypocrisy of objectivity, of apoliticism, of the innocence of study, is much more flagrant in the social sciences than elsewhere, and must be exposed.

An intellectual minority remains totally ineffectual if it submits, or even adapts, to the ghetto prepared for it.

While waiting for other actions, we will carry this debate to the conference for "defense" of sociologists, which should take place before Easter.[41]

—Daniel Cohn-Bendit, Jean-Pierre Duteuil,
Bertrand Gerard, Bernard Granautier

March 22 in Nanterre was marked, to begin with, by the second sitting, from 5 to 8 P.M., of the student-professor liaison committee (13 students, 13 professors) which was chaired by Jean Beaujeu, a Latin professor and assessor to the dean. Professor Beaujeu reported immediately on a request that had been made to the Ministry of the Interior in favor of Daniel Cohn-Bendit, who was threatened with expulsion. After passing in review various technical problems, the commission took up the latest incidents, the ones that had occurred during the class taught by Robert Francès and others, the most recent having taken place the same day: "an invasion of the first floor of the administrative building by thirty students"; on March 20 the partial exams had been sabotaged, and were later canceled. The student delegates were "cooperative," but declared at the same time that the sociology students considered the "teaching they were receiving in psychology was . . . elementary and lacked cohesion. . . ." This discontent "was being exploited by a handful of marginal students who had come to stir up disorder and had introduced a form of protest that most of the sociology students refused to accept." With regard to the bulletin recently put out at Nanterre[42] by the UNEF "actually this text represents only one or two individuals and does not really commit the UNEF." A. Touraine declared that in his opinion, "what they should do in order to put an end to intolerable disturbances was to isolate a small group from a majority that might have reasons for discontent." The examination that had been planned for March 20 should be reorganized and "it would be well to take severe measures that would permit identification of possible trouble makers, and also take immediate sanctions."[43]

Meanwhile, six militants from the *Comité Vietnam National,* among them a student at Nanterre, Xavier Langlade, suspected of having taken part in the window-breaking attack against American Express, had been arrested. They were released less than two days later, but rumors were flying in Nanterre: torture, threats of a long detention, etc. During the evening the *"enragés"* decided to act, and 142 of them occupied the Council hall. This was the beginning of the *Mouvement du 22 mars,* marked by an action that recreated the attack on the Moncada fortress, July 26, 1953. It was also the beginning of student power. But above all it marked decisive conversion towards French objectives of the force that had been acquired in the struggle in favor of the Third World and Vietnam. Here is the account of the facts as given on March 26 to the faculty assembly. It will be noted that the assembly made every effort to find a "counter-terrorist" reply to a type of student "terrorism" that had principally consisted in pledges of a psychological nature.[44]

That same day the *Mouvement du 22 mars* put out a first leaflet which contained the themes that were to be developed later (in April) in its bulletin, as well as those that had already been outlined in *Why Sociologists?*[45] "Militants are not picked up during demonstrations but in their homes. For us, these phenomena are not accidental; they correspond to an offensive on the part of capitalism which is in the throes of modernism and rationalization. In order to achieve this goal, the ruling class has to apply its oppression on every level:

—reconsideration of the workers' rights of assembly,
—integration of the Social Security administration,[46]
—automatization and cybernetization of our society,
—introduction of psycho-sociological techniques into business in order to smooth over class conflicts (some of us are being trained for this job).

Capitalism is through with subtleties. We must drop demonstration techniques, which can accomplish nothing more. Harold Wilson, who is a socialist, forces England to accept what de Gaulle forces on us. The time is past for such peaceful demonstrations as the one being organized by the snesup. for next Thursday, with goals that attack nothing in our society.

The important thing for us is to be able to discuss these problems at the University and to carry on our action there."

Document 16

Faculty Assembly, Academic Year 1967–1968, 4th Session

The Dean opened the session at 5:15 P.M.

He related the incidents that had taken place on Friday, March
22. Following certain partial actions that took place during mid-term
partial examinations, a group of students had occupied the Council
Hall on Friday evening. The reason given was the arrest of several students (one a former Nanterre student) accused of being responsible for
attacks on American property in Paris. During the day (Friday) various writings had appeared on the *faculté* walls. Monday and Tuesday
several demonstrations had confirmed *a determination to keep the*
faculté *from functioning*. This is a new situation and a particularly serious one. Calm can only be restored with the active cooperation of
everybody, teachers and students alike. Each in his own domain, by
keeping informed and informing others, will contribute to isolating a
small, active minority.

THE ASSESSOR TELLS WHAT HE HAS SEEN

After the meeting of the student-teacher commission, which bears witness to the existence of a dialogue, M. Beaujeu met with a hundred or
so students on the ground floor of B building. About 8:30 P.M., over
his protest, the demonstrators went upstairs and succeeded in entering
the Council Hall, where they held a political discussion as well as a
picnic.

In agreement with Rector Chalin, M. Beaujeu decided not to
call the police, a solution that would have given undue publicity to the
event and caused other students to side with this group.

After the demonstrators had left, about 1:30 A.M., the hall did
not appear to have been badly damaged by this incursion. In any case,
no systematic material destruction had taken place.[47]

A concert being held that evening was not disturbed other than
by speeches made during the intermission and at the end.

It is M. Beaujeu's opinion that this demonstration is of a political
nature. To be sure, the expression of ideologies that seek destruction of
society do not concern us. But *if this protest leads to destruction of the*

University, then we must act. Now there are at least three groups who seem to be working towards this specific goal. These are the CLER, the JCR, and an "anarchist" nucleus.

FURTHER INFORMATION CAME TO LIGHT DURING THE DISCUSSION

The Dean read a statement by the administrative staff, which refuses to work under conditions of insecurity. He also read a motion by student delegates from several disciplines, who dissociate themselves from Friday's demonstrations.

M. Anzieu: the boycotting of a mid-term examination in psychology (in the philosophy and sociology series), the subject of which was called "scandalous," was occasionally enforced by violence. The test had to be canceled.

M. Bastié:[48] students had entered certain administrative premises, tampered with the files, broken a door handle, and pulled out telephone wires.

The Assembly was unanimous *in condemning this type of demonstration,* but there were differences of opinion as to what response to make:

A. Call the police, teacher and *faculté* Assembly patience having reached its limit.

B. Combine a repressive inside action, at the University, with an information campaign that would arouse the more serious students.

C. Avoid repression and seek a solution in a dialogue with the students.

The discussion crystallized around five possible types of action (identity checks at the *faculté* gates being materially impossible):

1. Legal action: for destruction of public buildings.

2. Self-defense: hard to organize. In any case, this risked leading to serious incidents.

3. Creation of an autonomous police force for service inside the *faculté;* this being above all a matter of budget.

4. Academic action: a decision to be taken on April 1 on the case of a student who had been referred to the University Council[49] in January, this procedure is therefore possible but long, names and precise facts would be needed. (Several Assembly members moved that the Ministry should be urged to give disciplinary powers to the *facultés,* permitting rapid, effective procedure.)

5. Suspension of all teaching: (*faculté* closing cannot be done by the Dean or by the Assembly). It could be short and symbolic or continue until the return of normal functioning conditions.

6. Inform public opinion: the idea of a press conference,[50] with both professor and student members of the student-teacher commissions, was easily agreed upon.

M. Beaujeu raised the problem of freedom of access to University grounds and the uncertain frontiers between the public thoroughfares and the grounds. If they did not have their own police, they would inevitably he obliged to consider the *faculté* grounds and the public thoroughfare as one and the same.

A vote was taken giving the Dean the mission to suspend classes, without delay, for a limited period of time. The vote of the Assembly was 46 to 14, with 5 abstaining votes.

> —The Dean, Pierre Grappin; The Secretary of this sitting, Jean-Claude Boyer; General Secretary, Christian Rivière. *Faculté des Lettres et Sciences Humaines,* Nanterre, March 26, 1968.

Following the March 22 affair, classes were suspended in Nanterre from 7 P.M. on Thursday, March 28 until Monday, April 1. This suspension coincided more or less with the national campaign of action organized by the UNEF from March 27 through March 29: "Students everywhere should question their professors as to what they can do next year and what is the useful purpose of their work. A general movement in the University can prevent revival of 'selection,' put an end to students being sent up blind alleys, and to a policy for which it is always the students who pay the piper. The Minister must realize that, finally, students want their demands satisfied. We ask this for the last time. Otherwise, resumption of classes will be very, very difficult. It may even not take place."[51] The *Mouvement d'action universitaire* (MAU), whose leaders (J.-L. Péninou and M. Kravetz, among others) were to play an important role, although somewhat outside the student mass, held its first meeting on March 29. News from Nanterre was received with a certain scepticism.[52] During the period when Nanterre was closed three new facts had come to light: (1) the Communist teachers and members of the administrative staff took a stand which conformed strictly to the party line; (2) without siding with the *"enragés,"* a growing number of instructors and assistant professors took a separate, though moderate, position from that of the majority of the titular professors, as witness a motion adopted by the French Department; and (3) at an Assembly meeting there was much clearer realization of the gravity of the situation. Some concessions were made, the principal one being, that the students were given free use of a meeting-room, and there were contestations.

Document 17

Communiqué

On Recent Events, Issued by the Communist Teacher and Personnel Cell of the Faculté des Lettres

The Nanterre *faculté* has well over 11,000 students, and both material and pedagogical conditions have deteriorated.

Application of the Gaullist educational reform has resulted in depriving many students of any future prospects.

The deliberate government policy on educational matters is solely responsible for the so-called unrest that exists among the students.

This situation is being used by provocateur "groupuscules," whose methods we condemn. Just when the government is preparing to further undermine higher educational structures, the "groupuscules" are working to prevent all student organizing, as well as to mislead and paralyze the union movement.

With their methods they aim at discrediting the student movement and furthering the government's plans.

The Communist professors have confidence in the mass of students who, without having recourse to force, can silence a handful of provocateurs and, with the support of the UNEF,[53] which is the only real student union organization, restore an atmosphere to the *faculté* that will be favorable to study, joint discussion, and common action.

We are opposed to all measures of police or administrative repression.

We assert the right of all the students, as well as of the entire teaching staff, to express their political opinions and to participate in union action.

We demand construction of new buildings in Nanterre and new *facultés des Lettres*. We recommend democratic reorganization of the University, which is the only possible solution, and corresponds to the desires of both teachers and students.

—Nanterre, March 28, 1968.

Document 18

French Department

Twenty-seven assistant professors and instructors (out of a staff of 31), supported by several professors who had already been consulted, met together on Friday, March 29, 1968.

—They demand that University sanctuary be maintained.

—They are opposed to any police presence on the campus.

—They assert their hostility in principle to any intrusion of the police inside the campus and the *faculté*.

—They reassert the democratic right of the students to take part in free discussions of University, cultural, union, and political problems on *faculté* premises.

—They emphasize that this freedom should in no way limit the right of any student to pursue his studies under normal conditions, nor disturb in any way whatsoever the normal functioning of University institutions.

—They are resolved to develop joint discussion with all the students, without discrimination, in order to study their problems and demands and to try to define the conditions of a common action.

The Easter vacation (April 4–18) did not put an end to the action of the students. When classes started again on April 22 the *Mouvement du 22 mars* had put out a bulletin jestingly entitled "Bulletin No. 5494bis (Supplement to No. 5494). In addition to the two texts that follow, the bulletin includes a press review, a brief note on the role of examinations, two reports on the subject of the counter university (this term was taken over from the German movement), and the report of a "culture and creativity" commission:

> "Creativity is the most evenly distributed thing in the world, as proved by childhood. The characteristic of a child's ludic gestures is that they are poetry, that is to say, they achieve perfect harmony between the subjectivity they express and the world that confronts poetry as a possibility of its objectivization. This harmony is our revolutionary ideal. To allow it to exist again, to rediscover it, such is our program. Realization of the creativity of each person or, more exactly, the permanence of this creativity at every stage of life, is the truth that our revolution must try to achieve."

It also includes a report by a commission on "student struggle–worker struggle," another on anti-imperialist struggles, the words of the *Internationale,* and finally a recipe that later became famous (even though it is not apparently very good) for making a Molotov cocktail. The recipe was accompanied by the following note: "The administration has armor-plated the doors of the administration building."

There were deep eddies throughout the movement, and a large part of its "Maoist" members left because the movement did not adopt their theory that the Nanterre boiler room should become the "red base" of the revolution. The CLER became openly hostile.

Document 19

The Nature of the Nanterre Movement and Its Prospects

This issue of the bulletin will answer the following requirements:

1. The present movement feels that it must take stock of its position and ensure its continuity after the Easter vacation.

2. Accounts published on the one hand by the bourgeois press ("a few irresponsible people who are hampering the functioning of the University"; "revolution to the tune of the cha-cha"; "students led by a German Danton"), and on the other by the Communist press ("anarchists . . . who, as a result of their provocations, are objective allies of the government"), must be denounced by a restatement of what has happened.

Besides this editorial, this issue contains a press review and reports from the following commissions: the anti-imperialist struggle; opposition in the countries of Eastern Europe, culture and creativity, criticism of the University, and University criticism.

I. WHAT HAPPENED

During the first term a strike that broke out without any traditional, political, or union leadership brought out ten to twelve thousand *faculté* students on problems of improved working conditions. As a result, co-equal departmental commissions were set up which soon turned out to be fruitless.[54]

During the second term there occurred a series of sporadic incidents that indicated widespread uneasiness: a demonstration of solidarity with a student who was threatened with expulsion ended in a fight with the cops, who had been called in by the dean; scenes of disorder and uproar in several classes, etc. Furthermore, action by the boarders at the University dormitories (*Cité universitaire*) had resulted in abrogation of house regulations in February.

By the end of March a new phase was discernible:

—Psychology students boycotted their mid-term examinations;

—Four students distributed a handbill that challenged both the way sociology was being taught and the job openings it offered ("Why Sociologists?");[55]

—On Friday March 22, following the arrest of six anti-imperialist militants, a protest meeting was organized at the end of which it was voted to occupy the administration building. That same evening 150 students, at a meeting in the professors' council room, discussed a number of political problems until 2 A.M. Friday March 29 was set for an open-ended discussion on several political subjects.

When the University authorities saw the turn of events (active preparation for the discussions on the 29th, leaflets, speeches, a poster campaign, and writings on *faculté* walls) they grew anxious and began to set the staff against the students: the *faculté* bookstore was closed and there was a strike of disciplinary personnel. On Thursday the 28th, Dean Grappin ordered suspension of all classes and study groups until the following Monday. A meeting of 300 students decided to maintain the next day's action as a day of preparation for the political discussions, which were postponed until Tuesday, April 2.

On Friday the 29th, with a large police force surrounding the campus, 500 students participated in an opening meeting that took place in one of the *Cité universitaire* halls, after which commissions were set up for discussion of the subjects that had been chosen.

On Monday, April 1, the second-year sociology students (first cycle) decided to boycott their mid-term examinations, then voted a motion denouncing sociology as an ideology. At the same time there were differences of opinion on the professorial level between members of the liberal arts department (Social Sciences and Letters), who favored giving the students a place to meet[56] and the reactionaries (History), who demanded that the "leaders" should be arrested.

The Tuesday, June 2 event was a success. The administration was unable to prevent 1500 people from occupying B1 amphitheater for a "get-together" meeting, nor did the corporatists and fascists prevent commission sessions from taking place in C building classrooms. The final plenary assembly, in which 800 students and a few assistants took part, decided to continue the movement and to publish the present bulletin.

II. THE NATURE OF THE MOVEMENT

The Nanterre movement is quite definitely politicized. Contrary to the "corporatist" spirit of the November strike, it gives priority to such nonunion themes as "No to police repression, for a counter university, freedom of political speech and action in the *faculté*," etc. At the same time it has turned out to be in the minority and is aware of this fact; several speakers have denounced the illusions of the slogan "defense of the common interests of all students." In Nanterre it is clear that many accept higher education as initiation into an upper echelon position in a bourgeois business firm. So a nucleus has emerged composed of some 300 "extremists" who are capable of mobilizing a thousand out of the twelve thousand students enrolled in the *faculté*.

The activities they have organized have hastened the awareness of some: rather than stage "provocations," the idea has been to force latent authoritarianism to come out into the open (cf. carloads of crs ready for action) by showing what the proposed "dialogues" really are. As soon as certain problems appear, dialogue is replaced by blackjacks. Political awareness, but also active participation on the part of all who, until then were paralyzed by "groupuscule' ineffectualness and the routine of traditional protests that took the form of petitions and silent marches. In the end, students and professors had to go different ways when the repressive mechanism got under way. It was interesting to see the uec demanding a well-functioning bourgeois University, or certain "leftist," not to say "Marxist," professors frightened to see their status challenged in this bourgeois University.

It is necessary to insist on the originality of the movement that has been set in motion—originality, that is, in the French context. To begin with, the work has been accomplished in common, without regard for "groupuscule" opposition. There is no question of arbitrarily decreeing their futility. A process is under way, however, in the course of which differences will emerge through theoretical and practical confrontation with reality, rather than through quarrels between cliques about semantics. Already peculiarities of terminology are under scrutiny insofar as they represent rigid and unaltered perceptions of reality that function as a means of demarcation from other "groupuscules" and not as instruments of scientific analysis. Moreover, we are determined *to avoid co-option by any one political group as well as by the administration* and liberal teachers, who believe in "talking things over" and protest made between four walls (cf. Dean Grappin's proposal).

Certain new problems have come up, in particular: the problem of more direct and effectual refusal of a class university; denunciation of a type of knowledge that is neutral and objective, and also of its fragmentation; questioning with regard to the objective position we are intended to occupy in the present division of labor; junction with the fighting workers, etc.

Simultaneously, original forms of action have been developed, such as improvised meetings inside the *faculté,* occupation of classrooms to hold our discussions, interruptions during classes and lectures, boycotting examinations, political signs and posters in the lecture halls, takeover of the loudspeakers now monopolized by the administration.

Lastly, the movement shows its vitality through two additional features: an abundance of tendencies, and the fact that practice comes before theory. On the multiplicity of tendencies, commission reports are eloquent, and after all, there's no reason for scorn in the fact that side by side with straight political thinking there should be an article on "culture and creativity." As for the precedence of practice over theory, we will confine our remarks to recalling that nobody knows very well what is happening, but that to talk of "folklore" or "anarchist provocation" does not solve the problem. The "student struggle" commission will have to meet it head on: how considerable is the number of contradictions raised by monopolistic capitalism in the educational sector? What prospects does this open up?

On this question of prospects we shall limit ourselves to describing the tendencies that are presently identifiable.

III. PROSPECTS

After having defined, above all negatively (refusal of institutionalization, of "groupuscule" divisions, of blacklists) and formally (freedom of political expression), in order to work out a line of action, the movement will have to reexamine all the problems and, at the same time, reflect upon its own causes. While Dean Grappin is satisfied with arguments that are worthy of the *France-Soir* article on affective isolation and the University *vase clos,* we consider that beneath these apparent causes are hidden more profound realities. Is it possible to give an account of these events by mixing two or three facts taken at random: a lot of activists influenced by sds disturbances in Germany, the anxiety of some of them about job openings, the tense atmosphere in the different departments where there existed a confrontation between assistants and professors, etc.?

We must therefore go further and try to isolate as scientifically as possible the structural factors of the disturbances.

For the immediate future, continuity of the movement will depend on our capacity to set ourselves concrete goals during the third term, and for next year. Several tendencies have already appeared with regard to the concept of a counter university. Should direct action be increased in the University? Should we, in a more reformist way, bring in a larger fraction of students by using less radical directives? Or should we reject the idea of specifically *student* action and give priority to direct support for the workers? Finally, should we try to conciliate joining with the worker struggle and autonomous development of our own activities?

In this aftermath of an attempt on the life of the revolutionary Rudi Dutschke, an attempt perpetrated by German neo-Nazis with the tacit approval of the pro-American German ruling class, it is our hope in bringing out this bulletin to contribute however modestly to extending student agitation to other *facultés* in order that, as in Germany, criticism of the University may lead to radical, permanent political action within the framework of the counter university.

Document 20

Student and Worker Struggles in the Eastern Countries

At first the commission was merely informative, since certain members knew nothing at all about what was going on in the Eastern countries and had come simply to find out. The commission then decided that to study the problem of worker and student struggles in the Eastern countries amounted to posing the problem of governmental authority in those countries.

The commission was divided on this point: certain members considered these countries to be authentic socialist governments, while others considered them to be bureaucratic governments; on the other hand there were those who felt that bureaucracy was a caste, and some who felt that it was a class.[57] These are the problems the committee decided to discuss and concerning which it plans to make a written statement.

On April 22 there was a meeting of the *faculté* council.[58] Its discussions concerned an unusually violent motion, and it took some very serious decisions that had already been outlined at the March 30 council assembly. These were: (a) creation of a *faculté* police force, (b) creation of a University tribunal that would sit in Nanterre, and (c) designation of all open campus grounds as a public thoroughfare (that is, subject to police supervision). In other words, relations between faculty and students were to be settled by force, and this decision had been taken without the students having been warned of the measures under discussion. . . . In reply to the open terrorism of a group of students, a majority of the professors had voted to use clandestine terrorism. What was really serious was that the following motion was made by professors among whom some, undoubtedly, were well known conservatives (such as, Jacqueline Duchemin, François Crouzet . . .), but others were men from the Left.[59] Later, one of those who signed the document wrote a most interesting a posteriori analysis of the Nanterre phenomenon.[60] It is a fact that this day marked the final break.

Document 21

Faculty Council, Academic Year 1967–1968, 10th Session

The Council meeting opened at 5 p.m. with Dean Grappin presiding. It unanimously approved the minutes of the preceding meeting. Before taking up the items on the agenda, Mme Duchemin read the following statement:

"As this third term begins the undersigned professors, being determined to put an end to the doings of a group whose use of violence and provocation is discrediting the *faculté* and destroying the achievements of four years of effort, convinced that they are expressing the resolve of an all but unanimous number of teachers, students, and personnel, surprised at the inadequacies of the responsible authorities and regretting that the decisions taken at the last *faculté* council meeting (March 30, 1968) should not have been put into effect,

1. urge the dean, himself, to take the necessary measures and obtain from the higher authorities the necessary means to unmask and punish the trouble makers,

2. declare that should the aforementioned council decisions remain inoperative, and the indispensable conditions for work and security not yet be restored by Monday, April 29, they will quit their posts as of that date. [Signed] D. Anzieu, J. Bastié, A. Blanc,[61] A. Chastagnol,[62] F. Crouzet, J. Duchemin, H. Elhaï, R. Francès, J. Heers,[63] I. Maier,[64] F. Mauro,[65] A. Micha, P. Pélissier,[66] R. Rémond,[67] P. Riché,[68] A. Rondeau, P. Sagave,[69] P. Vernière."[70]

This motion and another introduced by M. Ricoeur (and withdrawn by him at the end of the council) gave rise to lengthy discussion.

Three proposals were adopted during the meeting:

1. The council asks that a University security force be created without delay, subject to the dean's orders (25 votes for, 5 votes against, 6 abstentions).

2. The council asks that a University disciplinary council be created for all the institutions of higher education in Nanterre, having the same authority and powers as the University council, and with the participation of student delegates (32 votes for, 1 vote against, 2 abstentions).

3. The council asks that all open campus grounds be declared public thoroughfares (19 votes for, 7 against, 8 abstentions).

At 8 P.M., discussion of the agenda not having started, the council members decided to adjourn and meet again on Monday April 29 at 4 P.M. (just before the faculty assembly, which was set for 6 P.M.).

—The Dean, Pierre Grappin; The Recording Secretary, Alain Lerond; The General Secretary, Christian Rivière, *Faculté des Lettres et Sciences Humaines,* Nanterre, April 22, 1968.

On April 25 the PC and the UEC, taking advantage of the freedom granted by the Dean, tried to organize a meeting with the participation of the Communist Deputy, Pierre Juquin, their leading specialist on University matters. The meeting was sabotaged by some "Marxist-Leninist" students from Paris, and P. Juquin, who was given the epithet of a "PC Lecanuet,"[71] was not able to speak. Shortly afterward some trouble broke out, attributable to the CLER, during a meeting at which Laurent Schwartz and André Gorz were speaking. Thanks to D. Cohn-Bendit, Schwartz was able to say what he had to say:[72] "After his speech, if we consider that Laurent Schwartz is an s.o.b., we'll tell him: Mr. Schwartz, you're an s.o.b." In Toulouse students from the *faculté des Lettres* who had occupied a hall on the 23rd,[73] founded the *Mouvement du 25 avril* along the lines of the *22 mars.* Two SNESup. motions printed here are also dated the same day; the first, of a general nature, is resolutely "centrist," while the second, which was approved by 18 out of 25 votes in the philosophy, sociology, and psychology departments, takes the side of the student movement, conceived as one aspect of the "revolutionary class struggle."

Document 22

The University Is in a State of Crisis

There's a shortage of job openings: both cadres and workers are unemployed.

Content, structures and teaching methods are not adapted to today's needs.

The output of the University is disastrous.

The Paris *facultés* are on the point of collapse as a result of the crowds of students, and lack of new buildings.

The living and working conditions of the students are deteriorating.
The students are not sharing in University management.

AGAINST GOVERNMENT POLICY
FOR DEMOCRATIC REFORM
WHAT DO THE COMMUNISTS PROPOSE?

For a régime in which all students can study full time.
For real student orientation.
For teaching that is relevant to life.
For renewal of teaching methods.
For co-management of the University.
For obtaining from the government the necessary financing and
number of teachers.

*The French Communist Party (faculty and administrative staff
cell), the union of Communist students of the Nanterre faculté, invite
you to take part in a*

ROUND-TABLE DISCUSSION
THURSDAY APRIL 25
AT 5 P.M.

at the *faculté des Lettres*—Amphitheatre D 1—Pierre Juquin, agrégé
de l'Université, Member of the central committee of the PCF, and
Gérard Bras, member of the federal board of the UECF, secretary of the
city of Nanterre, will speak.

Document 23

At a meeting on April 25 the coordinating committee of the SNESup.
sections again called on all students to enter into a critical, constructive dialogue, with a view to action aimed at expanding and transforming the University.

It was decided to discuss all the demands that are of interest to
both the students and the teaching staff at Nanterre.

With this confrontation in prospect, it urges all students to respect everybody's freedom of speech, to avoid all violence, and to see
to it that the classes, study groups, and examinations take place without interference.

—*Faculté des Lettres et Sciences Humaines* at Nanterre, SNESup.,
April 25, 1968.

Document 24

The SNESup. section of *Nanterre-Sciences Humaines* (*Philo, Psycho, Socio*), meeting in General Assembly, Thursday, April 25th, declares that:

1. The student movement is the expression of a genuine, general crisis in our society.

2. The present University may be characterized as a class University:
   —because of the type of students it caters to;
   —because of the aims assigned to it: selection of cadres in terms of the imperatives of an expanding society, that is to say, in terms of the goals of the French ruling class, in the framework of world competition;
   —because of the content and system of cultural and ideological values that it transmits;
   —because of the pedagogical relationships and the modes of control and sanction it is based on.

3. Although the contradictions of culture and pedagogy imply a critical analysis of the class University, the concepts and contents of a critical culture and pedagogy remain to be formulated with, as starting point, an analysis of class in the framework of a specific, theoretical study.

4. University critical practice is inseparable from a generalized social critical practice. It must hinge upon all the other aspects of the revolutionary class struggle; to begin with, therefore, upon the worker struggle.

5. The Nanterre-*Sciences humaines* section calls on all teachers to collectively investigate these problems, and to look for specific ways of acting upon them.

6. The Nanterre-*Sciences humaines* section will undertake to find forms of cooperation with the student movement in the framework of the counter university.

—Excerpt from the *Bulletin du Syndicat National de l'enseignement supérieur*, May, 1968.

On April 29 two texts, very different as to spirit, were adopted by a "general assembly" of assistants and assistant professors who, quite evidently, were swinging over to the student side.

Document 25

Excerpt from the Minutes of the Faculté *Council Meeting*

The teaching body has unanimously expressed its determination to see
to it that examinations take place under normal conditions.
     Written tests will begin on Wednesday, May 22.

        —Nanterre *Faculté des Lettres et Sciences Humaines,* April 29, 1968.

Document 26

Motion of the Assembly of Nanterre
Assistants and Assistant Professors

The general assembly of assistants and assistant professors, at a meeting that took place in Nanterre on Monday, April 29, 1968,[74]
     1. Recognizes that there exists a real state of crisis in the tradi-
tional University structures, both from the economic and pedagogical
standpoints, and from the standpoint of social aims. This crisis will not
be settled by applying the plan of technocratic elimination we have
been promised.
     2. Notes that student disturbances, by their very violence, high-
light these problems, which are serious, and concern all of us, students
and teachers alike.
     3. Declares that it favors a University policy which is not content
to asphyxiate the problems raised, by neutralizing or repressing the
student movement, but which demonstrates, through ways to be discussed, this critical solidarity—that is, solidarity within the crisis—between students and teachers.
     This assembly asks that a meeting of the *faculté* assembly be
held before the *faculté* council meets, with participation of all the assistants and of a student delegation.
     It asks for publication *in extenso* of the entire minutes, for dis-
tribution to all faculty members.
     The assembly declares that it opposes the setting up of any sort
of permanent police force inside the *faculté.*
     The assembly considers that examinations should take place nor-
mally, and protests against any attempt to sabotage them. It refuses to
supervise holding of examinations in the presence of police inside the
faculté.[75]

The assembly declares its opposition to any plan to close the *faculté*.

On Thursday, May 2, René Rémond's class in contemporary history was interrupted by some *"enragés"* who asked to occupy his amphitheatre. Somebody threw a bench in the direction of the rostrum. This incident, with others, led the dean to decide to suspend all teaching *sine die*. Eight Nanterre students (among them Daniel Cohn-Bendit and Michel Pourny, leader of the FER) were referred to the University disciplinary council.[76] Then *Occident* announced its intention of "ridding the Sorbonne of Marxists." Actually, on the morning of May 2, somebody set fire to the Sorbonne premises of the FGEL.[77] Meanwhile, at the Censier annex of the Paris *Faculté des Lettres* a leaflet made its contribution to the project for boycotting examinations by publishing a mock resolution supposed to have been adopted by Sorbonne faculty members. However, the dean stopped its distribution.

The next morning, in *l'Humanité,* Georges Marchais denounced the "dirty business" of the group led by the German anarchist Cohn-Bendit, and recalled the German[78] origin and presence in the United States of Herbert Marcuse, intellectual guide, if not of the Nanterre students, in any case of those in Berlin.

Document 27

FOR THE FIRST TIME IN THE HISTORY
OF THE UNIVERSITY
*The Sorbonne faculty have announced publicly
their intention of refusing to mark
examination papers this year!*[79]

On the initiative of the Sorbonne section of the SNESUP., an important meeting, presided over by the dean, of all assistants, assistant professors, titular and other professors attached to the Paris *Faculté des Lettres,* took place Tuesday evening in the salle Louis Liard. This is the first time that a general gathering of Sorbonne professors has been open to all the assistants! But the most striking feature of the meeting is, above all, that it should have taken place in the presence of student observers, representing all the political movements and unions at the Sorbonne. It was almost a revolution!

This is a far cry from the *faculté* assembly's refusal to receive the student delegates on November 18. A far cry from the mandarinate that a few *"enragés"* continue to denounce! This permits us to measure the depth of the evolution that has taken place among the teachers confronted with the University crisis and with the government's policy.

The discussion was long but fertile. It was as though each one were vying with the others to find new motives, all of them justifiable, for the final decision, which was adopted with unaccustomed unanimity.

Following are some excerpts from the resolution voted on Tuesday:

The Sorbonne teachers, assistants, and professors, unionized or nonunionized, at a general assembly meeting on Tuesday, April 30 in the salle Louis Liard[80] at the Sorbonne, being conscious of the important mission of higher education to educate and to mold, and being desirous of ensuring continuation of this fundamental mission in the best interests of all concerned, note that throughout the year it has been impossible for them to accomplish their task under proper conditions. . . . They regret that the indispensable means for regular functioning of the University should not have been placed at the disposal of those who frequent it. In addition, they consider that the recent reorganization of higher education imposed upon the University is of such a nature as to hamper discharge of its scientific and pedagogical functions, and that it is therefore extremely untimely and harmful. . . . Consequently, they are of the opinion that, under the present circumstances of penury and incoherence, any attempt at verification of a student's knowledge risks being a mere illusion. Members of the Sorbonne faculty firmly assert that teachers should not be expected to stanch the holes in government policy, nor should students have to bear the brunt of them. They refuse to validate through the expedient of final examinations the lamentable consequences of the situation in the University. . . .

But even more, perhaps, they want to point out the general malaise from which everybody connected with the University suffers, beginning with the students. This is the context in which Nanterre students are protesting, with a vigor and courage that command respect, the conditions that obtain there. . . . The only way to remedy the present critical situation in the University is by completely overhauling the entire institution, and to begin with by reexamining the teaching methods, which are based on an intolerable system of "selection" and hierarchical rating. . . . The Sorbonne faculty, in complete awareness of the responsibilities of their function, and of the implications of their decision, announce publicly their intention of refusing to mark examination papers for the June and October 1968 sessions. All candidates will be considered to have passed. . . .

They declare that they are prepared to discuss this matter in the lecture halls, with the students, and examine with them the necessary means for carrying out this project, as well as for their common defense.

STUDENTS

IF YOU DON'T BELIEVE IT GO ASK THEM

AND COME AND TELL US HOW IT WENT!

Although this solution would be the best, the most honorable, and the most effective, if the teachers refuse to assume their responsibilities, a lot of students have already shown that they want to assume theirs.

During the meetings and discussions that have taken place since the beginning of the campaign of information and preparation for action on the subject of examinations, the students have emphasized the need to come as near as possible to radical confrontation on the subject of the examination system. A certain number of proposals have been made, some of which follow.

PROPOSAL I

Systematic sabotage of test papers

1. Pilfering, misappropriation, or destruction of examination subjects: either through third party complicity beforehand (and in this case, of course, immediate distribution to candidates) or forcibly, during the test (one possible risk: change of subjects).

2. Circulation of corrected papers during the test: this action should start at the end of the second hour (you can't leave the room until the end of the first hour, and it takes about an hour to get a corrected paper ready) so that multigraphed copies of the corrected papers would have to be distributed, or they would be dictated from outside.

3. Invasion and occupation of the examination rooms, with a certain number of teachers participating. Quite evidently, too, students who have been victims of the iniquitous equivalence system are not going to want to retake examinations they have already passed, but that they would normally have had to pass this year. This proposal is only valid if the students decide to remain more than an hour in the occupied examination hall.

PROPOSAL II

Destruction, misappropriation, or temporary withholding of individual administrative files.

This action requires a sense of minutia and responsibility. For *Lettres,* the files are kept at Censier in a room that is easily accessible.

There are many safe places where these files can be stored and kept in good condition.

PROPOSAL III

Systematic destruction of results as they are published; strike or general boycott of examinations.

This requires the agreement of all concerned as well as powerful resources, but there is no doubt that it is the objective to be aimed at; however, numerous variations on this general theme of action could be proposed.

PROPOSAL IV

Interruption of oral examinations which, as we all know, are public.

It is not yet the moment to publish all the other proposals. However, both teachers and students should know that discussion has started on the subject. We should publish, at the most, a well founded criticism of examinations and of the capitalist University. We should refrain from all venturesome projects, but successfully carry out everything that thoughtful, unitary action will permit us to achieve.

Notes

1. Paradoxically, *Socialisme ou Barbarie* had disappeared in 1965; a dissident group (since 1963) had been publishing the periodical *Pouvoir Ouvrier*, the tone of which was resolutely working class. During the May events, *Pouvoir Ouvrier* put out two commercially printed issues. See also D. Mothé, *Journal d'un ouvrier*, Paris, 1958.

2. Who published the review *l'Internationale situationniste*. No. 11 of this review (October 1967) contained a document on the Strasburg affair with press notices. See also *Le Monde*, November 26, 1966; December 9, 1966 (article by F. Gaussen); January 12, and 15–16, 1967; March 6 and 9, 1967; April 15 and 18, 1967; and Ph. Nazaire, "Dix jours qui ébranlèrent Strasbourg," *Christianisme social*, 3–4, 1968.

3. This is a return to the Hegelian-Marxist myth of the end, if not of history, at least of prehistory.

4. An expression in vogue during May.

5. In addition, we may recall the declaration made by Cohn-Bendit: "Most useful would be . . . to publish an anthology of the best texts that appeared in *Socialisme ou Barbarie, l'Internationale situationniste, Information et Correspondance ouvrière, Noir et Rouge, Recherches libertaires,* and, to a lesser degree, in the Trotskyist reviews." *Le Gauchisme, remède à la maladie sénile du communisme,* p. 18. On *Socialisme ou Barbarie,* see the discussion between G. Genette, E. Morin, and Cl. Lefort in *Arguments,* No. 4, June–September 1957; R. Estivals devoted to *l'Internationale situationniste* a good part of his article, "De l'avant-garde esthétique à la révolution de mai," *Communications,* No. 12, 1968. Like *Socialisme ou Barbarie, l'Internationale situationniste,* founded in 1957, made radical criticism both

of capitalism and of bureaucracy but, following in the footsteps of Henri Lefebvre, the accent was placed on the analysis of industrial society as a spectacle. The spectacle being the moment "when merchandise has come to be the total occupation of social life" (G. Debord).

Only creative spontaneity, examples of which have been given by workers' councils, can create "situations"—that is to say, "concrete constructions with the momentary impression of life" which lead to the appearance of a "parallel society" and "the end of prehistory." Although *l'Internationale situationniste*, like *Socialisme ou Barbarie*, rejects the Leninist conception of the party, it nevertheless had its interdictions and its expulsions like any other "groupuscule." On the IS and its role during May, see J. L. Brau, *Cours, camarade . . .* , pp. 67–71, 162–166; E. Brau, *le Situationnisme ou la nouvelle internationale*, Debresse, Paris, 1968; R. Viénet, *Enragés et situationnistes dans le mouvement des occupations*, Gallimard ("official" point of view with collection of documents).

6. And also several intellectuals grouped around Daniel Guérin. The "six days war" had provoked violent confrontations between intellectuals who were in the same camp during May.

7. Concerning the different "groupuscules," cf. below, Chapter IV.

8. The CLER considered that the NLF had capitulated before the bourgeoisie and had betrayed the Vietnamese revolution.

9. Demonstration in which the JCR participated.

10. *Avant-Garde Jeunesse*, No. 12, May 1968. The language is the same in Italy and in the United States: "Two, Three, Many Columbias" was a title used by Tom Hayden, one of the founders of Students for a Democratic Society, *Ramparts*, June 11, 1968, after the Columbia revolt (end of April to beginning of May).

11. Belgian Trotskyite, economist, and theoretician, editor-in-chief of *La Gauche*.

12. *Falce Martello* (The Hammer and the Sickle), group of young Italian "leftists" close to the JCR. The Italian Socialist Party of Proletarian Unity (PSIUP) broke with the Nenni party when it merged with the Social Democratic Party.

13. This is the origin of the Paris slogan for May 6–7: "We are a 'group-uscule' . . ."

14. Cf. below, pp. 85 ff.

15. A photo illustrating another article devoted to Poland, emphasizes the fact that Peter Brandt, SDS militant, participated in a demonstration of support for the Polish students.

16. A reference to successive strikes at Rhodiaceta (since March 2, 1967) is found in the book by Ph. Bauchard and M. Bruzek, *Le Syndicalisme à l'épreuve*, pp. 160–165, but *no* allusion to the violent events at Caen, Redon, etc.

17. In this domain, no "polite resolutions," no petition as to fundamentals, however solemn, can accomplish anything against the social hierarchy of the educational system. Cf. J.-C. Passeron, in G. Antoine and J.-C. Passeron, *la Réforme de l'université*, Paris, 1966, pp. 201–205.

18. A *lycée* principal who was not very well disposed toward the Leftists wrote, after May: "When I explain to a child's family that I can't take him because he doesn't live in the zone from which the pupils for that *lycée* are recruited, I feel like a gendarme or a customs inspector. But when I'm obliged to refuse a prospective pupil who answers to all the requirements, for lack of room, then I feel more like a shopkeeper during the German occupation." Robert Bréchon, *La fin des lycées*, p. 40, Paris, 1970.

19. Cf. F. Gaussen and Guy Herzlich, "Le rêve de Nanterre," *Le Monde*,

May 7, 1968; A. Touraine in Ph. Labro, *Ce n'est qu'un début*, pp. 38–47; Episté-mon, *Ces idées qui ont ébranlé la France, Nanterre novembre 1967–juin 1968*, Paris 1968; H. Lefebvre, *l'Irruption de Nanterre au sommet;* Cohn-Bendit, *Le gau-chisme* . . . , pp. 28–56. There is a good account of the principal events in L. Rioux and R. Backmann, *op. cit.*, pp. 40–87. See especially A. Touraine, *le Mouve-ment de mai* . . . , pp. 96–125, J. Bertolino, *les Trublions*, pp. 55–82 and 225–382, R. Lourau, "Nanterre 1968, La transe institutionelle," *Autogestion*, No. 7 (January 1969), repeated in his *l'Instituant contre l'institué*, pp. 155–169.

20. Cf. above, p. 1070.

21. Gilbert Badia, professor at Nanterre and member of the Communist Party, estimated that a quarter or a third of the students at Nanterre ended by joining the movement launched March 22, 1968. He rightly considered this propor-tion a large one. (*Démocratie nouvelle*, June–July, 1968, p. 63).

22. Prouvost heads the most important woollen industries group in France. He also owns *Le Figaro*.

23. Theoretically correct but, in fact, the student movement gave the *faculté* an opportunity to ignore them and in this way to act independently.

24. The "blacklist" is a myth. This was not the case as regards the police.

25. Demand for democracy at the lowest echelon, which is also typical of the *"enragé"* movement.

26. Claude Estier has given his own account of these contacts with the Nanterre students (for the most part members of the UNEF) in *Journal d'un Fédéré*, Paris, 1970, pp. 199–202.

27. "Combat Committees," "Youth Demonstration" (*en masse*) are the style of the CLER, the future FER. Cf. below, pp. 253 ff.

28. Former Dean and acting Dean of the *Faculté de Droit* and the *Faculté des Sciences*.

29. The solemn opening of the school year at the University of Paris was protected by a large police force.

30. "Secrétaire d'état à la jeunesse et aux sports."

31. National Committee of Welfare Organizations, School and University Athletic Organization.

32. Appearance of the request for open-book examinations.

33. See the testimony of R. Francès, in the special students' number of *les Lettres Françaises*, May 15, 1968.

34. R. Aron, *Dix-huit leçons sur la société industrielle*, Paris 1960.

35. Didier Anzieu, psychology professor, whose account of the Nanterre events appeared under the pseudonym "Epistémon."

36. January 4–11, 1968, A. Geismar took part in it.

37. The author of *The American Challenge*, a volume which seemed to be a breviary for technocrats, had been booed by students in Madrid.

38. Because the students of IPES, future secondary school teachers, actually work for a *maîtrise*, whereas the *licence* had been conceived by the Fouchet Plan as a source of teachers for the lower classes of the secondary schools (*premier cycle*). Esprit, Paris, May 1968.

39. The Langevin-Wallon plan, which had been adopted by an official com-mission chaired successively by Paul Langevin and Henri Wallon, was an ambitious program for transforming National Education. It assumed, for instance, that all primary teachers would hold the *licence*.

40. At the Caen seminar, M. Philippe Olmer, new Director for Higher Edu-cation, had proposed a sort of "secondarization" of the first years of higher edu-cation.

41. Partial, slightly revised translation from the above-mentioned collection by A. Cockburn and R. Blackburn, *Student Power,* pp. 373–378. First published in *Esprit,* Paris, May 1968.

42. Cf. above, pp. 104–107, excerpts from this bulletin.

43. All quotations are from the minutes of the commission, dated March 29 and signed by a representative of the students and teachers respectively.

44. There were at Nanterre student groups helmeted and armed with slings and iron bars. The CLER, among others, was conspicuous in this connection, and the fascist group, *Occident,* with methods of its own, later provoked violent counter-actions. It is therefore useless to deny the existence of student terrorism. Even so, no students or professors were seriously hurt as a result of this terrorism. But it is also impossible to compare, as has often been done, the highly calculated violence of Nanterre with police violence, and still more impossible to call the *"enragés"* students "Nazis." Concerning the beginning of the *Mouvement du 22 mars,* see their book: *Ce n'est qu'un début, continuons le combat,* "Cahiers libres," No. 124, pp. 15–18, and especially Cohn-Bendit's *le Gauchisme* . . . , pp. 30–56, in which passages are quoted at length; the text voted during the night of March 22–23 is also quoted in L. Rioux and R. Backmann, *op. cit.,* pp. 50–51; R. Viénet points out that the *"enragés"* broke with the movement from the very beginning and made it a rule to write their slogans on all the walls (*op. cit.,* p. 34).

45. Cf. above, p. 132, *passim.*

46. An allusion to the "Decrees" that reduced working class representation in the Social Security divisions.

47. This statement did not prevent the legend of enormous pillaging from spreading. Cf. *Paris-Presse* of March 30: "The damages . . . add up to some fifty million old francs."

48. Jean Bastié, professor of geography.

49. The *"situationist"* Gérard Bigorgne; cf. below, p. 162.

50. *"21–27,"* *l'Etudiant de France,* publication of the UNEF, supplement to No. 19, March 1968. This press conference did not take place.

51. Cf. *Mouvement du 22 mars, Ce n'est qu'un debut* . . . , p. 19.

52. This appeal to the UNEF against the *"enragés"* was to be one of the two lines adopted by the Communist Party during the May crisis, the line taken particularly by R. Garaudy; cf. below, pp. 284–286 and pp. 555 ff.

53. This refers, naturally, to D. Cohn-Bendit.

54. Cf. above, pp. 104 ff.

55. Cf. above, p. 121.

56. Allusion to the designation of a room for political meetings.

57. The first position is that of the Trotskyites, the second of the anarchists, and the third of the followers of *Socialisme ou Barbarie* and of *Pouvoir Ouvrier.* We note that the Maoist thesis "restoration of capitalism" is not mentioned, and that, inversely, the Chinese problem is not posed.

58. In which only full professors take part.

59. Thus, A. Micha, professor of French, who on May 4 (after the closing of the Sorbonne and the beginning of the repression) wrote a letter to *Le Monde* against "the most stupid intellectual left in the world" and "those little hooligans who call themselves students," which was not published until the 9th (the edition dated the 10th) and which, moreover, appeared to approve of the massive police repression of the 6th and the days that followed.

60. D. Anzieu, under the pseudonym "Epistémon"; but this book does not mention the role played by its author, who signed the proposal but was absent the day it was discussed. Among the other signers of the motion some, such as H.

Elhaï, geography professor, are known for their professional conscientiousness and the absolute devotion they show their students.

61. André Blanc, professor of geography.

62. André Chastognol, professor of ancient history.

63. Jacques Heers, professor of mediaeval history.

64. Ida Maier, professor of Italian.

65. Frédéric Mauro, professor of history.

66. Paul Pélissier, professor of geography.

67. René Rémond, professor of contemporary history.

68. Pierre Riché, professor of mediaeval history.

69. Pierre Sagave, professor of German.

70. Paul Vernière, professor of French.

71. Which is a rather good description (personal account). The 3rd of April, at the meeting of the Nanterre cell, Guy Leclerc, an instructor at Nanterre and former contributor to *l'Humanité,* had warned P. Juquin against such a meeting: "Hundreds of students have been exasperated by the articles in *l'Humanité* signed Charles Silvestre, later joined by Georges Bouvard, who was equally unpopular." It had been decided that the cell would make a definite decision on April 18, but that day *l'Humanité* placed the Nanterre Communists before a *fait accompli* by announcing the meeting for the 25th (G. Leclerc's testimony before a delegation of PCF leaders on June 3). Cohn-Bendit and his friends, without defending P. Juquin, insisted in vain that he be permitted to speak. Already, on November 25, during the strike, the Communist mayor of Nanterre had been booed; cf. Ch. Charrière, *le Printemps des enragés,* p. 31.

72. In the *Nouvel Observateur* of November 1, 1967, Laurent Schwartz had taken a position in favor of a hierarchization of the universities and educational institutions and for a kind of selection which, in his opinion, would be the only way of avoiding selection by pure and simple elimination, such as in fact is practiced.

73. They were for the most part militants of the National Vietnam Committee.

74. This motion represents in reality only a minority of instructors and assistant professors. According to an intermural bulletin of the SGEN (May 10, 1968) the figures are the following: 54 present out of 202; about thirty votes for the motion. On May 3, eight instructors and assistant professors took the initiative for a motion of "support to Dean Grappin in his action to ensure respect for freedom of speech and education in the *Faculté des Lettres.*" One of the signers, Guy Serbat, was a Resistance hero, former Lt. Col. of the FFI, commander of the regiment "La Marseillaise" during the liberation of Marseilles, former member of the Communist Party; another, Claude Willard, is one of the authors of the official (and falsified) history of the French Communist Party. Merely to recall this fact gives an idea of the confusion that reigned in people's minds.

75. One may ask if these two sentences are not contradictory, because it was clear, at that date, that a number of examinations would be sabotaged.

76. They appeared on May 6; the verdict would never be pronounced.

77. *"Fédération des groupes d'études de Lettres."*

78. In retrospect this "denunciation" is all the more piquant, in view of details that came to light in 1970 in connection with the expulsion from the PCF of Charles Tillon (former Communist resistance leader), and according to which

Georges Marchais had in reality neglected to combat the Nazi occupants and had even agreed to go work in a German factory.

79. Leaflet drafted by militants of the *Mouvement d'action universitaire* (MAU).

80. The salle Louis Liard is known to be the place where candidates for a Doctor's degree appear before a jury to defend their theses.

II

Growth of the Movement
(MAY 3-15)

It would be artificial to make premature connection between the Nanterre movement and events at the Sorbonne. While the Nanterre *"enragés"* were protesting, above all, against a certain type of teaching, no serious incidents of the kinds already mentioned had occurred in the vastly more respectful Sorbonne. Beginning on May 3, the protest of an increasing number of students was directed against the police, who actually had been called in by the academic authorities. Whereas in Nanterre the slogan had been "Professors, you are too old," at the Sorbonne, on the morning of May 6, there were shouts in chorus of "Profs not cops," and cries of "CRS—SS" (identifying the riot police with Nazi ss troops) followed *la Grappignole* (a parody combining the revolutionary song "La Carmagnole" with the name of the Nanterre Dean, Grappin). By the afternoon of May 6, many members of the Sorbonne faculty, and even more from the Halles aux vins (Science) faculty, were demonstrating with the students.

On the morning of May 3, the fact that Nanterre had been closed and that students of the *22 mars* group had been summoned to appear before the disciplinary council prompted student militants to hold a meeting in the Sorbonne courtyard. An *Occident* commando had set fire to the headquarters of the *Faculté des Lettres* Federation of Study Groups, with the result that the atmosphere in which this meeting took place was a tense one. In answer to the call to arms sent out by the UNEF, militants of the JCR, FER, and MAU participated. The latter distributed a leaflet which is interesting for several reasons: it contains the first call for the May 6th demonstration and, above all, shows the rapid spread of typically Nanterre themes to the Sorbonne, especially the violent attack against "mandarins" and "pundits."[1] There is also the same error as regards the number of students summoned to appear before the University council: 18 instead of 8 (other documents give the figure as 7).

Document 28

A Trial at the Sorbonne

Dean Grappin of Nanterre has brought charges before the University council against 18 (*sic*) Nanterre students. These comrades, who are members of the *Mouvement du 22 mars,* run the risk of being expelled from the University.

The official reasons: assault and battery, insults to lecturers and professors while performing their duties.

The real reasons: by taking disciplinary measures against the so-called leaders, the University bureaucracy wants to bring pressure on the Nanterre students, to intimidate them and break up their movement.

ACADEMIC VESTALS

COULD IT BE THAT YOU ARE AFRAID INSIDE YOUR TEMPLE?

Today, the racist newspaper *Minute* states: "In the present turmoil, this Cohn-Bendit must be picked up by the scruff of the neck (. . .) and in case the authorities are not up to doing it, we know a certain number of young Frenchmen who are *itching* to accomplish this gesture for the common welfare."

The same day, at 8 o'clock in the morning, these same "young Frenchmen" left their mark on the walls of the Sorbonne ⊕ when they set fire to the headquarters of the FGEL.

Yesterday, the government and its courts started legal action against Danny Cohn-Bendit.

Now, academic bureaucracy, several measures behind as usual, is falling into step with the government and with *Minute.*

DEAR DEAN, DEAR MANDARINS, THE REPRESSIVE FORCE YOU
WANT TO MAKE USE OF TODAY IS THE OTHER SIDE
OF THE SERVILE IMPOTENCE YOU MANIFESTED
YESTERDAY:

You *accept* all that the students reject, you *give in* only when the students *oblige* you to do so: you have accepted the *Fouchet Plan,* you have accepted the *Peyrefitte proposals,* what else will you accept? You have been asked to act and you have only *talked.* You have been asked to be *teachers* and you are nothing but *pundits;* behind your *façade* of neutrality and autonomy, you are nothing but *pillars* of the bourgeois University. Dear Dean, dear Mandarins, do not consider this insulting, do not look upon it as extravagance. It had to be said because it is so.

Also, in bringing our comrades to trial, you will appear as the *principal accused*. We do not believe that it is still possible to speak of misunderstanding between the students and yourselves. Because, very fortunately, although there are many mandarins, professors still exist and they judge you the way we judge you.

DEAR DEAN, DEAR MANDARINS, IN BRINGING ACTION AGAINST 18
NANTERRE STUDENTS, YOU WANT TO PUT ALL STUDENTS
ON TRIAL.
DO NOT EXPECT TO DIVIDE US
YOU WILL NOT SUCCEED: WE HAVE WAITED A LONG TIME
TOO LONG A TIME
AND WE HAVE BEEN IGNORED, BY YOU, AS WELL AS BY
THE GOVERNMENT

Monday, for this trial, as also for the examinations, you will have the support, if needed, of the police force, of the stupidities of the press, and of bourgeois opinion: but, against you, there will be many teachers and the great majority of the students.

MONDAY, AT THIS TRIAL, WE WILL ALL ANSWER PRESENT. MONDAY,
WE WILL TURN THE TABLES ON YOUR LAWSUIT AND WE WILL TURN
YOU INTO THE PRINCIPAL ACCUSED.

*Everybody, Students and Professors, is urged
to be present at the Sorbonne with our comrades
from Nanterre.*

MONDAY, MAY 6, FROM 9:00 A.M. ON

—*Mouvement d'action universitaire*, May 3.

In spite of the many motives for mobilization and the arrival at the Sorbonne of the *22 mars* militants, the meeting was not very well attended—a few hundred people at the most. A new feature was that the meeting, which broke up at about one o'clock, was resumed at two. Militants of the groups already mentioned took the floor again, plus representatives of the PSU and Communist students. Still more surprising was the fact that whereas the UNEF had stationed its marshals inside the Sorbonne in anticipation of a fascist coup, the students who attended the meeting did not disperse, but improvised a discussion on current political problems in front of the Sorbonne chapel.

Soon the situation began to grow tense; word was passed that an *Occident* group was in the neighborhood; then the police arrived. A stormy interview took place with the rector's secretary, M. Bartoli, ending up with veiled threats on the part of the authorities who demanded the removal of the "pretorian guards" (term used by the rector's secretary to describe the student marshals, who were armed with their traditional ax-handles). A few minutes later the ampitheaters and the Sorbonne library were closed, and the *Union des étudiants communistes* began to distribute the following leaflet: "Leftist leaders are making a pretext of govermental neglect and speculating on the discontent of the students to try to obstruct the functioning of the *facultés* and prevent the students from working and taking their examinations." Meanwhile, some of the marshals began to hammer out the *Komintern Call* with their "weapons."

At 4:45 P.M., without the slightest official or officious summons, police squads led by M. Bartoli, entered the Sorbonne courtyard by way of the rue des Ecoles. The students, who had decided that they would offer no resistance, were quickly surrounded by government forces (Paris policemen, monitors in khaki, *gendarmes mobiles*). Although it was promised that they would be allowed to evacuate the Sorbonne voluntarily, actually the trapped students began to be picked up immediately. This operation continued until about 7 P.M.; since there was no room in the police cars, the girls were allowed to leave unmolested. The demonstration that broke out spontaneously on the Place de la Sorbonne, to shouts of "Free our comrades," brought sharp repression from the very start (5:30 P.M.) and soon the first paving stones were being thrown. This spontaneity is all the more remarkable since the large majority of student leaders were being held prisoner inside the Sorbonne, except for some of the militants of the *Fédération des étudiants révolutionnaires* who, as soon as the demonstration got under way, repeatedly called for disbandment.

As of that first Friday the militant students were aware of a political split. For the first time, without any party directives, the Latin Quarter began to mobilize. From then on the immediate goal, over and above satisfaction of urgent demands, was to enter into contact with the workers. This contact, which had started on May 11, during the "night of the barricades," and been materialized by the May 13 demonstration, achieved its political conclusion with occupation of the Sud-Aviation factory on May 14 and with occupation of the Renault factory in Cléon on the afternoon of May 15. What had been historical shadow play—the mimetic enthusiasm at the Sorbonne —had suddenly emerged on a front that was at once more classical and more determinant of the class struggle, which was the labor front.

On the morning of May 4, both labor unions and student movements felt that police repression had set a new process in motion. The following leaflet, which appeared during the forenoon, and had all the earmarks of the MAU, insisted on the necessity for grass roots organization that the situation had revealed. It also showed how the conscious intervention of the most politicized among the militants tended to capitalize on what, for the moment, was nothing more than a protest movement. A second leaflet, not included here, emphasized particularly organization of student information, and by Saturday the idea of a combat newspaper that would be put out by all the organizations participating in the struggle was in the air. This was *Action,* which appeared on May 7.

Document 29

So That the Revolt Will Not Be a One-Day Flash in the Pan—

how to form an action committee

WHY ACTION COMMITTEES?
Because, in the vast student revolt movement, crystallized by events in the Latin Quarter on Friday, it was proved that numerous students who were not members of union or political organizations wanted to participate in the action.

Because the structures of the UNEF union are neither sufficient nor well adapted.[2] The movement of revolt against academic bureaucracy and the Gaullist government is not concerned with political-trade union cleavages. It must be a movement of militants, belonging to the militants.

Because one of the great weaknesses of our new movement is its absence of organization. Political militants are dispersed in countless groups, others are awaiting orders from an inexistent leadership. The lying press, the University mandarins, the government cops, all secretly hope that, tomorrow, order will be restored. Let us show them that our revolt is not a one-day affair.

To extend the revolt started on Friday, we must organize ourselves into action committees at the grass roots.

HOW TO CREATE A COMMITTEE
First case: your faculté *is closed.* To begin with, contact your fellow-students in the lecture hall by telephone or letter; meet together; de-

cide on a leaflet, a form of action; make contact with other action committees or with the provisional coordination committees. Arrange meetings with members of your committee for demonstrations.

Second case: your faculté *is not yet closed.* Meet in the lecture halls, on University premises according to majors, in the lecture halls according to class year. Encourage the mass of students to organize into action committees. Set up headquarters. Do not be satisfied with having the strike respected. Put up posters on what is happening, on what must be done. Force the professors to say where they stand. Win the support of the workers to whom the press lies daily. But, as long as the University is not closed by the *gardes-mobiles* or the CRS, meet inside the University. In this way we will give evidence of what is meant by political freedom of speech for students within the University.

IN ANY CASE

—*Take the initiative!*

—*Contact the provisional coordinating action committees!*

Everybody, come to the Latin Quarter Monday morning where the *agrégation* examination will take place and the disciplinary council will meet.

May 4.

The next leaflet, dated May 5, reacts against accusations made by the press and stresses particularly the problem of self-defense in view of police brutality. On Saturday the 4th and Sunday the 5th, the MAU was extremely active. Its militants called for a counter-attack, without waiting for directives—which were slow in coming—from the National Committee of the UNEF. It was evident here too that the term "action committees" was a new one, a new organizational form in this milieu: the chief problem was to organize the grass roots. The following text is one of the first to give the Paris phenomenon an international perspective.

Document 30

A Handful of Agitators?

"Riots in the Latin Quarter," "the *'enragés'* on the rampage," etc. For the press, from *l'Humanité* to *l'Aurore,* Friday's events are the work of a "handful of students," "trouble makers," and "agitators."

The newspapers state that "400 hotheads have gone too far" and they call them Public Enemy No. 1.

THE PRESS LIES AND TRIES TO EXCITE THE POPULATION AGAINST THE STU-
DENTS. IN EFFECT, WHAT REALLY DID HAPPEN?

On Friday, several hundred students met together in the Sorbonne:

Not only to protect the Sorbonne against the repeated attacks of the neo-Nazi commandos who had already attacked isolated students and set fire to the headquarters of organizations during the week.

But also to inform the students about the closing of the Nanterre *faculté* and about the appearance of 7 students from Nanterre before a University tribunal on Monday.

At the beginning of the afternoon, at the Sorbonne, discussions were taking place in an absolutely calm atmosphere.

Suddenly, for the first time in many years, helmeted and armed policemen invaded the Sorbonne at the request of the Rector, Jean Roche. Refusing to react to the evident provocation that the police intrusion represented, the students agreed to leave the premises quietly, if let alone. The students (527) were surrounded by policemen armed with rifles, and all of them were pushed into police cars.

Spontaneously, outside the Sorbonne, young people, *lycée* students, passersby, and other students protested against these mass arrests and were violently taken to task by the police:

"In one corner a student was holding his arm. He was bent double. Three CRS came back and clubbed him again, while the young girl who was with him screamed in terror: 'Don't do that! Stop hitting him, he is in pain!' . . . 'Stop . . . you're crazy,' " shouted a woman of about 50, trembling and bewildered. . . . Some CRS ran at her and clubbed her with all their might. . . ."

That was how *Paris-jour* described the events. However, in its editorial, *Paris-jour* considered the students as the "enemy no. 1," in total contradiction to the description it had given of the attitude of the police.

Le Figaro ignored the events and attacked the students but not the police:

"Students, these young people? They are answerable to the police court rather than to the University."

Le Parisien libéré followed suit: "Public opinion is beginning to be aroused and it understands less and less why a few dozen students . . ." etc.

WHY THIS REPRESSION?

The press, the radio, the government, through disciplinary, administrative, and police measures, are trying to intimidate the students.

By bringing charges, by making rapid on-the-spot judgments, the government and the bureaucratic University, having ignored student demands for years, want to break up their movement by striking at the so-called leaders.

Government propaganda is trying to present what in reality is a profound movement for the reexamination of the Gaullist University, as mere agitation artificially kept alive by a few *"enragés,"* whom it would suffice to liquidate summarily.

If this movement is so artificial, how can we explain the fact that it has a general character, and that everywhere, from Berlin to Rome, students are refusing to accept a University that is imposed upon them, whose aims are to make them into docile instruments of the regime and of its economy, for exploitation of the people.

The government knows that with this refusal students are questioning the power of the bourgeoisie and its bureaucracy in every sector of society.

This is why the government wants to isolate the students from other sectors of the population and from the workers.

THIS IS WHY THE POLICE PROVOKED, ATTACKED, AND CLUBBED INDISCRIMINATELY.

AT THE SORBONNE, DESPITE GUARANTEES, STUDENTS MEETING QUIETLY WERE HANDED OVER BODILY TO THE POLICE.

UNDER THESE CIRCUMSTANCES, STUDENTS ON THE OUTSIDE DID NOT WANT TO HAVE THE SAME EXPERIENCE: IT WAS NORMAL THAT WE SHOULD DEFEND OURSELVES.

WE WILL NOT LET OURSELVES BE MUZZLED BY ADMINISTRATIVE, DISCIPLINARY, AND POLICE REPRESSION. WE CANNOT LEAVE THESE MEASURES UNANSWERED.

This is why we call upon the population to reject the lies of the press and to support us.

This is why we call on students to organize committees, to answer back on every level, everywhere, during the next few days and particularly from Monday on, when seven of our comrades from Nanterre will be appearing before a disciplinary council.

Latest news: Jean Clément, president of the Richelieu center,[3] has been sentenced to two months imprisonment (without reprieve) along with four other comrades.

—*Mouvement d'action universitaire.*

During the day of Sunday the 5th, the UNEF published a leaflet. But it had a critical reception, the militants of the UNEF's national board being completely snowed under—all the more so since some of them, who were members of the PSU, had to take part in a national congress of PSU students that was being held the same day. The result was that the leaflet, because of its physical aspect, its contents, and the way it was worded, was more in the line of the *Fédération des étudiants révolutionnaires* (whose militants had had it printed,[4]) than in that of the UNEF board.

Document 31

Call to the Population

Police violence erupted in savage repression against the students during the evening of Friday, May 3: 596 arrests, hundreds of injured. Like the workers at Caen and elsewhere, students, passersby, even *lycée* students were victims of fierce repression.

In effect, their struggle is fundamentally the same: workers reject the society that exploits them, students reject a University that tends to make them the docile leaders of a system founded upon exploitation, sometimes even the direct accomplices of this exploitation.

The reactionary press aims at presenting the student movement as a revolt of privileged youth and seeks to cut us off from our natural allies. The bourgeoisie knows that it is with the workers and only with them that the students can win. Against this wall of lies the students must make known to the public the motives of their struggle.

THE BOURGEOISIE SEEKS TO ISOLATE
AND TO DIVIDE THE MOVEMENT.
Our answer must be immediate; here is why:

THE UNEF PROPOSES THAT THE UNIONS OF TEACHERS AND WORKERS RETURN TO THE UNIFYING PROCESS WHICH ACTUALLY FUNCTIONED DURING THE DEMONSTRATION:

Workers, lycée *and University students have spontaneously responded, with the* UNEF, *to police aggression.*

Against police repression,
Against the reactionary press,
Against the bourgeois University,

GENERAL STRIKE FROM MONDAY ON, AND UNTIL THE LIBERATION
OF ALL OUR COMRADES; EVERYBODY PARTICIPATE IN THE DEMON-
STRATION IN THE LATIN QUARTER ON MONDAY AT 6:30 P.M.

Students, organize basic UNEF combat committees in your
facultés, by departments or by class year, to continue the struggle, particularly in view of the coming examinations. Permanent headquarters
will be set up from now on by the UNEF in order to organize formation of these committees. Comrades injured in the course of the demonstrations or witnesses of police aggression, are asked to get in touch
with the UNEF.

                                        —*Union nationale des étudiants de France* [May 5].

After the order for a general strike had been launched by the
UNEF and by the SNESUP. ("the national board of SNESUP., in solidarity
with the students, calls on all members of the faculties of higher education to participate in a general strike in all the universities"), reactions
began to appear in the provinces; as witness this leaflet from Clermont-Ferrand, dated May 5, which here again bears the stamp of the
FER.

Document 32

AGEC[5] *Inform*

Halt Repression!

For the first time in the history of the University, the Sorbonne has
been invaded by police, to prevent the meeting for solidarity with the
Nanterre students organized by the UNEF. "Although no incident had
occurred during the meeting" (communiqué of the Sorbonne *Lettres*
department of the SNESUP.), nearly 600 students were arrested.

The *gardes-mobiles* came inside the Sorbonne and forced the
demonstrators to evacuate the premises in small groups which were
directed toward Black Marias. . . ."

Students who happened to be outside the Sorbonne protesting
against this deliberate violation of the fundamental right of assembly,
spontaneously demonstrated throughout the Latin Quarter, where
they were chased and brutally hit by the *gardes-mobiles* and the so-
called *"gardiens de la paix."*

The CRS were leading the fight. They even charged into the halls of apartment houses, invaded several hotels and came out with young people whom they beat up while the public booed. Because of the general reprobation, they stopped, but one of them was heard to say to another, "You won't lose anything by waiting. . . ."

The police reaction reached its climax when the order was given to "clear everything." Blackjacks held high, the CRS attacked, hitting with all their might in all directions. Old women were caught in the general turmoil. A passing motorist shouted his indignation. CRS swooped down on his car and tried to pull him out of it, hitting him while he was still seated. They succeeded at last in getting him out of the vehicle, his face bloodied. . . .

This brutal repression has been in the making for several weeks, the result of a systematic campaign of intoxication and calls for police intervention via the press, the radio, and the television. The student movement is presented as being the action of a "minority of *'enragés.'* "

Rector Roche: "a small group of students."

Dean Grappin: "the excesses of a few."

Minister Peyrefitte: "a handful of trouble makers. . . ."

On May 3, 1968, Paris students provided proof that the struggle is not just the affair of a minority. Their spontaneous demonstration brought out more than 2,000 students.

Reform and Blackjacks

The Government has shown, through the use of blackjacks, that it will not stop at any means in order *to liquidate the student movement* before the examination period, when its plan to eliminate hundreds of thousands of us will be implemented.

After the closing of Nanterre (for which the FNEF congratulates itself!), the blackjacking in the Latin Quarter, the closing of the Sorbonne, the forbidding of the UNEF Paris demonstration on Monday, May 6, *how far will the government go* to muzzle the students and liquidate their union movement? How repressive will M. Fouchet, Minister of the Interior, become, in order to have "his" reforms applied?

Students, we should not let ourselves be intimidated by repression and threats!

Occident has asserted its intention to "clean up the University!"

Students, we must organize a rebuttal, we must defend our organization, the UNEF!

SOLIDARITY

With our jailed comrades!

With our comrades who are fighting to protect freedom to unionize!

NO

To police repression!
To mass elimination!

The Syndicat national de l'enseignement supérieur (FEN) *"in solidarity with the students, calls on the faculty in higher education to strike, in all universities."*

L'UNEF calls on all students to join the

GENERAL STRIKE

MONDAY, MAY 6, 1968

—May 5, 1968.

On the evening of Sunday the 5th, four students were tried and given prison terms. The official UNEF demonstration was to take place at 6:30 P.M. This directive was a retreat, however, because on Friday the 3rd an order had gone out for everybody to meet at the Sorbonne at 9 A.M., when Cohn-Bendit and seven students from Nanterre had been ordered to appear before the University disciplinary council. After long negotiations, they entered the Council chamber together, accompanied by their lawyers and professors, after singing the *Internationale*. D. Pourny, one of the leaders of the FER, refused to recognize his "judges" and left.[6]

Actually, on Monday the 6th, the mobilization was so large that by 9 A.M. the demonstration had started on the fringes of the Latin Quarter. Indeed, the number of students taking part in the demonstration (about 8000) bears witness to their unusual combativeness, and it went on uninterruptedly until the meeting at Denfert-Rochereau at 6:30 P.M., which brought out some 20,000 people. The day was further punctuated by a meeting at noon at the *Halle aux vins* and some violent clashes, which were accompanied by the first barricades[7] (composed, for the most part, of cars parked crosswise to hold off police attacks). About 4 P.M., on the rue Saint-Jacques, and that same evening on the Boulevard Saint-Germain, the first anarchist groups carrying black flags made their appearance. Four hundred twenty-two persons were picked up for questioning. Two leaflets, one put out by the MAU, the other by the *22 mars* movement, insist respectively upon the academic, intellectual aspects of the situation, and the social and international dimensions of the struggle. A SNESUP. communiqué, which appeared during the day, called on the entire teaching body to join the street demonstration. The first text calling on young workers to join the students that we have been able to find was put out by the independent Movement of Youth Hostels, an anarchist-oriented organization composed of young factory workers and other employees.

Document 33

The Working Population of Paris

This morning, the Latin Quarter is in a state of siege.

Yesterday, students were given severe prison sentences.

Indeed, for four days now, the press has been lying, slandering the students, attempting to discredit their struggle and to separate them from the rest of the population.

IN EFFECT, WHAT REALLY HAPPENED ON FRIDAY?

[The text then quotes Document No. 30.]

They [the newspapers] aim at presenting what is in reality a deeply rooted movement to reexamine the Gaullist University, as agitation artificially kept alive by some few *"enragés"* whom it would suffice to liquidate summarily.

If this movement is so artificial, how can we explain the fact that it has a general character and that everywhere, from Berlin to Rome, students are refusing to accept a university imposed upon them, whose aims are to make them the *docile instruments of the regime,* of its economy and for the exploitation of the people.

Because that, in fact, is what they want to make of us: good exploiters, specialized idiots in the service of the employers. That, we refuse.

And the government knows very well that this refusal implicates the power of the bourgeoisie in every sector of society.

This is why the police, after having indiscriminately provoked, attacked, and blackjacked students and passersby, want to make a tiny minority of *"enragés,"* who are supposed to have assaulted peaceful policemen who had come there by chance, responsible.

WHO WILL BE CONVINCED THAT SO MANY COPS ARE NECESSARY TO GET THE BETTER OF A HANDFUL OF AGITATORS?

The government wants to end the student revolt because it wants a University which will obey orders and students who will fall into line.

But the students are not going to let themselves be muzzled by administrative, disciplinary, and police repression.

FROM TODAY ON, TOGETHER WITH THE PROFESSORS,
THEY ARE ORGANIZING FOR A REBUTTAL.
THEY COUNT ON THE SUPPORT OF THE WORKING POPULATION OF PARIS.

Refuse the lies of the government and of the press, keep informed through the militants who are handing out these leaflets, talk with them, protect them against police repression.

OURS IS A COMMON STRUGGLE

—*Mouvement d'action universitaire* [May 6].

Document 34

A Flash in the Pan or the Beginning of a Fire?

Why

526 arrests,
13 prison sentences,
more than 100 injured,
7 students brought before the disciplinary council, student arrests all day Sunday,
threats of deportation,
lock-outs in the *facultés,*
a xenophobian and racist press campaign,
raids by fascist gangs,
general police mobilization (concentration of provincial police forces for Paris duty—all leaves cancelled . . .),
thousands of armed cops who transformed the center of Paris into a fortress.

Could it be that the bourgeoisie is beginning to be afraid?

As during the strikes in Caen, Saint-Nazaire, Redon, and Rhodiaceta, the bourgeoisie has understood the danger.[8]

Because from now on, students are using the same fighting methods as the most combative sectors of the working class. By showing up the authoritarian nature of the University, students are in the process of radicalizing their struggle.

The bourgeoisie realizes that it is vulnerable when confronted with the combined fighting forces of workers and students. Consequently, it seeks to distort the facts by slandering the action of the students, and by saying nothing about that of the workers, to repress their movement through violence, before it is too late.

To continue this fight in order to win it means grouping to-gether all those who are ready to fight, combining their energies, and uniting their forces.

The struggle of the Caen workers, of the Redon workers, of those in Rhodiaceta, of young people; the struggle of teachers and students at their places of work, in their cities, must be one and the same struggle.

To isolate one fighting sector is to abandon it to the lash of repression in spite of its resistance and the courage of its militants.

The battles of these last months, of these last days, and of today, prove that the principal and most urgent task is to forge the instruments of a common fight.

The outbursts of anger on the part of workers, students, and young people must not be rapidly extinguished flashes in the pan.

We must organize.

We must maintain contact with the workers, the university and lycée students, in our neighborhoods and at our places of work.

Just as it is impossible to stop the fight once it has started, at the gates of a factory or of a university, it is also impossible to confine it to one country.

LONG LIVE INTERNATIONAL WORKER SOLIDARITY,
LONG LIVE THE STRUGGLE OF THE VIETNAMESE PEOPLE,
LONG LIVE THE STRUGGLE OF WORKERS AND STUDENTS.

—*Mouvement du 22 mars,* Nanterre, May 6.

Document 35

The situation of the demonstrations is getting worse every minute; consequently, the SNESUP. calls upon the entire teaching staff of each University to assume its direct responsibilities—that is to say, to demonstrate in the streets with their students.

—Paris, May 6, 1968.

Document 36

Solidarity of Young Workers with the Students

The students refuse:

To be tomorrow's leaders, accomplices of capitalistic exploitation,

To be the future cops of the bourgeoisie, which is why they question the values of the existing society.

YOUNG WORKERS!
THE STUDENTS' STRUGGLE JOINS WITH THE STRUGGLE
OF YOUNG WORKERS
CULTURE MUST NOT REMAIN A PRIVILEGE
OF THE BOURGEOISIE

The *Mouvement indépendant des auberges de la jeunesse* (Paris area):
Rebels against police repression (in order to be aware of its significance).
Demands real freedom of speech as well as the liberation of jailed militants.
Urges all its militants to call on all union organizations for supporting action.
Calls on its members to support the demands of the students.

—*Mouvement indépendant des auberges de la jeunesse,* May 6, 1968.

The Nanterre *"enragés"* (in reality a few students to the "left" of the *22 mars* movement related to the "Situationist International") distributed a leaflet which more or less attacked "co-option" (before it happened) on the part of the various "groupuscules," including the *22 mars!*

Document 37

The Bellyache[9]

Comrades,
In spite of the avowed collusion between the UEC Stalinists and the reactionaries, last Friday's terrific brawls prove that the students in the struggle are beginning to acquire a conscience they did not have until then: when violence begins, reform is about to end.

The University Council which met today, May 6, will have met in vain: this antiquated form of repression can do nothing against street violence. The expulsion of our comrade Gérard Bigorgne for five years from all French universities—about which nothing was said in the entire press or by any of the "groupuscules" and student associations—and the exclusion that today threatens our comrade René Riesel and six other Nanterre students, constitute nevertheless a way for the university authorities to turn them over to the police.

In the face of repression, the struggle that is bound to come will have to maintain its methods of violent action, which for the moment are its only strength. But above all, it must give the student leaders food for thought. Because there are not only the cops; there are also the lies of the various Trotskyist "groupuscules" (jcr, fer, vo), pro-Chinese (ujc(m-l), Maoist Vietnam Committees (cvb) and anarchists à-la-Cohn-Bendit. Let's settle our own affairs.

The example of the comrades arrested Friday at the Sorbonne who mutinied in the police car that took them away is one to follow.[10] As long as there are only three cops to a Black Maria, we know what to do. The precedent of Brigadier Brunet, who was trepanned yesterday, will be judged: Death to the Pigs!

Already, violence is shutting the traps of the little "groupuscule" leaders; merely to contest the bourgeois University is meaningless when *the entire society must be destroyed.*

LONG LIVE THE ZENGAKUREN![11]

LONG LIVE THE COMMITTEE OF PUBLIC SAFETY FOR VANDALISTS (Bordeaux)!

LONG LIVE THE ENRAGÉS!

LONG LIVE THE SOCIAL REVOLUTION!

LONG LIVE THE I.S.!

LONG LIVE THE ANGRY STUDENTS WHO BROUGHT OUT THIS LEAFLET DISTRIBUTED BY THEIR COMRADES FROM NANTERRE ON MAY 6, 1968.

On May 7 the UNEF and the SNESup. put out a new directive for a demonstration at Denfert-Rochereau, at 6:30 P.M. The Student Union launched the "three points" that were to serve as directives until May 10. Precise technical advice appeared in the UNEF text for protection of demonstrators against the different types of tear gas bombs. (In this connection, the term "chlorine" or "sulphur" bomb is scientifically inaccurate; it was nevertheless very generally used to designate devices that in fact proved to be injurious.[12]) The UNEF then published an appeal to union organizations, and after SNES (secondary school teachers), the *Syndicat général de l'education nationale* (CFDT) joined the movement. The demonstration at Denfert, the original goal of which was to have been either the ORTF (radio) or the Sorbonne, brought out between thirty and forty thousand persons who, after walking as far as the Arc de Triomphe (*Etoile*), returned to the rue de Rennes, where the police charged.

Document 38

UNEF

Yesterday, Monday, May 6, once again the police brutally repressed student demonstrations in Paris, as well as in numerous provincial cities. These demonstrations were protesting against the imprisonment and penalization of militant students and union organizations, as well as against the attitude of the administration and of the police, which tend to turn the University into a battlefield.

Because of this brutality, hundreds of university faculty members, in answer to the call of the SNESup., staged a street demonstration as evidence of effective support, as already shown both in Paris and in the provinces by their determination during the strike.

At the same time, Minister Peyrefitte pretended to be making overtures for a "dialogue."

The attitude of the students and of a large part of the faculty is clear: there can be no dialogue in the present situation; there can be no dialogue between blackjackers and blackjacked.

The University administration and the government have voluntarily created an unparalleled state of violence, and they alone are responsible. Consequently, the only way out of the situation is the following:

1. To withdraw administrative, legal, and University charges against students; to declare null and void the current investigations; to liberate all prisoners.

2. To remove police forces from all University premises and their vicinity.

3. To end lockouts in University institutions.

If precise and immediate measures are taken which give satisfaction on these three points, and therefore allow a return to a normal state of affairs, discussion can then take place on the following points: political and union freedoms at the University, and rejection of selection commissions.

At present, students cannot let themselves be battered down by police violence. They must pursue and intensify their action:

By a general strike in all Paris institutions, distribution of leaflets and of the UNEF newspaper (*Action*) explaining the movement, its origin, and its scope.

Tuesday, May 7 at 6:30 P.M., meet at Denfert-Rochereau

A FEW PRECAUTIONS AGAINST GRENADES

Two types of grenades:

Not very dangerous tear gas grenades.

Fragmentation grenades based on sulphur or chlorine.

Rumicine

1 pill at the beginning of the demonstration,

1 pill when the grenades are thrown.

Lemon

wet a handkerchief with it,

suck on it.

Bicarbonate of soda

around the eyes,

in diluted form on a handkerchief.

Goggles

motorcycle or ski, or a swimming mask.

VARIOUS PROTECTIVE MEASURES

Gloves and helmet (stuffed caps are preferable; actually, people with helmets are the first to be chased)

Newspapers around the body

Garbage can cover as a shield

High shoes or basketball shoes

THE COPS SPURT ACID LIQUIDS
THAT BURN LUNGS AND FACE!

—[May 7].

Document 39

Communiqué

The *Syndicat général de l'éducation nationale* (CFDT) considering that the explosion of violence in the student milieu is the sign of a serious crisis in the University, worsened by threats of elimination based on arbitrary grading, holds the opinion that the definition of true guidance and diversification of teaching methods implies free discussion between representatives of faculty, students, and administration, and demands as an immediate prerequisite to this discussion:

a) removal of police forces from the Latin Quarter;

b) reopening of University premises for resumption of the academic year and of examinations;

c) liberation of students before the dates set, and general measures to restore calm;

d) organization of an elected student representation to university bodies.

The SGEN and the *Union régionale parisienne* CFDT are in contact with government representatives: among others, the police department, concerning these matters.

The CFDT—at the request of the SGEN—is placing its legal service at the disposal of the arrested students.

—Paris, May 7, 1968.

As early as Sunday the 5th, and even more so by Tuesday the 7th, the UJC(m-l) students, in their own name or over the signature of "defense committees against repression," proposed a different tactic from the one that had been decided on by the UNEF and the other groups, which was, for the students to go into working class neighborhoods. In Paris and in the provinces, "committees in support of the people's struggle" were organized by these militants.

Document 40

And Now, to the Factories!

Call to action by the UJC(m-l) *and "Serve the People" Clubs*
Anger is rumbling among the masses. A million out of work. Starvation wages. Fascist repression at Dassault, Citroën, Simca, and in many other plants. The CRS against workers' and peasants' demonstrations in Le Mans, Redon, and Caen.

For several months now, popular revolts have been breaking out against the employers and Gaullism.

Everywhere the reformist party machines, the revisionist leadership of the PCF, and the bureaucratic leadership of the CGT have striven to break the mass movement in Rhodiaceta, at Schwartz-Hautmont, Aluvac, the ceramic factories of Alès, and in many other places. But more and more the CGT and the PCF organizers have been checkmated and unmasked by the mass movement. More and more the masses are becoming conscious of these maneuvers which aim at crushing the class struggle in the factories in order to canalize action in favor of reformist objectives and, above all, of parliamentary debates.

On the occasion of student demonstrations, with violent police repression, popular pressure made itself felt: on Monday and especially Tuesday, workers and young laborers came to demonstrate in the streets with the students. This worker participation reflects the deep-seated anger that exists among the broad masses of the working class against Gaullism, which is a regime of unemployment and misery, and against revisionism, which is a reactionary trick for demobilizing the masses.

The masses want to fight against Gaullism.

On the question of street demonstrations, their slogans, and their itineraries: from now on we must take up the fight against the obstacles erected by the reformists, we must help the masses to overcome these and to clear a way towards the revolutionary class struggle.

Three reactionary forces have leagued together in order to repress and check the revolutionary mass movement.

Gaullism has repeatedly hurled its aggressive troops against the populace, the students, and the workers.

The social democrats (PSU, SFIO, Trotskyites, and the executive committee of the UNEF) were quick to try to turn the student movement to account. Their goals are to keep the students isolated from the working class and limit the movement to reformist objectives: "structural reforms" for the University, openings for young cadres, etc. These objectives are reflected in the reactionary political line followed these past days by the UNEF officers: at all costs keep the students in the Latin Quarter; limit slogans to absurd student demands, incapable of uniting students with the broad masses of workers and peasants.

The revisionists of the PCF and of the CGT leadership began by brutally attacking the student movement, revealing their true counter-revolutionary nature. The anger of the masses exploded against these traitors, who are police accomplices. Frightened, they have retreated a bit and rallied to the operation of their social democratic friends to limit the movement's objectives to the three points laid down by the UNEF officers. That is, the revisionists pretend that the workers are demonstrating for academic freedoms.

This is not true: the workers are demonstrating because they want to fight against Gaullism, a regime of unemployment and misery, because they want to make an end to repression. One flag only can unite the broad masses of workers, poor peasants, and students:

The overthrow of Gaullism.

The conquest of freedom for the broad masses of the people.

Control over the exploiters.

Let us sweep away the reformist slogans, which are purely academic, as well as the small revisionist and social democratic groups who are working together in an attempt to prevent us from having access to the masses of the people and to the revolution!

We must leave the bourgeois neighborhoods, which are not our concern. We must go to the factories and to the working class neighborhoods to join with the workers.

DOWN WITH GAULLISM

FREEDOM FOR THE MASSES OF THE PEOPLE!

—UJC(m-l), *cercles "servir le peuple,"* Tuesday, May 7, 1968.
Printed leaflet.

On May 8, the UNEF and the SNESUP. called for a meeting at 6:30 P.M. at the *Halle aux vins,* in which the Paris SNES joined.[13] Alain Geismar announced that students and teachers would sleep at the Sorbonne, while at the National Assembly, Alain Peyrefitte let it be understood that the Sorbonne might be reopened. The *Union des étudiants communistes* also sent out notices. The meeting ended with a demonstration in the Latin Quarter that was severely held in check, as much by the student marshals as by the forces from police headquarters. The movement became generalized in university cities, as witness, among a hundred other documents, the following leaflet used in Lyons. Meanwhile, large worker, peasant, and student demonstrations were taking place in the West (Le Mans, Rennes, Lorient, Brest, and above all, Nantes).

Document 41

Students, Men and Women

With only a few days to go before exams, the Gaullist government is keeping the *facultés* closed, the Latin Quarter is still under police control, students are in prison. This situation is intolerable.

THE UNION DES ÉTUDIANTS COMMUNISTES DE FRANCE
calls on all students to assemble at 6:30 P.M. [this evening], Wednesday, May 8, at the *Halle aux vins* to demand of the government:

An end to police repression.
Immediate withdrawal of police forces.

Freedom and amnesty for those who are in prison.

Immediate reopening of all the *facultés*.

Guarantees that examinations will be held in orderly fashion.

An emergency plan and special grants to satisfy student demands.

The *lycée* sectors of the UJCF and the UJFF have issued a similar call.

—*Union des étudiants communistes de France.*

During the day of Wednesday certain signs showed the impact of the demonstrations in various sectors, such as, in the CGT (minority) unions, *lycées,* etc.

Document 42

In the Last Analysis, the Future Belongs to the Young People . . . !

Aware of the problems of youth, as much for students as for workers, the workers in artistic bronzes[14] have always fought against governmental neglect in matters of national education and against attacks on democratic and trade union freedoms.

Our union approves and supports, without reservation, the action and demands of the students who are joining in the class struggle of workers and peasants.

The Monopoly State, which fears the workers' fight, wants to isolate the students from the working class and from the general population in order to be in a better position to blackjack them.

The government alone bears the responsibility for the *violence;*

Saint-Germain recalls Charonne[15]; only a united struggle of workers, peasants, and students will bring about the failure of Gaullist repression and will satisfy our demands:

—Withdrawal of police forces from the *facultés* and reopening of same.

—Lifting of sanctions taken against the students.

—Dismissal of charges and respect for academic immunity.

—Democratic and worker reforms for National Education (primary, secondary, technical, and university).

—Repeal of judgments.

—Return to a 40-hour week without salary losses.
—A halt to unemployment! Guaranteed jobs.
—Salary increases.
—Union and political freedoms.

TO THE WORKING POPULATION OF OUR AREA
ANSWER THE CALL FOR UNITED ACTION

—*Syndicat du bronze d'art* CGT–FSM, May 8, 1968.

Document 43[16]

This morning, May 8, a wildcat strike, spontaneously declared to support the demands of Paris students, took place at the *Lycée Georges Clemenceau* in Villemomble (Paris suburb).

The striking students demand:
—Evacuation of the police from school premises.
—Amnesty for indicted students.
—Reopening of the *facultés*.
As lycée *students, we consider that we can present the following* demands:
—Freedom of speech and discussion within the institution.
—Decent sports and school installations, adapted to needs.
—Collaboration between teachers and *lycée* students.
—Need to reform the *baccalauréat* examination.
—No arbitrary restriction for university entrance.

We propose:
—The formation of a liaison committee between teachers and pupils.
—Greater student participation in the administration of the *lycée* and real power for student representatives within the inner council.
—Delivery of the present motion, unanimously approved by participants in the strike, to the rector's office, to the academic supervisors, and to the different *lycées* in this area.

In view of the constantly growing mobilization, the action committees and the *22 mars* movement put out a reminder on the subject of necessary forms of organization and political "musts." The first text contains a reference to the NLF in South Vietnam. The second had existed since May 4 in an earlier form.[17] The following version was revised after the May 6 demonstration.

Document 44

Call from the Action Committees

Comrades,

The Council of Ministers is hesitating, but has not yet given in. It has even adopted a warlike tone. For five days now, students have been holding their own against the most tremendous police mobilization the Latin Quarter has ever witnessed. Friday, 5000; Monday, we were between 15,000 and 20,000; Tuesday, we were 50,000 at the Arc de Triomphe. But anyone could see that on Monday as well as on Tuesday, *the organizing was not equal to the magnificent turnout we obtained.*

Political groups, which are too divided and too numerous, cannot suffice. Nevertheless, we must organize for the fight in the streets; we must organize in the lecture halls, for demonstrations as well as for propaganda among the workers.

The only adequate form of organization is creation *of action committees, at the grass roots, all together, for action.*

1. We must reinforce the splendid unity

achieved these last few days. In spite of the lies of the press on Saturday, in spite of the furious attacks against the "leftists" and University and *lycée* students, young people knew which side they were on: against the police, with the students.

The mass of those who demonstrated are shouting their indignation against all those who condemned them, whether they were from *Le Figaro, l'Humanité,* or *le Parisien libéré.* But they want to remain together, not to be spread out in countless political groups.

THE MASS OF DEMONSTRATORS IS RIGHT!
LET US PRESERVE THE UNITY ACHIEVED IN THE STREETS!

2. We must reinforce our action

in the streets, against the police, in the neighborhoods, with the workers. Some think that the police, the police headquarters, and the

government cannot give in. But they're wrong! We can defeat the
police. Nothing can resist resolute masses for long. Yesterday evening,
Peyrefitte and Grimaud were panic-stricken, overwhelmed. They hardly
succeeded in holding the Latin Quarter. They were obliged to leave
most of Paris unguarded. By accentuating our pressure, by increasing
our action, we can:

—Liberate University premises and surrounding areas.

—Liberate all our comrades.

—Get the lockout at the *facs* annulled.

—Force the academic chief, Roche, to resign.

—Obtain complete freedom of political expression in the *facs*.

But we must not forget: to win the workers' support is at least
as important as to hold the streets against police barbarism. In Brittany
today, workers and peasants are on strike and are demonstrating. We
are with them. We help each other mutually.

It is difficult to construct a barricade, but it is more difficult still
to organize the overall combat with its countless indissolubly linked
forms: propaganda, information, and demonstrations.

For this, on the other side of the world, the NLF is showing us
how to do it: since yesterday, it is in control of a majority of the
Saigon districts and is victoriously resisting the attacks of the American
imperialists. But they can do this because they have organized the
mass of the population.

*As an unorganized mass we can create incidents and one or two
days of riots.*

*As an organized mass we can make the government withdraw
its police and its accomplices.*

3. How are action committees created?

If you are a group of comrades, form a committee, draw up your
own leaflet, set a place for daily meetings, make dates for demonstrations. Contact the provisional coordination committee of the AC's
(Action Committees), and name a liaison delegate.

If you are alone, contact the coordination committee and other
comrades (by telephone or by special delivery letter).

Each committee will meet daily.

Each committee will plan its own propaganda among the workers.

Keep together in demonstrations and in actual fighting.

KEEP UP THE FIGHT COMRADES
TOGETHER, WE CAN WIN

—The Action Committees, Wednesday, May 8, 1968.

Document 45

Press + University + Cops + Employers = Repression

Why are the students "enragés"?
The newspapers speak of the *"enragés"* as gilded youths who kill time by giving vent to violence and vandalism.
What is the purpose of these articles?
They have only one:
   To separate students from workers;
   To ridicule their fight;
   To isolate them, the better to gag them.
Are the 3000 students who came up against the police on Friday for five hours really the handful of troublemakers about whom the Minister of National Education, Peyrefitte, has spoken?

NO

We are fighting (wounded, 948 arrests, the disciplinary council for 8 of us, threats of deportation, and fines) BECAUSE WE REFUSE TO BECOME:

Professors, to serve an arbitrarily selective educational policy for which the children of the working classes will bear the consequences.

Sociologists, manufacturers of slogans for governmental election campaigns.

Psychologists, responsible for making "workers' teams" function to further the interests of the employers.

Scientists, whose research work will be used in the exclusive interests of a profit-oriented economy.

   WE REFUSE *this "watchdog" future;*
   WE REFUSE *the courses that teach us to be these things;*
   WE REFUSE EXAMINATIONS AND DEGREES
which reward those who have accepted to become a part of the system;
   WE REFUSE *to be recruited by these maffias;*
   WE REFUSE TO IMPROVE THE BOURGEOIS UNIVERSITY;
   WE WANT TO TRANSFORM IT RADICALLY
in order that from now on it will train intellectuals who fight on the side of the workers and not against them.

From struggles conducted this year by the workers in the main industrial sectors, we have learned new fighting methods and have understood the necessity for taking our combat outside the confines of the University.

We want the interests of the working class to be defended at the University as well. Those who want to separate us from the workers are going against the interests of the working class and of those who want to fight beside them.

On Friday, May 3 and Monday, May 6 we did not face repression alone: we were joined by workers and passersby. *We were fighting together.*

> WHEREVER YOU ARE, OR WHEREVER WE ARE
> LET US ALL MOBILIZE
> AGAINST BOURGEOIS REPRESSION
> AGAINST POLICE REPRESSION
> LET US ORGANIZE TO CONTINUE THE FIGHT!

—*Mouvement du 22 mars,* Nanterre [May 7 or 8].

The *faculté* at Nanterre was reopened under police supervision, and the Wednesday, May 8 demonstration fizzled out. The trade unions and political parties, having refused to join any but a "calm" demonstration, a dislocation announcement was made in front of the Luxembourg, in the presence of the police. In fact, the order to dislocate was actually given by an FER militant. During the day of May 9, the leaders of the UNEF openly acknowledged their mistakes at an impromptu meeting on the *Place de la Sorbonne.* The JCR meeting that evening turned into a free-for-all discussion among the various currents that composed the movement. The following account appeared in the May 15 issue of *Voix ouvrière* (Trotskyist).

Document 46

A Student Meeting

Although less dramatic than the violent demonstrations that preceded or followed it, the meeting of Thursday, May 9, held by the revolutionary students at the Mutualité, was characteristic of the atmosphere that has prevailed for a week now among Paris students.

Representatives of the SDS, who were to have addressed their French comrades in the name of the German student organization, were absent from the meeting, the French police having stopped them at the Orly airport.

But this petty measure was quite useless. It served only to increase a bit more the students' anger against the cops and the govern-

ment, anger for which there were, nevertheless, many other more important grounds. The success of the meeting was no less great. It was
due not to such and such a speaker, but to the circumstances under
which it was held. And if the police thought that such a measure
could intimidate those who participated in the meeting, it meant that
they had badly estimated the anger in the Latin Quarter. The twelve
hours of fighting waged against the students the preceding Monday
should have acquainted them with the students' determination. The
night of Friday to Saturday has perhaps convinced them of it.

A representative of sds succeeded, nevertheless, in speaking to
the 5000 students crowded into the meeting hall of the *Mutualité*. He
had simply taken a different route from that taken by his fellow
members.

This meeting had been planned for a long time by the *Jeunesse
communiste révolutionnaire*. Its goal was to get support from the
French students for the struggle of their German comrades. However,
much earlier than anyone had foreseen, and due to events, their own
struggle was the central topic.

On that very afternoon the jcr had proposed to the students
massed in front of the closed and cop-guarded Sorbonne, the use of
their hall, since the object of the meeting had changed. After several
speeches that had been originally scheduled, the floor was turned over
to those who wanted to speak on the present struggle (at least in principle; in reality, due to lack of time, more than twenty persons who
were to have spoken could not do so).

Three themes dominated the discussions: international solidarity
for students' struggles, discredit of the pcf among the French students,
the necessity for tying in the student struggle with that of the workers.

The solidarity of student struggles on an international scale—
this was the original object of the jcr meeting—was discussed by
foreign student representatives, Italian, German, Spanish (the latter
received special applause), as also by Greek, Portuguese, and Dutch
students. Some described the struggles in their own country. All said
that they were in full solidarity with the struggle of French students.
The *Internationale,* sung at the end of the meeting, was no outworn
rite but the expression of a feeling shared by all present.

Apparent throughout the discussions was the total disrepute of
the pcf in the student milieu. In the afternoon in front of the Sorbonne, Louis Aragon had been ridiculed by the students, who had
asked him to prove the solidarity he pretended to express by serving
as intermediary in order that the students should obtain a page of
l'Humanité to rectify the lies this newspaper had spread against their

movement. The "national poet" of the PCF disappeared without answering. He then had a communiqué published by the *France-Presse* news agency, in which he asserted that he had not pledged himself to do this. In reality, none of the students present had ever expected he would.

In the evening almost all the speakers stigmatized the party's policy. Many called it by its true name: Stalinism; some—pro-Chinese, representatives of the UJC(m-l) or of the PCMLF—used the term "revisionism." In any case the invective of first one then the other, as well as the reactions in the hall, proved one thing: among the students the myth of the PCF as representing the working class had suffered a terrible blow from which, undoubtedly, it would not soon recover. The only speaker who tried to defend it could not finish his speech, being interrupted by booing from the audience, despite requests from the chairman to let him speak.

But the theme that quite evidently dominated the discussions was the necessary liaison between the struggle of the students and that of the working class. All the speakers vigorously expressed this.

However, it was also the theme concerning which differences of opinion between the various tendencies reappeared most clearly. There is nothing surprising about this since it is the essential problem of the student movement as a whole, as well as of the various tendencies and groups who headed this movement. Should the movement address the workers, as Cohn-Bendit proposed, through meetings at the factory gates, including taking the risk of confronting the political and trade union bureaucracies that topped them? Or should students, on the contrary, place themselves "at the service of the workers," as the UJC(m-l) representative asserted? Finally, should they vote for a motion asking Séguy to launch a general strike, as was suggested by a CGT militant worker, quite evidently influenced by the OCI line?

These different viewpoints (there were others, but it would be too long to point out all their shadings) show clearly what is the essential question today for the revolutionary student movement.

The atmosphere of the meeting, its style, the enthusiasm and determination reflected in the various speeches, as well as in the audience reactions, were all symptomatic. Not only was a veritable mass movement created last week in the Latin Quarter—the fight against the police, the number of participants at all the demonstrations have shown this—but for the first time in France, such a mass movement, at least for the greater part, was under the leadership of extreme left tendencies. Certainly this is a movement limited to a specific social stratum distinctive from the class whose interests this extreme left wishes to represent, i.e., the working class. Nevertheless, in the last week something has changed in French politics. The 5000 participants in last Thursday's meeting gave proof of it.

—*Voix ouvrière*, May 15, 1968.

The historic appeal of the Strasburg students is also dated May 9. To be noted is the formula of "student council" modeled on that of "workers' councils."

Document 47

Notice

For the first time in their history, the students meeting in the STU-DENT COUNCIL, May 9, 1968, on the premises of the University, decided:

1. To start discussions that will be circulated in all the Strasburg *facultés* and throughout France, with the purpose of making the strike and the occupation of the premises effective.

2. To continue the unlimited strike at the call of the UNEF.

(a) Until our imprisoned comrades have been freed, with complete amnesty;

(b) until actual recognition of our existence as a STUDENT COUNCIL, with all THE POWERS THAT ARE HEREAFTER OURS, the present government will have to treat with us on all matters that concern our future and the future of the University. Our COUNCILS will remain vigilant in order to thwart all attempts at co-option of the deep changes that our movement is beginning to put into effect through its very existence.

3. We call upon our comrades in all the universities in France

(a) To set up student councils;

(b) to undertake radical and constructive criticism of the University and of the society in which it functions, especially consideration of the examination system, that could perhaps lead to a boycott in order to obtain satisfaction of our immediate demands.

4. We call on the national committees of the teachers' unions and of the working class trade unions to join us in our action.

—*Conseil étudiant de Strasbourg*, May 9, 1968.

As a logical consequence of the growing alignment on the part of the political parties and union machines, on May 10, an inter-union declaration proposed support demonstrations to take place on May 14. However, the events of that evening changed this decision.

The UNEF, the SNESUP, and the *Mouvement du 22 mars* called for another demonstration at Denfert-Rochereau on the evening of the 10th. Meanwhile, the FER organized a meeting at the Mutualité.

Document 48

Joint Declaration

The serious events of which the University is the theater have greatly disturbed public opinion; police repression directed against students and professors is provoking the indignation of workers against the regime.

Problems such as educational reforms to benefit the workers, full employment, transformation of the economic system by and for the people, constitute so many fundamental demands.

The grievances and struggles of the workers, like those of students, teachers, and other categories of the working population, challenge this policy; for they too frequently come up against the same methods of police repression and violation of trade-union and democratic freedoms.

In the name of solidarity and the common aspirations that unite workers, students, and teachers, the representatives of the CGT, of the CFDT, of the UNEF, of the UGE, and of the FEN have decided to organize, on May 14, in every large French city, joint demonstrations:

For amnesty of all convicted demonstrators

For trade union and political freedoms

They urge the leaders of their respective organizations to decide upon the forms of action that will result, for the Paris region, in a powerful joint demonstration in Paris.

—Paris, May 10, 1968.

Document 49

University Students, Men and Women, Lycée Students, Young Workers

At the moment when students in Prague, Warsaw, Berlin, Madrid, Algiers, New York, Tokyo, and Rome were fighting in the streets against the forces of order and reaction, in Paris, on April 27 and 28, 200 delegates representing 1100 militants, headed by young revolutionaries (*Révoltes*) and the Liaison Committee of Revolutionary Students, announced the formation of a

FEDERATION DES ETUDIANTS REVOLUTIONNAIRES

University students, men and women, *lycée* students, young workers,

At the moment when imperialism is striking at youth and the working class with "blood and iron," when Stalinist bureaucracy is striking at and imprisoning students and workers fighting for socialism and worker councils, when student combats augur huge confrontations, on an international scale, between the working classes and imperialism, between the working classes and Stalinist bureaucracy, the revolutionary students declared:

At the moment when de Gaulle is planning to make the working class and, to begin with, young workers and young intellectuals, pay the price for the rationalization of French economy, at the moment when layoffs are increasing, when unemployment is hitting hundreds of thousands of young workers, when Peyrefitte is preparing to exclude 300,000 students from the University, the *Fédération des étudiants révolutionnaires* declares:

DOWN WITH IMPERIALISM!
DOWN WITH STALINISM!
LONG LIVE SOCIALISM!
Resistance is possible, we must organize it.

WE MUST INSIST UPON THE JOINT DEMONSTRATION
OF YOUNG PEOPLE IN PARIS!

University students, men and women, *lycée* students, young workers,

On April 27 and 28 the *Fédération des étudiants révolutionnaires* came out in favor of formation of the *Organisation révolutionnaire de la jeunesse* and of the *Internationale révolutionnaire de la jeunesse*.

On April 27 and 28 the *Fédération des étudiants révolutionnaires* declared that it casts its lot with the fight led by young revolutionaries grouped around the periodical *Révoltes* in order to *assemble 3,500 young people at the Mutualité on June 29 and 30.*

The *Fédération des étudiants révolutionnaires* calls on hundreds of thousands of students to fight for socialism, against capitalism, against reformist and Stalinist bureaucracies, by joining its ranks.

The *Fédération des étudiants révolutionnaires* calls on students to fight by the thousands under the flag of socialism!

The FER calls on students by the thousands to help build the revolutionary youth organization.

The FER *calls all Paris students to its joint proclamation meeting on May 10 in Paris at 8:30 P.M., at the Mutualité.*

EVERYBODY COME TO THE FER MEETING
Friday, May 10 at 8:30 P.M., at the Mutualité
chaired by Christian de Bresson, National Secretary of the FER
Patrick Leu, young revolutionary worker
J. L. Argentin, member of the national board of the FER
Charles Berg in the name of the National Committee of Young Revolutionaries

[Previous to May 6; still being distributed on the 10th]
(printed leaflet).

Document 50

The Fight Continues

The Closing of Nanterre and of the Sorbonne
Repression in the Latin Quarter
By way of answer: *More and more numerous demonstrations, Tuesday evening 50,000 students and workers marched as far as the Arc de Triomphe.*

And yet, on Wednesday evening, those who answered the call of l'UNEF found themselves inflicted with another traditional meeting. Loudspeakers for the "officials," "jawboning" that opened up no perspectives, and to end with, a long walk that finished without explanations with a call for dispersion in spite of the obvious discontent of most of the demonstrators, and at the risk of breaking up the movement.

During all this time the press, with shadings and varied tactics, misrepresented the facts, lied about the movement's objectives and, as in Berlin and in Rome . . ., tried to pit workers against students.

To avoid the recurrence of a dangerous mistake like that of Wednesday evening at the Luxembourg.

To avoid all other maneuvers.

To expand our movement.

To deepen and define our objectives.

1. Liberation of university premises and surrounding areas.

2. Liberation of all our comrades still in prison, and annulment of penalties.

3. Annulment of *faculté* lockouts.

4. Resignation of those responsible for police intrusion into the Sorbonne courtyard: Rector Roche having acted upon the request of Dean Durry.[18]

5. Complete freedom of political expression in the *facultés.* In order to popularize our struggle among the workers,

WE MUST ORGANIZE: CREATE ACTION COMMITTEES
*Everybody at Denfert-Rochereau Friday evening
at 6:30* P.M.

—Les Comités d'action du 3 mai 1968.

In spite of the demonstration, the *Fédération des étudiants révolutionnaires* went through with its meeting. After heading towards the Santé prison, the procession, which had been joined by numerous *lycée* students and included (this fact was unusual) a large contingent of students from the schools of medicine, pharmacy, and law, was oriented, as a result of police pressure, towards the Latin Quarter; once there, the slogan "occupy the Quarter" could be heard. Negotiations on the three points with rector Roche and vice rector Chalin were started, but broke down because of the uncompromising attitude of the ministry. The result of these talks was awaited with mingled joy and anguish. Quite spontaneously, in a mood of conviviality and by way of a compromise between the activism of a few and the desire of others to avoid any incidents with the police, some sixty barricades were built, a few of which were effective, but most of which were hardly more than piles of paving stones. Towards midnight the participants in the FER meeting came to join the demonstration carrying a red flag and shouting, "Half a million workers in the Latin Quarter!" After one of their spokesmen had asked the demonstrators to disperse, the FER partisans went on their way. A UNEF leaflet gives an account of these events, and a later leaflet, brought out by the "action committees," emphasized the repressive techniques that were used when the barricades were destroyed, beginning at 2:15 A.M. on May 11.

Document 51

The Truth About the Events
of the Night of May 10–11

For a week now students have been fighting against police repression at the University.

Before engaging in any discussion, the UNEF has laid down three preliminary points, which are:

—To stop all legal and administrative action and to free all demonstrators who are in prison.

—To withdraw the police from the University area.

—To reopen the *facultés*.

During the two previous demonstrations (Tuesday and Wednesday), the UNEF clearly showed that it does not intend to seek violent confrontation with the police.

Again, the day before yesterday, the UNEF instructions were precise: we did not want to bear the responsibility for violence; the demonstrators were supposed to refrain from all provocation toward the police. They were to occupy the Latin Quarter and form discussion groups, at the same time that they prepared to defend themselves, if need be, against an attack by the considerable police forces massed around the Sorbonne.

INSTRUCTIONS WERE RESPECTED

For almost four hours students occupied the Latin Quarter, calmly, while awaiting a public reply from the government.

They have had this reply.

At 2:15 A.M. police forces brutally attacked the demonstrators, using not only simple tear gas bombs, but also chlorine and ammonia bombs, incendiary and blast grenades.

The brutality of the repression was such that there were many injured. At this time it is difficult to give a definite figure.

After having cleared a street, the CRS carefully visited every house to drag out demonstrators who had sought refuge there.

Many injured demonstrators were beaten up in the police cars.

Nothing was done to facilitate the task of first aid groups: indeed, on the contrary.

Greater savagery was never witnessed!

WHO IS RESPONSIBLE? WHO GIVES THE ORDERS?
Faced with police repression, the students will not surrender.

Faced with blackjacks and grenades, the students reassert their demands with a force that is all the greater since they know that they are less and less alone.

They ask the people and the workers to support them.

Students, workers,

EVERYBODY TAKE PART IN THE GENERAL STRIKE
AND IN MONDAY'S DEMONSTRATION

The UNEF leaflet distributed by the *Syndicat national des chercheurs scientifiques* (FEN).

Flash:

AMNESTY, AN END TO REPRESSION, UNITY OF WORKERS AND STUDENTS, JOB OPENINGS FOR YOUNG PEOPLE, JOB SECURITY, DEMOCRACY.

Everybody come to the demonstration at the Place de la République, Monday, May 13, at 3:00 P.M.

—Call put out by the the CGT, FEN, CFDT, UNEF [May 11].

Document 52

War Gas!

Material Used by the CRS
for Repression of Demonstrators

—Offensive hand grenades (a powerful blast).

—Incendiary grenades (which burn skin and eyes).

Combat gas *C.N.* and *C.B.* (based on chlorine and bromide compounds already currently used by Americans in Vietnam; they cause asphyxia and death).

—Disabling gas.

These devices have been used this week in the Latin Quarter for attacks in cafés, in the subway, buses, stores, and apartment houses.

Now, It Is Clear!

We are the guinea pigs for the experiments of a sadistic police who already has Charonne and the tortures in Algeria to its credit.

Thousands of youth who came to demonstrate have been harried, tracked down, bestially beaten.

We know that already there have been:
—injured who were blackjacked on stretchers,
—members of the Red Cross (Hôpital Curie) systematically harried wherever they went,
—doctors beaten (rue Gay-Lussac),
—people weak from loss of blood in police stations (Panthéon),
—injured to whom the police refused medical care for more than twenty-four hours,
—torn limbs requiring amputation,
—people in a coma,
—serious eye lesions,
—a student whose throat was slit by a cop on a windowpane (24 rue Gay-Lussac),
—probable dead.

All these facts have been carefully suppressed by the government and the press.

They have tried to impose silence in the name of medical secrecy by fabricating false medical reports.

The strike of medical students, the protests of professors, the UNEF press conference on the means of repression used by the police, that of the doctors from the Saint-Antoine Hospital, the spontaneous testimony of 50 doctors who had offered medical aid, prove that the medical profession will not allow itself to be muzzled by police repression.

Paris, May 12 (AFP)
During a press conference held yesterday evening (Sunday) in an amphitheater of the *Faculté des Sciences,* Dr. Kahn, professor of medicine, protested against the use of a particularly toxic gas during the demonstrations in the Latin Quarter.

The professor revealed that his observations of many students, together with a personal investigation, had enabled him to identify it absolutely as chlorobenzalmalomonitride, more commonly called *C.S.* or *C.B.*

This gas, according to Dr. Kahn, which is used by the police in the United States as well as by American troops in Vietnam, is said to attack the human hepatic and renal centers and, in the laboratory, to have been proved fatal to animals that have been given concentrated doses.

But what is serious, added Professor Kahn, is that they have been able to use such a gas during forty-eight hours in Paris without

warning the medical authorities, whereas no known antidotes exist
in France at this time against this compound. (AFP, 10:41 P.M.)

It is not possible to discuss
with assassins and liars

WE ARE CONTINUING STREET ACTION AND OCCUPATION OF THE FACULTÉS,[19]
UNTIL GRIMAUD AND FOUCHET RESIGN!

—The May 3 Action Committees, Monday, 2:00 A.M.

The May 13 call for an inter-union demonstration, which
brought out nearly a thousand people, was preceded by a series of
protests from inhabitants of the Latin Quarter and environs, Communist municipalities (the Nanterre municipality, which shortly before
had quoted Georges Marchais' May 3 article, was particularly vigorous), and *faculté* professors, among others. In the provinces, reactions
of support were immediate, as shown by the following leaflet from
Marseilles, where even the "Union des jeunes filles de France," a
Communist organization, although refusing to take part in the
strike, took over the formula of "action committees." M. Gaston De-
ferre, Mayor of Marseilles, somewhat absentmindedly helped to put
up a streamer on which was written "CRS = SS."

Document 53

Declaration of the Nanterre Municipality

During the night of Friday to Saturday, the police continued to
carry out an ever greater and fiercer repression against Paris students,
causing injuries to hundreds and, among those injured, a rather large
number were seriously so.

Once again, instead of taking measures which could satisfy the
justifiable discontent of the students, the Gaullist government ordered
its police to use every means of repression against them, including
offensive weapons.

The Nanterre municipality condemns once more, and vigorously,
the action of the government and of its police, and assures the students
of the Nanterre *faculté,* as well as all university and *lycée* students,
of its complete solidarity.

This is why the municipality demands:
—Cessation of police repression immediately and totally.

—Withdrawal of police forces from University premises and vicinity.

—Cessation of legal actions against students and immediate freeing of those imprisoned.

—Reopening, under normal conditions, of the *facultés,* permitting examinations to take place.

The municipality invites the working population to manifest to those responsible for the government, the *préfet,* the Minister of National Education, using every means (resolutions, petitions, delegations, etc.), their solidarity with the students in order to force the government to give the students and the University the indispensable means of providing an education in conformity with the necessities of our times, and of establishing a democratic life in the *facultés* and the professional schools.

—Nanterre, May 11, 1968.

Document 54

Resolution of the Sorbonne-Lettres *Teaching Staff*

The assembly of the Paris-Sorbonne *Faculté des Lettres et Sciences Humaines* decided that in view of the deeply disturbing events that had just taken place it was indispensable to convoke the whole of the teaching staff, professors, lecturers, assistant professors, and instructors to an emergency general assembly chaired by the Dean.

The assembly believes it is its duty to recommend the following measures, which it considers to be inseparable and extremely urgent:

1. Release of university and *lycée* students arrested or under investigation, and general amnesty covering all the events that have occurred since May 3;

2. Departure of the police from the Latin Quarter;

3. Reopening of the Sorbonne and the normal resumption of courses and other University activities once the two preceding conditions are fulfilled.

On this point the assembly has confidence in all its students and counts on them to see to it that freedom of university activities shall be assured at the *faculté.*

Lastly, it asks the adoption of an urgency procedure for the presentation of an amnesty law to the National Assembly.

—Paris, May 11, 1968.

Document 55

CRS = SS

Another Charonne in Paris

During the night, at the same time that rector Roche was receiving a delegation of students and teachers in an attempt to negotiate conditions for reestablishing order, 50,000 demonstrators, university and *lycée* students, teachers, and workers, occupied the Latin Quarter.

Until 2:15 A.M., the demonstration took place without any incident. It was at 2:17 A.M., even before the negotiations had ended, that the government decided to "clean up" the Latin Quarter.

There was then a generalized, deliberate attack by the police. Results:

—Thousands of injured, among whom some ten are in very serious condition.

—First aid teams systematically attacked by the police.

—The injured remained for hours without attention, the police having forbidden their evacuation.

THESE METHODS OF REPRESSION ARE THOSE OF A CIVIL WAR.

The Paris population has already shown that it is on the side of the students.

Professors Schwartz and Cartan[20] have resigned from the French University.

WORKERS, UNIVERSITY AND LYCÉE STUDENTS, TEACHERS, let us all show our solidarity against the massacre of the Paris demonstrators:

Starting at noon
everybody on the Canebière in front of the AGEM
DO NOT LISTEN TO THE LIES OF THE GOVERNMENT RADIO!

—SNESup., UNEF [Marseilles, May 11].

Document 56

JEUNES FILLES
we must defend our demands

As students of the girls' *lycées* and *collèges* (secondary schools) we represent thousands who have not the right to a genuine professional training. We represent thousands who remain idle. Gaullist France of 1968 offers young people: *unemployment.*

THE GOVERNMENT IS RESPONSIBLE FOR THIS SITUATION

On demands as important as professional outlets, the fight against unemployment, the democratic reform of education and, for young girls, nondiscrimination, technical education for women is out of date since 90 percent of it consists in sewing, selling, and office work. Victory will only be the result of action by millions of young students of *lycées, collèges,* and universities, and by the entire body of manual and intellectual workers.

We are right to demonstrate our discontent because we have other demands; we are right to claim better conditions for professional education (e.g., the Lycée Marie-Curie, built for 700 students, now has 2,000! Some courses are cancelled for the 3rd trimester because the premises are used for examinations).

Have we discussed and sought to obtain satisfaction of these legitimate demands?

Some of us advocate a strike. Certainly it is a means of making ourselves heard. But is this going to solve our problems? And won't our demands come up again soon? What will happen when we resume our studies? Striking is the ultimate weapon. Workers have recourse to strikes only when they have exhausted all other forms of action. This is why, before embarking upon a long strike, we must use other forms of action:

—Set up action committees *for the defense of our demands.*

—Make a list of our grievances, bring it in a delegation to the director: the representative of the administration.

—Demonstrate before or after the courses or proceed with limited stoppages in our work.

If, after all that, we do not obtain satisfaction, then we will discuss a strike which, in order to be victorious, must be undertaken with a maximum number of students of the *lycées* and *collèges.*

The *Union des jeunes filles de France* is carrying on an active campaign for genuine professional training giving access to all the modern professions (engineers, technicians, architects, lawyers, electronic specialists, etc.). These demands will only be achieved through application of the *democratic reform of education.*

FOR THAT, WE URGE YOU:

—To participate in the youth delegations that will bring numerous petitions to the *préfecture* at the beginning of June.

—To join the ranks of the *Union des jeunes filles de France.*

—[Marseilles, May 11].

On Saturday at 5 P.M., the *Censier* annex of the *Faculté des Lettres* was occupied at the instigation of the MAU. This slogan to "occupy the *facultés*" soon spread through the entire University.

Document 57

General Call to the Population

Information on the Occupation of Censier

We, the action committees of May 3, have been occupying the Censier center of the Paris *fac des Lettres* since Saturday at 5 P.M. We are discussing there in commissions and in general assemblies. We want to inform the public that these discussions are free and democratic.

For us, it is a question of obtaining satisfaction on the following points:

—reopening of University premises,

—total evacuation of the police,

—freedom and amnesty for all our comrades,

—cessation of all arrests (again on Sunday), and total freedom of political expression at the *faculté* and in the streets.

For that we will fight as long as it is necessary, and we call on all Paris workers to support us.

But it should not be forgotten that over and above satisfaction on these points we are fighting against a University in the service of the bourgeoisie, and against a bourgeois-capitalist dominated society. In a particularly spectacular way, this society in the last few days has shown what it really is: a society of blackjacks, tear gas, incendiary, offensive, and chlorine grenades.

Workers do not know the problems of education and of the University well enough, for the good reason that capitalist society has always taken pains to keep these problems out of their reach.

To remedy that, we invite all of you to discuss, to ask for information and explanations from the students of the University and *lycées,* and from the teachers.

On the other hand, teachers do not know the problems of workers well enough.

It is important for real unity among all of us to be developed in action as well as in discussion. This unity will only be achieved if we continue to act and speak democratically.

The students and workers who went to fight on the barricades will not permit any force whatsoever to keep them from expressing themselves and from acting against the bourgeois University and against a society that is dominated by the bourgeoisie.

PREPARE TO OCCUPY THE FACS.

ORGANIZE INTO ACTION COMMITTEES.

HEADQUARTERS FOR THE MAY 3 COMMITTEES.

Everybody come on Monday to the demonstration of support for the student struggle, Monday 1:30 P.M., Gare de l'Est.

—Censier Center of the *fac des Lettres* [May 12].

Meanwhile, negotiations between the Americans and the Vietnamese were about to begin in Paris on May 13, a fact which appeared to constitute a foreign policy victory for General de Gaulle. The *Comités Vietnam de base,* identified with the UJC(m-l), wanted to organize a demonstration to take place on Sunday, May 12. It should be pointed out that the principle of negotiations was not, however, criticized. Finally, the demonstration was called off.[21]

Document 58

The Vietnamese People Will Win!

"The Vietnamese people have a deep love for peace, but not for just any peace! Peace with independence and freedom." Hô Chi Minh.

At this moment, panic reigns among the American imperialists. The Vietnamese people are victoriously pursuing their general offensive.

Practically all the rural zones are liberated; in the cities, millions of patriots are rising against the occupant.

The revolutionary government has been brought to power in Hué and Saigon.

Entrenched in their bases, besieged on all sides,

THE AMERICAN IMPERIALISTS HAVE NOT LONG TO GO!!!

The pro-Yankee press of our country, the radio, television, all news sources tend to distract the attention of the French people from the victories of the Vietnamese people, to make them believe that the Americans are "invincible," that they are proving their "good will" by having accepted to begin talks.

But they have not been successful in hiding that the beginning of talks is the proof of the military and political defeat of the American imperialists.

The beginning of talks is also a victory for the Vietnamese people.

Since May 5, the freedom fighters are once again pounding the imperialists and their lackeys in their last sanctuaries: in the heart of the cities. In insurgent Saigon, the flag of freedom is flying over the popular quarters. The regime of the traitors, Thieu and Ky, is in the throes of death.

Each hour that passes brings the Vietnamese people closer to final victory.

As long as the American imperialists do not completely stop their aggression,

THE VIETNAMESE PEOPLE WILL NOT LAY DOWN THEIR ARMS!
The anti-imperialist movement of the Vietnam comités de base calls on all anti-imperialists, all sincere friends of the Vietnamese people to come to a mass demonstration of support and complete solidarity with the representatives of the Democratic Republic of Vietnam and with the political program of the National Liberation Front of South-Vietnam, and to denounce the duplicity of the Yankee aggressors' maneuvers.
Everybody come to the Hotel Lutétia
(where the representatives of the Vietnamese people are staying)
Sunday, May 12 at 5:00 p.m.!

—Anti-imperialist movement of the *Vietnam comités de base*
[May 11].

On May 11 and 13 the Strasburg students continued their "thrust." We have added to the Strasburg documents a Paris text (of unknown origin, but probably situationist), which seems to be a reply to their statement.

The *22 mars* group put out a very violent leaflet calling for a demonstration and, on May 13, the UNEF, the SNESUP. and the national committees of the big unions marched with the *22 mars* in Paris. In the provinces the demonstrations were largely unitary, but it should be carefully noted that the leaders in Marseilles insisted on the demonstrators remaining grouped "according to their original places" in the procession. Disregarding the CGT's order, at the instigation of D. Cohn-Bendit, several thousand students went on to the *Champs-de-Mars* where they held a meeting. Then, the Sorbonne having been liberated by the police, it was occupied immediately afterward. On May 11, at 11:15 P.M., Prime Minister Pompidou, who had just returned from Afghanistan, practically capitulated by giving in to the three fundamental demands of the UNEF and the SNESUP., which were: free the students who were in prison, evacuate the police from the Sorbonne, and reopen the *facultés*. The movement had now been made to exceed its own goals.

Document 59

Autonomy for the University of Strasburg

put out by the press service

MAY 11 DECLARATION OF AUTONOMY

The Student Council proclaims:

Autonomy for the University of Strasburg with respect to the entire present government, the one and only authority responsible for police repression in Paris and for the total deterioration of the University situation. From now on, with the cooperation of professors who wish to associate themselves with the Council, it will take in hand the entire functioning of the autonomous University of Strasburg.

We invite all the universities in France to make the same decision and respectively to proclaim their autonomy, rejecting in this way all authority of the present government.

—Declaration of the first Student Council of Strasburg,
May 11, 1968, at 7 A.M.

Manifesto of the First Student Council at 3 P.M. on May 13

By proclaiming the autonomy of their University on Saturday, May 11, the first student council of Strasburg demonstrated from the very first its independence with respect to a government which has completely failed in its task, as much in the matter of National Education as on the level of domestic policy, and whose police repressions are most striking.

In a period of transition, it seems necessary to preserve a skeleton framework, particularly in administrative and financial matters.

The student council, with the voluntary participation of students and professors, will now develop criticism of the University and gradual organization of the autonomy of this University, in line with the general orientation as defined.

This autonomy is the only means the students and professors have to calmly develop fundamental criticism of the University, independent of governmental and administrative restraints.

Letter from Rector Bayen, May 14, 1968

At the instigation of the rector, president of the University Council, a collective telephone interview took place Tuesday, May 14, 1968 from 10:15 to 10:45 A.M. between the minister of National Education, the president of the University Council, and the deans of the seven *facultés*.

The representatives of the University of Strasburg made concrete proposals as regards the content of University autonomy.

The minister agreed that the University of Strasburg should explore the possibilities of such an autonomy and give it a trial.

The University Council, in which elected delegates of the students will be called upon to participate, will meet within 48 hours to define the terms for this experiment.

—Maurice Bayen.

Reply to M. Bayen's Letter, May 14, 1968, 11:40 P.M.

The student council of the Autonomous University of Strasburg declares that in the official document signed by rector Bayen and relative to the interview which took place during the morning of May 14, 1968 between the rector, the 7 deans, and M. Peyrefitte, the student council, founded on direct democracy, is not recognized.

Furthermore, since the University of Strasburg is no longer at the present time the only one concerned with University autonomy, the reply to this text, whatever it may be, will be given only when all the French universities that have declared themselves autonomous have consulted together.

Finally, this reply will be transmitted only to M. Peyrefitte's successor.

—The Student Council of the Autonomous University of Strasburg.

Document 60

In Paris, we have demonstrated and we have constructed barricades. The students in Strasburg have drawn the one and only natural consequence: Saturday, at 7 A.M., they occupied the University premises and, alone, officially proclaimed the autonomy of the University of Strasburg.

Paris students, we are a sorry lot: in spite of our barricades we admit that the government is right, by wasting our time forming "committees" according to discipline, still fascinated by professorial authority and dazzled by the unscrupulous guild-socialist ambitions of "groupuscule" specialists.

ONLY STUDENT COUNCILS EXIST

The decision is ours, we have only to take it. The professors, if they so desire, can side with our decisions.

WE OURSELVES SHOULD PROCLAIM THE UNIVERSITY OF PARIS AUTONOMOUS

This is not an empty phrase: it is the principle of a work program with which all must collaborate. In any case, it is the slogan *sine qua non* for the resumption of any kind of work.

—[May 12?]

Document 61

Against the Police State We Must Continue the Fight

Following in the footsteps of the workers of Caen, Mulhouse, Le Mans, Redon, and the Rhodiaceta, during the night of Friday, May 10, 1968, University and *lycée* students, teachers, and workers who demonstrated against police state repression, fought in the streets for several hours against 10,000 cops. The bourgeoisie tried to crush a form of protest and demands that directly threatens the regime. The repression was fierce, the resistance tenacious. The cops used all means: incendiary bombs, deadly gases (*C.B.* and *C.S.* gas are forbidden by international agreements and unknown to the medical services), chlorine grenades, bullets made of hard plastic. The demonstrators and the population were asphyxiated by the gases, wounded by gunflash, beaten with bludgeons and blackjacks, pursued into apartment houses, given the "third degree" in the police stations, arrested by the hundreds. Red Cross first aid stations were sacked; wounded on stretchers were beaten hard.

The demonstrators, fully supported by the inhabitants of the Latin Quarter, met this violence with political determination; at the barricades the mercenaries of the bourgeoisie were treated to the delights of Molotov cocktails and a shower of paving stones. Several hundreds of them were put out of commission. Students and workers will not forget this lesson.

Faced with this resistance and increasing support from the working masses, the police state is forced to retreat and would appear to be giving in to the three conditions the demonstrators have posed as prerequisites to any discussion. But the basic problems remain unsolved.

The fight against police repression is the fight against the police state and against capitalist exploitation. The cops are nothing but the flunkies of de Gaulle and de Gaulle is nothing but the current flunkey of the bourgeoisie.

In the present stage of the struggle, we demand as a prerequisite to the resumption of University life:

—The definitive release of all demonstrators who are being held, whether students or workers, French or foreigners, and including those whom the bourgeoisie has described as "looters."

—The immediate and final cessation of legal and administrative action because of political activity, whatever the pretext.

On the other hand, since we have proof of criminal acts committed by the cops during the night of Friday, we demand as a new prerequisite:

—The resignation of the killer, *Grimaud,* Chief of Police, chief of the Paris coppers.

—The resignation of the killer, *Fouchet,* Minister of the Interior and number one cop in France.

For such acts not to be repeated it is necessary:

—To start a legal investigation of police crimes, with the participation of representatives of the demonstrators side by side with the magistrates of bourgeois "justice."

—To *disarm* the CRS = ss, the *gardes-mobiles* and other detachments specialized in repression.

It is clear that the bourgeoisie will not want to disarm their executioners.

We will force them to do so through our action.

To make an end to repression, workers and students must win their freedom in the streets. As long as the cops are armed, students and workers must organize their self-defense in order victoriously to resist organized repression.

DOWN WITH THE POLICE STATE   DOWN WITH CAPITALISM
FOR SOCIALISM
WORKERS AND STUDENTS, WE MUST FIGHT IN THE STREETS

EVERYBODY COME TO THE DEMONSTRATION, MONDAY, MAY 13, 1968
Gare de l'Est, at 1:30 P.M.

—*Mouvement du 22 mars* [May 12?].

During the evening of May 13, the Sorbonne, which was now occupied, was opened to workers.

Document 62

The Sorbonne Is Open to Workers At All Times

The general assembly of May 13 has decided that the University of Paris is declared an autonomous people's university, open, day and night, at all times, to all workers.

The University of Paris will henceforth be administered by the occupation and administration committees constituted by workers, students and teachers.

Document 63

Text Drafted Jointly by "Worker-Student" Commissions

(*during the night of May 13-14, 1968, while occupying the Sorbonne*)

1. *One very positive point:* difficult but fruitful discussion between workers and students at the Sorbonne.
2. In solidarity, they call for continuation of the common struggle against the primarily responsible element, which is Gaullism, as representative of the capitalist power structure; minimum platform to start with the resignations of Fouchet and Grimaud.
3. *Accepted principle:* in cooperation with the workers' unions, institution of a freely circulating information service and continual two-way discussion within the union sections; direct contacts for meetings in working class circles.
4. For this it is indispensable that students should be represented by their own elected delegates.
5. Creation of a new type of teaching, really accessible to the working class.

Headquarters for the commission on "Worker-Student Relations," open 24 hours a day, staircase C, 2nd floor, 1st door to the right, at the Sorbonne.

COME ONE, COME ALL

The other *facultés* followed the movement: Medicine, *Faculté des Sciences* in Toulouse, etc., when they had not already preceded it, as in Strasburg.

Document 64

Toulouse Faculté des Sciences

Order for a sit-in strike was given on the morning of Saturday, May 11.

Sunday, May 12: discussions in the lecture halls with workers and with the inhabitants of Toulouse (about 700 to 800 people). The CFDT had called on the inhabitants of Toulouse and its environs, and on the workers, to come to the *fac des Sciences* to discuss and to learn about the student movement (the call appeared in the local press). The open assembly decided late Sunday afternoon to put out directives for a strike on Monday and to meet in open assembly during the morning.

Monday, May 13: the directives for a general strike were followed by almost all of the teaching staff and students of the *fac* (more than 95 percent). The open assemblies held in the morning debated basic problems and decided to extend the strike to Tuesday the 14th.

Afternoon: demonstration in the city with union organizations: 25,000 demonstrators (40,000 according to *La Dépêche*).

Tuesday, May 14: the assemblies in session at 10:00 A.M. decided:

To extend the strike until Saturday, inclusive.

To postpone examinations for 2 weeks.

Afternoon: discussions on the following three themes:

1. University administration.

2. Problem of examinations and pedagogical methods; teaching content.

3. Justification of the University.

About 3,000 to 4,000 students, teachers, and research workers actively participated in these discussions, which continued the next day.

In addition, at the end of the morning and at the request of the open assemblies, the dean explained the functioning of the *faculté*. He was asked to convoke the *faculté* assembly with students present.

Today, the movement has become so broad that its bases appear to be uncertain, that is to say, all the students are far from being conscious of the necessity for a radical contestation of the University and of society. In spite of everything, we can be optimistic as to the evolution of events; no doubt, it would be desirable to be in closer contact with Paris.

GOOD LUCK TO YOUR CONTINUED ACTION

—*Le mouvement du 25 avril*[22] (*fac des Sciences*) [May 14].

On the morning of May 14 the first leaflet addressed to the workers was distributed at Censier. In it the theme "Your struggle is also ours" was clearly stated. The same day the Sud-Aviation workers occupied the Nantes factory, and those at Rhodiaceta did the same. The coordinating council of action committees, made up for the most part of MAU militants, tried to draw a certain number of conclusions from these events. This printed leaflet, which also appeared in a shorter, *ronéotype* version, criticized both the political groups, which as members of the action committee recommended that they should organize under political leadership, and the *Mouvement du 22 mars,* which opposed any organized structure.

Document 65

ACTION COMMITTEE
"WORKER-STUDENT STRUGGLE"
CENSIER CENTER, PARIS 5^{e}

Workers
Parisians
After one week of continuous fighting, Paris students took possession of the Sorbonne last night. We have decided to remain in control. Until now we have had a bourgeois education imposed upon us, the contents of which we could not refuse, and which only prepared us to be future cadres and tools of your exploitation.

The experience of these last days has shown us the inefficiency of traditional means of action and convinced us that only mass action led by the grass roots can force the government to retreat.

We have not simply asked for increased space, budget, and teaching personnel; we have asked ourselves: why this space, why this budget, why these professors?

There Are Many Resemblances between Your Problems and Ours
Who decides the norms and the work rhythms? Who decides the goals

for production and the type of production? Everywhere the regulation is the same: we're asked to execute orders. Unions and opposition parties propose nothing that is fundamentally different. It is always a minority who decides for you, in production as well as in society.

THE STRUGGLE MUST BE ORGANIZED AT THE GRASS ROOTS

—[May 14].

Document 66

Call for Action

Since Friday, May 3, tens of thousands of University and *lycée* students, teachers, and young workers have embarked upon a new kind of combat both in the streets and in the *facultés*.

Having started by questioning through the use of direct action the content and methods of the bourgeois University at Nanterre, today the movement is considering the problem of how to overthrow the Gaullist regime.

How Did We Reach That Point?
The ground swell provoked by the attempt on the part of the government and of the French University authorities forcefully to break up the disturbances that were slowly developing, has causes that it would be well to inquire into and to understand. The resistance and the combative spirit of the students provoked a sort of enthusiasm in favor of people who dared to resist the CRS, *gardes-mobiles,* and other police. Certainly workers were affected by the brutality of police repression, but it was the fact of seeing students not behaving like sheep and resisting by fighting that was new. Towards evening on Monday the 6th, young workers had started to fight alongside the students. The bitterness and cold anger provoked by years of police harassment and daily vexations, exploded. Anti-strike repression, CRS in the factories, cop raids against young people in the suburbs, all the daily manifestations of a State founded mainly on the power of its police, all that has started up again. Suddenly freed by the announcement of the fight, many have come to join the students "against the cops." Among the numerous possibilities of attack against a ten-year-old regime, which is at once the symbol of all French bourgeois conservatism and of attempts made within its ranks to "modernize" the exploitation of workers, hatred of the police, hatred of repression, have supplied the principal motor for action. A lesson to meditate upon!

The Uncertainty of the Moment

3,000 on May 3, 15,000 on the 6th, 40,000 the 7th, and more than 10,000 behind the barricades the 10th, we were more than a million on May 13 for the general strike. And yet . . . since May 13, uneasiness has grown. The words "burial" (of the movment), "co-option" (by the parliamentary political parties) are constantly being used. Many fear that the belated, halfhearted support given us by the leaders of the national unions is a kiss of death. The *facs* are occupied and the Sorbonne is occupied, but nothing is settled for all that, and Pompidou is playing the role of the "saviour returned from afar."

This period of uncertainty is the natural consequence of two essential characteristics of the movement: its lack of organization and its weakness as regards a program. At the same time that these two elements guarantee us against the mental paralysis and sectarianism of many extreme left groups, they risk bogging the whole movement if we are not careful.

Two Currents

From the numerous discussions of these last three days, two currents have in fact emerged. On the one hand there are those who wish to profit from the "University crisis" to have the existing government bring about "University reforms." These are usually the same people who would easily accept seeing the Sorbonne occupation turn into ridiculous old-fashioned folklore. On the other hand there are those who, during the week of the barricades, revived hope of revolutionary action. The latter want overthrow of the regime more than they do "co-management of the University," an alliance with workers more than an alliance with the "eminent professors" who only yesterday declared themselves our enemies, and today have become mealy-mouthed "friends." The occupation of Rhodiaceta on Tuesday morning and of Sud-Aviation at Nantes today show the way.

There is no question of systematically opposing all the University demands to the general political demands. All are legitimate and necessary. It is a question of priority according to importance.

Politics First

The same two currents emerge with respect to the place of action. On the one hand, there are those who agree to settle down in the *facultés* in order to resume a "normal life," only "improved." On the other, there are those who wish to transform our reconquered *facultés* into bases for action directed toward the outside. Faced with the cops, we

were obliged to say, "The Sorbonne for the students." Now that we
have it, we must say, "The Sorbonne for the workers." We ought to
use our conquered *facultés* as red bases from which the movement is
being organized, from which propaganda groups leave for the suburbs
and working class quarters, where the progress of the struggle is being
evaluated daily. Now, we must . . .

Go to the Working Class
Not to organize it ourselves, but to profit from the wide hearing that
our courage has given us and to explain the need to overthrow the
regime. In the suburbs we must go and make known the truth about
our struggle, say why we are against capitalism. We must also go to
learn there the concrete truth about what we know only from books:
the exploitation of work. Lastly, we must now recapture the streets,
because that is where confrontation takes place and where we will
join up with the workers.

The Sorbonne Is Our Base; It Is Not the Battlefield
There are three currents of thinking on the question of organization.
The first want to profit from the situation only to strengthen their
own group, but do not realize that if the masses refuse to join it, this
is not entirely due to their weak politicization but to their refusal to
be involved in sectarian quarrels or opportunist parliamentarianism.
Others propose to organize as little as possible so as to preserve the
movement's creative spontaneity. These comrades are also mistaken
because they do not understand that although it is possible to organize
500 people spontaneously to build a barricade, it is totally impossible
to overthrow the regime with the same number. We must organize at
the grass roots, in action, for action.

Action Committees Everywhere
Their form can vary: a disciplinary base, a base for small neighborhoods, a base where people work, etc., but they must have this in common: they are small units, 10 to 30 people, because if they are intended
for discussion, they are above all intended for action. When there is a
meeting of 200 people, break it up into 10 committees!
  —Each committee meets every day or every other day.
  —Each committee sends a delegate to the daily Coordination
    meeting at 2 P.M. at the Sorbonne, Staircase C, 1st Floor (at
    6 P.M. for those who cannot come at 2 P.M.).
  —Each committee enters into contact with the neighboring com-

mittees (for example: all the 15th arrondissement committees, or all elementary school teachers' committees, or all "Science" committees, etc.) in order to establish an intermediary coordination.

—Each committee works out its own activity and signs it.

—Each committee gives its opinion on what should be done and posts it.

—Individuals should not wait to be given instructions: they should collect some comrades, then enter into contact with the coordination committee.

—Committee members take part in discussions in the lecture halls, in the commissions, etc., but this does not replace participation in their own committees. The function of these discussions is to raise the general level of awareness through interchange of ideas, without taboos, on all subjects, but that is all; they are not the place for organizing action.

No to University reformism and to apolitical folklore. We must open the way to revolutionary contestation of the regime.

—Coordination of Action Committees [May 15, 1968] (printed leaflet).

On May 15 the Odéon was occupied.[23] While the Sorbonne was becoming the fortress of the movement, the strike was spreading, especially at Cléon. On the afternoon of May 16, the Renault-Billancourt plant went on strike.

This ended the first act. Between the May 3 demonstration and May 16 the movement had gradually extended throughout the University and had now suddenly broken out in the factories. The initiative was no longer in the hands of the student movement.

Document 67

The Imagination Seizes Power

The revolutionary struggle of workers and students, which started in the streets, now extends to places of work and to the pseudo-values of the consumer society. Yesterday Sud-Aviation in Nantes, today the so-called "Theater of France": the Odéon.

The theater, the movies, painting, literature, etc., have become industries monopolized by an "élite" for the purpose of alienation and commercialism.

> *Sabotage the cultural industry.*
> *Occupy and destroy the institutions.*
> *Re-invent life.*
> ART IS YOU!
> THE REVOLUTION IS YOU!
> ENTRANCE FREE
> *to the ex-Theater of France, from today on.*
>
> —CAR, May 16, 1968.

Notes

1. On the first demonstration of what later became the MAU, cf. above, Chapter I, p. 102.

2. The Paris sections of the UNEF-*Lettres* (Nanterre and Sorbonne) were organized according to discipline (geography, languages, philosophy, etc.) and confederated according to *faculté*. The large number of Paris students and this complex, multilevel structure resulted in the union's being a rather heavy mechanism.

3. Centre Richelieu: the center for Catholic students of the *Faculté des Lettres*.

4. And for which they later took responsibility; cf. below, Chapter IV, p. 256.

5. General Association of Clermont Students (controlled by the FER).

6. The text of the open letter he sent to his judges, and to which the FER gave wide circulation, is translated in John Gretton's *Students and Workers,* p. 109.

7. The beginnings of a barricade had been set up on the Boulevard Saint-Michel on the evening of May 3.

8. These strikes were accompanied by heavy fighting with the police (especially in Caen); cf. above, Chapter I, pp. 85 ff.

9. On the back of the leaflet are the names and addresses of the members of the Paris university council with the following: "It's your turn, comrades!"

10. During the day of May 3 a group of militants actually did escape from a police car.

11. Zengakuren: Japanese student association, divided into several fractions; its members have long experience in street fighting.

12. Cf. the press conference and testimony of Professor M.-F. Kahn in the UNEF-SNESup., *Livre noir des journées de mai,* le Seuil, Paris, 1968, pp. 84–91.

13. At that time people believed in the reopening of the Sorbonne, which the minister, Alain Peyrefitte, had hinted might take place the following day.

14. This union, like the correctors' union, is a very small minority in the CGT.

15. Allusion to the murder of 9 Paris workers (February 8, 1962 in the Charonne subway station). This police action, under Roger Frey, Minister of the Interior, has remained symbolic. The same is not true of the anti-Algerian pogrom of October 17, 1961, which was much more brutal and is never referred to directly. Paul Rozenberg wrote (*Vivere in Maggio,* p. 28): "The leftist militants had forgotten neither Charonne nor the Algerians who were driven into the Seine."

This last statement is only true of adult militants. We found no allusion to this tragedy in any of the leaflets.

16. A leaflet in longhand reproduced by duplicator.

17. Cf. this first version in M. Perrot, M. Rebérioux, J. Maitron, *La Sorbonne par elle-même* (*Mouvement social*, No. 64, pp. 47–48).

18. This action committee leaflet is one of the few to underline Dean Durry's responsibility for the entrance of policemen into the Sorbonne. Later the Dean denied any part in this operation.

19. In reality the occupation of the *facultés* had hardly started, but this slogan made it possible to relaunch the movement in spite of the concessions made by Premier Pompidou on the evening of the 11th. Many other distortions of reality may be noted in this text.

20. It was 4 o'clock in the morning of May 11th when Henri Cartan and Laurent Schwartz, after having called on the Minister of the Interior to stop the repression, handed in their resignations from the University. Cf. also the account by Alfred Kastler, Nobel prize winner, in Philippe Labro, *Ce n'est qu'un début*, Paris, 1968, pp. 81–87.

21. Cf. M. Kravetz (with the collaboration of R. Bellour and A. Karsenty), *l'Insurrection étudiante*, "Cours nouveau," 10/18, pp. 415–426.

22. Movement constituted on the same bases as the Paris 22 *mars*. Concerning this movement we only know of the not very explicit article by one of its members, Maurice Blanc, in *Frères du Monde*, No. 52 (1968), pp. 111–116; see also, on events in Toulouse, Jean Lacouture, *Le Monde*, May 17, 1968.

23. For the *Odéon*, cf. *Odéon est ouvert*, by Christian Bouyer, which is interesting for its atmosphere, wall writings and photographic documents. The political evolution of the occupation, the rapid abandonment of the theater by the CAR, close to the 22 *mars* group, which had occupied it originally, are not shown. The volume by Ph. Ravignant, *la Prise de l'Odéon*, Stock, Paris, 1968, is more complete, but also slightly mad. On June 5, *La Tribune du 22 mars* denounced the "merdier épouvantable" (the frightful shit pile) that the Odéon had become, and the participation in the occupation of extreme rightist elements.

III

The Student Movement in the Strike
(MAY 16-31)

The second act seemed longer: time did not pass so quickly, the demonstrations did not follow one another, day after day, as they had in early May.

On the level of the student movement, an immense attempt was being made to capitalize on events. The "action committees" were formally structured, the occupied *facultés* organized, the new structures given thoughtful analysis. However, from the very beginning there were two movements: one daytime movement, in the *facultés,* with reformist or utopian general assemblies, and one all-night movement composed of action committees and other political groups, who were desperately bending all their energies in the direction of the working class.

Corresponding to this dual student movement, each part of which risked knowing nothing about the other, was the long, slow movement of the striking masses, which culminated in a curious, climactic trade union-employer round table on Monday, May 27. While the student commune was re-enacting the Petrograd Soviet, the union machines were re-enacting the Matignon agreements, which the presence of Benoit Frachon brought closer.[1]

The final episode, dating from Monday the 27th to Friday the 31st, was characterized by both latency and rebound: the latency of a strike which the union leaders intended should be without prospects, and the rebound of the metal workers, who refused to believe that the whole thing could end on an increase in salary.

Actually the movement passed through two tempi which overlapped but had different rhythms. The blended tempi of the May 20 factory and *lycée* occupations, which go together; the separate tempi of the combined half race, half demonstration against Cohn-Bendit's expulsion, the rage that marked the evening and night of May 23–24, the nervous security of the Charléty meeting on the 27th. . . . Also separate were the tempi of the workers' combat, in a rhythm held steady and controlled by the labor union machines: i.e., the demonstrations of May 24 and May 29.

This duality expressed very well the ambiguity of the movement and also its doom to failure. The May 10 barricades forced May 13 on the union leaders, and the May 25 negotiations left the students alone again until the Gaullist reply on May 30 and the retaking of the Sorbonne by the police on June 16.

As the strikes spread, on May 16 and 17, worker-student committees, which served as discussion and liaison groups and took up collections, began to organize. By the evening of the 16th, hundreds of students had gone to Billancourt and talked with young workers in front of the gates of the Renault plant. On the 17th a demonstration was planned to take place outside the ORTF, but it was called off as a result of pressure from, among others, the CGT, whose Renault cell advised against any movement on the part of the students in the direction of Billancourt. Elsewhere during the evening action committees organized a hundred or so meetings in the Paris area, but with only moderate success. On the evening of May 16 Premier Pompidou, sensing that the nature of the danger was changing, had denounced the "subversive" movement led by the *"enragés"* (D. Cohn-Bendit, A. Geismar, J. Sauvageot) whom the television—hoping to embarrass them—had shown to the public. On the morning of the 17th the CGT decided to cancel the young workers' festival that was to have been held in Pantin, an eastern suburb.

Document 68

Students-Workers

It has been stated that our demands were specifically student demands and had nothing to do with those of the workers. This is not true.

The press and other media intentionally minimize the importance of the fight. Faced with this fact, we ourselves have decided to replace this inadequate news service.

The workers have taken up the fight in Caen and Redon, and the Sud-Aviation workers in Nantes are occupying their factory. And now, at Renault, as well as among newspaper distributors (*Messageries de la Presse*), workers are fighting for objective news reporting. This is only a beginning; the fight goes on! Students, everywhere, are backing them.

Workers are for freedom to unionize and for freedom of the press inside the shops.

Students are for freedom of speech and political discussion in the University.

They are for the end of capitalism, a slogan they have taken from the working class movement itself.

ALL THIS UNITES US

Under the present university regime, students are trained to become cop-cadres of your factories. You want to force students to become the oppressors of the workers. From now on, students refuse to play this role.

Today it is indispensable for students and workers to join together and to understand each other if they want to work out common goals.

Workers, the students will go into your factories and into your neighborhoods. Workers, the universities are open to you. Ask for information!

JOIN THE WORKER-STUDENT ACTION COMMITTEE
Sorbonne-Staircase A-1st floor

—[May 16, 1968].

Document 69

Workers, Students

In Caen, Le Mans, and Redon, workers and peasants have been fighting; the ORTF has said nothing or has lied.

In Paris, students and young workers have demonstrated against the Gaullist police state; the ORTF has systematically minimized these events and has lied. Newscasting is a government monopoly; parliamentary opposition can do nothing about it.

Nevertheless, after the barricades the ORTF was obliged to concede several crumbs of information, thanks also to pressure from the staff.

Through news channels, the government is making every effort to hide, isolate, and ridicule our struggle.

Today, the government must continue to retreat.

The right to news.
Control of the ORTF by the workers.

Freedom of speech at the ORTF *for those who are fighting.*
EVERYBODY COME TO THE ORTF AT 7 P.M.
rue Cognacq-Jay
FRIDAY, MAY 17.

—CAL, UNEF, *Mouvement du 22 mars* (Nanterre), with the support of
the SNESUP. [May 16] (printed leaflet).

Document 70

After the call to demonstrate in front of the ORTF this evening, and due
to the pressure of its staff, we have been able to obtain time on television for the leaders of the student and university movement. We believe now that the determining feature of the situation is the fact that
workers who are occupying numerous factories have now joined the
fight. We are united with them just as we are united with the movement decided upon by the ORTF staff.

The fighting workers should also be able to express themselves
in public.

We have therefore changed our call to demonstrate this evening
in front of the ORTF building into a call for concrete support of the
workers' fight by first participating in meetings, especially in the Paris
suburbs and, specifically, with the striking workers.

—UNEF-SNESup, May 17, 1968, 2:30 A.M.

On the 18th, while the strike was still spreading, three Trotskyist
organizations grouped together in a permanent committee. These
were: the International Communist Party, the JCR, and *Voix ouvrière,*
which were later joined by the "Pablist" groups. Efforts to organize
and give form to the action committees continued. The *Etats Généraux*
of the University, called by the UNEF, turned out to be simply an information meeting.

That same evening, fascist groups demonstrated at the Étoile
(Arc de Triomphe).

By May 19 the strike had spread to the SNCF and the RATP. The
same day, General de Gaulle, back from Rumania, where he had
spoken highly of educational "selection," pronounced his famous dic-
tum: "Yes to reform, no to *chienlit!*"[2] To which the students immediately replied: "He's *chienlit* himself." While the Marxist-Leninists, who
had disappeared from the Latin Quarter from May 8 to 13, organized

a big meeting at the Mutualité, to which busloads of delegates came from the provinces (some even from as far as Lyons), in Nanterre *chienlit* took the form of a festival in honor of student-worker unity.

Document 71

The Red Flag of the Workers Is Flying Over Renault

Down with the Gaullist anti-people regime!
For ten years the working class has fought step by step to achieve unity in each factory, to defend in each company living standards which have systematically been attacked by big capital. The workers' struggles have held back the employers' offensive, but the division of their forces, the policy of collaboration between the classes which has become the rule *even at the level of the* CGT *confederal leadership,* has prevented the mass struggle from leading to the fall of the anti-people class regime of unemployment and want.

For the last month progressive students, who reject the bourgeois University, who want to enter the people's camp in its struggle against the employers' regime, have thrown all their forces into the battle.

Through their stubbornness, their resolve, their determination to link their fight to that of the working class, which is the main force in the fight against big capital and its government, the mass of progressive students has been able to strike a very hard blow at Gaullism. The workers have understood this: the progressive current in the student movement reflects the people's determination to fight and its determination to make an end of Gaullism. The resolve of progressive students has reminded the workers that only combative action pays. Today the class collaborationist unions who were urging workers to demonstrate calmly and with dignity in order to get nothing but charity, the same unions that sabotaged the mass struggle in Caen, at the Rhodia factory in Lyons, in Schwartz-Haumont and Aluvac, in the Alès ceramic plant, at Dassault and at Renault, *today they can no longer resist the pressure of the working masses.*

The banner of the fight is now in the hands of the proletariat.
The leaders of the PCF and the CGT began by basely attacking the progressive students' movement, using the same terms as the government; then, when the workers demonstrated their determination massively to intervene and lead the fight against capital and its government, the CGT

and PCF leaders called a strike based on lower middle class university slogans. But the workers had understood: they threw all their weight into the fight.

The government wants repression: Pompidou has just said so. The government is panic stricken. Repression against the workers and progressive students, repression against the true Communists, who are battling for the victory of the people, will change nothing. Hatred of the people for their class enemy will be ten times greater.

An immense force is arising today. *The people will win!*

AGAINST UNEMPLOYMENT, STARVATION WAGES,
FIENDISH WORK RHYTHMS.
AGAINST REPRESSION BY POLICE AND EMPLOYERS.
FREEDOM FOR THE PEOPLE!

Call issued by the Communist work groups, the *Union des jeunesses communistes (marxistes-léninistes)*, the *"Servir le peuple"* circles, the *Mouvement de soutien aux luttes du peuple,* and the *Comités de défense contre la répression.*

MEETING, SUNDAY, MAY 19TH
3:30 P.M. at the Mutualité

—*Servir le peuple.*

Document 72

Join Us on Sunday, May 19

From the 3rd to the 10th of May, students, supported by workers, demonstrated in the streets against the bourgeois University because they refused to become the cadres and cops of production.

The Gaullist government has had to give in: the *facultés* are now occupied by the students who are organizing free committees for discussion and political action.

But we do not wish to remain by ourselves; we know that alone the students will not be able to change society or even the University.

This is why, within the framework of a day for open discussion and information, we ask workers and their families to participate in the activities that have been organized.

SUNDAY, MAY 19 FROM 2 P.M. ON, AT THE FACULTÉ:
—Jazz
—Movies

—Documentary exhibit on repression
—Discussions
—*Day nursery.*

—*Mouvement du 22 mars*, Nanterre *Faculté des Lettres*
(Gare de La Folie) [May 18, 1968?].

On May 20 the FEN issued an order for a strike to begin on May 22, which risked interrupting the talks already started between *lycée* students and their professors. This was clearly understood by the normal-school students in Aix-en-Provence.

Document 73

The Aix-en-Provence Normal School

To Lycée *Students* (*boys and girls*)
The FEN is asking for schools to be closed for an unlimited time starting Wednesday, May 22. Through this measure it expects to completely end all classes. This endangers the movement for reform already begun by our commissions. We ask you to avoid being dispersed by setting up working committees in your *lycées* during the strike and afterwards.

All grades (pre-baccalauréat) have organized commissions for educational reform, the results of which will be communicated to you by our information groups with a view to closer collaboration between all *lycées*.

EFFECTIVENESS REQUIRES
EVERYBODY'S COOPERATION

—Committee for Reform of the Pre-bac, May 21, 1968.

On May 22, while discussions were beginning in the National Assembly on a parliamentary censure motion—later voted down—that had been planned before the events and hastily brought up to date, the CGT, followed by the CFDT, announced that it was ready to negotiate with M. Pompidou's government.[3] The same day it was learned that Daniel Cohn-Bendit, who had left for a short visit in Germany, had been refused permission to re-enter France. A demonstration took place later that day to the cry of "We are all German Jews!" There was a clash in the rue de Solférino, in front of the Gaullist organization headquarters, and the following day, other more serious incidents took place from

6:30 P.M. on in the Latin Quarter. On both sides there was talk of "provocation" and "provocateurs." Certain "unidentified" participants seemed to be responsible for these events.

Document 74

No to Police Authority

A residence permit for Cohn-Bendit!
The strike committee of the Paris *Faculté des Sciences* supports the call of the UNEF and the SNESUP. and the *Mouvement du 22 mars.*

RENDEZ-VOUS AT THE HALLE AUX VINS
at 6:30 P.M. (Tour 32)
ALL COME TO THE DEMONSTRATION
Wednesday, May 22 at 7 P.M., Boulevard Saint-Michel

Oppose the expulsion measure against Cohn-Bendit.

This measure will undoubtedly appear as a diversion, to say the least, concerning which the government has no doubt once more failed to estimate the risks involved.—(*Le Monde,* Thursday, May 23, 1968).

—[May 22, 1968].

Document 75

Where Do the Provocateurs Come From?

Fouchet has declared
"On good authority, I know that troublemakers who are not students mingle with the demonstrators. . . . To cope with this danger, the Minister of the Interior urges you not to mingle thoughtlessly with provocateurs."

"On good authority" we do indeed learn:
> —That the government decided to send important police forces to the Place Saint-Michel when nothing justified it.
> —That, *at the same time,* the government sent provocateurs (ex-prisoners, delinquents, who were promised pardons) in order to start a fight against the police.

THIS MANEUVER WAS CARRIED OUT WITHOUT EVEN THE KNOWLEDGE
OF THE POLICE.

Why?

Because the government is not sure of the police and can control them
only by creating an insurrectional climate.

Because the government, in fomenting chaos, wants to justify
general repression.

—Worker-Student Action Committee [Censier, May 24, 1968].

On Friday, May 24, in Paris, while the CGT was organizing two
local demonstrations, which took place calmly at the Bastille and on
the Place Balard, the UNEF, the CAL's, and the *Mouvement du 22 mars*
called for one big demonstration at the Gare de Lyon, to take place at
6:30 P.M. The leaflet brought out by the *Mouvement du 22 mars,*
"Your Struggle Is Ours," was considered sufficiently characteristic to
be picked up in Marseilles by the *Mouvement du 11 mai*. The CGT marshals succeeded in preventing any possible junction between the student and the union processions. The students were, however, joined by
many groups of young workers and young unemployed, by anarchistic
groups, and even by "gangs" such as are found in all large housing
complexes. A police block set up very quickly on the right bank kept
the demonstrators from reaching the Hôtel de Ville (City Hall). Then,
some of them began to build barricades while other groups occupied
the Bourse (Stock Exchange) and set fire to it. In the *Mouvement du
22 mars* there were those who wanted to occupy the Finance and Justice Ministries, and they accused the UNEF marshals (who were not
very apparent) as well as the PSU marshals, of preventing them from
doing it. On the Place de l'Opéra, it was a member of the JCR who
urged them to return to the Latin Quarter.[4] On the Boulevard Saint-
Michel, while the first incidents were breaking out in the rue de Lyon,
barricades began to reappear, some more symbolic than real.[5] The Sorbonne was turned into part hospital, part fortress, and the night was
spent in an atmosphere of tear gas. One demonstrator, a sympathizer
of an extreme rightist movement, was killed in Paris, and the autopsy
showed that he had been hit by a grenade (although this fact was not
made known for a long time). A police officer was killed in Lyons,
where similar events took place, by a truck loaded with paving stones
on the Lafayette Bridge. That day some thought that the fate of the
regime was in the balance. But it was more a time of repression, even
of "rat hunting." On the 25th an action committee leaflet made an accounting, and a UJC(m-l) leaflet brought out in Lyons was severely

critical. Actually, by the evening of the 24th, the Lyons movement had practically ceased to exist. On the student side, a certain apprehension began to show, mingled with a need for explanation, as witness this text from Lyons, and also, with a rejection of the ministerial accusations concerning the role of the "riff-raff." The cgt and the pc condemned, at first brutally, then more subtly, the actions of "certain irresponsible persons." On the 24th at 8 p.m. a speech by General de Gaulle announcing a referendum on the subject of "participation" was received with indifference, not to say sarcasm—"Everything he says is screwy"—and humor, while at the Gare de Lyon demonstrators waved their handkerchiefs and called, "Adieu, de Gaulle!" Large peasant demonstrations were taking place throughout France, but liaison with the worker and student activities proved very hard to establish.[6]

Document 76

While the combat movement of all manual and intellectual workers continues to spread to the entire population throughout the country,

While the problem of the responsibility and power of workers is constantly being posed on every level,

While in the Chamber of Deputies, successive debates won by the government allow it to pass a law that amnesties murderers as well as demonstrators and keeps the latter from obtaining reparations for wrongs done them,

The government is acting:
> —It has decreed the expulsion of a militant student, the first attempt at repression against the demonstrators.
> —It has sent the crs against workers occupying their places of work.
> —It has concluded an agreement with the employers in an attempt to settle University problems and the economic and social crisis.

—At the same time it has proposed two-way talks, negotiations. We cannot let the first attempts at repression take place. Failure of parliamentary action cannot be the conclusion of the workers' struggle. We cannot allow them to disregard what is essential to everybody: the responsibility of the workers, their authority to make decisions, their ability to look out for their own interests.

Also, at the moment when the government is trying to weaken our struggle by dividing the students and by attempting to separate them from the workers, it is important to produce substantial proof that students and workers remain united and determined to pursue the struggle.

This is why the UNEF asks all university and *lycée* students and teachers to participate in the meeting arranged for Friday, May 24 at 6:30 P.M. at the Gare de Lyon.

This is why the UNEF asks all the workers to take part in this demonstration in large numbers.

FRIDAY, MAY 24
6:30 P.M.

—UNEF

Document 77

Students, Men and Women

The struggle of the workers and the students is extraordinarily powerful. The Gaullist government is at bay: it has already agreed to open discussions on the satisfaction of workers' demands.

Since the strength of the joint combat of the working class and the students makes impossible any provocation or attempt at division,

We call on all students, men and women, to join in the large demonstration organized at the instigation of the CGT.

Everybody come to the Place Balard at 4 P.M.

—*Union des étudiants communistes de France* [May 24, 1968].

Document 78

Your Struggle Is Ours!

We are occupying the *facultés;* you are occupying the factories. Are we both fighting for the same thing?

Ten percent of the students in higher education are sons of workers. Are we fighting so that there will be a higher percentage, for a democratic reform of the University? It would be better, but it is not the most important thing. These sons of workers will become students like any others. That a son of a worker might become a director is not in our program. We want to do away with the separation between workers, laborers, and managers.

There are students who, upon leaving the University, do not find employment. Are we fighting for them to find it? For a good employment policy for graduates? It would be better, but it is not the most essential thing. These graduates in psychology or sociology will become the selectors, the "psycho-technicians," the guidance leaders who will try to plan your working conditions; graduates in mathematics will become the engineers who will construct more productive and more unbearable machines for you.

Why are we, students from the bourgeoisie, criticizing capitalist society? For the son of a worker to become a student means leaving his class. For the son of a bourgeois, it can be the occasion for getting to know the true nature of his class, to question himself concerning the social function for which he is intended, concerning the organization of society and his place in it.

We refuse to be scholars cut off from social reality. We refuse to be used for the benefit of the ruling class. We want to do away with the separation between carrying out work and planning and organizing it. We want to construct a classless society; the goal of your struggle is the same.

You demand a minimum salary of 1,000 francs [about $210 monthly] in the Paris area, retirement at 60, and a 40-hour week at the same salary now paid for a 48-hour week.

These demands are fair and they are not new. Nevertheless, they seem to have no connection with our goals. But in fact, you are occupying the factories, you are taking the employers as hostages, you are striking without previous notice. These forms of fighting have been made possible through long, stubbornly led action inside the factories, and also thanks to the recent combat of the students.

These struggles are more radical than your legitimate demands because they do not only seek the betterment of the workers' lot within the capitalist system, they imply the destruction of this system. They are political in the true sense of the word; you are not fighting to have the Prime Minister replaced, but so the employer will no longer be in power, either in the factory or in society. The form of your struggle presents us, students, with a model of truly socialist action: appropriation of the means of production and the power of decision by the workers.

Your fight and our fight are convergent. All that separates one from the other must be destroyed (habit, the press, etc.). The occupied factories and *facultés* must join together.

LONG LIVE OUR JOINT STRUGGLE!
Everybody come to the four meetings and to the demonstration at the
Gare de Lyon, *today, Friday, May 24, 1968 at* 7 P.M.

—*Mouvement du 22 mars.*

Document 79

What Is to Be Done?

The extraordinary combativity shown by the workers, the University and *lycée* students and the peasants who, for almost two weeks now, have been giving tireless response to the repressive forces of the capitalist state, has reduced to nothing the plans and structures of traditional working class organizations.

The question of government authority has now been posed. It is not a question of replacing one government by another, or even one regime by another; it is a question of establishing the authority of the whole working class over all of society, the abolition of the class society.

Any lesser goal would betray the deep meaning of this movement.

For more than a week, workers have been occupying the factories, and students, the *facultés;* peasants, who are victims of the absurdities of capitalist markets, are joining them in the struggle.

The red flag of the working class, not that of a party, is waving everywhere. The grass roots are beginning to organize and are developing immense capacities for initiative.

The government is retracting, trying through negotiation to reconquer the country and wrest from the workers what they have won so far, while surreptitiously preparing the repression. The red flag must continue to wave over the factories. For this, the workers must organize their own authority, now.

Occupation of the *facultés* and of the factories was accomplished in an orderly fashion and with a minimum of violence. But violence is inevitable as long as the threat of losing everything they have won weighs on the working masses, and as long as the repressive authority of the government subsists.

Order reigns in the streets and the workers are capable of maintaining it if the forces of repression do not try to destroy their organization, their strength, and what they have won.

Faced with the power of the working class, which is organizing (whereas the capitalist bourgeois power is being destroyed in the factories), the continued existence of government authority constitutes a permanent threat of bloody disorders and civil war.

The very sources of this power structure must be destroyed now by organizing working class power everywhere.

The workers are occupying the factories, but they have not yet collectively taken possession of them. What we must do now is to transform the strike, to make it active, taking as example the post office employees in several cities who are keeping communications open for the strikers.

The workers should generalize the grass roots organizing that is beginning to appear in certain factories. They should meet uninterruptedly at their places of work, discuss the line their action will take, and delegate spokesmen in order to ensure the coordination on factory, regional, and national levels that is indispensable.

Organized in this way, they will be able to resume factory production for the benefit of the whole national community. They should guarantee security, transportation, and supplies for the cities; they should produce industrial goods for the cities and the countryside, in exchange for the agricultural products which the peasants have begun to furnish free of charge to the strikers.

In this way, by setting up a proletarian social order, the workers will reassure the lower and middle bourgeois strata, who for the moment are hesitant and disturbed by a violence they do not understand. It is, however, in their interest to join the workers, the slight advantages that capitalists grant them being absurd compared to the immense advantages that can be offered them by the society that is becoming visible before our very eyes.

Workers, organize at the grass roots in order to retain control of the fight.

Repressive authority will not be overthrown simply by disorganized demonstrations and barricades in Paris, even if they become generalized.

The source of the power structure must be destroyed by making the bourgeoisie useless, by our taking over the organization of production and distribution in the country.

Then the government will have to give in.

The strikers should set up road blocks and control the circulation of goods and people. They should establish liaisons with army recruits. By the firmness of their attitude they should discourage governmental provocation and bring about dissolution of the repressive machinery by guaranteeing the integrity and security of all policemen and soldiers who come over to the side of the workers.

The workers must prepare themselves by organizing their power to crush any attempt at repression, by organizing armed response to any provocation.

When the workers organize, the armed forces of the government can do nothing against them.

Only activity desired and organized by the workers themselves will put an end to the crisis of the present society by reestablishing man's domination over his principal activity, which is work.

—Worker-Student Action Committee
[Censier, May 25, 1968].

Document 80

Why There Is Slander

Another night of barricades. Once again repression broke loose against students and workers.

The government is trying to smear the demonstrators by speaking of "riff-raff"; newspapers and radio have mentioned the presence of non-students.

"Non-students?" Certainly! Thousands of teachers and workers preferred to demonstrate with the students rather than follow the traditional CGT parades.

SLANDER POURS IN FROM ALL SIDES.

"There is something shady," said the Minister. "There is something shady," asserted the CGT.

IT'S TRUE. THERE IS SOMETHING SHADY.

Why is it that the police prevented 40,000 demonstrators who met at the Gare de Lyon from entering the Place de la Bastille when a few hours before, this same Place was occupied by CGT demonstrators? Why is it that all along the two CGT processions there was not a single cop, when impressive CRS forces immediately surrounded the demonstration organized by the UNEF, provoking confrontation and foreseeable consequences?

Why is it that the CGT and PC leaders, on that very day, had called this demonstration a provocation? Didn't this denunciation amount to giving the police a free hand, to justifying repression in advance? Why is it that in Lyons (according to the radio and newspapers) the cgt leaders in one factory turned over to the police young people who had come to ask the workers to help the students who were fighting on the barricades? What explanations can be given for these slanderous statements put out at the same time by the Gaullist government and by certain cgt leaders?

THE INTENTION IS TO ISOLATE THE MOST COMBATIVE SECTOR OF
STUDENTS AND WORKERS FROM THE STRIKING MASSES.

It means presenting them as poor boobs who are either looking for a fight for its own sake or letting themselves be maneuvered by agitators hidden in their ranks. For the government, the interest in this operation is clear: to prevent the general strike from ending with the fall of Gaullism and, at the same time, to crush the most determined elements: those who want to open up the road to socialism.

For the bureaucrats, heads of the pc and the cgt, their interest is also clear: to have their militants avoid the contagion of revolutionary ideas. Because these machine politicians have long since ceased to believe—if they ever did so—in the possibility of a revolutionary transformation of society which would substitute worker power for capitalist power. What's more, they do not dare encourage the present movement to the point of collapse of the Gaullist regime.

Workers, students, do not let yourselves be hoaxed by the government's campaign of lies, led by certain leaders of the pc *and the* cgt, *by the press and radio.*

OPPOSE EVERYWHERE THOSE WHO WANT
TO STIFLE THE REVOLUTIONARY CONTENT OF THE
PRESENT MOVEMENT THROUGH SLANDER,
EXPLAIN TO YOUR COMRADES THE GOAL OF
THE OPERATION THAT AIMS TO REINCARCERATE US
BEHIND THE WALLS OF CONFORMITY AND
ACCEPTANCE OF THE CAPITALIST SOCIAL ORDER.

—Worker-Student Action Committees, Censier [May 25, 1968].

Document 81

Stop the Provocators

Students have occupied the *facultés*.
Workers have occupied the factories.
Everywhere workers are organizing, consolidating their strikes.

Friday, tens of thousands of demonstrators in Paris, hundreds of thousands throughout France asserted their determination to fight to the end.

The government has turned its cops on them.

The government has no more universities, no more factories, no transport, no radio; it has only its cops to defend it.

THE GOVERNMENT ITSELF IS THE REAL PROVOCATOR!

It's de Gaulle, calling for a plebiscite by using civil war as blackmail.

It's Pompidou, decreeing police terror today.

It's Fouchet, hurling his racist hatred against the "riff-raff."

THEY ARE THE PROVOCATORS!

The riff-raff is this collection of privileged people who cling to power against the popular will.

The provocators are the ones who have nothing left but blackjacks and grenades as their sole legitimacy.

They are the ones who organized massacre and rat hunting all during the night of Friday to Saturday, in the name of law and order.

Against provocation, one answer only: Unity in action of workers and students; organization of the combat so that the popular will will triumph.

WE MUST JOIN THE ACTION COMMITTEES!

WE MUST FORGE NEW ONES!

ACTION COMMITTEE COORDINATION
Sorbonne, staircase C, 1st Floor

—May 25, 1968.

Document 82

Position of the Movement for Support of Last Night's Demonstration

NO to police repression.
NO to demonstrations and violence that have no political content.
YES to just revolt against the machinery of repression.

We protest against the violence of "bourgeois mercenaries" who, as in Paris, used chlorine grenades, tear gas bombs, and even offensive grenades to force back the demonstrators, at the same time avoiding contact with them. After the demonstration there were raids against individual pedestrians and passing cars, accompanied by very tough third degree measures in the police stations. In particular, rat hunts took place in the Algerian quarters, with arbitrary roundups and outrageously brutal violence. Once again, immigrant workers were subjected to disgraceful fascist and racist repression.

Nevertheless, we take issue with this demonstration for having no political content. The backers of the demonstration claimed to follow the Paris example without having assessed its true implications, and a certain number of provocators were merely looking for a fight, hoping in this way to give the working class a lesson.

This demonstration is lagging as regards the fight of the working class masses because it polarizes attention on very secondary aspects of the present juncture—that is, on police repression and the actions of those who are trying to mislead the struggle of the mass strike movement and destroy its unity.

The positive aspect of this demonstration, however, was represented by justified revolt against police repression. Immigrant workers, young social outcasts (the ones the bourgeoisie calls "toughs" or "hoods") are the victims of continual harassment, bourgeois exploitation, and police repression. They are also unorganized. They have therefore used the channel of violent demonstration to express their legitimate revolt.

Our position is obviously the same as regards the demonstration of the same type planned for this evening [Saturday].

REFUSE IRRESPONSIBLE PROVOCATION WITH NO POLITICAL CONTENT!
LONG LIVE THE MASS STRIKE MOVEMENT!
STUDENTS MUST SERVE THE WORKERS' STRUGGLE!

—[Lyons, May 25, 1968].

Document 83

Concerning the Riff-Raff

Capitalist society creates, through repression and unemployment, a state of general violence. Students and workers are revolting against the permanent violence of a regime of competition and shortages, supported by the authoritarianism of government, business, and the University.

The greatest victims of this violence are the hundreds of thousands of unemployed, especially young people without work and workers affected by reconversion. They are the very same ones whom Minister Fouchet calls "riff-raff" and "hoods."

We protest this attempt at division and defamation, which aims at isolating the demonstrators from the workers of all categories who are occupying their plants, their offices, and their universities.

The government does not yet dare fire on workers.

The government does not yet dare fire on students.

It is looking for pretexts for a fascist repression against the entire movement of dissent by falsely distinguishing between "good demonstrators" and "riff-raff."

Since the government has lost all control over the students, this maneuver aims at preparing an armed and bloody aggression, because the government is neither capable of answering the demands of the great mass of workers or of enforcing its own "law and order."

For the same reasons, the government is engaging in a series of police provocations (such as the transformation of the Gare de Lyon into a police trap during the big demonstration of workers and students on May 24) which, together with divisionary tactics, compose a plan that would result in making the workers accomplices in the massacre of some of their own people.

Workers, office workers, professors, students, and peasants: we all belong to what the government dares to call riff-raff. We are occupying the factories! the offices! the universities! the streets!

> *Our strength is irresistible.*

—Action Committee of Preparatory Research Training (Social Sciences);
—Revolutionary Action Committee of the Center for Sociological Studies (CNRS);
—Action Committee of the Laboratory of Industrial Sociology
[May 25, 1968].

Document 84

Barricades: How? Why?

This commission met in an attempt to analyze the present situation of the student movement after the events of Friday, May 24th, in Lyons, particularly.

I. WITH RESPECT TO THE DEMONSTRATION
There has been an attempt to determine the demonstrators' actual participation, responsibilities, and motivations.

Among the participants, two categories stand out: the most politicized (workers following their union lines), and workers, intellectual or manual, who envisaged refusal of society and rejected University or social domination.

With regard to the responsibilities for organizing the demonstration, the security setup was severely criticized.

On the other hand, *exploitation of gangs of young people* by certain students who were said to have used these adolescents for political aims and grievances was brought up. . . . So we must clearly recognize that these young people, who form a so-called subproletariat, non-unionized and very often unemployed, have the best of reasons to revolt and to engage in violence. They felt immediately concerned by the present movement and, particularly, by Friday evening's mass demonstration of dissatisfaction.

In the same way, immigrant workers felt concerned as workers, leaving aside their political option (ambiguity of the use of red flags and of *The Internationale*).

There was therefore no exploitation of young people. It was the revolt of all these workers that was expressed and not their actual persons that were exploited. The demonstrators' motivations are varied. First of all, people spoke of a "visceral" event, which is supposed to have consisted in various calls for violent demonstrations—that is, a certain amount of provocation and incitement. But the demonstration planned by the AGEL and the *Mouvement du 22 mars,* in answer to the call of the UNEF and the SNESUP., remained essentially peaceful in its form and slogans (cf. the article dated May 25 in the *Journal du Rhône*).

On the one hand, an *element of hesitation* and uncertainty as to the attitude to take contributed to the disorganization and panic. In addition, there was an element of unawareness. Motivations of this sort are no longer rational, no longer canalized politically and socially, which explains to a great extent the disorganization of the fights that consisted in a use of dynamic force by people who did not know exactly what the situation was. As for the will to fight, it seems that the great majority had no intention of doing so, even though many did participate in the fighting.

An experience of this kind shows a determination to depart from all forms of security setups and traditional demonstrations. It allowed those who were revolting against any sort of internal organization and for whom violence is a solution, to regroup. The risk of such a group becoming fascistic does exist.

II. THE SITUATION THAT FOLLOWED THESE EVENTS LEADS US TO
EXAMINE THE STATE OF THE STUDENT MOVEMENT

We note disorganization of the movement and demobilization of students due:

—to police threats, which provoked public panic, hostility towards the students, and fear among students themselves (the state of psychological hysteria in Lyons, which was without any reliable information, is a proof);

—to settlement of immediate University problems (examinations);

—to transport strikes;

—to individual family opposition;

—*to the impression of uselessness of committee work sessions.*

There is a disassociation between Committee work, which remains on a university and theoretical basis, and the work of liaison with the workers.

The committees no longer see the general direction of their work, and this results in a certain lack of interest for this kind of activity. Two movements have been created which, although they set out with the same intention, are not always convergent. They stem:

—From the shock due to the demonstration: the actual events were more serious than the consequences that had been foreseen. The phenomenon can be more wholly and directly social. There is a lag between becoming aware theoretically and comprehension of what happened.

—From diversification of opinions, therefore, of actions. The movement has no precise preconceived policies. With this general statement, we feel the need of a security setup and committee work that will permit us to give a precise definition of the direction of the movement.

This then, is the *negative aspect* of the present situation (absence of structures for the movement, which carries with it a risk of fascism). But the student movement remains combative; it remains the center of contestation and reinforces a certain number of tendencies on the level of the working class struggle. It remains, therefore, a pole of contestation which reinforces the others (for example, radicalization of the position of the working class grass roots).

From these positive and negative aspects is derived the ambiguity of the student movement's situation:

—On the one hand, the fact of having sparked the flame of contestation.

—On the other, a slowing up of action due to police repression, which used the demonstration as a pretext, and which made it possible to discern the risk of fascism.

III. BY WHICH MEANS AND AT WHICH LEVELS CAN THIS
      FASCIST PENETRATION TAKE PLACE?

From a short analysis of the period that preceded the inauguration of Nazism in Germany, it can be stated that, in addition to the economic crisis, which reduced many people to unemployment, there was a struggle within the working class that provoked a demobilization of revolutionary forces and benefited the nationalist forces. This is the process of division of working class forces.

At present
On the middle class level, people can lose hope in the working class, which is itself hardly organized for assuming power (despite union organizations representative of the working masses). They have insufficient strength to organize themselves and have few prospects in the future society. This situation of uncertainty makes them receptive to fascist reasoning.

On the working class level, people are also at loose ends. The most politicized among them will not be satisfied with agreements made between the unions and the government, because their criticism is on another level than that of material demands (wages, hours, various working conditions). People, therefore, will break with their former organizations, but no organization at present is capable of bringing them together. The disillusionment runs the risk of making them vulnerable to the attraction of fascism. This risk is all the greater since, even within the CGT there is opposition between the more dynamic, more flexible federations, who pose more fundamental problems, and the confederation itself.

On the student level, there is the police threat, which because it provokes panic reflects the lack of confidence, the separation between the revolutionary nature of the minority, and the less supple attitude of the majority. On these three levels it is the separation of forces and the lack of planning for a later organization which, because it leaves people hesitant, can render them receptive to fascist influence.

For us, therefore, Friday's demonstration marked an important stage in the present movement; but this stage is above all a moment for clearly examining the continuation of our struggle and deciding what forms it will take. We must systematically continue to work with the outside (that is to say, with workers, both skilled and unskilled, and with peasants).

An increased number of talks and meetings, whether during or outside working hours, not only on the organizational level, but especially between militant students and workers, is the only way to plan our common struggle in the coming days.

> —AGEL *Mouvement du 22 mars,* Committee meeting at the *Faculté des Lettres* [Lyons, May 27, 1968].

On May 25 the UNEF spelled out its immediate demands in a long statement and announced a day of protest for Monday the 27th. The meeting that was taking place at the Ministry of Social Affairs, rue de Grenelle, between the government, the unions, and the employers (CGT, CFDT, FO, CGC, FEN, CFTC, CNPF, CPME) was still going on.

Document 85

The UNEF Declaration

Following the events of the last three weeks, and particularly these last few days, in all the University cities in France—notably in Paris; taking into account the situation, the distortions made by official news releases or by those controlled by the government, we want to clarify the following points:

1. *The police and the government are entirely responsible for the incidents that have just occurred, and the* UNEF *declares its solidarity with all the victims of the forces of repression.*

These incidents arise from the government's intentional tendency to create an objectively explosive and provocatory situation for the students and for the workers fighting with them: the UNEF declares its entire solidarity with victims of police repression, on whatever occasion it is used.

2. *The* UNEF *proposes to designate Monday, May 27, as a day for big demonstrations throughout the nation.*

The attitude of the police makes them entirely responsible for all confrontations. Particularly today and tomorrow, the presence of large forces in the Latin Quarter, their constant comings and goings, the way they disperse all groups, are so many provocations: if incidents occur, the government must know that it causes them.

The UNEF makes no call for demonstrations today or tomorrow.

As a counter-measure it proposes that all Paris and provincial militants make Monday, May 27 a national day for demonstrations, to be held after 5 P.M.

3. *The university struggle has meaning only if it is integrated with the larger struggle; there will be no dialogue with a government that refuses to recognize the meaning of this common struggle.*

For a long time now the UNEF has emphasized that the University struggle is meaningless unless it becomes a part of the framework of confrontation and combat against the capitalist regime: true democratization of education can only exist in liaison with an overthrow of production relationships and the transformation of economic structures by and for the workers.

It is very evident that on all these points the government and General de Gaulle are unwilling to consider the nature of our combat and that they see it only from the standpoint of perpetuation of the present system.

Therefore, we consider that there can be no dialogue with the regime.

4. *The University, in any case, is taking in hand its own affairs.*

On May 17, 1968, the UNEF proposed to all students and professors four precise points on which pressure may be brought to bear.

The decisions freely taken by the student body are in broad agreement with proposals made by the UNEF. Wherever possible, particularly in the *facultés* henceforth under co-equal administration (teacher-student), we must now conclude and actually inaugurate the right of veto on all decisions taken. In reality, only control over decisions will make it possible to ensure permanent University confrontation. Wherever universities are autonomous, all deviation towards any sort of private administration of the *facultés* must be fought against. Autonomy also means that the University should be widely opened to workers.

The UNEF therefore calls on all its militants and the whole student body to apply their own decisions from now on.

It also calls for postponement of all examinations until September.

5. *For an even stronger liaison between the University struggle and the struggle of workers and peasants.*

The UNEF welcomes the actual junction of striking workers with students which took place in Paris on May 24, as well as in many provincial University cities, in the factories, and in the *facultés*. In all these cases tens of thousands of striking workers have joined the students.

The UNEF sends its warmest greetings to all workers engaged in the battle with their unions. Because it believes in the importance of keeping a united student-worker front, it asks workers' unions:

—To maintain the same solid front in face of government repression. As it happens, the refusal to give Daniel Cohn-Bendit a residence permit is precisely a decisive element of this repression.

—To remember that our position is a simple one: never, and in no way, do we intend to give lessons to working class organizations, but on the other hand, none will be accepted with regard to the student struggle.

Permanent discussions exist at the grass roots between students and workers. To the extent that the aforementioned points are clearly understood, the UNEF proposes that the same discussions be begun on all levels with the workers' union organizations.

The degree to which action carried out in Paris has been reproduced in the provinces has made extension to the workers' sector possible.

At present, and with the same concern for developing the movement, the UNEF calls on all students in all University cities to increase their activities:

—for continuation of our university combat,
—for union of students and workers,
—for their common victory.

—National Committee of the UNEF, May 25, 1968. (Printed leaflet.)

On Sunday the 26th, negotiations between the unions and the government were still going on. The provincial sections of the UNEF were also getting ready for the Monday event. The following leaflet put out by the General Student Association in Nantes is interesting both for its style and for its historical references.

Document 86

Worker-Student Unity

For a year now, the AGEN has constantly asserted that the destruction of capitalist society could be accomplished only through worker-student unity. In fact: (1) the Paris riots, the fundamental reexamination of the bourgeois University through occupation of the *facs* and theaters, on the one hand; and (2) occupation of factories and all places of work, on the other, are merely the actual implementation, through appropriate means, of a struggle that is capable of completely transforming society.

The government and the venal press make no mistake, for they are trying to impose, at all cost, worker-student division:
On Friday, May 24, two demonstrations took place in Paris on the same afternoon:

— one by the CGT, at the Place de la Bastille, went off uneventfully, there being no police repression;
— the other, at the Gare de Lyon, organized by the UNEF, the SNEsup., the *Mouvement du 22 mars,* and the action committees, was instantly attacked by the CRS and the *gardes-mobiles.*

The newspapers are trying, among other things, to split the demonstrators' unity by creating false categories such as: non-students, riffraff, foreigners (German Jews), etc. Nevertheless, we would be betraying the students if we did not warn them against a danger that is greater than division, and that is: co-option of a movement which is evidently going beyond the simple framework of traditional economic demands of wages, formulation of union rights, etc., and which from now on can pose the problem of workers' assuming control of their way of life. This danger is substantiated by top level national union-employer-government negotiations, which pretend to be the outcome and the end of the limited general strike spontaneously begun in the factories.

This danger was also foreshadowed by the maneuvers of the PCF and of the FGDs, which are trying to set up a type of coalition of which the betrayal of the Spanish Republicans in 1938, and Munich, were logical consequences. A complete change of society was implicitly present in the forms of student combat from the beginning; then, in the forms of worker combat, which go further than prospects of partial reform within the system. The revolution of the present society will be complete or it will not take place, which seems to frighten M. Georges Séguy, General Secretary of the CGT:

The movement, placed under the vigilance of the workers, is indeed too strong for there to be any question of arresting it through such empty formulas as self-management, civilization reforms, and other inventions which would end in relegating immediate demands to the background. (*Le Monde,* May 22nd).

For the above-mentioned reasons which, moreover, are given concrete form by the contents of this declaration, we have not signed the joint interunion leaflet. In effect, this leaflet condemns "the national Gaullist revival," but is unwilling to work out a possible plan for satisfying the announced demands, in this case, the step from:
  "immediate satisfaction of demands" to "demands
  for immediate demobilization"
is quickly taken.

To achieve a true worker-student unity, it would be well for *l'Humanité,* the CGT, and the PCF to stop their attacks against the UNEF (declared irresponsible) and against such militant revolutionary comrades as Cohn-Bendit (*"agent provocateur* in the pay of Pompidou"). We can envisage political polemics, but not of a xenophobian and racist nature (German Jew[7]).

Contrary to the PCF, which refuses to participate in the UNEF demonstrations on a national level for the above-mentioned reasons, the AGEN calls on you to take part in Nantes in

THE MONDAY, MAY 27 DEMONSTRATION
Starting 9:30 A.M., rue Ricordeau.

The demonstration will show students and workers confronting the police state, side by side.

For your information, here are the slogans of the 80,000 demonstrators on the night of Friday to Saturday in Paris:

To hell with national borders,
The power is in the streets.
This is just a beginning; we must continue the fight.

—The AGEN–UNEF [Nantes, May 25, 1968].

On Monday the unions, representatives of the government and of the employers' associations, meeting in the rue de Grenelle, drew up a report that was immediately rejected by the Renault workers,[8] then, by the rest of the metal workers.

The slogan of a "popular government" got off to a fresh start, and the CGT organized twelve meetings in Paris and in the suburbs.

The demonstration planned by the UNEF and controlled for the most part by the PSU, took place in the Charléty stadium with between fifty and sixty thousand people present. The *Mouvement du 22 mars* did not join it out of opposition to "union co-option"[9] and organized its own neighborhood demonstrations, which received little notice. In point of fact, in the march to Charléty there were many *22 mars* militants as well as Marxist-Leninist militants (the PCMLF, unlike the UJC(m-l), called on its members to demonstrate). Following is the article denouncing the meeting that appeared in *la Cause du Peuple* of May 29. This faction remained a minority.

The presence at Charléty of Pierre Mendès-France, the fact that André Barjonet, who had just resigned from a leading position in the CGT, spoke, led many to believe that a decisive political corner had been turned.

Document 87

CHARLETY: AGAINST
*the anti-*CGT-*ism and anti-Communism
of Social Democracy*
LONG LIVE THE CGT!

Big Business is not afraid of its friends Séguy and Krasucki. It knows that they can be counted on to compose their differences at the expense of the fighting workers. But Big Business is afraid of the CGT; it is afraid of the militant traditions of the class struggle; it knows that the working class will not give up the weapons it has forged in the course of 70 years of struggle. It is afraid of the thousands of militants actively defending class struggle issues, particularly since they are opposed to a Confederation sell-out. Therefore, the CGT must be destroyed *at the grass roots,* where reformist leaders are ineffectual. Big Capital is going to play all sides. It is putting the reformists, Séguy and Krasucki, at the head, and is proposing to the workers, who are disgusted by this leadership, a petty bourgeois current with revolutionistic terminology that is profiting from the forms of the students' determined combat. And it is the CFDT that will head this current.

Anti-CGT-*ism* and traditional anti-Communism à la CFDT are being offered to workers who refuse the revisionist leadership of the PCF and the CGT.

The petty bourgeois social democratic operation led by the CFDT and the UNEF is supposed to do this dirty job.

At the Charléty meeting, before 25,000 people, the CFDT, which was the star of the meeting, declared it had fought during the negotiations for authority and democracy of the workers in the factories and for management by the workers of their own economy.

With a fat subsidy from our Big Business government, the CFDT has for many years enjoyed the luxury of implicitly attacking the class collaboration of the CGT leadership, and of talking themselves hoarse

about the struggle to be carried out with the students, for achieving a
. . . socialist society!

Barjonet is making propaganda for the theory of his new PSU
friends, according to which the dual power structure and reformist
humbug of student power in the University and workers' power in the
factory must be enforced.

FO, a scab union founded by the CIA, is even more eloquent on
the subject of "economic and social democracy which is not to be negotiated, but must be fought for."

No, you reformists and demagogues of the CFDT and the PSU; no,
you FO scabs! The millions of angry workers opposing Séguy and his
accomplices will not join your ranks!

Proletarian unionists are mobilizing large masses of workers to
reconquer their CGT unions, which are dedicated to the class struggle
and eliminate the quitters and traitors on every level.

An unusual event for Paris was a call directed to the peasants.
The effort to break out of the "University ghetto" went hand in hand
with an effort to break out of the "Paris ghetto," and Paris students
left for the provinces to try to mobilize the peasants and find food for
the strikers. In certain provincial cities, such as Nantes, this worker-
peasant liaison, through the intermediary of the students, was quite
successful.[10]

Document 88

Peasants

Ever since the barricades, students and workers have joined together in
a common struggle.

In order that our hard-working people may really participate in
the economic, social, and political life of the country,

Peasants, there is no agricultural policy.
The Common Market makes decisions without consulting
the peasants.
Financing is insufficient.
Who guarantees your income?
For a quick, real, and effectual solution

LET'S ALL ACT TOGETHER!

The ten million strikers, who are determined to fight till the end,
ask the peasants to support them.

Feed the strikers and their families—how?
By depositing your farm products in cooperative centers.

WE WILL HAVE THEM DISTRIBUTED.
EVERYBODY AT THE SORBONNE!!!
Workers—students—peasants are expecting you

—"Student-worker" Liaison Committee [May 27, 1968].

On May 28, Mitterrand came out in favor of a provisional leftist government. The Federation and the Communist Party had a consultation; Geismar resigned from the central committee of the SNESup.; a meeting of action committees from the *"22 mars"* and the JCR, with various well-known militants, among whom were the pro-Chinese Gilbert Mury and the pro-Castro Jean-Pierre Vigier, failed in its attempt to set up a joint revolutionary party. A few days later, a not very strong "working committee" was the result.[11]

On the 29th, in order to contribute to a "political change denoting social progress and democracy," the Communist Party and the CGT organized a demonstration at 3 P.M., from the Bastille to the Gare Saint-Lazare. The other union heads refused to take part, and the UNEF had insisted that as a prerequisite the CGT would formally protest the refusal to allow Cohn-Bendit to return to France. This demonstration was attended by several hundred thousand people, among whom were many students. In addition to the USC, several student groups, including the JCR and the Coordinating Committee of the "action committees," officially called on their members to take part. De Gaulle flew off to Colombey via Baden-Baden. Pierre Mendès-France accepted the hypothesis of a government to be headed by himself, as representing a union of the left.

Document 89

Why We Are Going to the CGT Demonstration

Recently, at the Gare de Lyon and at Charléty, whatever may have been the intentions of certain people, we were together, students and workers, to demonstrate against the Gaullist government.

Today, whatever the intentions of the others, we are going to demonstrate together, workers and students, against the Gaullist government.

We remain united in the struggle,
and we reject all divisive maneuvers:

—*because grass roots* unity in action is our best weapon against the Gaullist government and capitalist exploitation,

—*because* the demands of the workers and those of the students call for overthrow of the bourgeois system,

—*because* our revolutionary struggle, which is the same on all fronts, needs more than ever unity of action at the grass roots.

When the workers take to the streets,
we students stand shoulder to shoulder with them.
We are responsible for our actions
and we are proving it to ourselves.

EVERYBODY COME TO THE DEMONSTRATION
3 P.M.—*Bastille*

—EPHE Action Committee, Preparatory Training for
Social Science Research, Paris, May 27, 1968.

Document 90 (other side of the above leaflet)

Clarification

Where do the divisive maneuvers come from?

RECENTLY
When the worker-student demonstration took place at the Gare de Lyon, the leaders of the CGT refused to be associated with it.

RECENTLY
Again, at Charléty, there were 50,000 of us, workers and students, among whom were numerous CGT union members, without the support of CGT leadership.

TODAY
The heads of the CFDT and FO, on the pretext that the UNEF is not participating, have not called for a demonstration.

But the UNEF leadership, even though it is right to demand that the CGT heads must withdraw their accusation of irresponsibility and accept the student struggle on student terms, should have understood that OUR PLACE IS WITH THE WORKERS, whatever the mistakes of union leaders who urge them to take to the streets.

—Political Action Committee, Preparatory Training for
Social Science Research, May 29, 1968.

On May 30 at 4:30 P.M., there was a speech by de Gaulle followed by a huge "patriotic" anti-communist demonstration at 6 P.M. The referendum was "postponed" and the Assembly dissolved. The following action committee leaflet is especially interesting because of its evident determination to set up the structures of a dual authority. At this stage of the movement it seemed strangely dephased. The anarchist-surrealist leaflet that closes this long series, by virtue of its very disillusionment, is an acknowledgment of an evident fact: the bourgeoisie was alive and well, and all direct political exits were blocked.

Document 91

He Talks and Talks . . .

After having laboriously set the stage, de Gaulle just issued a warning to the country. Using senile anti-communism, he invoked threats of forceful overthrow of the government and of civil war with the intention of provoking in his favor a great wave of national panic.

BUT WHOM CAN HE STILL FRIGHTEN?

Certainly not the workers who are occupying the factories. Certainly not the students who are occupying the *facultés*. And, in reality, what can this dying regime do against millions and millions of striking workers?

*The violent tone used by de Gaulle is one
of impotent rage confronted by the popular will.*

The only supporters the government has left are its henchmen in the "civil action committees." It has nothing left to defend it but its cops. The workers and students know how to handle the cops. They have proved it.

De Gaulle can keep on barking. Opposing the regime he embodies, the force of the student-worker combat is irresistible. We must organize this force systematically in action committees that unite workers, students, and the people in each neighborhood and in the surrounding districts.

We must strengthen our organization through unity, at the grass roots and through action. We must support and popularize the workers' defense of their places of work. We must organize, right now, new forms of people's power in the factories, universities, neighborhoods and surrounding districts.

All action committees must get together with the strike committees in the surrounding factories, discuss the objectives and forms of
people's power on all levels and, from now on, do everything possible:

—*by keeping* certain indispensable public services going (house-
hold garbage collection, transport, etc.);

—*by maintaining* the food supply of the population through direct contacts with producers' cooperatives;

—*by ourselves taking over* the means of informing the people
about the workers' struggle in order to put an end to the lies of the
bourgeois press.

Only through organization of this struggle and of these activities
will we be able to guarantee satisfaction and defense of workers' demands and give true content to the people's government which we
want to promulgate.

GAULLISM IS NOW NOTHING BUT A GHOST.

THE PEOPLE ARE NOT AFRAID OF GHOSTS.

WE WILL WIN.

—Action Committee Coordination, 28, rue Serpente, Paris 6°
[May 30, 1968].

Document 92

The Paris sewers disgorged their tricolored rats
when the leader blew the bugle of the well-behaved
the well-protected
by the well-trained blackjackers and machine-gunners
of the Sacred Order.
All the rats painted with the Lorraine Cross vomited
their patriotic phlegm:
"France for the French."
"Let us erect frontiers bristling with fire and sword."
"The Jews in Dachau."
"We must pray together to the god of the capital-quilted bourgeois."
"Brothers, we must rekindle the flame of century-old passions."
And they cry: *"Vive la France,"*
but they think,
these buck-filled paunches do,
"Vive our big money."
Unknown soldier of their Arch of Bloody Triumphs,
arise,

let your anger rise;
a general? no;
young man of good family? no;
just a poor little guy from the people,
factory, or countryside; fatigue, oppression,
arise,
unknown soldier, your body in splinters,
reject their foul flowering of flags and banners,
soaked in the sweat and blood of your brothers,
the workers;
arise,
little guy with the splintered jaw,
and throw
over their crowd of fear-stinking rats
the great red flame
of *The Internationale*.

—[May 31, 1968?]

Notes

1. The press later underlined the fact: "M. Frachon, you participated in the Matignon agreements."

2. *La Chienlit:* D. Singer translates this as "dirty mess," and adds the following note (*op. cit.*, p. 173, n. 11): *"Chienlit* means literally "he who shits in bed." It originally referred to the gay dog returning from the party so drunk as to foul his bed. Its meaning then was "masquerade." Now it is used as a loose and vulgar equivalent for disorder. This word was used for the first time to describe the student movement by the fascist weekly, *Minute.* General de Gaulle took it over on his return from Rumania on May 19. The Littré dictionary for 1873 gives the following definition: "Name that children and the general populace use to designate the masqueraders that crowd the streets on Lenten feast days."

3. Which Georges Séguy had already made clear on the preceding day.

4. Cf. Cohn-Bendit, *le Gauchisme* . . . , pp. 74–76.

5. For instance, at the request of the security services of the Sorbonne, an anarchist barricade on the rue de la Sorbonne was obliged to occupy only half the street in order to permit first-aid cars to pass.

6. See the concrete example of the Vendôme region in G. Chaffard, *les Orages de mai,* Calmann-Lévy, 1968, pp. 97–98. The peasant arbitrator of a conflict between workers and milk producers was elected a centrist party deputy on June 30. A few indications are found in Nos. 71 (April–May) and 72 (June–July) of the review *Paysans,* and in Bernard Lambert's book, *Les Paysans dans la lutte des classes,* collection Politique, Seuil, Paris, 1970.

7. Actually, "German anarchist."

8. What happened at Renault on the morning of Monday the 27th, remains controversial; according to J. Ferniot, *Mort d'une révolution,* pp. 121–126,

the CGT and the PC were as of then resolved to continue the strike locally. But it is hard to understand that Georges Séguy and Benoit Frachon should have run the risk of being booed. The different suppositions are analyzed by G. Lefranc, who draws no conclusions, however, in *Le Mouvement syndical* . . . , Paris, 1969, p. 238.

9. Cf. Cohn-Bendit, *le Gauchisme* . . . , pp. 76–77; however, on p. 78, he writes, "At no moment thereafter was there a mobilization as large, on objectives as radical, as on May 24 and 27."

10. See below, Chapter VI, pp. 379–380 and above p. 214.

11. See below, Chapter IV, pp. 307–315.

IV

"Groupuscules" or Action Leadership?

"I recall the amused astonishment of my students one day when, during a discussion of genders and 'literary structures,' I set out to demonstrate for them that all revolutionary myths were descended from the same archetypal fairy tale, 'Sleeping Beauty.' On the evening of May 13, in the liberated Sorbonne, one of my students said to me: 'The Sleeping Beauty is awake, but there are too many princes, and which one is Prince Charming?' "

—Paul Rozenberg, *Vivere in Maggio.*

The slogan, "We are a 'groupuscule,' a dozen *'enragés,'* " was first used on May 6, then picked up and generalized during the "long march" of May 7. It seemed particularly derisive with regard to those who, in the PCF or elsewhere, blamed the student disturbances on the action of a few leftist "groupuscules," but also to those members of the aforementioned "groupuscules," who claimed that they were the sole depositories of revolutionary truth. In the introduction, at the beginning of the present volume, an attempt has been made to describe the role of the "groupuscules" and other revolutionary organizations by showing how they both helped and hindered the essentially pedagogical and practical action of a movement like the *22 mars* in Nanterre or the *25 avril* in Toulouse. We should simply like to clarify a few points in order to make the texts more intelligible.

Naturally, the small student organizations were all opposed to the action of the fascist-oriented students in *Occident* which, although it was actually limited, had enormous mythological importance. They also opposed, in an obviously quite different way, the *Union des étudiants communistes,* the traditional organization of leftist students, which is considered to be a negative pole of reference. (The socialist students, however, may be considered negligible,[1] while the PSU students (ESU) are important only to the extent—which is real—that they control certain sectors and the leadership of the UNEF).

Finally, they oppose one another, at times, term for term. This is the case, for instance, among the organizations that have grown out of the rivalries that divide French Trotskyites. It is impossible to understand the action of the FER without referring back to the JCR and to the opposition of the "Lambertists" and the "Frankists" which dates, officially, from 1951. More generally, the FER, as also for different reasons the UJC(m-l), regards with the same contempt everything it does not control.

The JCR, the FER, the UJC(m-l), the UEC, and, to a lesser degree, the ESU are the only organizations that are really important. This should be borne in mind provided room is left for the countless "Doctors in Revolution" who, however foreign to the student movement, swamped the *facultés* with their leaflets and pamphlets. Although hardly important in themselves, the anarchist groups were important for the quality of their contribution both to the formulation of demands and to the demonstrations.[2]

Three kinds of organizations tried to transcend the "groupuscule" situation. The traditional union organizations, that is, the UNEF and the SNESup., at times succeeded in being a meeting-ground for action, while at others they were nothing more than a closed circuit of old rivalries. An attempt was made, probably prematurely, to unify in one "Revolutionary Movement" the principal groups that worked together in a common action. On the contrary, the *Mouvement du 22 mars* brought together, independently of doctrines and sects, militants of extremely diverse origins and numerous students who were entirely foreign to the sectarian world. The Pompidou government, as was its way, treated the "groupuscules" and the *Mouvement du 22 mars* as a whole, by dissolving them all by decree on June 12.

Lastly, and although they are not represented in the following pages (they will be found elsewhere, however), it should be recalled here what an important role was played—even though partly clandestine, and especially in the *Coordination des Comités d'Action*—by the *Mouvement d'action universitaire* (MAU), and the attempts at direct democracy, with no organization of any kind (even the *Mouvement du 22 mars* was a "groupuscule" in their eyes) sparked, particularly in Strasburg, by the "situationists."

The JCR

The *Jeunesse communiste révolutionnaire* (JCR), which was founded in Paris in early 1966, after a long incubation period, in the *secteur Lettres* of the *Union des étudiants communistes,* had opposed the support given by the PCF to Mitterrand's candidacy and formed close ties with the Trotskyist group (PCI) of which P. Frank was the moving spirit. Among all the "groupuscules," it is probably the one that tried most coherently to restore the Leninist-Trotskyist concept of a party founded on "democratic centralism." Its militants played a decisive role in the formation and development of the *Comité Vietnam national* (CVN), and generally in all radical forms of "Third World" action (Castroism and Guevaraism). Certain of its founders, in fact, had played an outstanding role in support of the FLN during the last months of the Algerian war. In Nanterre, its militants had helped found the *Mouvement du 22 mars,* which was forced out by its own polemics in June, on the very subject of a revolutionary "party." The priority orientation towards the Third World was somewhat diminished just before the May events, under the impetus particularly of the German student movement.

In May the JCR was at the heart of the movement, but at no time could it have claimed either to have started or to be leading it. Its name will appear frequently throughout this book; following are two characteristic texts. In the first, the JCR defines its position with regard to the principal "leftist" organizations; in the second, it undertakes a critique of the Communist attitude—a theme of which it never tires.

At the end of 1968, the JCR became the "Ligue Communiste," and one of its leaders, Alain Krivine, was a candidate for the presidency in the elections of June 1, 1969.

Document 93

Students' Struggles and Workers' Struggles

I. THE HISTORIC ROLE OF THE PROLETARIAT

In France, the student movement has proved that it has a political maturity which is probably greater than that of the Italian and German movements. The presence of a deeply rooted and well constructed workers' movement helps explain this. Here, contrary to the *Nouvel Observateur's* claims, Marcusian ideology plays only a secondary role. Avant-garde militants are almost unanimous in recognizing the historic role of the working class as analyzed by Marxist theory.

But today this comprehension goes well beyond the limited circle of political militants. The student masses, through their concrete experience, have explored the limitations and extent of their action. At the time of the Nanterre protest strike[3] they understood that their basic demands could be satisfied only if they were backed by a powerful ally. At the time of the street fighting and barricades they discovered that their struggle against the bourgeois state and its repressive police could be successfully carried out only if some powerful force able to solve all capitalist contradictions would relay them. From now on, the historic role of the proletariat is no longer a simple conceptual abstraction, but a practically proved necessity.

In order to achieve this necessary junction between the students' struggle and the workers' struggle, a historically proved solution exists: this is the regrouping of avant-garde militants, without distinction of social origin, within a revolutionary party. In such a party "any distinction between workers and intellectuals must be eradicated" (Lenin). And the majority of the militant students agree that their place would be in such a party if it existed.

But today, when the big working class parties no longer have anything revolutionary about them, must we be content to wait for the "grass roots," who are by definition healthy, to get rid of the pontiffs and bureaucrats, and meanwhile train and arm for the "great day" elite theorists who do not fight? Numerous groups, "groupuscules," and even smaller groups have worn themselves to the bone over this problem.

II. PARASITES AND MENIALS

The originality of the present movement resides in the fact that it attempts to solve this formerly unsurmountable problem concretely. To get out of the rut, avant-garde militants have had to refuse several attitudes taken by one group or another, on the grounds that they were unworkable.

1. Political Parasitism

In the absence of mass fighting, a student organization, the CLER (today qualitatively changed into the FER—in the sense of regression and not of progress), had become specialized in the use of the political gadget that took the form of motions and objectives. Roughly, it meant addressing such verbal summons to trade union and political organizations, "objectively traitors to our class interests" as: "Are you in favor of strike committees?" of "general demonstrations?" of "3,500 young people at the Mutualité?" etc.

And if the answer (often predictable) was no, they denounced the bureaucrats. On the basis of these successive denunciations it is always possible to recruit a few discontented or embittered segments—

that is, to feed on the tail ends and leftovers of other people's struggles. (Which perhaps explains the mediocrity of the CLER membership.) This is what is called political parasitism: inflating the ego through a process of denunciations, an escalation which can only exist with respect to others, to the detriment of political initiative proper.

But this only concerns a decadent movement whose survival was linked to stagnation of the struggle. When history begins its march these elements fall out and disappear. Symbolically, therefore, they have left the barricades which they consider criminal and unsound.

Far more interesting is the reasoning confirmed by the formula:

2. *"Serve the People"*[4]

Since these are people who lay claim to Marxism-Leninism, with heavy parenthetical support, we shall refer to Lenin without dogmatism. Here reference is not a simple scholastic procedure; it is justified by the situation itself. During the years 1898–1902 there existed no revolutionary party in Russia, so that in combatting various currents in the working class movement, Lenin was working to construct one. And at that time, too, "groupuscules" flourished with their reformist, populist, economist variations. Today, given the political and organizational social-democratization of the PC, it is not surprising to see a whole diversified range of groups appear which at times repeat, with slight variations, the events of earlier years.

Our m-l comrades say that we must serve the people, we must place ourselves under the authority of the workers, otherwise the student movement is a reactionary one. But who represents the authority of the workers? It is not their (r) organizations (read "revisionist"), and everybody is in agreement on this point. Then it would be the individual problem we meet in the bread lines, or at the factory gates.

For a Leninism that is well understood, if not well compiled, such an attitude has something monstrous about it. Lenin recognized that the atomized, isolated worker is not a bearer of class consciousness; he is, at the most, a spokesman for the limited, fragmented, corporatist interests of this or that particular fraction of the proletariat. Class consciousness is not something spontaneous and inherent to the proletariat; it can only come to it "from the outside." "The history of every country confirms that, by itself, the working class can only achieve a trade-unionist consciousness (. . .). And the trade-unionist policy is the bourgeois policy of the working class" (Lenin).

Lenin also declared that all those who imagine that the worker movement is capable of working out an independent ideology by itself, provided they can wrest their fate from the hands of the rulers, are wrong. Because socialism and the class struggle first appear on parallel lines and do not produce each other. Socialist awareness can appear only on a basis of profound scientific knowledge of society as a whole. (Lenin, quoting Kautsky). Spontaneous development of the worker movement only leads to its subordination to bourgeois ideology: "trade-unionism is the ideological subjection of workers by the bourgeoisie."

In a very condensed form, at the time of the three articles in *Rabochaya Gazeta* and even before *What Is To Be Done?*, Lenin furnished the fundamental answer:

> "What is the class struggle? When workers confront
> their employers, it is only a weak embryo. The workers'
> struggle only becomes a class struggle when all the avant-
> garde representatives of the whole working class are
> aware of forming one single class and begin to act, not
> against such or such an employer, but against the entire
> class of the capitalists and against the government which
> supports it. 'Every class struggle is a political struggle.'
> It would be wrong to understand these famous words
> of Marx in this sense that every action of workers against
> their employers is always a political struggle. They must be
> understood as follows: the workers' struggle against the
> capitalists becomes necessarily a political action to the extent
> that it becomes a class struggle."

Today, simply to declare that the task of progressive students is to serve the workers is to give proof of a total lack of comprehension of the historical and crucial role of the student movement. In 1902 there appeared people who, Lenin said, "got down on their knees, religiously, to contemplate the rear of the Russian proletariat." We wager that our proletariat-minded mandarins, after forty years of Stalinism, will not find the rear of the French proletariat any shinier than that of its Slav counterpart.

To be content to announce that the proletariat alone is resolved to pursue the fight to the end, is to be content with a theoretical abstraction when we have a concrete political problem to solve; it is taking politics as a simple reflection of the economy; it is, once more, to reduce Marxism to the rank of everyday "economism." In the same way that it was stupid to place ourselves at the service of the Vietnamese, because the Vietnamese cannot judge for us our own possibilities for action, it would have been criminal for the avant-gardes to have the students serve the workers instead of using the student movement as a political detector to reveal society as a whole.

> "In the era of imperialism, in every branch of social
> life, we see inflammable matter accumulating and numerous
> causes for conflict, crisis, and deterioration of the class
> struggle being created. We do not know, we cannot know, in
> this mass of sparks which are now flying from all
> directions, which spark will be able to start the fire in the
> sense of a particular awakening of the masses. We must
> therefore put into action the Communist principles of
> preparing all terrains, even the oldest, the most amorphous, the
> most sterile in appearance; otherwise we shall not be
> equal to our task, we shall be exclusive, we shall not be
> in possession of all the weapons at our disposal."

III. FROM THEORY TO PRACTICE

Just when the working class movement is placed on a terrain chosen by Gaullism, by making of the working class a simple protest force and by transforming demonstrations into simple performances, the student movement has pushed the government and the Left up against the wall, not only verbally but actually, in the streets and in view of everyone, by means of its determined fight and because it has rejected the methods of the traditional political parties. By mobilizing independently at the risk of cutting itself off from "the class," it has created genuine areas of concurrence through street demonstrations, through the barricades, through occupation of the *facultés,* where more and more numerous workers have come to fight and to talk. Therefore, it is neither with the apparatus nor with isolated individuals that union with the working class has been made, but through action, with the avant-garde militants of the working class.

This is why, for us, the great demonstration of May 13 is a success. Anybody who still had illusions about the political and trade-union machines may be disappointed, but anybody who had no illusions should be satisfied. By subjecting the government to its first important defeat through street confrontation, we compelled the unions to organize the demonstration they had not wanted, or did not know how to organize, against the decrees. "Things are moving," and that is what is important. The million workers who marched on May 13, even if they returned to the fold, did not come out for nothing. They became conscious of their strength; they showed their determination to express themselves; they no longer consider students as *"gauchistes enragés."* This is so much gained.

At present, by continuing its action, the student movement can speed up the crisis of the regime and of the leftist parties. We are no longer arguing about problems that only concern the university, but for the resignation of Fouchet and Grimaud, that is to say, against the Gaullist government itself. In the long run this struggle leaves two possible exits which we must now bear in mind:

1. Either a fascist orientation of the regime, certain beginnings of which have been noticed these past weeks. And the danger is considerable. In a difficult economic context, the possibility must be envisaged all the more seriously since "the democratic forces" offer no real political guarantee to counterbalance it.

2. Or, the coming to power of a united Left. However, the troika Waldeck-Mollet-Mitterrand will not come to power as a result of a simple parliamentary operation, but on the basis of a real mass mobilization. A regime with Wilsonian leanings coming to power under these circumstances would, in time, increase the indifference of militant workers towards it. Then, various constituent elements of a revolutionary party would stand out much more clearly (opposition currents in the PC, workers' and teachers' unions, various adult groups, youth organizations).

These are the results and prospects offered by the student struggle which, led by avant-garde militants and conceived on non-party lines, has unbolted and unblocked the political situation. From now on, a militant juncture, not a careerist or parisitical one, with the workers' struggle, has become possible.

—D. B. [Daniel Ben Saïd]

N.B.: All the citations from Lenin are taken from the *Three Articles in the* Rabochaya Gazeta, from *What Is To Be Done?,* and from *Infantile Disorder.* They are given without page reference to induce digest fans to read the complete texts.

—Excerpt from *Avant-garde jeunesse,* No. 13 special, May 18.

Document 94

When Leftism Seized Control of the Masses . . .

On May 3, a few dozen leftist provocators, who "objectively play the government's game," were arrested in the Sorbonne courtyard. Undoubtedly some were allowed to escape: that very day the escalation of "irresponsible" leftist provocation and police repression began. Within a few days the provocators became tens of thousands of demonstrators, students, teachers, and young workers. We must acknowledge the facts: leftists, isolated from the masses, sparked the most tremendous mass mobilization ever seen in France in the university milieu. After a new "provocation"—the night of the barricades—they were victorious: the government gave in on all points.

What is more, the extent of this struggle gave rise to profound reactions in the great mass of workers who saw in it the beginning of the fall of Gaullism. On May 1 less than 100,000 demonstrators answered the call of the CGT for the traditional République-Bastille march.[5] On May 13 a million workers went out into the streets, not only to declare their solidarity with the students but also to make their own demands. For everyone it is clear that what is being challenged is the regime; the example of the students shows that the government can be made to retreat. Since then, the struggle has widened: permanent occupation of the *facultés* by the students, and especially, the workers' struggles have started up again. After the Sorbonne, red flags are now waving over the factories of Sud-Aviation, over Renault, and over hundreds of others. The regime is shaky: what it must confront now is no longer sterile parliamentary discussion prearranged for ORTF publicity, but also the supreme weapon of the proletariat: unlimited strikes with occupation of factories.

Where Was the Party?

Where was the Party during these decisive days? To be honest: it was not there. Let us reread *l'Humanité*. On May 3, in an article packed with lies, Marchais denounced the pseudo-revolutionaries united in what they called the *"Mouvement du 22 mars Nanterre,"* led by "the German anarchist Cohn-Bendit,"* "whose activities are contrary to the interests of the student masses and favor fascist provocation." "These false revolutionaries must be energetically exposed because, objectively, they serve the interests of the Gaullist government and the big capitalist monopolies," added peremptorily our clear-sighted organizational secretary. He later declared:

"Quite evidently, we do not confuse the small leftist 'groupuscules' of trouble makers, agitating in the universities, with the mass of the students."

The same afternoon the arrests of the principal leftist leaders

---

* At the UEC, it is rumored that he is paid by the government, but nobody says that he is Jewish: we are not in Warsaw.

and the spontaneous reaction of several thousand students took place. It was the first violent confrontation of students with government cops. Next day's *l'Huma* was a real feast; Georges Bouvard was indignant:

"But how shall we describe the people who brought about this situation through their irresponsible actions, their violence and insults? . . . The students are in a position to verify where the government really recruits its best allies, how you can play their game and at the same time call yourself a 'super-revolutionary.' "

The UEC, a highly representative "groupuscule" in the student milieu, declared in conjunction with the Paris Federation:

"They [the leftists] facilitate the attempt on the part of the government, the press, radio, and television to isolate the students from the population. Through their unsound slogans, through their conception of the violent action of 'small groups,' they offer no concrete viewpoint and hinder massive mobilization of students, which alone can make the government retreat."

The Nanterre municipality joined in the chorus with its remote-controlled refrain:

"Certain 'groupuscules' composed, in general, of sons of the upper bourgeoisie and led by the German anarchist Cohn-Bendit, make a pretext* of governmental deficiencies to indulge in actions aiming to prevent the normal functioning of the *faculté* (destruction of premises, interruption of courses, proposal to boycott examinations, etc.)."

On Monday, May 6, Georges Bouvard deplored the fact that orders for an unlimited strike had been given by the UNEF and the SNESup. How could they study for examinations under these conditions! He reassured his readers, however, by enumerating the cities where the order will not be followed—without specifying that these cities are those where the General Student Associations are in the hands of the UEC comrades or of the "apolitical" FNEF.

While this gabble was going on the movement was being organized, and on Monday evening there were 15,000 demonstrators who

---

* The Leftists really take just anything as a pretext. Friday, they were even armed with ax handles and iron bars "under the pretext" (*l'Huma* of May 4) of repelling an attack by *Occident* which really took place, whether G. B. likes it or not. In the same vein we call attention to a UEC leaflet distributed on May 6: "leftists and fascists play the game of the government." Undoubtedly all pretexts are good for the government as well: "We cannot allow the government to use as a pretext the behavior of a tiny minority to (. . .) unleash police repression." In brief, if there had been no leftists there would have been no repression. This is certainly true. There would have been no movement, either.

met the police head-on with recognized courage. The Party militants were amazed: nothing they had read in *l'Huma* had allowed them to guess the breadth of the movement. The next day *l'Huma* headlined: "The government is responsible!" And for several days their position with respect to the leftists was toned down; they even went so far as to write that the government was completely responsible. Except that through its policy the government had favored the actions of irresponsible groups, whereas, for G. Bouvard:

"The just cause of the students and of the University has no better defenders than the Communists."

It is easy to write in the columns of *l'Huma;* it is unfortunately much more difficult to defend oneself on the field of action. After the demonstrations of Tuesday and Wednesday evenings—demonstrations which by now had brought out nearly 30,000 students and members of the faculty—the BP dispatched the liberal intellectual, Aragon, to try to renew contact with this movement. Aragon was whistled at by some thousand or so students who were holding a spontaneous meeting on the Boul'Mich: Aragon proffered his tender heart to the students, but refused to express himself on the subject of the articles in *l'Humanité.*

In point of fact, the corner was apparently turned on Wednesday. In the morning the Party's declaration, published in *l'Huma,* spoke again ". . . of actions on the part of adventurers whose ideas offer no prospects for the students and have nothing in common with a true movement for future progress or with a true revolutionary movement."

In the evening the Communist students, followed by the Federal Bureau, called for a demonstration. As of the next day the Leftists disappeared from *l'Humanité.* On the other hand their numbers increased in the streets: Friday evening 50,000 demonstrators arrived in the Latin Quarter, and the barricades rose spontaneously despite the efforts of several party-line militants lost in the general throng—that is, about a hundred UEC militants—who shouted themselves hoarse: "No paving stones!" But it was to no avail, confronted with this leftist tornado. That evening the provocators were tens of thousands and our worthy comrades went to bed. At 2:15 A.M., 15,000 demonstrators were attacked by the cops. The battle lasted a long time: thousands of CRS and *gardes-mobiles* needed three hours to overcome the resistance. During this time new appeals against the repression arrived from all sides, even from priests. But not from the Party. The Party could have threatened the government with the anger of the workers, thrown its enormous weight into the balance, in the face of the repression. None of this happened. A logical position, certainly: they had already denounced the provocators; they were not going to support them now—this would have been, objectively, playing the government's game. But the position was untenable, so untenable that finally they had to rally to the anarchist proposal during the night of the general strike.

In the morning the demonstrators were worn out but victorious all the same: the government had had to give in. The government understood that the student movement had dislocated the political situation in the country. Young workers by the thousands had participated in the student demonstrations, an entire potential of hostility to the regime had been revealed and given new forms of expression; the government then tried to temporize, to limit the movement to the students. But by giving in it gave further proof to the workers that fighting pays. Faced with this tidal wave of sympathy for the student struggle, the Party had no other choice left: it had applied what restraints it could and yet a mass movement "of unparalleled size" existed; the Party would have to head it. As of Saturday morning (after 6 A.M.), the Communist militants were at work: the Party and the CGT called for a general strike and for a national demonstration on Monday.

This was like a thunderclap: repercussions of the student struggle had gone beyond all expectations of the participants. For the great masses the student struggle had shown the way. During the following days several plants went out on strike with occupation of the shops. The procedure was the same each time: spontaneously, young workers called for strikes with occupation. The news spread like wildfire in the shops. The unions could do nothing but let things take their course and, since they had not condemned the shop occupations, they claimed credit for them.

L'Huma of Wednesday the 15th, on page 9, went so far towards neutrality as to relate the occupation of Sud-Aviation, but the fact that 100,000 signatures for the repeal of the Decrees had been sent to the National Assembly was given ten times more space. . . . The CGT gave no order for a general strike, but the strike was becoming generalized on its own. On May 17 the CCN of the CGT asserted: "The action undertaken on the initiative (sic) of the CGT and with other union organizations has created a new situation and is of exceptional importance."

We will return to this new situation, but we now know, thanks to *l'Huma,* that the Party was not the obstetrician. Where was the

Party? One step behind the masses. Does the new position, *ipso facto,* place us in the advance guard?

—Excerpt from the *roneotype* pamphlet *Where Was the Party?*
(May 21).

The FER

On April 28, 1968, the *Comité de liaison des étudiants révolutionnaires* (CLER) set up the *Fédération des étudiants révolutionnaires* (FER). The CLER itself was created in 1961 by militants of the "Internationalist Communist Organization for Reconstruction of the Fourth International," known as Lambertist Trotskyites, from the name of their militant leader. Lambert was also a permanent member of the Paris area branch of the Social Security and Family Allowance *Force Ouvrière* union, which had a large worker basis in Nantes, where in May it played an essential role. In the Latin Quarter and in the associations that the CLER controlled (the Sorbonne philosophy group, the AG in Clermont and in Besançon, among others), its impact was an original one. Part of this originality is explained by the rivalries that divide the Trotskyist organizations, term for term, from one another. Example: during the Algerian war the OCI supported Messali Hadj's MNA, whereas the Frankists helped the FLN; the OCI and the CLER were both opposed to the FLN, which they accused of betraying the Vietnamese revolution. With its military type of organization, the CLER was inclined to sabotage UNEF meetings when they were controlled by others than themselves. Like the Marxist-Leninists, the FER militants were violently "worker-oriented" and did not believe in the existence of a student movement as such. Although often savagely critical of union leadership, they did not challenge the unions but tried to defend them—that is, to take them over or oblige them to go along by "forcing them to call a national demonstration" that would bring "500,000 workers to the Latin Quarter," or "2,000,000 workers to the Elysée," slogans that were spread abroad by remarkable mass speakers. The FER's theoretical model apparently was furnished by Trotsky himself who, during the thirties, wavered between an all-out offensive attitude and a defensive one with a solid worker and democratic front. Like Marceau Pivert in *le Populaire* of June 1936, *Révoltes* came out on May 22 with the following headline: "Anything is possible." (Trotsky wrote at that time: "The French Revolution has begun.") During the May movement the FER was opposed to demonstrations considered to be venturesome or petty bourgeois, including the one that took place on May 3 and at the barricades on the night of May 10-11. It fought determinedly, however, to impose a "centralized strike committee"—if need be by creating it fictitiously—and frequently took refuge behind the UNEF's defense committees. The style of its publications and leaflets was extremely characteristic, and throughout France an FER leaflet was recognizable at first glance from its typographical presentation: systematic use of stencilled capitals on mimeographed leaflets, with boldface type scattered throughout the text, as well as a personality cult of its own leaders. For instance, in the June 1968 *l'Etudiant Révolutionnaire,* No. 1—as well as in many other FER publications—an account of the May 7 demonstration is accompanied by a photograph with the following caption: "C. de Bresson, FER national secretary, one of the first to be wounded." There is also continual repetition of the same slogans and directives.

Following is the account by one of the FER leaders, Claude Chisserey, justifying the attitude of his organization. In the accompanying leaflet FER directives are circulated without mention of their origin.

On July 4, 1970, the *Conseil d'Etat* annulled the dissolution measure banning *Révoltes,* the OCI (having in the meantime become the Trotskyist Organization), and the FER (having in the meantime become the *Alliance des jeunes pour le socialisme* (AJS)). The supreme administrative tribunal considered that governmental authority had not established that these groups had participated in the riots of May–June 1968.

Document 95

LONG LIVE THE JOINT FIGHT OF WORKERS AND STUDENTS,
LONG LIVE THE WORKERS AT SUD-AVIATION!
WE MUST ORGANIZE FOR COMPLETE VICTORY
OVER THE GOVERNMENT!

On Friday, May 3, while the police were invading the Sorbonne and arresting militant students, the following slogan was heard, and could be heard for more than a week, in the Latin Quarter: "Free our comrades!"[6]

The confrontation lasted several hours. As on January 26th in Caen, young *lycée* and University students, with young workers, took to the streets against the police.

From that time on it was evident that this student combat was not simply a combat of students based on specifically university problems, but a real class combat of students and both young and older workers against the bourgeois government.

For many years the liaison committee of revolutionary students has fought inside student circles against the petty bourgeois theories that tend to isolate students from the working class. The student fight against the Fouchet reform or against "selection" is the equivalent of the workers' fight against the Ve Plan and against the decrees dismantling Social Security.

Since the end of the Algerian war this fight by revolutionary students has been the hard fight of the defense of Marxism against all the ideologies that would like to re-examine the class struggle theory for the benefit of "psycho-sociology," which gives priority to interpersonal psychological relationships.

That was the time when the reigning "house psycho-sociologist" was Lapassade, who is now trying to stage a comeback.

That was the time when the forgers of the "Péninou and Kravetz" policy were leading the UNEF, and leading it to ruin.[7]

That was the time when these customers wanted to "democratically" exclude the militants of the CLER from the UNEF.

That was the time when these same customers wanted to experiment with "group dynamics," explaining to all and sundry that "small groups" encouraged people to express themselves democratically and that this desire for democracy led them to question the regime.

That unutterable fraud Lapassade wrote that a "democratic University" would then lead to the fall of the Gaullist regime.

That was the time when we were already explaining, "There is no student problem, but general problems having student aspects *which are expressed in terms of class struggle.*"

Student Aspects of General Problems

That was the time when we were already explaining that it is not psychology that is the motor of history, but the class struggle.

That was the time when we were already explaining that the UNEF must be defended more than ever.

On that Friday, May 3, when the fight broke out, the Nanterre *Mouvement du 22 mars* was already declaring, "The UNEF is a whore; the unions are brothels."

On that Friday, May 3, these anarchists questioned the necessity of unions as the organizations best suited to defend the elementary interests of the workers. In fact, these characters deny the necessity of class organization of the proletariat. They prefer small discussion groups because in effect, for them, the class struggle does not exist; all that counts is communication between individuals of good will.

This orientation, which aims at re-examining the organizations that have been created and built up during dozens of years of struggle, is fundamentally reactionary. It denies the leading role of the proletariat in the revolutionary struggle and wants to make intellectuals the enlightened leaders of the proletariat. In fact it reintroduces the notion of an "elite" giving advice to the proletariat and acting in their name; in fact it reintroduces purely and simply the notion of bureaucracy, which, however, it pretends to combat.

These petty bourgeois think that the proletariat is fundamentally alienated and reactionary and that, therefore, commando actions or provocatory actions are necessary. They refuse to fight inside the masses, to organize them and help them mobilize against the bourgeois government. They identify the working class with Stalinist bureaucracy and in fact play the game of the latter when they try to separate the student struggle from that of the workers. They refuse to fight in order to challenge Stalinist political leadership of the proletariat. All they do is take over what the Strasburg situationists were doing, moreover, as a joke.

The *Fédération des étudiants révolutionnaires,* in its proclamation manifesto, stigmatizes the idea of University criticism, intended to bring students to participate with the "authorities" in making the selection plans the bourgeoisie needs. The *Fédération des étudiants révolutionnaires* is fighting for the defense of the UNEF, which is and must remain the organization of the mass of students. Yes, the UNEF must and will live.

The UNEF *Must and Will Live*

To begin with, on the national scale the UNEF has been the framework in which the fight was organized. As of Sunday, May 5, the UNEF sent out a justified *Call to the Population*[8] which said, "The bourgeoisie is trying to isolate and divide the movement. The response must be immediate. This is why the UNEF proposes that teachers' and workers' unions again use the unitary procedure that was worked out during the demonstration: workers, *lycée* and University students, together with the UNEF, spontaneously replied to police aggression. . . . General strike, as of Monday, and until all our comrades are freed. Participate massively in the demonstration in the Latin Quarter on Monday at 6:30 P.M. Students, organize in your *facultés* into UNEF grass roots combat committees, according to disciplines and class year, to continue the fight, particularly because of the coming examinations."

The FER supported this call unconditionally, mimeographed it, and distributed it in factories in the Paris area. On Monday, at 6:30 P.M., starting from Denfert-Rochereau, 15,000 demonstrators marched to the Latin Quarter, where once again there was confrontation with police forces and about twenty FER members were injured.

On Tuesday, at 5:30 P.M., at Denfert-Rochereau, there were 20,000 demonstrators who marched towards Port-Royal, where the pro-Chinese wanted to go to "working class neighborhoods," while Cohn-Bendit's anarchists wanted to have mini-demonstrations. Together with the UNEF leaders, the FER postponed that day's confrontation and led the demonstration to the Champs-Elysées, where 50,000 young people and workers, red flags waving, sang *The Internationale*. The situation was becoming clear; it was the workers' turn to act.

On Wednesday morning Geismar, secretary of the SNESUP., "proudly" announced: "Tonight we will occupy the Sorbonne" (either you are a revolutionary or you are not). But meanwhile negotiations with union leaders, without calling the workers to a general strike, were slowing up mobilization.

On Wednesday evening the demonstration began with an incident: the PCF leaders, having made their turn "to the left," wanted to head the demonstration, but they were unable to do so.

Occupation of the Sorbonne?
The march began with all this ambiguity: Geismar had called for "occupation of the Sorbonne," whereas he was expecting a telephone call from the rector during the entire demonstration. When the demonstration reached the Luxembourg it had two possible solutions: either to confront the police without being strong enough to occupy the Sorbonne, or to march for hours while waiting for the hypothetical telephone call from the rector. In both cases it meant breaking up the movement. The confrontation had to be postponed. It was the time for organizing and constructing the movement, for joining the workers.

For this reason, the only realistic position was the one taken by the FER leaders calling for dispersion and for organization of strike committees that would elect their delegates.

One of the lessons of the movement is that this movement must be structured, and in structuring it we must construct the revolutionary party and the revolutionary youth organization, which involves the FER. *Without a revolutionary party there will be no victory.*

This is why, although underlining the importance of a spontaneous mass movement, the FER underlines the importance of *political organization*. In no case will we agree to dissolve our organization in the name of unity, as everybody is asking us to do. We know that we represent the only force capable of organizing the struggle of the students and the workers.

We will not imitate the JCR, which has fused with the so-called "true mass movement," making short shrift of the teachings of the workers' movement and Bolshevism, whose authority, however, it claims to recognize.

For this reason the FER has stuck to its May 10 meeting. Throughout this fighting we must maintain and strengthen revolutionary organization.

500,000 *Workers in the Latin Quarter*

On Friday, May 10, after the meeting of the FER, the FER marched in procession to the only realistic slogan: "500,000 workers in the Latin Quarter," while a lot of irresponsible characters à la Cohn-Bendit "were digging up paving stones and at the same time avoiding provocation." All night long the police charged; the result was butchery. Students and workers battled until dawn.

At 5 A.M., Cohn-Bendit called for help: "The workers' national unions should call for a general strike."

This is what impotent petty bourgeois talk leads to.

The workers' answer was such that the union leaders did call for a general strike.[9]

A million workers demonstrated in Paris. In the provinces the *préfectures* were the targets.

The fight continued.

In Nantes the workers occupied the Sud-Aviation plant.

At the Sorbonne it was a field day.

Revolutionary combat consists above all in bringing together the avant-garde, constructing a revolutionary organization, and organizing a framework of class organizers.

After the FER meeting we will prepare for May 25 and 26, when delegates from the coordinating committees for the realization of a single workers' front, on a national scale, will discuss action and at what point the FER will be involved.

The fight continues.

Organize strike committees.

Elect your delegates.

We must construct a revolutionary youth organization.

We must develop the FER as an indispensable instrument for future struggles.

—Claude Chisserey; excerpt from *Révoltes*, No. 19, May 15, 1968.

Document 96

CALL FROM THE STEERING COMMITTEE
for the defense of the UNEF *and the fight against repression,*
    to all students, of all tendencies, unionized or not.

The alternative after de Gaulle's speech is clear: either socialism or fascism.

That is to say, either reinforcement of the struggle of all workers, students, and teachers, or the rise of fascism and the institution of a police state.

After this speech, are working class unions going to play the game of the bourgeoisie by abandoning every form of united action? Will they count on elections to obtain abrogation of the Decrees and the fall of the bourgeois government?

Faced with the fierce repression that has now started, the national headquarters of the UNEF has proposed organization of a general demonstration by all workers, students, and teachers: this is the immediate prospect for combat.

Faced with these alternatives—reinforcement of the struggle or rise of fascism—militants, students, and workers must react promptly. The only answer to reinforcement of de Gaulle's reactionary policy is in the ever increasing unification of the student and worker struggles.

This is why student militants of all tendencies, unionized or not, have decided to create

A STEERING COMMITTEE FOR DEFENSE OF THE UNEF
AND FOR COMBATTING REPRESSION

This committee will assume the task of reinforcing union organizations and the UNEF; it has delegated the UNEF, together with the leaders of workers' unions, to achieve:

—Unification of the struggle through *elected strike committees subject to dismissal at any time* by general assemblies;

—Federation of these strike committees *into a single national committee* whose task would be to organize a united response through:

—*A general demonstration in front of the Elysée with two mil-*

> *lion workers and, in the provinces, in front of the* préfectures *with 100,000 workers;*
>
> —Creation of groups for self-defense against fascist gangs and the regime's increasingly fascist character, in order to defend the factories and *facultés,* protect meetings, and respond to fascist provocation.

The militants assembled together have decided:

to elect in each *faculté* responsible people (subject to dismissal at any time) who will head this committee and have as their first duty to organize meetings in each *faculté* (Tuesday, June 4, at 2 P.M., in the *Humanités* building at the INSA) and prepare a possible General Assembly for Tuesday at 5 P.M. at the *Faculté des Lettres,*

to join the national liaison committee for the defense of the UNEF, constituted on March 31st in Paris by 140 responsible union militants,[10]

to become unionized under the UNEF,

to print a leaflet with the present call and to subscribe to its printing,

to keep an office open daily to the public at the *Faculté des Lettres.*

Join the steering committee for the defense of the UNEF *and the struggle against repression*—History Room No. 3, 5 P.M., Tuesday, June 4, at the *Faculté des Lettres.*

> —Steering Committee for the Defense of the UNEF and for combating Repression [Sorbonne].

The Pro-Chinese

There was a veritable myth about the "Chinese" aspects of the May Revolution, a myth which was encouraged by the bourgeois press, by the press and cables from Peking, and by everybody who identified the May movement with the "cultural revolution." But when we examine the real role of the "pro-Chinese" organizations, we find that we can disregard entirely the *Centre Marxiste-Léniniste de France,* which had become known for positions that favored the *Front National* and General de Gaulle.[11]

Nor should much more importance be attached to the *Parti communiste marxiste-léniniste de France* (*l'Humanité Nouvelle*), which set up a stand in the Sorbonne courtyard, even though it was the only organization recognized by Peking and possessed, especially at the Berliet plant in Lyons, an indisputably working class substructure. An example of the grandiloquent style of the manifestos put out by its "central committee" will follow, nevertheless. The PCLMF was "aware of its responsibilities"—all the more "aware," in fact, since they were actually rather light. Its influence among students, though practically nonexistent in Paris, was important in certain provincial cities such as Grenoble and Lyons. It became more important, however, after the return to school in the autumn of 1968, with the title of its new periodical, *L'Humanité rouge.*

The *Union des jeunesses communistes (marxiste-léniniste)* was created in 1966, after two years of preparation, among the *Ecole Normale Supérieure* group of the *Union des étudiants communistes.* Somewhat paradoxically, the most purely ideological version of Marxism that French intellectuals have had access to grew out of a scientific criticism of the ideological deviations of Marxism and a rehabilitation of theory undertaken by the philosopher Louis Althusser. What in fact is "Mao Tse-tung's thought" if not ideology in a state of chemical purity?

The m-l militants did not want to be considered revolutionary students, being uninterested in the student movement as such;[12] what they wanted, according to the title of one of their publications, was to *Servir le peuple,* and many of their leaders were former students of the *Grandes Ecoles,* who abandoned their studies to take factory jobs. "Students, mass uprising," announced the first issue of *La Cause du peuple* (May 1, 1968): "By putting ourselves under the leadership of the broad working masses we can learn what their fighting needs are and try to respond to them: we will learn from them, they will be our professors." Already, before the May movement, the m-l militants had given assistance to the wildcat strikes in Caen, Redon, and Le Mans; and in Nanterre, where they set up a "red base" in the furnace room of the *Faculté des Lettres,* they had tried to operate in the heart of the nearby foreign-workers slums.[13] As we said before, their first reaction to the May movement was worker-oriented.[14] A projected draft for self-criticism, written in June, and which covers the period from May 10 to 14, bears quoting:

> "During this period we neglected the role of sparking the
> Latin Quarter explosion, and underestimated the role that
> during the first stage could be played by the movement of
> violent anti-Gaullist revolt launched by students and other
> young people. . . . The anti-Gaullist battle broke out
> quite suddenly, not on the themes of oppression of the

working class, starvation wages, or unemployment, but on the
theme of criticism of decadent teaching methods, which
rapidly enlarged into revolutionary criticism of the ideology
and culture of our moribund imperialist society. We
were not prepared for a cultural revolution of such
proportions, either in our work with young people and
students or in the organization of our propaganda services.
This led us to describe as petty bourgeois and anti-worker
certain positions on the ideological struggle that had genuine
revolutionary significance, however, both for the working
class and in particular for the young people."

The same document expresses regret at the sectarianism with
which the m-l had regarded "French anti-Stalinism," described,
above all, as "anti-Thorezism." Once the strike movement was under
way the m-l militants did an immense job in the factories, where they
set up numerous support activities, practically made a daily paper of
La Cause du Peuple, carried out an original propaganda campaign by
means of wall posters, and took personal risks—as witness the death
in Flins on June 10 of Gilles Tautin, a *lycée* student.

At times this work was accomplished with the help of the
Mouvement du 22 mars. The ideological and practical content of this
propaganda was, however, very peculiar: the UJC(m-l) was re-enacting what it believed the PCF had been at the peak of its glory back in
1934–1936. Its language was what a "real" communist's language
should be: "Yes! to popular government!" (This is a PCF slogan),
but they added: "No to Mitterrand!" "Against the advocates of a sell-
out. For the class struggle. Long live the CGT" was the headline of
the May 1 issue of *Servir le Peuple.* The sectarianism with regard to
the CFDT was the same as that of the PCF at its height. Indeed this
imitation went so far that the UJC(m-l), like the PCF, adopted the
system of satellite organizations. Officially *La Cause du Peuple* was
not a UJC(m-l) publication, but spoke for the Movement of Support
for the People's Struggle and, beginning on May 23, it even became a
"Popular Front journal" because the m-l's, although knowing what
the 1936 electoral alliance had been, were about to publish in the June
1 issue of *La Cause du Peuple* a "proposal for a Popular Front program." By the same token, they later published in Flins a paper called
l'Unité Ouvrière in the name of the "proletarian trade-unionists"
(CGT) at the Renault plant. Using the tried and tested PCF technique,
the "Chinese propaganda," properly speaking, that appeared in these
papers, was extremely circumspect.

Following is a historical account, written by militants and left unfinished, of how the ujc(m-l) started. It is a typical leaflet, to be added to those we have already included here, of the *mouvement de soutien aux luttes du peuple,* and of the anti-repression defense committees.

La Cause du Peuple, after the return to school in the fall of 1968, became the paper of the *Gauche Prolétarienne,* which took in certain elements of the *Mouvement du 22 mars* and of the ujc(m-l).

Document 97

LONG LIVE SIT-INS

LONG LIVE UNLIMITED STRIKES

Workers and students, block maneuvers!

We must organize at the grass roots and through action!

There are no straight roads in the world; we must be ready to follow a tortuous path, without trying to obtain things cheaply. We must not imagine that one fine day all the reactionaries will fall down on their knees of their own accord. Briefly, the future is bright, but our road is tortuous. We still have many difficulties ahead which must not be neglected. By uniting with all the people in a common effort, we will certainly be able to surmount them all and achieve victory.

—Mao Tse-tung.

THE SPARK HAS SET FIRE TO THE PLAIN

The first revolutionary victory of the students has served as an example to avant-garde workers. It opens up new perspectives for the workers' struggles. In many companies workers are becoming a problem for the union higher-ups: they are going on strike and staging sit-ins like the students in the *facultés,* particularly at the Sorbonne. There even exist a certain number of honest union leaders who refuse any longer to bow to the class collaboration line of the confederation leaders, and who firmly take the lead of the masses to engage in the class struggle. In Nantes (Sud-Aviation), in Flins and Boulogne-Billancourt (Renault), in Cléon, in Le Mans, etc., the fight has started. In other words, the alliance of revolutionary intellectuals and the working class is becoming a reality in action against monopoly power. The parliamentary, peaceful line of the revisionist and reformist leaders has been shown up: in effect, only the firm fight of the grass roots and revolutionary proletarian violence can put up vigorous resistance to the counter-revolutionary violence of the bourgeois class in power.

THE FIGHT WILL BE LONG, DANGEROUS, DIFFICULT,
BUT IT WILL BE VICTORIOUS

The Marxist-Leninist Communist Party of France, conscious of its responsibilities, warns all strikers, students, or workers against the maneuvers of monopoly power. The threatening speech of the bank director Pompidou, Prime Minister, made the night of May 16, can preface an attempt at massive repression of a fascist nature. On the other hand, the intrigues of the revisionist leaders of the PCF and of the CGT tend to serve the interests of the bourgeoisie to preserve the established order. Already, many revisionist bureaucrats, disguised as workers, are circulating among the strikers, particularly at the Sorbonne, to sow the seeds of discord and to sabotage the unanimous desire for unity that exists at the grass roots. They fear above all the mass movement and the only forms of fighting which have given results: that is, sit-ins, as in 1936. Meanwhile, they are trying to introduce the resigned and de-activating line by means of which they have oriented and hemmed in the working class for years.

The PCMLF also warns the workers and students who are fighting against the intrigues of social democracy and the power of the monopolies, that the latter are trying, with the active help of the revisionist leaders of the PCF and the CGT, to make the movement fall into ruin by orienting it into sterile discussions of a reformist nature on technical and secondary problems.

ONLY GRASS ROOTS UNITY IN ACTION CAN LEAD
TO A COMMON VICTORY OF ALL INTELLECTUAL AND MANUAL WORKERS

Workers and students, the only true unity is the unity achieved in the fight. People who have but one slogan, which is dispersion; who hide during the street fighting or at the barricades and then jump on the bandwagon in order to sidetrack it; who try to stir up workers against students; who smear the revolutionary leaders with their lies—are all nothing but divisionists, spokesmen for the bourgeoisie, and they will be swept away in the fight. We must never forget the class struggle; we must judge by actions and not words.

Workers and students, join or form action committees at the grass roots, which must be created everywhere, in the neighborhoods, in the factories, in the *facultés,* etc.

Against monopoly power.

Against the decadent capitalist system.

For a radical change in the economic and political system.

For a government of the people, in the service of the people, opening the road to socialism.

The militants of the PCMLF are fighting shoulder to shoulder with the workers and students. They are actively participating in the committees which exist or are being created.

Workers and students, join the fight of the Marxist-Leninist Communist Party of France; join its ranks.

Long live the fighting unity of workers and students; we must organize at the grass roots and in action; we must be vigilant against all maneuvering.

—Paris, May 17, 1968, *le comité central du parti communiste marxiste-léninste de France.*

Document 98

How Was the Young Communist Union (Marxist-Leninist) Started?

The inception of our organization antedates its public appearance, which took place at the time of the big split in the UEC in the autumn of 1966. Our organization was started in February–March 1966, when a direct political offensive against the revisionism of the PCF was launched during the meeting of the Central Committee at Argenteuil. At the same time, the clandestine organizations of the Marxist-Leninists in the UEC were simultaneously created (Marxist-Leninist cells that were leading larger fractions and organizing a systematic fight against the revisionists in the UEC grass root circles, sections, and cities).

But the inception of our organization, properly speaking, was preceded by long preparation in the UEC which involved study, propaganda, and planning. Through a complicated internal struggle led according to the principles of the mass line in the UEC, this paved the way for beginning a Marxist-Leninist organization among the students and the youth. We propose here to analyze these preliminary stages of the work done by the Marxist-Leninists in the UEC.

I. FIRST STAGE: THE D'ULM CIRCLE AND THE MARXIST STUDY MOVEMENT
    AT THE ECOLE NORMALE SUPERIEURE, RUE D'ULM

Beginning January 1964, in the d'Ulm Circle of the *Union des étudiants communistes,* under the influence of the Marxist philosopher, Althusser, a certain number of Communist students in this group started a comprehensive study of Marx's *Capital,* together with the other Marxist-Leninist classics. At that time, the d'Ulm Circle was not at all homogeneous, nor was it Marxist-Leninist. Certain of its members were Leftists influenced by Trotskyism and the anarch-syndicalist theses that were current in the student union; others were rightist partisans of Liberalism, or of free expression in artistic matters, and produced "esthetic" work of a bourgeois type. Still others formed a group which actively launched a movement to study the Marxist classics. Among those who set out to study Marxism seriously, under Althusser's influence, a certain unity existed, but this unity was superficial and the underlying contradictions later led to its division. Actually there were three positions that were more or less evident in this group.

First Position
A certain number of constituents who participated actively in the study movement were only Communists in name; they were interested in Marxism from a "theoretical" point of view, but had no desire to put themselves in the position of the proletariat, to participate actively in the class struggle, or to serve the proletariat and the people. Their interests were the academic interests of a small circle, not those of revolutionary intellectuals but of future bourgeois university authorities. They developed a harmful "theory" according to which the only "practice" that "theoreticians" must have is "theoretical practice[15]"; they concealed the fact that a revolutionary intellectual must join scientific theory to contact with the popular masses, that the theoretical work of revolutionary intellectuals has as its objective the revolutionary practice of transforming society.

Their theory denied the fundamental role of proletariat organization in the centralization of correct thinking among the masses. Basically, the principal function of this theory was to jusitfy the position of the bourgeois class of these intellectuals, who went in for theory without a goal, without taking revolution in France as their goal. This first group participated in the movement of Marxist-Leninist classical studies but had no role in the political battle that developed later in the Union of Communist Students; it did not participate in the inside struggle in the Communist organization. A united front existed between this group and the budding Marxist-Leninist nucleus during a certain period (roughly until the middle of 1966). This united front was established on the basis of the recognized importance of theoretical work and theoretical training and the minute and systematic study of Marxist-Leninist classics. Other points of agreement were: (a) criticism of the absence of theoretical work in the PCF and its ideological deterioration; (b) the struggle against eclectic, humanist, and revisionist ideologies, which were gaining more and more influence in the French Communist organizations. Lastly, there existed points of agreement between this group and the budding Marxist-Leninist nucleus on points of method of dialectic materialism and on the analysis of certain concepts of *Capital*. This united front permitted:

1) Inauguration of a periodical by the group of Communist students at the rue d'Ulm Normal School (*Les Cahiers marxistes-léninistes*).

2) Existence of a supporting Communist organization to serve as a basis from which the Marxist-Leninist nucleus undertook infiltration of the UEC and could participate, as of February 1965 (VIIIe UEC Congress), in the leadership of the whole revisionist student organization. The first important divisions in the united front between these intellectuals and the budding Marxist-Leninist nucleus were already apparent in October 1964, when the board of the d'Ulm Circle made a "self-criticism" during which the conceptions of these intellectuals, the separation they made between theoretical work and revolutionary practice, were combatted. Serious criticism was made also of people who sharpened their theoretical tools without ever using them, without ever placing them at the service of the proletariat and of the revolution. This "self-criticism" provoked violent discussion for a certain time, and there were fierce contradictions. Actually, real unity of thought was not restored between these intellectuals and the budding Marxist-Leninist nucleus. The relationship of forces demanded, however, that unity be maintained in order that the d'Ulm Circle could serve as a supporting base in the fight that the Marxist-Leninist nucleus was preparing to lead within the UEC.

The Marxist-Leninist nucleus succeeded in having accepted a group work-project that provided for investigations of workers' and peasants' struggles in France, active participation on the part of the group in the political fights within the UEC, orientation of its ideological work towards concrete analyses, documented study of the class struggle in France, and continuation of the movement for study of Marxist-Leninist classics and of propaganda for theoretical training of Communist militants. *Les Cahiers marxistes-léninistes* were created on this basis (in the autumn of 1965). We shall return to them later.[16]

Unity of action in the movement for study of the classics of Marxism and of propaganda for theoretical training, as well as in press organization, was maintained more or less satisfactorily between this group of intellectuals and the budding Marxist-Leninist nucleus, and the former agreed, however passively, to support the Marxist-Leninist positions in the internal struggle. Contradictions appeared, however,

between the different tendencies, contradictions that were reflected by
the strangely diversified aspect of the first five issues of *les Cahiers
marxistes-léninistes*. In fact, the last issue of the first series of *les
Cahiers marxistes-léninistes* (No. 5), dated May 1965, terminated the
period of unity. The group of bourgeois intellectuals ceased to participate actively in the work of the Circle in the autumn of 1965 and, at
the end of 1965, a new attempt at collaboration ended in a bitter crisis
in January–February 1966. After lengthy discussions, the actual majority of the d'Ulm Circle, which had regrouped around the Marxist-
Leninist nucleus, ideologically defied the bourgeois positions on questions of theory and conception of the role of intellectuals. It was at
this moment that seizure of power by the revolutionary proletarian
Left and defeat of the bourgeois current in the d'Ulm Circle may be
said to have taken place. At that moment, and already for some time,
the center of the work of the Marxist-Leninists had been moving
towards the *Union des étudiants communistes* as a whole, and our
clandestine organization was about to enter upon a period of large
scale expansion. After assumption of power by the revolutionary proletarian Left in the d'Ulm Circle, the intellectuals whose participation
in the movement for Marxist studies had taken a bourgeois position
of academic authority definitely withdrew from the work of the d'Ulm
Circle, which became essentially Marxist-Leninist. None of the bour-
geois-based intellectuals who had participated in the movement for
study of the Marxist-Leninist classics took part in the creation of the
clandestine Marxist-Leninist organization, and they were never members of our organization.

Second Position

A second current participated at one time in the study movement, in
the form of collaboration with No. 5 of *les Cahiers marxistes-léninistes:*
this current, contrary to the first, wanted to bring about a revolution
and to combat imperialism, and it endeavored to take practical measures
to do so. But in spite of a creditable revolutionary position and genuine
knowledge, this current had a politically mistaken basis, which was a
petty bourgeois revolutionary ideology (Castroism). This current participated only very briefly in the work of the d'Ulm Circle, had no part
in the foundation of our organization, and was never part of it.[17]

Third Position

In the course of the year 1964, the Marxist-Leninist nucleus was set up
inside the movement for Marxist studies in the d'Ulm Circle, on the

basis of varied experiences. It later waged an internal struggle and, by merging with other forces, prepared the launching of our organization. This nucleus was composed of comrades who were enthusiastic about the theory and practice of the Chinese revolution, the laws of continuous revolution in stages, and the methods of ideological transformation and revolutionization used in China. These comrades studied particularly the stages of socialist transformation in agriculture, the system of people's communes, the ideological transformation of the masses who determine a revolution with respect to production. They also studied the dialectics of class struggle and the problems of strategy and tactics posed by progression from one stage to the other. They strove to assimilate the principle that seemed fundamental to them— that is, the mass line—and they tried to seize aspects of it in specified concrete circumstances. These comrades also attached great importance to determination of a correct proletarian ideology as a productive force, and, in *Pékin Information,* they analyzed different examples of inventions rooted in the experience of the masses in their fight for production.

Having been obliged to study the class struggle in the countries dominated by imperialism, these comrades became convinced of the accuracy of the principles of "counting on one's own strength," "taking agriculture as a base and industry as a leading factor," applying the mass line, etc. They understood the reactionary nature of imperialist "aid" to these countries as a means of shameless exploitation. They acquired the conviction that the Chinese way was the right way for the entire world, and that profound knowledge of it was necessary.

To achieve this, these comrades attentively studied *Pékin Information* and the works of comrade Mao Tse-tung, particularly *The Analysis of Classes in Chinese Society, The Investigation in the Hounan, The Introduction to Investigation in the Countryside, On Agricultural Cooperation,* as well as philosophical works, particularly *On Contradiction.*

Enthusiastic study of the theory and practice of the Chinese Revolution was the basis upon which the unity of thought of an entire small nucleus of comrades who constituted the initial nucleus of our organization, was forged during 1964. These comrades were also in agreement with the theories concerning the general line of the Communist movement as expressed in the 25-Point letter. But they considered that this letter could be adopted as a sound political basis only through a process of assimilation of the theory and practice of the Chinese Revolution.

It seemed to them that the theory and practice of the Chinese Revolution were about to settle a certain number of questions left open by the earlier development of the revolutionary movement, and that they would decisively enrich the theoretical store and experience bequeathed by Marx and Lenin. This seemed to them to be the basis for "correct" thinking, without which any position in the discussions of the international Communist movement could only be superficial. This idea was to guide their educational work and their Marxist-Leninist propaganda.

It should be added that when all the questions that these comrades had particularly studied were rendered magnificently topical by the Great Proletarian Cultural Revolution, they felt tremendous enthusiasm and were immensely encouraged to continue their struggle. They understood that what they had more or less clearly formulated as a primordial necessity for assimilating the theory and practice of revolution was nothing other than the principle of "putting Mao Tse-tung's thought in a position of command," and they held to this principle even more firmly.

The big split in the *Union des étudiants communistes* was based mainly on the question of the Great Proletarian Cultural Revolution, as well as, understandably, on overall problems concerning the International Communist movement's line and the Communist movement in France. The revisionist traitors who were leading the UEC were unmasked and beaten by the mass of Communist militants in this organization principally on the question of the Great Proletarian Cultural Revolution. We believe that this was a good thing, that it helped our organization to found its activity on sound bases and to acquire a correct manner of working.

More generally, we believe, on the basis of our experience and the study of facts, that the 25-Point letter only permits us to draw a firm line of demarcation on the condition that we remain closely linked to the assimilation of Marxism-Leninism and of Mao Tse-tung's thought, as it appeared clearly in the Great Proletarian Cultural Revolution.

Finally, it is the Great Proletarian Cultural Revolution that provides the bases for a profound, unalterable, and definitive line of demarcation between the revolutionary Marxism-Leninism of our time and all the variations of revisionism. We believe that the assimilation of Mao Tse-tung's thought in the light of the Great Proletarian Cultural Revolution is the touchstone of a "correct" theory according to which the Great Proletarian Cultural Revolution opens up an entirely new epoch in the International Communist movement.

These were the different currents that made up the d'Ulm Circle in 1964 and, at the beginning of 1965, launched the movement for Marxist-Leninist classical studies, called the campaign for "theoretical training" inside the Communist organization. *Les Cahiers marxistes-léninistes* constituted an important weapon for this campaign beginning with its first issue. Certainly, as we have already indicated, the first five issues of this *roneotype* publication were not Marxist-Leninist but reflected the heterogeneity of the group that headed the study movement. Certain texts were school exercises written in obscure language; others were first essays on Marxist analysis of concrete situations in which right ideas coexisted with instances of tactical concealment and unilateral judgments. Other texts were erroneous from the political point of view, and others reflected a mechanical application of theoretical Marxist principles. Nevertheless, on the whole, despite all these faults, this publication was from the beginning a serious, carefully edited publication in which certain Marxist theories were presented in detail and were of a kind to incite its readers (principally Communist students) to make an effort towards thoughtful analysis of important questions of Marxism. This is why it played a very important role in the awareness of a certain number of Communist students. It also became a rallying point for partisans with a background of serious theoretical training and thinking on Marxism-Leninism, and constituted the first weapon used by the initial Marxist-Leninist nucleus in its internal struggle, a weapon which adequately prepared the ground for later steps in the fight of the Marxist-Leninists inside the UEC.

It should also be pointed out that from the beginning the administrative and material management of this publication, *roneotyped* and financed by contributions from members of the d'Ulm Circle, was taken on by the small Marxist-Leninist nucleus. The latter patiently undertook the accumulation of financial support necessary for the internal struggle and for the split. They helped finance other UEC grassroots organizations and laid the first bases for material equipment (*roneos,* printing materials, etc.) which guaranteed organizational independence for the Marxist-Leninists within the revisionist organization.

A last point deserves to be underlined: the intellectuals who participated in the Marxist study movement on a bourgeois position did not want to take part in politics. This allowed the Marxist-Leninist nucleus to assume direction of the d'Ulm Circle organization from the beginning, to represent them in organizational meetings, to have themselves elected to higher institutions, and to have the Circle adopt tactical positions which supported the Marxist-Leninists in their internal struggle. This helped the Marxist-Leninists considerably in their ideological, political, and organizational fight against the revisionist direction of the UEC.

—Excerpt from *Servir le peuple*, No. 4, August 15, 1967.

Document 99

Long Live the Union of the Workers and the Students Working for Them!

For one week, students resolutely fought against the counter-revolutionary violence of the CRS, *gardes mobiles* and other cops. Their fight showed the fundamentally repressive and anti-popular nature of the Gaullist government.

In the meantime the blackjacks and grenades that hit the students are the same that knocked out and wounded the workers in Redon, Le Mans, and Caen. The workers have always had to fight against oppression on the part of the bourgeoisie; for ten years they have confronted the Gaullist blackjacks and iniquitous measures for organizing unemployment, increasing work rhythms, and lowering wages.

The workers are the main target of bourgeois oppression.

They represent the main force which will provoke the fall of the anti-popular Gaullist government.

WORKERS AND STUDENTS ARE SUBJECTED TO GAULLIST OPPRESSION.
HOW CAN THEY UNITE IN ORDER TO OVERTHROW IT?

The Mitterrand type of pink[18] gives a reactionary answer to this question. Although they shout their indignation as soon as workers hit back at the CRS, they also noisily applaud the student actions. They show their true faces in attempting to force on the workers reformist directives referring to the University. They want the workers to fight for a Sorbonne which trains their exploiters. What an absurdity! What a sinister plot!

The objective of the pinks and of their reformist accomplices was, first of all, to limit the movement of student revolt to reformist demands and demonstrations in the Latin Quarter; secondly, to make the workers a *contributing force* to the struggle of the petty bourgeoisie. All in order to prepare a reactionary-oriented solution to Gaullism.

The workers and progressive students do not want this kind of unity!

The workers want to profit from the present situation in which Gaullism is weakened, in order to fight on the basis of their class demands:

AGAINST UNEMPLOYMENT, STARVATION WAGES, FIENDISH WORK RHYTHMS, DOWN WITH THE ANTI-POPULAR GAULLIST POWER! FREEDOM FOR THE PEOPLE!

These solgans can ensure a broad mobilization of the popular masses. On these points, the workers can attract large sections of the population and particularly progressive students who want to help them.

That is the true form for unity of workers and progressive students.[19]

LONG LIVE THE UNITY OF WORKERS AND PROGRESSIVE STUDENTS! LONG LIVE WORKER LEADERSHIP OF THE POPULAR STRUGGLE! DOWN WITH THE DICTATORSHIP OF THE MONOPOLIES, DOWN WITH THE GAULLIST GOVERNMENT! FREEDOM FOR THE PEOPLE!

—Mouvement de soutien aux luttes du peuple, Comités de défense contre la répression [May 10th?].

The ESU

Like the Communist students, the PSU students had had many sources of conflict with the leaders of their party, and expulsions for reasons of "Leftism" or Trotskyism had been frequent. In 1968, to the extent that they controlled the UNEF leaders as well as several General Assemblies, the ESU were able to play an important role, as for instance in Lyons, where they were the moving spirits behind *le Journal du Rhône,* in cooperation with the CFDT and the Lyons General Student Association, or in Clermont-Ferrand where they tried to take over the General Assembly from the FER.[20] Their own role was much harder to discern, in spite of the importance that the PSU appeared to assume at the time of the Charléty meeting (May 27), and perhaps because of the rather equivocal nature of the party's action, which was at once "electoralist" and "revolutionary." We give here a Lyons leaflet that antedates the movement a bit and criticizes the *Mouvement de soutien à la cause du peuple* (generally called *soutien aux luttes du peuple*) and a leaflet from Clermont-Ferrand dated the day that followed the first barricades.[21]

Document 100

With Regard to the Movement for Support of "The People's Cause"

At the *Faculté des Lettres* a movement has just been created, the goal of which will be to obtain student support for the working class struggle. This movement which continues the work undertaken several months ago by members of the ujc(m-l) has a very positive aspect. Students can never be too aware of the workers' lot. Lulled by the rose-tinted propaganda of neocapitalism, they are constantly being told that the affluent society is just around the corner. As though the very essence of the scandal of the acknowledged 500,000 unemployed, under-employment, regional economic crises, mad urbanization, etc., were not to be found in the capitalist system. This movement has had the merit of introducing information about social conflicts into the *Faculté*.

However, our approval stops there.

At first the movement declared that it wanted to be put "under the leadership of the workers." This is really a curious statement on the part of its activists, all students, whose organization happens not to have the slightest foothold among the workers and is desperately seeking the means for converting them to the virtues of Maoist thought.

But above all, the professorial hierarchy of the *Faculté des Lettres* can rejoice at the rash of proclamations of support for the workers' cause that has appeared on union billboards. The interest of the politicized minority of students having been diverted, the University can continue to quietly fulfill its duties of training docile specialized nitwits intended for industry and the consumer society that serve the bourgeoisie.[22]

Undoubtedly it can rightly be considered that the leftist parties that now represent the working class are hardly combative. We are also critical of them. How absurd seem discussions of formulas for a governmental program that involves a subtle dosage between unifying and divisive tactics at the very moment when the workers and peasants of Le Mans, Redon, la Rhodia, Caen . . . are revolting. But we reject escapism. We must support the workers' fight without flinching. For our role is not to give advice, even if we say the contrary.

Our concern is to fight the bourgeois University, to put the great machine of intellectual oppression on the side of the workers. But to mention the role which the University fulfills in society is not sufficient; it must be replaced.

As in Nanterre, it is a matter of denouncing examinations. In *Lettres,* for instance, these examinations sanction submission to the outworn values of ruling class "culture."

Psychologists are the future cops in social conflicts: philosophers, the watchdogs of morals (Paul Nizan *dixit*); student teachers, memory machines, not pedagogues.

As in Berlin, it is a question of going towards the critical counter-University by allying ourselves with the progressive fraction of the teaching body and the intelligentsia.

The University is now playing and will be playing an ever greater role in the production of scientific and technical know-how as it progressively places itself at the disposal of organizational capitalism. We may therefore consider that students participate directly in the class struggle, and that, by enforcing their refusal of social "selection" and their demands for genuine access to scientific knowledge, they are helping the workers more effectively than by applying a facile and thus far impotent worker-oriented policy.

SOLIDARITY WITH THE WORKERS!
NO TO A UNIVERSITY IN THE SERVICE OF THE BOURGEOISIE!

—*Etudiants socialistes unifiés* [Lyons, end of April].

Document 101

ESU

Last Night in the Latin Quarter

After the failure of the hoax carried out by the Ministry, the CRS, without notice, threw chlorine and incendiary grenades and beat up students who were massed in the Latin Quarter, and until then, had maintained absolute calm and composure. No comment necessary.

YOU WILL GIVE THE ANSWER!

Students, men and women:

This morning, in the light of last night's events, after a discussion with certain professors of the SNESup. and SGENsup. who participated in the strike picketing, the ESU made the following proposal to the AGEC:[23]

Postponement of the June examinations until September with a possibility for trying again in October in case of not passing.

This proposal was accepted right away by the AGEC, whose president immediately went to the professors of the *Faculté des Lettres* to ask them to bring up the question before the *Faculté* council.

If this decision is taken, we hope that all the students freed of all University obligations will join us spontaneously to fight against police repression and in this way obtain the three conditions proposed by the UNEF and the SNESup.

We call on all the AGE in France to adopt this plan and we are considering other forms of action.

The students of PCMLF and of the FER have spontaneously joined us. We expect support from all the other progressive forces that we have not yet been able to contact.

EVERYBODY COME THIS AFTERNOON AT 4 P.M. TO THE
FACULTÉ DES LETTRES.

—[Clermont-Ferrand, May 11].

The Anarchists

The appearance on May 6 of the black flag on the first Paris barricades, and the polemics this gave rise to, constituted one of the important facts of the May movement. There is no doubt that anarchist thinking, to which Cohn-Bendit was personally committed, had a profound influence on this revolution, concerning which it has been emphasized to what extent it had returned to the revolutionary trade-union ideas of the early 20th century[24]—to start with, the idea of worker management. Similarly, the regionalist orientation frequently adopted by the movement was greatly indebted to the traditions of Proudhon and Bakunin. In their written statements, however, the anarchist groups, properly speaking, were not always as successful as these forebears.[25] There follow a leaflet from Marseilles brought out by a small group of young people, and a lyrical reply to the accusations made by the Minister, Fouchet (May 25 at 2 A.M.), against the "riff-raff" that Paris was invited to "vomit." In the first of these leaflets, the tone of opposition to all predominantly "worker-oriented" thinking should be noted.

Document 102

Young People Are No Longer Fighting Alone

After having called students "rich men's sons" and *"enragés,"* the property-owning, conservative-minded class is beginning to have its problems.

After the insults, they admit that "important reforms" must be carried out in the domain of education, in professional training, and in openings for young people.

A wave of concern that borders on panic has seized these gentlemen. How is violence to be avoided, how is the uneasiness to be dissipated?

But "violence" is the basis of a society founded on the exploitation and servitude of man:

Beyond the revolt of the student world, the importance of which is growing quantitatively and qualitatively every day, *the entire governmental system is in question!*

THE AGE-OLD FIGHT FOR FREEDOM IS TODAY

TAKING ON NEW DIMENSIONS!

Faced with the breadth of the 22 *mars* movement, the political parties and the national unions, paralyzed in a verbal and sterile opposition to the Government, are preparing to "stick" to the students.

We welcome the enormous contribution of the workers to the students' action, but we urge them to remain firm in their determination.

We urge them to reinforce their unity, to maintain their vigilance, to avoid any attempt at infiltration on the part of political parties (however "large" they might be).

Young people do not need to be "headed" by anybody. During this spring of 1968 they have demonstrated their strength, their maturity, and the manner in which they are able to solve the problems of our time.

—Group FA 3, *Bakounine de la fédération anarchiste,* Marseilles, May 12.

Document 103

M. Fouchet, chief steward for panic and hypocrisy, commander of mercenaries, State weathercock and Elysée garbage can, M. Fouchet recalls Vaillant, Ravachol, and Bonnot's gang [19th century French anarchists]. Snug in the armchair used by so many earlier persecutors, he has rejuvenated the old scapegoat: the anarchist has succeeded the Jew; riff-raff is now his synonym. Tremble, shopkeepers! Lock yourselves in, foolhardy onlookers! Anarchists are on the prowl. A bomb in one hand and equality in the other, they conceal themselves in the crowd to incite to murder. Worse, the man with the black flag has attacked the Stock Exchange;[26] he has desecrated the temple. Up till now, hierarchic turmoil could be repressed without terror. The people's blood, which at one time stained the red flag, had become the color of a pale rose. It still had thorns, but we were less fearful of injury, which was limited to reform! And now the throne is unsteady. Another enemy is not content with a few nationalizations. He refuses money in its slaveholder form. He is the devil. M. Fouchet is preparing, then, a new inquisition, with its torture and its informers. He is seeking to arouse the venom of ordinary people about a concept that is beyond them. What could be more anti-progressive?

But nobody in this country, with the exception of the blood-thirsty fossils of nationalism, wants a return to the Nazi winters when an entire race was sacrificed on the altar of Power. Despite the calls for lynching, there will be no witch hunts, even against the ministerial agitators who are trying to provoke it. The black flag has never been soiled by being spit upon, but contact with M. Fouchet's cadaver would make a corrupt rag of it. It will not be used as a shroud. M. Fouchet can die like a dog.

—The Anarchists [May 25].

The Right

A specifically rightist current has never ceased to exist in student circles, either inside the *Fédération nationale des étudiants de France,* or in the former majority of the UNEF. This current was expressed in May inside many organizations, certain of which took over the word "revolutionary" as in the case of the *Conseil étudiant de France;* while others (among them the *Comité étudiant pour les libertés universitaires,* one of whose texts follows) combined an intensive fight against "subversion" with activity oriented towards technocratic reform of the University.[27]

It was characteristic of the rightists' thinking that they attributed all revolutionary movements to a conspiracy. The following text offers a good example of the mania for interpretation, the *"enragés"* being accused in it of forcing strong-arm men to speak for the opposition in order to ridicule it.

Document 104

How to Organize Revolution

1. Mixture of real demands with idealistic principles of permanent protest in order to obtain a well dosed combination of respecta-

bility and subversion, which attracts undecided people, as well as all uninformed opponents, into the current.

2. Sudden introduction of structures and exceptional procedures in order to liquidate the non-revolutionary organizations and authorities normally responsible: improvised or hastily elected commissions, provisional committees, strike committees, deliberative assemblies.

3. Permanent activity of these custom-made structures in order to have everybody participate in them, even those who are opposed. Discussions in which everybody will want to defend his project without taking into consideration that he is inundated by unacceptable positions and is therefore keeping the revolutionary movement going. No intellectual respite. Long night sessions for brainwashing, for neutralizing all thinking inside a vague idealism.

4. Reform is not the goal; it is the means by which revolutionary action is conveyed.

5. Innumerable assemblies with a democratic outward appearance, during which speaking time is given to all who want it with the help of a widely circulating microphone.

6. Chairmanship given to men who belong to the movement but who are second in rank.

7. A few agitators or plants in strategic parts of the hall.

8. Stooges speaking in the name of the opposition in order to ridicule it.

9. A sturdy commissar and accomplished democratic champion drowned in the heart of the discussion in order to control the game and put the train back on the tracks if necessary.

10. No voting when an opponent has just got up to speak.

11. No voting on a definite point but always on vague ideas about which everybody thinks they can agree.

12. The steering committees of assemblies or committees or commissions choose themselves.

13. No discussion permitted on the representativeness of the groups in power, with shifting of prime movers from group to group, without informing others.

14. Leaflets containing only what is wanted discussed in the assembly, and which elude the points that have already been seriously discussed.

15. Obligatory solidarity every time a decision is to be taken to eliminate unreliable people by calling them enemies of the cause.

16. Taking the floor without indication of political color and, even less so, of apolitical color.[28]

17. Full power wrested from the crowd in order to be able to proceed.

18. Diversions by provoking difficulties on problems that are simple for everybody; then, after a vote which entails no commitments, dissolve the assembly.

19. Voting after exhaustion of opponents, late at night.[29]

20. Tense atmosphere in order to accelerate progress towards the boiling point of the participants. Overheating operations repeated until explosion of the masses, who are thereby prepared for any violent action that may occur.

RAPID LISTING OF THESE POINTS OF MARXIST TECHNIQUE
BRINGS OUT THE TACTICS TO BE OPPOSED.

1. Do not participate in any way in demonstrations inspired by revolutionary groups.

2. Observe the men who are reacting normally but confusedly in order to take them aside and enlighten them as much about the true problems as about the methods to be used.

3. Systematize training of volunteer help through work meetings between periods of action.

4. Find out what people can do, in order to organize them for possible action.

5. Commissars must not push themselves forward, in order to be able to devote more attention to essential matters.[30]

—*Comité étudiant pour les libertés universitaires* [distributed at Nanterre, particularly among professors, May 30].

Fascist Students

We shall give two texts that represent the fascist current inside the University. It should also be pointed out that in May, and practically until the end of the movement, the *Action Française* students and those belonging to genuinely fascist groups (*Rivarol, Occident, Jeune révolution*) were able to express themselves freely and carry on their propaganda at the *Faculté de Droit* and at the *Institut d'études politiques.* One text comes from *Occident;* the other from *Jeune révolution,* an organization that stems from the OAS, headed by Captain Sergent. It is interesting to see how carefully they fit into the "revolutionary" language mold.

Document 105

What Does Occident *Want?*

The Nationalists did not wait for March 22, 1968, to oppose the regime. From the very beginning the Nationalists have fought it. Many among them have been victims of systematic repression: imprisoned, even shot.

At that time the Communists played the role of informers paid by the regime by publishing names and photographs of Nationalist leaders in their newspapers. Only recently *l'Humanité* was protected by the CRS, while from the upper floors Communist provocators threw *lead blocks* and *bottles of acid* at our militants in the streets.

The Nationalists therefore have the right, more than any others, to speak out in the name of students in revolt against the government's attitude.

The *Occident* movement, having been favorable from the very beginning to the student struggle against the government and to the strike, has, on the other hand, firmly decided to oppose the seizure of the movement by extreme left groups for the satisfaction of demands. These groups are congenitally incapable of anything but fruitless, endless discussions; they would only cause the students to lose the benefits of the last weeks' fighting, and ridicule them in the eyes of public opinion.

STUDENTS HAVE NO USE FOR THE BUFFOONERY AT THE ODÉON
OR THE ORGIES AT THE SORBONNE!

Students!

Do not let parlor terrorists who have broken with the *faculté* dictate your future!

If, tomorrow, France becomes a popular democracy, there will be no question of reforms or of confrontation. All you students will be able to do will be to comply with the orders of political commissars without being able yourselves to choose either your profession or your fate.

IT IS NOW THAT YOU MUST FIGHT!
JOIN US!
BECOME A MEMBER OF THE "OCCIDENT" MOVEMENT!

—[About May 20].

Document 106

Mouvement Jeune Révolution

The crisis that the country is now going through is not only dramatic. It is also complex, and, at least in its first stage, has assumed an aspect that might sow confusion in many minds. In effect, superficially it appears to be a confrontation between the Gaullist government and the forces of the extreme left supported by the Communist Party—in spite of the initial reservations of the latter. It could thus seem at first view to substantiate the false dilemma dear to Gaullists and once set forth by Malraux: The Communists or us. . . .

Faced with this situation the *mouvement Jeune révolution* has issued a formal warning to all its members and sympathizers, as well as to all young people concerned about building the future and social structures, avoiding at once both Gaullist and Marxist rigidity: the choice proposed is faked; the dilemma is a trap and we refuse to let ourselves be caught in it. We must go beyond the present confrontation and not let ourselves be forced to play the game of one or the other of the apparent antagonists.

This implies a certain number of *imperative condemnations.* First of all, condemnation of the primary reaction which has led certain people to take their places ostensibly on the side of the so-called "forces of order" through fear of Communism. Gaullist "order" is only a *caricature of order,* and it is precisely what has led to the present situation. What is more, any alliance with it would not only be immoral but stupid: it would only profit the government still in power, which alone is armed to utilize it and to harvest the fruits for its exclusive profit. If these gentlemen lack CRS, they should look for them elsewhere than among us!

On the other hand there is certainly a convergence of views between our movement and the profound reaction in the student world in its confrontation with a society which has become incapable of defending essential values and of promoting veritable structures for the future.

The second formal condemnation aims at those who have nothing to suggest to this society but archaic formulas: the red flag and the *Internationale,* expressing only a *caricature of confrontation*—one which consists in proposing as a remedy an even more worn out system, that has ended in total bankruptcy everywhere people have undertaken to apply it. Marxist old men should not take over from Gaullist old men, and above all, not in the name of youth. . . .

Besides, on this point French students must take into consideration the action and desires of their comrades on the other side of the iron curtain who are now fighting against a social system and a rigid education that looks forward only to ensuring total control through dictatorial power over people's minds as well as their bodies.

Having said this, it is essential to underline that the movement of student demands is *profoundly just*.

The justness of their aspirations is precisely what gives the movement a breadth incommensurate with the true importance of the various groups who have successively tried to "co-opt" it. For ourselves, without having tried to "head" the operation politically, certain among us having been on the barricades too, we can testify to the true atmosphere of this movement.

We reject the present system of educational organization, rooted in fifty years of ultra-conservatism and lacking the slightest concern whatsoever for adaptation to a modern economic society.

And we also reject it—we must define this clearly—because it is the reflection of a totalitarian albeit incoherent society, which leaves no place for ideals while preaching and applying entirely incorrect economic concepts. For us the economy must serve mankind: consumption should be dictated by need and not the contrary.

Consequently, the *mouvement Jeune révolution:*

—orders its militants to reject any collusion with the government in the repression of a revolt which this government itself has provoked;

—denounces attempts at co-option of the student movement made by the backers of the dictatorial bankrupt regime, beginning with the Communist Party;

—proclaims the necessity for a general reform of the French university system in the direction, however, of the humanist tradition suited to western societies and by rejecting Communist totalitarianism and surrealist buffoonery, as well as the present routine;

—undertakes continuation of its fight without respite and whatever the circumstances, for the instauration of a new society capable of proposing definite aims and ideals to a youth which rejects the various types of materialism that are all anybody has to propose just now.

—*le mouvement Jeune révolution* [end of May].

The UEC

The Union of Communist Students, although remaining the most numerous overall student organization in France, had been reduced—at least in Paris—to the state of mere "groupuscule" by the dissensions that followed the appearance in 1966 of the JCR and the UJC(m-l) (not to mention those members who left because they favored Italian or Castroist ideas); and, more generally, by the attitude of the PCF, which was reluctant to admit that student problems might first concern the students themselves. Nevertheless, as of May 7, the UEC militants took part in the march from Denfert-Rochereau to the Étoile, which was a backdown from the violent condemnations that had been pronounced by the Party after the events of May 3 and 6. On May 8, their alliance was official.[31] Militant Communists took part in the work of the commissions and action committees, although they were often ill at ease in this type of body. They did everything they could to make maximum use of the possibilities for maneuvering that the Party line left them: as for instance, the UEC in Clermont-Ferrand published on May 22 an article by Roger Garaudy which had appeared in *l'Humanité* on the 15th, showing understanding for the "human uprising" that the student movement represented.[32] The fact remains, however, that the Communist leaders had done a lot to deserve the epithet that D. Cohn-Bendit hurled at them on the evening of May 13, when he called them "Stalinist scoundrels." Also, the position of the Communist students became uncomfortable after Georges Séguy's declarations on May 19 against the *Mouvement du 22 mars,* and the Party's approval of its leader's expulsion from France. At the Sorbonne their position was in fact almost untenable, at least after the sharp condemnation of the May 24 and 27 demonstrations, and association with the proposed elections.

The following leaflet entitled "For a Democratic University" is inspired, with an adapted vocabulary, by the Communist Party reform plan, which justifies their attitude toward elections.

Document 107

For a Democratic University

The adaptations achieved by the government in the name of urgent and desirable modernization all converged in fact to make the University subservient to the needs of an economic and financial feudal system.

Gaullist policy is contrary to the interests of the students, to the interests of the workers and of the nation.

Gaullist reform increases the obstacles separating the people from cultural life; living conditions are deteriorating with, for example, student unemployment, the latest Social Security reforms, and reforms of University social services.

The government policy limits democratic freedom at the University and favors extended control on the part of the financial powers over cultural matters.

The Gaullist policy refuses the large subsidies necessary for the present development of the University. Despite increases, the National Education budget remains well under its needs.

The government's policy is coherent and clever, but it is a class policy as well as a reactionary policy.

At the University, as throughout the country, it is an anti-social policy marked by difficult living conditions (unemployment, low wages, attacks against Social Security, insufficient numbers and amounts of scholarships, elimination of students of humble origin).

This is an anti-democratic policy marked with the seal of personal power, a policy characterized in the country by monopolization of the ORTF, reduction of union freedoms, and, in the University, by questioning of union and political freedoms in the *facultés,* in student residences, and in the lecture halls.

THIS IS WHY:

We must ask for a democratic reform of the University closely allying professional training and general education, theory and practice. It should achieve unity of teaching, research, and the economy, unhampered by private monopolies, and planned according to the needs of the nation.

This University will give a mass education accessible to all who have the capacity for it, and favoring higher education for young people of humble origin, through grants for study and a genuine cultural policy.

This modern University will abolish hasty orientation. It will cover a common period of preparation, of initiation and orientation for all students. Flexible structures will allow for changes in orientation.

Training and nomination of a large number of teachers, construction of suitable and well-equipped premises, will permit application of modern teaching methods.

The University will receive the necessary funding to ensure the best training of the largest possible number of students, i.e., 6% of the national income.

In addition, the University must take its place in a social, national, and international context. In effect, it suffers from the servitudes imposed by military research; it needs free development of scientific and technical exchanges with all countries.

This is why all students must unite to enforce a self-governing,[33] democratic University, and to give students a real position in society. All our intellectual education must serve our moral and civic training through the cultivation of a spirit of criticism and free investigation.

For civic and moral training, an experience of economic life is indispensable. From the start of moral training, education will make us aware that work is the source of all material and cultural conquest. It must teach us respect for work, manual as well as intellectual, and respect for young workers. Civic training, which the self-governed and democratic University will offer us, will interest us and introduce us to economic problems. It will prepare us actively to use the fruits of science and technique for the well-being of man.

Democratic education will have as a point of departure the idea that the connection between education and economic practice has as its principal goal not direct increase of production in a given function, but the general training of men in all branches, both as producers and as citizens. This connection with the economy under various aspects has the value of an educational principle for students. To foresee the future needs of the nation is one of the conditions for increased productivity.

The ways and means for carrying out such suggestions would be studied in cooperation with the unions.

Development of these struggles will contribute to hastening the disappearance of monopoly power and the advent of a true democracy opening the way to socialism. There is room for students in this struggle at the side of workers and of other democratic forces. This democracy will be a stable and lasting regime which will rely on a common program with advanced social content, corresponding to the deep aspirations of the masses.

—*Union des étudiants communistes*, Marseilles, May 21, 1968.

Document 108

Why Elections?

Faced with this movement of a size unparalleled in our country's history, de Gaulle owed it to himself to act. As he usually does, he began by choosing the field of action that was most favorable to him.

First of all, he played the card of ministerial resignations (Peyrefitte) and promises for reforms, hoping that these measures would calm public opinion.

The extension of the movement to settle grievances restrained him from going farther and calling for a vote of confidence—a veritable blank check—by means of a referendum. Faced with firm opposition on the left and the reservations of other non-Gaullist reactionaries, faced also with the poor reception from public opinion, de Gaulle had to acknowledge the facts: the "trick" of the referendum-plebiscite was becoming somewhat stale. He had to abandon this project.

From that time on his intentions became evident. He increased provocations by allowing it to be believed, for instance, that once dissolved the government could be had for the taking. He hoped that in this way the opposition would drift into venturesome undertakings, permitting him under these conditions to intervene brutally as the custodian of legality. De Gaulle was aiming purely and simply at a military dictatorship. His visit to General Massu and other commanding officers, in order to ensure loyalty on the part of the military, shows that the so-called collapse of authority was only a maneuver.

The working class, its trade-union organizations and its Party, by keeping cool and refusing to give in to provocation, avoided merciless repression, which would have compromised their accession to power for a long time to come.

Dissolution of a Chamber in which he had, to be sure, a very close but unconditional majority and recourse to new legislative elections was, therefore, the only possible way out for de Gaulle.

From the beginning of the May crisis the French Communist Party had every reason to engage in the electoral battle with confidence and hope.

Actually, it is undeniable that Gaullism is bankrupt in the eyes of public opinion. The immense strike movement involving ten million manual and intellectual workers[34] is an admission of failure for the social and university policies of the government. From both business and the universities, we hear the same unanimous shout: Enough!

Enough of a regime incapable of solving the present and future problems that face the nation. "Ten years is enough!" This was the slogan taken up by millions of demonstrators in all of France and in particular in the imposing demonstrations of May 13 and 29 in Paris, each one of which brought out nearly a million people. In the same way the 300,000 workers who have joined the CGT since the beginning of the strikes have likewise objectively taken a position against the regime.

As for the French Communist Party, which is strong in the just fight it has waged against the Gaullist government for ten years, strong because of the total support that it has given to the important movements for workers' demands, strong in its correct past and present analyses, it has greatly increased its already considerable influence: 17,000 Frenchmen have joined it in one month. This will be evident on the electoral level. Ever since '58, the Party has continued to increase its percentage of votes during the various elections. The number of Communist Deputies in the National Assembly went from 10 in 1958, to 42 in 1962, and 73 in 1967. The protest movement of this recent period can only accelerate this progress. Under these conditions we can really look forward to a victory of the Left: in '67, 54 Gaullist Deputies grabbed their seats with less than 500 votes over the opposition candidate, who was generally the Communist candidate.

Because the Gaullist government is conscious of this situation, it fears elections. This is why it is reviving primitive anti-communism and collecting around it a mob composed of all the reactionary and even fascist forces in the country. This is why it will not let any occasion pass, if offered by sufficiently serious disturbance, to cancel these elections and have recourse to "other means," which the General has already considered, and which would lead to a military dictatorship. For that, the government will not retreat before any possibility of provocation to create disorder and cancel the elections. Up till now the cool-headedness of the militant working class and the responsible attitude of its trade-union organizations and of its Party, have thwarted his calculations. We must follow this example and remain vigilant to thwart any provocation, which would only serve the government.

Under these conditions, elections are not a "betrayal," but the best and *only* means in the present situation to give concrete form to the legitimate discontent of the French people with regard to the Gaullist regime.

By voting Communist on June 23, these elections offer in effect a real possibility for them to assert their desire to obtain a guarantee of durable results, and an affirmative response must be made to the other aspirations of manual and intellectual workers. Thus in order to prevent "granting" of a reform which, once more, would only correspond to the exigencies of Big Capital, in order, on the contrary, to ensure adoption of the reforms proposed by the students and teachers in support of a truly democratic government, the students and the workers should vote Communist on the first ballot.

To vote Communist on June 23 is to refuse to lend oneself to the maneuvers of politicians that would take us back to a past when leftist governments applied rightist policies.

In reality, there is no progressive leftist policy without active Communist collaboration. The only democratic way out, therefore, implies a union of forces of the Left which will lead to a popular government of democratic union, supported by large masses of the people and applying a common governmental program.

To vote Communist on June 23 is a means of contributing to the mobilization of democratic forces and ensuring the accession to power of a government in which the Communists will have their share of responsibilities.

—Excerpt from *Challenge,* publication of the English Circle of the UEC
[beginning of June].

Among the Others

The Sorbonne was a particularly favorable terrain for distribution of propaganda material by all sorts of groups, and it would take a much larger book than this one to do justice to all that was circulated by the various Trotskyist groups or by their descendent, *le Communiste,* publication of the so-called "revolutionary tendency of the French Communist Party," which distributed El Fatah propaganda; *la Lutte communiste,* with editorials by J. Posadas, policy maker for the "Latin American committee" of the Fourth International, and very close to Chinese positions; *la Voie,* offshoot of the *Voix communiste,* which published some interesting pamphlets;[35] *la Voix ouvrière,* which had a small factory foothold, and whose militants have often been victimized by Stalinists; *Pouvoir Ouvrier,* offshoot of *Socialisme ou Barbarie,* and which, justifiably, has seen confirmation of many of its analyses.

Here we shall only give two examples. It is well known that sects are faced with a dual and (only apparently) contradictory temptation: the claim to hold a monopoly of truth, and therefore to pose as learned doctors of Revolution—this is what was expressed with total ingenuousness in a leaflet put out by the "parti communiste international," a group inspired by the violently anti-bureaucratic ideas of A. Bordiga—former leader (until 1923) of the Italian Communist Party—or to argue as though one were already identified with the united mass movement, as a "Pablist" inspired paper did.[36]

Document 109

Students!

A simple comparison of the number of injured on the side of the student demonstrators with those on the side of the police offers eloquent proof that it is not a matter of the usual peaceful marches organized by a democratic opposition. The demonstrators are not bleating sheep, they are returning blow for blow and are showing energetic solidarity with their imprisoned comrades: revolutionaries worthy of the name can only salute these facts with joy and hope; but they see in it *the only clearly positive aspect of this student turmoil.*

The government and its parliamentary opposition certainly react entirely differently. The government is having them blackjacked; it is there for that. The opposition (the PCF at the head) regrets that the government is blackjacking, but explains complacently that it is also the fault of "leftist provocators." The PCF and the CGT stigmatize these *"petty bourgeois leftists"* who disturb democratic order, and they cite the "worker movement" as an example. Many students are potentially petty bourgeois, it is true; it is also true that those among them who want to serve the proletarian revolution should study the more-than-a-century-old history of the worker movement. But *which* worker movement? Marx said: The worker movement is revolutionary or it is nothing. The "worker movement" today is therefore nothing; the PCF and the CGT are taking pains to direct any inclination toward revolt on the part of the workers to petty bourgeois demands; to be precise—pacifism, parliamentarianism, patriotism, reformism, fragmented strikes limited in time—after having banished forever the prospect of class revolution.

The government is also saying that the crisis must be solved and that its solution is the Fouchet Plan. The opposition is protesting: it needs a *democratic* reform. For the PCF, therefore, the solution exists (If only the united Left triumphs in the next elections!), but violence is to be condemned. The PCF is still more demagogic than the government, although quite as attached to law and order.

The "University crisis" that has been evidenced in the big industrialized countries is a dual one. It is commonly said that the type of education given is unadapted to the demands of modern life; that is to say, to the necessities of modern capitalism, to put it bluntly. This is true, and government and opposition are on this point roughly in agreement. But that is not all! Technological development has brought with it prolongation of schooling; the fear of increased unemployment and the demagogery of the democratization of education did the rest. University enrollment is overcrowded, particularly in certain disciplines, given the needs of capitalist society. The real goad of student disturbances, therefore, is the spectre of unemployment, the perpetuation of anguishing uncertainty about the future. Behind this goad certain students perceived in a still unclear and often even entirely distorted way, but perceived nevertheless, the symptoms. These are the symptoms of world imperialism which kills, pillages, crushes, and stultifies humanity, and whose capitals are Washington as well as Moscow, Bonn as well as Paris. Certain students, then, even began to understand that a student is the future "cadre" of this putrefying society and that the sacred culture that they were made to gulp down is the ideology of a decadent ruling class; since putrescence smells bad, they showed their disgust.

This awareness remains nevertheless confused, and only touches a minority while the student mass remains attached to its cultivated petty bourgeois privileges. It therefore offers a favorable terrain for the maneuvering of democratic opposition which has scented a possible electoral boon. The PCF and the CGT, both recently hostile, are now taking the students' defense. The meaning of the Fouchet Reform is clear: we must manufacture at the lowest possible cost only the necessary number of "cultivated" servants of Capital. The leftist parties and University organizations are protesting in the name of "eternal values," or of the needs of an idealized society; they forget that the mass is made up of exploited wage earners, that if there are unskilled laborers it is because capitalist society must have unskilled laborers, and not because these laborers have not had sufficient education. This is so true that all their beautiful talk boils down to the old recipe for "social advancement": "that nobody should be prevented by his social origin from becoming a bourgeois." This is their slogan.

The only real social problem is that of the abolition of the wage earner: the only means of emancipation, the Communist revolution, and not this demagogic, democratic University which would allow the sons of workers to become bourgeois (admitting for a moment that this would be seriously possible!) with no change in the existence of exploited workers and of bourgeois exploiters in the rest of society. Quite evidently the means for emancipation no longer reside in this hazy notion of "self-government" of the University we want to reform.

Alienation of the wage earning classes is not due to their lack of culture but to the demands of production for profit and the social division of work this imposes. We do not demand their access to bourgeois culture but we do demand abolition of capitalist production relationships. We do not ask that the exploitation of which these classes are the victims should be perfected—which is the only goal of the "educational reform" generally mentioned. On the contrary, we are making a radical criticism of bourgeois culture by showing that its only aim is to hide the sordid realities of bourgeois civilization.

One of the goals of our party is to oppose the school system of the bourgeoisie and to educate young people who will be intellectually freed of every form of prejudice, determined to work for transformation of the economic bases of society, and *ready to sacrifice all individual interests to revolutionary action.* To bourgeois culture we must oppose revolutionary theory, which the bourgeois University will never make known. The party of the proletariat must do this, and the role of the students—if they do not want to be accomplices of class repression—is to militate in its ranks. Then they will cease to be *students* gropingly searching for an illusory solution to the University crisis, but *militants* in the revolutionary cause of the world proletariat.

—International Communist Party[37] (*Programme communiste*)
[May 8th?].

Document 110

On Being a Guevara Follower in France

Many young people are attracted by the Cuban and Latin American revolutions; certain of us simply by the exotic aspect of revolutionaries with long hair, long beards, and cigars—in short, it is the nonconformist human aspect that attracts these young people. Others are attracted because they understand the political importance of revolution on a continent which is one of the pillars of American imperialist wealth. What is certain is that this very type of guerrilla is popular among large sectors of young people, whether they are politically organized or not.

A certain number of militants in youth organizations understand the reasons for the guerrilla in Latin America. They understand that the guerrilla is "the fundamental way to seize power" in the large majority of Latin American countries because of the social-economic conditions in these countries. But few understand all the implications of this new form of struggle. Few understand the new relationships it introduces between avant-garde and mass action. Few understand what the Cubans mean when they propose the following new idea: *The Party is not the condition of revolution; on the contrary, it is the revolution which is the condition for forming the Party.* The Cuban comrades have arrived at this conclusion on the basis of their own experience, but also on that of the other current revolutions in Latin America:

> —In Cuba the revolution took place without (and even outside) the Party. The embryo of the present Communist party was constituted in the struggle, around the Sierra Maestra militants.

> —In Guatemala, another example, it is the guerrillas of the rebel armed forces under César Montes, and of the November 13th Revolutionary Movement under Yon Sosa, who constitute the present Guatemalan avant-garde and the rudiments of the future revolutionary party.

It is quite superficial to explain these phenomena by the simple reformism of the Communist parties in these two countries. Otherwise we would not understand that this phenomenon could also apply to all the other tendencies in the worker movement. The case of Bolivia is conclusive in this respect. Neither the pro-Soviet nor the pro-Chinese CP's, nor the Revolutionary Workers' Party (Trotskyist) had a fundamentally different attitude at the time of the fight led by the Army of National Liberation (ELN)[38] and by Che Guevara. They all expressed solidarity, but none made a move. For years, all three had been disputing for the revolutionary title, but none had actually chosen to fight for the overthrow of the Barrientos dictatorship and the instauration of Socialism in Bolivia. On the other hand, militants of various origins, weary of discussion, threw themselves into action. And in spite of a first battle lost, in spite of the tremendous loss that the assassination of Che Guevara represented, it was these militants of the ELN who formed the true Bolivian revolutionary avant-garde. It was toward them that the miners turned; it was around them that the students organized their demonstrations. In fact the true revolutionaries of every organization, as well as a part of the masses, identified with the guerrilla action.

The explanation is therefore more complex and at the same time simpler than merely to throw all the blame on this or that organization. *The masses only trust the revolutionaries who are ready to die for their ideas.* The various political ideas proposed to them are too numerous, the failures have been too many for the masses still to follow blindly one organization rather than another. They will only follow those who in deed and in action show the accuracy of their line.

Let us say right away that it is not a matter of "theorizing" *ad aeternum.* This new situation is naturally linked to the concrete political conditions that now exist in the Latin American and, more generally, in the world revolutionary movement, especially in the Communist movement.

But in France? To a great extent the problem of the avant-garde is posed in the same terms, at least on the level of young people. We are faced with a good dozen organizations, all of which claim to be revolutionary and socialist: UEC, JCR, Révoltes, pro-Chinese, etc. Each of these organizations, with only several hundred militants apiece, claims to be in possession of the Truth and often wants to impose it on others by force. For example, in student circles the energies of these organizations are more often dedicated to fighting one another, even physically, than to developing true mass action. Even for organizations that repudiate violence among revolutionary militants, militant activity is reduced essentially to talking about revolution, but not acting. These two attitudes are, in effect, the consequence of a line, conscious or unconscious, which gives priority to development of the organization rather than to development of a mass movement. This explains that the mass organizations (CAL, CVN, UNEF) should be considered above all as means for recruitment for political organizations rather than for mobilization of the masses. There are here two factors which we found in Latin America: (1) dispersion of revolutionary militants; (2) claim of each organization to be sole representative of the avant-garde.

In this situation action alone is effective, for it allows a bringing together of all those who in the different organizations are really revolutionaries and who do not give priority to "shop interests" over the real struggle against our society.

But to be a follower of Guevara in France also means to combat every aspect of class oppression, to question all the values of bourgeois society. Because to be revolutionary, it is not enough to be favorable to revolution in Asia or in Latin America. Global criticism is necessary.

This assumes, too, that action itself takes forms which break with the values of our society and, in the end, with bourgeois legality. This is what our German SDS comrades have understood and applied. In fact it means devising mass activities and forms of action which oblige the existing structures to reveal themselves to the great mass of young people by pushing them, through pure and simple repression, to respond. In France as in Latin America, as long as the mass movement does not fundamentally question the class structure the exploiters will remain within an orthodox "reformism" which, in exchange, demobilizes the masses. On the other hand, whenever they make a frontal attack on the system this "reformism" reveals its true nature, which as a result makes it possible to raise the level of mass mobilization.

—Pierre. Excerpt from *Front,* No. 1, *Bulletin des comités d'initiative pour un Front révolutionnaire de la jeunesse* [May].

Unity or Diversity of the UNEF

All during the month of May and until the last big student demonstration, which took place on May 11, the UNEF gave the impression, in spite of weak membership and the criticisms it incurred on the part of the *Mouvement du 22 mars,* of being able at least to designate where the student demonstrations would take place and to set the general tone of the demands. A *22 mars* speaker at a meeting at the *Cité Universitaire* on May 25 declared: "The reason we started the Nanterre movement was to oppose the UNEF. And if we have kept it going at the Sorbonne and elsewhere, but especially in the streets, it is in spite of the dilatory maneuvers and attempts to negotiate on the part of the UNEF, which the government is trying to bolster up against us. Pompidou wants to make the UNEF into a student CGT. Watch out for the UNEF."[39] The following text, in its very confusion, expresses all this quite well. The same thing was true in certain provincial cities, such as Lyons, for instance; elsewhere the UNEF was merely the spokesman for different sects: for the FER in Clermont, which protested against an attempt to overthrow the executive committee of the General Association of Clermont Students that, according to their account of the facts, strangely resembled their own regular attempts at taking control by force; and in Lille, for the UEC, which protested through the General Association against the demonstrations that took place on May 24 and 27 (Charléty).

Document III

The UNEF *Proposes . . .*

Considering the extension of the student-worker movement in Paris and in the provinces, considering the results of the first discussions that have taken place in the *facultés* today, the national committee of the UNEF believes that its duty is to outline a first summary and to contribute proposals in order to relaunch discussion and action in all the universities in France. In any case, one phenomenon is irreversible: the radical contestation of the University is inseparable from the contestation of established government. In other words, now and henceforth, the struggle is political.

At present when new prospects are opening up for the movement started by the students (occupation of factories by the workers), we must fight against any attempt to mire it, either by limiting it to University objectives only, or by leaving the junction to Sorbonne courtyard theorists. This is why we must participate in the dynamic movement of social contestation, especially by developing in the University the potential for redressment of grievances that has appeared there. It is therefore of prime importance to propose objectives that respond to this analysis.

As of now, four essential objectives can be proposed to the student movement:

1. Immediate instauration of real student power in the *facultés* with right of veto on all decisions taken.

2. Subject to this first point: University and *faculté* autonomy.

3. Extension of the struggle to all the sectors that propagate the ruling ideology—that is to say, the mass media.

4. A real liaison with the workers' and peasants' struggle by posing the problem of the same kind of government contestation inside business and professional structures.

These four essential points are necessary conditions for the solution of others (examinations, "selection," political and union freedom in the *facultés, lycées,* and elsewhere).[40]

I. STUDENT POWER

Whether through the counter university, through predominantly student commissions, or through a complete change in *faculté* assemblies, what counts is that the student movement must maintain control of all decisions taken in the University. Whatever the structures to be discussed with the grass roots, it is the students' right of veto which will allow all decisions taken to become operational and prevent any co-option.

This demand must become operational immediately, and it alone justifies continuation of the strike.

We know, nevertheless, that in a capitalist regime this kind of power can only be temporary.

II. UNIVERSITY AUTONOMY

Without student power, this autonomy is a lure since it amounts to giving authority to the mandarins who govern us. On the other hand, without autonomy student power is a lure, since the government and the administration retain considerable powers of control. Autonomy means that all decisions taken by the students in liaison with the teachers are immediately applicable.

III. EXTENSION OF THE FIGHT TO ALL IDEOLOGICAL SECTORS

The bourgeoisie is trying to drown the movement through mass media channels; it is therefore through these channels that we must make our actions known and understood. This means that all news that plays into the hands of the government must be combatted: whether in the form of newscasts (the ORTF, peripheral stations) or in the press. No newspaper should go out if it gives false news. This action must be planned in close cooperation with journalists and printers. In the same way as youth and cultural centers, the theaters of the entire artistic sector must join the battle for the creation of a new kind of popular culture.

IV. LIAISON BETWEEN THE STUDENT AND WORKER STRUGGLES

The fall of the present government can be accomplished only if the fight is led by the workers themselves. This means that the principal force for social transformation remains the working class. The workers must take over their own fates and from now on attack the employers' power in the factories. This supposes, on our part, systematic participation in the discussions that are taking place in the working class in order to contribute our point of view and not to give them lessons. Inversely, all discussions taking place in universities under student control must be open to workers.

Clarification of these four points will allow us to influence the situation and to put through other demands that concern us:

1. *Boycott of traditional examinations*

which only serve to eliminate students as a result of an educational failure; a first synthesis of the discussions makes it possible to formulate the following principles:

a) There is no question of making students bear the brunt of contestation of examinations. This means that it is unthinkable that they should lose the benefit of their year, and that it is also unthinkable that examinations should disadvantage militants who were fighting while others stayed quietly at home, or students who are wounded as opposed to those in good health.[41]

Since questioning examinations is linked to total educational change, this means that any discussion on the control of knowledge is subordinated to it. What counts in the present circumstances is:
—student control of all procedures for examinations or any other manner of giving diplomas;
—change of content, in a certain number of domains, of any tests given;
—student control of all decisions.

b) There is no question of permitting examinations and national competitions to take place in their usual form:
—we propose transforming the CAPES competition into an examination: this means that the established quota of openings[42] will not be taken into consideration;
—for the *baccalauréat:* it is unthinkable that the *baccalauréat* should take place in its traditional form. As a minimum, we propose that *lycée* students should exercise power of control and that all candidates should be able to take the oral examinations.

2. *Political and union freedoms*
are a fact in the *facultés.* They must also become a fact on the campus (with student power having a right of veto), in the *Grandes Ecoles* and *lycées.* On this subject the UNEF declares itself not only in solidarity with the CAL but solemnly announces that it will participate in the struggle for recognition of the CAL in the *lycées* and for their complete freedom of expression and action.

3. *No "selection"*
for admission to and courses in higher education. Since complete educational change is an absolute prerequisite, we reject all "selection" of whatever nature.

What Should Be Done Right Now?
1. It is essential to continue discussion of fundamental issues in every domain and on every level. But from now on, the UNEF calls on its militants immediately to seize control of university institutions. If discussions with the teachers remain necessary, the right of veto on all decisions taken is the only valid guarantee.

The control to be set up in terms of relative strength can only be given to the combat, strike, or action committees that have actually led the action during these last ten days. Wherever the relative strength is not favorable we must have recourse to parallel structures (the counter university or others) in order to maintain pressure that would make it possible to obstruct the functioning of the traditional University. This line, which is applicable under present circumstances, can be altered according to the evolution of our relative strength.

2. Proclamation of autonomy must be demanded now. But this proclamation must be made only if the first point (right of veto) has been obtained, and with all the necessary guarantees that this autonomy will not bring about a reinforcement of the conservative and technocratic professional fraction.

3. The mass media battle must be waged in every university city. This means that no regional newspaper can come out if it has not accurately presented information concerning our struggle. Demonstrations, occupation of premises, boycott of distribution, etc., will be organized in collaboration with newspaper workers.

The battle in the cultural sector can also be waged with young workers in order to orient the activity of youth and cultural centers toward combat (occupations, organization of political discussions, etc.).

As regards other sectors of cultural life, participation will take place in agreement with artists who have taken a stand against bourgeois culture.

4. Occupation of factories by the workers has already begun. Our role is to broaden the campaign of political explanation to prevent the government and the reactionaries from separating the student and worker struggles. The UNEF militants will therefore take part in the meetings, assemblies, and demonstrations decided upon by the workers, this participation being considered by us as a priority.

This series of proposals has been introduced into the free discussions that have been going on for several days now in the university.

—The National Board of the UNEF [May 16].

Document 112

AGEC—*Information*

Attack on the Union

Extremely serious events took place yesterday evening at the *Fac des Lettres*. The Coordinating Committee, which represents nothing on the union level as regards the UNEF, took the initiative of calling a "general assembly" of UNEF militants. The meeting was announced during the *Lettres* student assembly for immediately afterwards, at half past twelve at night.[43]

In the course of this meeting members of the Coordinating Committee arrogated to themselves the right to question the AGEC leadership, and clearly admitted that they intended to call the union leadership to account. They forced a vote to declare the meeting legal and to convoke an AGEC General Assembly within forty-eight hours.

Thus, disregarding all the statutes of the UNEF and of the AGEC, these members of the Coordinating Committee tried to perpetrate a real takeover. Because the democratically obtained local leadership does not suit them politically, they have consciously chosen to destroy the union just when the fight is becoming crucial and the union is consequently more than ever necessary.

We recall briefly that only the board of the *Lettres* student union is qualified—under certain specific conditions—to convoke a General Assembly of *Lettres* and that a board no longer exists. Some members of the coordinating committee had themselves appointed . . . by this illegal assembly, to head the *Lettres* student union!

All students must realize the responsibility assumed by those who have become the liquidators of the union; they must unite to continue the fight and back the union, over and above all the factional quarrels to which certain persons have sacrificed student interest.

Flash: Some UNEF militants from the *Fac de Droit* [Law School] were prevented from distributing a union leaflet by people who said they were from the union. Just when the union is more than ever necessary, since the students have a chance of satisfying their demands, those who have tried from the beginning to sabotage the student movement are today seeking to destroy the union *very quickly*. It is hardly necessary to point out that yesterday's illegal meeting took nothing but illegal decisions.

To Prepare for Victory
Everybody United Behind the Union!

May 20.

Document 113

Everyone Must Be Able to Decide

This leaflet is not customary. In reply to the urgent request of numerous militants who want a "complete" explanation of the reasons for what has been presented to the national UNEF leadership as a "knifing" by the AGEL, the AGEL board has drafted and published this leaflet. The students will judge.

Ever since the beginning of the movement started by the students, union organizations in higher education: AGEL (UNEF) and the Lille Sections of the SNESUP. have always assumed the responsibilities that devolved upon them. Some divergencies as to the strategy and structure to be followed have arisen between union organizations of the University of Lille and their national leaderships. As far as the AGEL is concerned, it has always considered that in order to be effective, that is to say, to achieve true, positive transformations of the student situation, action should respect the following basic principles.

I. AT ALL TIMES DECISIONS FOR ACTION ARE TAKEN BY ITS LEADERS

This democratic principle should be particularly respected at a time when a very large number of students, until then unorganized and excluded from action for redress of grievances, are mobilizing in large numbers, preparing to attack the "old university" in order to create a "new university."

It was imperative that students themselves should be able to talk about their problems, speak out on the question of examinations, discuss with professors the "internal" changes to be made in teaching, and express their opinions about the forms to be given "co-management."

In this way, dents have been made in the system by students and professors through the momentum of their impressive and determined mass movement.

It would be a mistake to minimize the movement's gains:

—*de facto* union and political freedoms,

—teaching changes decided upon in co-equal commissions of students and professors,

—a step forward toward co-management of the institutions (tensions still subsist, however, in a number of them, and victory on this point may still be obtained, the *Facultés des Lettres* and *des Sciences* being the most advanced).

II. ACTION IS BEING LED BY THE STUDENT MASS IN A UNITED,
   CALM, AND RESOLUTE FIGHT FOR CLEAR OBJECTIVES

The relative strength between students fighting for their objectives and their opponents really depends on three factors:

—*The number of students engaged in action* (which explains the systematic disparagement on the part of governmental propaganda, of "commitment," and calls to the "unorganized").

—*The cohesion of their fight* (it is not for nothing that the government is determined to divide student unionism).

—*The support students receive from the public* (hence government seizure of news media).

This explains why the AGEL has tried to achieve these three conditions to the best of its abilities. It has the right to assert today that this attitude has brought Lille students as much, if not more, real success as elsewhere, and this, by ensuring the solidest bases for the pursuit of action. Through their calm determination, Lille students have won the support of the public, and their union organization is reaching a considerable audience.

This also explains why it should have definitively refused strict obedience to directives given by the national leaders of the UNEF and of SNESUP. (like many AGE's on the national level). After having twice asked in vain for a national meeting to coordinate action, the AGEL decided not to ally itself with the UNEF and the SNESUP. demonstration directives, for Friday, May 24, and Monday, May 27. As regards the Friday, May 24 demonstration, the objective of which was questionable, they let it be rumored that it would be impossible for the organizers to avoid violent encounters with the police (we do not want a policy of "martyrs"), or to avoid these being used to change the nature of the student struggle and turn against them a large part of the public, whose support we had won. Events have proved that we were right— unfortunately—as regards the demonstration on Monday, May 27; it was not yet the day when clearly expressed demands would obtain satisfaction. Subsequently, although the support given the Paris demonstration by a certain number of organizations allowed it to take place without violence, it also gave it a rather ambiguous character by the fact that it went from actually inoffensive generalities on "socialism," to scornful criticism of the demands for which nine million strikers are fighting and which were called "dietary."

III. THE STUDENT UNION IS ORGANIZING THE STRUGGLE FOR SATISFACTION
OF STUDENT DEMANDS BY WHATEVER POLITICAL GROUP IS IN POWER

Let us summarize in a few words the platform for demands proposed by the AGE (cf. project for a resolution distributed to all participants in the general assemblies of the *corpos*):

—abandonment of all eliminatory measures,
—recognition of union and political freedoms,
—drafting by all interested parties of a project for a democratic educational reform, to be applied,
—necessary funding: 25% of the budget for National Education.
—immediate demands.

Each of these demands, which some might call "lukewarm,"

means forcing the government to make political decisions, calls into question general policy orientations (even though this is not our objective). For example, to increase the funding for National Education necessarily calls into question general allocation of the budget and requires expansion of the nation's wealth.

To clearly pose these demands to whatever political group is in power is to permit the students to discern for themselves the true nature of this power. We must denounce the "pseudo-revolutionary phrase" of those who declare that to enter into negotiations is a waste of time.[44]

On the other hand, the union cannot neglect the people's rights, especially in a period like the present one, when police repression is aimed at students: the demands made by all the students are an example. Nor can the union neglect the broad options that concern the entire nation. For example, the problem of the jobs open to students, that is to say, educational planning, is quite evidently linked to the real long-term needs of the country's economy. In this sense union action is also political. The students' interest in the "mino" (minority) conception of the UNEF[45] coincides with the national interest and objectively justifies worker solidarity. To take only two simple examples: students who demand an education the content of which would be such as to ensure them real professional training, as well as the possibility of adapting themselves to development of the sciences and techniques, are naturally in solidarity with the workers who are fighting for guaranteed employment and wages. Workers, whose sons only represent 10% of the students, are in solidarity with the students who are demanding study allowances and abolition of all the mechanisms that organize social segregation in the University. This also justifies the unity of inter-union action to which the AGEL has always attached the greatest importance. The "majos" (majority) who *say* the contrary know this very well, being themselves amply subsidized by the government.

The role of the union is to see to it that in this general context the students' interests should be taken into account. It differs from a political party in that each student remains free to choose between the different existing political organizations.

To summarize, and above all, in the present circumstances of great political instability, our force is in maintaining our demands and in imposing their satisfaction on whatever government there may be. This firmness is the only guarantee that students will not be cheated of the results of their combat.

Concretely, the AGEL proposes for discussion among union or

non-union students a platform of demands that will be common to the
entire student body in all disciplines.

This platform, which has been printed, is being distributed to
all AG participants in the *corpos* or schools. These *corpo* AG's should be
able, in our opinion:

1. to set up and adopt a platform of demands relative to the
problems of the students in the *corpo;*

2. to make a statement on the platform of demands proposed by
the AGE which, if correct, must be an expression on the highest plane
of the demands suited to the students in each discipline;

3. to make a statement on the ways and means proposed for
action in order to carry it out on a local as well as on a national level.

These proposals, which are in accordance with the above-stated
principles, open up new prospects for action, which belong in the context of continuity, but on a higher level than the action carried out
thus far. A certain number of recent occurrences—to begin with, the
decision of the striking workers taken yesterday (Monday) to continue
their action in order to make the government yield much more than it
had accepted during the weekend negotiations; the fact that a certain
number of AGE seem to share the AGEL's viewpoint as to the tactic to be
adopted; that the General Secretary of the SNESUP. should have had to
resign[46]—allow us to hope that student action may finally be destined
to support clear demands, the satisfaction of which would achieve real
democratization of the University.

A perceptible evolution of the national situation also allows us
to hope for an effective union of student-teacher-worker struggles that
would be expressed through a united front facing the government
which, let us not forget, has not played its last card, far from it.

—AGEL, Tuesday, May 28, 1968.

Conflict Inside the SNESUP.

The majority among the members of the SNESUP., an organization comprising about one-fourth of the higher education teaching body, was
founded on an actual alliance between sincerely reform-minded teachers (among them many Communist teachers) who thought that reforms
would only be achieved through the autonomous action of academics,
and others (the most representative was Alain Geismar) no less concerned with reforms, but who considered that, if need be, they would

"take to the streets" to obtain the necessary transformations. This alliance was in fact opposed to the orthodox Communists, who wanted the union to confine itself to action concerned with purely union demands, leaving the task of formulating projects for reform to the leftist political forces (PC and FGDS). On May 24, during the union congress, a motion that originated with the Communists, couched in prudent terms but in fact asking for association with the CGT demonstrations, carried more votes than did a motion of support for the line of the National Committee. This success was ephemeral, however. The congress was interrupted and its participants were supposed to join the student demonstration. One of the authors of the first motion, Herzberg, was elected General Secretary of the SNESUP. Meanwhile, on May 27, Alain Geismar had resigned. From the beginning the cleavage had been very evident: in the provinces particularly, the activity of the Paris committee had frequently been seriously questioned and the "classical" academics supported the orthodox Communists. The result was that at the Besançon *Faculté des Lettres* the directive for an unlimited strike sent out after the closing of the Sorbonne was rejected as unrealistic, and the section unanimously decided on an eight-day strike.[47]

But the paradox of the SNESUP. is perhaps to have appeared to be in the eyes of the public, and thanks particularly to the actual presence of Alain Geismar in the demonstrations and on the radio and television, a student organization (which explains its inclusion here); whereas, in reality, it was and could only be a teaching union. This ambiguity is also responsible in part for the conflicts that beset it, and that at the time of the Congress of March 14-16, 1969, ended up in the overthrow of the "leftist" majority by elements activated by the PCF.

Document 114

Motions Discussed at the SNESUP. Congress (May 24, 1968)

Motion No. 1
(Herzberg, Bennaroche)
At a time when workers, teachers, and students are carrying out their fight for recognition everywhere of union and political freedoms, along with their other demands, the expulsion order pronounced against Daniel Cohn-Bendit is a deliberate provocation by the government to provoke the students to anger and to permit further repression. The

SNESup. reaffirms that the teachers in higher education will tolerate no discrimination between the militants of the movement, whatever divergencies may exist among them. Workers, teachers, and students are engaged in an unprecedented strike movement. After the defeat of censure in Parliament they will find a way out of the political blind alley resulting from the absence of parliamentary-type solutions through a unified fight, especially against repression.

On the above bases the SNESup. Congress has authorized the union leadership to promote the meeting in Paris on May 24, 1968. *1,363 yeas.*

Motion No. 2
(Mohon, Innocent, Lecaille, Mouillaud)
The Congress considers that the oppositions and divergencies that have appeared, either between organizations or within the union, should not oppose the existence of a common front, which is the most urgent demand for the present.

It takes cognizance of the existence of different demonstrations for this afternoon. It delegates its General Secretary to do everything possible in order that this afternoon's demonstrations should be organized in common. It calls on all union organizations to show a spirit of the greatest unity, in order to reach an agreement.

The SNESup. Congress has delegated the National Board and the General Secretary to make every effort today and in the coming weeks to discuss with the union organizations of the working class the forms and means of future struggles which it would be advisable to organize in a spirit of broad union. *1,548 yeas.*

Closing Motion
(proposed by J. M. Lévy)
The SNESup. Congress:
    —*Takes cognizance* of the positive discussion that took place during the day of May 23, 1968, and of decisions made during the morning of May 24, 1968.
    —*Considers that,* as a result of events over which it had no control (demonstrations during the night of May 23–24, 1968, organizational difficulties in the provinces due to the general strike; activities of the National Board outside the Congress for preparation of the demonstrations of the evening of the 24th), continuation of the discussions could not take place under normal conditions and no significant decision is possible.

—*Decides in consequence:*

1. not to conclude the discussion on orientation by a vote, but to send the motions on the floor to all the sections;

2. to retain the outgoing action committee (CA) and National Board (BN), on the basis of yesterday's vote on the BN's activity report;

3. to authorize the national leadership to convoke an assembly of section secretaries as soon as circumstances permit, and to prepare as soon as possible the convocation of a regular Congress in the near future which would make a decision on union orientation and renew its leadership;

4. to pronounce this emergency Congress closed. *2,180 yeas, 743 nays,* and *13 abstentions.*

A Revolutionary Movement?

A former member of the PCF central committee, Jean-Pierre Vigier, who was also a leader of the *Comité Vietnam National,* had accepted legal responsibility for the newspaper *Action,* and he made no secret of his intention to organize a Castro-type movement in France. With this in view, an ephemeral *mouvement du 3 mai* was created at the Sorbonne. On May 28, a first attempt at coordination brought together, in addition to J.-P. Vigier and S. Depaquit (who had both been expelled from the PC on the 26th), A. Barjonet, A. Geismar, and G. Mury (a member of the PCMLF). This attempt failed. A second one, on June 1, led to a call for action and formation of a "planning committee" that included, in addition to J.-P. Vigier, members of the SNESup. (J.-P. Deléage), of the JCR (A. Krivine, D. Ben Saïd),[48] of the PCI ("Frankist" Trotskyite) (D. Lequenne), of the CGT Renault union (R. Benoît), and of the CAL's (J.-L. Weissberg). A second call, voted June 10, stated: "What was sorely lacking in May 1968 was unity among the revolutionaries, a sense of oneness in the common struggle. This cannot be achieved through well-meant resolutions but requires experience and discussion in common. Today, militant revolutionary workers, particularly those who belong to the PCF and to the CGT, must be given a real choice between revolution and reformist practice." And yet, no later than the evening of June 1, during a press conference held by the *Mouvement du 22 mars,* an argument took place between J.-P. Vigier and D. Ben Saïd (JCR leader and member of the *22 mars*) on

the one hand, and D. Cohn-Bendit on the other, as to the advisability
of creating such a movement "at the summit."

Document 115

A Revolutionary Movement for Today or Tomorrow
(Excerpts from the press conference
held by the *Mouvement du 22 mars* on June 1 at the Sorbonne)

D. COHN-BENDIT: The press conference taking place today is not a text
formulated by a Central Committee, but by a General Assembly of the
Mouvement du 22 mars, which took place this evening—that is to say,
breaking with all press conferences, whether of the Board of Directors
of the French Employers Association, of the Federation and Board of
Directors of the Federation of the Left or of the Board of Directors of
the PC. It was not a Board of Directors which took the decisions, but
the grass roots of the *Mouvement du 22 mars* who will speak for themselves; that is, that there will be differences of opinion today and we
are going to show them clearly. We are not playing the game of unity;
what we want is to show clearly that a movement such as the one that
has developed in France has come from the grass roots, and that in
every truly democratic movement—based on worker democracy—there
are differences of opinion, but these differences constitute the only possibility of overcoming the contradictions of the system.

We are quite aware that in France today there is a campaign to
demoralize the working class; this campaign of demoralization is orchestrated by the radio and the press. From such big headlines as
"Back to Work," they want people to believe that work has started
again. Example: they tell us that at Villeurbanne work has been resumed; it is true, as General de Gaulle would say, that in Villeurbanne
200 women paraded behind the French flag for a return to work; but
this company employs 5,000 people, so we would have to know if they
said in the news releases that there were 200 people who paraded with
the flag for return to work, or whether it was 4,800 people who refused
to return to work.

We are not saying that there might not be small companies
which are beginning, or which want, to return to work; but the government knows very well that that is not the problem; the problem
is to get the big companies running again, because it's the big companies that create the social climate. And so we come to the third problem, which is the problem of the strike. Obviously today, with headlines

such as "The Revolution Has Ended," they are trying to make us believe that the problem has been settled. To begin with, a very simple declaration must be made: nobody among us has ever claimed that the problem of the Revolution could be settled in one evening, or in one night: we are not romantics who believe that the Revolution took place overnight just because we built barricades.

What we are saying is, that today people want a revolutionary order. This revolutionary order is not only the order of the general strike, but it is the possibility of taking over production for the benefit of the working class. Some would like to substitute this order for the bourgeois order by means of elections. We are against all organizations which today are ready to abandon the fight in order to let bourgeois elections take place in an orderly fashion.

We say that for us it is not a matter of posing the problem of elections on all occasions but of continuing our revolutionary action— that is to say, of setting up overall concurrent authority in the factories (as was said about supplies) that will allow us to continue the fight as long as the workers themselves decide to continue the fight, and not as long as the leaders, whoever they may be, want to continue the fight.

Organize for the Revolution

Therefore, we are posing a problem here that is fundamental: the problem of revolutionary organization. Today we had a big meeting, with the launching of a revolutionary movement; on this subject we should say that there were present at this meeting several speakers from the JCR or from the Fourth International. Our aim is not controversy. We have comrades like Daniel Ben Saïd, who participated in the *Mouvement du 22 mars,* and who participated in this evening's meeting; this means that there are differences of opinion within the *Mouvement du 22 mars* on the party and on revolutionary organization, and that these differences are going to be discussed at the grass roots. We are aware that a problem of revolutionary organization has arisen among us today, that is to say a problem of coordinating all the action committees, whether revolutionary action committees, Sorbonne or Censier action committees, or action committees of the *Mouvement du 22 mars.*

What we are saying is that this move to create a movement has been initiated from above, and not at the base: we are not interested in re-posing the problem in terms of structuring the avant-garde; what is really needed is a technical organization that would see to it that all information is filtered through all the action committees. As a matter of fact, we condemn this move today—part of the *Mouvement du 22 mars* does, in any case—because it seems premature to us, and

because the problem has not yet been seriously discussed at the grass
roots. We know this may still take a certain time, but we know too
that it is the only real chance of discovering flexible forms of revolutionary action, unlike the rigid ones that all the revolutionary movements in France have produced thus far. In other words, we will invent
forms of organization involving a larger number of neighborhood and
factory AC's. These AC's are the foundation we propose for continuation
of the struggle. At the same time they will make possible a liaison between all the revolutionary movements.

Against Bureaucracy for Organization

D. BEN SAÏD: I believe that we have the opportunity this evening to
thrash out a basic problem.

Do the differences among us come from a problem of principle,
from a point of principle on the questions of organization? At the
Mutualité meeting (May 9), we were in agreement, and during the
entire genesis of the *Mouvement du 22 mars* we were in agreement.
As a political militant I was in agreement during those early days of
the movement in saying that we needed very flexible structures, complete spontaneity, total responsibility, and freedom for militants to
organize, to initiate projects, to propose political objectives—all at the
grass roots. But I do not—and this is a personal standpoint which commits no movement—I do not make lack of organization a permanent
principle. I believe that however much the informal character of the
movement has allowed this movement to grow, develop, and broaden
out as it has today, for several reasons, I believe that the political juncture requires a minimum of organization. This has become evident in
several committee discussions where at first any proposal of organization was rejected *a priori* as bureaucratic; then, as we became aware of
the enemy with whom we were faced and of the means at his disposal,
we saw that we could not continue in the same way and that a minimum of organization was necessary to continue the fight. Danny says
that we are in agreement on that; so I believe that on the point of
principle there is agreement.

The Committees

The important thing is to see just what in the present situation mo-
tivates and is the basis of our disagreement. I believe that we have
here a subject for very broad discussion; that tonight's fundamental
discussion, in my opinion, is perhaps the ambiguous nature of the
grass roots AC's. There are two sorts of committees: there are the committees that constitute the embryo, or at least the driving element in

the creation of organs of dual power, constituted by the strike committees, which are to a certain extent the neighborhood AC's inasmuch as they assume the task of ensuring supplies and control speculation and prices. Actually these committees are broad, soviet-type structures; all currents are represented at the grass roots and they play the role of dual power structures for better or for worse—but they do tend to play it, and they are a kind of committee and have the nature of a committee.

Similarly, superimposed or even within these committees, there is another type of organization which constitutes a reassembling of avant-garde militants on relatively homogeneous bases; I am not saying in total political agreement, but avant-garde militants who have in common an outlook on socialist revolution, certain fundamental principles—even theoretical ones, and who consider themselves as a minimum regrouping of avant-garde militants. I consider that these two types of regrouping have neither the same task nor the same future.

Against Manipulation

As regards the Charléty operation: we went to Charléty telling ourselves that for the first time, independent of the CGT and the PC, 50,000 avant-garde militants had come out who claimed to be socialists, and that was a fundamentally positive point. But underneath we saw the party maneuvers, we saw Mendès-France brought back in the wings at Charléty—so this political operation was denounced, and rightly so. But denunciation is not enough today; today we have proved that against the PC, and against the PSU and the reformists, there existed a really revolutionary force that had originated in the streets and in action. But this force, because of its lack of organization, does not constitute a pole of possible reference and the revolutionary militants were obliged to follow the UNEF initiatives.

It is a matter then of regrouping the avant-garde militants. A little while ago I participated in a meeting which called for such a regrouping. It is a matter of regrouping the avant-garde militants.

I should point out that that is not the main structure, the source from which all the grass roots organizations will stem, the way generations do from above. The revolutionary militants who must construct this movement are not old militants who have been able to resurface thanks to this operation; they are really people who have come together at the grass roots of the AC's and are ready to go further. They are even ready for the ebb tide, which can come within a few months if there is repression.

The Committees Have the Floor

D. COHN-BENDIT: What we are saying today is that to create this organization before there has been a broad discussion in the movement is a fundamental error; I am not saying that there must not be organization and we are aware of this problem; nor is it a matter of saying that by condemning today's initiative we condemn all organization, that we want simply to remain with the AC's, as they exist today. And Daniel's [Ben Saïd] criticism is entirely right when he says that if there is an ebb tide, the AC's risk being emptied of their content. But today the AC's are not without content; today they exist and first of all, through these AC's, discussion must be carried on. Actually these AC's will not remain committees with 150 to 200 members as they are today; they will become smaller. From that point on we shall really see the strength of the revolutionary movement, because we all know that any revolutionary movement in our consumer society becomes all at once a "show" movement that people watch; that is to say, that to participate in action is the thing to do, and we know quite well that many AC's were discouraged at first and frightened after General de Gaulle's speech because, actually, it was a threat. But it is the duty of revolutionary militants to continue in the AC's in order to avert this fear, because today these AC's are not yet without content; they can still formulate a line.

Ebb Tide

We are not afraid of ebb tide because it is at ebb tide that the revolutionary militants who desire to continue the struggle will stay on. These are the militants we will gather together when that time comes. But the present period is still euphoric: lots of people are able to join a movement; it is easy for any movement whatsoever, for any "groupuscule," to go fishing.

I think that we must not be afraid of difficulties, precisely so that an organization having every possibility for expression, for all revolutionary movements, might be set up. And perhaps there will be two of them; this does not mean that there will be two opposed revolutionary movements, but two revolutionary movements which will continue to have their own political lines, yet will be able to act together.

It is true that today the problem is much more laborious than any spectacular action like the action of the barricades, and that it is just as important. This is why I propose that organizational discussion should really take place in all the committees. And then we shall see if, actually, the grass roots' demand—the demand of the different movements—corresponds to a form of organization such as has been proposed for this evening, whether we will reconsider our position.

The Critical Mass

VIGIER: I personally agree with Ben Saïd and not with Cohn-Bendit. Our differences are not about the general political question. One of the remarkable aspects of this movement is its political convergence: rejection of elections, rejection of co-option. But I do not agree with him on the question of organization. Danny claims that organization is premature, whereas we have said this evening that we thought it was urgent.

Why? For three reasons. First of all because, faced with the Gaullist threat, it is extremely important, as I see it, immediately to present public opinion with a sufficient revolutionary critical mass to rally the mass of young workers, the mass of revolutionaries who today are ready to leave the neo-social-democratic line presented by the parliamentarist parties of the respectful opposition to H.R.M. de Gaulle, and who want to find another line. And we must not forget that the French working class—the mass of Communist militants and militants unionists of the CGT—are accustomed to work as a mass and that they need to belong to a sufficiently large organization in order to be able to lead their revolutionary action in the factories.

A *"communarde"* line containing a certain number of the ideas that Danny discussed this evening is apparent, and one of the essential tasks of the new MR (*Mouvement Révolutionnaire*) will be to organize theoretical research within the free confrontation of the revolutionary currents that will converge there.

Danny Cohn-Bendit says that it has been done from above; but I think it had to be done in part in order to unblock the present situation as well as the spontaneous bureaucracies that today refuse any political line, any political discussion.

The Cost of Time

WEBER[49]: Comrades, I will not repeat what comrades Ben Saïd and Vigier have just said. I believe that the disagreement which places us in opposition to Daniel Cohn-Bendit—I have just been corrected, to a part of the *Mouvement du 22 mars*—is not so much one of principle as one of method. With increasing emphasis they state that the present situation is a revolutionary one. They state it, but for a good number of comrades—and I hope that the *Mouvement du 22 mars* is not to be

counted among them—this assertion remains an abstract one which
has no bearing on the conduct of revolutionary militants.

Comrades, I agree perfectly with the part of the *Mouvement du
22 mars* that agrees with Daniel Cohn-Bendit; I agree to the measure
and to the method it proposes and I have this to say: this method is a
correct one in an absolutely calm period of the class struggle; in a normal period, in a natural period, in a period when events evolve slowly,
in a period when revolutionaries can take their time. In a period such
as ours, in a period of revolution such as the one we are living in, time
is not passing simply day by day, hour by hour—each minute counts
enormously. I believe that it is just plain common sense that there is
an acceleration of time which is quite considerable.

We Must Decide

Comrades, in the revolutionary period we are living in, each hour is
precious and we have no time for taking credit, we have no time to be
over-democratic; there are moments when we must know how to make
decisions, there are moments when we must even take the responsibility,
as revolutionary militants, of hastening the processes which are too slow.
(Applause) And on this subject, comrades, I would like to point out
the following: from the moment when the center of gravity of the fight
left the *facultés* and the student movement for the factories and the
worker movement, from this moment things changed completely. From
the moment when the center of gravity left the *facultés* for the factories, the problem that faced us was and is the following: either the
reformist organizations, the traditional organizations of the worker
movement—the Communist Party and the CGT—will be able to do
what they want and force the torrent back between its banks, or else
the student movement and the avant-garde will be capable of achieving
for themselves the organizational strength that will still permit them
to influence events.

The Workers Decide

D. COHN-BENDIT: For the moment it is not a question, in my opinion,
of saying whether we are socialists, libertarians, uncompromising Communists, or *"enragés"* Communists. It is a matter of saying whether,
yes or no, we can continue a revolutionary fight in France today—that
is to say, if we are ready *not* to enter into the game of false legality, as
I said, but to carry on the workers' fight as long as the workers continue to fight. It is actually not for us to decide if the workers must
continue; it is for them: it is they who will decide this in their factories. What we can do—and there is still the problem of our so-called

opposition to the Communist Party and to the CGT, I believe that now the assertion that we are playing the game of the Gaullist government, that we are hand in glove with the Gaullist government, collapsed after the last demonstration—what we are saying, and I believe that we will show it here this evening, is that differences of opinion do not and have never prevented a movement from continuing. So actually it is not differences with the Communist Party that prevent us from being in liaison (if we continue the action and if the worker movement continues the action), it is not a matter of our being followed by the working class; rather it is a matter for us to be in solidarity with the working class in the fight, as long as it does fight. We are saying that actually events are moving very fast. We did not say that it will take weeks and weeks before we can get organized; [here followed four incomprehensible lines] . . . but we repeat that it is not, and it is a good thing that the comrades should have posed it, and, first of all, that perhaps, to pose something, the only way was to create the problem of organization.

Very well. But from today on it is not, I believe, important to set a problem now, to say: we must go fast, very, very fast because the others are going very fast. In any case we know that the revolutionary movement has, you might say, certain barriers, that is, that it will not be able to develop endlessly because there exist traditional working class organizations; what we know therefore is that the revolutionary movement, by frequently taking the initiative, has been able to launch various movements, which is why it is called the spearhead. . . .

The "Internationale"

There is yet another problem we have to take up, which is the problem of the universities. I believe that we will have to pose the problem of relaunching the summer universities, to make all the Paris universities into reception centers for all the revolutionary youth in the world; that is to say, to force the government to let young German and Italian revolutionaries come to France, those who want to discuss with us in the *facultés*—because we can use the *facultés* as bases, dormitories, etc. —the revolutionary problems that exist on a European level. We now have a situation which allows us to occupy all the universities; let's make of these universities the European bases for discussion during the entire summer in order to develop the revolutionary movement on a European scale.

—Excerpt from *Action*, No. 4, June 5.*

* A more complete version of this discussion has been given by Jean-Louis Brau in *Cours camarade*, pp. 310–315.

An Anti-"Groupuscule": The *Mouvement du 22 Mars*

We have already watched the *Mouvement du 22 mars* emerge and go into action. It is represented here by two texts: a definition of its aims and forms of action, and a critical account (particularly as regards the Marxist-Leninists) of a militant experiment in a working class group. These texts are not always perfectly coherent as regards each other; the worker-oriented tone of the projected manifesto is patent, while the two last texts leave room for a more thoughtful view of action in the factory. As they stand, however, they define the thing that gives the movement its exceptional originality, which is its pedagogical attempt to create everywhere—outside established groups, outside university or union hierarchies,—collective speech areas in which the "implicit knowledge" of each group, whether student or worker, might become manifest. In point of fact, it is the first practical, modern attempt to create an anti-Leninist revolutionary movement, if need be by playing the author of *State and Revolution* against the author of *What Is To Be Done?*—which is a charter adapted to the conditions of the struggle in Russia at the time of the Czars, but which a catastrophic evolution has imposed little by little on all revolutionary movements. In other words, this was a first attempt, in an industrial society, to go beyond the Bolshevik model, usually considered as the one and only revolutionary model.

Obviously this attempt did not immediately resolve the contradictions between actual freedom of speech and the risk of manipulation by overt leaders and over-clever speakers, or between the constraints of action and permanent discussion. It is likewise hard to consider as mere lunatic babble such ideas as that of "rise" and "fall" of the government.[50] On the contrary, experience has shown that they were fundamental; this does not make them clear for all that. But the *22 mars* experiment, because it went beyond the other "groupuscules"—all of whom, more or less on a microscopic scale, were playing the Leninist card—remained the real gain of the May revolution. It should doubtless be pointed out that this was true only in the Paris area. In Lyons, or in Besançon, the *22 mars* was merely the emblem that designated one "groupuscule" among others.

Document 116

The *Mouvement du 22 mars* stems from a test of strength that took place in Nanterre in response to police provocation: the arrest of comrades because of their militant action in favor of the NLF in Vietnam.

Having begun in action, the 22 *mars* is at present based on a certain number of principles:

1. Revolutionary unity is achieved directly, in action and not around a political line or an ideology.

2. The preliminary condition of any revolutionary action is the right of everyone to speak.

The masses only act when they themselves speak directly, without intermediaries or representatives. This carries with it

—absolute plurality of tendencies and their right to be voiced;

—revocability of those who are answerable and rejection of any monopoly of news and knowledge.

3. This right of the masses to speak and act implies that they now create their own organs of expression and action:

—action committees at the grass roots, autonomous with respect to any political or union organization whatsoever.

4. Practical destruction of all types of partitioning prescribed by bourgeois society:

—abolition of cooperative-type divisions (student, worker, peasant, intellectual);

—abolition of the division of labor and of partitioning between manual and intellectual work;

—destruction of all hierarchy and all privileges for leaders founded on pseudo position or pseudo knowledge.

5. Worker management in business and industry on the basis of worker power, which can only be the power of grass roots committees.

Until now the 22 *mars* methods for action have been essentially:

—active political contestation: poster campaigns, political meetings;

—blocking the functioning of bourgeois institutions by occupying premises, sabotaging examinations (that is to say, the means for selecting future cadres for the bourgeoisie: its cops);

—combatting repression by direct action in the streets: meetings, demos, barricades, etc.;

—organization of the struggle: creation of revolutionary action committees, neighborhood committees, etc.

On all levels the struggle is revolutionary only if it attacks bourgeois and capitalist government and tends toward its destruction: for example, worker management is inseparable from abolition of bourgeois government.

These methods for action have value only as examples. They can in no case be systematized: in fact, the *Mouvement du 22 mars* denies

the existence of models for revolutionary action because it is the study
of local conditions that allows us to find suitable forms of action.

—[May]

Document 117

Apropos of an Experiment Made in a Plant by a Group of 22 Mars Comrades

We are not coming into the plants to "raise the level of workers'
awareness," to "make them aware" of the treason of the PC machine,
or even, "to put over" our ideas.

Such a concept implies that we have a monopoly of the truth
and that it is our duty to convey it to the workers. In reality, things
do not happen this way: the workers already know that the CGT only
"represents" their economic interests within bourgeois society, that it is
betraying the revolution.

The essential objective is that the workers themselves should be
able to express and speak of this implicit knowledge.

It therefore seems to us that our function as 22 *mars* militants
must be to allow the workers to speak outside the union machine.

Two mistakes must be avoided at all costs:

First, the one made by our Marxist-Leninist comrades, who
come with a series of pre-established plans:

1. "Serve the People":[51] that is to say, to present themselves
as sort of charitable clerics: "What can we do for you?" This orientation led certain m-l comrades to start "listening" to workers in a
certain way that made them implicitly or explicitly approve of the
worst stupidities simply because they were said by workers: for example, that all students are petty-bourgeois, etc. In our opinion, this
kind of non-leadership of the psycho-sociological type is the very
opposite of a political listening post, which demands that we commit
ourselves, that we show ourselves in such a way as to be placed in
a position not to tell "the truth," but to interpret the truth that appears
in the speech of the workers themselves.

2. "Students should place themselves under the leadership of
the working class": except that at present the working class *as a class*
is merely the class that is represented within bourgeois society by its
organizations. Such a directive, under present conditions, means:
placing oneself under the leadership of the CGT and the Party.

3. "Long live the CGT" is more than a mistake, it is a counter-

revolutionary policy to call for strengthening of the CGT at a moment when it appears to be the worst tool for oppression and alienation of the working class.

With regard to this, both our m-l and JCR comrades are making the mistake that consists in calling on grass roots union members (the "good guys") as opposed to their bureaucratic leadership. Experience has shown that the CGT functions as an institutional whole and that militants or delegates of the CGT remain prisoners of the logic of the organization.

The whole problem is to designate a collective speech area (the explicit objectives of which are neither for nor against the CGT) that might eventually be the place for contesting the machine.

We are not dealing with "rational" individuals who choose the "right" position, but with institutions and groups that have their own logic and their own function in a whole, and who super-determine the thoughts and wills of the individuals who are part of it: "They think, therefore I am."

Second, the mistake made by certain *22 mars* comrades who believed themselves obliged to answer questions asked by representatives of the machine, in meetings organized by them.

Meetings of this kind become transformed into dialogues (between deaf people) between "worker representatives" (i.e., the bureaucracies) and "student representatives" (i.e., the *22 mars* militants).

Such dialogues, taking place on terrain chosen by the machine, have as principle function—without the knowledge of the comrades who let themselves be taken in—the prevention of any possibility of independent expression at the grass roots. In our opinion, at the end of the meeting which took place at Elisabethville just before the clash with the CRS, Geismar and the *22 mars* comrades let themselves be caught in this trap. They spoke "in the name" of the *22 mars* and of the students; they told the truth after the CGT's lies, whereas, it was a unique opportunity to force the machine to recognize that *any* worker should be able to use the mike and to set up a sort of permanent meeting based on direct democracy.

Not having done this permitted the CGT to end the "debate" by saying: "we have let everybody express himself, now let's get down to work," etc. Fine—except that it just so happened that the workers were the only ones who could not really speak!

What then is the reference for *22 mars* militants when they get up to speak, if they want to be listened to other than passively by the workers? It is not only because the *22 mars* is supposed to be characterized by the actions it undertakes, or because it does not cultivate "small ideological differences." It is essentially because at its best it is a place where the floor is not monopolized by either the leaders or by grass roots "representatives" (independently of all reference to a so-called democracy of which the exterior signs are: the AG, election of governing bodies, reports and minutes, votes, etc.).

When all is said and done, our participation in the discussion has no other aim than to allow workers to forge a similar tool for themselves.

They will then have the possibility, despite bureaucratic machines, to express the true reasons for their strike and to invent their own methods of action.

This tool, as well as these methods of action, cannot be given them from the outside. Nevertheless, there is no question of our listening passively to the workers and then returning their own image to them, which is the same as that forged by the Party and the union. "The workers have the floor" cannot be a slogan. In the present structure of the CGT there will always be workers to say that they have nothing to add to what has been said in their name by the union representatives. There are no ready-made directions for use: it is a matter of inventing on the spot, at the opportune moment, the concrete initiative that will allow designation of this "speech area" for the workers *to become a fact.* The process that will then be thrown into gear and taken over by a nucleus of workers inside the plants is the only one that can effectively break the inhibiting hold of the organizations.

—Excerpt from *Tribune du 22 mars,* June 8.

Notes

1. Although their national secretary, Thierry Pfister, had published in *Le Monde* dated May 8, a relatively comprehensive article with regard to leftist students, at a date when *le Populaire* was hardly less violent than *l'Humanité;* but nobody read it.

2. In an otherwise hasty and mediocre book (J. A. Penent, *Un printemps rouge et noir,* pp. 13–26) there is a rather apt characterization of certain "groupuscules"; R. Gombin's book, *Le Projet Révolutionnaire,* although apparently scientific, with a large number of precise references, turns out to be a bit disappointing, having been written without inside experience of the events.

3. November 17–25, 1967.

4. Title of the principal publication of the *Union des jeunesses (marxiste-léniniste) de France.*

5. In reality this march was the first to have been authorized since the

banning of the traditional May 1 procession by the Laniel government in 1954. Its relatively tense atmosphere had struck most observers.

6. In fact the FER refused to participate in the May 3 demonstration, but on May 16 had the honor of organizing the first student march to the Renault plants; cf. D. Singer, *Prelude to Revolution,* p. 153, n. 1.

7. Péninou and Kravetz, former leaders of the FGEL, moving spirits of the MAU.

8. This refers to the call actually written by the FER, and which appears above, Chapter II, pp. 155–156.

9. This sentence seems to contradict the preceding one.

10. This refers, of course, to a committee composed exclusively of FER members, and constituted on the occasion of an attempted raid against the UNEF leadership.

11. In the documentation which we have assembled we have found only one CMLF leaflet written in Lyons. The "Parti communiste révolutionnaire de France" by V. Keukidjian, which published the *Cahiers du communisme révolutionnaire* and called itself Marxist, Leninist, and Stalinist, can be completely ignored.

12. The m-l militants are the most sensitive of all to the arguments of P. Bourdieu and J.-C. Passeron, who accused the students of being the "heirs" to the culture of the privileged classes. At the time of the revolt at Stanford in June 1968, which ended in a student victory and a general amnesty, a Maoist professor declared: "Your movement is an attempt on the part of the ultra-privileged to obtain other privileges. If you are serious, your main political action must take place outside the campus." Cf. *The Washington Post* of June 30, 1968.

13. We must also recall the role of the m-l militants in the action of the *Comités Vietnam de base,* and in the first action committees of the *lycée* students: the grass roots committees were distinguished from the national CVN organization by their determination to work from the grass roots and thus to place themselves "at the service" of the Vietnamese people. Cf. above, Chapter I, p. 72, the criticism of this action made by the JCR, a member of the CVN.

14. Cf. above, Chapter II, pp. 201–205 (French edition only).

15. Allusion to L. Althusser and to his direct disciples. On the notion of "theoretical practice," cf. the article by J. Deprun in *Raison Présente,* No. 6, January–March 1968.

16. It will be noted that there is nothing said here about the *Cahiers pour l'analyse,* a review influenced by the disciples of L. Althusser and J. Lacan at the *Ecole Normale Supérieure.*

17. Wrong, to our knowledge.

18. Note the "populist" terminology.

19. Note here the use of the classic Communist vocabulary.

20. Cf. below, Chapter IV, pp. 299–300.

21. It should be said here, since this mistake is frequently made, that Alain Geismar was no longer a member of the PSU in May 1968 (contrary to what may be read on p. 258 of J. Gretton's *Students and Workers,* or in G. Lefranc, *Le Mouvement syndical,* p. 229), and that in spite of what Gretton further writes, Pierre Mendès-France *was* a member of the PSU.

22. These ideas are very close to those developed by the MAU and the Nanterre movement.

23. *Association générale des étudiants de Clermont.*

24. Cf. J. Julliard, in *Esprit,* June–July 1968; see also Paul Goodman, "The Black Flag of Anarchism," *The New York Times Magazine,* July 14, 1968. Ma-

deleine Rebérioux, "La constante libertaire dans la tradition populaire française," *Politique aujourd'hui,* March 1970.

25. See nevertheless the very fine text reproduced above, pp. 236–238.

26. A fire was started at the Stock Exchange (*Bourse*) on May 24.

27. Cf. below, Chapter VIII, p. 493.

28. It is difficult to understand what an "apolitical color" might be.

29. This tactic was used effectively; it is by no means characteristic of the *"enragés,"* but on the contrary, quite traditional.

30. This concern for clandestinity explains, counteractively, the interpretations given the student movement with its "strongarm men" and its concealed organizers. This text was broadly distributed in a form usually limited to its first seventeen "points." The Neuilly Civic Action Committee sent it out at the beginning of June with the following title: "How the Masses Were Taken In"— How to Organize Revolution. (Excerpt from the Mao Tse-tung book, which makes it possible to understand present events.) As for M. Marcellin, Minister of the Interior, he coldly reproduced these seventeen points in his book, *L'Ordre public et les groupes révolutionnaires* (Plon, 1969, p. 106) attributing them to revolutionary students. This false report having been denounced, there followed a discussion (*Le Monde,* May 25–26, 1969).

31. Cf. above, p. 168.

32. R. Garaudy had also been behind the resolution of the Political Bureau, dated May 12. Cf. below, Chapter IX, p. 555.

33. This concession to the vocabulary of the May Revolution must be pointed out.

34. This figure, which was generally cited in May, was somewhat reduced after the elections (nine million, according to René Andrieu, Editor-in-Chief of *l'Humanité,* in *le Nouvel Observateur,* 15–22 September 1968). There was the same evolution on the part of the CGT. On June 15 its National Confederation Board sent greetings to the "ten million workers, men and women, who for three to four weeks had taken part in the general strike movement . . ." (*le Peuple,* special issue, p. 132); while Henri Krasucki, Secretary of the CGT speaks of "nine million" (preface to the book by Maurice Cohen, *Le Bilan social de l'année 1968,* Paris, 1969, p. 5). The data analyzed by Gérard Adam: "Étude statistique des grèves de mai–juin 1968," *Revue de sciences politiques* 20.2 (February 1970), pp. 105–119, give the figure of six million strikers, not including the teaching body and the rest of the civil service workers. The striking *lycée* and University students are of course not deducted from this figure.

35. *Révolte étudiante, mouvement politique, chute du pouvoir?,* May 23; *Elections bourgeoises ou Action révolutionnaire,* June 17.

36. The Bordiguists published a pamphlet, "Principaux tracts diffusés par le Parti Communiste International (programme communiste) en mai 1968," Marseilles, 1968 (stencil), in which our document is dated May 15, which we consider to be highly improbable since no allusion is made in it either to the night of the barricades or to the events of May 13.

37. Trotskyist tendency led by Michel Raptis (Pablo), who played an important role on behalf of the NLF during the Algerian Revolution and during the first period of self-management. In 1965 the *Pablists* (publication: *Sous le drapeau du socialisme*) separated from the *Frankistes:* placing the accent on self-management, they favor the Yugoslav experience and deeply oppose the Chinese Communist Party. They have also published a pamphlet, *Situation révolutionnaire en*

France? Their official title is *"Tendance marxiste révolutionnaire de la quatrième Internationale."*

38. *Ejercito de Liberacion Nacional.*

39. Cf. *Le Monde* of May 28. This definition of government policy, even though out of date, is not entirely incorrect as regards the first fortnight in May. But the UNEF tried to resist this temptation, which was also proposed by certain PCF leaders (among them, R. Garaudy).

40. Four points that followed the three points of the first few days.

41. The *Mouvement du 22 mars* had proposed that injured students be passed without examinations. The UNEF did not entirely back this rather curious suggestion, but its comments are totally lacking in precision.

42. Which presumes that through a fundamental change the teachers in secondary education would be recruited on the strength of their degree (as are part of the elementary school teachers) and not through competitive examinations.

43. This coordinating committee, which was a result of the May events, was made up especially of ESU and JCR militants.

44. This text was made public right after the Grenelle Agreements were signed.

45. We recall that the "minos," the old Left minority of the UNEF, won out in 1956.

46. Alain Geismar resigned on May 27.

47. On the same day, however, the majority of the section rejected a condemnation of "student agitation, at least as it developed from directives given in advance by various groups [they do not say 'groupuscules'] at the Nanterre *faculté."*

48. The JCR later resigned from the "planning committee."

49. Leader of the JCR.

50. Cf. below, Chapter VI, p. 378.

51. Cf. the texts printed above, pp. 265 ff.

V

Forms and Means of Action

The May–June movement broke with every type of political practice that had characterized French society since the big strikes in 1947–1948, and even since the Liberation. The only time anything like it had seemed possible was in connection with the Algerian war, and then on an infinitely smaller scale.[1] From a practical standpoint this break was felt in the invention or reinvention of forms of action such as "tough" demonstrations, occupation of University buildings, strikes *plus* occupation, and autonomous means of expression. These new forms of action were not manifestations of "avant-gardist" directives, but assertions of a collective consensus which was trying to respond directly and immediately to the problems of the moment. Through a certain type of violence the movement showed up social and police repression; through occupation of the *facultés* it confirmed student sovereignty over study premises; lastly, through a new type of action publications and other press forms, it tried to show and express non-parliamentary democracy functioning in a "state of nature."

Violence

The problem of violence provided the original break: for the first time, after being attacked by the police on May 3, students counterattacked and, at the same time, rediscovered the use of paving stones. Like the *Sciences-Pô* student, whose text follows, each one of them on this occasion could indulge in his own "reflections on violence."

The rapidity of events made it impossible to canalize and control violent confrontation once the political decision had been taken to resist police violence. "Everybody his own marshal," Cohn-Bendit said on the evening of May 10, and the next day Jacques Sauvageot added, "Molotov cocktails are one element of the situation."

The fact is that in the political process, as analysis by the 22 *mars* militants showed, violence occurs on two different levels (and is possible on a third). At the level of "exposure of repressive structures," by such actions as signs denouncing the presence of police in the *faculté,* writing on *faculté* walls, etc., in order: a) to show up the repressive solidarity between *faculté* and governmental authorities, and b) to demonstrate that the cloistered world of the *faculté* does not escape the essential dominants of a class society and its particular aspect, which is police repression.[2] On this level the action of the Nanterre students took its examples from the students of the German SDS: as for instance, Rudi Dutschke's interruptions of a West German Protestant church service to speak on Vietnam. This is not in fact a matter of violence against persons, but of violence against things: at this stage the institution being denounced responds immediately.[3]

The use of violence in a pedagogical sense (where through a concrete example militants see the internal, implicit characteristics of the system) is fundamentally different from violence conceived as self-defense.

The violence of the barricades was no longer merely a proof, it was a political response to a political problem—occupation of the streets. On May 10 the militants who refused to disperse when ordered to do so by the police, broke with the tacit rule that consists of disbanding a demonstration before confronting the police. This break created a second political trauma even greater than the one that had been caused by occupation of the *facultés.* At this particular juncture the thousands of students and young workers attacked by the police stood for much more than just themselves, and actually the order for a general strike on the 13th stemmed directly from this confrontation.

Under these conditions, and once the dynamics of self-defense had been primed, the militants were bound to rationalize and politicize their problems. Organization of self-defense at Flins was set up through a political, concrete liaison with militant workers: it was in the symbiosis of the "technical" experience of the students faced with police attacks, and of the political determination of militant workers that this liaison took place. Generally speaking, in spite of this theorization of the problem of self-defense, resistance was largely spontaneous.

The leaflets that follow, containing advice and suggestions for militants, lack precision and are often contradictory. In fact, in the matter of self-defense, they present two conflicting positions that are expressions of more general political "lines":

1. The *"22 mars"* position: the problem of self-defense concerns all militants; in concrete situations solutions are found spontaneously.

2. The position of the various political groups: self-defense can only be the result of a well-constructed organization. Otherwise it can lead to contradictory or even dangerous actions (example: police trap barricades).

The leaflet entitled "Reflections on Violence" will be followed by one in which resistance to police violence is presented in both its practical and political dimensions. Lastly, it should be recalled that although "CRS-SS" was the characteristic slogan of a generation that had no knowledge of the German ss (or of the Algiers "paras"), the students tried several times to appeal to their "CRS comrades" in a document picked up the day the Sorbonne was retaken, in one addressed to "security workers" before the night of the barricades, in a leaflet entitled "CRS, They're Deceiving You," which got little distribution; and in another, printed at the Odéon (3,000 copies), that was later scattered about in front of local police stations.[4]

Document 118

Reflections on Violence

by R. Billon

Violence is one of the questions of the day. On page one of the newspapers, first in the hit parade of the month's chatter.

It is the main subject for indignation on the part of that category of pompous bipeds who feign astonishment that our "fine young people" should leave Sheila for Marcuse or for Che Guevara.

This odd species, which alas is not yet about to disappear, always finds in its glorious past or in its long experience, arguments as respectable as they are irrefutable to stigmatize the ill-considered excesses of the students. Inspired by good intentions, soaked in humanism the way others are in alcohol, it protests solely against the violence of "certain *enragés*," against "Germano-Zionist" mongrels, the student "mob," those "little bourgeois intellectual bums" who play at being revolutionaries and amuse themselves by smashing cars or punching the noses of the police.

The only reason they build barricades is in order not to take their examinations, believe me! What they need is a good war! They should all be sent to the reform school!

Actually, to tell the truth, a real provocation to murder directed at the gentlest of upper class school boys.

Having said this, the above-mentioned zoological species finds it normal to send its sycophants to clean up the Latin Quarter by means of countless "gadgets" and combat gas!

We'll fix this riff-raff of students and workers! We'll fix these bed-fouling trouble makers! And modestly veil the sickening scenes taking place in police stations, or at the Beaujon interrogation Center. That's not nice, and it's improper to speak about it. "Besides, you know, over-reaction of this kind is, of course, too bad, but it's inevitable. . . ."

But the big scandal for this strain of cattle is less the violence done to people than the attacks on that tin calf of our civilization, the sacrosanct jalopy. The bourgeois press that reflects this state of mind clearly proved this after these nights of tears and suffering, by touching sensitive souls with the dramatic tale of the deaths of dozens of those piles of scrap metal. A hundred or so wounded was merely the revolt of overexcited peasants on the loose! But a dozen burnt-out cars is an insurrection, it is the devastating flood of nihilism, an obscene, traumatizing gesture, the negation of all values.

And why be surprised, why not see in it the good conscience of these crusaders for public morality: they are the ones who vilify the indecencies of non-reproductive love while accepting permanent rape of the individual conscience and personality through publicity. Morals must not be confused with commerce. All exhibitions of the anatomy are innocent if they eulogize the youthfulness and airiness of a "brief" or other "panty"; all the ways to make love, standing, seated, in front, in back, or on the side, are displayable, if they remind the participants that there is a time for everything, and that a good watch is necessary if we want to be on time for our jobs.

Morality: comrade, if you locate any such cancerous
ectoplasm, don't hesitate to set fire to it.

—Excerpt from *Renaissance, 68,* Information Bulletin No. 7 of *Sciences Pô* (School of Political Science), May 30, 1968.

Document 119

How to Avoid Blackjacking

Material
Carry in your pocket *from the very start* of any demonstration:
    —A pair of motorcycle spectacles (about $1.00).

—A surgery mask: either the kind used by surgeons, or one you
make yourself of cotton gauze dressing 20″ long and 8″ wide
(comes in rolls) with a wad of absorbent cotton in the middle.

—If you "feel" the need to put the mask in place, it is necessary
to tie the two ends of the gauze in the back of your neck.

If possible, get yourself a motorcycle helmet or just any plain
aluminum container stuffed with newspapers and equipped with
some sort of chin strap—even though this object for elementary protection may be considered by some as an offensive instrument. To avoid
a warrior-like or ridiculous appearance in the eyes of the general
public, carry this instrument on your belt. Besides it will be the
best way to expose *provocateurs*.

—Contrary to what you might think, you must wear very full
clothing or top garments: raincoats, capes, old-fashioned long
coats, duffle coats, etc.

—Instead of ordinary shoes, wear well-fitted boots, *espadrilles,*
or tennis shoes, but to avoid being easily recognizable, particularly at night, don't make them so white they're like a
brand on the rear end of a sheep.

—Protect your shoulders and a part of the back of your neck
with comfortable-sized newspapers like *France-Soir,* or *Figare-
muche* [*Le Figaro*] by opening them at the middle of the
theater and movie page and folding them once lengthwise,
then a second time, in the shape of a very wide open "V,"
in order for it to cling to the form of your shoulders. Then slip
the two ends into the upper part of your sleeves and let the
"point" formed by the last fold fall well over the base of your
neck. The thickness should correspond to your blackjackable
epidermis, that is, about 25 sheets of bourgeois press.

A few things to remember when the police, who are more
attentive to orders than to the dictates of courage, feel "obliged" to
intervene from behind their little 14th of July knickknacks.

A city like Paris is more thickly wooded than a virgin forest.

A man on foot *advances much faster* than any kind of vehicle.

At all cost, avoid letting yourself get caught in a police trap
(free access to the Pont-Neuf during the night of the 24th, for instance).

Avoid also being *pinned down*.

Once the first shock of psychological action was over, during the
first demonstrations, the *barricades were mediaeval.*

A pretext for provocation used by the police.

They are absolutely no protection.

They quickly antagonize people.

Despite the equipment and enormous means of the "other side" they are weighted down with their own material.

They are old and want to reach retirement age as peacefully as possible.

They work for dough while each one of us is fighting to live like a man and not like a mercenary of any kind whatsoever.

Dispersion

Everybody must know *before* the demonstration what he must do *afterwards, where and how* he is supposed to break up.

In order to avoid rat hunts, systematic blackjacking, and kidnapping of isolated persons (those who wear white shoes, for instance), break up in groups of 50 to 100 maximum at an intermediary meeting place where adequate decisions will be made.

This dispersion must take place in the form of a star and with very jagged curves even if the police try to canalize, in order to avoid a police trap. The most recent events prove that the police are practically powerless when faced with very mobile groups who disperse throughout the entire city.

Up to the present, given their currently respected status as sanctuaries, the various *facultés* have never been used as fortresses, but as bases.

These are the places where you fortify your ideals, where you sleep, you rest, you eat, you talk.

On the other hand, a certain vigilance must be applied to spotting undesirable characters who worm their way into the buildings: all kinds of provocators, passersby, bums, plainclothesmen, nuts, etc., in order to be able to throw them out at the first warning (check for, among other things, mikes, ties, *boutonnières,* transmitters, etc.).

Demonstration

In case this demonstration can no longer take place in a normal procession:

Use the outline sketched under the heading *Dispersion.* Each small autonomous group must then be equipped with transistors and have two or three liaison men.

Work in sectors with autonomous demonstration groups around a fixed point and in a radius of 500 yards around this point, in such a way as always to be able to come together again. In principle, it is then the police who are pinned down and who become vulnerable, especially if you are careful to make them appear ridiculous. It is better to ridicule them than to insult them (paint, shit, honey, stink balls by the dozen, etc.).

Make them look like something out of a carnival.

Make people laugh at them with you.

Absolutely *avoid* useless destruction.

Explain the student movement each time it is possible to do so, using *very simple language.*

Give figures: We are so many, there are so many unemployed, a room costs so much; there are so many students from worker families, etc.

With regard to individuals in the Communist Party and certain national union boards: *do not attack these organizations generally, but only the individuals in question.*

In spite of the bitterness we feel: *continue to stress unity with workers and peasants.*

Try to explain and *convince* any man or group of men, from the postmaster to the policeman, not forgetting firemen and road workers, particularly government employees.

For this, avoid being partial; let the others speak first and refute later.

A few absolutely irrefutable ideas:

Nothing that is happening among the workers would have happened without the student revolt; but nothing would have happened either if the economic situation on the human level had not become unbearable to everybody at the *same time.* The movement is a youth movement and youth forms a class in the same way as the traditional classes because a large part of their present and future situations converge upon a tremendous question mark. Analysis by old people is an analysis based on experience, whereas we must invent new structures.

—[About May 24, 1968, distributed especially at
the demonstration of the 29th.]

Document 120

MEMBERS OF THE POLICE FORCE
*You have no real possibility
for striking or for protesting*

Bourgeois society obliges members of the police force to exert fierce repression on students and other workers, which the police have no right to evade under threat of unemployment.

But this same bourgeoisie, in its press, is the first to condemn the violence for which it is itself responsible.

MEMBERS OF THE POLICE FORCE
DON'T LET YOURSELVES BE FOOLED ANY LONGER

—CAR [Odéon, May 16, 1968].

Document 121

CRS, Gardes-Mobiles, *You Are Being Duped!*

Yes, the government is making dupes of you just as it is of us: Peyrefitte promised that if Wednesday's demonstration took place calmly, the Sorbonne would open on Thursday. Nothing happened, but the Sorbonne is still closed.

What, then, does the government want? It is clear that it wants further confrontations, that it is looking for an escalation of violence. With this goal, the government is using you to repress the demands of those who are asking for a University open to sons of workers, which could receive your children too.

This concerns you.

The students are resolved to fight to the end to achieve victory for their demands!

Refuse to be the blind agents of fascist repression!

Don't oppose those who are fighting for a democratic university.

—University Action Committee [May 9, 1968, distributed the 10th].

Occupation of the *Facultés*

The second political break brought about by the movement consisted in occupation of *faculté* buildings, which began on the evening of the 11th in Paris, at Censier, and on the 13th at the Sorbonne. An action committee leaflet dated May 14 furnished historical justification for these occupations: "in 1936, workers occupied the factories—in 1968, students occupied the *facultés*." This new form of action was sparked by the June 1936 occupations, but certain foreign examples, especially Italian, contributed to making this model even more timely. The goal of these occupations was not merely protest and reorganization of the

University. They wanted to be more political, to become an open University in which workers, students, and teachers would compare their experiences. The following belated text (produced by the occupation committee) illustrates retrospectively the political intention of the militants who were occupying the Sorbonne.

Document 122

The Evening of May 13

After a week of fighting, when we reoccupied the Sorbonne, we also knew that it would never be the same again. These events ushered in a new era for the University.

While the general strike and factory occupations were developing, hundreds of thousands of students were occupying all the universities in order to organize them as red bases for support of the worker struggle and as centers for analysis and discussion of University problems.

Today, now that the majority of workers has momentarily returned to work, where do we stand? Assemblies, commissions, and committees almost everywhere have discussed University reform, the principles that should govern its functioning, and the type of teaching that could go on there.

We have witnessed the collapse of academic authority, the disappearance of Rectors, the retirement of Deans. Being now in charge, we have heard professors, former lords of the manor, former owners, protesting their sudden desire for dialogue!

At the same time that we opened the University to the problems and tasks of the moment, we set to work in the firm desire to make a clean sweep. But we are still far from having done it. Some texts have been prepared, but they are very incomplete; some ideas have come forth, but they remain still only in outline.

In any case, everybody knows that under present conditions a simple reform of University structures will solve none of the problems posed. By declaring the Sorbonne a people's University we have done nothing, all told, but express this idea: before making changes within the University, we must know for whom and for what it will serve.

More than seven centuries were needed for the priests, then the bourgeoisie, to build their University. It is normal that in one month, when there was so much to do, we should not have succeeded in setting up this workers' University we all want, all the more so since the magnificent combat of the workers, which strengthened our power in the *facultés,* is momentarily obliged to fall back.

That is why our job is not to organize another university year, but to prepare ourselves for the movement's second wind. That is also why we make the following proposals:

1. That the end of the old University regime and all the institutional forms it entailed be officially recognized, as well as our determination never to return to them.

2. That the Sorbonne cease to function as a University during the coming months in order to allow serious study of the various problems under discussion. Demolishing five centuries is well worth six months of study.

3. That the Sorbonne be declared a "University in the Service of the Revolution."

a) That during six months, not only university reform should be studied at the Sorbonne, but especially all the political questions that condition it. The general problems facing society will be analyzed, studied, and discussed. Seminars will be organized, investigations will be made. The collaboration of informed persons will be requested. Reports will be worked out. At the Sorbonne, discussions will take place on social housing, employers' power, underdevelopment as well as imperialist wars, publicity, and immigrant workers.

b) That the Sorbonne should be one of the bases from which the daily action of militants is organized. That here the latter can meet to draw the first conclusions concerning the actions undertaken.

c) That students from all the European universities be invited to the Sorbonne during the summer. In Berlin, Rome, Turin, Madrid, Barcelona, everywhere in Europe, students have carried on struggles similar to ours during the past months. Today the time has come for them to exchange their experiences and to coordinate their action. This summer the Sorbonne will be the site of our cooperation.

d) That the Sorbonne be a center open to workers, skilled and unskilled, peasants, and office workers desirous either of giving their opinion on the University of tomorrow, or on the problems under discussion, or of using the Sorbonne for their own struggles against capitalism in their factories or in their professions.

4. That the Sorbonne should be run during these six months by a council composed of students, teachers, and members of the staff, who would be revocable at all times and replaceable in rotation. This council would be in charge of administrative and technical management (with coordination within the *faculté*) and of defense, if re-

quired. It would be assisted by any group considered useful by the different assemblies. All the administrative resources in the *faculté* will be placed at its disposal; this implies that no budgetary impediments to the normal functioning of the "Sorbonne in the Service of the Revolution" will be accepted.

All who are in agreement with these proposals are asked to demonstrate everywhere, to proclaim these ideas, discuss them, define them, and promote discussions in all the assemblies and commissions. Thousands should join the "Committee for the Sorbonne in the Service of the Revolution," which will prepare a large Constituent Assembly to take place within a few days, in agreement with the present Occupation Committee and the steering committees of the assemblies for each discipline.

THE OLD UNIVERSITY REGIME IS DEAD
HELP CONSTRUCT A NEW ORDER!

—[Distributed June 11, published in *Action*, No. 9, June 13].

Actually, with the movement on the wane, the discussions that had led a certain number of militants to agree on such a text had been extremely keen. Following are some of the first texts to describe the Sorbonne occupation[5] and show the "organized spontaneity" that prevailed there. From the first day the question of the material organization of the occupation was up for discussion. This occupation had been made possible by the existence of certain general services, such as the duplicating service, in which the occupation committee (first described as a "technical" body) proceeded from a general assembly composed of some 5,000 people who met every evening in the main lecture hall and, every evening, re-elected an occupation committee.[6] The major political theme of the moment was that the *faculté* should be open—a place where workers and students together might seek and find new political solutions to their problems.

Document 123

Whether or not you are connected with the University, you can discuss what you want with anybody you want. But coordination with the OCCUPATION COMMITTEE and the GENERAL ASSEMBLY allows for wider discussion.

If the subjects posted do not suit you, organize a discussion yourselves in the following manner:

a) Find an empty room.

b) Put up a sign indicating the subject.

c) Inform the OCCUPATION COMMITTEE OF THE SORBONNE (Staircase C, 1st Floor: Léon Robin Library). Give details: place, subject, time discussion will begin, so that we can answer requests for information.

d) In order that the results of the discussion may be publicized,
—*Write a motion* which you will present to the general assembly.

—*Write a leaflet* which you can have distributed in the Sorbonne. For typing and printing, see the SECRETARIAL OFFICE (Staircase C, 1st Floor, in the hall on your left).

e) Give 50 copies of this leaflet to the Press Office (Staircase C, 1st Fl. Philosophy Professors' Office) and to the Coordination Committee.

f) Inform the OCCUPATION COMMITTEE when you have finished using the room.

—[May 14, 1968].

Document 124

1936: Workers Were Occupying the Factories
1968: Students Are Occupying the Facultés

Today the bourgeois University is collapsing. Action committees have been created in the *facultés,* which are finally open to workers, in order to pursue the fight begun on the barricades.

The goal of these committees is:
—*To give information about the true circumstances of the repression by exposing the lies of the bourgeois press.*
—*To re-define forms for a common struggle against oppression in all its forms; inside as well as outside the University.*
—*To militate against the exploitation of which workers and students are victims.*

Today we have upset the government by giving it "the hardest slap of its career," and by reasserting unity of students and workers.

The government has given in on minor points; we are only beginning our common fight.

There exists
—*an action committee*

—*a coordinating committee*
—*a* CLIF *(comité de liaisons interfacs)* open to everybody.

YOU BELONG WITH US

COME IN LARGE NUMBERS TO THE FACULTÉS

—Action Committee [May 14, 1968, 2 P.M.].

Very soon general service problems began to accumulate: information inside the Sorbonne had to be organized, available lecture halls found, food had to be brought in for the militants on permanent duty. The occupation committee, which was re-elected every day, was not able to guarantee continuity, in addition to which situationist factions had gained a certain influence. On Thursday the 16th, the latter distributed a leaflet denouncing the "bureaucrats" who disagreed with their slogans and working methods. On the evening of Friday the 17th the occupation committee, having received a minority vote, was replaced by a new committee composed of former leaders of the FGEL (Sorbonne UNEF section) and militants of the MAU, the JCR, and the UJC(m-l). The FER, which refused to participate, defended the position taken by a strike committee from the union sections. The may 19 report gives the "situationist" version of the facts.

Document 125

Existing Services[7]

ENTRANCE HALL OF THE MAIN AMPHI
Reception, information (afternoons only).
STAIRCASE C
At the foot of the staircase.
Information, guidance.
1st floor left.
Room 1: assignment of lecture halls.
Room 2: coordination.
Room 3: reception and liaison (red armband).
Room 4: main office.
1st floor right.
Room 2: inter-*faculté* liaison (CLIF).
Rooms 3 and 4: liaison with *lycée* students (CAL).
2nd floor left.

1st room to the right: cultural services (organization of movies, concerts, music hall, theater, etc.).

2nd room to the left: press.

3rd room to the right: liaison with workers.

MAIN HALL RUE DES ECOLES.

Food and drinks.

CENTER COURT OPPOSITE THE CHAPEL.

Red Cross.

2nd floor right.

Room 3: investigation of repression.

—[May 16th?]

Document 126

Report on the Occupation of the Sorbonne

Occupation of the Sorbonne, which began on Monday May 13, inaugurated a new period in the crisis of modern society. Events now taking place in France foreshadow the return of the proletarian revolutionary movement in every country. What had already progressed from theory to street fighting has now gone on to a struggle for power over the means of production. Enlightened capitalism believed that it had finished with the class struggle, but it started up again! The proletariat no longer existed: here it is again!

By giving up the Sorbonne the government counted on pacifying the student revolt, which from inside its barricades had been able to hold a Paris quarter an entire night, and the police had had great difficulty in retaking it. The Sorbonne was turned over to the students so that they might finally discuss their University problems in peace. But the occupants immediately decided to open it to the public for free discussion on general problems of society. It became, therefore, the blueprint for a *council* in which the students themselves, having ceased to be students, emerged from their own wretchedness.[8]

To be sure, the occupation was never total: certain remnants of administrative premises and a chapel were tolerated.[9] Nor was democracy ever complete: the future technocrats of the UNEF union claimed that they were making themselves useful while other political bureaucrats wanted to manipulate things. Worker participation remained very fragmentary and soon the presence of non-students began to be questioned. Many students, professors, journalists, or morons from other professions, came just to look on.

In spite of all these deficiencies, which are not astonishing given the fact of the contradiction between the breadth of the project and the limited number of students, the example of what was best in such a situation immediately took on an explosive significance. Workers saw free discussion taking place, search for radical criticism, direct democracy, rights to be seized. Even limited to a Sorbonne freed from the government, it was the program of the revolution choosing its own forms. The day after the occupation of the Sorbonne, the Sud-Aviation workers in Nantes occupied their plant. On the third day, Thursday the 16th, the Renault plants in Cléon and Flins were occupied, the movement beginning at the NMPP and at Boulogne-Billancourt, starting in Shop 70. By the end of the week 100 factories were occupied while the wave of strikes, accepted but never launched by the union bureaucracies, had paralyzed the railroads and was evolving towards a general strike.

The only authority in the Sorbonne was the general assembly of its occupants. At its first session, on May 14, amidst a certain confusion, it had elected an occupation committee of 15 members renewable daily by the general assembly. Only one of these delegates belonging to the group of Nanterre and Paris *"enragés"* had proposed a program: defense of direct democracy in the Sorbonne and absolute power of the worker councils as a final objective. The next day's general assembly voted to retain the entire occupation committee, which had been unable to do anything until then. Actually, all the technical organisms that had installed themselves in the Sorbonne were following the directives of an occult, so-called "coordination" committee composed of volunteer and oppressively moderating organizers responsible to no one. One hour after the occupation committee had been re-elected, one of the "coordinators" privately tried to declare it dissolved. A direct appeal to the grass roots, made in the courtyard of the Sorbonne, brought out a protest movement that obliged this manipulator to retract. The next day, Thursday the 16th, thirteen members of the occupation committee having disappeared, two comrades only, one of whom was the member of the *"enragés"* group, found themselves vested with the only delegation of authority accepted by the general assembly, whereas the seriousness of the moment called for immediate decisions. Democracy was constantly being flouted inside the Sorbonne, and outside factory occupation was spreading. The occupation committee, which was gathering around itself everybody it could collect among the Sorbonne occupants determined to maintain democracy, sent out a call at 3 P.M. for "occupation of all the factories in France and creation of worker councils." To obtain distribution of this call, the occupation committee had to re-establish at the same time democratic functioning of the Sorbonne. It had to occupy, or recreate along the same lines, all the services that were supposed to be under its authority: a centrally located loudspeaker, printing, inter-*faculté* liaison and security. It ignored the complaints of the spokesmen for various political groups (JCR, Maoists, etc.) by recalling that it was responsible to the general assembly only. It had intended to make a report the same evening, but the Sorbonne occupants having unanimously decided to march that day, for the first time, to Renault-Billancourt (occupation of which had meanwhile been confirmed) the assembly meeting was postponed until the following day, at 2 P.M.

During the night, while thousands of comrades were at Billancourt, some unidentified persons improvised a general assembly, which broke up of its own accord when the occupation committee, having learned of its existence, sent two delegates to remind it of its illegal nature.

On Friday, the 17th at 2 P.M., the regular assembly found its rostrum occupied for some time by fake marshals belonging to the FER, and, in addition, had to interrupt the meeting for a second march on Billancourt at 5 P.M.

That same evening, at 9 P.M., the occupation committee could at last give an accounting of its activities. It was absolutely unable, however, to obtain any discussion or a vote on its activity report, and especially, on its call for occupation of factories, for which the assembly did not assume responsibility either of disavowal or approval. Faced with this degree of indifference, the occupation committee could only withdraw. The assembly also proved incapable of protesting against a further invasion of the rostrum by FER troops, whose putsch appeared to aim at a provisional alliance of JCR and UNEF bureaucrats. The advocates of direct democracy realized that there was nothing more for them to do at the Sorbonne, and they promptly let it be known.

At the very moment when the example of the occupation began to be followed in the factories, it collapsed at the Sorbonne. This was all the more serious in that the workers had against them an infinitely more entrenched bureaucracy than that of the student amateurs or Leftists. Besides, the leftist bureaucrats, who were playing the game of the CGT in order to be recognized by them as a small marginal entity, abstractly separated the workers from students who "didn't need to give them any lessons." But in fact the students had already given the workers a lesson by their very occupation of the Sorbonne and by allowing real democratic discussion to exist for a brief moment.

Bureaucrats all tell us demogogically that the working class has reached its majority, in order to hide the fact that it is enchained, first of all by them (at present, or else in their expectations, according to the initials). They compare their false seriousness to the "festive" atmosphere in the Sorbonne, but it was precisely this festive atmosphere that contained the only real seriousness, that is, radical criticism of prevailing conditions.

The student struggle is now outdistanced. But even more outdistanced are all the substitute bureaucratic leaders who think it's clever to pretend respect for the Stalinists, just when the CGT and the so-called Communist Party are trembling. The outcome of the present crisis is in the hands of the workers themselves, if they can succeed in obtaining through occupation of their factories what University occupation has only been able to outline.

The comrades who supported the first Sorbonne occupation: the *"Comité Enragés-Internationale situationniste,"* a certain number of workers, and a few students—have set up a council for maintaining the occupations: maintaining the occupations being evidently conceivable only through its quantitative and qualitative extension, which must not spare any existing regime.

—*Conseil pour le maintien des occupations,* Paris, May 19, 1968.

The following motion presented at the Sorbonne General Assembly on May 20 shows the political intention on the part of the occupation committee to make the *faculté* a center for combative action. In point of fact, in spite of condemnation by the co-equal committees, a dual authority *was* gradually set up inside the Sorbonne: the political authority of the occupation committee, and the academic authority of the section assemblies (languages, philosophy, sociology, history, etc.). These two authorities, which were soon on the most distant of terms, were quickly in sharp contradiction with each other— all the more so since the Sorbonne general assemblies (the "political" ones) degenerated very rapidly, and the occupation committee was no longer able to organize them.[10]

Document 127

The Movement Recalls That . . .

1. Occupation of the *facultés* constitutes only one particular and circumstantial aspect of its activity.

2. Occupation and the tasks accomplished while it lasted must serve the general struggle against the capitalist system.

The occupation responds to the following political objectives:
1. To momentarily neutralize university functioning in order to neutralize capitalist university legality.
2. To organize university faculty and students for a radical contestation of society and of the university.
3. To constitute a base for the movement.

The faculté *being a place for:*
—organizing the movement into action committees;
—discussion within the movement and with the outside;
—preparation for activities to be carried out.

In this way, the occupation of the *facultés,* having taken on a new dimension during the development of the worker movement, constitutes in itself a showdown of strength which can lead to two situations:

a) Either collapse of the movement and reopening of the *facultés,* whether they are reformed or not;

b) Or, purely and simply, overthrow of the regime.

The occupation of the *facultés* in liaison with the development of the worker movement must therefore be extended, prolonged, and organized.

Considering:
—that the political objective is really the overthrow of the regime by the workers, and that the occupation must be carried out within this political framework;

—that, in fact, education will only answer the needs of the population when the people have actually defeated the capitalist government;

—that reorganization of the University being inconceivable outside this framework, it must not be achieved, consequently, only by the people who are working for it at the present time, but by all the workers together.

Reform of the capitalist University will be opposed and creation of "co-equal committees" will consequently be boycotted.

Exposes Generally
attempts to lead the movement astray, orchestrated by certain professors whose aim is to force the movement into the narrow frame-

work of University reformism, such as student folklore, by which the occupations risk being submerged.

Recalls

that the essential task of the students is to join the working class struggle against the regime.

This motion was voted by the Sorbonne AG on Monday, May 20, 1968.

The occupation committee bore the brunt of the different Sorbonne services, concerning which the following texts give an idea. Actually, however, it was unable to control them. The situationist-run restaurant, which was headed by a male cook with a predominantly female staff, functioned fairly well (in spite of unavoidable disorder). But outside the Sorbonne certain people were anxious, among them the president of a consumer education association, which circulated a leaflet describing a few elementary rules of diet.

The most aware among the militants were haunted by the possibility of another Reichstag fire, given the particularly favorable terrain offered by the Sorbonne library and the laboratories of the *Faculté des Sciences*. Several fires did break out, one of which damaged the rector's quarters rather seriously. Little feudalities sprang up around such essential activities as the restaurant service, the medical service (momentarily headed by a crook), and even the cleaning service! The best known was the one that developed under the name of "Rapid Action Commandos" (known as the Katangans,[11] after the notorious Congo mercenaries), and who, having made arrangements with other services (medical), threatened the occupation committee's authority. Putting them out was only possible thanks to the help of a "committee of young unemployed," led by a strange figure who had played a far from clear role during the Algerian war.[12] Even then, in spite of the pressure exerted by union organizations (SNESUP., Sorbonne) and the teachers and students responsible for security, the occupation committee refused to convert to a role of offshoot of the student-teacher general assemblies.

Document 128

Proposal for Interior Organization of the Sorbonne

Commissions

1. Each one must have a chairman, two spokesmen, and one secretary.

2. The time for work and discussion must be limited.

3. The number of participants in the commission must not be more than 40 people.

4. Before each meeting the commission must present its agenda of subjects to be discussed.

5. During the session the doors of the room must remain closed to the public.

6. Once elected, the spokesmen for the commissions must register with the *occupation committee* and with the *coordinating committee for commissions*. This same rule holds for the chairman of the commission.

7. When the commission has finished its work and adopted certain points, it must make its report to the committees and then submit it to the general assembly.

8. Security measures should be in force outside each meeting room.

The Assembly

1. The one and only role of the general assembly is to vote on decisions taken by the different commissions.

2. These decisions must be presented by the spokesmen from each commission.

3. To maintain order, more people than the lecture hall can hold must not be allowed in. Consequently, security measures must be in force at the entrance to the assembly hall.

The Committees

1. Creation of a reception committee for workers.

2. Of an information committee.

3. Of a committee to coordinate the work of the commissions.

4. The PC (*Poste de Commandement*) or Headquarters, of the security system must remain in contact with these three committees and with the Sorbonne occupation committee.

5. The committees, the security system, the medical services, and the dormitories are permanent.

Permanent Services

1. Occupation Committee.

2. Information Committee.

3. Security System.

4. Dormitory.

5. Medical service.
6. Reception service for public relations.
7. *Permanence* (General inquiry service).

—[May 15, 1968].

Document 129

Comrades,

THE FILTH, THE LACK OF HYGIENE, AND THEIR CONSEQUENCES ARE OBVIOUSLY ONE OF THE ARGUMENTS THE GAULLIST GOVERNMENT INTENDS TO USE TO WREST THE SORBONNE FROM THE STUDENTS.

—*Hygiene and disinfection measures will be taken by the occupation committee in agreement with the sanitary services.*

—*We must all understand the significance of this action, not only because of its evident practical consequences, but also and especially because of its* POLITICAL SIGNIFICANCE.

WE MUST ALL PARTICIPATE IN THIS IN A RESPONSIBLE AND EFFECTIVE WAY.

—*By accepting the hygiene and disinfection measures.*

—*By observing bodily hygiene.*

—*By designating in each committee, in each group, whether organized or not, comrades who will be responsible for hygiene and cleanliness, who will point out the problems, explain to their comrades the importance of this effort, and give direct help to the comrades in the cleaning, hygiene, and health services in carrying out their work.*

EFFECTIVE ACTION IS ONLY POSSIBLE IF EVERYBODY PARTICIPATES!

—[about May 20, 1968].

Document 130

NOON	Sat.	Sun.	Mon.	Tues.	Wed.	Thurs.	Fri.	NOON
			CENTER-SORBONNE		MEAL TICKET			
	Valid from.................... to							
	Committee or service							
EVENING	Sat.	Sun.	Mon.	Tues.	Wed.	Thurs.	Fri.	EVENING

Document 131

Be Careful of Sandwiches!

To keep up, you must eat well and not expensively.

In order to avoid malnutrition, do not forget to eat every day at least

| *1 glass of milk* | or 1 oz. of cheese |
| | or 1 yoghurt |

at least

| *1 ripe fruit* | or 1 lettuce salad |
| | or 1 fruit juice |

According to what you have on hand, you will then be able to eat *sandwiches* and *canned goods* to reach the 2,000 or 2,500 calories necessary per day.

—*Union Fédérale de la Consommation,* or, Federal Consumer's Union, 13, rue Férou, Paris VIe [about May 27, 1968].

Document 132

Today Free Distribution of LSD, Hashish . . .

Cops have introduced into the neighborhood as well as into the *facs,* L.S.D., kief, and hashish, which they are distributing generously free of charge.

The Purpose
to prove that the students and workers fighting against Gaullism and the bourgeoisie are nothing but irresponsible drug addicts and not revolutionaries.

We must forestall these maneuvers.

Stop the provocators!
Stop coppers disguised as drug addicts!

WE DON'T NEED HALLUCINATORY DRUGS
FOR OUR REVOLUTION!
THE CREATIVE SPONTANEITY OF SOCIALISM
IS ENOUGH FOR US.

—*Comité d'action révolutionnaire* [June 10, 1968?]

Document 133

Hunting score (in CRS) set up by the "Katangans" after the events of the evening of May 23: number of CRS knocked out:

> 5 with paving stones
> 4 with blackjacks
> 1 with bare fists

Whereas problems of security were not numerous at the *Halle aux Vins* (*Faculté des Sciences*) or at the *Faculté de Médecine*, they were the focal point of the material organization of the Sorbonne, which was entirely in the hands of the students. Except for the *Faculté des Lettres secrétariat*, the administration had left, and cooperation with the occupation committee had practically ceased. The very layout of the premises, the existence of a sector of the *Faculté des Sciences* left unguarded by scientists, the vastness of the cellars—concerning which there were all kinds of rumors—presented serious problems. The security system (at first "spontaneous" and headed nobody knew by whom) was purged several times, with the less identifiable elements re-grouping in the CIR (*Commando d'intervention rapide,* or "Katangans"), from which all inside security responsibility was withdrawn. After being finally abolished, it was reconstituted on a union basis, principally from UNEF and SNESup. union sections of the History Department (students, lecturers, instructors, and a few professors). However, because of the existence of the CIR, plus the uncertain authority of the occupation committee and their own weakness, the UNEF and the SNESup. declined to assume full responsibility for this latter group. In addition to the problems presented by the occupation there were others, posed by the myths that attached to the Sorbonne and according to which all sorts of people had taken refuge there including thieves and lunatics, not to mention intelligence agents, police, and informers. Nor did the provincial *facultés* escape this problem, as may be seen in a document from Lyons. Occupation of the Odéon Theatre, however, was a special case.

Document 134

Communiqué[13]

Yesterday evening, June 10, students demonstrated in the Latin Quarter against police repression in Flins; by doing this they demonstrated their solidarity with the victims in Meulan. All night long the students came up against police violence. The Sorbonne, little by little, took on the appearance of a fortress: windows giving on the streets were open, facilitating the shooting of grenades into the building, people on the roofs, numerous "Molotov cocktails," without any security guarantee (a mere cigarette could set a large part of the Sorbonne on fire).

At 7 in the morning the police stormed the door of 17 rue de la Sorbonne using offense grenades. There was no way to oppose them. Even without trying to occupy the Sorbonne, it was very easy for them to renew their attack, which this time was much more deadly.

Under these conditions the demonstration planned for this evening must not and can not keep the Sorbonne from playing the role during demonstrations that it has constantly played during the events: shelter for the injured, refuge for the demonstrators. The Sorbonne must therefore remain a place of refuge and debate for all militants. Consequently, it is absolutely necessary to avoid all provocations or irresponsible acts such as:

—throwing anything from rooftops or upper floors of the *faculté* in the direction of the police;

—manufacture of dangerous projectiles inside the Sorbonne.

The inter-union Sorbonne security system, insofar as its means allow, will see to it that the necessary protective measures are taken. All militants are invited to help in this task.

Any irresponsible act endangers our common security and compromises the future of the movement.

—UNEF Sorbonne Occupation Committee [June 11, 1968].

Document 135

After a Month's Occupation of the Faculté des Lettres *in Lyons.*

For the last month the *Faculté des Lettres* has been in the limelight of the news in Lyons, where there have been all sorts of rumors. Faced with a great number of erroneous assertions and news exploited for partisan purposes, it seems possible to make a first summary of what has happened and been achieved since the red flag was hoisted.

I. Deep and Irreversible Transformations Have Caused Dad's Old-Time University to Disappear

1. A profound change in people's attitudes.

Events in Nanterre and Paris, the considerations they have given rise to, the questioning of conventional viewpoints, all have furnished an extraordinary opportunity for many students living in the cloistered world of their studies, and indifferent to union or political questions, to acquire a greater awareness of their significance. Certain individuals have come to the fore: some have attained the point of all-out confrontation with capitalist society (March 22); others, of demand for profound reforms. In any case, nothing will ever be the same again.

Teachers are overjoyed at the changes in human relationships that have accompanied this movement: instead of an unorganized and amorphous mass, they are increasingly finding themselves faced with responsible students.

2. Work of the Commissions.

Here everybody—student or teacher—may express himself freely.

Commissions on the level of the entire faculté, which are concerned with important questions (University and political society at the University, re-organization of the *faculté*, etc.).

Commissions on the level of the different University disciplines which, in addition to the same problems, are concerned with reform of curricula, with teaching content, and with student-teacher relationships.

Lastly, commissions oriented towards the outside, open to everybody, such as the art and revolution commission, which works on popular cultural problems in collaboration with Planchon and Maréchal,[14] or the commission of immigrant workers that groups union members, students, and elementary school teachers.

To this should be added a series of discussions on the most varied subjects and a reaching out towards the life of the community, already expressed through students working in the different neighborhoods, or in youth centers.

As for support for the workers, it has not yielded what the students themselves had expected: their generally bourgeois origin, as also their lack of political and trade-union training, caused them too often to adopt "pro-worker" attitudes that were well meaning and generous but too intellectual and naïvely elated. However, there will remain—and this is fundamental—a deep awareness of the problems of our time.

3. Re-Examination of the Recent Past.

—Re-examination of a type of education with a *traditional* content that is too far removed from present-day problems.

—Re-examination of *authoritarian* teaching methods by which professors imposed their knowledge on the students: the latter intend to participate in their education by means of free discussions which do not exclude debate.

Furthermore, a whole generation is beginning to become aware of the need to reform education as a whole, and is preparing to provide a new type of teachers.

—Re-examination of structures that are centralizing and suffocating for individuals, in favor of ideas for University autonomy and for co-equal student-professor commissions (that imply student participation on every level of responsibility).

—Re-examination of the University's role in society and of its bourgeois nature: from now on it must fulfill the critical function that corresponds to its *raison d'être,* and must become a University for the entire population.

On numerous points all this is still in the project stage, but the work done is already far-reaching. Nothing could be less true than to believe that students are still concerned with the problem of examinations, which has long since been settled. On this subject it should be pointed out that nobody has been disadvantaged by their being postponed until September, since a session on "special cases" (decided upon by the co-equal student-professor commissions) is planned for this week.

II. Difficulties and Problems Encountered by the Faculté.

In spite of the serious work that has been done, we must not ignore some enormous difficulties.

1. The events of the past weeks have descended upon a student body and, to a large extent, on a teaching body, both of which were loosely structured.

On the one hand a very small politicized minority (extreme-leftist organizations); on the other an unorganized, atomized mass and a UNEF having had little influence in *Lettres* for a long time. Creative spontaneity, which was the source of the student movement, ran the risk of giving out and of finding its first gains hard to consolidate, all the more so since at the beginning events had had a tendency to increase this lack of organization: many students reacted by refusing coordinated activities and any sort of structuration (*Mouvement du 22 mars*).

This explains the impression of good-natured anarchy that many have noted. But now, most of them have become aware of the need to be organized in order not to leave the student body isolated before the threat of a new authoritarian governmental reform, and submerged, when school starts again, by the flood of today's absentees.

2. Security in the *faculté* has nevertheless created very serious concern.

Occupation of the buildings, plus their permanently open state, implied an effective security system capable of checking everybody who came in: but neither the unorganized students nor the teachers were prepared for such responsibilities.

Moreover, events (particularly the demonstrations) led to invasion of the *faculté* by various elements the people in Lyons now know by the generic name of "tramps" (unemployed youth, "hoods," and other maladjusted members of our society). To these should be added a certain number of destructive students or outsiders: some come to steal, others through anarchistic ideals, who have actually caused much more damage than the "tramps," who are always accused. Furthermore, it should be observed that the most serious destruction was carried out by the fascist elements who came to attack the *faculté* on Tuesday, June 4, 1968 (quai Claude-Bernard).

The security system, which was badly organized, was not able to avoid these depredations in a *faculté* that is very difficult to supervise and to control. Besides, an ill-advised conception of total solidarity among all the occupants made any energetic measures for eliminating undesirable elements impossible.

This is why we had to resign ourselves to evacuating a part of the valuable material. But it is untrue to say that the *faculté* has been abandoned. Every day commissions take place there, and the problem of security itself is on the way to a definitive solution.

In Conclusion

The task of reorganization and reconstruction, although made more difficult by the above-mentioned drawbacks, is progressing rapidly. The bases for the coming school year have been laid down and provisional organisms for the new University we all hope to see are being set up.

—UDCFDT of the Rhône Dept., Lyons, June 17, 1968.
(*Union Départemental de la Confédération Française Démocratique du Travail*). *Document written by three militants of the* SGEN (CFDT *Supérieur*), *among whom is Baumont* (UD Councilman).

Document 136

After the events of these last days;
After police occupation of the Latin Quarter and of Nanterre;

After the barricades on the night of May 10 and the fierce police repression;

After the general strike of May 13 and the Sorbonne occupation;

Last night when the performance of the Théâtre des Nations ended, a group of artists, theatrical people, students, and workers, constituting a revolutionary action committee, occupied the Théâtre de France-Odéon, which symbolizes a type of bourgeois culture that they contest fundamentally in the same way that they do capitalist society.

As soon as the theater was occupied commissions, open to all, were created to undertake the task of analyzing our refusal to accept distribution of consumer-theater, and the possibilities offered by the new situation to develop an art for combat.

This is evidently only a first step, and we urgently ask professionals in the theatrical business, in liaison with the workers and students, to join us and also to take similar initiatives in their own places of work.

IN ORDER TO CONTINUE THIS MOVEMENT
WE URGE YOU ALL TO COME
to the *ex-Théâtre de France* this evening, Thursday
May 16, at midnight

—[Nanterre, May 16, 1968].

At the *Faculté de Médecine,* as well as in all the other *facultés,* the same problems arose, with the difference that they were rather less dramatic than at the Sorbonne. On June 17, the day after the evacuation of the Sorbonne, Censier [*Faculté des Lettres*] voted to adopt a federative type of organization that gave equal representation to general assemblies according to discipline, and to action or technical committees. Problems regarding the authority of the permanent delegation were posed in the same terms—with perhaps even greater difficulty —as at the Sorbonne.

Document 137

Do You Know Who Is Running This Occupied Faculté?

"Services that were already set up," you will reply, and consider that well and good. In reality, some *fifty* of your exhausted comrades have been performing the vital functions in this house on a permanent basis.

Fifty who, whether in the coordination commission, the press and secretarial services, running the duplicators, or anywhere else, are getting only two, three, or four hours of sleep a night!!!

This situation has become untenable, and is in contradiction with productive and effective work.

Equally serious is the fact that your comrades who are working like this for everybody haven't the time to assume their duties as students and adults responsible for their own fates as this revolution has proclaimed them to be. They cannot participate in general assemblies and commissions, and, absurdly enough, those who print this paper and the leaflets do not even know what they contain, have not had time to read them!!!

Your comrades who receive you at the office, at the duplicator, etc., are not professional administrators sprung up during the confusion that accompanied our settling here.

Ours is not a set and rigid administration.

We do not want to re-create inside these walls a society like the one we condemn!

There are always responsibilities to be assumed, ideas to be proposed, services to be rendered.

We keep saying that our discussions are positive, which is true. But this can only last, and the world can only be told about it, if each person conscientiously gives the maximum of himself both intellectually and physically.

The coordination commission impatiently awaits:
   —your ideas
   —your two hands
   —all your constructive proposals
Do not allow a minority among us to become exhausted by work which may seem secondary to you, but which is essential!!!

Once more, we are all
RESPONSIBLE!!!

—Excerpt from the *Journal du comité d'information de la faculté de Médecine de Paris,* No. 9, May 26, 1968.

An article in the newspaper *Action* dated June 14 furnished the following conclusion about this occupation of the Sorbonne: occupation of the *facultés* was a political weapon that was directly contingent upon the political juncture. On June 16 the government could afford to have the Sorbonne evacuated.

Document 138

The Sorbonne: Against Provocation

Yesterday and this morning, the press campaign against the Sorbonne had taken on new proportions. The radio and newspapers have found in this subject a dreamed-up diversion with which to conceal the murders in Flins and Sochaux.

The government-owned radio stations, which day in and day out give only the government line, have permitted the "Katangans" to speak. This morning *Paris-Jour* devoted the first page, plus a double page of photographs, to them. The sensational press has found a sensation cut to its size.

Radio-Luxembourg is talking about epidemics when everybody at the Sorbonne knows that this is not true.

We will not permit such provocations to develop.

Cleaning the Sorbonne and getting rid of the people who are the source of the provocations the government wants is only one of our tasks. This is the meaning of the decisions taken yesterday by the Sorbonne occupation committee.

For several weeks now the University commissions have been thinking about setting up a "Popular Summer University" which, in all the universities, and principally in the Latin Quarter, would permit us to examine thoroughly the lessons of our movement. The Sorbonne would become preeminently the place for these discussions and political analyses—more necessary today than ever, for workers as well as for students—in order to continue the struggle. University reform will not be accomplished in one day, isolated from other political problems of society. In the next few days a general assembly will take place at the Sorbonne, attended by students and teachers who have been working on these projects for several weeks.

To bring together workers and students at the Sorbonne, participating in these discussions, for several months, is our political answer to press accusations of nihilism. We refuse to be put in the category of general news items, which is where the press and the government would like to try to contain us.

Communiqué of the Sorbonne Occupation Committee

After the press campaign started against the Sorbonne, which aims at discrediting our movement, the occupation committee states:

1. A certain number of irresponsible groups who are neither stu-

dents nor workers are taking advantage of the situation that has arisen these last few days to enforce what is practically police control in certain parts of the Sorbonne.

2. The sanitary situation of the Sorbonne is bad. This is due to the unbelievable dilapidation of the premises, which necessitates urgent measures. These can only be taken, however, after a certain number of rooms and staircases have been vacated.

Consequently, the occupation committee has decided, in agreement with various organizations of students and teachers, to progressively close the entire Sorbonne with the exception of the courtyard, the five lecture halls leading to the hall of the Library, and Staircase C. This closing will last 48 hours in order to clean and disinfect the entire premises. For several days the occupation committee has been trying to have this measure accepted amicably by groups who were adamantly opposed. Due to their refusal, the committee calls on all militants to help keep the Sorbonne for the struggle.

We refuse to authorize any longer the existence of a pretext for the government to intervene with its crs.

—Excerpt from *Action*, No. 10, June 14.

The Action Committees

By the evening of May 3 a problem faced the militant students: how should they take advantage of the sudden student mobilization to confront repression? By the 14th, the mau had launched the "action committee" formula,[15] while members of the ujc(m-l), who were already the moving spirits of the Maoist Vietnam Committees, launched "defense committees against repression," and members of the 22 *mars* set up "revolutionary action committees." The term "action committees" rapidly became popular,[16] to such an extent that on May 21 the Communist Party launched its own "action committees for a popular democratic government," which were accompanied by the "popular action committees" of the psu.

Where did the formula come from? As long ago as February, subsequent to the *Lycée Condorcet* affair, *lycée* action committees (cal)[17] had made their appearance. The German student movement also had its "action committees"[18] and the mau militants, who were very close to the sds, may have played the role of transmitters. Further back, in 1935, the Komintern had suggested creation of "action committees" to give mass support to the Popular Fronts, but this had not been done.[19]

Still further back, it was not the 1917 Soviets (composed of elected delegates) but the 1905 St. Petersburg Soviet (composed of militants) who used the term "action committees." In 1968 this designated bodies that differed from one another, certain being mere discussion groups, or study committees. There was only one at the *Faculté des Lettres* in Besançon, but several dozens were set up at the Sorbonne. Certain of them were organized on a neighborhood basis; others according to place of study, or work. As a rule they all had something in common, that being lack of hierarchy, spontaneous creation and dissolution, an alternating presidency. While the general assemblies were the legislative bodies of democracy in the *facultés,* the action committees were the planners. Having originated in the strike, they kept it from remaining passive.

The stage of struggle against repression, and such immediate goals as the resignation of the Minister of the Interior, Fouchet, and of the Chief of Police, Grimaud, having been left behind with the extension of the movement, the action committees started a direct attack against the government, and most of the political groups (except for the FER and the UEC[20]) later became integrated into the action committees, bringing even their quarrels with them.[21]

The bureau for coordination of action committees, in order to avoid their dispersion in vague political directions, tried to get a minimum platform adopted.

Document *139*

The action committees were created as a result of the people's occupation of the *facultés* on the evening of May 13.

They are the result of our awareness of our possibilities for common action.

They group together militants from diverse political and union origins.

Their goal is to go beyond the stage of traditional demands.

They are the expression of the fundamental democratic need of the masses.

The student struggle is what has made it possible to unblock the political situation.

Today, workers and students are fighting to recast the structure of society.

They are not seeking to attain their goals through questionable commissions, but through occupation of work premises and, if need be, through grass roots defensive action against all forms of repression.

This combat has shown that the middle classes, the workers and the students will have to work on a broad political level, with radically new perspectives.

In order to increase the efficacy of their participation, the action committees have adopted as a basis the following minimum agreement:

The action committees, which are open to everybody, group together and coordinate the grass-roots movements that are engaged in the same action. They do not aspire to play a parliamentary role, but to set up groups for analysis and information.—*To create national coordination of action committees, at the same time that they respect their autonomy and see to it that interrelations on all levels are established.*

—To create active solidarity with students and workers.

—To contribute to setting up worker power.

Today the vote of a coordinating body has proved to be necessary. It was decided, during a general assembly, that it would be composed of delegates from the different districts.

At present the districts are arbitrarily constituted; they require reorganization by the action committees themselves.

—The Coordinating Committee for the Paris Region [May 15?].

On May 19 and especially on May 23, during a "general assembly," the action committees tried to formulate their position with regard to two crucial problems dictating their action: 1) organization, and 2) a political platform.

Document 140

Political Platform Proposed
at the General Assembly of May 23

Whereas, the generalized movement for factory occupation, spontaneously started by the workers, demonstrates the workers' high level of combativity;

Whereas, consequently, the problem posed today is that of authority;

Whereas, within this power relationship we cannot accept the capitulation of union leaders who, by advocating negotiation with the Gaullist government, thereby legalize a government which is completely discredited;

Whereas, the agreements concluded between the union leaders are, in addition, a complete backdown from the demands set forth in the factories by the workers themselves;

The action committees have decided to continue and also intensify the fight that they have undertaken in the streets, on the basis of the following provisional, minimum agreement:

1. Rejection of the Gaullist regime and of any other bourgeois government in favor of setting up a workers' government.

2. Proletarian internationalism, and particularly complete support for Cohn-Bendit, who has been expelled from France; unity of action and solidarity with foreign workers in France, who are the principal targets of repression.

3. Popularization and extension of direct action groups: CA's, the strike committees set up in factories, neighborhoods, *lycées,* CET's, and *facultés,* comprising both unionized and non-unionized persons joined together in the same anti-capitalist struggle.

4. In view of the generalized mobilization and combativity of the working class and the students, refusal of any agreement that

—endorses the Gaullist regime, or

—breaks up the movement in a period of rising revolutionary mood.

5. The importance given to new forms of parliamentary struggle as being the decisive element for any victory and symbolized by the slogan: "The power is in the streets."

6. The necessity to foresee and organize self-defense for militants faced with possible repression when the movement is on the wane.

7. The necessity for national coordination of committees. On this point, proposals:

a) that the newspaper *Action* be the paper of the CA's[22] with, if possible, correspondents in the factories; b) on the bases expressed above, that a provisional collective group be elected right away and entrusted with:

—carrying out the immediate tasks of coordination and organization of the demonstration to take place on Friday, May 24, 1968;

—organizing for Monday, May 27, 1968, an AG of the CA's, at which delegates will be commissioned, on the basis of this project, to set up a minimum platform defining the objectives of the CA's.

On this basis to elect a renewable and "transferable" leadership, to define the lines for organization and coordination of the CA's.

The agreement that appeared to have been made on the preceding resolution did not prevent the political currents from continuing to clash inside the committees; several proposals and platforms opposed one another in a confrontation which at times became violent, as evidenced by the JCR document that follows.

Document 141

A Political Platform Project for the Action Committees

The student struggle, by making a direct frontal attack on the government itself, has made it possible to unblock a political situation which in spite of the difficult nature of the present economic juncture (cf. the movements in Caen, Le Mans, Redon) was following the rhythm of traditional parliamentary political life with its parades, petitions, censure motions, and election campaigns.

But the student struggle against repression is only one aspect of the frontal attack led by all workers seeking to overthrow the social and economic structures of capitalist society.

It is not through vain negotiations that students have succeeded in paralyzing the universities and preventing application of the Fouchet Plan, but by combining fighting with occupation.

The workers did not launch the struggle by way of the Toutée and Grégoire commissions, or in the Economic and Social Council, but by occupying all places of work. They have done this by direct and, when necessary, violent fighting against all forms of repression, regimentation, or class collaboration.

This struggle has shown that the middle classes and the workers generally can be won over at a broad political level, offering radically new prospects, and not through action that is limited to the various slogans for merely satisfying the grievances of these social strata.

The generalized movement of factory occupations, started spontaneously by the workers, gives evidence of the combativity of the workers, particularly of young workers.

All the legitimate demands of the workers can in no case be satisfied by a bourgeois government.

For this reason today's problem is to overthrow the government. In a power relationship of this kind, we cannot accept the capitulation implied in the union directives which, by advocating negotiation with the Gaullist government, legitimize its existence.

Furthermore, the agreements concluded between the union leaders are far from meeting the demands set forth in the factories themselves by the workers.

Criticism of union leaders does not imply criticism of unions as organizations, but merely:

—the need for effective supervision of the leadership by the workers;

—the inadequacy of this type of organization for responding to the situation created by the governmental crisis.

The action committees are not a political party but a movement composed of militants of different political and union origin. They stem from the current unitary movement from which sectarian and bureaucratic attitudes have been banished and in which complete democracy must be observed. On the political level the action committees are a manifestation of the fundamental democratic needs of the masses, who are expressing themselves today.

In order to increase the effectiveness of their political participation, the committees have adopted the following minimum agreement as a basis:

1. Rejection of the Gaullist regime and of any other bourgeois government, in favor of instauration of worker power.

2. In view of the general mobilization and combativity of the working class, and of the students, refusal of any agreement that:

—puts back in the saddle the Gaullist regime and the power of the employers, both of which are tottering as a result of the worker-student fight;

—does not contain any serious guarantees against a return to the past;

—gives up part of the demands considered essential by the workers;

—was arrived at one sector at a time, or one business establishment at a time.

3. The importance given to extra-parliamentary forms of struggle as being decisive elements for winning, and particularly the combative assertion of determination on the part of unskilled workers, students, peasants, and workers generally, in street actions, as well as the general strike with factory occupations that have been organized by workers into an active combat tool, at the service of the strikers.

4. The re-grouping and coordination into action committees set up in factories, in many neighborhoods, in school and University buildings, by militants, unionized or not, all engaged in the same anti-capitalist combat.

5. The action committees do not aim to play an electoral or parliamentary role the way the traditional political parties do, but to promote combat groups set up by the workers against capitalist au-

thority, along the lines of the strike committees elected by worker assemblies.

6. Organization of resistance to repression proves our refusal to yield to the government's attempts to liquidate the strikes, the mass movements, or the militants themselves.

7. Active solidarity with foreign workers and students in France, who are special targets for repression.

8. The need for a national coordination of action committees which respects their autonomy, consequently the need to define objectives and means. For this, the following proposals:

a)   Starting with the demands actually made by the workers, bring out the political nature of their struggle which tends towards the overthrow of capitalist power.

b)   Active participation in the struggle against the government, especially:

— encourage direct liaisons between strike committees.

— be responsible for circulation of news between business establishments and among the public, by making known the decisions of the striking workers.

— actively collaborate in a possible takeover of the means of production by the workers, to consolidate the struggle.

— combat the insidious propaganda being carried on among the people through press, radio, and TV by the capitalist forces, and instigate demonstrations of solidarity.

The action committee movement, in an assembly of delegates or in a coordination committee, can send out a call for action and demonstrations.

Each action committee will decide for itself whether it will or will not be associated with these Paris or national political plans.

—[Discussed at the AG on June 2, 1968, probably before May 30.]

Document 142

The Charléty meeting and the UNEF demonstrations had revealed a current which, although at times confused, was determined to fight for a socialist revolution. In order to transform this current into a force, it appeared necessary to organize it and give it form. Almost spontaneously students, *lycée* students, and young workers, who had been thrown together in the fight, and were bound by ties of actual or assumed common experience on the barricades, reorganized into action committees, according to neighborhood, school, or factory.

The almost unanimously accepted function of these committees was to constitute or encourage in each neighborhood, place of work, etc., a nucleus of dual power by assuming responsibility for supplies, information, coordination of strike pickets, and control of speculation.

Quite evidently, in this case, these committees should be conceived of as broad *action* committees, bringing together *all revolutionary tendencies* into soviet-type bodies. Discussion was directly linked to the needs dictated by action, and through a phenomenon of natural selection those who were most able to find solutions to the political problems of the moment turned out to be the real, not the bureaucratic, moving spirits of the committees. In the beginning, political agreement, as in the case of the *Mouvement du 22 mars,* was not a prerequisite for actions that were to result from a wide confrontation of various lines, but an agreement that had been gradually liberated from the imperatives of intervening.

On the other hand, since the revolutionary current in gestation implied the danger of miscarriage there was no question of remaining in the tow of other people's undertakings. At Charléty, underneath the at first eminently positive aspect of the demonstration, one felt the personality of Mendès, who had been brought there in the baggage of the PSU. Two days later the UNEF, by refusing to go to the CGT demonstration with its own slogans, gave guarantees for FO and the CFDT, thereby seeming to confirm the *de facto* alliance outlined at Charléty.

In both cases, to be content with denouncing the operation or to regret it without being able to do anything about it amounted to contemplating one's own impotence, to remaining subject to hollow labels devoid of content, whereas the living forces are in the action committees. It became evident from these experiences that we needed serious *political coordination* precisely mandated to coordinate the committees, to supervise their actual existence, and to take overall initiatives: this leadership being of course revocable with each AG (the solution of technical coordination being nothing but a maneuver on the part of microphone monopolizers or of an unrevocable AG chairman trying to preserve the prerogatives of a spontaneous bureaucracy).

The AG of the committees, which met on Sunday, June 2, at the Sorbonne, was the occasion to carry out these two objectives: unification of the committees and political coordination. All the conditions were favorable since the *22 mars* and the *Comités de Soutien aux Luttes du Peuple* were present. The operation even began under felicitous auspices since agreement was unanimous on the text for the poster "The Bourgeoisie is Afraid." The delegates from the twelfth district took advantage of this agreement to ask for unification of signatures under the name: *"Mouvement des Comités d'Action de la Région Parisienne."* This proposal was voted unanimously except for three votes, in spite of reservations on the part of the 22 *mars* representative. We then explained that this was only a first step, and that it was necessary to obtain grass roots fusion of all militants in the action committees in order to work together and, through action, explore the possibilities for political agreement, while rigorously respecting working class democracy in the committees.

This amounted to asking for unification of the mass movement alone, while remaining distinct from the political groups (UJC[m-l], FER, JCR, VO). Either the 22 *mars* would dissolve into a mass movement which would then include and transcend it, or it would be constituted as a district avant-garde political group, in the same way as the "groupuscules" it denounced. Either the *"comités de soutien aux luttes du peuple"* would dissolve into the general movement or they would openly declare themselves the mass branch of the UJC(m-l), desirous of building up its mass for maneuver by nibbling away at the movement from within instead of trying to develop it.

Failing which, it became evident that each "groupuscule" was going to constitute its own *cordon sanitaire* of committees, its own federation of committees, and repeat, on a larger scale, the mosaic of "groupuscules." Failing which, those who claim that they want to fight to the end were nothing but double-talking demagogues, already preoccupied with drawing up the balance sheet of events for the benefit of their own show or their own clique; that is to say, they consider that the game is up and the time has come to capitalize on the fruits of their efforts.

Unfortunately, ignoring the vote of the general assembly which they even deceived, the 22 *mars* and the *comités de soutien aux luttes du peuple* left their names on the poster, having imposed them not by political discussion but in the offices of the print shop.

This is not only political dishonesty, it is compromising for the unification of the committees, and already it is tearing the movement apart; it is looking ahead to a day of accounting and division of spoils, it is seeking to guarantee and sanction the signatures of the "groupuscules," by that of the mass movement.

Let us hope that the committee militants will be able to reintroduce the usages that until now have permitted the movement to succeed. Let us hope that an end will be made to these practices and that we will operate according to the principle that we still recognize: unity at the grass roots and in action.[23]

—*La Jeunesse communiste révolutionnaire, Aujourd'hui*, No. 6, June 4–5.

The Movement Press: The Example of *Action*

The student movement could not get along without its own press. *Le Monde*,[24] needless to say, could not fill this need, besides which, it had made a violent about-face in its June 12 issue. *Combat,* as usual, published practically anything, mostly favorable articles, but also Gaullist articles, articles by former OAS members, almost all of them violently anti-communist. It could serve as a convenient platform but it was not a mouthpiece. As for the *Enragé,* while it was very widely read in student circles, it was above all a good advertisement for its publisher, J.-J. Pauvert, and the mention of an "action committee" in its first issue was a mere blind.[25]

Action, on the contrary, was an unquestionable success for the movement. Whereas the student press (particularly "21–27," the UNEF mouthpiece) was moribund, this latter paper quickly assumed the role of platform for the movement, with a practically daily circulation of 30,000. The first issue, which appeared on May 7 with illustrations by Siné and Wolinski, was exclusively centered on the students. But already, in the article entitled "Why Are We Fighting?" (see below), there was a reminder of the workers in Caen and Redon. The slogan featured was "The Latin Quarter for Students." In the second issue, which appeared May 13 and was circulated during the demonstration, there was a call put out by the UNEF, the SNESUP, the *Mouvement du 22 mars,* and the CAL's to set up action committees "to force Grimaud and Fouchet to resign" through a campaign that would organize a "public political trial, by the people, of the men who were responsible for the repression." The third issue, dated May 21, was able to announce the demonstration that went out to the Renault factory: "For the first time in France a student demonstration went to a factory occupied by workers." From June 5, that is, after the ebb tide had started, and until July 1 (No. 20), *Action* appeared five days a week and was the mouthpiece of the strike as long as it lasted, and then of radical denunciation of Gaullism (No. 7, June 11: "De Gaulle: I will say for all to hear that the police have done their entire duty and done it very well." Assassin—Assassin—Assassin, wounded demonstrator's head). *Action* was certainly the only paper that was still demanding the withdrawal of the Chief of State (No. 8, dated June 12). *Action* was also the only paper that tried to carry on a campaign against the "electoralism" of the left. Politically, too, *Action* avoided to a very large extent the tone of a coterie. The FER did not collaborate with it, and the "Marxist-Leninists" (who had their own daily, *La Cause du Peuple*), although present, were discreetly so. The editor of *Action,* J.-P. Vigier, was also the moving spirit of the "planning committee for a revolutionary movement"; and yet *Action* published the polemics instigated by D. Cohn-Bendit *against* this movement.[26] *Action* was technically very well done, and it succeeded in blending pure polemics (drawings and photographs) with militant cultural information.[27] The call for immediate action (No. 7, dated June 11) was from beginning to end a call for that evening's demonstration: an account of the death of Gilles Tautin, an article illustrated with photographs of Flins, etc. *Action* was undoubtedly the underground paper that had been outlined during the Algerian war[28] but that had not materialized for lack of readers.[29]

Although it was eminently the movement paper, *Action* was not alone. Countless multigraphed or printed papers appeared, put out either on a *faculté* or a *lycée* basis (such as *Scienlit* at the Halle aux Vins, le *Mouvement* at Censier—from which we publish an editorial), or on a local basis. The need for expression in order to convince others and to act, was certainly one of the characteristics of the movement, which was a word revolution. The press was of course only one of its modes of expression; graffitti, "wall newspapers" (which were the work of the "Marxist-Leninists"), and, even more, the superb poster series published by the Beaux-Arts schools, especially in Paris, Caen, Montpellier, Lyons, and Marseilles,[30] were a breakaway from the dreary series usually to be found in the worker movements in Eastern as well as in Western Europe, showing a peasant grasping the hand of a worker against a rising sun background. Posters, too, like the press, recovered their "turbulence and aggressiveness" (Bachelard); they, too, restored meaning to the phrase "freedom of speech."

Document 143

Why We Are Fighting

The Reasons for the Revolt
It is not with pleasure that students are confronting the gardes-mobiles helmeted and armed to the teeth. It is not with pleasure that, at the period of examinations, students are responding to police violence.

It is never out of pleasure that one fights someone stronger than oneself.

For years students have been protesting the authoritarian methods that the government wanted to force upon them. Calmly, they protested against the Fouchet Reform, then against the Peyrefitte measures. For years, calmly, but also in an atmosphere of general indifference, the government ignored their protests just as it ignored the workers' protests. For years these protests remained vain and without response.

Today, the students are resisting.

Their only crime is to reject a University the sole goal of which is to train future bosses and docile tools for the economy. Their only crime is to reject an authoritarian and hierarchical social system which rejects any radical opposition; this means refusing to be the servants of this system.

For this crime alone, they are being rewarded by blackjacks and prison sentences.

University and *lycée* students have rallied and faced repression, because they want to defend themselves against police repression and the bourgeois government; the students are in a state of legitimate defense.

What you are also being led to believe is that this is merely a matter of the released inhibitions of a handful of isolated agitators who, of course, come from Nanterre, the source of all evil. Recourse to "nanterrorism" explains nothing. The government is easily reassured: the Nanterre "trouble makers" are not and never have been isolated. If this were not true, how may we explain the fact that students all over Europe are demonstrating? Where there is general unrest there are general causes.

All Over Europe

To stop the student revolt, beheading Nanterre would not be enough: the revolt that has now started in Paris has no boundaries; in Berlin, thousands of students have checkmated a strong reactionary governmental authority. The sds too was only a small handful of agitators; today it represents the only large movement opposed to growing fascism in Western Germany. In Italy, thousands of students have enforced their right to question the social system. They have responded to violent repression through demonstrations that were even more violent than those of last Friday. In Spain, England, Brazil; in Louvain,[31] throughout Europe and the world, students have taken to the streets to confront the forces of bourgeois "order." Everywhere, even in Paris, the violence of the repression has shown that governments are afraid of these movements, apparently so weak, but which have nevertheless begun to upset the existing order. However, press campaigns have tried to isolate and discredit the movements: it is not thanks to any particular love on the part of journalists that student revolts have made the front page of the newspapers. On the contrary, their only aim is to proportion the hate campaign to the potential danger to the social order.

The Same Combat

In Paris and in Nanterre they are not fighting alone; they are not fighting only for themselves. In Germany, on May first, tens of thousands of students and workers were *together,* on the initiative of the sds, in the first anti-capitalist demonstration that has taken place in Berlin since Naziism. The "handful of agitators" became a mass movement. Those who are combating the capitalist University stood shoulder to shoulder with those who are combating capitalist exploitation.

In France we also know that our fight has only begun; we know that youth is sensitive to the capitalist crisis and to the crisis of imperialism oppressing people in Vietnam, in Latin America, everywhere in the Third World. In Redon, in Caen, young workers are revolting violently, more violently than we are. On that subject the press, which is attacking us today, has remained silent. In spite of the government, in spite of the silence and the manipulations of its servile press, our struggle and theirs will converge.

Today students are becoming aware of what they are being trained for: to be managers for the existing economic system, paid to make it function in the best possible way. Their fight concerns all workers because it is also the workers' fight: they refuse to become professors in the service of an educational system which chooses the sons of the bourgeoisie and eliminates the others; sociologists who manufacture slogans for governmental election campaigns; psychologists responsible for making "worker teams function" in the best interest of the employers; managers responsible for applying against the workers a system to which they themselves are subjected.

Young people in the high schools, universities, and from the working class reject the future offered them by today's society; they reject unemployment, which is becoming a growing threat; they reject today's University, which gives them only worthless, ultra-specialized training and which, under the pretext of "selection," reserves know-how for sons of the bourgeoisie, and is but a tool for repression of all non-conformist ideas in the interest of the ruling class.

When young people resort to violent revolt, they are conscious of making this rejection stand out more clearly; they are conscious that their fight can give results only if the workers understand its meaning and make it their own. This is why today we are continuing the fight; this is why we appeal to you.

—Excerpt from *Action*, No. 1, May 7, 1968.

Document 144

Organizing Freedom

1. The absence of formal leadership was what attracted the major part of the student and worker demonstrators until May 13. Their constant concern not to be "co-opted" by any outside committee had no other significance than that of personally taking in hand their own fates.

2. For several hours on May 13 the presence of central committee leaders cast a mood of immense disappointment over the movement.

3. What is true on the national level is just as true on the level of preconstituted leadership in the Latin Quarter. All attempts at co-option by the "groupuscules," or by their militants, were severely opposed despite the fact that the broadest democracy had permitted everyone to express himself and to convince the crowd.

4. Freedom of speech was, in fact, the principal characteristic of the movement in student circles, but it also had strong attraction for both the young and older worker groups, even though they were greatly surprised by it. This freedom, which was imposed by the mass on those who tried to confiscate it for their own benefit, is the evident sign of an extraordinarily high level of awareness, even if it is accompanied by momentarily embarrassing aspects. The obsession with the risk of bureaucracy sometimes carries with it rejection of any kind of organization—which *is* necessary, nevertheless.

5. The categorical and persistent refusal to delegate any power whatsoever to anyone explains the success of the general assemblies among the students, and the organizational difficulties encountered by the professional organizers who, because of this fact, had nothing left to organize, since the people to be organized did not want it done by others than themselves—that is to say, in their own way, by the movement itself.

6. This same refusal explains the extraordinary reluctance on the part of those present at any assembly merely to tolerate a chairman, made necessary nevertheless by the very real differences of awareness. Voting was refused for the same reason.

7. But it should be noted that every time there was a majority of

workers working with a minority of students, the problems of organization solved themselves without any bureaucracy being set up.

8. At first the refusal to organize bureaucratically led to general refusal of any kind of organization. Once this was put into practice there was no more problem: organization is accomplished in and through the movement itself, of which it is only one aspect. The movement has no need of professional leaders or guides: it leads itself in the only possible direction, because reality does not permit it to choose among several paths.

9. Firsthand information is the commodity the most in demand in the movement because each one of its members wants to be able to make up his mind himself, with full knowledge of the facts.

10. Coordination is the second unsatisfied demand. This demand, which cuts across the preceding one, shows a general concern for anti-bureaucracy in seeking a solution to the problem of effectiveness.

11. Confident that the movement is the best possible approach to the socialist society we want to build, the desire has many times been manifested that it should continue to be so. Any undertakings that did not take this desire into account would fail, because they would lead to inevitable separation and consequently could only reproduce within themselves separate categories that would prefigure future social classes. Quite certainly this would not be acceptable to the majority.

—Excerpt from *Le Mouvement*, No. 3 (June),
published at Censier, about June 4.

Notes

1. Cf. above, Introduction pp. 4–8.

2. Cf. *Mouvement du 22 mars, Ce n'est qu'un début continuons le combat,* pp. 117–125.

3. On this point see Chapter I, pp. 128–131.

4. For appeals to soldiers see, among others, J. C. Perrot, M. Perrot, M. Rebérioux, J. Maitron, *La Sorbonne par elle-même,* pp. 139–140; J. P. Simon, *la Révolution par elle-même,* pp. 81 and pp. 104–105.

5. See above, Chapter II, p. 196, the leaflets circulated during the night of May 13–14.

6. For a more detailed choice of texts concerning the Sorbonne, see *La Sorbonne par elle-même.*

7. It should be noted that no mention is made of security services.

8. On the situationist vocabulary, cf. above, p. 66 and below, pp. 413 ff.

9. Against which someone had written: "How can one think freely in the shadow of a chapel?"

10. For a realistic picture of the occupied Sorbonne at this time, cf. J. La-couture, "Une République libertaire au quartier Latin," *Le Monde,* May 21, 1968.

11. See below, Chapter VI, p. 396.

12. He appeared under the name of Olivier Mamerloy in the novel by Françoise d'Eaubonne, *Jusqu'à la gauche,* Paris, 1964.

13. This text, which was actually written by members of the inter-union security service, was not distributed because of the occupation committee's veto. See the documents giving evidence of these problems in *La Sorbonne par elle-même.*

14. Avant-garde theatre directors in Lyons.

15. Cf. above, Chapter II, pp. 187–188.

16. Cf. above p. 187 the document from Marseilles dated May 11.

17. See below, Chapter IX, pp. 536–548.

18. Cf. S. Bosc and J.-M. Bouguereau, *les Temps Modernes,* July 1968, pp. 38–40.

19. *La Quatrième Internationale* for June 1968 published an article by Trotsky, dated November 26, 1935 on this subject.

20. Individual Communists were numerous, however, in the action com-mittees. Moreover, the UEC set up its own action committees.

21. The term "coordination of action committees," appearing as the signature on many leaflets, must not be taken too literally. It stood for a partially super-imposed body and, until May 25, was an offshoot of the MAU. After this date it was essentially controlled by the JCR. The left-wing elements who were opposed to this control grouped together in a permanent mobilization commission with head-quarters at the Beaux Arts. Cf. A. Geismar, S. July, E. Morane, op. cit., pp. 220–221. For a critical evaluation of the role of the "action committee," cf. especially, D. Singer, *Prelude to Revolution,* pp. 269–275.

22. Cf. below, p. 364.

23. For a contrasting view of these facts, cf. A. Geismar, S. July, E. Morane, op. cit., pp. 219–221.

24. For the attitude of *Le Monde,* as seen by a Communist academic, see the analysis by Jean Girault in *Le Monde, Humanisme, objectivité et politique,* by Aimé Guedj and Jean Girault. Collection *Notre Temps, Editions Sociales,* Paris, 1969.

25. No. 1: the address given (that of J.-J. Pauvert) is also that of the "action committee," 8, rue de Nesle. In No. 2, mention of the action committee disappeared and J.-J. Pauvert's name appeared. In the provinces, various *Enragés* (in Caen and in Rouen) were authentic publications of the movement.

26. Cf. above Chapter IV, pp. 308–315.

27. Cf., for instance, the article in No. 9 on the factory councils in Turin in 1920.

28. *Témoignage et Documents* and *Vérité-Liberté;* cf. above, Introduction, p. 5. By seizing *Action* No. 22 (July 18, 1968), the government returned to a tradition that also goes back to the Algerian War. And it is hard to understand why, in 1970, *La Cause du Peuple* should be regularly seized, in view of a court's refusal to forbid its appearance.

29. *Action* did not always avoid "phony" stories, and from May 6 on, they were one of the features of the movement; but how about the announcement of General de Gaulle's departure by the "leading newspapers" and the radio? How-ever, certain assertions or questions that passed for phony stories (for instance, concerning the mutiny on the aircraft carrier *Clemenceau,* No. 10, July 14) were perhaps more serious than appeared.

30. The collection published by Claude Tchou, *Affiches mai 1968,* prefaced by J. Cassou, "omitted posters that might suggest a call for violence, as well as those having a defamatory character with regard to private or official persons"; it is only very partially representative. As for the intellectual honesty of the procedure . . .

31. It should be noted that this list does not include Eastern countries, but *Action* abandoned this limitation. No. 22, dated July 18, 1968, contains a very interesting "letter from Prague."

VI

June: Ebb Tide

From May 31 (actually, from May 30 at 4:30 P.M.) until June 18, there was no doubt that the movement's ebb tide had set in. While all over France Gaullist demonstrations were becoming more numerous, resistance on the part of the metal workers in Paris, Sochaux, and Lyons assumed epic proportions in the eyes of the students. Flins too seemed like a symbol of hope. But signs of progressive, though not "victorious" (as *l'Humanité* stated), return to work were evident. The Montparnasse demonstration on Saturday, June 1 was to be the last peaceful march, the one that took place during the night of June 11–12 being marked by a confrontation between the police and young people burning official election panels. The "June days" followed a process that was symmetrical, only inversely, with those of May: fewer and fewer people were participating in the actions until the meeting at the Halle aux Vins on June 17, the day after the retaking of the Sorbonne. Compared with the May 8 meeting, this one was pretty bitter.

In spite of the blows it had received, particularly the dissolution on June 12 of the revolutionary student groups, the movement was not wholly aware of this ebb tide. The people's printing atelier at the *Ecole des Beaux-Arts* reached its peak of production in June, until it was closed by the police on June 27. Little by little, however, although tardily, the action committees adopted a less spectacular way of working, oriented now toward reform, now toward organization of the apocalypse. Meanwhile the Gaullist style triumphed, and the left-wing parties attributed responsibility for their electoral disaster to the revolutionaries.

On June 1, to assert its determination to pursue the movement, the UNEF organized a demonstration in front of the Gare Montparnasse where, to shouts of "elections are treason!" it brought out 40,000 people.[1] The "committee for coordination of action committees" supported this type of slogan, while an unsigned leaflet, after analyzing the political juncture, offered a series of suggestions that included both those of the action committees (self-defense) and those of the FER: the national strike committee.

Document 145

UNEF

Since early May, the most powerful mass movement that France has ever known has continued to grow. By occupying the factories, workers aim to impose their authority in industry as well as on the whole of society. By occupying the *facultés,* students are demonstrating their determination to radically transform society.

The breadth of the movement has been such that the bourgeoisie became frightened and is now trying to pull itself together by rallying around a government which was breaking down. Its game consists in trying to canalize the present movement, with a view to elections in which the employers' money and election combinations will allow it to save the essentials.

We cannot fall into such a trap. Only real worker authority in the factories and in society can guarantee lasting satisfaction of our demands. Otherwise the rise in prices and employer repression will quickly reduce to nothing the few advantages that have been won. When the mass of workers decided to pursue their action they understood this very well. They will not give in to threats and intimidation; they have already begun to organize to take over production in the factories, and they will continue the fight.

The consultations requested by the UNEF for the last three days, with a view to organizing a broad inter-union demonstration, could not take place. Certain people seem to have no concrete outlook beyond preparing for the elections. This is not our objective; a popular movement of this kind cannot get bogged down in any electoral operation whatsoever. The UNEF is therefore taking the initiative of calling on students, teachers, and workers to come to a large demonstration on Saturday, June 1, and is inviting the union organizations to join in this call.

DOWN WITH GAULLISM! POWER TO THE WORKERS!
THE FIGHT CONTINUES!

4 P.M. Meet at the *Place du 18 juin.*

—[June 1].

Document 146

Elections: A Delusion and a Snare

In order to break up the movement of 10 million strikers who threatened to overthrow the Gaullist government, the latter has decreed a reelection of Parliament as the only response to the unsatisfied demands of the workers. *These elections are therefore a counter-revolutionary maneuver* aiming to make the workers accept the legality of their oppression. However, in spite of union and political directives which deliberately play the game of the government by submitting to bourgeois legality, the majority of the workers and students have understood that elections will solve no problems.

If the movement has succeeded in undermining the authority of the employers, it is because it has developed independently of Parliament. This Parliament is nothing but a weapon of the bourgeoisie, which uses it when it wants. It is not the workers' weapon. The workers' weapons are the mass struggle and the general strike.

ELECTIONS ARE USEFUL FOR THE BOURGEOISIE!

They crush the mass movement. They are falsified through electoral gerrymandering, through monopoly of the news media, and through repression. They are a delusion and a snare with which the ruling class expects to lull the workers and students with illusions. They are a pretext for enforcing the legality of our oppressors. In short, for workers and students, the elections are a farce for which they will have to bear the brunt, as usual. *The bourgeois are not going to relinquish their authority through the ballot boxes; it must be wrested from them in the factories and in the streets.*

The regime has yet to be overthrown.

THE FIGHT CONTINUES.

AGAINST LIES: GET THE FACTS; AGAINST REPRESSION: ORGANIZE.

POWER IS NOT IN THE BALLOT BOXES, IT MUST BE SEIZED IN
THE FACTORIES.

Join the Action Committees.

—Bureau for Coordination of Action Committees [May 31].

Monday, June 3 was marked by a return to work in the banks and in the mines, as also by voting, instigated by the RATP and SNCF unions. The ORTF inter-union broke with its ministry, while the JCR and the 22 *mars* made contradictory analyses of the ebb tide that had set in. As always in periods of wane, the "organisateurs" proved to be more clearsighted than the "spontanéistes."

Document 147

De Gaulle gave a firm response to PC hesitations and shillyshallying, thereby sowing panic among political general staffs. He responded by faithfully defending his job: then came the Gaullist demonstration on the Champs-Elysées.

The CGT leaders, who had changed attitudes several times, were now in the position of being forced to accept or refuse confrontations. Although at first they had underlined the strictly economic aspect of the strike, Séguy, Krasucki, and others like them, hard pressed by the grass roots after the workers had refused to ratify the negotiations, organized Wednesday's big demonstration of force with political slogans ("popular government!"). The corner was turned.

But the bourgeoisie was prompt to counter, having been made uneasy by a Mendès solution that stemmed from an occupation movement, and believing (rightly or not) that this last card would be of little advantage, faced with an organized popular movement. The bourgeoisie closed ranks behind the General-President, symbol of the maintenance of bourgeois law and order.

In this way de Gaulle cut short all maneuverings on the part of the political machines. His speech gave notice: the present struggle is a typical class struggle; if confrontation becomes necessary, the bourgeois government will do its duty. The CGT and the Communist Party having been driven into a corner took a new turn the very next day, after the Bastille-Saint-Lazare demonstration. The PC, which was politically unprepared for the insurrection, did not want it—even feared it, to an extent that worried the Soviet Union, for whom de Gaulle was a friend, thus clearly demonstrating its political and organizational social-democratic nature.

After de Gaulle's speech the CGT abandoned all political demands by again confining itself to the economic aspect of the fight, even giving in on this ground (repeal of the decrees as a prerequisite for any negotiation was thrown out). This being the case, by presenting the legal solution of elections as the goal of the fight, the working class leaders surrendered to the government and admitted their defeat. Worse still, through a policy of negotiation by sectors, they left the way open to the "carrot and stick" policy advocated by de Gaulle.

The government must now give satisfaction—temporarily—to

the "justified demands" of serious students and workers and, at the same time, prepare the repression against the diehards, the impenitent troublemakers and the riff-raff, or rather the *chienlit*. It must help restore order in the factories and in the *facultés,* at the price of temporary concessions, the better to liquidate the most resolute and combative elements.

Until the elections Gaullism can present itself as champion of the maintenance of law and order through parliamentary means; it can even appear to be liberal. But if elections confirm the "popular support" that Gaullism claims, it will take advantage of the ebb tide, demobilization, and vacations to become all the more repressive toward the tail end of the movement and the last strikers.

Today, whether the movement is being stabilized or is on the wane, we must clearly understand that it is entering upon a phase of organization in which its soundest features remain intact. We must understand that the bourgeoisie has only a slight margin of maneuver, on the economic and political level, in which to solve the crisis. In order to profit from this slight margin, we must act. The month we have just lived through is only the first flareup of a historical crisis which, after twenty years of relative stability, is weakening all of Western capitalism. We must prepare ourselves for the struggles to come by organizing and reassembling the revolutionary militants who have appeared during the fighting. We must explain to them the scope and limitations of the combats that have taken place, in order to avoid demoralization and build up the strength needed to launch future combats.

If all these elements are understood, we must carefully watch next Tuesday's events. If there is a mass return to work in certain determinant sectors, especially transport, it would be irresponsible, by waving the banner of a "hell and high-water" philosophy, to encourage the irreconcilables to fight one last ditch battle, with the risks this would entail. The most combative militants would become exhausted and demoralized in rear guard fights, and would be all the more exposed to repression, since they would be more isolated.

This is why, to the extent that we are presently entering into a time of temporary reflux, political organization and explanation must now have priority over agitation, properly speaking. We must show through our propaganda action just what happened, as well as what could have happened. We must show that socialism in France is not a utopia, that it could have been set up at the end of these May days if the political and organizational bases that they implied had been achieved by the entire worker movement.

Lastly, it is now clear that the spontaneousness of the masses can not suffice to make a movement end by seizure of revolutionary power. Revolution is a science to be learned. Its preparation through the organization of a true revolutionary movement has become the fundamental task of today, if we do not want everything that has happened to be lost for the future.

—*La Jeunesse communiste révolutionnaire, Aujourd'hui*, No. 5 [June 3].

Document 148

"Counter-Revolution Is a Science to Be Learned"

The specific action of the *Mouvement du 22 mars* cannot be reduced to direct confrontation with governmental authority or to rediscovery of violent forms. It has not been the straw that breaks the camel's back, the catalyzer, etc. Whatever a certain number of the sociological-minded may think, the "consumer society" by no means reduces the potentialities for violence in present day society. These potentialities have simply been reduced, fragmented, and integrated.

The specific action of the *22 mars* is to have *politically* thwarted the canalizing methods of government institutions, the unions, and the Party [Communist].

"Normally," when the cops prevent entry into a building like the Sorbonne, we negotiate, we withdraw, we protest, or we make motions. "Normally," there are people there to play the game of this negotiation: representatives of the UNEF, unions, elected delegates, etc. In this case, the mechanism has not worked. In his text Coudray seems to consider that most workers—except for an avant-garde of young workers—are fundamentally accomplices of union bureaucracy.[2] In fact, there are no alternative solutions at their disposal. Occupation of the factories has followed the illegal occupation of the Sorbonne and other public buildings.

The lack of authorized spokesmen for the student movement is paralleled by the fact that numerous workers refuse Séguy's preliminary agreement.

Today, those who like to speak in terms of periods of rise and fall, have decreed general withdrawal and are beginning to count their marbles, which explains the calls for a return to discipline, to organization, to long-term perspectives. . . . In fact, the protest movement is absolutely not in retreat. It is searching for new ways and means, new weapons. When all is said and done the "groupuscules" who claim to be capitalizing on the avant-garde are behaving like watchdogs of the union bureaucracies. They want to canalize a movement between organizational outlines that have been proved a failure. The reactionary ideology of a pyramidal organization has already begun to proliferate: the cc, the bp, the *secretariat,* the avant-garde party, the mass organizations or "transmission belts," etc.

An original form of revolutionary organization is trying to find itself in the struggle, as well as in an effort to frustrate the maneuvers of the "very experienced specialists" in revolutionary organization, who claim to dispose of an ideological capital, of absolute know-how, and from whom the masses should expect everything. A takeover of the action committees by these rigid militants, who have shown themselves incapable of understanding the struggle in its development and have several times, under different pretexts, tried to go against it, would mean disorganization and, in the long run, retreat.

Not only must the *22 mars* not give in to the blackmail of so-called democratic-centralist integration of grass roots committees, but it must defend the right of these committees to remain independent of all structures that are seeking to top them.

To federate grass roots committees would make sense only at a much later stage, at the moment when it would be a question of setting up one of the structures for seizing power on regional and national levels. Today the grass roots committees are pursuing a guerrilla-type action; to try to unify them too soon would undoubtedly mean sterilizing them.[3] A coordinating structure that leaves the possibility for full extension of the committees, and especially for freedom of speech and creativeness at the grass roots—which remains the essential weapon of the revolutionary movement—is something quite different.

—Excerpt from *Tribune du 22 mars,* June 5.

On Tuesday, June 4, work was resumed in the arsenals and at the edf. The *Tribune du 22 mars* published accounts of a few typical provincial situations that take on a nostalgic exemplariness.

Document 149

Rennes

Creation of an inter-union front (cgt, fo, cfdt) was achieved on May 31 with occupation of the hall transformed for the occasion into a Neighborhood House. The Mayor placed it at their disposal.

Students and workers meet there for:
—discussion of the strikes,
—criticism of capitalism,
—cultural evenings,
—history of the Commune,
—readings of excerpts from Brecht's works,
—organization of supply committees.

Furthermore, on June first there was agreement with the Rector giving the strikers access to University restaurants; this was obtained by the unions and action committees (suggested by the tryout in Nanterre). The municipality is making a contribution of 1 franc per meal, which makes lunch cost the striker 2 francs.

Organization of supplies has only just begun. At the beginning peasants, out of solidarity, donated rabbits, poultry. . . . Transport difficulties were considerable (gas, vehicles). Twin-city arrangements were made with the different communes of the Ille-et-Vilaine department.

Meat was brought down to cost price; calf's liver at 7 francs a kilo (70 cents a pound), and new potatoes at 50 centimes a kilo (10 cents a pound).

Distribution is being made in the occupied factories, unfortunately as yet only on a very small scale.

The peasants have asked striking workers for help with the hay, and technical school pupils to help them repair agricultural machines.

Have set up food stocking one day in advance in the villages, to simplify collection.

Actors have begun to give newscasts, using living theater techniques, which seem to have a great impact.

Tours

In Tours, which is a reactionary city (70% of the votes go to the deputy-mayor Royer), the movement has undoubtedly been out of line both because of its starting date and of the extent of its evolution in comparison with the rest of the country.

In this respect, the situation of the Michelin plant offers a good example: repression there is severe; union membership is very weak; fighting traditions are practically non-existent. The strike, started at the instigation of a minority, took the form of occupation and organization of hard-line picketing. There were no foreigners (Portuguese or Yugoslavs) among the non-strikers. But the strike was very quickly broken up by the employers and the scabs, with the aid of a locomotive. It was only after work started again, and not during reoccupation of the premises, that CGT pickets responsible for the non-functioning of electricity in the plant cut off the electric power for a short time.

After having been occupied, the University was abandoned at the request of the professors and of the AGET. The ESU members who control the AGET bogged down the movement on the question of examinations and co-management. The situation is very different in the secondary schools where the CAL's are very strong and often become CAR's. The CAR's work with the militant anarchist-syndicalist railroad workers, who seem to have retained a certain influence over the evolution of the fight. The result was that after de Gaulle's speech they had the railway station occupied, as well as the freight depot, to which they retreated with dogs and iron bars. They are organizing self-defense and occupation, installing dormitories in sleeping cars. They say they are ready to intervene in places threatened by the police or by the Gaullists.

Last Friday a unitary demonstration brought out 6,000 people. Students supported by the CAL's were able to put over the slogan "power to the workers" in reply to the CGT's "popular government" directive. With this, the *m-l*'s [*marxiste-léniniste*] may be said to have left the student ranks to join those of the CGT.

—Excerpt from *Tribune du 22 mars*, June 4.

Document 150

The Nantes Commune

Sometimes thought precedes action and ends, exhausted, beyond reality. This is what happens at the hallucinating forums that take place in the amphis of the Sorbonne or at the Odéon. But sometimes action precedes thought and one might be tempted to say precedes language. This is what has happened in the Nantes Commune. Whereas in Paris, without believing in it too much, we are urging constitution of a dual power—that is to say, the power of the masses, of the self-organizing grass roots confronted with established authority; whereas we are calling for self-management—it already exists on the municipal level, or at least a promising outline of it exists, in Nantes. Here is a city about which one can say that it is in the advance guard of the revolutionary struggle. An inter-union committee has its headquarters in the city hall and practically runs the city. It is in charge not only of the distribution of water, gas, and electricity, but also of obtaining food supplies for all the strikers, in cooperation with peasant organizations and neighboring villages. Moreover, for several days duly certified gasoline and food coupons were distributed by this inter-union committee. Better still, the committee controls prices in the city, and delegates visit the markets and retail stores to force shopkeepers to hold their prices. That is what is meant by dual power. They have also formed neighborhood committees and in cooperation with the nearby villages, have undertaken to supply the strikers' families with the basic products. The peasants, especially those in the CDJA, sell at cost price—that is to say, we are witnessing concretely, even though on a reduced scale, the disappearance of middlemen!

Dual power, then; but the originality of Nantes does not stop there. One thing is surprising, and for that very reason encouraging: this is a real and concrete alliance among workers, peasants, and students— that is, between the revolutionary classes and the revolutionary students. This alliance has been formed especially at the grass roots; the students and workers are going to help the peasants with their work, the students are supporting the picket lines of the striking workers, everybody is acting practically hand in hand. But the alliance exists also on the organizational level. At the *Intersyndical* there are the CGT, the CFDT, CGT-FO, FEN, the UNEF (controlled by the "anars," the CDJA[4] and the FDSEA[5]).

A thought comes to mind when one has seen and understood the reality of the Nantes Commune. Here is the solution; this is the revolutionary action that should be carried out everywhere now! If there were 10 or 20 Nantes in France and in Europe, Gaullist administration, and capitalism along with it, would collapse. If there were 10 or 20 Nantes, the revolution would really take place, concretely, at the grass roots, for good. If there were 10 or 20 Nantes, we would not have to reckon with the established bureaucracies, we would be able to avoid the monstrous hoax, the monstrous co-option of a revolution "de palais" (under the circumstances, the *Palais Bourbon* [National Assembly building]) bringing the left to seize this administrative authority, to which we oppose this other authority, the authority of the masses and direct democracy. The revolution will be a revolution of the masses, not a coup d'etat between bureaucracies.

—Excerpt from *Tribune du 22 mars,* June 5.

On Wednesday, June 5 and Thursday, June 6, return to work became more and more general, involving the RATP, the postal workers, the miners, and the SNCF. The CRS were still occupying the Renault factory at Flins when Alain Geismar and a student from the *22 mars* spoke on the morning of the 7th at Elizabethville.

Document 151

Flins: Determined to Resist

Just when several striking sectors are going back to work, after satisfaction of certain grievances and pledges on the part of the parliamentary left to the Gaullist government, *the bourgeoisie has chosen to strike at the most enlightened part of the working class in order to crush the revolutionary action under way.*

At the Renault plant in Flins, the CRS first invaded the plant, attacking the picket line with the help of some twenty halftracks, which drove into the gates at almost 40 miles an hour. 3,000 CRS are now occupying the plant. But the workers have organized their reply.

In answer to their call, several thousand workers and students assembled in front of the plant at 5 A.M. The workers decided to pursue the fight until their demands had been satisfied. About 10:30 A.M. the cops charged. They immediately used high power grenades on the front picket lines, which fell into place facing the massed *gardes mobiles.*

Twenty demonstrators were injured. The cops charged again, while the demonstrators were bombarded from a helicopter.

The fight will continue. *The future of the revolutionary process is at stake in Flins.*

—Excerpt from *Tribune du 22 mars,* June 7, 1968.

"The Gaullist government is seeking and fomenting disorder and to this end they are being greatly helped by Trotskyist, anarchist-Maoist, and other leftist groups." This leaflet, dated June 7 and brought out by the Renault section of the PCF, shows how the CGT and the PC welcomed the students. During the late afternoon a march left the Sorbonne and the Halle aux vins, headed for the Gare Saint-Lazare: "Liberate Flins! No cops in Flins!" were the slogans. About 7 P.M. the marchers were joined by CFDT workers and a delegation from the *Etats Généraux du Cinéma.* The demonstrators hoped to get a special train for Flins. The station loudspeakers warned against provocation. The demonstrators then went to the Porte de Saint-Cloud to ask for transport from the bus terminal, but without success. General de Gaulle's radio-television interview with Michel Droit on the evening of June 7 left the students cold. The next day, with *l'Humanité* denouncing the "Geismar groups," that is, the students who had succeeded in reaching Flins, the rat hunts started, with the police picking up all those who had anything youthful about them. The *Mouvement du 22 mars* recounted the facts.

That same day several primary school teachers, in protest against the back-to-work order, occupied the headquarters of the *Fédération de l'Education Nationale* (FEN). In the evening, Georges Pompidou launched a violent attack against secondary school professors, most of whom returned to work on June 10 or 11.

Document 152

Flins: Self-Defense

> The fault lies with the bourgeoisie; the fight is exemplary.
> Thousands of CRS have invaded Flins.
> THE RESPONSE WAS IMMEDIATE: THE STRIKE WILL CONTINUE.
> Worker-student solidarity has been demonstrated.
> At the request of Flins workers and in answer to the call of the *Mouvement du 22 mars,* the *Mouvement de soutien aux luttes du peuple,* and of the action committees, hundreds of Parisians came on Friday at 5 A.M. to support the fight, facing the CRS.
> A meeting showed the workers' determination, after which they left for the picket line to organize the fight.
> *3,000 CRS charged with offensive grenades.*
> A day of combat in which 5,000 workers and several hundred students opposed repression.
> *Solidarity is being organized.*
> In answer to the Renault workers' call for self-defense in Flins, workers and students, re-organized in committees for action and combat, are mobilizing.
> *Today, Saturday, tomorrow, and Monday,* they will be in Flins to help with self-defense and with procuring supplies.
> This is not a call for verbal solidarity or for an outing, *but for really organizing the defense of Flins, which is the focal point of the working class.*
>
> MOBILIZE IN YOUR NEIGHBORHOOD!
> FORM SELF-DEFENSE GROUPS!

ALL UNITED IN THE FIGHT!
ALL UNITED AGAINST REPRESSION!

—Mouvement du 22 mars, June 8, 1968.

On the 9th and 10th the rat hunts were still going on. Concurrently, the repression was accentuated by arbitrary expulsion of foreigners. The following *22 mars* text gives a glimpse of this general atmosphere.

Document 153

In Flins, on this 10th day of June, the police reign supreme.

6:30 A.M.—About *a hundred comrades at the* CFDT *headquarters in Les Mureaux. There are also the* CGT *comrades.* Discussion by small groups in the headquarters garden. Arrival of cops, some forty of whom block all exits. The comrades are facing the cops, their backs to the wall. The cops advance. Some comrades try to jump behind into the gardens of the adjoining houses, since the CRS were not yet there. One or two comrades say: "No provocation, everybody stay together so that there'll be no isolated rat hunts." *80 comrades were picked up this way.* They were not given the third degree immediately, but a little later, because we could hear their screams of pain. Then the rat hunts started in the streets of Les Mureaux. The cops pursued the "students" (all those who appeared to be students), who were the only ones arrested. The workers let them do it. For instance, a small police car stopped in the middle of a group of several hundred workers, trying to arrest a young man among them. The same young man later was chased by a half-dozen cops running at full speed in front of their paddy wagon. He was obliged to keep shouting for 250 yards, before a door was opened and he found refuge in somebody's house. The cops then went to look for him for a quarter of an hour, searching the vicinity carefully. The young comrade succeeded in escaping on foot into the woods, but the whole city was surrounded; it was impossible to leave. All the cars with "75" on their plates ["75" refers to Paris] had their tires punctured, their windshields broken. On the way out, the same comrade had been stopped by motor-cops in a jeep, armed with machine gun pistols.

Other comrades tell the following: The buses going to Renault-Flins were almost empty, but some were carrying workers. Since the cops were inside the plant, they told the workers, "Now we are here,

we don't need you. . . ." The cops refused to leave. The workers said,
"In that case, we will stay in the garden; we are not working." Then
the cops attacked them. The workers fell back to the paint shop; there
were between six to seven hundred of them. They put up a hard fight.
The cops shot off tear gas grenades at them. After a certain time, half
the comrades had passed out.

9 to 11 o'clock—We arrived in cars after proceeding with a series
of precautionary operations. The *gardes-mobiles* were on the super-
highway bridges, well before the Les Mureaux exit. Apparently,
they were announcing by telephone the arrival of suspected cars. In
front of the CRS post on the highway (3 to 5 miles before Les Mureaux)
identity papers were being "examined" by men with machine guns. In
Les Mureaux, the streets were crowded, but there was no meeting, just
small groups discussing. In Elisabethville, on the Place de l'Etoile, there
were small, scattered groups in the streets. "What's happening?" "We
don't know. There was supposed to be a meeting at 8 o'clock; the delegates haven't come! We're waiting." Someone thought they had arrested
the CFDT delegate.

10 o'clock—A motorcycle cop passed with a radio set on his motorcycle. At the barrier on the school corner, in front of the factory, a
group of about one hundred persons composed of young people and
workers asked, "What's going on?" Nobody knew. Someone said, with
regard to the meeting, that something must have happened at the factory, but he didn't know what. Lots of cops on the other side of the
barrier. Until 11 o'clock, nothing. As soon as we left Elisabethville we
noticed that the whole region was blanketed. Gendarmes at the crossroads of National Road 13 leading into the freeway; the entire length
of the water works; behind Flins; near the small wood, on foot; an
armed gendarme every ten yards; radio cars. In a quarter of an hour,
on the West Freeway going toward Flins, six convoys of some ten
trucks each were going up filled with CRS. At the Porte de Saint-Cloud,
at the exit of the freeway, cops started chasing everybody they considered suspect. Anyone who even resembled a student was stopped.

Pursuit of students and rat hunting were continuous. Although
by noon access to Elisabethville as well as to Les Mureaux was relatively easy, it was practically impossible to remain in the streets. There
was a permanent police car patrol, even inside the workers' housing
complex, where a certain complicity allowed the students being pursued
to take refuge in people's homes.

The police maneuver was to separate the students from the workers, to consider them the only trouble makers. But this maneuver was
self-defeating because of an atmosphere of a veritable state of siege;

students were arrested in large numbers. Against the psychosis of fear which has tended to take hold, the working class population is reacting and trying to organize its own protection: lookout posts at their windows, bicycle tours of inspection, as well as protection of students who have escaped arrest.

FLINS HAS BECOME A FORBIDDEN AREA;
THERE TOO, THE GOVERNMENT IS PREPARING THE PARLIAMENTARY ELECTIONS.

—*Mouvement du 22 mars,* June 10.

On June 10, an eighteen-year-old *lycée* student, Gilles Tautin, was drowned as a result of a police raid. That evening a demonstration broke out spontaneously in the Latin Quarter. Following is the testimony of Jean Terrel, former president of the *Cartel des Ecoles Normales Supérieures,* as well as of the UNEF.[6] Gilles Tautin's funeral procession, supervised from a helicopter, was followed by 5,000 people, singing softly the *Internationale* and *Le Chant des Martyrs.*

Document 154

Open Letter to Newspaper Editors

To the Editor-in-Chief:

I was one of the militants of the *Mouvement de soutien aux luttes du peuple,* who were brutally attacked by the police yesterday at Les Mureaux. In view of the plot of lies and smears orchestrated by the bourgeoisie through its press and radio, the facts should be made known.

We were sitting to one side on the grass, discussing the work we had to do to support the strikers. This was at the far end of an island. We were talking about examination of identity papers when two groups of police charged us, *brandishing their rifle butts.* Certain of them even had makeshift arms such as pieces of hose or wood.

The police said that we did not have a clear conscience. But today every militant knows what cop accusations are. Charging with rifle butts is a funny way to verify a person's identity.

People also say that, panic stricken, we jumped into the water. There was no question of panic. We dived in because, faced with police brutality, we had no other way out, real rat hunts having taken place all day long in Les Mureaux. According to the Mayor himself, young people had been pursued into municipal, union, and even Church premises. We knew all that. We preferred the Seine to being blackjacked. Actually, the police wanted both the Seine and blackjacks. We were attacked to shouts of "into the water! Everyone into the tub!" The comrades who were too slow in diving were pushed into the water with rifle butts. On the other side of the Seine, the cops were waiting for us, ready to shoot. On three occasions comrades who had been too prompt to flee were stopped with shouts of "Halt, or I fire!"

One comrade was shoved into the water with a rifle butt. We saw Gilles sink. We shouted: "Stop, someone is drowning!" The gendarmes remained impassive, more concerned with stopping us on the bank than with giving "assistance to a person in danger" [as French law requires].

By this time people had begun to gather on the bank and were shouting their anger and indignation at the gendarmes. Paving stones began to fly. If they had not run very fast, the police would have been lynched. The gendarme who clubbed a comrade as he came out of the water was formally recognized. The Mayor of Les Mureaux took his number.

These are some of the facts that have not been reported by any newspaper. I draw from this two conclusions:

1. The bourgeois press and radio, without any investigation among participants and witnesses, has started a vile campaign of calumnies and lies.

2. Our comrade died assassinated. Assassinated by de Gaulle's cops.

> —Jean Terrel, former president of the UNEF, militant of the *Union des jeunesses communistes (marxistes-léninistes)*.
> Excerpt from *La Cause du peuple,* No. 15, June 12.

On June 11, with the situation becoming more tense, a worker was killed by gunshot in Sochaux, and another died while trying to escape from the CRS. A call for a demonstration at the Gare de l'Est, in protest against the repression, was sent out by the UNEF, the CAL's, and the action committees. In spite of what appeared on certain leaflets, neither the SNESUP. nor the CFDT had officially backed the call. The police tried to prevent the demonstrations from forming, and all night long there were violent clashes at the barricades almost everywhere. A UJC(m-l) leaflet gave the conclusions to be drawn from Gilles Tautin's assassination.

Then *Le Monde,* which had supported the student movement thus far, more or less, criticized it sharply in an editorial by Hubert

Beuve-Méry (Editor-in-Chief), while B. Girod de l'Ain, in the same
newspaper, exposed the *"bateau ivre"* that the Sorbonne had become,
and made public the existence there of so-called "Katangans,"[7] a group
in which a would-be former Katangan mercenary and a few ex-oas
men had joined up with what were mostly victims of unemployment
from the sub-proletariat. A violent press campaign that went from
Paris-Jour to *l'Humanité* followed.

Document 155

Everybody in Support of Flins: to Continue the Fight Is to Assert the Power of the Workers

A police state has taken over in Flins, believing that it can crush the
strikers' resistance and stop the movement. The confrontation is a
violent one, but Flins is not isolated.

RENAULT, CLEON AND BILLANCOURT,
PEUGEOT (IN SOCHAUX),
CITROEN,
WILL NOT GIVE UP.

On the contrary, working class determination to keep on fighting
is taking on a new impetus. For workers and students, Flins is becoming the exposed nerve of the class struggle.

Monday, June 10th, third day of repression. At the beginning, in
the buses going to the plant, the CRS, their weapons slung over their
shoulders, were "rat hunting" students. Students, jammed into police
cars, were transported to Beaujon.

NOBODY WILL GO BACK TO WORK!

All day long at Les Mureaux, 10,000 CRS on patrol; in the city
tension was growing. Workers and students were fraternizing; those
who were tracked down were being taken in by the inhabitants. During the afternoon a meeting of young people took place on the island.
The CRS attacked. *An 18-year-old* lycée *pupil, a political militant, is
dead! Knocked senseless by blows from a rifle butt, he was thrown into
the mud bank, and drowned.* A young girl was revived just in time to
save her.

The government has entered upon a new stage of repression: we
must enter upon a new stage of the struggle.

We must generalize response on all fronts
Against repression
In solidarity with the strike, which will continue!

EVERYBODY COME TO THE DEMONSTRATION, TUESDAY JUNE 11TH
AT 7 P.M. GARE DE L'EST.

—Coordinating Committee of Action Committees [June 11].

Calling for this demonstration are: the UNEF, the SNESup., CAL, CFDT, and the Action Committees.

Document 156

A comrade is dead. A young *lycée* student, Gilles Tautin, from the *Lycée Mallarmé*. A militant of the *Mouvement de soutien aux luttes du peuple*. A militant of the *Union des jeunesses communistes (marxistes-léninistes)*. He died in Flins.

He died blackjacked by the cops, drowned. Other comrades have not yet come back. All day long hundreds of young people were being chased, hunted, and arrested. And the Flins proletariat, yes or no, were they killed? We will find out. Hundreds of proletarians were wounded. Gilles is a witness for them all.

Who killed our comrade? The cops and the Gaullist dictatorship. This government of assassins horrifies the people. This government, which is the legal agent of the exploiters, is loathed by workers, peasants, intellectuals, and by the entire working population. Our people rose up against this government. The strength of millions of proletarians taking over the factories weakened the authority of the exploiters, and the capitalists were trembling. Today, their government would like to make the people pay, make them forget that they are an invincible force. It would like to divide them, repress them. It will not be able to do it.

The Gaullist government hoped that "law and order" would be restored. Had it not promised legislative elections? Yes, elections in order for work to start again. For work to start again before satisfaction of the workers' demands. Elections in order for the workers to return to their factories under the pressure of the scabs, the cops, and the CDR's. Elections in order to subdue the people. And when workers resist, as they did at Citroën and Renault, the government of assassins sends its CRS.

But like all reactionaries, the Gaullist government underestimates the people's strength: the working class is resisting, and the youth and the people generally are supporting the bastions of proletarian resistance. In Flins workers, students, and all the inhabitants are united, united for the victory of the same cause, which is the people's cause.

Who helped the government in its task of division and repression? The anti-worker and the anti-people police. The great masses of our country saw them at work: the FO leaders licking the ministers' boots, the CFDT leaders who signed all the capitulation agreements and who succeeded in presenting their candidate, a retired anti-communist politician, Mendès-France, at a time when the working class was fighting for satisfaction of all its demands and for a people's government. Lastly, the leaders of the CGT confederation, and the clique of PCF politicians.

The attitude of the CGT confederation leaders was disgraceful. They called for a return to work, by means of secret balloting and lies. They sabotaged the self-defense of the factories. They opened the gates of Flins to the CRS. *In order for the elections to take place, they disarmed the working class and armed the assassins in Flins.*

What did the Board of the CGT confederation and *l'Humanité* say on June 7, 1968?

"The government has neglected to designate the true instigators of trouble and provocation whose machinations, including the refusal to go back to work, are covered up by an odd complacency on the part of the government."

The government answered this call: it killed our comrade.

Our comrade is dead. Those responsible for his assassination are the Gaullist government and its accomplices in the confederal board of the CGT and among the PCF leaders. Our comrade died to serve the people. He died for union of the Youth Movement and the Worker Movement. He went to Flins to put himself under the authority of the workers and the proletarian unionists of the CGT, because he was part of a political organization that began in the heart of the working class masses. The organization was proud to have among its members defenders of the CGT and of the proletariat. He was a young militant who defended the working class cause and the class struggle cause of the great CGT, which are indissolubly linked together. He did not confuse the traitors of the confederation's board with the hundreds of thousands of CGT militants, who are ardent defenders of the working class cause. It should be known for what and for whom he died: *for the working class, for the* CGT *class struggle, for the party of revolutionary prole-*

tarians that he helped to set up, *for the people*. In his mind he had engraved the teachings of the great guide of World Revolution, comrade Mao Tse-tung: *Serve the People*.

Comrade, from now on your name is inseparable from the people's revolution, from the springtime of our people!

We swear to you that we will follow the path you have marked out with your blood. The blood of proletarians, the blood of our *lycée* comrade, of those who died without the people's knowledge, is for us all *the blood of martyrs*. Martyrs to the people's revolution. It rouses our hatred, which is enormous—as great as the suffering inflicted upon the people by their exploiters.

> *Comrades, gather around the red flag*
> *of proletarian resistance,*
> *of the people's revolution, of communism*
> UNITED UNTIL VICTORY!

—Proletarian Unionists CGT. *Mouvement de soutien aux luttes du peuple. Union des jeunesses communistes (marxistes-léninistes)* and organizations along the lines of *"Servir le Peuple"* [June 11 A.M.]. (*printed leaflet bordered in black*)

On the morning of Wednesday, June 12, all demonstrations were forbidden and the extreme leftist organizations were disbanded by the government: FER, JCR, VO, UJC(m-l), *Mouvement du 22 mars;* these were followed later by the PCMLF, the OCI, and the PCI. The disbanded movements called for a demonstration which soon turned into a meeting at the *Cité universitaire*.

Document 157

Communiqué

Wednesday, June 12

The government is brandishing the threat of repression at the demonstration on the rights of immigrant workers in France. We are demanding that their rights be recognized and that discrimination cease.

While awaiting clarification of other means of responding to governmental attempts to crush the workers' struggle, we are maintaining our decision to defend immigrant workers. We do not intend

to fall into the police provocations of the bourgeois government. Consequently, we invite workers and students to hold a gathering in the
> *Gardens of the Cité universitaire internationale,*
> *Boulevard Jourdan, at 8* P.M.,

to protest, as planned, against all forms of discrimination against foreigners, and to demand that deportation measures taken with respect to certain of our comrades be rescinded.

> —Action Committees, *Mouvement de soutien aux luttes du peuple;*
> *Mouvement du 22 mars.*

On June 13 the Sorbonne was gradually closed for cleaning and reorganization by the students.[8] On the 14th, at dawn, after an eventful night, the "Katangans" were evicted, as much through persuasive as through violent means. The Odéon [Theatre] was surrounded and retaken by the police, while at the Renault factory it was decided to vote on whether or not there would be a return to work on the 17th. On the 14th there was a meeting of the "Steering Committee for a Revolutionary Movement."[9] During this same period, in the national committee of the CGT confederation, Georges Séguy devoted much of his analysis to savage criticism of the leftist movements and congratulated himself on his own wisdom.

Document 158

The Fight Continues

To be relieved of its responsibility, the government is prohibiting revolutionary organizations. This measure is the logical consequence of the policy of intimidation of the masses announced by de Gaulle in his May 30 speech. Whereas the government brutally attacks the worker-student resistance centers in Flins, Sochaux, and Paris, it wants to blame the consequences of the brutality of its repression on movements which have refused to be fooled by promises of elections.

These police measures will not be enough to solve the serious social problems raised by the crisis. The fight continues. Today we are taking advantage of an electoral period in order to launch an important campaign for political explanation of the May events.

STOP REPRESSION
RESCIND THE INTERDICTIONS

Everybody come to the meeting organized by the
Steering Committee for a Revolutionary Movement.

FRIDAY, JUNE 14, AT 8:30 P.M. HALL OF THE MUTUALITÉ
(*Métro: Maubert-Mutualité*)

Speakers, under the chairmanship of J.-P. Vigier:
M. Heurgon, J. Sauvageot, A. Krivine, G. Bloch, J. Grynbaum, B.
Herzberg.

—(Printed leaflet.)

On June 15 and 16, the Sorbonne was still being cleaned by the
students. On the 16th, in the early afternoon, it was suddenly surrounded by police forces. They claimed to be seeking information concerning a young man taken from the Sorbonne infirmary, who had
been hospitalized at the Hôtel-Dieu for a knife wound received in the
neighborhood of the Odéon. A communiqué from the National Board
of the SNESup. exposed—with some exaggerations (it is not true that the
last occupiers had all been molested)—the circumstances of this takeover. By the end of the afternoon, fighting had broken out pretty generally from the Latin Quarter to Saint-Sulpice.

Document 159

The National Board of the SNESup. *Communicates*

The representative delegated by the National Board of the SNESup to
the Sorbonne wishes to make public the following facts, which he personally witnessed.

1. At the time the events I am describing took place, the Sorbonne was calm and orderly.

2. The wounded person sent to the Hôtel-Dieu hospital had been
brought to the Sorbonne infirmary during the night from the outside.
A certain number of sick or wounded in the neighborhood had in fact
been brought to the Sorbonne infirmary since the beginning of the recent events. During this same night of June 15–16 other sick or
wounded persons were brought to the Sorbonne infirmary from outside and sent to hospitals, without their cases having been exploited in
a similar scandalous and clearly provocative way.

3. A commission investigating this point had already started its
work inside the Sorbonne. Its functioning was interrupted by the threat

of police invasion, then by the invasion itself. Nevertheless, while this commission was in session, a certain number of policemen were able to enter the Sorbonne.

4. The functioning of this investigating commission had been accepted and even desired, on the absolute condition that the Sorbonne occupation by students, teachers, and those who had come to join them would be fully and unconditionally maintained, and that the police would immediately evacuate the Latin Quarter. The police replied to this by suddenly appearing in large numbers inside the Sorbonne, through two entrances.

5. While the investigating commission was still in the Sorbonne, the police began to surround the buildings.

6. Vice Rector Chalin did not at any time propose, solicit, call for, or accept a police incursion to the Sorbonne. Questioned in my presence by police authorities about what he would do if actual control of the Sorbonne were left to him, he replied that he would immediately throw it wide open, without restrictions or control.

7. The last occupants of the Sorbonne were ejected forcibly. Among them were the Dean of the *Faculté des Lettres,* M. Las Vergnas, and several other Sorbonne faculty members. All were molested by the police (the representative of the National Board of the SNESUP. received a blow from a police helmet) and were searched on leaving.

—Paris, June 16, 1968.

On Monday the metal workers, especially those at the Renault factory, returned to work. A meeting was organized (wihout participation of the UNEF) at the Halle aux Vins. It was only sparsely attended. The same day, the newspaper *Action* gave a detailed account of how the Sorbonne was retaken.

Document 160

A Plot Against the Sorbonne

For several days . . . the press and radio have been the best allies of the government. Friday, Saturday, and Sunday, one page by Del Duca and a radio bulletin by Paoli were worth a hundred grenades for Gaullism, while the RTL was worth a squadron of *gardes-mobiles.*

The murders in Flins and Sochaux last week had been left unmentioned. The press had more important things to do: it talked about the "Katangans"; and, besides, Guéna, the Minister of Information, had himself said, "These deaths were merely the result of tragic accidents."

It was time for elections. The CRS had left Sochaux; continuing strikes were no longer mentioned. Most of them had "ended." The principal topic was "back to work" and the press was not going to strike any discordant notes. There remained only one shadow in the picture: the students and the Sorbonne.

OPERATION "KATANGA"

In order to bring things to a head, the government launched its first operation: Operation "Katanga," which netted a relative failure, the students and workers who were occupying the Sorbonne having reacted in time. Thursday evening, when they read *Paris-Presse,* they understood that the "Kantangan" affair, which had been entirely trumped up by the authorities, would be the first pretext for intervention; to foil this provocation it was therefore necessary to act before Friday morning. When our *Action* headline read: *Sorbonne: Beware of Provocation,* we had not been mistaken. On Friday the morning had hardly begun when the police invaded the Odéon, the rear guards applying intimidation and swinging their blackjacks as far as the corner of the rue de la Sorbonne! From 5:30 on, the students and workers had been routing out the Katangan "légionnaires."

Beginning Friday, in the press and radio, the counter-attack got under way, and the Katangans were no longer mentioned. One single theme: the students are cleaning up the Sorbonne, and the CRS the Odéon. *Le Parisien-libéré,* which is never the most contemptible, had a headline reading: "The Sorbonne Disinfected, the Odéon Evacuated by the Police," with the subtitle: "M. Georges Pompidou declares that wisdom is on the way." *L'Aurore,* to which these few weeks had not even taught the difference between a blackjack and a broom, headlined: *"Big Sweep-out at the Sorbonne . . . and at the Odéon.*

The radio, thanks to a greater flexibility in its reactions, continually harped on the same themes: the good students are getting rid of the riff-raff, or *chienlit,* which this time no longer means the "Katangans" but everybody who is not a student. According to the radio, the situation seemed to be the following: now that the "groupuscules" have been declared illegal and that foreign agitators have been deported or parked in camps in the Massif Central, the "nice" students, having got rid of the mob and of subversion, will be able to discuss educational reform. To the workers it was implied that "the strikes are finished! Order has been restored. For you workers, what happens now at the

University no longer concerns you, and the students are right to proceed to 'serious,' 'concrete' matters. . . ."

The warning was clear; so were the political objectives: isolate students from workers a little bit more and facilitate development of reformist currents in the University. Simultaneously, with its release of General Salan, the government was making gratuitous promises of University reform, while the Minister of National Education, M. Ortoli, was making declarations which, in the light of police occupation of the Sorbonne, were really witty: to the effect that "today it should simply be understood that I am ready to engage in new undertakings in the broadest, the most objective, the most open-minded spirit of concertation. . . ."

But whereas the press gorged itself with Salan's declarations and Bidault's lecture tour, Pierre Charpy in *Paris-Presse* of Saturday evening pointed a policeman's finger: "The government hopes to succeed (. . .) by outflanking the remaining Paris pockets with 'reasonable' *facultés,* especially in the provinces. But this may still be an illusion on the part of the government with regard to the Sorbonne." He went on to explain: "Things being what they are, the new occupation committee will quietly proceed with creation of a 'people's summer university.'" That same morning Raymond Aron had drawn his conclusions in *Le Figaro:* "It remains to be seen if the bourgeois government will support a revolutionary school system, and what type of employment, outside of being guerrillas, students trained for permanent contestation will find." The answer was not long in coming.

SUNDAY: SECOND OPERATION

On the RTL, the 1 P.M. newscast announced that there had been fighting at the Sorbonne; that during the night a young man was seriously injured; that an investigation had been started and that the police had taken over the Sorbonne. Those who listened to their transistor radios and have read *Paris-Presse* and *France-Soir* for the last few days, can have no doubts: the police are intervening against the "riff-raff." With slight variations the other radio stations broadcast pretty much the same tune. However the tone changed somewhat as the afternoon wore on. At 4 P.M. there was an announcement that the "murder" had not taken place at the Sorbonne, but in the vicinity of the Carrefour de l'Odéon. The police were not supposed to have taken over the Sorbonne, but merely to have surrounded it. Police Commissioner Grimaud was supposed to have "negotiated" with the Sorbonne occupation committee, which was said to have agreed to a court investigation at the Sorbonne. The occupation committee telephoned a declaration rectifying all these points to the radio stations, who made only faint allusion to this fact.

A little later, there was an announcement that the Hôtel-Dieu hospital had no knowledge of the arrival of the wounded person. The maneuver was foiled; the pretext had now become completely inconsistent in proportion to the number of police involved, but nobody expressed surprise. A little later, about 5:30 P.M., Pompidou put the dots on the i's and the pretext where it belonged, by declaring, "It had to be done." Raymond Aron had been listened to. A little before 6 P.M. radio newscasters announced that "in spite of the agreements made between the occupation committee and the police, fights have been provoked inside and outside the Sorbonne by outside elements."

The false report, according to which an agreement was supposed to have been made between the police and the occupation committee, was repeatedly insistently. No mention was made of any communiqués put out by the occupation committee itself.

In its evening edition the *Journal du Dimanche* explained with striking brevity how the police had entered the Sorbonne: "5:50 P.M., a scuffle occurred; the police entered the Sorbonne."

For the *Journal du Dimanche,* everything is crystal clear.

—Action, No. 11, June 17.

On June 17 a plenary assembly of the *faculté* teaching body raised a protest. A Sorbonne professor, who was the secretary of the *Syndicat Autonome des Facultés des Lettres,*[10] announced that together with a certain number of his colleagues, he refused to take part in the discussion. He left the hall, followed by two or three others, amid general booing. A scrimmage ensued, during which the same professor called a woman instructor a "bitch"; academic courtesy was put to a severe test.

Document 161

Notes Taken on June 17th by an Assistant Professor
Who Participated in the Sorbonne Plenary Assembly.

A certain number of faculty members were not present at the Plenary Assembly of the *Faculté* (R. Polin,[11] Mrs. J. de Romilly,[12] F. Chamoux,[13] etc.). After the reading of the Deloffre communiqué, Deloffre, Stoetzel,[14] and a third person started toward the exit, followed by people standing behind the last rows of the Plenary Assembly (Le Bonniec,[15] Miss Bontemps, a Latin assistant professor, etc.).

There was some booing and several incidents occurred. A teacher stopped Deloffre as he was leaving to say, "Monsieur, you are a dishonor to the University." On his way out Deloffre jostled the people standing in the rear. After Mme. Gabet, a French instructor, protested against the jostling, he came back to where she was standing, called her a *"garce"* ("bitch"), and stepped on her toes. An assistant professor, M. Chauvet, protested in the hall.

June 18: the Gaullist style triumphed, even in the revolutionary student movements, as witness the "June 18 calls" we collected.

Document 162

Call Made on June 18, 1968[16]

The leaders who have been at the head of the French army since May 13, 1958, have formed a government. This government, alleging our defeat, has made contact with the OAS leaders in order to make us stop the fight.

Assuredly we have been submerged by the enemy's mechanized strength on the ground, in the air, and through hertzian waves.

Infinitely more than their number and their matériel, it is the hammer of boots on television screens and the mass poison spread by press and radio that is making us withdraw.

The obvious complicities and the rapid recourse to illegality are what have shocked us and brought us to the point we have reached today.

But has the last word been said? Must hope vanish? Is withdrawal definitive? No.

Speaking to you in full knowledge of the facts, we tell you that nothing is lost for the revolution.

We still have many possibilities of achieving victory one day, because students are not alone; they have the whole working class with them. They can unite with it to resist and to continue the fight. Together, we students and workers will be able to liberate and turn to account the immense industry of the factories, as well as the *facultés*.

This revolution is not limited to our country. This revolution has not been settled by the May events.

This revolution is a world revolution. All the mistakes, all the delays, do not prevent the fact that there exist in the universe all the means for crushing our enemies.

Although we are vulnerable today because of our mechanical weakness, we will win eventually through our superior revolutionary strength. Herein lies the fate of the world.

The *Mouvement du 22 mars* invites all revolutionaries who are on French territory, or who should happen to come there, with or without arms, workers and students, to organize.

Whatever happens, the flame of popular resistance must not die, and it will not die.

Tomorrow, as today, we will continue to speak.

—*Le Mouvement du 22 mars.*

Document 163

To All Fathers and Mothers in France

In four years of combat on its own soil, France freed itself from foreign oppression; however in 24 years of apparent freedom, France has not been able to free itself of its internal oppressions.

The fortuitous governmental team of the last ten years of absolute power has abdicated its most sacred duty, which is to ensure a moral order for the French nation and to offer an example of this order to its own youth.

The desire for participation paraded by the chief of state is a typical imposture, as witness the aggression committed against the Sorbonne, which is a symbol of world youth revolution.

Yet nothing is lost!

Nothing is lost because this revolution stems from man's innermost heart and soul.

In the "free" universe, tremendous forces have not yet made their contribution.

One day these forces will crush the enemy; on that day, France must be present at the victory: she will then recover her true freedom and her true grandeur.

This is our goal, our only goal.

This is why we urge all fathers and mothers in France to join their children in an action for renovation of French society.

Our country is in deadly peril; we must express our determination to fight within the legal process, which is the only means left to us. We must vote and urge others to vote by casting a blank ballot on the first round of the June 23, 1968, legislative elections. This will make it possible to distinguish between the live forces of the nation and the Electoral Body.

LONG LIVE GENEROUS FRANCE.

—The Council of Resistance to "Economic and Social" Oppression
[Censier], June 18, 1968.

Notes

1. Having returned on May 28, D. Cohn-Bendit participated in the demonstration.

2. Cf. J.-M. Coudray (theoretician of *Socialisme ou Barbarie*), "La révolution anticipée," in E. Morin, Cl. Lefort, J.-M. Coudray, *la Brèche*, p. 116: "It is of capital importance to say loudly and calmly: in May 1968, in France, the industrial proletariat was not the revolutionary avant-garde of society, but its ponderous rear guard." This *roneotype* text, distributed at the Sorbonne, is dated May 30.

3. Cf. above p. 311, already.

4. *Centre départemental des jeunes agriculteurs,* led by the former MRP Deputy, PSU militant, B. Lambert, who has since published a book entitled *Les Paysans dans la lutte de classe,* cited above in Chapter III, note 6. On the "Nantes Commune" see also *les Cahiers de mai,* No. 1, June 15, 1968; Yannick Güin, *La Commune de Nantes,* les Cahiers libres, No. 154, Maspero, Paris, 1964; and Philippe Gallard, "Le second pouvoir du mai nantais," *Politique Aujourd'hui,* August–September and October, 1969.

5. *Fédération des syndicats d'exploitants agricoles* (Federation of Farmers' Unions).

6. Other testimony in J.-Ph. Talbo, *La Grève à Flins,* pp. 67–74.

7. Issue dated June 12. On the "Katangans," see also above, Chapter V, pp. 343–346.

8. On the problems of the Sorbonne, see also above, Chapter V, pp. 332 ff.

9. See above, Chapter IV, pp. 307–316.

10. J. Deloffre, French professor. At the time of the retaking of the Sorbonne, the SNESUP. had proposed a boycott of the baccalauréat examination by higher education faculty members. The Autonomous Union immediately pointed out that its members were ready to act as chairmen of the juries. A member of the Autonomous Union and a professor of Greek history at the Sorbonne, H. Van Effenterre, after having shown that the spokesmen for the Autonomous Union had not been legally elected, concluded,

"I personally detest violence and war; I like neither disorder nor negligence, but I must bear witness to the seriousness, the generosity, and the keen creative effort of the colleagues and students whom I have seen at work. . . . If one day a new University can be built, it will be much more with them than with the ones who have learned nothing and forgotten nothing, and who seem to delight in going back to give their courses in police vans. At the moment when the vanquished of a beautiful dream are taking leave of the old Sorbonne, I prefer not

to be on the side of those victors." Concerning this controversial discussion, cf.
Le Monde, June 19, 20, and 21.

    11. Philosophy professor.

    12. Greek professor.

    13. Greek professor.

    14. Psychology professor.

    15. Latin professor.

    16. A similar call, imitating the Gaullist call of June 19, is reproduced on
the cover of the book on the *Mouvement du 22 mars, Ce n'est qu'un début, continuons le combat.*

VII

Words, Myths, and Themes

Few exercises are as difficult and ambiguous as the one that consists in reconstituting the student movement thematically. Computers would be needed to determine its exact linguistic nature;[1] but there would remain the problem of knowing which texts to analyze. Was the student movement expressed in the wall writings collected before the police cleaned the walls,[2] in the situationist comic strips, in the minutes of the reform commissions, or in the leaflets that a certain number of psychopaths distributed at the Sorbonne? The real difficulty, however, lies elsewhere. The student movement continued to hide its true reality, even from itself, by borrowing the physiognomy and terminology of a proletarian movement.[3] This is what Pierre Bourdieu would call its "proletaroid" aspect. Here is a 22 *mars* militant testifying on the subject of the first night of the barricades: "That night there was a guy who started phantasizing at about three in the morning. It started with a doctor, I think, who said there were ten thousand workers at Strasburg-Saint-Denis ready to march on the barricades. Everybody believed him and guys in the street started hugging each other. The revolution's started! Terrific! You saw fellows in the front line facing the gas for an hour and when they dropped they just lay there. It was incredible."[4] Among the 350-odd posters brought out by the people's atelier at the *Ecole des Beaux Arts,* hardly any made allusion to the existence of a student movement; almost all of them, in fact, were in the line of the political struggle against the Gaullist regime, with glorification of the working class struggle. This is why the slogan of the Marxist-Leninists, *Servir le Peuple,* even though in practice it ended with ultra-minority directives such as the one dated May 5: "Everybody come to Saint-Denis,"[5] corresponded nonetheless to an expectancy. The leaflet dated May 24: "Your struggle is ours"[6] corresponded perfectly to the student movement's experience, if not to that of the worker movement. Actually the degree of awareness was not the same in both cases, and one might say that whereas self-management was the "conscious" of the student movement, it was only the "unconscious" of the worker movement, except in the minority case of certain ultra-modern factories.

More generally it may be said that the student movement hesitated when faced with what was, however, its most marked characteristic, that is, its desire for *disorder* in the face of established order, and its refusal to plan for the future. In all his speeches, D. Cohn-Bendit insisted on this point, whereas if we read the "groupuscule" press, for instance, it is difficult to believe that the society to be built is not already in blueprint. What is clear, however, is that "the fact that the movement could not formulate proposals or projects for society in general in no way disqualified it, because the movement was only structured and only formulated projects in terms of the problems it encountered; and the problem of a global model for society had not been posed. Or else, if it had been posed, it would only have been in the old terms, which the movement rejected."[7]

In the following pages there will be no question of omitting this proletarian mythology[8] on the pretext of arriving at a chemically pure student movement. To do this would make the student movement itself incomprehensible. It is more a matter of placing the movement "in situation" in order to show, as it were, how its language expresses now the Same, now the Other.

A Student Account

Although the students were not always able to define the meaning of their movement, they were remarkably good at telling about it.[9] For the most part the accounts that appeared in the general press, or in the books that have been published to date, were by Paris students. The following, told by a Strasburg student, covers the period from May 6 to May 24. The reader should remember that although at the beginning the Paris public was in genuine sympathy with the movement, this sympathy was, on the contrary, practically non-existent in many provincial cities, including Strasburg.

Document 164

Excerpt from an Open Letter from a Strasburg Student to the Public

On Monday, May 6, 1,500 students gathered in the *aula* of the University Palace to protest against police interventions in the Latin Quarter.

A solidarity meeting with the students in Paris. Certain persons exposed the contradictions the French University is faced with: graduates are not finding jobs, the number of examination failures is fixed in advance, and yet, the country lacks cadres. . . . In the University, the weight of the administrative machine, which is entirely subject to ministerial authority, takes routine for granted and paralyzes all spirit of initiative. From the first day, the bases for criticism of the University were set up. Demonstrations took place in the streets in protest against the slanted information contained in the *Dernières Nouvelles d'Alsace,* which was placed under police protection.

Tuesday, there were 2,500 of us. Each one arrived disgusted by events in the Latin Quarter and discovered that his uneasiness, his problems, and his confused anguish were shared by his fellow students. This new demonstration encountered a new police barrier Rue de la Nuée-Bleue. It was more difficult for the student marshals to make the demonstrators go to the *facultés* than on the preceding day.

The strike hardened in the Fac. des Lettres *and it was decided to occupy the buildings.* The movement has been spreading progressively to all the *facultés* during the week. This occupation may seem symbolic, but its consequences are tremendous: there are no more classes, and discussions have been started with participation of students and professors. From criticism of the University they quickly came to criticism of society.

Events move fast. The students are constituting themselves into a Student Council founded on direct democracy; in assemblies of 2,000 to 3,000 people, each one can freely take the floor. All decisions relative to the University are within the jurisdiction of the Student Council, which votes on them. From this council to autonomy was only one step. The manifesto of autonomy refuses discussion with all who seek to save the pieces of the system it rejects.[10]

The manifesto inaugurates a long period of analysis. This University, which has been gradually built up since Napoleon's time, cannot be arbitrarily or hastily replaced. Everything has to be re-created. Everything has to be reconsidered. What structure could the Student Council be given without deviating from direct democracy? Can delegates be named without losing the sense of individual responsibility? And student-professor commissions? Yes, but certain professors feel outdistanced; will they not have a tendency to use their maturity and their speaking experience to co-opt the movement?

And yet, a more important and more urgent problem will appear: examinations. Many think they must refuse examinations. Can the movement, can this impulse for spontaneous and sincere thinking be crushed by cramming? Are examinations possible at this time? Examinations are a symbol of the entire educational system that is being challenged. They are the pillars of injustice within the University, the tools of selection. However, others—many others—need examinations. And while some are working hard to set up a way of avoiding the loss of a year at the same time that they refuse traditional examinations, the government has understood that this is a sensitive point. But refusal of examinations is an irreversible act which commits all the students. The point of examinations is a painful one and the government is going to profit from it to intervene, to try to reach many students—that is, all who are hesitating, who have not yet understood, or who need examinations. It warns them that to boycott examinations is to lose one year. In Paris it is promoting the formation of "spontaneous movements," which declare themselves reasonable, refuse the boycott in the name of the rejected structures, and are invited to tell their story on the radio and television.

The strike is spreading to the workers. Students have their share of responsibility in the instigation of this movement. For what are they responsible? All tendencies are represented in the student movement. There is no question of our imposing a party program. What we must do is to make an honest and serious criticism of the University, and therefore of society.

Nobody can set up a political program in three weeks. Besides, this is not the students' role. What they want to do is to refuse the stultification, the alienating conditions that cause the loss of all political conscience, all human conscience: an ORTF that considers a speaker's smile more important than the objectivity of the news. Instead of education, people are given games to distract them from their own lives: they must admire "stars"; they must discuss the "hit parade" rather than the Prime Minister; they must be more excited about the latest ski champion than about Social Security. And the champion is presented to every Frenchman on the front page of his newspaper with additional trimmings: he will even be decorated with the Legion of Honor. This is what we call "consumer culture." All that glitters is thrown to the people in abundance, and this diverts them from real problems in order to allow a minority to act without supervision. But as soon as someone denounces this game and, in spite of everything, becomes aware of what is alienating men every moment, he gets blackjacked.

The regime knows very well what students are denouncing. It has already sought to divide and neutralize them through its intervention on the subject of examinations. It has wanted to discredit them in the eyes of public opinion; "you see the ones who are refusing to take examinations, they are the slackers. . . ."

But students have understood the danger. They are refusing to talk with the government. Therefore the government is undertaking a vast operation to separate students from the rest of the nation. It is going to drive them to violence by provoking them. After having assured itself of the neutrality of the workers' unions, the government launched the Cohn-Bendit affair.[11]

A propaganda campaign has made an agitator out of him. If he shouts, they howl. Why he is shouting, nobody knows. It's no wonder that students are obliged to shout in order to make themselves heard. But now Cohn-Bendit is an agitator, a provocator. "Europe No. 1," thanks to its radio-telephone cars, was able to bear witness to the fact that this agitator called for calm on the barricades in the Rue Gay-Lussac. What of it! To avoid recurrence of such unfortunate incidents they forbid the use of radio-telephones.

Whether they are in agreement or not with Cohn-Bendit's ideas, students cannot accept repression against one of their own. And even though he is German, he is the spokesman for a sector of French students. They may or may not agree with his ideas on society, but they have felt that the measures taken against Cohn-Bendit constituted just one more provocation to drive them to violence, and in this way to cut them off from other people.

What are the police doing in the Latin Quarter? Would there have been barricades if the CRS had not been there? Where is the provocation?

On Friday, May 24, they did better. The worker demonstrations paraded in Paris without seeing a single CRS. A student demonstration, and there are hundreds of CRS. Barricades, charges. . . . The success of the demonstration went beyond all the hopes of the government. Students attacked the *Bourse;* that is something Frenchmen won't understand; they see in it only the specter of anarchy; they are afraid de Gaulle will leave. Friday evening in Strasburg, 2,000 students heard the news that the police were attacking. A spontaneous demonstration of solidarity was decided upon by the students, who felt that they were being ridiculed. This was revolt. It was a gut reaction. There was talk of building a symbolic barricade. Everybody knows the disproportion of a police attack.

I have never been a militant, either in a union or in a party. Two months ago I did not understand very well what I read in the press on the subject of the Nanterre students. At the Place du Corbeau I was not behind the barricade but beside it. Perhaps I was afraid. I was not at all convinced, because I had never seen the CRS attack without notice, break arms with rifle butts, as was the case that night in Strasburg. However, I understand perfectly the 300 who were on the barricade, and I feel that no student who is aware of things has the right to be unconcerned about their gesture.

I hope the public will understand this act and that it will judge it at its true value. I hope that the public will accept discussion with the students.

—Excerpt from *Non-Retour*, theoretical review of the May Revolution (Strasburg), No. 1, June 7, 1968.

Why Students?

This question, which seems so natural in the United States, or even in Germany, to a direct disciple of H. Marcuse, familiar with the idea that revolutions are born of the actions of marginal elements in society, met with reluctant response in France.[12] Here are two factors of explanation: one from the *Faculté des Lettres* in Caen, which attempts to remove the "proletarian" complex of the students,[13] and another, which tries to find Marxist terminology to explain and justify the revolt of a part of the "middle classes."

Document 165

Which Revolution?

The students have provoked a revolution in the University. Their action has made it possible to expose to the eyes of all, the repressive function of our institutions. They began by questioning the authority of the university administration and of the professors, and they soon found themselves confronted by the CRS. They have proved that the Rector is responsible to the police *préfet*. At the same time their action revealed the unity of grievances of all groups subject to exploitation and oppression. In answer to the movement started in Nanterre and continued at the Sorbonne, in answer to police aggression, workers, office workers, cadres, journalists, research workers, and writers have all entered the fight.

Nevertheless, since the strikes have mobilized the working class, students are prey to a strange uneasiness. They vaguely feel that the revolutionary initiative no longer belongs to them. They would like to demonstrate their active solidarity with the workers, but must deal with the national unions and, more particularly, the CGT, which asks them not to interfere in affairs that do not concern them. When they succeed in persuading themselves that this attitude is not that of all workers, they nevertheless remain aware that many of the latter consider their demands with contempt and themselves as petty bourgeois. Consequently, students dream of placing their movement under the leadership of the working class, but they are beginning to be disillusioned, because the fraction of this class which they think ought to back them is silent (at least for the moment); the mass is indifferent or hostile, and organization leaders send them back into the University ghettos. This disillusionment, in fact, increased when it appeared that numerous students who joined the movement late were more concerned with organizing details within the framework of the old system, more concerned, for example, with finding a solution to the problem of examinations, than with understanding the political significance of the revolt already under way.

Certain of the more advanced among them were then inclined to rationalize in terms of an alternative of all or nothing. They say either the revolution will overthrow capitalism and the old University will disappear, or no reforms will be enforced. With this prospect, often without hope, they persist in offering their services to the workers. They assume a bad conscience, which the leaders of the workers' unions seek to accuse them of, unfairly; they are on the point of being ashamed of their own demands, and of their presence on the social scene in the role of students.

It is essential for students to free themselves of this bad conscience; they should agree to show their true colors and state the direction of their action, because this action, even though it is carried out in a definite place in society, has a universal truth, a truth which can be recognized in all the other places where the struggle has started.

At first, and above all, students must understand that the problems posed in industry are not entirely different from those posed in the University. It is true that within the framework of industry, workers endure the principle of exploitation, that the ownership of the means of production is in the hands of a particular social stratum, and that the decisive combat is taking place within the framework of the production process. But it is no less true that a change in the system of ownership—that is to say, the conquest by a government bureaucracy of the management of production—would not put an end to exploitation. What characterizes the structure of businesses, in fact, is at once the division between capital and the working force, the division between those in power and those who are powerless, and the division between those who have knowledge and those who are deprived of it. Workers (and with them, office workers and technicians) are exploited to the extent that they are reduced to the pure and simple function of executants, excluded from the decisions that determine the fate of the community and, to the extent too that it is made impossible for them to judge with full knowledge of the facts, the ends and means of management.[14]

Monopolization of capital is accompanied everywhere by monopolization of power and of the news media. And yet, this is where the student revolt has an exemplary value; it attacks those who pretend to be the custodians of authority and knowledge. It attacks those who, in their collective practice, teach obedience and conformism along with general knowledge.

Rather than scrutinize closely the relationships that unite the University with other sectors of social activity, it is essential to declare that the same structures are enforced everywhere with slight variations, and that they are supported everywhere by the same mental structures that forbid the creativity of individuals and of groups; that the University is pre-eminently the place where these mental structures are formulated and maintained; and that to upset them within the framework of the University is necessarily to upset them in the whole of society—even though we do not know how this fire spreads.

We already see signs of this upheaval in the protests that are pouring in from every direction, not only in the working class, but among the cadres, in the press, radio, and television, among artists and writers, and even among Catholic, Jewish,[15] and Protestant youth, who are suddenly rebelling against an oppressive theology!

The student fight is breaking down all barriers; no matter if it develops in a specific, predominantly petty bourgeois milieu, its effects interest all society.

Besides, all has not yet been said, and people are simply reciting a literal and badly interpreted Marxism when they subordinate all action to its insertion into the bourgeois-proletarian antagonism. This antagonism itself is derived from an economic, social, and political structure: any impairment of this structure, from whatever source, has revolutionary significance.

Therefore, students must not be afraid to speak out and, instead of looking for leadership where it does not exist, they must clearly state the principles that are valid in all industrial societies of our time, and in all oppressed social groups.

They Must Proclaim That They Are Fighting
—To take over collectively the affairs that concern them, that is to say, for *self-management.*
—To destroy *the hierarchies* that are paralyzing the initiative of groups and of individuals.
—To force those who hold authority or, upon whom it has been conferred, *to make regular reports.*
—To spread information and ideas throughout the entire social body.
—To break down partitioning which, under the guise of demands for technical division of work and knowledge, isolates the categories of students and teachers from one another.
—*To open the University* to all who are at present excluded from it.
—To obtain recognition of the plurality of tendencies and of schools of thought, as a law of democracy.

By asserting these principles, students can address themselves freely to the workers; they do not claim to have a program for reconstructing society; even less, to define a policy in the conventional sense of the term; they are not giving lessons; they recognize that each group has the right to define its demands and its fighting methods, as it understands them; they speak only the universal language of revolution; they realize that they have learned it to a large extent from the worker movement; they know enough about it, however, to make themselves understood and to understand others.

—Excerpt from *l'Enragé* (Caen), No. 1 [end of May].

Document 166

An Example: The Students

The University has a special nature in that it latently condenses several causes of poor functioning.

At the same time that it transmits technical knowledge, it has a specific role in the transmission of systems of value. A first source of contradiction appears when a system of values is not adequate to the task; at the level of students who apprehend it, the possibility of this contradiction is already a source of distress. This is quite visible in the case of sociologists or psycho-sociologists (educated in the values of the "purity" of research and the neutrality of science, and who risk being employed to serve the interests of the capitalist regime).

In order to reduce this contradiction, the perfect solution within the framework of the present system would be complete bureaucratization (total separation of tasks) accompanied by a corresponding division in education (complete specialization). But this solution encounters limitations and, in fact, the threat of contradiction is permanent. Actually, the division of tasks is in perpetual evolution and there will always be tasks to which no system of values instilled by the University will correspond. At present, the differences are aggravated by absence of study guidance, and by a system of selection through failure, which imposes indiscriminately upon each student the system of values corresponding essentially to the traditional tasks for which higher education prepares, i.e., research and teaching.

This being the case, students seized upon the need of this difference felt by the majority, as a necessary aberration of the system. They thus escape more easily into individual interiorization of the sense of failure, and can question the system collectively.

Furthermore, just now, the conservatism of University structures leads to juxtaposition of the values of liberalism (the former dominating ideology) and of technocracy. The result is that the system of values prevailing at the University is in itself contradictory because it is heterogeneous. Instead of playing its role of universal advocate, it can bring out the arbitrary nature of all the dominating values and therefore lead spontaneously to a contestation which, though it comprises nihilistic aspects, can also emerge upon a revolutionary criticism of the system, thanks to the elements of analysis it contains.

There are, therefore, among students, and particularly among certain students, specific causes that have brought their revolt to this point of intensity. And it would be vain to believe that it will spread to the entire population through the simple effect of writing devastating slogans on the walls of the cities. But it is possible to postulate that what has moved us to action—the contradictions and the dissatisfactions that motivate us, our hatred of lies, our anger in the face of this rigid world—exist also in other forms practically everywhere around us; and that to various extents, according to their class situations, people will be able to rise to the need to change society.

—Excerpt from: *The Student Movement Between the Struggle Against Exploitation of the Proletariat and Criticism of the Consumer Society,* pamphlet published by *le Centre révolutionnaire d'intervention et de recherche* (CRIR[16]), May 15, 1968.

Derision

Another way of answering the question: "Why Students?" was to use systematic derision. This was done in the texts signed *Les Inconnus* that were posted in the *Rue des Ecoles* at the start of the Sorbonne occupation, and were very likely of Situationist origin. The following is the beginning of these texts, to which we have added a leaflet summarizing the lyricism, delirium, and violence of the *Situationist International,* and its glorification of all juvenile revolt.

Document 167

To hell with your pity.[17] Hypocrites applaud the mere name of "workers." They coddle us; they beam upon us . . . and they continue to live thanks to our work. We ourselves are not proud to be workers. The people who try to paint a halo about our prison are the same who tomorrow will test us psychologically and dictate our work rhythms.

You called us to the Sorbonne but we were unable to talk about our real problems; you are only interested in problems concerning Gaullism. That's a conversation for specialists.

The "Revolution," as you say, is not a political act with specific laws that will take place . . . one of these days. It is a change to be introduced *immediately* in every detail of life.

The Consumer Society

This is the society in which, thus far, men have fought to ensure their survival.

We are at a moment when, thanks to the development of the means of production, and consequently to the multiplication of objects, competition with its declared goal of appropriation is losing its principal reason for existing, the vital forces through which men can attain full achievement having been liberated.

The malaise of our civilization is the conflict that results from this tendency to appropriate for ourselves, by means of domination, the objects of our environment, at the same time that we suffer from being confined in our role of objects of production or of consumption.

The civilization of scarcity was one of fear and exclusive rights. With its disappearance new powers are appearing which are leading men to seek contact with other men over and above the taboos, the laws and the structures we have known thus far.

With the destruction of privilege, old social institutions like the family will disintegrate entirely, but already this destruction is taking place.

Everybody talks about contestation of the bourgeois University, and yet what is radical is the contestation of all privilege. Even if it were "autonomous" the University would continue to exist within the framework of the division of labor: that is to say, to be the property of the privileged.

The abolition of class is more than the abolition of Gaullism. Simultaneously with destruction of repressive institutions, students must pursue their action to the end, and do away with themselves as a class. This is the only example of their good faith that they can give us workers.

The unions in the plants (and we know what we are talking about) are only good for bargaining about the value of the workers' manpower. We cannot imagine that one day they might be able to fight effectively against the hierarchical society they nevertheless keep going. The struggle for abolition of privileges will necessarily end in a struggle against the unions. Men who fight for complete emancipation have nothing to do with flags, structures, or speeches. When they form a group, they maintain their autonomy . . . which is the only way to keep from being knifed in the back. This lesson has been understood by those who have nothing more to lose (according to the old criteria of values).

Your subjugation to the system is above all your fear of the un-known.

You must all have positions, honors, and power, because it is the only way to be recognized.

But you will croak as a result because this leads you to boredom and isolation.

Formerly, to have a full stomach was a sign of life!
Now it is a sign of death!

The best picture of comfort is given by the CRS . . .
    well-nourished   well-housed   well-trained
                                        They restore
                                        order.
What are you after? What are you after? Aren't you in favor
of order?

For those who hesitate to leave their jobs and to live outside the law, there is a lot to be gained by wandering through the vast world in search of new human relationships (meaning non-aggressive), to meet men who are not solely concerned with the effort to blend into everyday uniformity, who reject work, bosses and family as being so many restraints.

On the contrary, to accept to live within the competitive system, to fight in order to make a place for oneself in the great assembly of frogs, is consequently to be haunted by fear, to repress indispensable vital aspirations, to live in order to die!

Everything ties in together: we believe in culture because in this system it is synonymous with advantages. . . . How then can we avoid letting ourselves be lulled by such illusions as hierarchy, order, discipline, examinations. . . . What can students do with the Sorbonne, tell me, Madame? Exactly what they can do with society:
    —if they accept it entirely, with the implications we know, the *faculté* is a good foster mother to them.
    —if they refuse it completely, they have only to get out of it; that is to say, refuse any compromise with any class structure.

On worker-student pseudo-solidarity.

Must we remind students that workers took to the streets primarily to fight against police repression?

To ask workers to back the students means defining right now the exact bases upon which an agreement can be reached, if the workers are not to be used as a mass to be maneuvered.

Within this framework, is it a matter of "using" them in order to obtain a reformed University, which would be just as detrimental to them as the present University (as a privileged person or a future

privileged person, can a student consider himself the equal of a worker?)
or, is it a matter of looking forward to a common struggle against all
forms of inequality (which supposes denouncing education to the extent that it gives students a possibility for later becoming members of
the middle classes, like denouncing any hierarchic position in a company organization)?

Radical contestation of the University, as of society, is contestation of all privileges,
> —if students only want a reform of the University regime, bour-
> geois society can give it to them.
> —if students want a "counter university," this too can be achieved
> within the framework of a class society.
> —if students want the disappearance of all forms of repression,
> they can only get it through destruction of the consumer so-
> ciety, which is based on the principle of appropriation.

To consider global contestation of the University is to denounce
all the privileges enjoyed by the students (or to be enjoyed later). At
the same time it is denouncing all class society.

At this stage we must look forward to the overthrow not only of
University structures, but of all social structures.

Radical contestation of the University is to reject it as a real
value.

LOOK OUT! THE WORKERS ARE LEAVING!

There were few enough of them who came to rub elbows with the
students in their temple; now, they are going to leave because this
affair of the Sorbonne occupation does not concern them. Those proletarians who without the directives of their national unions came here
to seek a solution to the old problems of the division of society into
classes will never accept new gods, new leaders, and new liars. It is
possible that one day they will have to fight against the leaders of the
new student movement!

—*Les Inconnus* [Anonymous], Paris, May 16, 1968.

Document 167a

Against Student-Worker Pseudo-Solidarity

1. The development of numerous worker-oriented actions should
not create any illusions. This is only a worker-student pseudo-solidar-

ity, based on a rigid conception of the class struggle (to place oneself
at the service of the workers or to educate the workers) which only
tends to reduce the problems of students and the middle classes to
those of the workers. All these movements will collapse after the
period of sentimental revolutionary excitement is over, or they will be
reduced to a community of masochist students, assuming their estate
by licking the behinds of the proletariat with their rough tongues. As
for the proletariat, they can go to hell. The counter university and
placing oneself at the service of the workers are positions that do not
depart from the schemas of a class society.

2. The only possible support is that of a movement which
denies itself as a student movement; which prepares its own disappearance and that of all students to the extent that they are a *separate,
privileged* stratum. This is why any reconstruction of an autonomous
or counter university is merely a safeguard for division of labor, and
for the bases of exploitation (the asinine profs are not wrong when
they pair off with left-winging students: they know that, in any case, the
latter will keep their jobs, and therefore their power). Only this negation can permit a broadening of the basis of the fight which, for the
moment, boils down to a struggle against police repression. This
solidarity, which could be extended to repression in general (culture,
militaristic organization of work), is insufficient.

3. Student privileges to be exposed, denounced, and destroyed,
in order for students to disappear as such, are:

—*The privilege of knowledge:* University knowledge is nothing
but social knowledge; there is no technical or scientific sphere
which could miraculously escape the class struggle. It is necessary to abolish private property of knowledge, which is the
basis of the secondary power exercised by cadres, technicians,
and academics. As long as we do not abolish it, workers will
respect and admire our knowledge, our way of speaking, . . .
and submit to the intellectual-manual hierarchy.

—*The privilege of free time, leisure, and culture:* being a student
offers more possibilities than others for believing oneself free,
creative, available. . . . So long as we do not denounce the
faked, alienated creativity of the people who take themselves
for the artistic avant-garde, so long as we do not denounce
culture as contemplation of what is fictitiously experienced, the
means for playing a role and being played by it, to conceal
boredom, we will remain students, trying to achieve the great-

est possible power, despite the will, when it is not the sole intention, to bring about an actual junction with the proletariat.

—Rue Bonaparte Action Committee, *Les Inconnus,* Paris, May 20, 1968.

Document 168

The Spit on the Offering!

"Enragés *of All Countries, Unite!"*
 Comrades,
 The rage for living that unfurled over the Latin Quarter, flashed
upon the screen of history like one of those prodigious outbursts of
joy that clutch the throats of a world in which the guarantee of no
longer dying of hunger is exchanged for the certainty of croaking
from boredom. The blood of cops is heady, and precious are the
moments when life emerges so intensely from the cesspools of inau-
thenticity to wipe elegantly more than one runny humanist nose. Freed
at last from the matrix of restraint and isolation, this time our all-too-
long unsatisfied desires have treated themselves to a fine slice of
pleasure. *This is only the beginning, so pass the word!* Once again,
the peanut leftist politicians have known how to restore order better
than anyone. But this is only a postponement in the diabolical dance
that conveys the premonitory symptoms. Everywhere, in the red dawn
of insurrectional festivities, the old twilight world of East and West
is flickering in its braziers. Tokyo! Berlin! Los Angeles! Prague! Turin!
Warsaw! Stockholm! From now on the shock waves sent out by these
ironic flare-ups of anger are beginning to interfere in the petrified scene
of everyday life, sweeping aside any impediment to their dionysian
excesses.

 The splendid scuffles that set fire to several Parisian nights,
shitted up the entire lot of CGT—PCF—PSU—FGDS—CFTC—FO—SNESup.
leaders and other blockheads of the same ilk. Having begun by vomit-
ing the most insane nonsense with regard to the insurrectional turn
of events that was quickly taken by the student revolt, the reformist
canaille was quick to take it over, after having filthily strangled it with
the help of that scheming whore of a UNEF, for political ends that are
well known for their redundant triviality. Between the angry hordes
who held the barricades and the bleating flocks of May 13, there had
only been time for decay, cleverly orchestrated by the vermin who keep
alive among the naïve—too naïve—masses the all but weak-minded

belief that another governmental balloon would change anything. *They are making fools of us! They won't make fools of us for long!*

In the stinking fascination of "dialogue" we recognize the ultimate disguise of combined repression–co-option. Fetid breath beneath a drooling smile, a sordid police meanness—that's been updated: an outstretched hand extending the blackjack while yesterday's and today's spectacular deep-freeze culture asphyxiates far more surely than tear gas. *Let's spit on the offering!* Let's spit on the dialoguing rascals and their shabby reforms, which certain people might be weak enough to accept. Once people's minds have calmed down, what's in store for us is the stagnant swamp water of servility.

In view of the fact that on May 13–14–15–16, an attempt at *direct democracy at the grass roots* was set up in the occupied *facultés,* we must therefore support and propagate far and wide anti-bureaucratic agitation, in order for it to spread to the working class, which is always being hierarchically throttled by the riff-raff of union bigshots. Active minorities, which are nuclei of clear-sighted resistance, must start permanent guerrilla harassment from key zones, against the government, whose general strategy conceals in a negative form the essential aspects of the system to be destroyed—a wonderful way to get at its very marrow, which gives us strength while it grows weaker. When it becomes the object of pitiless, subversive play, the social machine abounds with exciting resources to be exploited. Sabotage, lies, embezzlement, fraud, boycotts . . . let *joyous creativity* be unconfined!—a diabolical storm of illicit delights—and many a taste and talent will be revealed! It will all end one day by again taking to the streets.

Wildcat strikes and healthy rage, when they occur, will have to recognize one another in their most ethereal crystallizations. Beautiful as a paving stone on a cop's mug, murder, in the last resort, blooms within the confines of sublime efficacy. As for pillaging and other fine freelance operations, they should be considered as the great deeds of our struggle toward actually surpassing the world of merchandise and "thingified" social relationships. In front of store windows—those deforming mirrors in which our human image is lost, made rigid by money—our eye has too often met only things and their cost-price. *Enough of that!* The reborn revolutionary forces will achieve clear awareness of their struggle only in and through such a *praxis.* There is no better product for removing ideological mouldiness!

Whereas for a very long time no radical contestation has straddled the ossified nag of the old bureaucratic machines of the left, suddenly there has appeared a rivalry of farcical lies in the mire of the "little chiefs" of the Trotskyist "groupuscules" (JCR, FER, VO), pro-Chinese (UJC(m-l), CV *base*) and the anarchists à la Cohn-Bendit.

Let's settle our own affairs! Under the thumb of moth-eaten leaders, unity will never be anything but submission. The revolutionary project should actually become what it already was substantially, and its global coherence should show through its successive concretizations like the immanence of the whole to its parts. Let all beware! What is lost in partial contestation returns to the oppressive function of the old world. A senile blunder if there ever was one. More criticism of the bourgeois University makes people laugh, except for its connection with the entire class society that we must abolish—that is, transcend dialectically through and for generalized *self-management*—at its very core. This is the base, vast human prostitution of alienated work. *Death to all wage-earning! Death to subsistence living!* Don't you already hear the halloo sounding in the distance? We're on your trail, old world; you're out of breath! We'll finish off your old carcass!

LONG LIVE THE ZENGAKUREN [JAPAN]!
LONG LIVE THE ENRAGÉS [NANTERRE]!
LONG LIVE THE SITUATIONIST INTERNATIONAL!
LONG LIVE THE VANDALISTES [BORDEAUX]!
LONG LIVE THE COMMITTEE FOR PUBLIC SALVATION!
LONG LIVE THE REVOLUTION OF DAILY LIFE![18]

—The *Enragés* from Montgeron [about May 20, 1968].

The Revolutionary Tradition

Inevitably, the May movement was looking for ancestors: 1789, 1848, 1917, the Chinese Revolution, June 1936, and, above all, the Paris Commune[19] were recalled to a point of obsession, most often to be adapted to the needs of each "groupuscule's" ideology. We present an example taken from the Marxist-Leninist press, but they abounded everywhere. The *Association Générale des Etudiants* in Lyons showed greater originality by publishing extracts from an article written in 1919 by Rosa Luxembourg, arguing against the principle of a National Assembly, in favor of an assembly of workers' councils.[20] We give here the text in which a future architect of the *Ecole des Beaux Arts,* taking June 1936 as a point of departure, tried to set down his thoughts on the significance of his profession.

Document 169

A hundred years ago the French working class rose up against the bourgeoisie: that was the *Commune*. Against misery, for freedom, the rifles of Parisian workers repulsed the attacks of the bourgeoisie. They fought to overthrow the dictatorial power of the employers. For the first time in the world, workers rose up to overthrow the bourgeoisie. Their attack was aimed at heaven; Paris was the first city freed by the proletariat; the bourgeois were driven out.

At Versailles, profiteers, panic-stricken when faced with the loss of their privileges, could only think of one weapon: to have the German armies open the gates of Paris. It was through their opened breach that the government of profiteers re-entered Paris.

In the same way, today, the government of the employers is panic-stricken; it sees rising up in front of it the powerful army of ten million strikers; it sees around the strikers the support of the entire people. Today it is faced by a commune that is a thousand times more powerful than the first.

On the verge of their loss, the employers and their spokesman, de Gaulle, are preparing to launch their attacks against the workers' fortresses: the occupied factories. They are sending their cops, their fascist gangs, and the army. Why this attack? Because they feel in their very flesh that the principal obstacle is the occupation of the factories and that this constitutes the workers' position of strength.

Confrontation with the workers in the factories cannot take place simply. Once the mass of workers is assembled, once the factory gates are closed, the gates will not be reopened for the employers, even if they come surrounded by cops.

The employers are looking for people who will open the gates for them and they are finding them! These people are the capitulators, the panickers, the ones who spend their days demoralizing the workers, wanting them to give in, not in favor of complete victory, but of a little lollypop: elections.

De Gaulle, who has his back to the wall, says: "Stop the fighting and you will have elections." The PCF and CGT leaders, betraying the last bit of confidence the masses had in them, grovel before him in complete surrender, declaring: "This is what we have been asking for, for a long time. It is a great victory. Now we are going to do everything we can to reopen the factories." In the eyes of the grandsons of the people of the Commune, the PCF is nothing else but the party of the *Versaillais*.

—Excerpt from *La Cause du Peuple*, No. 8, June 2, 1968.

Document 170

An Interpretation of the Events of 1936

After the triumph of the Popular Front in the legislative elections, the workers occupied a large number of factories. Left-wing intellectuals talked of making culture available to the workers.

The "wildcat" movement extended beyond the parties, but did not provoke a fundamental upheaval in the political game. Because it was economically ill timed, it transformed into failure the apparently brilliant success of popular demands. Nevertheless, 1936 gave a new dimension to the strategy of workers' struggles.

The fascist threat, the policy of deflation, German rearmament, and soon the Civil War in Spain, explained the formation of the Popular Front and its success in the elections of April 26 and May 3, 1936. Its program was to develop the purchasing power of the masses and take the measures against the oligarchy of the "200 families" that would make a currency devaluation unnecessary. The law-and-order party had as its only argument the example of the disturbances in Spain, after the victory of a Popular Front.

In June Léon Blum was asked to form a new cabinet. The Communists promised their support, but refused to participate in the government. They were afraid that the influence of the Radical Party in the Senate would prevent any changes in the French economic and social structures.

This did not placate the law-and-order party, which feared that the Communists would outbid them, and also detested the personality of the "intransigent Marxist" Blum.

Although Blum did not take power until June, strikes and factory occupations had broken out as early as May 26: approximately 60,000 strikers demanded new regulations governing overtime and piece-work, paid vacations, a minimum wage, general increases in wages, application of a 40-hour week, and the nomination of worker delegates to confer with the employers. In June there were 1,500,000 strikers. Application of the new labor statute, resulting from the Laws of June 1936, met with difficulties. In July disorders broke out in the countryside.

In this atmosphere of revolt and defiance, which overwhelmed the political party machines, the government tried to carry out its program. Out of respect for the rules of the parliamentary game and the political tendencies that had resulted from the balloting, Léon Blum was not able to make a clean sweep. There was no question of revolution.

The Matignon Agreements, signed on June 7 by both worker and employer delegates, accepted the principal demands of the workers: the 40-hour week, paid vacations, collective contracts, workers' delegates, union rights, a 15% increase for at least the lowest wages. Nevertheless, social agitation continued until the end of June. The banks were not nationalized, and only the statute of the Bank of France was altered. On the other hand, ownership of factories manufacturing war materials, principally aeronautics, became a government monopoly.

This wave of worker successes finally encountered an unfavorable economic and financial juncture. The French population had aged due to a considerable slowing down of the birthrate after the [first] war. Consequently, the number of workers was insufficient to ensure economic expansion, which, besides, had declined in several sectors.

Gold exports and the deficit in public finances forced the government to devaluate the franc in October 1936, but without success. The cost of living increased during the winter, while production diminished, paralyzed by application of the 40-hour week, reduction in worker output per hour, and by lack of confidence on the part of the capitalists and those with savings accounts. Capital export began to accelerate and the commercial deficit was growing. But—final paradox—in spite of and no doubt because of, the reduction in working time, unemployment hardly diminished.

Then, in January 1937, Léon Blum declared the need of a "pause." He did away with restraining measures against capital investment and reduced expenditures for big public works. Railroad fares were increased. On June 14, after a prolonged slump, the government asked for "powers permitting it to take the necessary measures by decree for reconstitution of public finances, as well as for protection of savings, the currency, and public credit." Defeated, the Blum government resigned. Between 1937 and 1938 the Popular Front disbanded.

What Lessons Are To Be Drawn From This Failure? Elementary:

1. That worker demands, as long as they are within an established framework, have no chance for real success during an unfavorable economic juncture; only expansion and full employment permit an increase in wages without neutralizing the benefits derived through

an equivalent increase in prices. If we consider the present situation, these two conditions are not fulfilled: the threat to throw open the borders can, at a pinch, limit an increase in prices (although not those for public services) but, on the other hand, it can precipitate the bankruptcy or merger of several companies and therefore increase unemployment and, consequently, a revolutionary public (socialist or fascist) at the same time that it weakens the unions.

2. The other remark concerns the dimensions of union demands. They have always been about working conditions (medical inspection, labor inspection, delegates, joint production committees) on the one hand, and on the other, payment for the work that is done. The events of 1936 enforced acceptance of the idea *in principle* that it is not enough to increase wages in order to improve the lives of workers. They should also obtain a decrease in the number of working hours. From this standpoint, the 40-hour week, which could not really be respected (overtime, a second job)—first of all because of the rather serious lack of manpower and then because of the need of workers to increase consumption—had less importance than paid vacations. The latter really changed the worker's way of life and sowed the seeds of a "leisure society" as well as of a "consumer society." This being the case, the demands had two axes: money, and the amount of free time polarized attention more than conditions and interest of the work. Life was no longer all work, but what could be done outside it.

Employers and unions agreed on these terms to explain the movement of revolt at the grass roots. Things are going to happen now as they did earlier at Rhodiaceta.

3. As students of the ex-ENSBA[21] what can we expect from an evolution of worker demands? That to the two present dimensions of their living conditions, *money and time,* a third will be added: *space,* its free ownership and the use to be made of it. What advantage is there, actually, for workers to obtain $x\%$ more, and a reduction in working time of half an hour, if a real estate and urbanism policy forces additional travel on them, which takes both their time and their money? If they have to go to the movies to see pleasant landscapes and buy a car in order to get away?

These orientations (particularly the second), by broadening the awareness of the workers, would encourage them to make their influence felt more widely than through union action, in their own strictest interests. These new aspirations can, in effect, find expression and solutions only on a political level.

—J. Chazot [about May 25, 1968].

Self-Management and a Republic of Councils

After having been denounced as an "empty formula" by Georges Séguy (May 24), and half-heartedly taken up by the CFDT, self-management (and the organisms it implied—that is, student councils and worker councils), became one of the key words of the movement.[22] "We must take this society and turn it inside out like a glove" was the slogan of *Perspectives Syndicalistes,* and it undoubtedly did express one of the temptations of the movement, particularly among sociology, psychology, and philosophy students. "The Sorbonne should belong to the students and the factories to the workers," was what the Sorbonne student-worker action committee never tired of repeating, even after the movement had started to ebb. The situationists set up a "council to maintain occupation" which, in their inimitable Hegelianistic-Marxist terminology, expatiated on the same themes. At the height of the ebb tide the *22 mars* militants warned against facile, equivocal verbalism.[23]

Document 171

In-fighting Between Individuals, Local Groups or Cliques Is Now Out of Place

We must take this society and turn it inside out like a glove!

In one night, the students got France out of its political lethargy.

They did more: they started a revolutionary process which will easily sweep aside the capitalist authority if the working class associates itself wholeheartedly with their action.

The action of the workers who are now striking at their places of work constitutes a hope and an example.

The time has come to silence all individualism and to weld the entire worker movement to the student movement.

But the time has also come to go beyond programs geared solely to the demands of the Left, and to define sound bases for a real program for edification of Socialism.

Since neither the parties nor the unions have thought it necessary until now to think in terms of revolution, the students, in collaboration with the worker movement, must buckle down to this task, the importance and urgency of which are obvious.

*This will be the best way to unite all the ideological families of
the worker movement, if each has the revolutionary intelligence
to state its proposals in terms of the present circumstances and
no longer in the name of its intellectual guides.*

—*Perspectives Syndicalistes* [about May 20, 1968].

Document 172

We Are Continuing the Fight

Our goal is evidently not to destroy present structures without proposing anything new, contrary to what Gaullist slander is insinuating.

The absence today of a leader at the head of our movement corresponds to its very nature. It is not a matter of knowing who will
lead us all, but how all of us will form one single head. More precisely, there is no question of any political or union organization whatsoever, constituted before the formation of the movement, taking it
over.

The unity of this movement must not and cannot come from the
premature presence of a celebrity at its head,[24] but from the unity of
aspirations of the workers, peasants, and students.

These aspirations can take concrete form within the framework
of grass roots committees, thanks to discussions in small groups.

These committees will then progressively abandon the inevitable
differences that may have appeared among them.

UNITY MUST COME FROM THE GRASS ROOTS AND NOT FROM A
PREMATURE LEADER WHO COULD NOT NOW TAKE INTO CON-
SIDERATION THE ASPIRATIONS OF ALL THE WORKERS.

But this unitary task will encounter the worst sort of outside
difficulties and cannot be accomplished without actual control of the
streets, which is where contestation and political discussion take place.
Pompidou has understood this very well when he claims to grant us
everything except the streets.

Nevertheless, difficulties can also come from the inside. We must
protect ourselves in fact from unthinking anti-Gaullism which could
encourage some among us to believe that the problem would be automatically settled with the departure of de Gaulle and his government.

The movement cannot back a co-option operation of the Popular
Front or transitional government type.[25] In fact, concessions of a ma-

terial nature which we might obtain would in no way change the scandalous nature of present-day society. Besides, they would very quickly be absorbed by an increase in the cost of living organized by the employers.

This is why the ultimate weapon of all workers fighting for the revolution is direct management of their means of communication and production.

An additional step must be taken!

Comrades, the occupation of factories must now mean that you are capable of making them function without the bourgeois infrastructure that was exploiting you. The revolutionary movement must now be allowed to live, develop, and organize production under your control. In this way you will deprive capitalism of its instrument of oppression. You must ensure production and distribution, so that the entire working class can prove that a worker authority which owns its means of production, can set up a real socialist economy.

Self-management as an economic and social system has as its goal fully to achieve free participation in production and consumption through individual and collective responsibility. This is therefore a system created above all for human beings, to serve them and not to oppress them.

Practically, for working class comrades, self-management consists in having their factories function by and for themselves and, consequently, in doing away with the hierarchy of salaries as well as with the idea of employees and employers.

They should set up worker councils elected by themselves to carry out the decisions of everyone together. These councils should be in close relationship with the councils of other companies on regional, national, and international levels. The members of these worker councils are elected for a determinate period and tasks are to be rotated. We must in fact avoid the re-creation of a bureaucracy which would tend to set up a leadership and thus re-create a repressive power.

We must show that worker management in business is the power to do better for everybody, what the capitalists were scandalously doing for a few. We must follow our comrades of the csf in Brest, who have been pointing the way for several days.

On the other hand we must create new trade structures that would allow us to do without the numerous and varied intermediaries who take a totally unjustifiable profit, to the detriment of the worker and the consumer (wholesale dealers, banks, brokers, etc.).

Comrades, we must see it through. We are occupying the *facultés,* government agencies, and factories. . . .

We must stay there and make them function for ourselves as soon as possible, because capitalism is trying to starve us.

We must show that we are responsible for the enormous movement we have launched.

We must not fall into the trap of sterile discussions; we must not let ourselves be impressed by the slander and threats of an old man who claims to represent France, without taking into account its inhabitants.

Capitalism is afraid; it is showing its true face, which is fascism. But the power is there for the taking.

LET'S TAKE IT!

—Student-Worker Action Committee [May 28, 1968, according to
the authors of the CAR-Sorbonne pamphlet; June 2nd, according to
our source].

Document 173

To All Workers

Comrades,

What we have already done in France is haunting all Europe and will soon threaten the ruling classes throughout the world, from the bureaucrats in Moscow and Peking to the millionaires in Washington and Tokyo. *In the same way that we set Paris dancing,* the international proletariat will storm the capitals of every country in the world, of all the citadels of alienation. Occupation of factories and public buildings all over the country has not only jammed the economy, but above all it has brought about a general contestation of society. A deep-seated movement is leading almost every sector of the population to desire a different life. From now on this is a revolutionary movement in which all that is lacking is *awareness of what has already been done,* in order that we might really possess this revolution.

What are the forces that will try to save capitalism? The regime will fall unless it tries to maintain itself through the threat of recourse to arms, and even through immediate armed repression (accompanied by a hypothetical reference to elections, which could only take place after capitulation of the movement). As for the potential power of the Left, it too will try to defend the old world through concessions, and through force. The so-called Communist Party, the Party of the Stalinist bureaucrats, which has fought against the movement from the beginning, and which began to reckon with the fall of Gaullism only when it realized it was no longer able to be its principal protector, would in this case be the best guardian of this "popular government."

Such a transitional government would really be a form of "Kerenskiism" only if the Stalinists were beaten. This will depend essentially upon the awareness and capacity for autonomous organization of the workers: those who have already turned down the absurd agreements that so gratified the union leaders will discover that they can not "obtain" much more within the framework of the existing economy, but that they can take everything by transforming all the bases for their own benefit. The employers can hardly pay more; but they can disappear.

The present movement did not become "politicized" by going beyond the miserable union demands on wages and retirement allowances, improperly presented as "social questions." It is beyond politics: it poses the social question in its simple truth. The revolution that has been in preparation for more than a century is here. It can assert itself only in its own forms. It is already too late for a bureaucratic-revolutionary patching up. When a man like André Barjonet, newly de-Stalinized, calls for formation of a common organization which would bring together "all the authentic forces of the revolution . . . those who claim to be following Trotsky, Mao, anarchy, and situationism," we can only recall that today those who follow Trotsky or Mao, to say nothing of the pitiful "Anarchist Federation," have nothing to do with the present revolution. The bureaucrats can now change their minds as to what, for them, is "authentically revolutionary"; but authentic revolution need not change its condemnation of bureaucracy.

Just now, with the power they hold and with the parties and unions everybody knows, the workers have no other choice than direct seizure of the economy and of every aspect of reconstruction of social life by the unitary grass roots committees. In this way they can assert their autonomy with regard to any sort of political-unionist leadership, ensure their self-defense, and federate themselves on a regional and national scale. If they do this, they should represent the only real authority in the country—that is, the authority of the *worker councils*. Failing this—because it "is either revolutionary or nothing"—the proletariat would again become a passive object. It would return to its television sets.

What defines the authority of the councils? Dissolution of all outside authority; direct, total democracy; practical unification of decision and execution; delegates who may be revoked at any moment by their constituents; abolition of hierarchy and of independent specializations; deliberate management and transformation of all the conditions of a liberated life; permanent creative participation on the part of the masses; internationalist extension and coordination. The present demands are not the least. Self-management is nothing less. *Beware of co-opters* of every kind of modernist tendency—even to priests, who begin by talking about self-management—even about worker councils —without granting this *minimum,* because in reality they want to save their bureaucratic jobs, the privileges of their intellectual specializations, or their future as little chiefs.

Actually, what is needed now has been needed ever since the beginning of the proletarian revolutionary project. It has always been a matter of working class autonomy. We have been fighting for abolition of the wage system, of marketable production, and of government. We wanted to make history consciously, to abolish all separations, "everything that exists independently of individuals." The proletarian revolution has spontaneously outlined its adequate forms in the councils: in Saint Petersburg in 1905, as well as in Turin in 1920, in Catalonia in 1936, and in Budapest in 1956. Each time, survival of the old society or formation of new exploiting classes was accompanied by abolition of the councils. Today the working class knows its enemies and has its own methods of action. "The revolutionary organization has had to learn that it can no longer combat alienation with alienated forms" (*La Société du Spectacle*).[26] Worker councils are clearly the only solution, since all other forms of revolutionary struggle have ended in the contrary of what they wanted.

> —*Comité enragés-internationale situationniste; Conseil pour le maintien des occupations,* May 30, 1968 [printed leaflet].

Document 174

Self-Management and Narcissism

Self-management, like all slogans, can be served with any kind of sauce. From Lapassade to de Gaulle, from the CFDT to the anarchists. Self-management of what? To speak of self-management alone, independently of the context, is a device. It becomes a sort of moral principle, a commitment according to which on one's own accord, by oneself, one will manage the entity of such and such a group or enterprise. The effectiveness of such a slogan depends no doubt on its powers of self-delusion. The designation in each situation of the corresponding institutional object is a criterion which should make it possible to clarify the question.

Self-management of a school or a university is limited by their objective dependence with respect to the Government, to a method of financing, to the political commitment of the users, etc. It can only be a slogan for temporary agitation, which in the long run risks remaining somewhat confusionist if it is not part of a revolutionary, coherent outlook. The self-management of a factory or of a shop also risks being co-opted by the psycho-sociological reformist ideology which considers that "inter-relational" problems must be treated by group techniques,[27] for instance "training-groups" among technicians, managers, employers, etc. For workers such techniques are too "expensive."

In imagination we contest the hierarchy. In fact, not only do we not lay hands on it, we rediscover in it a modernist base, we invest it with a style and a lackadaisical or other kind of morality. The province of self-management of a business implies actual control of both production and planning: investments, work organization, commercial relations, etc. Due to this fact, a workers' collective which "adopted self-management" in a factory would have to solve innumerable problems with the outside. This would be lasting and viable only if this outside were itself organized along lines of self-management. An isolated post office would not be able to live long under a regime of self-management and, in fact, the entire machinery of production is interpenetrating, the way telephone exchanges are. Experiments in self-management during the strikes, organization of the production sectors of a factory *in answer to the workers' needs,* or of supplies and self-defense, are all very important indicative experiences. They show possibilities for going beyond the grievance levels of the struggle and point the way for organization of a revolutionary society during a *transitional period.* But it is evident that they cannot furnish clear and satisfactory answers to the types of production relationships, or to the types of structures adapted to a society that has expropriated the economic and political powers of the bourgeoisie in a highly developed economy.

Worker control, in fact, poses fundamental political problems as soon as it touches upon institutional objects that contest the economic infrastructure. A self-managed lecture hall is undoubtedly an excellent pedagogical solution, whereas a branch of industry taken under direct control by workers immediately presents a whole series of economic, political, and social problems on both a national and an international level. If the workers do not assume these problems in a way that is beyond the competence of the bureaucratic leaders of today's parties and unions, pure economic self-management risks becoming a myth and ending in the dead end of dissolution.

To speak of political self-management is perhaps also a delusive, all-purpose formula, politics being fundamentally the adjustment of a group with respect to other groups in a global perspective, whether spelled out or not. Self-management as a political slogan is not an end in itself. The problem is to define on each organizational level both the type of relationships and forms to be furthered and the type of authority to be set up. The slogan of self-management can become a smoke screen slogan if it generally replaces responses differentiated for different levels and for different sectors, in terms of their real complexity.

Transformation of governmental authority, transformation of the management of a branch of industry, organization of a lecture hall, or contestation of bureaucratic unionism, are entirely different things, which must be considered separately. We must be careful lest the slogan of self-management, which has proved to be correct in contestation of bureaucratic structures on the university level, should be co-opted by reformist ideologists and politicians. There is no "general philosophy" of self-management, applicable everywhere and in all the situations created by the establishment of a dual authority, by the institution of a democratic revolutionary control, by a perspective of worker power, by the setting up of systems of coordination and regulation between the various fighting sectors.

If a theoretical clarification of the scope and limitations of self-management is not made in time, this "slogan" will become compromised in the reformist sense and will be rejected by the workers, in favor, perhaps, of other formulas of the "democratic centralist" type, which are immediately co-optable by every form of dogmatism of the Communist movement.

—Excerpt from *Tribune du 22 mars,* June 8.

Beyond the Proletariat

The student revolution also tried to reach the victims of the social regime, those who exist either on this side of, or beyond, the traditional class struggle: the sub-proletariat, members of the "mob,"[28] victims of unemployment. The question of the sub-proletariat, or "lumpen-proletariat," assumed all the more importance in that representatives of these social categories (among them a certain number of rather dubious characters) were present on the barricades, and the "Katangans" in Paris, the "drudgers" in Lyons, and the "slum-belters" in Nantes, were collaborating with the security services inside the facultés, at times, under student leadership, at others, in opposition to them. The "Katangans" were put out of the Sorbonne at dawn on June 14th, both because they were really terrorizing the students and were themselves apparently being manipulated from the outside, and because of a reflex in favor of order and morality.[29] Although the presence of women and their complete participation was permanent, the movement gave only occasional consideration to the position of women in society.[30] The text that follows was put out by a feminist association.

Document 175

Sub-proletarian Status

The sub-proletariat, 3 million people in France

In France, more than three million men, women, and children—French sub-proletarians or immigrant workers—live in emergency housing,[31] miserable neighborhoods, and shanty towns.

They are the most evident sign of the way a society based on profit and competition ends by reducing human beings to the role of solvent consumers, and because of this fact, neglecting their most elementary rights.

Hostages of grievances, never beneficiaries

At the same time, they demonstrate that not only the beneficiaries of the system, but many of those who today air their dissatisfaction are capable of indifference and disregard when faced with an injustice that does not affect them directly and consideration of which might risk being prejudicial to their own demands.

Intolerable conditions:
  no housing,
  not always the right to manage one's own family, jobs that no one wants.
  Salaries under

In reality, each one of us should examine his own conscience. Although we are witnesses to this modern slavery, what have we done thus far for the thousands of people living on our doorsteps in intolerable conditions? Today, we no longer accept a situation in which the government, municipalities, political parties, unions, and private organizations serve individual interests to the detriment of the people.

the guaranteed minimum,
    educational retardment that handicaps children starting school; 90% never complete the primary grades;
    no access to professional training,
    no political power . . .

But who are the people? Within the framework of the defense of the working class, what role have we given to this vast French sub-proletariat that has remained outside the expansion, condemned to odd jobs, to a precarious life, victims of what is actually veritable segregation on all levels of political, economic, social, professional, cultural, and spiritual activity. And in the political struggle, what position has been given the sub-proletariat in our programming?

How many among us have chosen the part of resignation, of seeking refuge in our powerlessness to solve a problem concerning which we know very well, in reality, that it challenges not only a political regime and individual interests, but also an entire scale of values and the economic system that stems from it.

The sub-proletariat has received no answer from us other than laws—such as the Debré law on urbanization of shanty towns—laws that have become ineffective for lack of necessary funds, but above all because they were not supported by a public opinion willing to assume responsibility for their application, based on adequate preliminary study.

Together, let us act in solidarity with the sub-proletariat and refuse to allow it to serve as a hostage for demands that only end in increasing the luck of the lucky.

The movement *Science et service* is issuing a manifesto. It has no other aim than to make its voice heard and let it be understood that the sub-proletarians, who are the most completely crushed by the system, must be the criterion and the lever of our action; they must be introduced to participation in the *management of their own fates.*

—*Mouvement Science et service* [date unknown].

Document 176

Women students,

You were on the barricades, the police charged and blackjacked you just as they did the men students, your comrades.

You participate in the discussions, in the work of the commissions, in the large public demonstrations.

Girls' *lycées* and women's institutions have at times brought in other establishments and, among the ten million strikers, the women workers also have their place.

However, during these decisive days, either in large gatherings or on radio and television, no woman spokesman has appeared.

In the negotiations between unions, employers, and government, no one formally demanded equal wages for women and men, no one mentioned the creation of collective services and day nurseries[32] to lighten the burden of women in their dual workday.

In the enormous discussion which is taking place throughout the country, in the great contestation of structures and values, no voice has been raised to declare that change in relationships between men also implied change in relationships between men and women.

Students and young people in general want the same ethics for girls and boys. This is one aspect of change. But it is only one aspect.

We must break with other taboos.

The society to be built must be the work of women as well as of men; it must give all women equal opportunity with men.

If you are in agreement with the above, what are you willing to do about it? Come to discuss it with us.

—*Mouvement démocratique féminin* (Stand is in the Sorbonne courtyard) [date unknown].

Regionalism

Another characteristic feature of the movement was its interest in reviving regional life. This was evident in the plans for University reconstruction,[33] as well as in the existence at the Sorbonne of a very active "committee for regional socialist revolution,"[34] which was set up on May 16 and promulgated the theories advanced by Robert Lafont.[35] One day the announcement "We need a Breton autonomist" was broadcast over a Sorbonne loudspeaker. The PSU devoted part of its propaganda to the slogan: "De-colonize the Provinces."

Document 177

A Leaflet Put Out by the Action Committee
for Regional Socialist Revolution

REGIONAL SOCIALIST STRUGGLES

For the last ten years or so, regional struggles have become more and more vigorous. With respect to each action on grievances, it is possible to perceive changes in the strategy applied.

1. The Basque Country

Struggle is almost inexistent. Complete depoliticization. Business is shaky and agriculture is on the decline. Capitalism has taken over the Basque country without encountering any contestation. The left-wing parties have attempted no structural analysis. Basque organizations emphasize that no action is possible other than in liaison with the Spanish Basque country, which is highly industrialized and is one of the main forces of contestation of the Franco regime.

2. Brittany

Three phases mark the peasant struggle: the vegetable zone in 1960–1962, the chicken war in 1966, and the pork war in 1967. In each case, contestation followed capitalist aggression and remained on the level of a professional defense reflex. A certain number of things became evident. In 1960–1962: farming on too small a scale (GAEC[36]), marketing organizations that are a rationalization of exploitation and commercialization.[37] In 1966: awareness of dependence on distant European markets. Realization of domination by the big cereal regions as a result of chicken feed requirements. In 1968: increased awareness, accentuated by the fact that encouragement by the government—that is to say, by the political representatives of capitalism—to produce chickens and pigs, clashed with the capitalist structures themselves.

On the worker level, Brittany constitutes a zone with a strong worker tradition, Nantes-Saint-Nazaire and small centers.[38] For several years now, the struggles have been toughening. Hennebont, Fougères, and Redon give evidence of the existence of a combative working class.

More important is the fact that these worker struggles have been mobilized around grievances of workers, small farmers and the middle classes.

3. Corsica

Tougher and tougher demonstrations have taken place against the vignette [automobile tax], against nuclear experiments, for keeping the mines working, and against agricultural colonization.

The parties on the left, especially the PC, have supported these various demands. They have supported the emotional content of each contestation while repeating the classic party line. No global view has ever been presented, out of mistrust of an ethnic tinge.

The content of all these demands is not entirely socialist since there exists no political organization that would attempt to insert the regional combat into the global socialist struggle.

—From *Urbu*, No. 6, June 1968.

International Dimensions

Both in its terminology and, to a large extent, in practice, the movement was internationalist. There were numerous speeches at the Sorbonne in Italian, Spanish, and Portuguese, intended for foreign workers, and actually, foreign students participated both in the demonstrations and in the activities of the different commissions. In institutions where they were especially numerous, the number of participants was at least in proportion to the number of enrollments. The "Tri-Continental" committee for the Sorbonne, two of whose texts follow, continued the action started before May in support of revolution in Latin America, and circulated information on the spread of the movement in Third World countries. The Middle-East conflict was responsible for a few clashes. However, at the time of the Belleville incident that opposed Jews and Arabs (June 2–3), bilingual posters in French and Arabic urged both groups to turn against their common enemy.[39] Through leaflets and posters ("Frontiers = Repression") a campaign against the symbols of petty nationalism was undertaken. The foreign students, who were given a place to themselves at Censier, were entirely free to get in touch with their French comrades. However, this spirit of international solidarity disappeared with the rest of the movement, and during the last two weeks in June, foreign students and intellectuals were deported without any special protests being made.

Document 178

Tri-Continental Committee

Africa, Asia, Latin America

The nature of the French student and worker movement is based on contestation of the infrastructure and the superstructure of capitalist society.

This contestation must be expressed by us, through total commitment over and beyond all frontiers.

In effect, to contest capitalist structures within a national framework is also to contest the international relations set up by these structures.

Proletarian internationalism is the expression of this commitment. It is not a problem of law, since law is the expression of these contested structures.

Nor is this internationalism an abstract idea. It is a way to lead the offensive against our own regimes, whose allegiance is bound to international capitalism. Every attack on capitalist structures in Western countries is of invaluable help to the national liberation movements and to the socialist revolutions in Africa, Asia, and Latin America.

Our tasks must therefore be carried out within this framework.

The committee should inform French manual and intellectual workers of the ties that exist between their present struggle and the struggle of oppressed peoples, because the exploiters are the same: capitalism and imperialism. It should keep them informed about the development of the people's struggles in Asia, Africa, and Latin America.[40]

The committee must serve the revolutionary movement now developing in France, the result of which, to a large extent, will govern the solution to the problems of the three continents; that is to say, the struggle for socialist revolution on the three continents and throughout the world.

Its help is two-fold.

—Complete participation in the revolutionary movement, on the same basis as all French militants.

—Specific participation, which must take place through information and recruitment, carried out among foreign workers and students (the modalities and means of which should be studied), in agreement with the objectives of the present French revolutionary movement.

—Tri-Continental Committees [end of May?].

Document *179*

For Abolition of the Status of Foreigners in France

A very large number of foreigners—for the most part workers and students—live, work, and are exploited in France and, having no alternative, they generously participate in the struggles of the French workers and students.

These foreigners come under an oppressive special statute[41] which subjects them to almost permanent special police checks and threats, which we, Frenchmen, avoid simply because of our nationality.[42]

This concept of "nationality" is profoundly reactionary. Men work, are exploited, dream, and fight for their freedom in a specific geographic and social context; there, they have every right.

Foreign students and workers, who are even more oppressed than the French, should enjoy in France the same political rights that we do: the right to strike, to demonstrate, to vote (if they so desire).

The example of the Commune, in which the Minister of Labor was a Hungarian worker named Fraenkel, and the military chief a Polish worker named Dombrowski, should be recalled. For not only does actual segregation of foreigners exist in France, on professional and academic levels, it also exists in workers' political and union organizations. This anti-foreign segregation, which has been widely expressed by a certain part of the press[43] during the recent events, is however only the social reflection of an oppressive jurisdiction.

The latter may be summarized in three points.

1. The "residence-card"—or foreigner's identity document, which is subject to frequent renewal. This constitutes in reality a permanent police check.

2. The "work-card"—this document allows a foreigner to be exploited in a trade without it being possible for him to exercise any other; it must also be renewed very often. In reality it is an unspeakable encroachment on the right of freedom to work.

3. Threats of "deportation from French territory" for the slightest offense. These threats weigh upon foreigners quite arbitrarily, and are mercilessly applied for the most futile reasons. It so happens that a good many of the foreigners who come to France come not only to look for a land to work in, but believe they will find a land of liberty. What they find is a police state.

And that concerns us.

Join us in demanding abolition of the "residence-card," of the "work-card," and of the harsh jurisdiction against foreigners.

They have a right to everything, just like yourself.

—Worker-Student Action Committees [beginning of June 1968].

Document 180

CAAF

Since the crisis, national frontiers have been closed to young people. The government thinks it is protecting itself through measures borrowed from counter-revolutionary recipes of the 19th century.

THIS MANEUVER WILL NOT SUCCEED

The ideas of May 1968 will not be stopped by a roadblock or a *képi. Young people will not be stopped any more than will ideas.*

The revolution we are fighting for will only be definitively achieved if it invades Europe.

Our struggle demands the abolition of national frontiers.

MEETING WEDNESDAY JUNE 5 AT 5 P.M.

Amphitheater 240 of the Faculté de Droit (Assas)

AGAINST DEPORTATION OF OUR FOREIGN COMRADES.

AGAINST CLOSING OF FRONTIERS.

FOR A UNIVERSITY WITHOUT FRONTIERS.

—*Comité d'action pour l'abolition des frontières* (CAAF) [June 3, 1968].

Document 181

Foreigners Address the French

Foreign workers and students are taking part in the struggle led by their French comrades because they are aware that this struggle is also theirs.

Consequently, they believe that it is their right to urge you all to realize that only international solidarity among workers, peasants, and students will make it possible to change the very harsh way of life that capital and imperialism impose upon them.

In this connection, foreign comrades wish to denounce the economic, social, political, and cultural discrimination of which they are victims—discrimination that can only weaken the struggle of the French working class.

> *The committee of foreign workers and students calls on you to come to the Sorbonne to hold a general assembly on the position of foreigners in France. The* AG *will be called upon to make a statement on a new statute for foreigners.*
> Sorbonne, Amphitheater Guizot—Thursday, May 23—8 P.M.

—Committee for Foreigners, Censier, Room 410 [May 22, 1968].

Document 182

American Permanent Committee

The French Students' Movement calls into question the dominant values of capitalist society. Like their comrades in Rome, Milan, Berlin, at Columbia and Berkeley, the students of Paris have challenged the institutions of bourgeois-imperialist society and fought its police in the streets. Although each struggle has unique characteristics, they have begun to form a common experience. Many of the foreign students currently in Paris have participated in struggles in their own countries and in France and may have useful experience to contribute, and can learn from their French comrades the important lessons of Paris. We want to enter a dialogue.

A group of American students have established a permanent committee at the Censier Center to exchange ideas. Although discussion will be informal (in French and English), interesting topics might be:

1. student movements in the United States, both campus and nationwide (SDSA).

2. attempts of students to organize workers.

3. in the light of the "co-optation" attempts by liberal reforming professors and a frightened Pompidou, the discussion could also treat the American model for the technocratic university, and the danger of the liberal programs proposed, for example, at Caen in 1966.

4. we plan to establish a news link-up with the USA which will make available to a student readership of over two million *honest* information about the important events that we are living here. (All forms of information connected to any phase of the student movement is urgently requested.)

SOLIDARITY!

Censier Center, Rm. 216, from 2–4 P.M., and from 8–12 P.M.

13, rue Santeuil, 5° (Metro: Censier-Daubenton)

—[May 17, 1968?] [Original English text]

To Change Life

"People who talk about revolution and clean struggle without any
explicit reference to daily life, without understanding what is subversive about love or what is positive about refusing coercion, have
corpses in their mouths."[44] This situationist wall text, which figured
both in Strasburg and in Paris, summarized marvelously well what
was no doubt the highest ambition and the most evident success of the
movement. For tens of thousands of students, the revolution actually
did "change life," and brought with it a breakaway from family restraints. The May 10 barricades were a real festivity, and the night the
Sorbonne was occupied, with its singing, piano, and jazz, was sublime,
in the Stendhalian sense of the word. The Sorbonne was decorated
with works by Calder and Giacometti, and the *facultés,* which had
been experienced (with some mythology) as pure instruments of repression, became the theater (with some inverse mythology) of a great
emotional release, not to say sexual liberation. All of this could hardly
concern anybody but the students, and this is one of the obvious limitations of the movement when isolated in time: "only those who benefit from a 'consumer society' can really criticize it." Another limitation
was the rapid, hard-to-avoid deterioration of joy into intoxication, and
a fake doctor (who was also a real crook) proposed to set up an
abortion center at the Sorbonne.

The movement found its poetry in posters and wall texts, in syn-
copated slogans on "jerk" rhythms, and in demonstrations. "Wild-dog
Fouchet, liberate the Sorbonne," "This is only a beginning, keep up
the fight." Literary expression[45] was inevitably indebted to the past: to
surrealism, even to Apollinaire's calligrams. The Freud–Che Guevara
action committee developed the theories of Fourier, Reich, and Marcuse
on liberating the passions, in contradiction to the Freudian defense of
sublimation.

In this respect, however, the most important manifestos of the
movement were the series of "theses" produced by the commission entitled "We are on our way" (Censier, Room 453). Widely distributed,
prominently posted at the *Ecole des Beaux Arts,* and duplicated in

Lyons, they summarize perfectly both its ambitions and its contradictions.[46]

Document 183

Join the Revolutionary Commune of the Imagination

The cultural revolution cannot adapt itself to the economic and juridical structures of bourgeois society because it constitutes only one of the multiple aspects of the revolutionary movement.

In this connection, the so-called *avant-garde* theaters, which, in order not to miss Saturday night's box-office receipts, really were in the back-to-work *avant-garde,* furnished clear proof. As a result, revolutionary students and artists, responding to the call of the CRAC, interrupted shows in the name of solidarity with the strikers at Flins and at the ORTF, and publicly denounced the use that the commercial system could make of Art, whether *avant-garde* or not, and of ideology, whether to the left or elsewhere.

At present the government is actively engaged in neutralizing the movement of worker contestation and the germs of revolution it contains.

Ideologists, official artists, and the whole capitalist system of production and distribution of art and theater—among them, the union organizations established within the system—are contributing to this operation both by sabotaging the workers' strike and by urging the public to return to the fake world of commercialized dreams.

STUDENTS—ARTISTS—WORKERS

We must crack open the bourgeois cultural system. We decree a Revolutionary Commune of the Imagination.

The Latin Quarter is a ghetto of a very cunning species which keeps culture in confinement for the benefit of the few, and commercializes it in limited editions. This is a ghetto of intellectual complacency where sheep demand the brand marks they wear on their haunches.

We must break our degrading chains.

We must occupy together the territories reserved for private paradises of cultural alienation.

We must rid the area of certain restricted spots where conditioned or tolerated products of the cultural system—theater, movies, and art galleries—are sold pell-mell to a few privileged persons.

We must open up the streets—the *facultés*—the *lycées*—to creation and invention.

We must welcome on the ruins of its Pantheons all who have been excluded, the poor and oppressed of bourgeois culture.

We must transform our ghetto into a fortress of freedom and imagination.

We must liberate the creative forces that our society represses, together with all the workers.

COMRADES, THE REVOLUTION TAKES PLACE EVERY DAY
IT IS A FESTIVITY, AN EXPLOSION
WHICH LIBERATES PEOPLE'S ENERGIES
WE MUST ORGANIZE—WE MUST INVENT OUR MEANS OF ACTION
WE MUST COMBINE OUR ENERGIES!

For free exercise of the imagination in the streets. For transformation of the Sorbonne

into an International Revolutionary Center for cultural agitation, open to all workers and self-managed by its participants, who would have the following minimum program:

—*enforce, coordinate, and support* subversion and destruction of the bourgeois cultural order wherever there is guerrilla cultural action, such as is beginning to break out in our industrialized capitalist societies;

—*impose and materialize,* in new forms of civilization, the creative and revolutionary forces transmitted by workers in cities and in the countryside, and smothered and suppressed by the bourgeois cultural system;

—*achieve,* as much on a practical as on a theoretical level, the launching of limited self-management operations, in preparation for generalized self-management of society.

For occupation of all the theaters

in the Latin Quarter, and for their utilization as operational bases for transforming outside space into a vast stage with infinite possibilities, on which each person becomes both actor and author of collective social-dramatic events.

For occupation of all movie houses, art galleries, and dance halls

and their conversion into operational bases for taking over all urban space: walls, sidewalks, streets, roads, rivers, and sky, as settings for images, sound, and plastic expression, in a huge sketch based on permanent invention and at the service of everyone.

FOR APPLICATION OF THE IMAGINATION
TO THE SERVICE OF THE REVOLUTION

*Form groups and enter into theoretical and practical action within
the* CRI (Commandos de Recherches et d'Intervention). *Enroll in
the* CRAC.

—(*Comité Révolutionnaire d'Agitation Culturelle*), Free Sorbonne–
Odéon [June 11, 1968?].

Document 184

The Revolution Is Continuing . . .

Comrades,

Government propaganda, the CGT's *attitude, the delaying tactics
of those who are reorganizing their political groups, have caused some
people to doubt in the future of the movement of revolt begun May 3.*

*But the revolution must go on, and its nature is not put into
question by this sabotage. Analysis of the themes of our revolt, the
courage of the demonstrators, and their quality, prove that only the
traditional character of our analyses makes us doubt in the revolution.*

THIS IS WHY THE REVOLUTION WILL CONTINUE

1. Against the existing economic and socio-psychological system, we
must pursue a *revolutionary struggle,* through revolutionary actions,
on the basis of alliances defined as a result of the following analysis.

a) A revolutionary action

is a contesting action which shows young people and workers
the implicit or explicit violence of the established system.

It must be:

—politically right, that is to say, easily explained to young people
and workers, and not constitute a gratuitous provocation.

—a contestation—that is to say, it must openly flout a taboo of
the system.

—debunking, by forcing the permanent and implicit repression
of the bourgeois system to show its real face.

b) A revolutionary alliance

combines all the forces of true contestation of the system, that is
to say, the people who are fundamentally excluded from its benefits:
young people and workers.

2. A social system is the *repressive organization* of barriers built by
the "haves" against the exploited "have nots." From the system of
slavery to socialist societies, these barriers have never been lacking,
under the most varied forms.

a) Private ownership

of the means of production is an essential barrier of capitalist societies.

b) Bureaucracy

is an essential barrier of the socialist system.

c) "Diplomania"

is an essential barrier in all developed societies.

d) Education

is an essential barrier in all social systems. Anguish is associated with the Father, who will become the Professor, the Sergeant-Major, the Boss, the Bemedaled Gentleman, the Noble Old Man.

3. Anguish linked to the educational system, later takes the form of a search for security: titles, "social success," enjoyment of prestige, an aggressive attitude or superior paternalism.

a) The "consumer society"

offers consumer models which are experienced like a system of signs that secure and ensure prestige or integration into the group.

b) Sexual repression

which is principally applied to young people and

—ensures continuation of the anguish mechanisms.

—allows canalization of non-liberated energy toward the objectives of the "haves" (war).

4. The functioning of such a system must necessarily provoke *violent tensions* between the "haves" and the excluded. Nevertheless, nothing allows us to foresee absolutely a social-economic group in which awareness of exclusion and the dissatisfaction that results from it, prevail over the fear of losing the few advantages that have been acquired.

a) In the system as a whole

it is the *workers* who are the most excluded, who are the victims of unemployment or of economic exploitation.

b) In all social strata

it is the young people who are the most excluded and who most resent the repressions inflicted upon them by the "haves."

Young apprentices are even more exploited than common laborers.

Lycée and University students find themselves uselessly confronted with giant mountains of knowledge to be absorbed.

Young artists must surmount countless difficulties in order to replace the older ones who hang on.

5. We saw during the week of May 3–10, the gathering of the *front of those who are excluded* from the system: the unemployed, young workers, *lycée* and University students, apprentices, intellectuals re-

buffed by the consumer society, "beatniks" in revolt, graduates discovering their role of "watchdogs," jobless young people.
a) In order to reconstitute this front
  we must continue the revolution we have started, and *which is
submerged at the present* by those who have been given a function
within the system: rigid national unions, co-opting professors, established political parties, workers who, though veterans of the social
struggle, are now family men who lack combativeness.
b) In the struggle against the existing economic and social-psychologi-
cal system
  we must give up the idea that only workers are revolutionary;
this is the road to "wait and see."
  We must advance with the allies we have made during the police
repression.
  The real revolutionaries are neither the students themselves, the
illusory "student class," nor the workers, who too often are caught up
in habits of petty comfort and fascinated by consumer delusions.
  The revolutionaries are all who are crushed or excluded by an
inhuman system.
c) The struggle must set as its *final objective*
  the instauration of a socialist system in which, through the destruction of barriers, everybody's creativity will be given free rein.
  This objective implies a revolution not only in production relationships, but in everybody's way of living, manner of thinking, human
relationships, and conception of sexual life.
d) The struggle must set as *tactical objectives* for the student movement in its present situation, revolutionary actions that re-launch contestation of authority. It must:
  —protest against the corrupt atmosphere of the city of Paris and
    the accompanying sexual repression: demand liberation of the
    Luxembourg Gardens, to be open 24 hours a day for young
    people and workers. From the Sorbonne to the rue d'Assas,
    we must organize a permanent campus with revolutionary so-
    cial evenings.
  —ape and ridicule government censorship: we must forbid the
    sale in the Latin Quarter of newspapers which refuse to pub-
    lish the communiqués of the revolutionary movement.
  —fight against psychological conditioning: by means of hoots
    and booing we must force theater managers to replace pub-
    licity and newsreels by debunking documentaries that are
    not subject to preliminary government censorship.

—increase solidarity with the workers: propose to cooperate with those who are occupying their factories, to get them started again for the sole benefit of the workers. More symbolically, the students can suggest simply decorating a factory wall: the workers being in their own work-place have a right to choose their decorator.

6. The revolution, which is the sum of all the grievances that have accumulated justifiably, must necessarily constitute their outlet. Fascism risks being the only alternative.

The revolution is at a critical point. It lacks neither troops nor raison-d'être. Enormous forces have risen up in its name. Today, unemployed, young workers, lycée and university students must play their part in this necessary revolution.

—"Freud–Che Guevara" Action Committee [May 19, 1968?].

Document 185

We Are on Our Way

First Series: Amnesty for Blinded Eyes[47]
Students and Workers,

For more than a week we demonstrated in large numbers and, when necessary, we fought determinedly. At that time, we believed that our situation could change. Today the working masses have profited from our exemplary movement to demand satisfaction of old "corporative" and salary grievances. These are necessary, but not sufficient—too much or not enough!

Too much because they are impossible of achievement in the present state of the structures that they are implicitly contesting.

Not enough because they are addressed to an authority which has in effect been abolished—which therefore no longer has any real power—and which is being asked for reforms.

And here is what we have to record today: hundreds of injured and mutilated, to go back this side of where we started.

This we refuse to accept; we want the hope engendered by the demonstrations of these last days to find its expression in an irreversible movement.

Our ideological choice is clear; the barricades are necessary but not sufficient; leaflets cannot replace political thought, or slogans achievements.

The following text is intended to be the start of a program.
It is intended to be a basis for thought and action.
It is not a doctrine nor even a manifesto.
But it must become that.

CALL TO THE POPULATION

Students and Workers: we must not let ourselves be fooled again. We must become aware of what we have all done hastily and in the streets.

Students, we must look sharply and not allow ourselves to be co-opted, assimilated, or "understood," with our petty problems which are considered to be the problems of "minors," of conscience-stricken well-to-do and "non-proletarians."

Let us state clearly what we want; we must take the time to know what we want.

Thesis 1. There is no more "student problem." The student is an outdated concept. We are privileged—not economically, but because we alone have the time and physical and material possibilities of becoming aware of our situation and of that of society.

Non-proletarians we are indeed, but above all, we are passive and unproductive consumers of "goods" and "culture."

To be a proletarian is neither a value nor a future. May proletarians become real workers with all the rights that this entails. May students cease to be privileged beneficiaries of culture, and future exploiters, and restore immediately to society in the form of professional guidance what society has given them as individuals.[48]

Thesis 2. Students, let us not allow ourselves to be cut off from professors and other "classes" of society. Nor must we allow ourselves to be confined in a so-called student class with its economic and social problems of integration.

Thesis 3. Formerly, we were only a small minority necessarily capable of being integrated. We are now an over-large non-assimilable "minority," yet maintaining the status of the old minority. This is the contradiction in which we, sons of the bourgeoisie, are placed. *We are no longer assured of our future role of exploiters,* which is the origin of our revolutionary strength. We must not let it slip away from us.

Let's abolish ourselves: let's become workers so that all workers may become privileged, with the right to knowledge, culture, and the choice of their own fates.

Thesis 4. Henceforth we are workers like any others. We are an immediate and future "capital" for society, not a promise of succession for the ruling class.

Thesis 5. Students, stop being parasites, even temporary ones. Future exploiters and privileged consumers, from now on we must be true producers of goods, services, and knowledge.

Thesis 6. The unemployed student is dead; the night student too. Everybody will study if everybody produces, consumes, and studies at the same time.[49]

Thesis 7. Students and workers, we are rejecting the consumer society; we are wrong. Everybody must consume and produce so that everybody can consume the equivalent of what he produces.

Production and consumption must no longer be separated by distribution or by technical division of labor. You must accept this commonplace remark: the total number of workers can consume only what the total number of workers produce. The total number of workers must choose what they want to consume in order to know what they want to produce.

Thesis 8. Working class promotion to the bourgeois way of life, hidden and demonstrated by the fake demands attributed to it, has been an undertaking of modern capitalism which, in this way, has been able to divide the world in two: the "haves" and all those capable of becoming such within a more or less short time, being confronted by the "temporarily" excluded of this world, the so-called underdeveloped countries.[50]

Thesis 9. Students have become the proletarians of the bourgeoisie; workers have become the bourgeois of the Third World.

Thesis 10. Students and workers, you who enjoy privileges of all sorts, let us continue the fight for a radical change in all exploiting, oppressive, unauthentic societies.

Let us be what we are and want to become and not what they make of us in spite of ourselves.

Thesis 11. We must reject at the same time "a-politicism" and "revolutionism" as being basically identical. A few credits or wage increases will change nothing in our status of passive objects confronted with political, economic, and technical power.

Thesis 12. Revolution is not a luxury or even an art; it is a necessity when all other means are impossible.

Students and workers, you alone can accomplish this. Nobody will do it for you because nobody can.

Thesis 13. If our situation leads us to violence, it is because all society commits violence against us. We must reject the violence of "the good life" committed against everybody—a scandalous "good life" of overtime, of bargaining for our labor and our vital strength, in exchange for a few baubles in black and white or in color, their only further use being to reduce us to slavery by depriving us of our humanity.

Thesis 14. Students and workers, from now on we reject this vicious cycle and this slow death. We demand and we will see to it that all workers obtain, on every level of responsibility for consumption produced and production consumed, the right to decide together and in solidarity all that concerns them as working human beings, in exchange for their services.

To work is to live one's life through a necessary free activity; division of labor is the exchange and human solidarity of services by means of techniques that have been mastered.

Thesis 15. Students and workers, we must accept the means to our ends. If we want a radical change in our condition, we will not obtain it through dialogue, because dialogue was broken off long ago. If we desire simple organization of our "privileges," or a few more baubles, we should not delude ourselves with revolution, because it will cost a lot.

Students and workers, let us choose—but we must choose quickly.

Thesis 16. We must be something else than the "characters" in a tragicomedy which is no longer even funny. We must be real actors.[51]

Thesis 17. To act is not to demand "the impossible"[52] within the present system; it means seeing to it that we no longer need to demand a role and our rights. This is making a gift of their sacrifices to charity and to good works.

Thesis 18. Let us reject the deaf men's dialogue of words, but let us also reject the dialogue of brutal and conventional force.

We must not take refuge either behind our demands or behind our barricades. We must attack!

Thesis 19. Let us assume our responsibilities toward ourselves and toward others. We must categorically reject the ideology of output and "progress," and of the pseudo-forces of the same name. Progress will be what we want it to be. We must reject the meshed entanglement of the "luxurious" and the "necessary," stereotyped needs, both imposed separately, so that every worker will force himself to work, in the name of the "natural laws" of the economy.

Thesis 20. Worker, decide with all the other workers, whether competent or not, the question of your output and of your own "market value."

Thesis 21. We must reject all the divisions perpetuated consciously or through necessity between the proletarian and the bourgeois. Proletarian, abolish yourself; become a full-fledged worker and there will be no more bourgeois, but only workers.

We must also reject the intellectual autonomy of technocrats. Once work was isolated from the person who did it, once this living contradiction between "product and consumption" was forged, it was necessary to valorize the only thing that remained—that is, raw *work, force, violence.* This made possible the separation of engineers from workers, creators from executants, the literary from the scientific, the "useful" from the "superfluous." It also permitted creation of a *hierarchy of "values"* and *authorities,* so that each one would be the informer of another, in order the better to direct all the workers in the most complete "liberty."

Thesis 22. Workers of every kind, we must not let ourselves be fooled. We must not confuse technical division of labor with the hierarchical division of authority and power. The first is necessary, the second is superfluous and must be replaced by an equal exchange between our work forces and our services within a liberated society.[53]

Thesis 23. We must also reject the division between *science* and *ideology,* the most pernicious of all, since we secrete it ourselves. We do not want to be passively governed by the "laws of science" any more than we do by those of the economy, or of technical imperatives. Science is an "art," the originality of which is to have possible applications outside itself. We must reject its delusive imperialism, which is a guarantee of all kinds of abuses and setbacks, also for itself, and we must replace it by a real choice among the possibilities it offers.

Thesis 24. We must also reject the facilities of revolutionary language as being an instrument of assimilation and refusal to pose problems. We must always ask *which* revolution is being discussed.

Thesis 25. When people ask us to say "where we are going," we should not answer. We are not in power, we do not need to be "positive," or justify our "excesses."

But if we do reply, that means also and especially that we *want* the means to our ends; that is to say, if not governmental authority, at least *an authority from which all forms of oppression and violence would be excluded as a basis for its existence and means for its survival.*

Thesis 26. We must no longer allow our aims to be assimilated by all kinds of tired revolutionaries or by existing institutions.

We desire and we demand that production and consumption be controlled by each other, and both of them by all of us, workers of the entire world, united in the same necessity to live and act in such a way that this necessity will cease to be alienating.

Thesis 27. The proletariat, and in its time the bourgeoisie, were once revolutionary—that is, they were unable to set up a dialogue other than by radically transforming society. People tried and are still trying to withdraw this power from the proletariat by dividing the workers and by trying to constitute a false "peaceful co-existence" of the bourgeoisie and the proletariat as opposed to the *hungry peoples of the world.* This "association of interests" is founded upon *racism* and the countless hierarchies of intellectual and financial work values. The whole attitude is justified by a 19th century ideology which has been willfully cut and thingified into extracts.

Thesis 28. Students are treated as privileged persons in order to integrate them into this industrial technocracy office for profit and "progress," by deluding them with economic-scientific imperatives. The importance of this appellation then becomes comprehensible. For the workers, these privileged persons can only be *petty-bourgeois provocators.* For the ruling class, they are *ungrateful, romantic trouble makers.*

The point of departure is different; the reasoning the same.

Thesis 29. The bourgeois revolution was juridical; the proletarian revolution was economic; *ours will be social and cultural,* so that men can be themselves and cease to be satisfied with a humanizing ideology.[54]

Thesis 30. Lastly, we must reject the ideologies of "complete" man, with their proposals of an ultimate goal—the end of history—made in the name of progress, the better to reject progression.

Workers and students, we are the revolutionary class, we are the bearers of the ruling ideology, because our goal is to abolish ourselves as a class and with us, all classes.

All we want to be is young workers. And that we can propose to thousands of "young workers," young or old, intellectual or manual, so that they can be like us and we like them.

Once more, we must abolish all privilege, all hidden barriers. To do this we will have to fight with all our strength and with every means at our disposal until a victory which could only be provisionally final is attained.

Send out this call again and again.
Become its author, correct it.
Distribute millions of copies of it.
Post it up; re-copy it.

And when we are all its authors, the old world will collapse and make room for the union of workers from all countries.

—[May 11].

We Are on Our Way

Second Series: University Reforms,
Teaching Reforms, Reforms of Society
Preamble. Since the barricades, there are no more students, no more professors, and soon there will be no more proletarians. We have exceeded our limitations in spontaneous action. We are all together. The point now is not to become separated again and to become aware of the new worker status we have granted ourselves without explicitly realizing it.

Article 1. Declaration of the rights of workers (ex-students, ex-professors, ex-workers).

Every professor of a certain knowledge—"know-how" or culture —is supposed to "repay" *as an individual* what he has received from society as "a privilege," in order that from now on this knowledge should no longer be a further ruling class privilege which, in spite of all good will and individual messianic attitudes, can only alienate and exploit workers generally.

Article 2. As of today, education is decreed as permanent—free— and obligatory at all ages.[55]

Article 3. Every student (or learner) will be requisitioned to fulfill the counterpart of his present advantages.

Every ex-student, having been taught, must become a teacher, while at the same time continuing to be taught.[56]

Article 4. Every ex-professor is maintained in his functions to which are added those of giving guidance to new "colleagues."

Article 5. Every worker who thus far has been deprived of "knowledge" is invited, whatever his present education or age, to become a *learner,* and soon, a teacher, in order to choose his own fate.

Article 6. The 40-hour week[57] is henceforth the maximum tolerated. All overtime will be used for education, self-improvement, cultural activities, and political discussion.

This overtime will be paid by the government as compensation for violence done to workers by depriving them of this "privilege."

This will also permit workers to meet all the financial commitments that they have already contracted, until such time as the worker-learner can himself become a worker-teacher.

Article 7. Any local educational unit (factory-school-ex-secondary-ex-University) will be administered by all the workers-teachers-learners together.

Article 8. All workers-teachers-learners will be elected, dismissed and promoted by their peers,[58] all decisions to be taken by a simple majority. All decisions of this kind will have immediate repercussions on remunerations over and above the base set by the following Article.

Article 9. Every worker-learner-teacher will be paid according to age and family "needs."

Article 9a. To radically transform a society does not mean to "proletarize" everybody. It means doing away with the very conditions of the existence of a proletariat. Therefore, no salary would be reduced as a result of *Article 9.*

Salary and income must not be confused.

Article 10. No more professors will be named from today. The crisis in recruiting professors is passed since every teacher will repay *at an equal cost of effort,* in the form of guidance and teaching, what he has been taught, on the level of his own proficiency, of course.

Article 11. No more *formal examinations* are necessary, the checking of knowledge being permanent, thanks to the fact that more than adequate guidance has been substituted for didactic and authoritarian teaching.

Examinations will be replaced by direct promotion (*Article 8*) decided by fellow workers-teachers-learners at the simple request of "the candidate."

No monitor or inspector of any kind is necessary any longer, checking being permanent on all levels and independent of any directional hierarchy, which, itself, is replaced by a "hierarchy" of responsibilities.

Article 12. For each self-managed economic-political-cultural unit of production and consumption of "goods" and "culture," an elected judicial commission will settle all litigation. This commission may itself be revoked by a simple majority vote of no confidence.

Article 13. All modalities for carrying out the above may be considered by whatever government is in power, present or future.

Article 14. This program is fundamental and minimum.

Article 15. This program will make it possible for university reform not to be merely a matter of organizing those enjoying "cultural privileges" and the advantages in kind that now accompany them.

Article 16. This utopia is perfectly achievable and will be much more "economical" than the present selective machine, or than the support society gives to 600,000 unproductive students during a minimum of three years. If it cannot be peacefully imposed through discussion of its application and contestation of its partial and inevitable incoherences, it will call on the "full powers" of the streets.

Closing Clauses[59]

The University cannot reform itself all alone and become a free "socializing" enclave in a society of economic, social, and cultural selection.

Education as a whole must be reconsidered and replaced by transmission of knowledge of every kind.

Transformation of the University cannot be achieved without radical transformation of the relationships between class–sub-class–privileged persons of all breeds.

We must be radical and, if discussion is refused, we must impose discussion through other means.

No one wants to lose his privileges. We must insist, either by mutual agreement or by force, that there be no more privileges, or that everybody should become "privileged." Let us have nothing to lose and therefore everything to gain, for everybody.

Reconsidering education is reconsidering society and mutually transforming them both.

Third Series: Preliminary Proposals for a Cultural Revolution
1. We are living in a pre-revolutionary period. A pre-revolutionary period is one that witnesses the birth of a new ideology: this remains to be created.
2. Utopians are people who believe that by being content to change social structures, man's spirit will change.
3. All critical struggle is political; critical politics is neither courage nor debauchery. It is a simple duty.
4. May everybody be carried away by his enthusiasm without feeling guilty, in order to relearn the meaning of what is human.
5. Let us take from what exists all that is good and has been disfigured.
6. Professors should return to find in education the satisfactions they often seek in vain in conventions, or elsewhere.
7. People who are afraid of "adventure" should know that they are merely afraid of change.
8. The intellectual, political, and social majority of young people has been established.

9. Anybody who does not understand should join in discussions. Everything can be explained to everybody.

10. Our paralyzed and archaic psychic structures should be scuttled to make place for the imagination of a new world.

11. We live in a critical period;[60] anyone who does not seize this fact can understand nothing about the world.

12. Stop the acceleration[61] of the sterilizing routine of all fragmented work.

13. All existing ideas are out of date and are to be reconsidered.

14. Change is not an end in itself; between rigidity and agitation there is sufficient margin for all who are willing to take the trouble to think.

15. Youth is a matter of mind and not of age.[62]

16. Every youthful spirit that is still free from overdetermined psychic patterns can imagine new ideas and be creative.

17. Only real autonomy makes creativity possible.

18. The idea of a generation conflict must disappear from the world: it is only a mask for the struggle for power.

19. If fathers truly play their role of fathers, the revolution will be evolution.

20. Any person who considers emotion as foreign to logical thought must rid himself right away of this idealist's vision.

21. All creation starts with an experienced emotion.

22. Personal re-discovery is indispensable for training the mind.

23. The difference between the ordinary person and genius is not the level of intelligence but the determination to go further.

24. Every new creation should include anti-paralyzing elements.

25. The men in established institutions—whether governmental or oppositional—must continue to take care of current business; they must furnish our daily bread. Tomorrow we will do it for them, and we will give them culture in addition.

26. All who are not responsible for taking care of current business should defrock, go out into the streets, and question their ways of thinking.

27. Eat and rest every day.

28. One should discuss everywhere and with everybody.

29. To be responsible and to think politically is everybody's right; it is not the privilege of a minority of the "initiated."

30. We should not be surprised by the chaos of ideas, nor should we smile at it. We must neither ridicule it nor take pleasure in it. It is the necessary condition for the emergence of new ideas.

31. The fathers of the regime should understand that autonomy is not

a hollow word; it presumes a sharing of power—that is to say, a change of its nature.

32. Let no one try to pin a label on the present movement; it has none and needs none. The movement creates itself with all those who come to join it, leaving behind them everything they believed until now.

33. People who refuse to understand should retire.

34. Build thousands of parking spaces so children can play marbles in the gutters.

35. Take the time to love and to learn to love.

36. Underneath the class struggle there is fundamentally a struggle for power.

37. Access to autonomy and shared power can come about peacefully if the fathers of the regime are good enough to play their role.

38. To learn to think again, we must scuttle ourselves as individuals, conditioned by a class.

39. Play!

40. Workers in all professions should continue to urge their organizations to abandon their passivity and, with the help of intellectual workers, promote progress toward autonomy.

41. Let's recover our sense of festivity.

42. The red flag . . . can die.
    The black flag, too.
    Painters must invent a thousand flags symbolizing research, effort, interior revolution, enthusiasm, and invention.

43. Musicians and poets must compose new songs.

44. May new vacations be invented for this summer, so the movement will not be interrupted.

45. Let's have open discussions every day, in the press, on radio and television.

46. Only the explosion of our present methods of thinking will permit us to re-invent a new world.

47. From the creativity of each one of us will come a new culture and a new ideology. The new manifesto that will result from it will be in perpetual fusion with it, thanks to the personal contribution of each one of us.

48. The strike is over. The counter-university and the action of criticism have already begun. The strike committees and others should be called constructive "autonomous business or university committees."

49. Nobody can achieve autonomy without having learned to go forward. Those who know how to go forward must first learn how to

teach it. Those who know how to go forward and teach, must teach it to others.

50. And all of that simply so that men may become themselves!

—Theses of the "We Are on Our Way" Commission (Excerpts),
Censier, Room 453 [May 11–30, 1968].

Notes

1. This work is now being carried out at the Linquistics Center of the *Ecole Normale Supérieure* in St. Cloud.

2. *Les Murs ont la parole,* W. Lewino and J. Schnapp, *l'Imagination au pouvoir.* The "spontaneous" nature of these writings should not give rise to illusions. The important writings at the Sorbonne were the work of a small number of people. Many were quotations, sometimes slightly changed. For instance, the Sorbonne inscription: "Godard, the biggest swine of the pro-Chinese Swiss" exists as: "Godard, the most famous among the pro-Chinese Swiss" in the article by René Viénet, *l'Internationale situationniste,* No. 11, October 1967, p. 35. As for the poster: "Let's leave the fear of red to horned beasts," this is a quotation from Victor Hugo.

3. This phenomenon is in no way isolated in history. The Algerian revolution borrowed—at least in its French language texts—the language of the French Revolution; cf. A. Mandouze, *la Révolution algérienne par les textes,* Paris, Maspero, 1960.

4. Ph. Labro, *Ce n'est qu'un début,* p. 65.

5. Cf. above, Chapter II, p. 196.

6. Cf. above, Chapter III, p. 215.

7. R. Marienstras, *Esprit,* June–July 1968, p. 1065; cf. too, J.-P. Peter, *l'Homme et la Société,* April–May–June 1968, p. 13: "A fig for structures! What can be constructed today that would not necessarily inherit from the old orders as long as one of their walls remains standing? This rejection of organization demonstrates a very vigilant and perspicacious distrust of all acquired conditioning and the contagion of old apparatuses."

8. Here is a characteristic example taken from a round-table discussion published by the review *Autogestion,* March–June 1968, p. 26. In it a student says, "As far as I am concerned, there was absolutely no question of having a maximum number of workers enter the University. On the contrary, I believe that this is what should be avoided, insofar as bringing them into the University means incorporating them even more into the system and encouraging them to prostitute themselves or rather to become alienated, to lose the very nature of their worker status." Would work in a factory not be alienating?

9. The most extraordinary account is perhaps that of a 22 *mars* militant, in Ph. Labro, *op. cit.,* pp. 48–77. See also, for instance, P. Peuchmaurd, *Plus vivants que jamais,* R. Laffont. Among accounts by teachers, perhaps the best are those by Paul Rozenberg on the beginnings of the movement (special "student number" of *les Lettres Françaises,* May 15, 1968); by Jean Chesneaux, "Vivre en mai," *les Lettres nouvelles,* September–October 1968, and by R. Jean, *la Pensée,* August–October 1968.

10. Cf. above, p. 240.

11. May 22. We recall Georges Séguy's question: "Cohn-Bendit, who's that?" To which someone replied on a Sorbonne wall: "Séguy, who's he?"

12. At least at the beginning of the movement. Naturally, when everything was over, discussions were more numerous. See particularly, the two "round-table discussions" published under this title in *l'Homme et la Société*, April–May–June 1968, pp. 3–48.

13. This text could be compared with that of Claude Lefort, a teacher at the *Faculté des Lettres* in Caen, in *La Brèche*, pp. 35–62.

14. This is the terminology of *Socialisme ou Barbarie*.

15. We recall, for instance, that on May 21 several dozen young Jews occupied the premises of the *Consistoire Israélite de France* to "contest the archaic and non-democratic structures of existing community institutions"; a few notes by A. Memmi in *l'Arche*, June–July 1968.

16. Group formed by former partisans of the "Italian" positions inside the UEC. This center is presented in the review *Hermès, Critique de la vie quotidienne*, October 1968.

17. It was the workers who were supposed to take the floor.

18. Cf. the analogous conclusion in the leaflet that appears above, Chapter II, p. 163.

19. The book by Henri Lefebvre, *la Proclamation de la Commune*, Paris, Gallimard, 1965, which defines the revolution as a festivity, undoubtedly had an influence. In Marseilles, the *Lycée Thiers* was re-baptized *Lycée "Commune de Paris."* Naturally, the May movement was immediately reflected, at first on the level of literature intended for a wide reading public, in interpretations of past revolutions; cf., for instance, Patrick Kessel, *Les Gauchistes de 89*, Collection 10/18, UGE, Paris, 1969 (anthology).

20. Text from the *Rote Fahne*, translated in *Partisans*, No. 41, March–April 1968.

21. *Ecole national supérieure des Beaux-Arts.*

22. After the Yugoslav and Algerian experiences, the slogan self-management, which, for a long time, was confined to small anarchist or anti-bureaucratic groups, and spread by such theoretical militants as D. Guérin, had assumed an entirely new importance, as shown by the review of this name, published by the Editions Anthropos, and which published a special number, 5–6, May–June 1968, on *l'Autogestion et la Révolution de mai*. The more classically Marxist, Trotskyist, or Maoist groups insisted with perspicacity on the existence of an entrenched State apparatus that the slogan self-management could not break up. See also on this subject: *Mai-Juin 1968, la Sorbonne par elle-même*, pp. 274–280.

23. Cf. above, Chapter VI, pp. 378–381.

24. Probable allusion to the presence of P. Mendès-France at Charléty on May 27.

25. Proposal made by F. Mitterrand on May 28.

26. This is the title of a book by the situationist Guy Debord, Buchet-Chastel, 1967, see p. 27.

27. Allusion to the theories, popularized by G. Lapassade, of Moreno, Lewin, and Rogers.

28. Cf. above, Chapter III, pp. 222–223, the leaflet "Concerning the riff-raff."

29. For glorification—in part mythological—of the role of the "lumpen" and of the "Katangans," cf. A. Geismar, S. July, E. Morane, *op. cit.*, pp. 324–335.

30. On masculine chauvinism in the movement, cf. Introduction, p. 47.

31. See the inquiry on "temporary housing" by Colette Pétonnet, *Ces gens-là*, Maspero, 1968.

32. In certain suburban *lycées*, the students, particularly the girl students, organized day-nurseries in order to make it possible for their professors to come to the *lycée*.

33. Cf. below, p. 503.

34. We lack information on the size of the regionalist movement in the University cities most directly concerned: Rennes, Montpellier, Aix, and Toulouse.

35. *La Révolution régionaliste*, Paris, 1967; see the discussion in *Esprit*, December 1968.

36. *Groupements autonomes d'exploitation coopératives.*

37. Allusion to the creation in 1962, after the demonstrations of the Breton peasants, of the *Fonds d'organisation et de régulation du marché* (FORMA). On all this see S. Mallet, *les Paysans contre le passé*, le Seuil, 1963.

38. But neither Nantes nor Saint-Nazaire is in the least "Breton-minded."

39. Text of one of these documents in J.-P. Simon, *La Révolution par elle-même*, pp. 155–156. See also A. Geismar, S. July, E. Morane, *op. cit.*, pp. 425–426. Members of the Betar (extreme right Zionist group) overdid the spirit of provocation to the point of entering the Sorbonne courtyard with a banner "Death to the Yids" (*Mort aux youpins*). Part of the Arab press saw in this movement the result of a Zionist and CIA plot, an attitude that is reflected in the behavior of a certain number of Arab students (from which we must except the Tunisian militants of the group "Perspectives").

D. Cohn-Bendit, nevertheless, had very clearly taken position against Israeli expansionism: cf. *la Révolte étudiante*, p. 70. A few associations of foreign students, known for their verboseness (students from Black Africa, Greeks, Arabs, et al.) in a leaflet, and without further information, attributed responsibility for the Belleville incidents to "Zionists and other provocators." A meeting on the Palestine question had been organized on May 15 at the Mutualité by groups favorable to the Arab cause. On the other hand, certain Jews did not like such slogans as "We are all German Jews!" One of them, A. Mandel, went so far as to write, "So far as I know, none of them went to be circumcised after the march," *l'Arche*, June–July 1968, p. 62.

40. The *Comité des Trois Continents* devoted considerable space (leaflets, pamphlets) to this information effort, but in the country where the revolution had perhaps contributed the most to inspiring the French students, which was Cuba, there was at first complete silence; cf. K. S. Karol, *Les Guerilleros au pouvoir*, Robert Laffont, Paris 1970, pp. 495–499 (*Guerrillas in Power*, Hill and Wang, New York, 1969). The Chinese press, on the contrary, reported the events in full, but presented them from the Maoist point of view.

41. The document reads "constructive."

42. A foreigner can be deported "in case of urgency" without any other form of due process. There were a number of such cases in June and July, and political opponents were sent back to their own countries.

43. Especially the fascist weekly *Minute*.

44. Once more, this is actually a quotation from R. Vaneigem, *Traité du savoir-vivre à l'usage des jeunes générations*, Paris, 1967, p. 19.

45. A very fine series of poems was published in *Le Monde* of June 1st. See *Poèmes de la révolution, mai 1968*, editions of the review *Caractères*, Paris, 1968.

46. Posted on a Sorbonne bulletin board in manuscript, at the end of the first week of occupation, these "theses" were then known as the "Sorbonne Char-

ter." They were published several times, notably in the collection *Quelle université? Quelle société?*, pp. 144–221, as well as in pamphlet form, in *Esprit*, August–September 1968, pp. 26–34. Their symbolical importance is such that there could be no question of leaving them out of this collection. Following the example of *Esprit*, we have cut repetitions.

47. "Blinded" because a number of students and demonstrators had become momentarily—and even in some cases definitely—blinded by "tear" gas.

48. The unusual feature of this formula must be pointed out, because the entire movement continued to ask if the concepts of "cadres," "leaders," and "exploiters," were not associated.

49. General student or eternal student?

50. A typically "Marcusian" theme: identification of the "fringes" of industrial societies with underdeveloped countries. We find it again in the text by the Freud–Che Guevara action committee.

51. But the vocabulary remains that of the theater.

52. Cf. the slogan: "Be realistic, demand the impossible."

53. This thesis summarizes perhaps the essence of the movement.

54. This cultural theme is taken up again and criticized in a later text (*Quelle université . . . ?*, pp. 164–168).

55. Cf. the preceding text, *Thesis 6*.

56. Fundamental theme on the abolition of the difference between teacher and pupil. Cf. Epistémon, *Ces idées qui ont ébranlé la France*, pp. 49 ff.

57. The Editions du Seuil text reads 30 hours.

58. From these words on, our text differs totally from that of the Editions du Seuil (*Quelle université? Quelle société?*, pp. 169–171) and appears to be taken from an earlier version.

59. This series does not figure in the versions of this text published thus far.

60. The Editions du Seuil text reads sensitive.

61. The Editions du Seuil text stops at this word.

62. Here we seem to have returned to the "wisdom of nations."

VIII

The "Ancien Régime"
and the University Revolution

The student movement having started in the *facultés* and finding itself in control of them, which was something of a surprise, was inevitably led to consider the question of what to do with them. On this point it encountered—and clashed with—the professors, who were not experiencing the problem at the same *tempo*. Indeed, a certain number of professors withdrew to a nostalgic Aventine, either out of wounded dignity or because they could not accept the idea of a *faculté* in which the students would feel perfectly at home. One Sorbonne professor,[1] a distinguished Hellenist, said, "The Germans occupied Paris, and I did not collaborate; the students are occupying the Sorbonne, and I will not collaborate."

Those professors—and there were many—who consented, if not to participate in the student movement itself (this was the case particularly of the assistant professors and instructors), at least to collaborate with the reform commissions and general disciplinary assemblies, were above all anxious to define as quickly as possible stable structures, undoubtedly very different from the old ones, if only in the role they assigned to the students inside the different departments and *faculté* assemblies, but which would allow the *facultés* to start functioning again as organs for research and transmission of knowledge. No doubt a large number of students—certainly the majority—shared this reasoning.

This was not however the general attitude of the students most actively involved in the movement, once the first dreaded hurdle of exams had been taken. Some, undoubtedly, wanted simply to prolong the delight, but for the greater part the motive was quite different. The principles they had agreed upon were so ambiguous that they were all living in anguished fear of being "co-opted": by the government, the leftist political parties, or the professors themselves. They were nearly all aware, too, that the ongoing discussion was taking place between "privileged persons," and that nothing could be done without those "outside the system" having their say.

While some were waiting for the revolutionary apocalypse, the power takeover that alone would allow creation of a popular university (for different reasons this was the attitude of both the FER and the UJC(m-l) militants), others, taking their cue from South American universities, sought to create a permanently disorganized situation that would permit permanent contestation (the case of a part of the JCR students); others still, on the principle "Be realistic, demand the impossible," took refuge in utopia. But almost no one among the students realized the imminence of a counter-current, which certain professors however clearly foresaw. Almost no one, either, realized that even the most "reasonable" reforms were nevertheless of a radical and utopian nature, since to apply them would mean practically doubling the National Education budget. It was only during the last days of the Sorbonne occupation, after the police intervention on June 16, that the common front outlined between May 3 and May 13 *appeared* to have re-formed.

During nearly the entire movement one feeling dominated the most committed among the students, and that was absolute refusal of all change of a technocratic nature for the University; refusal of both the former liberal University and of a University "adapted" to modern capitalist economy; refusal too of the "competitive" universities outlined in November 1966 at the Caen colloquy. Naturally on both sides enormous misconstruals were committed, the most evident being confusion between the terms *savoir* and *pouvoir:* knowledge and authority. The professors were tempted to confuse the two and to think that any concessions in matters of authority challenged their technical competence; while the students did just the opposite, and would readily have agreed, if pressed, that "student power" should automatically put students and professors on a plane of equality as regards knowledge, and in this way do away with the undoubtedly authoritarian aspects of the teacher-pupil relationship.

The same type of confusion characterized—in my opinion—the fundamental discussion between the supporters of "parity" (separate colleges for teachers and students) and those of "mixity," accompanied, if need be, by closed lists. Parity had been denounced before the events by the revolutionary students, and for good reasons;[2] in revolutionary periods, "mixity," or election of authorities by mixed assemblies of students and professors, obviously permits more rapid progress; but once the "back to normal" stage had been reached, would it not permit, even more than parity, "manipulation" of the students by the professors—all the more so, in fact, since the revolutionary students were not in the majority? The most radical students, however, were conscious of this, and much of their conduct is explained by their desire—which was the same as that of the 1848 revolutionaries, even of the Bolsheviks and the leftist social revolutionaries when they declared the Constituent Assembly dissolved—not to set up any institutions *before* the work of explanation and propaganda, and even a social mutation, had actually given them the majority.

It so happened that the "back to normal" or, if you prefer, the "counter-current," arrived with lightning speed. As long as the movement appeared all powerful it was threatened from within, by the professors, by all varieties of demagogues, by war-profiteers, and by young (or not so young) "sharks," who calculated that there would be vacancies to be filled. General de Gaulle had hardly finished speaking on May 30 when the reaction became perceptible,[3] and it was even more so after the reoccupation of the Sorbonne: the *faculté* councils knew how to fool the new assemblies, and the independent union of higher education, which thus far had kept very quiet, took a new lease on life and opposed everything that had been done until then.[4]

Meanwhile, a great deal had been done, to a point where on July 24 Edgar Faure, the Minister of National Education, very cleverly appeared to ratify the work that had been accomplished. It is not the aim of this chapter to list this work,[5] but to trace the sequence of events[6] and to bring to light the principles and difficulties of application and the different kinds of reactions they aroused.

The Fall of the *Ancien Régime*

Beginning May 11, the assembly of professors and associate professors of the Paris *Faculté des Lettres,* as an "exceptional" measure, was opened to instructors and assistant professors.[7] This first revolution was followed by a second, on the 18th, which was adoption of the principle of a co-equal commission of teachers and students. Through pressure on the part of the middle and lower echelons of the teaching body, and above all of the student movement, similar measures, with countless variations, were adopted almost everywhere.[8] In addition to the Sorbonne text, the following statutes were adopted very soon at Tours-Orléans (*Lettres*). In most cases, by May 18, the general principles had been adopted.

Document 186

Communiqué of May 18, 1968

The Dean of the Paris *Faculté des Lettres et Sciences Humaines* (Sorbonne), M. Marcel Durry, having reached the age limit and judging that in the present circumstances it was necessary because of the new situation to bring in new men, on the morning of May 18th consulted a plenary assembly of the *faculté* composed of full professors, assistant professors, and instructors.

This plenary assembly, to which the ordinary assembly of the *faculté* had delegated its powers, asked M. Las Vergnas, the Vice Dean, to be responsible for the functioning of the *faculté* until the creation of new structures with which the students would be associated.

Moreover, the plenary assembly, under the chairmanship of M. Las Vergnas, started by an exchange of views as to the methods and principles of organization of these new structures, which were to be the object of its planned deliberations.

In particular the plenary assembly of the *faculté* decided to constitute a co-equal commission of teachers and students composed of at least fifty members: the teachers to be elected in each section by secret ballot, by the plenary assembly of the section; the students to be elected according to the modalities adopted by the general assembly of each discipline. These modalities to be made public by means of press and radio.

This co-equal commission will be obliged to propose to the plenary assembly of the *faculté* within the week that follows the result of the aforementioned elections, the new *faculté* structures organized on the basis of the following principles:

—student representation, or co-management, according to the wishes expressed on every level;

—presence of all faculty members in all assemblies on every level;

—existence of permanent councils for the sections and the *facultés*, for which election modalities are to be determined;

—the plenary assemblies of the disciplines to meet before May 23, 1968, and the next meeting of the plenary assembly of the *faculté* set for May 30;

—the new structures to be submitted to a vote of the student general assemblies, according to sections.

In addition, as regards the examinations that should take place at the end of this school year, the plenary assembly of the *faculté* states the following:

The student and teacher movement is continuing to develop today within the framework of a wider movement. Examinations must therefore, in any case, be postponed to a later date.

It is neither desirable nor possible that this year's examinations should take place according to traditional methods, whether they take place this summer or not until the autumn. The sections themselves will decide on their modalities, in agreement with the general assemblies of the students in that discipline.

It goes without saying that this provisional organization would in no way prejudice the necessary recasting of the system for checking knowledge and the students' capacities.

The plenary assembly is considering creation of a special session for particular cases (among them, foreign students and students with deferments). The question of the entrance competition for IPES will be examined by the plenary assembly during its May 30 session.

Document 187

The *Faculté des Lettres et Sciences Humaines* is governed by the following institutions as of today, Wednesday, May 15, 1968.

I. SECTION

There exists a section assembly, meeting for:
1. Preparation for the coming year.
2. Examination of application files and drawing up of a preferential list submitted to the assembly.
3. Preparation for examinations.
4. Annual report.
5. Any urgent problems concerning section affairs.

Except for points 2 and 3 (which concern only the teachers), the section assembly is composed, proportionately, of all the section faculty members and of an equal number of section students, elected according to school year or course, in proportion to their number.

The minutes for the section assembly sessions are made public.

Students delegated to the section assembly can also sit on commissions.

The section head is elected among the professors, associate professors, assistant professors, and instructors[9] by the teaching body of the section.

II. THE PLENARY ASSEMBLY

It has supreme power.

It consists of the entire teaching body and an equal number of students, elected according to school year or course, in proportion to their number.

The plenary assembly meets with full rights four times a year and, in special session, upon the convocation of the Dean or the proposal of a third of its members.

Its decisions have weight only if at least two thirds of the faculty members and at least two thirds of the student delegates take part.

It is convoked and chaired by the Dean.

The agenda is prepared by the Dean, discussed and adopted at the beginning of the session. The Dean's proposal is communicated to everybody a week in advance; each participant can communicate to the Dean any suggestion for the agenda.

The minutes of the session are published.

III. COMMISSIONS

The plenary assembly elects specialized commissions, responsible to it, to handle social questions (scholarships, student allocations, etc.), budget, pedagogy, nominations, examinations, cultural policy, buildings, personnel. (Two elected representatives of the personnel are obliged to sit on this last commission.)

Each commission is composed of four faculty members and four students. The faculty members are elected by the teaching body, without discrimination among the different categories of teachers; the students are elected by their representatives to the plenary assembly.

IV. THE PERMANENT DELEGATION

The plenary assembly names a permanent delegation within its own ranks.

The permanent delegation is composed of the Dean and ten members: four section heads, elected by their peers on proposal by the Dean; one representative of the instructors elected by his peers on proposal by the Dean, and five students elected by and among the student delegates to the plenary assembly.

The spokesman for each commission must be consulted by the permanent delegation on all questions within the scope of his commission; he then takes part in the meeting of the permanent delegation.

V. THE DEAN

The Dean is elected for three years[10] among the professors and lecturers by the plenary assembly. He chairs the plenary assembly and convokes it as stipulated in Article 2. He presides over the permanent delegation.

Upon a motion of censure, the plenary assembly, on a majority vote of two thirds, can dismiss the Dean.

VI. THE UNIVERSITY DEPARTMENT OF LITERATURE

There exists for each discipline one single section including faculty members and students of the *Faculté des Lettres et Sciences Humaines* and of the University Department of Literature (see CLU).

The section head can be elected among faculty members working either in Tours or in Orléans. He is helped, for each section represented in Orléans, by an assistant working in the other establishment. This assistant is elected under the same conditions as the section head.

The Director of the CLU (University Department of Literature) is elected under the same conditions as the Dean. The Dean relinquishes his place to him and his right to vote in the permanent delegation on all questions specifically concerned with the CLU.

VII. APPLICATION

The first plenary assembly will take place before the 1968 summer vacation. Its delegates on every level will therefore be elected to serve only until the first plenary assembly of the 1968–1969 University year.

The Fall of a Mandarin:
Professor Soulié's Dismissal

On May 11 Doctor P. Vernant, *médecin des hôpitaux,* associate professor and assistant to Professor P. Soulié, the latter occupying the chair of cardiology at the *Hôpital Broussais* (Paris), circulated a petition against repression. On May 15 Professor Soulié took measures that amounted to dismissal of his assistant from the service and, on the 16th, the latter replied by letter[11] (Document 188). The example of the student movement served to strengthen and embolden the majority of those employed in the service and, on the 17th, there was a meeting of the entire personnel, during which Doctor Z., who is not a callow youth but a full-fledged *médecin des hôpitaux,* made the remarks contained in a document to follow. The next day a student from the action committee of the *Faculté de Médecine* informed Professor Soulié of his dismissal. We give his statement. Professor Soulié's reply, and a second declaration by Dr. Z. On May 22, in a secret ballot, a large majority of those attached to this service voted to set up group management. After May 30, Professor Soulié reconquered a part of his authority and, at the beginning of August, took advantage of this fact to dismiss from his service three research workers who had protested too vigorously against it.[12] Later still, eight doctors (one of them an associate professor) were dropped as of October 1;[13] out of solidarity, twelve others resigned from the service.

Document 188

Paris, May 16, 1968.

Dear Sir:

I am your senior assistant in the service, having not left it since 1952. I believed that because of this you had respect for and confidence in me.

I see now that this was not the case. Yesterday, before witnesses, you made remarks about me that I consider humiliating, and you reproached me, among other things, with having resorted to political activity in a service you called "yours."

It is true that last Saturday, indignant at the police violence in the Latin Quarter, together with other members of the hospital personnel, I circulated for signature a manifesto condemning the repressive methods of the police. I assume entire responsibility for this fact.

You then decided to prevent me from effectively performing my hospital duties by taking the following measures:

—discontinuation of my out-patient consultations,

—interdiction of access to the files of the patients,

—interdiction for me to communicate with patients whom I follow regularly,

—interdiction of my ward functions, which have now been entrusted to another assistant in the service. This situation prevents me from practicing my profession.

I therefore ask you:

1. to send me a written excuse;

2. to give each assistant in the service greater autonomy in the exercise of his functions;

3. to give students real participation in the activity of the service and in the organization of teaching;

4. to abolish this extreme hierarchization of the service by accepting regular meetings of all the active participants: doctors, students,

nurses, and secretaries, at which each one will be able to discuss freely the innumerable aspects of service affairs.

Without a positive reply to the four points in this letter, I will continue to come to the service every day, without participating in its activity, complying in this way with your directives, but I will not oppose any action or demonstration that this situation might create.

Believe me, I greatly regret having to write you such a letter, which I do at considerable cost, but which is dictated by my conception of hospital medical practice, my determination to contribute to a profound change in the archaic University structures, and the support shown me by a large number of service members.

Please believe me,

> Sincerely yours,
> Doctor Pierre Vernant,
> *médecin des hôpitaux,*
> associate professor.

Document 189

Contestation at the Hôpital Broussais

DOCTOR Z.: If you will permit me, I will summarize the discussion in the following way. There are three problems which have just been raised for you:

1. There is the problem of Vernant, who is present. This problem exists on two levels: medical and general. On the medical level the assistants, all those who participate in the work of the service, cannot, I believe, do otherwise than consider this gesture as surprising and shocking. I am obliged to say this. Vernant has been working here for fifteen years. He has assumed a lot of responsibilities. He has done much that honors the service and enhances its reputation, and to send him away like that, with only a day's notice, is inconceivable. Speaking generally, you have just heard what we think: there has been an abuse of power with regard to a freedom which, I still believe, was not used abusively.

2. The second problem concerns the way the service is structured, which is M. Soulié's personal problem. It is obvious for all those who work in this service that for years we have suffered from the really terrible authority—why not say it—that the chief wields over us. We have lived in terror, and this word is not too strong. It will make

young people smile to think that men of 45 like myself should speak of terror, but it really is the most suitable word. For we have lived in terror. We have been humiliated several times a week because we were ridiculed in front of the patients, or in front of the personnel, and because the structure of this system as it existed did not allow us to react; indeed, how often we had to grin and bear it! Really, there were scenes which will not interest those who do not belong to the service, but the scenes that took place in the library . . . where, really, you would have wept to see how we were treated; and the impossibility, I repeat, impossibility—perhaps a bit of cowardice too—but really we were treated the way a lord of other days would not have treated a slave. Consequently—there is something, and I am speaking really to the first row here, and I am not afraid to say it openly—this attitude has hurt me deeply, and I am not the only one, and it is largely responsible for today's outburst. I shall add too that, still as regards this extraordinary authority, it included not only the Cardiology service but many other things. It included teaching in the service, which never involved any discussion; everything took place in a monologue and we were never able to have a dialogue. And in the fifteen years of association with my chief, I have never been able to say to him, as man to man, what I wanted to say.

3. The Vernant problem is the match, and the other problems are the wick, because, really, we have a lot on our chests. So the third point is: what are the reactions to this affair going to be? As I was saying, it is extremely serious for us to meet here in M. Soulié's service, during his absence, and to say what we have just said. For this I assume complete responsibility and I expect things to be taken as follows: there is no question of settling accounts with our chief; nor is it a matter of hatred, etc. It is not that at all, and I am extremely sorry, because you can't live for fifteen years with someone of M. Soulié's stamp without liking him; but these two problems, the match and the wick, end in an explosion when there is a grenade at the end.

So that's that! That's what is going to happen, and the grenade is aimed, as I have just said, at this hospital structure which is stifling us, which is bad, which actually is a brake to all progress and all that is medically possible; which has been a brake for years, and to which we are attached out of routine, or befuddlement, by a thousand ties, like Gulliver when he had little threads attached to every finger. We are all prisoners, we are all becoming accomplices, to the extent that we climb the ladder of the system, which is an awful thing. Really, I think if we change it, if we reform it, or if we get rid of it, this will remain an extremely useful date in the history of medicine; and I strongly hope that everybody, as many as are here, will contribute to rendering to medicine this tremendous service by getting rid of these structures that so exasperate all of us.

—Excerpt from a recording of the meeting of the Cardiology Service
at the *Hôpital Broussais*, May 17.

Document 190

The Dismissal of Professor Soulié

STUDENT: We have been talking about an extraordinary situation and about the courage of the students. I represent here the student action committee. I remind you that the declarations you have just heard were adopted and unanimously voted on May 17 at 10 P.M., at the general commission of students, which includes all the medical students in Paris. Therefore, we consider here and now that the points decided upon in this motion are irreversible and must be considered final.

The first point we discussed was abolition of "Chairs," and I wish to inform you, Sir, of a motion voted with an absolute majority yesterday evening, May 17, 1968, at the general assembly of Paris medical students. Two points:

On the 1st point: within the context of the general measure recorded in the motion adopted at the May 17, 1968 general assembly, the chair of clinical vascular cardiology is abolished.

On the 2nd point: within the context of hospital-University reform, for which the modalities of application are still to be decided, there has been instituted at the head of the hospital services a collegial directorate elected by secret ballot, considered necessary by the students, and, mentioned moreover in this motion which we have unanimously adopted.

PROFESSOR SOULIE: No opposition.
THE STUDENT: Let me now say that there remains for us to build effectively. The foundations have been laid; we have had the courage to lay them, and now we shall have to reconstruct everything, and of course to work with those who have taught us.
P. SOULIE: We must start again at zero. Because if we leave a faculty scaffolding, we will fall into the same mistakes. You have assumed a task that is a heavy one, because men are automata, and you'll have difficulties. I hope you'll get the organization you dream of. But you

should have no illusions. If you had ever been present at what is called a *Faculté* Council . . .

THE STUDENT: There aren't any more! . . .

P. SOULIE: . . . the standard *Faculté* Council is a regular riot—to be exact, an unbelievable uproar; things that are supposed to be resolutions, that is to say, orders. . . . I know about resolutions! But you will need courage and perseverance, and you'll get, I believe, you'll succeed, after numerous obstacles, in setting up a different system.

I have told you what I think about the organization. I have suffered from it, not personally, but a certain number of young people present imagine that because I have not been able to name them to such or such a position, I have done nothing. If I gave you the details of the battles fought at 3 in the morning, when we were driving around trying to chase down this or that man, you would realize that members of the jury, even those who are not members, want to defend their own men. It's a terrible thing.

DOCTOR Z.: Sir, it's fifteen years now, as I was saying yesterday at the assembly called in this amphitheater where I said a lot of bad things about you, it's fifteen years now that I have been waiting for the opportunity to talk to you man to man. At last, here it is. What I want to express to you is neither hatred nor sympathy nor excuses: I will take the liberty of giving you an explanation, which I owe you.

Contrary to appearances, what is happening is not the result of actions that some of us are supposed to have taken against you; it is only the first result of an extraordinary action. It would have been unthinkable only a few days ago, and was planned by tens of thousands of students. This action, which is a real groundswell, is of such magnitude that I believe you still do not realize it. It appears to be irresistible. These young people, thanks to their courage, have had the good fortune that no generation before them had, the good fortune to be able to sweep aside everything that is cluttering up the ground so that they can build a house on it which they like and is the way they want it. In order to understand this action, this force, and this marvellous enthusiasm, one should have heard these boys discussing night and day for the last few days at the *faculté*. This action, which terrifies us older people a little and makes us anxious about the future, will not take place without difficulty and certainly not without some mistakes; but, in the end, the mistakes of youth are better than the mistakes of mature men.

I want to tell you in any case that at no moment was there on our part, or on that of the students, the least hatred against you; that you are only, excuse me, the first statue that is being knocked off its pedestal, but that soon you will be in good company.

I also want to tell you that this moment, which seemed to everybody to be necessarily a bitter, tragic one, can become a moment of marvellous joy if you realize that the decision taken yesterday to dismiss you is finally going to place you on an equal footing with all of us, it is going to allow Pierre Soulié finally to be himself, is going to permit him, because the wards and the files are open to him, finally to abandon all those overwhelming responsibilities that so weigh upon him (as you said a little while ago) and at last to join us in order to practice medicine.

—Excerpt from the recording made at Broussais, May 18.

The Examination Hurdle

As the preceding texts have shown, the problem of examinations was a dreaded hurdle for many of the students. For most of them the written session of the *agrégation* competition, which the first barricades had brought to a close, had already taken place. The candidates generally accepted to sit for the competition on condition that there would be a reform, and possibly even that the *agrégation* would be abolished. However, a strike against the oral session continued in certain sectors and was still being followed by a majority in mathematics in July. The written session of the CAPES[14] was turned down,[15] but the situation in the *facultés* was all the more difficult in that very early[16] a countercurrent in favor of examinations began to take shape. Students from underprivileged families could least afford to lose credit for their year's work, which certain of them insisted on, either sincerely, or out of demagogy. The solutions adopted were varied. In a few rare cases (Medical School, Marseilles) the examinations took place, but in most cases they were postponed until September. In Nanterre the year was finally validated after examination of the student's record according to a project introduced on May 17. At the Sorbonne however, only "special cases," which were strictly defined, were accepted for consideration.[17]

There follow, in addition to a very early text in favor of the boycott, two contradictory position statements by sociology students, and two calls for a strike by the CAPES, the second of which poses fundamental problems. The question of examinations also had an administrative aspect, as witness the leaflet from Clermont-Ferrand.

Document 191

Where Are You? What Are You Doing? Where Are You Going?

On May 3, at the Sorbonne, a thousand students had met in the court-yard to reply to attacks from the extreme right and to support their Nanterre comrades who were threatened with expulsion. Why were the *gardes mobiles* called in? Because questioning of the examination system, which had begun with leaflets, started up again in the form of free discussion.

Only the blackjack could answer criticism of the University authorities if this handful of *"enragés,"* whose disease risked being contagious, was to be quickly put down.

Spontaneously, students and passersby in the Quarter countered the brutal police repression.

More numerous every day, University students, *lycée* pupils, and young workers joined in the street fighting to drive the cops from the Sorbonne and liberate their comrades. Through action they organized and discovered their own strength, proving that the unity and resolve of a mass of people are invincible. For the first time, many started to think about the political problem. *Today,* after a merciless fight, which ended with barricades, the government has withdrawn, and we are occupying the Sorbonne. This occupation only makes sense if it constitutes a stage in the struggle being waged against repression. There can be no question of turning back: the University, which was only an instrument for "training" professors and passive cadres, has become and must remain a center for general contestation of society: a center for liaison between students and workers, for collective drafting of our fighting objectives.

We must remain vigilant: even though the hideous spectacle of police repression has left the Latin Quarter, and even though the thousands of discussions that have taken place day and night have roused enthusiasm, the government has not renounced its original aim, which was to restore order, to maintain the bourgeois University—even to reorganize it—in order to better adapt it to the needs of capitalism. Today, repression wears a new mask: it is called *dialogue, participation, reforms.*

Already, some students and professors who were absent or hostile during the recent fights, and either accomplices or victims of the illusion of a University degree, have come back to repair by every means the dismantled system. *Boycotting examinations* is not only a weapon with which to obtain the resignation of the ministers responsible for the brutality practiced on young people; it also gives indication of a breakdown of the entire University system, and of actual abolition of the repression that was practiced daily on thousands of students.

Students who are occupying the Sorbonne:
Refuse all compromise and all attempts at co-option.
No bureaucracy should head the movement, which is
your own.

A genuine University reform implies the overthrow of society as a whole. Refuse attempts at temporary repairs.

Don't indulge in fruitless talk; do your own organizing.
Join the May 3 action committees.
Create new action committees.

We are in favor of continuing the struggle by organizing discussions and action for the immediate future at the grass roots.

—A May 3rd Action Committee (*Lettres*) [May 15th?].

Document 192

Motion Voted by the General Assembly of Sociology Students (*May 1968*)

The Sorbonne sociology students, meeting in a general assembly on May 15, 1968 at 2 P.M., voted on the following motions:

I. All decisions regarding the future of the student movement must meet two political requirements:

1. Not to break up the mass student movement—we are all "*enragés*"!
2. Not to isolate students from workers.

The problem of examinations risks blocking the student movement. It can only be solved in terms of political options.

II. We refuse traditional examinations (which the crisis has made impossible and obsolete):

—"deriding examinations" (examinations given everybody), because we are opposed to privileges unworthy of the very idea of work in the University;
—pure and simple boycott (against the prospect of a lost year).

III. We propose:

No vacation for students!

Summer school in the University, which would be left open and occupied by students and workers.

New examinations in the autumn, to decide promotion to the next grade.

WORK THEMES

    1. Students and workers.

    2. Police repression and the police state.

    3. Critical analysis of the entire teaching system (primary, secondary, and higher education).

IV. The nature and organization of provisional examinations in the autumn will be decided in the course of this summer work.

According to modalities to be determined, they will concern essentially:

    1. The University program that was interrupted May 3.

    2. Results of the summer's work.

    3. A student's analysis of each discipline and its relation to society.

V. We, students and instructors, invite our professors to collaborate in organizing this work.

In order to carry out this critical analysis, we must form work and action groups which we hope will go beyond the confines of the Sorbonne and bring together workers, teachers, and students.

OPEN THE UNIVERSITY TO WORKERS

This motion was adopted by 328 *yeas*

to 85 *nays,*

and 103 *abstentions.*

Document 193

Toward "Co-option" or For the Movement?
(*action study*)

We are conscious that our position is moving in opposition to the pseudo-reflexive agitation of the majority of the students. Right here we want to tell our student comrades that they risk botching what has been so painfully achieved, i.e., the right to free speech and to self-management. Endless talk and agitation leading to hasty decisions taken in an atmosphere of euphoria will only make it easier for the administration and the government to "co-opt" the movement.

We reject the boycott as conceived under present conditions by the students and by certain professors who have seen an advantage in suddenly siding with the students. Actually, it would be putting ourselves in a difficult situation with regard to those of our comrades who *work* to pay for their studies; with regard to scholarship holders (it would be hopeless to expect any generosity toward boycotters on the part of the Ministry); with regard to those who have the obligation (often military) to finish their studies in June of this year; and with regard to all those—some for perfectly valid reasons—who expect to take the examinations whatever happens, even if it means calling in the CRS. The government will then have an easy victory by once more denouncing the divisions that exist among us. Lastly, it is clear that for certain students the boycott would be an unhoped-for validation of a purely fictitious University year.

We refuse to beg for any postponement or adjustments of the examinations, which the administration would surely grant out of paternalism, in order to "cool things down"—that is to say, to buy our future silence. There are rumors around that examinations will be held, and some are seriously asking if we can't have three questions at the oral session instead of one . . . in case we can't answer the first two . . . or why shouldn't each student propose the form of examination that suits him best . . . ? All that is only playing the game of the demagogical administration, which bides its time in the hope that lack of organization today will lead to disintegration tomorrow. Not knowing how to incorporate our strength into a representative, effective organization—thanks to a few obliging persons—we are going to run to a suddenly indulgent administration, which will open its arms to us—the better to smother us.

The answer will be that they want to maintain and safeguard their position of strength. We say, that's not the way to do it! Fear of giving the impression of capitulating has congealed the students in a purely magical, self-willed attitude that apparently aims at keeping up an artificially overemotional situation (ineffectual night work; feverish, endless discussions).

In our opinion, if the movement wants to succeed it should rest on far more coordinated, patient, and scientific study. How many students took the trouble at the beginning to read a minimum of exact analyses on the problem that concerns us? Furthermore, it is doubtful that the students who have prepared themselves *individually* for a particular form of examination (which we are contesting), will suddenly succeed in unanimously inventing a new type of "validation," even a temporary one. And can we logically exhaust ourselves in temporary construction when it is a matter of contesting an entire social system?

Polarizing ourselves in any sort of adjustment would be giving exaggerated importance to examinations in our present struggle for a new society. It would mean a return to a corporative situation, to an irresponsible "apolitical" attitude. In their desire to wrest for themselves a few easy adjustments, the students forget the fundamental meaning of the movement, which is to change institutions through a change of society. The government and the administration expect, nevertheless, and have in fact started, the "co-option" predicted in M. Maurice Duverger's analysis in *Le Monde* of May 16.

In conclusion, boycott, postponement, and adjustment of examinations are only premature, unsuitable, partial solutions; but above all —and this is more serious—they are security-seeking rear-guard actions that only reduce the ranks on the contestation front.

The work we must do is on this front, and nowhere else. It is an effort of *creative contestation* of the university system and of society. It concerns everybody: students of course, citizens undoubtedly.

Students on the level of stable commissions.

Citizens on the level of serious information, *which they must demand,* and of a compromising commitment.

ON THE INDIVIDUAL, UNION, AND POLITICAL
LEVELS . . . RESPONSIBILITIES MUST BE TAKEN
SEPARATELY.

—A group of second-year sociology students in Lyons; excerpt from
Point d'exclamation, liaison publication of the Lyons *Faculté des
Lettres,* No. 2 (May).

The Principles of 1968

The principles of 1968 are as brilliant—and as ambiguous—as those of 1789.

Autonomy (which some called independence) was proclaimed as early as May 9 in Strasburg, approved "as an experiment" by the Minister, and then immediately contested.[18] The word, which is in direct opposition to the old centralizing tradition in France (dating from Napoleonic and even pre-Napoleonic days), won the approval of both professors[19] and students. After Strasburg, others followed suit (Nanterre on May 14).

Co-management (which others called self-management) means in any case that for the students the University world was not a foreign one. This too was acknowledged everywhere, in spite of both covert and overt signs of resistance.

Contestation, which for certain professors was the mere right to scientific criticism, was for the students an assertion of their power inside the counter university; it was the symmetrical opposite of co-management.

Democracy fluctuated between democratic management of the universities and democratization of student enrollment, the one not necessarily implying the other.

Faculties open to workers was subject to wide interpretation, according to whether it was considered in terms of the immediate future, as it was in May (but it was the premises that were open and not, perforce, the universities as such), or whether it was viewed as a process of long duration. This refers us back to the idea of democratization.

These were the principles to be found in countless documents, among which we have chosen two: the "May University Manifesto" and the introduction written by law students to their pamphlet on the counter university. Here the principles are clearly presented, although certain ambiguities remain.

Document 194

May 1968 University Manifesto[20]

The University is refusing Napoleonic centralism, paralyzing conservatism, and egotistical Malthusianism. It asserts its determination to be in the forefront of the combat for democratization of society.

The revolution that it has started supports the right of all young people to participate effectively in decisions that affect the fate of the community. It is based on the following fundamental principles.

I. INDEPENDENCE AND CONTESTATION

a) The University is independent of private interests and autonomous as regards political authority. It nevertheless rejects all forms of corporative organization.

b) The University is a center of permanent reflection which permits contestation of society. Information and the discussions freely organized among students, teachers, and workers in the University constitute the fundamental means for implementing this contestation.

c) General regulations adapted to each establishment guarantee application of these principles.

d) This right of contestation is effectively guaranteed by the full exercise of union and political freedoms respecting minorities.

e) The Minister of National Education retains a power of overall conception of University policy and coordination.[21] His present duties will be completely transformed through wide decentralization of his powers in favor of establishments of higher education.

II. DEMOCRATIZATION

a) Society must be assured of free education on all levels.

b) Education is equally accessible to everybody, without recourse to any manner of selection which would maintain or accentuate social inequalities. Selection is combined with guidance and possibilities for reconversion on all levels.

c) The existence of private, paid institutions of higher education, with a monopoly in a branch of professional training, constitutes an obstacle to democratization.

d) The University is truly democratic only if it ensures real professional training at the same time avoiding premature specialization.

e) Democratization of the University implies:
—increased material and financial means,
—organization of a system of scholarships,
—modernized pedagogical methods,
—greater mobility and diversification of faculty recruiting.

f) Democratization implies lowering the voting age to 18.

III. SELF-MANAGEMENT

a) Higher education establishments are administered co-equally[22] by students and teachers. This self-management is not an end in itself. It particularly takes into account the needs of society as democratically defined by society itself.[23]

b) The funds due education by the government must be reckoned according to the demands of the national community expressed in middle and long term economic and social plans that have been democratically adopted, and application of which is obligatory.

Teacher-student organizations are represented when plans are being drawn up. The sums of money affected by these plans, once ratified for education, are mandatory for the political, executive, and legislative authorities in voting the annual budget. A co-equal student-teacher organization participates directly in the allocation of these funds, thereby guaranteeing the University's autonomy.

IV. THE DYNAMICS OF THE UNIVERSITY

a) The University is a center for social culture. Workers define with the University the conditions of their participation in these activities.

b) Aspiration toward constant progress is expressed in the University by:

—combined research and teaching,

—permanent education and regular re-training of workers and teachers. Periods of complete availability for study are provided for.

c) Students and teachers can regularly and freely question the content and form of the teaching offered.

d) Examinations and competitions will disappear in their present form, to be replaced by a continuous check of the quality of both individual and group work.

Revolution in the University is inseparable from the recasting of education on all levels.

Document 195

The Counter-University at the Law School (Faculté de Droit)

The Strike Committee was created as of May 6.

It immediately began to think about and act upon the subject of the University, its relationship to society, its internal organization, and the subjects that are taught there. The Committee did not want to favor one aspect of its activities at the expense of others. It has undertaken a complete reorganization of the *faculté* and is participating in the movement of national contestation to show its solidarity with the workers. The object of this pamphlet is to present a general view of its activities. It contains the results of a month of work and exchanges, the outline of a first report.

In order to understand the significance of the effort presented here, one should be familiar with the manner in which it was done.

From the beginning of the movement a certain number of committees were spontaneously created at Assas, at the Pantheon, and at Nanterre. After the May 13 demonstration they decided to meet day and night at the *faculté,* to define the bases for their action. Commissions were formed to work on various themes; they are open to every-body and meet twice a day. Periodically they make a summarized report which they have printed to serve as a basis for a future stage in their thinking. Little by little their action will tend to be less centered on the *faculté,* whether through the intermediary of action committees, circulation of an outside newspaper, or through collection of funds for the benefit of the strikers. Like the technical services, they elect three delegates and together these delegates form the commission to meet with the Strike Committee. This is the main organism for making decisions. It elects a joint action group.

The students meet regularly in a general assembly during which they report on their activities. The most important decisions are taken by the assembly.

It is the day and night duty of numerous technical services to allow this work to be done. The reception, duplicating, information, press, organization, and security services include several hundred students.

This organizational outline of the movement explains the plan of the pamphlet.

The first three parts are devoted to commission reports, which break down into the following three themes:

1. Relations between the University and society: what is the role of the University in society? What should be the liaisons between the two? How does the idea of work serve as a common basis for both?

2. Taking the *need* for a critical University[24] as point of departure, what should its structures and pedagogical methods be? What should the training of professors consist of? How should we proceed with orientation? How are we effectively to democratize the University?

3. Taking the *structures* of the critical University as point of departure, how are we to reinterpret and adjust the teaching of law and economy, whatever the scholastic level (capacity, doctorate)?

A fourth part is composed of a certain number of motions, reports, and political positions of the various commissions and the Strike Committee. It is a heterogeneous part as regards makeup, but it reveals an evolution through attempts to define the movement from its own elements.

In conclusion, it contains the program set up by the Strike Committee at the time of the elections; it also summarizes its present positions on the political and academic planes, taking into account the results obtained.

These reports, motions, and programs may appear unrealistic, even contradictory. The impression may exist of rediscovering already known results or of revealing reasoning that lacks coherence. There is nothing surprising about that. What counts here is less the result obtained than the cause and approach to this result. The creative effort we have undertaken proves in its very principle the necessity that exists for students to participate in the contestation, the organization, and the direction of the University. There is in this effort a negation of the bourgeois, reactionary University, and a refusal of a society that seeks to force its violence and its alienations upon those who contest it.

Here, therefore, we see the poles of the student movement: Student Power—Solidarity with the workers—Contestation. No doubt this last feature is just now the most visible; in any case, it serves as a basis and an enrichment for the other two.

What we are really expressing through the destruction of certain institutions and of certain ways of thinking is the need to go beyond them. In this alone we are contesting. We want continually to question what has been granted, we want to introduce a utopia inside the existing world. The students are faithful to Rimbaud in that they give first place to poetry in relation to action, and illuminate human projects with its light. They are retracing the steps of Marx by continually going from the necessary utopia to the necessary rationality.

Our movement is therefore profoundly political; it aims to create new political and social structures. Actually the insertion of new themes implies an option on the way society must be organized. In the true meaning of the word, it can only be political. Contestation is one of the features of this vision.

Contestation therefore appears at once as imagination and action, as both negative and positive. It can therefore be defined in two ways:

—it is a continual surpassing of what has been achieved;

—it is setting up structures that continually permit this surpassing.

It is from this viewpoint that this pamphlet must be read: in it may be found, conjointly the creation of the structures for contestation and the application of this contestation to existing society.

No doubt there is something strange about criticizing in order to reconstruct, about continually questioning each stage of one's thought and action, about mixing critical realism with the logic of surpassing, about systematically connecting the various levels of thought; in short, about defining a new value, which is freedom of man's spirit "in situation"—consequently, of contestation.

We did not invent the idea of contestation. We hope simply to have recalled its value. In any case we believe that it is this freedom of

the spirit "in situation" that constitutes the basis and the guarantee of
our work.

—Introduction to the pamphlet *l'Université critique*, published in June
by the Strike Committee of the Paris *Faculté de Droit* (Panthéon-
Assas-Nanterre).

Reforms and Reformism

No word was more depreciated in May and June than the word "reformist," unless it be "revolutionary." A distinction should therefore
be made, perhaps, between reformist action and a "reformist" attitude.
All action that has for its goal reorganization of existing structures,
however radical, is reformist—a statement to which many revolutionaries will retort that unless power is in the hands of the working class,
"reforms" serve only the interests of the bourgeoisie. The reform projected by the Paris medical students[25] (an outline of which follows)
is "revolutionary" in intention, although it undoubtedly does not solve
or even pose the problem of governmental authority, nor does it abolish
private practice. But by doing away with the "mandarinate"[26] and the
caste system, by entirely changing the human relationships that obtained in the hospitals (no mean achievement in the framework of
present-day society), such a plan can play a revolutionary role. A much
more classic type of reformism was the one advocated by the "student
committee for University freedoms" at the Paris *Faculté de Droit*.[27]
At the same time that it took over some of the movement's key words
—autonomy, co-management (or participation), which it could only
do thanks to the May explosion—it came out openly for close ties between the University and industry (on the U.S. model), in favor of the
principle of profitable return on research, and for student "co-partner-
ship" in the University in the sense that certain businesses offer "co-
partnership" to their workers. "Once these conditions are fulfilled, a
regional University which is keyed to local industry and largely financed by it, under the co-management of its professors, its students,
the industries, and the government, and being liberated from its former
cramped setting, could go on to a new development and become the
polarizing body of the region."[28] The manifesto of the CELU follows.

The program of the "student committee for a democratic University" (Besançon) represents another type of reformism. With its
technically well-presented projects and the reference to the "united
action of the working class and other strata of the nation, *under the
leadership of their union and political organizations,*" that is to say,

the very negation of what the movement stood for, the mark of the Communist Party may be recognized.[29] This committee, with the support of the majority of the *faculté* SNESup. section, obtained a very large majority of votes (759 out of 1,044) in the elections for a temporary steering committee (June 13), in spite of the boycott directive put out by the action committee.

Document 196

In What Respect Medical Students Are Revolutionary

During the second weekend in June, the Paris *Faculté de Médecine* had a White Book published summarizing the present state of the reform proposals. We shall try to show here the principal orientations as they have been presented in this publication and, on the other hand, to define the principal lines the work of the commissions will follow, using this platform as point of departure. However, we must underline right away two points: in the present state of affairs the student movement, and particularly proposals of a medical nature, may be interpreted in very different ways.

The reason medical students proclaimed "Student Power" was because they had decided to do everything in their "power" to give their country a proper health system. But only in the last month has the present situation been coherently questioned. We know what we want, but we can only say gradually how to put it into action. We would like the ideas set forth in this article to be discussed by all the members of the medical corps; we also hope to meet with new ideas for reform. The formulation of our proposals is not accompanied by irreversible crystallization; everything can be called into question. It should be known that students are also ready to listen.

There exist four lines of force in our reform:

The principle of autonomy
In the old University each decision had been taken at the highest level compatible with its importance. The principle of autonomy, on the contrary, implies that decisions be taken on the lowest level, taking into account the means involved. For example, each *faculté* must be able to choose its own ways of teaching and checking knowledge.

Abolition of the "mandarinate"
The present system placed an entire department or an entire section under the authority of one single person, with all that this entails in

the way of rigidity and waiting for the retirement of the head doctor-in-chief. Moreover, the method of choosing these all-powerful persons made it impossible to determine their qualities of organization (not to speak of human qualities, which represent a necessity for any hospital function) with therapeutic responsibility for everybody. Such training seems to us to be the only guarantee for the future security of the patient.

Abolition of the present competitions
This concerns particularly the internship: endlessly to learn the same question, fearing that one word changed might decrease the professor's "empathy" is in no way a preparation for research, for contact with patients, or for teaching.

Lastly, abolition of the present caste system
This sets two closed worlds, hospital and private practice, in opposition to each other. A doctor with a private practice must be able to partici-pate in teaching his future colleagues; he must be able to continue to learn himself, to follow and treat his patients, even when they are hospitalized.

THE NEW TEACHING PLAN FOR MEDICAL STUDIES

It comprises two main components: complete overthrow of peda-gogical principles and profound transformation of teaching structures. But only the new spirit that has allowed us to organize will be able, later, to make them effective. Otherwise, it is just an intellectual game, without meaning or value.

1. Pedagogical principles.
The teaching must be well thought out; the student should not receive finished products, authoritarian lectures, or duplicated copies of them: in this case, learning by heart is the only way. But this "absorption," as a general rule, is accompanied by quick forgetting.

On the other hand, thoughtful teaching requires coordination of the subjects taught: the physical bases for haemodynamics should be learned at the same time as heart anatomy and radiological evidence of shrunken valves.

A complete recasting of documents placed at the disposal of the student, which should allow *him* to make the synthesis of his knowl-edge, is necessary.

New ways of exploring knowledge are needed. We should lay greater store on true assimilation rather than on pure memorizing; at the same time that the student's knowledge is checked, the teacher too should feel concerned, because failure of his pupil might very well be imputable to him.

Self-teaching should exist: a student must understand what he is being taught: he must practically be placed in the position of a scholar who has discovered the new idea under consideration. We believe that to achieve this goal the principle of the seminar is useful. The seminar is a work group bringing together a restricted number of students, helped by a teacher. This group has as its object the study of a given problem. Each student gathers a part of the existing bibliography, analyzes it, and compares it with the results obtained by his fellow students. Then, through confronting a jury of specialists, the members of the seminar become aware of their possible incomprehension, therefore, of their non-assimilation of one aspect of the problem.

Along parallel lines, members of the seminar find themselves in the position of teachers with respect to others less advanced in their studies. Teaching thereby achieves one of the best verifications of knowledge. Thus, the student-teacher relationship is placed in a new, unrestrictive juxtaposition. Criticism no longer has a sanction value, but a value of productive exchange.

Progressive, permanent orientation. As a general rule, secondary school graduates enter medical school without knowing very well what they want to do. To help them determine their vocation, few facts have been made known to them in the course of their studies. In fact, all teaching, all information, should permit a future doctor to become more and more convinced of his real calling. In addition, teaching should not be abstract, but integrated within its real framework; the student must know right away at which moment and how he will be able to use his new knowledge. When he is confronted with situations that demand real exercise of his profession, a student orients himself progressively according to his tastes. The system must nevertheless be flexible enough for a late choice still to be possible.

2. Reform of Medical Studies.

The very spirit in which we want to work, real integration into the hospital and the laboratory, implies a longer academic year; that is, about ten months of real work.

Medical studies to be divided into three cycles:

The first cycle lasts a minimum of thirteen months. It comprises three principal periods:

Acquisition of fundamental bases and thinking processes that are useful for the remainder of the training years.

Practical training period of the nursing care type: the future doctor must know his patients as concretely as possible. Integration of students into medical teams, according to the three 8's system, should allow for this contact.

Reliable information on all medical and para-medical job openings. We want to make this first cycle a genuine "common trunk" for all those who will have to treat patients, in whatever capacity. Basic knowledge that is shared, and especially, shared Hippocratic human education, should make for better future coordination and do away with artificial antagonisms among those who are to take care of the same patient.

The second cycle will last a minimum of thirty months. At this stage, all students should have a hospital function similar to that of the present *"externat."*[30]

Teaching proceeds through integrated courses (certificates); that is to say, through concerted study of different sciences connected with a certain system, as we said before. There will be between ten and twenty courses constituting a common trunk of knowledge essential to every doctor, validation of all the certificates being necessary for entrance to the third cycle.

The third cycle will last a minimum of three years. The study plan is organized in the form of disciplines corresponding to the framework of former specializations, general medicine having an equal rank with other categories. At the same time there must exist a hospital training period with full time and remunerated therapeutic responsibility.

At the end of the third cycle—that is to say, at the time of receiving the title of Doctor—orientation is obligatory:

—private practice: a period of training under an established practitioner is desirable;

—a full time hospital post;

—a hospital post with part time presence, corresponding to the service of a medical attaché.

These orientations should be neither rigid nor definitive.

Examinations and Competitions.

Examinations and competitions, as they exist at present, should be abolished.

Knowledge checks should introduce, besides the quantitative notion of the mass of information that has been learned, the manner in which this "information" has actually been assimilated (qualitative notions). There should be more than one check during an allotted time, and the methods used should be varied. In the same way the old style competitions should be replaced by a selection that takes into account all the qualities required by the position applied for.

HOSPITAL-UNIVERSITY STRUCTURES

The spirit of this reform corresponds to several criticisms of the present structural setup:

—Excessive partitioning between the present services, which does not guarantee maximum use of skills.

—Dispersion of technical means, with poor results.

—Overcrowding of specialized services with patients who do not need them.

Because of these criticisms, the present reform proposals are looking beyond the specially favored hospital-university unit toward easy access to dispensaries, centers for preventive medicine, private practitioners, etc.

We propose that all training for treatment in a given geographical sector be grouped together in one single complex.

The concept of CHU (*Centre Hospitalo-Universitaire*) would then be replaced by that of SMU (*Secteur Médical Universitaire*). Of course this idea of SMU could be extended to the sectors that do not at present have a *faculté de médecine* or a medical school.

A patient should not be handed from one person to another, nor at each stage be treated by total strangers. These new structures should be in no way constraining; on the contrary, they should make the existing barriers more flexible.

At present, reform projects have been centered essentially on the CHU, as conceived by the "Debré Plan." The principal points that we will try to summarize are to be given reconsideration within the framework of the SMUs, during the coming weeks.

In spite of certain efforts a hospital-*faculté* duality still persists in day-to-day operation. However, the absolute necessity for closely interknit training-patient contact is evident. There should be real CHUS.

The CHUS have three essential functions: teaching, treatment, and research.

The function of *treatment* could be organized in the following manner:

—On the one hand, creation of an emergency medical-surgical unit; on the other, creation of a common pool where patients whose condition is not of an urgent nature will be hospitalized.

—In this common pool a series of departments will interpenetrate one another.

—A department is defined by a specialized hospital-university team that disposes of the means required for its activity. Certain departments can be medical-surgical, as for instance, cardiology, pneumology, etc. Each department is run by an executive board composed of representatives of all the workers: nursing, dietetic and maintenance personnel, according to a system based on responsibilities.

—At the head of this board there will be a coordinator whose role will be to apply the department's general policy as formulated by the members.

—The coordinator and the board will be re-elected periodically.

—Teaching will have a similar executive board. Teachers and students will be included in the board with students having a right of veto, modalities of which remain to be defined in order that it should not be conceived as a simple negative brake, that would prevent the CHU from functioning.

—Lastly, research, also administered by an executive board, must increase the number of its members. The integration of others than doctors and close cooperation with the other sectors of research must become effective.

—At the level of the CHU, general problems will be solved by a council, which will include, according to accepted proportions, all the coordinators of the CHU, representatives of professional and academic groups, and technicians. Attached to the CHU council and responsible to it will be an administrative staff.

—The manner of selecting future permanent members of the hospital-university team and of their subsequent promotion remains to be specified.

—It may be noted however that title and function will be dissociated, and that selection will be based upon an objective evaluation, the various qualities to refer to a period of several years. A mode of procedure, close to co-option, would appear to be desirable.

—If a member of a team is no longer able to fill his position, he must give it up. But in any case he remains in the treating team with another assignment and continues to receive a salary in keeping with his qualifications.

These are the principal orientations of the reform. Quite obviously they imply an entirely new direction in medicine and in teaching. We wanted a REVOLUTION because we considered that successive reforms could not really change anything. The snag we now face is putting it into practice. Having defined our principal options, we must now define how this new type of medicine can be achieved. We are aware of the difficulties that its application will meet with.

This is why we propose to promote our reforms gradually, providing for long transitional periods, and including by degrees all existing structures.

Our reform proposals will not be considered definitive until we have received assurance from responsible medical, juridical, and administrative authorities that it is possible to carry them out. From now on our work will be oriented essentially in this direction. But whatever the case, the spirit of our reform contains the necessity of making continual progress, without having to take to the streets. The structures we have set up must not be considered to be definitive, even after they have been implemented. It will be the duty of each one of us to see that both the teaching and the practice of medicine are subject to continual readaptation.

When the time comes at which all those involved feel responsible, we may consider that our revolution has succeeded.

DOCUMENTATION COMMITTEE OF THE STUDENTS OF THE FACULTÉ DE MÉDECINE DE PARIS, June 9, 1968.

—Supplement to *La Revue du Practicien*, No. 16, June 1, 1968
(printed leaflet).

Document 197

Revolution or University Reform?

An urgent call is being sent out to all student associations, to leaders of professional and union organizations, to local and regional authorities, and to members of parliament. We urge them, given the seriousness of the present crisis, to assume their responsibilities as citizens and carry out the necessary common actions according to the following principles.

Whatever the responsibilities of National Education and the government in the university crisis, whatever the extent of this university crisis, nothing could justify revolutionary exploitation of the situation for the sole aims of political groups.

Progress in social organization has never been obtained through overall contestation of society.

Committees improvised along revolutionary lines have always ended in totalitarian regimentation and not in citizen participation in the organization of their own society.

If we really want to achieve the general reform of the University that is needed we must work out plans for indispensable working conditions.

For instance:

A return to the normal course of activities in order to designate representative groups to work on preparation of the reforms, on the general as well as on the particular plane corresponding to each establishment.

Any group that talks about reform and does not itself contribute to achieving these conditions may be considered suspect because it conceals intentions other than those stated.

By refusing all equivocation and adhering to a certain number of clearly stated principles, each one of us must contribute to clarification of the situation, and organize accordingly.

This is why demands for the reforms to be undertaken must be clearly defined by those who reject revolutionary adventurism.

This is also why an urgent appeal must be made to the government by all the authorities who are conscious of their responsibilities in order to obtain formal agreement as to the terms and the agenda for the most urgent reforms. An orderly return to work of all public-spirited citizens will only take place after precise government guarantees have been given.

Once these guarantees are clearly confirmed, those who continued the agitation would, by this very fact, reveal their subversive maneuvering.

FOR SOLUTION OF UNIVERSITY PROBLEMS

We must denounce:

The "Fouchet Reform" which, far from solving the student situation, aggravates it.

Systematic overcrowding: university overcrowding, which is aggravated by urban, economic, and administrative overcrowding that creates explosive situations, and makes present institutions unsuitable. "Men are like apples; when piled together, they rot" (Mirabeau).

University overcrowding which, through centralization of the powers of decision in the hands of National Education, provokes on every level a lack of interest that favors the massive explosion of everybody's discontent:

—insufficiency of professional, technical, and commercial train-

ing, which contributes to overcrowding in higher education;[31]
—the purely pragmatic dimension of teaching that works to
the detriment of the disciplines of a universal education;
—the absence of real outlets on leaving school, because of the
overall statistical options in governmental planning.

We must orient ourselves toward:

Effective decentralization of University authority within the regional framework; giving the *facultés* and schools their legitimate
autonomy of decision as regards programs, recruiting professors, etc.

Genuine modernization: only consultation between professional
and regional organisms can result in adaptation of the curriculum to
real outlets in economic life.

For this:

A code of University immunities and freedoms should be
worked out, stipulating the indispensable juridical definitions, particularly a statute for students that would entitle them to "use of all
University facilities."

Specializations that will encourage a spirit of competition between the different establishments should be chosen.

Constitution of administrative councils to be composed of professors, representatives of professional organizations, of local and regional community organizations and, possibly, of the government, will
be encouraged. The role of these administrative councils will be to
plan effective coordination of available intellectual, technical, and
financial means with the existing professional outlets in order to
determine the most favorable teaching conditions.

Independent of these *faculté* and school governing councils—in
order the better to adjust the necessary reforms—co-equal student-
professor commissions, elected by proportional and secret representation upon presentation of a student card, should be created in each
establishment for solution of specifically student problems.[32]

—*Comité des étudiants pour les libertés universitaires,* June 17, 1968.

Sociological Criticism of Principles

At a meeting held May 12, researchers from the European Sociological
Center (P. Bourdieu, assistant director), wrote the following and, after
a few changes, had it signed by more than one hundred teachers and
researchers. It presents a sociological criticism, formulated before the
event, of the 1968 principles.[33]

Document 198

At the same time that the students through their courage were winning
a first battle, a group of teachers and researchers, meeting in Paris on
May 12, decided to call on all groups interested in democratic transformation of the French University to define the broad lines of a program, and to present for general discussion as soon as possible some
fundamental ideas and suggestions for orientation. It is less a matter of
reasserting grievances which are being confirmed or will be confirmed
in any case (the rights of students to participate in the management
and control of teaching, transformation of the nature of pedagogical
relations, freedom of speech and extracurricular activity inside the
facultés, etc.), than to state the *lacunae* that any program defined in
the institution by beneficiaries of the system is more than likely to
present.

It seems to us that participation of teachers and researchers in
a movement that they have followed rather than started could not,
without risk, be founded much longer on good will, whether it be the
"affection" teachers feel for their pupils, or legitimate indignation at
police repression. Actually, it appears to us that only an objective
analysis of University functioning and of its functions, both technical
and social, can serve as a basis for a *program of demands, that would
be sufficiently explicit and coherent to resist the attempts of technocratic or conservative co-option* that will not fail to increase. Consequently, it appears to us necessary to recall two fundamental facts
which, given the very conditions in which the movement was started,
risk being forgotten.

To start with, the principal victims of the present functioning
and organization of the school system are by definition outside the
system because of having been eliminated from it. Consequently, the
groups who did not make themselves heard during the University discussions that took place among beneficiaries of the system are the very
ones who should be most directly interested in a genuine transformation of the system—even if in present circumstances their exclusion
from the system prevents them from formulating their demands for
a system capable of integrating them.

Second, any questioning of school institutions that does not
fundamentally concern the function of elimination of the lower classes,
and through this the function of social conservation of the school system, is necessarily fictitious. Moreover, in spite of its apparent radicalism, all limited and superficial contestation results in displacing the

point at which criticism is applicable and in this way contributes to maintaining "the University order" as a mechanism for perpetuating "the social order." For this reason we must denounce attempts to reduce the present crisis to a generation conflict, as though belonging to the same age group—or even more, to the student world—could by magic erase the differences between the social classes.[34]

The first proposals, presented below, do not claim to constitute a complete program for University transformation, but only aim to illustrate several preferred orientations for a University policy. In fact, it is important to be armed against the dangers of technocratic utilization of the situation that has been created: if the University crisis is only a "malaise" linked to anxiety about job openings or to the frustrations imposed by a conservative pedagogical relationship, it is easy to present as a solution to every ailment a technocratic plan for the development of teaching in terms of the needs of the labor market only, or of fictitious concessions on student participation in University life. The changes that the student movement has introduced de facto into the *facultés*—and which can contribute to constitution of a *critical* attitude that can be extended beyond pedagogical relationships—have no chance of leaving a durable mark on University and social life unless relationships between the University and society undergo a radical transformation. By declaring the University "open to workers," even if this is only a symbolic and illusory gesture, the students have at least shown that they were aware of a problem which could be solved only by bringing pressure upon the mechanisms that forbid access of certain classes to higher education.[35]

I.

In the matter of promoting democratization, that is to say, setting up a policy that aims to neutralize as completely as possible the effects of the social mechanisms that ensure inequality and perpetuation of inequality with regard to school and culture, we must declare that:

1. The real scope of a transformation of the school system is measured by the degree to which *procedures for recruiting teachers and pupils* are transformed. This implies that the problem of higher education cannot be separated without mystification from the problems posed by organization of the other teaching orders. By limiting analysis and action to higher education (where everything is already decided and has been for a long time), all real transformation of education, including higher education, is excluded.

2. The real scope of any transformation of the school system is measured by its capacity for thwarting the purely school mechanisms

of elimination and exclusion as deferred elimination: for instance, democratization of admission into secondary schools remains fictitious as a result of the disparity between the establishments and sections that offer different opportunities to the children from different social classes. A technocratic policy of orientation, and even more of selection, would only perfect and guarantee the functioning of a system which provides traps or side tracks on all levels (from the CEGS to the IUTS[36]) for the use of the lower classes.

3. The real scope of a transformation of the school system is measured by the degree to which it succeeds in minimizing the effects of class inheritance through redefinition of the content handed down —that is to say, of the study courses, of the techniques for succession, and of the ways of controlling the effects of this succession.

4. The real scope of a transformation of relationships between the school system and the social system is measured by the degree to which it succeeds in stripping scholastic diplomas of their function of exclusive criterion of ability, at the same time that it ensures professional utilization of skills. Actually, today, a diploma constitutes one of the principal mechanisms opposed to application of the principle of "equal pay for equal work," by making it appear that work or workers, separated only by their school degrees, are not on equal footing. This phenomenon, which may be observed in all sectors of activity, is especially evident in education, which at all levels disposes of underpaid teachers who, because of the subtle differences between school degrees, are deprived of the rights that are logically attached to the functions they actually perform: for instance, those of teaching adjunct, CAPES holders, and high-ranking *agrégation* candidates in the *lycées;* or, in higher education, *chargés de cours* (outside teachers), *assistants* (instructors), *maitres-assistants* (assistant professors), and *chargés d'enseignement* (non-titular associate professors).

II.

As regards inclusion in the educational system of social demands for democratization and scientific demands for teaching and research, we must give priority to the mechanisms that govern the functioning of the traditional University.

1. Any attempts to change the pedagogy, curricula, work plans and techniques for transmission of knowledge that are not accompanied by transformation and even by abolition, when possible, of traditional examinations, remain necessarily unreal. Every time an examination cannot be replaced by a continual check (and in higher education, if there were enough faculty, it could be done most of the

time, since teachers would judge their own pupils) this fact should be stated in a clearly defined contract between teacher and pupil. The conditions having been fixed as a result of discussion, teachers would commit themselves to ask only what they had taught and would conform to a clearly defined model.[37] They would then be legitimately authorized to ask anything they had taught, that is to say, anything that explicitly defined the level of proficiency guaranteed by the diploma. The joint teacher-student collective from one discipline, if it had been constituted as a genuine unit for teaching and research, would rationally determine the types of tests, that is to say, in terms of training objectives and of social differences. Teachers in charge of checking results should be scientifically trained in techniques (not only in the art of testing) that permit control of acquired knowledge and of work furnished with reference to explicit criteria. Any mark being a personal judgment, it goes without saying that an examiner must be able to justify his markings if he is called upon to do so.

2. The profession of teacher (whether in kindergarten or in the University) must be defined, no longer merely according to traditional criteria of competence, but by one's gift of imparting to all, by means of *new* pedagogical techniques, what only a few (that is, the children of the privileged classes) derive from their family milieu.

3. Transformation of the way establishments of higher education function, particularly of the structural planning of a career and the distribution of authority inside teaching and research units, constitutes a prerequisite for all real transformation of pedagogical and scientific customs. Distribution of pedagogical and scientific functions and responsibilities must be carried out exclusively in terms of the competence attributed to each person by all the members of each teaching and research unit—which implies taking into account, on an equal footing, pedagogical aptitude and scientific achievement; and, consequently, abolishing exclusive, automatic references to a thesis or to any other degree (*grande école* or *agrégation*), even, and especially, to seniority.

On a short term basis, action should be concentrated from the very first on the obstacles to complete redefinition of pedagogy and scientific life that are constituted by the *agrégation* and the doctorate thesis as individual productions subject to archaic criteria. In short, it would mean looking for every possible way of overcoming the obstacles to realization of a better adjustment between ability and function by breaking down the institutional partitioning that prevents circulation of teachers and pupils between the various "orders" and the different domains of teaching and research.

III.

Technical formulation of the program for systematic transformation of the University in conformity with these principles can only be accomplished by *all the parties concerned,* that is to say, by representatives who really represent all the groups participating in the functioning of all the teaching divisions, from primary to higher education, and more particularly the social classes now excluded by the teaching system, as well as corresponding organizations.

The undersigned call on all the parties concerned, as defined above, to undertake without delay organization of the *états généraux* [states general] of teaching and research, and to prepare them through discussions between teachers and pupils, as well as by drawing up a written memorandum of claims and complaints.

The Utopian Logic of the Principles

It is well that there should exist a document that pursues the logic of the 1968 principles to its utmost conclusion. This was what was done by the *"Commission Nationale Inter-Disciplines,"* an offshoot of the *"Comité de liaison inter-facultés"* (CLIF) in session at the *Faculté de Droit-Assas.* The document was worked out in a curious atmosphere of tension by students, some of whom, particularly those from the *Institut d'Etudes Politiques,* were concerned above all with practical reforms, while others, philosophy students, stressed the importance of logical consistency. A few teachers took part in the discussions.[38] The basic text was frankly "technocracy minded," but as may be seen, it was the logic of the philosophers that won out. One of the latter (H. Wiseman) compared the position of the University, viewed in this way, to that of a church which receives its support from the community, and serves the community, yet owes nothing to the community. It will be noted too that the time factor has not been integrated into the edifice, with the result that democracy is promoted at the expense of democratization.

Document 199

The following document is the result of a long confrontation. The inter-departmental national commission, which for several weeks has brought together students, teachers, and alumni from different intellectual and geographical horizons,* has drafted it at the request of the work commissions of numerous general assemblies. It must receive their observations before the meetings and the indispensable national convention.

With the intention of avoiding ambiguous formulas and compromises between opposing tendencies, the commission confined itself to bringing out points of agreement.

Certain problems in scientific research, those of the first and second degrees, were only touched upon. Those concerning self-management and the system for checking the students' work are now being studied by the inter-departmental national commission.

These proposals are intended to liberate today's students and teachers, as well as all those who will take part in the life of the University, from an over-cumbersome apparatus. They outline the institutional, juridical, and financial framework of a federative system capable of grouping establishments with varied specialties. They have taken serious account of the conflicting situations indispensable to the development of society, to the University's exercise of its critical function, and to progress in scientific research.

IN FAVOR OF A STUDY OF THE UNIVERSITY'S MUTATION

The rigidity of the French educational system, its ultra-centralization, and its adaptation to an earlier society, have allowed it to resist all attempts in favor of serious reform for over a hundred and fifty years.

It collapsed all at once under the pressure of the movement of students and workers. Together, students and teachers are now seeking the principles for future structures. These must permit renewal and contestation that will be vested with a permanent nature.

Three fundamental principles have now become imperative: contestation, self-management, and autonomy.

Contestation

The University is a center for permanent study which permits the contestation of knowledge, of society, and of itself. Knowledge cannot be transmitted if it is sclerotic: research, by its very nature, questions all knowledge in order to renew it. It cannot be otherwise than critical

---

* Particularly, medicine, pharmacy, biology, mathematics, physics, chemistry, letters, philosophy, psychology, sociology, German, English, Law, Science, Economics, *Institut d'Etudes Politiques, Ecole des Hautes Etudes Commerciales, Ecole des Mines, Ecole des Travaux Publics, Institut Agronomique,* Dental Schools, CPREA (ex-art schools), *Conservatoire de Musique,* Schools for social workers, *Institut Pasteur,* CNRS, *Commissariat à l'Energie Atomique, Ecole Pratique des Hautes Etudes, Collège de France.*

of acquired learning and consequently of the finalities of economic and social life, which are necessarily linked to forms of knowledge.

This contestation must lead to concrete action. Conflicts between the conceptions that research questions and those it develops are inevitable.

The University cannot accept being a modern enterprise for manufacture of the cadres that society would ask of it; it must itself estimate the needs it satisfies, orient and create them, and freely choose its teaching, research, and training activities.[39]

On the other hand it is obliged to contribute to defining the future of the national community. Higher education, through representatives elected in all proceedings for planning economic and social development, must make its contribution to what is in prospect and foreseeable according to its own criteria, which are not necessarily those of economic profitability.

A new type of relationship will thus be established between the University and society that will progressively give meaning to the University's obligation to contest.

As regards the University itself, this obligation implies that the students and teachers could regularly and freely question both content and forms of teaching.

Free political information, freely organized information and discussions between students, teachers, and workers in the University, are indispensable to this contestation. A list of inside regulations governing each establishment of higher education should guarantee these principles, as well as the presence of and free expression for minorities.

Self-management

This permanent contestation cannot be undertaken solely by teachers or solely by students. They must work together. A new relationship between students and teachers, already perceptible in the present beginnings, must be progressively defined with this goal in view.

This relationship should take the form, for instance, of systematic liaison between teaching and research; association of advanced students with this dual activity; and self-management of teaching establishments that would confer power of conception and decision at all levels—upon the students and upon the teachers.

Autonomy[40]

The power of conception and decision for students and teachers would be an illusion if teaching in general and teaching establishments were not autonomous, which implies that each one be given responsibility for its own affairs.

This responsibility is inconceivable without the existence of organisms capable of neutralizing those outside forces that with the complicity of certain conservative and technocratic academics could, in fact, dispossess both students and teachers of the power of conception and decision in everything that concerns the functioning of the University.

On the other hand, legitimate revolt against a Napoleonic type of centralization should not allow us to forget that autonomy can begin only by setting up a purely University power capable of abiding by its own regulations and ensuring their respect. Because of the existence of a central authority emanating directly from the political power structure[41] that is being challenged, this University power implies organization from the grass roots up, and cooperation between establishments that mutually complement one another, coordinate their activities and their functioning, and federate within increasingly higher level procedures.

To ensure contestation by students and teachers together implies, to start with, a federative, autonomous organization. This organization will be defined only progressively, but it would be advisable to draw up a blueprint right away. The aim of the present text is merely to specify the institutional, juridical, and financial conditions without which autonomy for higher education is non-existent, and which it is therefore indispensable to impose as of now, in order to allow the movement to develop its energies and to assert itself through continuous creation.

I. GENERAL STRUCTURES

The Ministry of National Education is abolished as a ministry for scientific and administrative management of education.

The National Education structure no longer extends from the Ministry down to the primary grades; it is, on the contrary, a federative structure of autonomous establishments which group together or are coordinated from the base to the summit.

For higher education, the autonomous basic unit can be neither the University nor the *faculté*, but all the students and teachers together,* united in an evolving organization—a department† and

---

* Teaching being inseparable from research.

† The term "section" is not used here because it is too closely linked to the tradition of establishments having different divisions, whereas, on the contrary, it is a matter of creating autonomous organisms that will federate.

laboratory in the same discipline or establishment, in response to a function which cannot be attached to one single discipline.*

These basic units then federate into autonomous, geographically localized universities.

The autonomous universities, *lycées, collèges,* and other public establishments that could be created to run the primary schools would be coordinated according to modalities to be defined in each region,† and then on the national level.

In higher education, each autonomous basic unit is administered by an elected council which chooses an administrative and financial committee responsible only to itself. The council makes its own regulations for functioning. Specialized administrators may take part in purely executory or administrative tasks.

The elected delegates of the autonomous basic units constitute the council of the autonomous University; it chooses an administrative and financial committee responsible to itself alone. The council itself makes the regulations for its functioning.

The elected delegates of the establishments set up for primary education, the *lycées,* and autonomous universities, constitute the Regional Council for National Education.

The elected delegates of the Regional Councils constitute the Council for National Education. Each council makes the regulations for its own functioning.

Alongside this vertical cooperation, a horizontal cooperation should make it possible to surmount partitioning between disciplines, and to organize cooperation between autonomous organisms of the same university, or of different universities;‡ between universities in the same region, or in different regions; or even between university establishments in different countries.

Horizontal cooperation also means the possibility granted students and teachers to belong to several organisms, that is especially, to pursue their studies, teaching, and research simultaneously in several autonomous basic units.

Vigilance commissions will function at all levels of National Education. They will be representative of the total number of students

---

* *Collège,* CHU, etc. The departments place teachers at the disposal of the former, either full time or part time.

† The National Education regions do not coincide with the present *Académies.* [France is now divided into large academic regions called *Académies.*]

‡ For instance, departments of related disciplines or departments, using the same buildings.

and teachers, and necessarily distinct from the councils having power of decision or execution.

Their special role will be to receive the complaints of diverse autonomous basic units and universities, in order to present a united front to government recommendations or pressure groups, and to publish the research contracts of departments and laboratories.

The national commission will make a synthesis of the complaints it receives from the regional commissions and communicate them to all the interested parties. It will itself make no decisions.

II. AUTONOMY

Autonomy is not an end it itself but an instrument indispensable to the critical function of the University.

In the old University, each decision was taken on the highest level compatible with its importance. The principle of autonomy, on the contrary, implies that decisions should be made on the lowest possible level, taking into account the means involved: the department in preference to the autonomous University, the autonomous University in preference to national procedures.

This general rule for autonomy allows of only few exceptions.

1. *Students*

Each autonomous organism itself decides on which conditions it will accept students.

In any case, higher education being open to all according to the modalities designed to erase social inequalities, the law gives the following guarantees:

—every pupil, having validly terminated secondary school education,* has the right to pursue his studies in higher education,†

—every student has a right to a study grant that will vary above a certain level, according to whether or not he chooses other sources of revenue by participating in teaching or by entering professional life.

Autonomous organisms should allow students to pursue in one of them a school career begun in another.‡

Each university should be prepared to accept persons who have not received seçondary schooling, as also former students.

* The present *baccalauréat* will no longer guarantee this school level.

† Without a given school being obligatory for a student, or a student for a university.

‡ Certain study cycles, especially on the highest level, may be pursued successively in several universities. This is only conceivable if a new policy of regionalization and of territorial planning permits action against existing inequalities.

2. Teachers

Every teacher belongs to a department or a laboratory, even if this organism places him at the disposal of a CHU, a *collège,* an institute, etc.

The departments or laboratories freely define the conditions and duration of recruitment of teachers, as well as the role that they will be called upon to play in the new University—a role that is the result of the relationship between teachers and students created during the present work sessions of the general assemblies and joint commissions.

A few rules can nevertheless be set up by the autonomous University, especially with regard to the principle of the sabbatical year.

On the other hand, the law recognizes a national statute for teachers, ensuring them complete independence vis-à-vis all authorities, establishing a minimum salary for those whose career is teaching, and guaranteeing them employment security after they have taught a certain time. Teachers of foreign nationality are beneficiaries of this statute.

Lastly, universities agree to engage persons without academic background as associate teachers by virtue of their special capacities, and without requirements as regards diplomas.

3. Certificates

University life cannot be reduced to working for diplomas. Nevertheless, at each stage of school life every student has a right to a certificate confirming the value of his work.

The modalities for granting these certificates are freely determined by the autonomous universities, except for a common decision on the conditions required for the practice of certain professions.

Although the modalities for granting certain certificates are defined in common, it is nevertheless the task of the lowest echelon (department, laboratory, CHU, *collège,* etc.) to define its teaching methods and its activities for studies or research (example: teaching rhythms, complementary study training periods).

However, each University, for pedagogical reasons, must accept students who divide their time, successively, between University training and professional activities.

4. Self-management

Autonomous organisms are administered through self-management. Each one must state in its statutes the modalities for this self-management, particularly those that concern personnel participation.

On the other hand, two principles must be obligatory for everyone: the general assembly of students and teachers (including researchers) of a department, laboratory, *collège,* etc., freely elects those responsible for these departments or *collèges*. Also, upon their proposal, those responsible for the autonomous University are each one answerable for his management to the general assembly that elected him.

The University, in its role of permanent critic of society, must consult with outside authorities. It is the duty of each of the autonomous organisms to define the modalities for this type of consultation, with the reservation that wide publicity be given it lest this gesture toward the outside prevent the University from responding to its calling.

5. *Management*

In the old University system, the organisms that had juridical authority for decision making generally did not have the financial means for its implementation. For instance, the creation of new teaching subjects demanded a proposal by a *faculté,* ministerial authorization, the naming of teachers by the minister and the rectorate. Allocation of premises was also a prerogative of the ministry and the rectorate.

In an autonomous regime each autonomous organism will dispose of a financial allocation that will permit it to set up its program of activities and its budget without having to solicit either authorization or funds from the higher echelons. Allocations should therefore be made without specification.*

Apportionment of expenditures for personnel, equipment and running expenses to be carried out on each level. Checking by the upper echelon to take place only *a posteriori*. In the same way, the credits corresponding to the allocations that have been earmarked must be placed at the disposal of the beneficiaries automatically, without their having to account for their intended utilization, which would amount to restoring supervision by the upper echelon.

Lastly, credits that have not been used at the end of a given financial period will remain at the disposal of the beneficiary organisms.

But although autonomy avoids in this way any a priori outside control, it forces each autonomous establishment to itself organize all the more strict control of its expenditures, at the moment they occur. Each one must be provided with the services of an expert accountant,† who will assure the ordinator that the expenditures he incurs are legitimate and have been voted by his council, see to it that the necessary credits are at his disposal, make a periodic accounting of the state of

* With the reservation of a distinction between the credits that come from different budgets for equipment and for running expenses.

† Who would not be an employee of the Finance Ministry.

the treasury to the ordinator, and in this way permit him to make a report to the council.

III. FUNDING

The means to be employed by the educational authorities for achieving their goals are the subject of national education plans intended to highlight for consideration in the overall planning, all the National Education demands that have been set according to its own criteria, as well as to orient distribution of credits by the National Education Council.

Students and teachers (and technical personnel) are associated from the grass roots on, in the making of these plans. The National Education Council passes on them. Within national procedures a research council, composed of specialty councils from the laboratories, decides upon a plan that defines the needs of medium and long term research policies.

If necessary, after agreement among the different interested parties, each basic autonomous unit, each autonomous University, will be able to plan within its own council a pluri-annual development project with a specified budget. These projects will be examined by the autonomous University councils, by the regional councils, and then by the National Education Council which together, after the indispensable rounds have been made, will pursue the necessary arbitrations.

The credits received on the national level can only be sums that were not allocated before the National Education Council distributes them among the regions. This distribution takes place under the supervision of the National Vigilance Commission.

The regional councils distribute the credits received among the establishments created for primary schools, *lycées, collèges,* and autonomous universities. An autonomous University remains free as regards a possible redistribution of the credits attributed to it.

For investments on a national scale and corresponding credits for running expenses, the National Education Council can recommend priorities, which would seem justifiable on the national level, to regions, universities, or basic units, but only in the form of an opinion.

To avoid allowing research contracts to divert departments and laboratories from their academic role, it is advisable to confine these contracts within three limitations: a definite time limit, priority for contracts of general interest, and a ceiling to be set in terms of the total amount of credits assigned to research by the interested departments or laboratories.

Before they are signed, research contracts are communicated to the vigilance commissions, which publish them. They are then submitted for approval, according to the amounts involved, to the regional commissions or to a national commission, both elected by the departments and the research laboratories.

The council of each autonomous University determines the part of its autonomous budget to be directly self-managed for its usual services, and distributes the remaining credits among the autonomous budgets of the various basic units of the University.

These budgets are freely distributed in expenditures for personnel, equipment, and overhead. A record of expenditures required for remuneration of all personnel must be kept.

Several departments, laboratories, or other autonomous units can join together to administer in common their autonomous budgets.

These proposals do not claim to define either the university revolution or even the framework in which it will function. There is no more question of accepting a reform granted by the ministry than a plan agreed upon by a few leaders responsible for the student movement. The revolution will have to be defined progressively[42] through performance at the grass roots and permanent criticism of projects and achievements.

But this performance would be impossible if we did not very quickly set up a minimum of institutions: the institutions described above are provisional.

They are nevertheless commitments for the future. They indicate a definite break with the certainties of the past and with the restraining institutions imposed from above. The experience of the new relationship established between students and teachers will transform the University from top to bottom.

When the government seeks to interpret this action, students and teachers will have discovered a common language, the logic of the movement, and a common determination: to create the University every day in the rhythm of their research and discoveries, and to the extent of the development of permanent education, to open up for tomorrow's society a future that they will create together.

—National Inter-Discipline Commission, June 6, 1968.

Application and Criticism of the Principles

Actual application of the 1968 principles could not but raise new problems. The mere fact of participating in a *faculté* assembly did not abolish tensions: professors were anxious on this point, and students were disappointed to have only unimportant things to "manage." This is evident in a document from Caen (*Lettres*). Another, from Bordeaux, poses the problem of student veto rights. Some Sorbonne philosophers proposed a drastic solution which accepted the existence of a mixed co-equal "central coordination committee" from the *Faculté des Lettres,* but this committee, although charged with coordination, had neither power nor mandate. The delegates composing it were mandated by the general assembly, but with no relation to the co-equal committees that managed the sections. At the *Faculté des Sciences* of the Halle aux Vins, members of the University-Society commission, set up to determine the University's role in society, decided to pursue as far as possible their inquiry on the relationships of the University to industry and to atomic research. In this respect, their movement was related to the "radical" student and professor movement in the United States, and they even went so far as to question the neutrality of the most abstract mathematics. In Besançon a Marxist theologian replied in his own idiom to the election platform of the Communist-sponsored "Student Committee for a Democratic University," while in Strasburg the proclamation of autonomy changed nothing. Actually, at the *Faculté des Lettres* there was a break between students and professors,[43] and the principle of co-equal commissions was impugned.

Document 200

The Great Misunderstanding

When the student movement decided to question the structures of the old *faculté* assembly, it was convinced that it was revolutionary, and rightly so. Professor-student co-equality allowed the latter to engage in radical contestation of the setup they had been subjected to, and of the education they had received thus far.

This assembly having been constituted, they claimed victory: a victory over old structures, a victory over those who had erected or accepted them: they had a right to expect heated sessions with violent accusations and moving but firm defense. However, they were soon disappointed. Though the sessions were long and laborious they were passed in setting up legal texts, in writing amendments, and quarreling over points of detail. Consciously or not, the underlying confrontation was avoided through clever jurisprudence.

Let's clearly assert what everybody feels, but nobody says. There is a malaise over this assembly. And how could there not be? Even if, during a revolutionary period, everybody wanted to work for the general good, we quickly realize that everybody has not the same interest in it. Professors and students united . . . but united against whom? Against the professors. The old ones, certainly . . . but who are the new ones if not the former old ones? M. Leclaire[44] is overjoyed at the possibility of civic education being open to everybody in the *faculté*. But is he convinced that he understands this teaching the way the students who want it do?

The professors have risen to the defense of independence of high level research: this question is still on the table and even deserves to be seriously discussed. But shouldn't it be added that this high level research is supported by a small minority, even a tiny minority at the Caen *faculté*? The students want to benefit from this high level research, and it was in this context that they insisted on voting in the newly constituted permanent delegation, which could mean that they want some professional changes. However, they did not encounter any explicit opposition; the professors confined themselves to saying that they would vote "yes," explaining at the same time (as though excusing themselves) that they ought to vote "no." Certain professors, aware that sooner or later they would not be able to avoid the confrontation, left this assembly. We thank them for this. But the others? Is it possible that two weeks of "happenings" in their big house could have made them forget that they were professors?

The initial revolutionary project lapsed into a bastard reality as a result of a misunderstanding. The *faculté* assembly, which we wanted to transform, was only enlarged: discussions are longer, setting up projects and reports is more laborious. General interest has lost much by it, and student interest has gained nothing. If this misunderstanding is now a crucial point, in the next few days it can only become more so. Today's revolutionary temper will be followed by a so-called constructive tomorrow, but it will be without value, unless the malaise is exposed. Let us beware then of restating a false interpretation of the facts: it will not be direct democracy that will need challenging, but the retracted hypocrisy of those who now, while denying their entire past, continue to hark back to it.

—Excerpt from *l'Enragé* (Caen), No. 1 [end of May].

Document 201

Questions to Students, Assistants, and Professors,
to all who profit from their knowledge
to have a clear leftist conscience

The "University-Society" Commission has wanted to undertake a pro-found criticism of the University in its role of bourgeois University. In the course of its sessions, it has had the opportunity of hearing two eminent professors: Baruch and Godement.[45]

The first said of the "Army Research" reports, in referring to his field, which is the physics of solids: "In the *Ecole Normale Supérieure* laboratory, we do not work for the bomb; we only work on DRME[46] contracts (Ministry of the Armies) in fundamental research, and then . . . naturally, you have to go through with it if you want money, equipment, personnel (contractual of course), and if you want progress. . . ."

The second said of the relationships of mathematics to politics: "We have a choice: we are not obliged to work for IBM or for SEMA.[47] For myself, I chose pure math, as remote as possible from any applica-tion. Needless to say, it's not totally excluded; I can't help that."

So there we are! As you see, there is a place for everybody in the system and especially for people who refuse it. Very obviously, Gode-ment's "courage" seems more decent than Baruch's attitude, but both show how the bourgeois University perpetuates itself and what we must unmask through relentless criticism.

I. *Questions asked Baruch and his friends in the* Ecole Normale Supé-rieure *and other* faculté *laboratories and elsewhere, in physics, mathe-matics, and even in biology. To the assistants and research workers who profit from their contracts to make a career or quite simply to "live" and forget their clear leftist consciences.*

1. Are you willing for the co-equal committees to stick their noses into the so-called fundamental army research contracts, into their respective usefulness to the laboratory (how much waste?) and to the army (how many well-guarded secrets and additional occult power for the military?)

2. Are you willing for us to publish lists of these contracts and their subject matter and the financial sums they represent in your laboratories?

Why these questions? Because it is no longer possible for the students to close their eyes. Because they too must have a choice to make. Will you be able to convince them that they too will profit from them, as you say "everybody profits from them"? Will the students let themselves be corrupted like their academic elders? They are as yet only half-corrupted; you can fear that they will wage the fight that most of the others have abandoned.

II. *Questions asked Godement and several others (ourselves included).*
    1. What fight do you claim to be waging by quitting the game? What will people do who have no faculty chair?
    2. Why do you suppose society pays for (and attaches value to) such parasitism? Aren't you the clear conscience of the University? Thanks to your little corner of purity, won't it appear in the eyes of the worthy populace to be a world in which everything can be settled scientifically—the flawless world of experts who know all? What a fine prefiguration of the rational society toward which present-day progress is leading!

Isn't it this image that we must first destroy if we want scientists to play a different role in society, if we want power one day to be in the hands of the workers and not in those of experts?

Will you banish corruption and lies from this marvellous *faculté?* Corruption in the relationship between power and money:
    —the positions it hands out to assistants and research workers,
    —the travel opportunities it offers (scientific congresses),
    —the additional amounts to be earned (overtime, translations, private contracts, outside consultations).

Lies in everyday life, since it depends upon such relationships. Lying—that's honesty, scientific purity (know-how), paternalism between research workers, and on the part of research workers as regards technicians and students (co-management).

Are you willing to lead this contestation supported by all the details among all the students, all the researchers, whose eyes have been closed or who are willing to close them; and also, among workers who still respect this University and the people it trains: professors, engineers, doctors. . . .

Are you ready to describe how the following laboratories function:

Rocard (ENS geophysics)
Balkanski (Paris, *Fac des Sciences,* physics of solids)
Lederer (Orsay, biochemistry)
Malavard (Orsay, mechanics)
Delcroix (Orsay, physics of plasmas)

Benzecri (Paris, *Fac des Sciences,* statistics)
Blamont (Verrières, aeronomy)
Fetizon (Orsay, chemistry)
Normand (Sorbonne, chemistry)
Couteaux (Paris, *Fac des Sciences,* biology)
Julia (ENSCP,[48] chemistry)

This list does not claim to be either exhaustive or libellous. The laboratories cited have been chosen at random among the best known. A priori, they have no more relationship with the army and with industry than all the others; their chiefs have no more power than many others.

Let us take a little closer look. . . .

—The "University-Society" Commission of the Paris *Faculté des Sciences*
(Halle aux Vins), June 20.

N.B.: Baruch plays on the fact that one can work for the bomb without manufacturing it. Obviously they do not manufacture the bomb at the ENS, but various systems of control and detection are perfected there.

Document 202

The Cause of the Anti-program

The title "anti-program" needs to be explained. For everything "anti" is in bad odor, and the petty bourgeois keep repeating that it is "better to construct than to destroy," meaning: "constructing (capitalism) is better than destroying (it)." Our task is to overthrow an educational system, not to organize it.

Anti-program, therefore, and here is why:

1. The declaration of movement grievances appeared after, and in opposition to, the program of reforms proposed by the *faculté* SNESUP. and SGEN; after, and in opposition to, the CEUD platform. This delay has several causes. The first is that we followed the political line that resulted from our analysis of the University and of the present juncture: the implantation of the University in society does not allow us to believe that it can be changed from within; its social function determines its deeper structure; as long as the social structure remains the same, only the surface structures will be reformed; today, the workers' strike is the people's principal weapon against governmental au-

thority; all progressive groups have adopted the same line, which is to support the workers' struggle. This is why making plans for the so-called "new University" has thus far been the least of our worries; to be exact, for us, the University front has been for us a secondary front and still is. The second cause is that formulation of our demands was preceded by *research on the causes,* which the sNEsup. and the sGEN neglected to do in their zeal for assembling the *faculté's* "wheels within wheels." The results of our research were contained in various reports that were distributed at the *faculté* during the month of May.

2. An anti-program is not a counter-program. Because our proposals do not in fact constitute a program:

either in form, because we combat the illusion implied by the very idea of a program of reforms. In fact, it is a strict rule that all programs must conform to criteria of completion and coherence. Now we are obliged to maintain that *by definition* reforms cannot be complete, since they emphasize effects without touching causes; they cannot be coherent, since they affect a surface level the principle of which is elsewhere;

or, in content, because we do not intend to restore their balance to the capitalist system and the bourgeois University, by improving the way they function. The measures we propose have an opposite aim: we want to accentuate the imbalance of the University so that it will give way more easily when the next crisis comes and continue to give evidence of the contradictions of a certain moment in time; we want to clog its functioning, not by obstructing the communication of knowledge (a technical function) but by inserting at strategic points the grains of sand that will prevent free circulation of the ideology (a social function).

The University will not be transformed from within: under these conditions, all that is permissible to propose must be limited to a corpus of simple measures that derive directly from an avowed principle, which is to use and multiply the openings provided by the bourgeois University, in order to turn them against the system that makes it possible. It can disappear only with the disappearance of the system.

Criticism: The Secret of "Reasonable" Demands

The points in common in the reports of sNEsup. and sGEN professors on the one hand, and CEUD students on the other, are immediately evident. We shall make no distinction between these demands, labeling them "reasonable," which is what they want to deserve and which is their condemnation (under the dictatorship of the bourgeoisie we know who the "reasonable people" are: they are the ones who listen to reason).

In reading these "reasonable" demands, one characteristic feature stands out from the very first: the abundance of detail, the precision and complexity of the proposed rules, in contrast with the absence of principles that would furnish the key to them.

This leads us to think that everything takes place as though these detailed measures were precautions intended to *save* something that must remain implicit.

In order to recognize this "secret" it will suffice to note that the material effect of these measures will maintain the students in a situation very close to the one they have always occupied, which is that of being *part of a subject "corporation."*

This is clear, for instance, in the way elections for the various assemblies take place: in appearance the measures proposed (40 percent students, 40 percent faculty, 20 percent technical personnel) are perfectly fair, but it must be evident to everybody immediately that equal representation of faculty and students, the latter being dozens of times more numerous, is merely organized constitution of the students into a minority. What actually results is a system of electoral classes, each one of which elects the same number of representatives, but one of which contains a tiny minority and the other an overwhelming majority of voters. A similar system existed in history, which was the system in force in imperial Prussia, and that principle was based on property ownership.[49]

These "reasonable" demands seem to consider as evident that only technical types of classifications should be adhered to in organizing elections, that is, division into "corporations," teachers, students, and technical personnel. This cannot be taken for granted, however, and it entails precise effects: in particular, all principles of political grouping are made more difficult. "Political" is used in terms of University policy, which commits the ideas we hold concerning society, science, teaching, man himself.

Why has it seemed necessary to salvage a characteristic of the old University, i.e., student subjection?

Leaving aside easy explanations, it is clear that all this is due to the priority accorded technical functions and to their unwarranted transfer to the level of *faculté* policy.

If we ask why the principle of corporation, the reply would no doubt be that a division between those who teach and those who are taught is necessary. In the same way, if we were to ask why equality of proportions, the answer would refer to the "competence" of teachers who, being specialized in University questions, normally have preponderance.

And it is true that the University as an institution includes functions that are necessary: transmission of knowledge from teacher to pupil must take place there; material questions must be settled by technical specialists. But even more, these necessary functions are also non-interchangeable: it is impossible to substitute the agents of one for those of the other, and it is equally impossible to abolish entirely the technical "subordination" of those who learn to those who teach (it is demagogical to say that all teachers are students, and illusory to claim that students are teachers in their own way[50]). In addition the teaching personnel, like the administrative and technical personnel, is permanent, whereas the presence of the students is transitory.

But it does not follow that this technical division of labor should be the only principle on which to organize the *faculté* functioning, or that "subordination" should become dependence with regard to a hegemony.

Just as the necessity for technical guidance allows ordinary economy to achieve a set goal—perpetuation of the employer class—in the same way recourse to solely technical criteria for organization of the University will have one precise, easily recognizable effect: exclusion of politics.

The whole secret resides in the following point: that to the extent that it can be achieved, students must remain apolitical. But then that too is a policy in that it will increasingly strengthen the University's own ideological function. It is no longer merely a matter of not preparing students to combat the bourgeois exploitation for which they will serve as agents, but even more a desire to contribute *actively* to making them like that. Because it is well known that today the political indifference of technicians and scholars is the best guarantee of their availability.

This, then, is the aim of the organizational babble of this ventriloquial talk-talk: to maintain students in the status that "modern economy"—that is, neo-capitalism—wants them in, which is the status of petty bourgeois bound to ruling capitalism.

Since the subjection of students is self-perpetuating in the "reasonable University," in what does the democratic revolution, so vaunted for its merits and audacity, consist? In the fact that a redistribution of power within the teaching body has taken place: the non-titular faculty members (instructors, professors, etc.) have seized a large part of their prerogatives from the titular members. What better example than the choice of four representatives of the teaching body: an instructor, an assistant professor, an associate lecturer, and lastly, a full professor (the Dean). We note that the *lycée* teachers who fill occasional functions at the University are not included.

Here we have the best possible of worlds for *faculté* teaching unions: supernumerary students, complicity of administrative personnel, the real power in the hands of the faculty members who have carried out a democratic revolution *from within*.[51]

—Excerpt from *Antiprogramme du mouvement,* a *roneotype* pamphlet published by the *Centre Théorique Marxiste* of the Besançon *Faculté des Lettres,* June 11, 1968.

Document 203

The Teachers at the Faculté des Lettres *and Ourselves*

The first time the nature of the relationship between students and teachers was put into question was on Monday, May 6, when student power became an established fact. There were many teachers who out of mingled surprise and anxiety tried first to check the movement, then to co-opt it, when the flash-in-the-pan assumed the proportions of an immense conflagration; and when autonomy was proclaimed at the University of Strasburg, certain of them sincerely thought that they would be its sole beneficiaries.

For the greater part of the teachers, the content of the word "autonomy" is clear, and this gives us an opportunity to make as complete as possible a critical estimate of our study conditions, independent of government restraints and consequently, of any limitations in time.

Unfortunately for the others, the term autonomy hides desires and projects that can scarcely be acknowledged: is there a single "bigwig," jealous of his authority and prestige, who has not seen in it the chance he had been dreaming of to increase his prerogatives and exercise them quite independently without restraints of any sort? Have they, moreover, abandoned all hope of achieving these ends? They have not! Certain of them are waiting patiently behind the pillars of the University Palace for the situation to bog down and turn to their advantage. Others, believing in the virtues of demagogy, are abdicating in the firm hope that an army of bootlickers will reinstate them in the absolute power of their monarchies. Others still are past masters in the art of co-option; they work out their pseudo-organization plans, or their mini-reforms, and invite each student, personally and individually, to come and ratify them. Such dreams as these are terribly naive; they are nevertheless deeprooted: to such an extent, in fact, that certain unions have talked of "restoring University autonomy." Is this pure befuddlement? In any case, it gives evidence of a very revealing lapsus![52] These old fogies must finally understand, then, that the authoritarian teacher-pupil relationship between us is finished, and that more and more a relationship based on competence must take its place. To use an already much quoted formula: "professorial autonomy is merely decentralization (of authority)," and this is what we do not want, since it would replace one evil by another even more serious one.

Very fortunately, most of the faculty realize that the situation is irreversible and, better still, have stated that they are ready to support us. However, this close understanding between students and faculty has started to show signs of weakening and has just been put into question with regard to voting on the co-equal commissions. We are beginning to wonder, in fact, whether even if the faculty members have made up their minds as they wrote they had, they really do "unequivocally support the determination that, little by little, is being evidenced by the student movement." Determination to do what? To develop, in consultation with the faculty, the vast movement of criticism and contestation that has made its appearance inside the student-faculty council. As for the faculty, they see the relationship between students and teachers as an exchange of views between our delegates and theirs within the co-equal commissions. However the very principle of co-equal commissions calls for a certain number of comments.

Contact between students and teachers should offer two essential features: a) it should be in the form of a discussion—that is, of a free exchange of ideas between competent persons who are fully aware of the goals to be attained; b) in addition, it should take place on all levels of discussion: in study groups, in commissions, and finally in the student council, which we have already defined as the "strategic point" of all University criticism (however paradoxical this may seem to some). Because what matters above all is not so much the rapid results of the discussions as fully cognizant criticism—that is, when all is said and done, the give and take of ideas, which should be as intensive as possible. In a co-equal commission, however, just the opposite would happen: the discussion would assume the form of a confrontation and, instead of being on all levels, would take place at the summit. In this way, discussions on all levels would be replaced by a veritable confrontation at the summit; "free exchange of ideas" would be replaced by a confrontation of viewpoints, planned in advance, on the student council level as well as on the level of the faculty council, thus depriving both of all individual freedom of maneuver, which is indispensable to any real exchange of ideas.

It is easy to foresee that the student delegates to the co-equal council will come from the student council. This implicitly supposes the existence of a faculty council—that is, of a veritable seat of professorial power (from which the faculty delegates to the co-equal commission would be chosen) and which we categorically refuse to recognize since it would set itself up as a rival to student power.

The idea of a co-equal commission does not come from the students but from the professors, who little by little have forced it upon the minds of the students by using the following form of petty blackmail. Having decided that by participating in the student council they would not get what they wanted, and knowing perfectly well that discussion between students and faculty was indispensable (particularly as regards examinations), the faculty proposed their own terrain on which they would have the advantage—that is, a co-equal commission—in the hope that eventually the students would be obliged to accept: in fact, they emphasized the concreteness of their proposals, concreteness being manna for tired minds. So that is how it happened that as of May 16, the "professor" tablet of the co-equal commission diptych was ready (the number of delegates is 12, which at once sets 12 as the number of student delegates!).

The principle of a co-equal commission, as well as the powers conferred upon it, was voted on and adopted Tuesday, May 21 by a very weak majority (339 to 288). But more interesting than the vote itself is the little explanation that followed it, which may be summarized as follows: "What is there to prevent professors from taking part in the discussions of the student council and in those of the work commissions?" The few faculty members who did take part in the student council (you recognized them) made the following astonishing reply: "We fear we will be submerged in the student mass and will not succeed in making our viewpoint heard."

May I be permitted to tell them three things: the voting that has taken place during the last few days in the student council was very close, the last time there being a majority of about fifty votes. We figure that there are 120 teachers at the *Faculté des Lettres,* which means that they would have been numerically strong enough to overthrow the majority.

Numbers are the determining factor in a fascist-type regime, in which a good speaker can carry the crowds without having to furnish them any coherent arguments. The student council is not an assembly of sheep; students are responsible enough to base their judgments on solid arguments only: professor comrades, you can't make us believe that you had none!

Moreover, how can you judge in advance an experiment you have not made?

Besides, in case the student council should still not tempt you, who is preventing you from turning your entire attention to the work commissions, where you are conspicuous for your absence; what's more, you continue to keep to yourselves by creating your own commissions!

Teachers, one last question: do you sincerely believe that it is by each side remaining aloof in its own corner that we shall succeed in "constructing, on new bases, a community of teachers and students"?

Let us have proof, after all, that you know how to act unequivocally.

—J. J., May 21, 1968; excerpt from *Non-Retour,* a theoretical review of the May Revolution (Strasburg), No. 1, June 7, 1968.

The Nanterre Charter

The three documents of the Nanterre[53] action committee that close this dossier complete and transform the discussion of principles: none is abandoned, but all are reinterpreted and placed "in situation." The Nanterre Charter does not aim to rebuild society, nor does it make the introduction of Socialism a prerequisite for transforming the University; it does project a model for a University that can become an instrument for socialist change without expecting its salvation to derive from any historic (or prehistoric) "end." Declaring that "Plato, Shakespeare, Marx, and Freud were not the property of the bourgeois," the commission for "culture and contestation," uninfluenced by either the Chinese or the Stalinist model, did not discard "bourgeois culture." Nor did it cherish the illusions of the early twentieth century people's universities, or of the champions of democratization through extension of present University privileges to everyone. It posed the basic preconditions of communication, language, and the "sub-culture" that the consumer society imposes upon the working classes.

Lastly, a new type of higher education was proposed which was new in its faculty recruiting, in its anti-authoritarian orientation (left to the co-equal councils), in its way of entering into relations with the profession that precluded subordination to the company cadres, and in rational organization of work semesters founded on the principles of non-directive pedagogy. There is little chance that the Nanterre model will be adopted, but it summarizes the University revolution.

Document 204

Commission for Culture and Contestation

The Nanterre *faculté* has decided to become autonomous. At the same time it has granted itself the right to be open to all workers. Within the limits of this autonomy, the question of the access of workers to culture and of the transmission of culture toward the workers was very soon raised.

The discussion between workers and students, which was started by and on political issues, must also take place on the cultural terrain. During the work meetings, hesitation as to the concept of "culture" fluctuated between two poles: culture understood in the broad sense as an individual social experience that amalgamates ways of feeling, acting, and thinking . . . , and in a narrower sense, culture considered in terms of constituted, theorized knowledge, and as such capable of being transmitted.

We agreed that as a social experience culture characterizes a social class and that the absence of culture in the second sense is peculiar to the working class.

In fact, our intention is clear:

To seek, with the workers, the means of access to culture: how it can become a complementary instrument for criticism and contestation at the disposal of the working class against the ruling class in view of the fact that one of the aspects of class domination is precisely permanent use of cultural repression.

1. The ruling class refuses to give workers the culture it reserves for its students.

2. The ruling class organizes mass circulation of a sub-culture the function of which, under the guise of leisure and recreation, is to increase, far from the place and conditions of work, the alienation of the workers.

But students are contesting the culture they receive in the University. Is it a matter then of transmitting the same culture that they are questioning? Yes, because culture should not remain a privilege of the bourgeoisie. Plato, Shakespeare, Marx, and Freud are not the personal property of the bourgeoisie. What is being contested is not so much culture itself as the objectives assigned to it by the ruling class, and the state of ideological repression against the workers in which the bourgeoisie has situated and maintains culture. For these reasons the contradiction between contestation of this culture by students and the transmission of this culture that they propose to undertake remains a superficial one.

On the other hand, it is not superficial to say that repression by the ruling class is evidenced as regards language (expression and communication) with a force and efficacy that are scandalous:[54] the working class has only one possibility of expression, and that is political. This may or may not be stereotyped (as in the case of union, syndicalist, and political party speeches), but even this latter form of expression does not necessarily implicate language (example: strikes, factory occupations, the Paris Commune).

The interdiction imposed by the bourgeoisie on working class expression is so innerly suppressed by a large number of workers that it leads to a sort of self-censorship that keeps them from speaking. Our immediate task, therefore, consists in finding the means of removing this block which today makes speech impossible for workers and leaves their own words unspoken. To help workers break out of their "languageless" situation, to smash the inhuman repression that not disposing of speech exerts upon them (whereas language is the tie that binds humanity together), to say that the reason for the workers' position as regards speech lies in a class situation—this is our task.

Transmitting culture does not mean repeating the rigidity of the traditional pedagogical relationship, but rather making this transmission effective through work in common that is both real and concrete. This will call for means that are seldom used in the University, such as:

—Painting;
—Audio-visual equipment;
—Group work that will allow concrete creation and free expression of the creative impulse (for example: group composition of a scenario based on the barricades);
—Theatricals (group composition of a scenario to be played by a cast composed of students and young workers);
—Film making;
—Tape recordings of discussions and texts on philosophy and politics;
—Comparison between different forms of modern and traditional theater;
—Week-ends;
—Vacation periods (not necessarily on University premises) that would bring together young workers and students, etc.

Transmission of culture must not make us forget contestation. This contestation will be permanently guaranteed, it seems to us, by the social experience that workers will be able to use to advantage at any moment through critical resumption of our own student assertions and of the political position of the problem of culture.

This summarizes the work of the four commission meetings. For the moment, the commission is trying to implement the suggestions that seemed to be the most valid, several of which have been mentioned above.

—Tuesday, June 3.

Document 205

Commission on Form and Content of Teaching

Fundamental principles

1. Inauguration of a new teacher-pupil relationship that will permit:

a) contestation and challenging of teaching, from the point of view of both teachers and pupils.

b) collective as well as individual research and production.

2. Choice of orientation for students at the beginning of and during their school years.

3. Abolition of horizontal partitioning according to discipline and of vertical partitioning according to school year.

TEACHING METHODS

1. Objectives

Until the effects of a deep-reaching, indispensable reform of primary and secondary education are felt, it is advisable to avoid:

1. Authoritarian, arbitrary orientation.

2. Hasty, irreversible specialization.

3. Actual isolation of a student with respect to these problems and in his work.

4. Student passivity, which is encouraged by the teaching methods (lectures, study groups—*travaux pratiques*—that in no way fulfill their function, which should be to "arm" the students methodologically and critically); isolation and passivity, moreover, being the result of both the quantitative and qualitative weakness of the pedagogical assistance given.

Consequently, the University study cycle should fulfill two functions:

1. specialization carefully prepared through practical information concerning both the sphere and line of work;

2. acquisition of methodological tools of information, analysis, and expression, which are indispensable whatever the career to be chosen later ("workshops" for small groups on the chosen theme).

2. Pedagogical environment

a) The function of the seminar, which should not include more than 50 students, to be as follows:

—to transmit fundamental knowledge that is indispensable to later thorough study of a chosen sphere;

—to present the existing knowledge in this sphere;

—to point out the connections between this sphere and others;

—to prepare speculation on the probable evolution in this sphere (research prospects).

b) The workshop,[55] which should not include more than 25 students, is where students are introduced to methods of obtaining information, analysis and expression (e.g., bibliography, investigation, critical reading, knowledge of foreign languages, graphs, audio-visual techniques): and experience in the methods specific to this or other professions.

c) The work group is the collective or individual unit that is devoted to the theme of the seminar. It forms spontaneously within the workshop group.

3. Teachers-Pupils

a) *In the seminar:* the "dominant" role of the teacher, who conveys to the pupil a certain type of learning, a state of knowledge, and the provisional results of research, which the student assimilates through active checking. To avoid the solitary platform lecture, it would be necessary to tend toward participation by several teachers and more advanced students, who would alternate with one another; organize if possible a "shadow" course, or a carefully prepared seminar for criticism and appraisal, with the help, perhaps, of a teacher.

b) *In the workshop:* there are symmetrical roles of teacher and pupil, who work out together effective critical means of analysis and research. This means avoiding any kind of programmatic teaching, not announcing a possibility of partial research or a certain method applicable to the subject of the seminar, but carrying it out; the student himself should be encouraged to find and use the various methodological approaches to a given problem. In the environment of the workshop the more advanced students can furnish real proof of their pedagogical qualities by acting as monitors and tutors for the less advanced ones.

c) *Inside the work group:* the "dominant" role is that of the pupil who is developing his own work; teachers, monitors, or tutors act as adjustors or coordinators of the collective or individual work being done.

ORGANIZATION OF COURSES

1. *Information-Orientation: first year*

First stage: Information. Upon entering the *faculté* the student who so desires has an interview with one or several co-equal information councils, one or several of which exist for each discipline. The council is composed of a professor, an instructor or an associate professor, and two advanced students. According to the results of this interview the student organizes his work for the semester, or for the year, and chooses participation in three seminars.

Second stage: Orientation. At the end of a period that varies according to discipline and students (between one or two semesters), the student makes a report on his participation in the three seminars originally chosen. This report must be very flexibly conceived in order to make it possible: (a) to find out the student's preferences, abilities, and intrinsic qualities; (b) to circumscribe the difficulties encountered in one sphere or the other in order continually to readapt the means used for transmission of knowledge as well as the pedagogical methods applied; and (c) to check the fundamental knowledge acquired in the chosen sphere and determine whether it warrants continuing.

Third stage: Provisional choice. At the end of this period and possibly after consulting the co-equal information council, the student decides to take part in a seminar on his chosen discipline. This seminar, which takes place during the second semester, is reserved for students entering the *faculté*. The themes and subjects of the orientation seminars must allow the student to acquire individual and group work attitudes as well as a certain mastery of basic methods and knowledge.

Note on the co-equal information and orientation council:

The student who so desires should be given dual orientation by this council both for his studies and for his future profession. It is consequently desirable:

for the council to add to its number, should the need arise, persons of eminence from outside the University, or specialized psychologists;

for orientation to be permanent, because both the motivation for study and one's view of a profession can change during the University cycle.

2. *Specialization and Interdiscipline: seminar-semester units*

a) During the years that follow, students should have the possibility of specializing in a given field of knowledge and practice. However this specialization can only be obtained through interdisciplinary polyvalency, real specialists being trained at the crossroads of several disciplines. It is nevertheless essential, particularly as regards the future profession, for the study cycle to comprise a major discipline.

b) The University cycle is made up of semesters[56] (on leaving the University students must furnish proof of a certain number of study semesters after the first year of orientation); within certain limits the semesters may be either simultaneous or successive. Each seminar lasts one semester.

c) A student takes part in at least two seminars, one in his own discipline, the other as he chooses, but the possibilities of choice must increase as the student advances in the study cycle. This means that with only four or six study semesters, a student's "card" will be more restricted than if he has had eight or ten.

d) After the first year, with the possible help of the co-equal information council, a student enters into a study contract[57] covering a minimum of four semesters, any change in which will involve reorientation of the student. The idea of introducing a contract into the study cycle indicates that the student is responsible for his studies both to himself and to the groups he works with (teachers and students). The contract takes into account his stage of advancement, his capacities, his interests, and his level in this or that discipline.

e) Although the seminar-semester units may be either simultaneous or successive in the student's study cycle, it is certain that from the standpoint of teaching content they must follow one another according to progress in complexity and in specialization, without ever ceasing to represent autonomous units of teaching, research, and work.

ORGANIZATION OF TEACHING BRANCHES

Organization of the study cycle into seminar-semester units carries with it the risk of a certain dispersion of studies. To remedy this difficulty it would be advisable to apply the following system.

1. *In every teaching and research unit*

(department), one or several co-equal teacher-student commissions decides at the end of every academic year the content, progression, and breakdown of the various seminar-semester units for the coming year. We think that it is advisable to abandon the very idea of a *certificat,* which harks back, whether we will or no, to traditional teaching forms. In content, however, the *certificat* can constitute in certain cases a hypothesis for coordinating and harmonizing the various seminars and a useful administrative reference for the diplomas conferred at the end of the University cycle.

2. *On the* faculté *level*

are held meetings of a co-equal commission,[58] whose role is to coordinate the work of the departmental co-equal commissions both as regards the content and harmonization of the seminars from different disciplines, and as regards creation of interdisciplinary seminars. This coordination may affect only a few departments during a more or less long period of time (e.g., temporary organization of seminars in French, art history, and sociology, treating a common theme).

3. *Organization of teaching and research*

into seminar-semester units should allow every teacher to divide his or her participation in the teaching and research unit (department) into one period more directly devoted to teaching and one period more directly devoted to research; the teacher's research should partially constitute the basic material of his teaching.

4. *Permanent education*

in teaching and research units should permit the *faculté* to offer the possibility for anyone who so desires, to acquire or complete his cultural development; for supplementary professional training; and for re-orientation.

This problem of opening the *faculté* to outsiders brings up the question of teacher participation in the work of teaching, criticism, and contestation. It may be considered that dividing the teacher's time into teaching and research would facilitate the practical solution of this problem, providing however that this principle is safeguarded: participation in criticism and contestation should not be considered as a voluntary activity.

5. *Organization of student trial periods into professional activity*

should be obligatory for all disciplines: for certain of them in the form of research-field activity, which can easily be integrated into the normal study cycle; for others in the form of pedagogical work (teaching or guidance in workshops, work groups, or summer universities, as well as in cultural and leisure organizations); for still others in the form of work in industry or on the land.

THE TEACHING FUNCTION, DIPLOMA
CHECKS, AND RATIFICATION OF STUDIES

I.

The teaching profession is defined by one's capacity to transmit to everybody, through recourse to new pedagogical techniques, what a limited few owe to their family background. In addition to the final University diploma, the teacher should have pedagogical training begun at the start of the study cycle proper by participation either in workshops and work groups, in professional trial periods, or in specialized seminars organized within the disciplines that have teaching as their principal goal. This implies necessary changes in the career structure and in the distribution of power inside teaching and research units; in other words, the distribution of pedagogical and scientific assignments and responsibilities should be done exclusively in terms of the competence conceded each person by all the members of each teaching and research unit, equal consideration being accorded to pedagogical capacity and scientific work accomplished. Consequently, exclusive and automatic reference to a thesis or to any other titular degree—even, and above all, seniority—is abolished. For the time being, the *agrégation* examination and the doctorate thesis, representing individual work subject to archaic criteria, should be abolished as obstacles to any attempt at redefinition of pedagogy or of scientific activity.[59]

II.

The aim is to minimize the social and economic returns on University degrees: actually, a diploma constitutes one of the chief mechanisms preventing application of the "equal work, equal pay" principle by making workers who are separated only by their school degrees appear unequal (a phenomenon evident in both secondary and higher education). On leaving the University a student will be given a diploma automatically if he can furnish positive proof of his actual participation in a certain number of seminar-semester units.

University diplomas must be independent of the definition of professional outlets and, with this in view, it would be advisable to abolish the idea that teaching is the only outlet offered by the *Faculté des Lettres*. The suggestion follows that professional institutes should be created, with students working under contract, which would be specialized in these professions as well as teaching more general university subjects.

III.

Traditional examinations will be changed or abolished. They will be replaced by continual checking. This checking should be mentioned in the study contract in the form of a clearly defined commitment between teachers and students: a sort of statement of claims. The departmental co-equal commission should draft rationally conceived tests with a dual reference to training objectives and to the student public. The teachers assigned to checking results need to be scientifically trained in the techniques that will permit them to check the knowledge that has been acquired and the work that has been done, with reference to explicit criteria. The ultimate aim of this check is neither negative nor coercive, and there is no attempt to provoke the student's failure—that is to say, to cause him to be temporarily or definitively excluded from the University cycle. It is rather to decide with the student, in a positive way, if reorientation must be considered, at what moment, and in which direction.

—Interdisciplinary report, Nanterre, June 11, 1968.

Notes

1. The book by J. Perret, *Inquiète Sorbonne*, contains the evidence of a deeply hostile professor but one who insisted upon being present.

2. Cf. above, Chapter I, pp. 104–107.

3. The most characteristic evidence is given in a series of articles by Raymond Aron that appeared in *Le Figaro*, since republished and somewhat attenuated in *La Révolution Introuvable*. The articles dated May 15 and 16 are certainly not sympathetic to the student movement (their author nevertheless protested against the repression after the night of the barricades), but they end on a note which is not entirely pessimistic: "The present outburst carries with it, on the historical plane, more danger than hope; but the actors in the drama, rejecting conventional slogans and being situated outside the old parties, in spite of everything, offer an opportunity for total availability." Later, R. Aron had the occasion to regret that the old parties had lost their influence. The article dated May 29 is the disillusioned account of a liberal conservative who is an admirer of Tocqueville; the June 5 article is a rather clear historical exposé; that of June 6 denounces the "Castroist, Maoist, or PSU trouble makers" and declares that there are hardly any adults, "either in the PSU, the UNEF, or the SNESUP." From June 11 to 19, a series of articles, which was completed the 29th, condemned the "cultural revolution," the "institution of terrorism," and appeared to foresee—then to go along with and justify—the retaking of the Sorbonne by the police. R. Aron received more than a thousand letters of approval.

4. Cf. above, Chapter VI, p. 398.

5. A first outline was published by *Le Monde* on July 4. See the useful, if rather sketchy, documentation presented by *La Revue internationale, Les sciences de l'éducation pour l'ère nouvelle*, special issue, June–July 1968; the texts reproduced by the review *Sciences*, special issue 54–55, important for the *Ecole Polytechnique*, the *Faculté des Sciences d'Orsay*, the CNRS; *Esprit*, October 1968 (a very good choice), and especially *La Sorbonne par elle-même*, pp. 313 ff.

6. Although for the sake of convenience we give chronological accounts, these should not be taken too literally; the "stages" were often simultaneous.

7. Cf. above, Chapter II, p. 186, the text of the motion adopted.

8. As for instance the Clermont statutes (*Lettres*), which include three dis-

tinct assemblies: for teachers and research workers, for students, and for administrative and technical personnel; as well as a joint council. In Caen (*Lettres*), the council is replaced by a permanent joint delegation; in Brest (*Lettres*), a student can be Dean; at the *Faculté des Sciences* at the Halle aux Vins, in Lille (*Lettres*), and at the *Ecole des Hautes Etudes* (6th section), teachers and research workers are grouped in two categories, each of which elects its representatives; at Orsay (Sciences), the Dean is free to choose his cabinet but is responsible to a joint bureau, etc.

9. Previously he had to be a titular professor.

10. And no longer only among the professors.

11. See the controversy between the two doctors in *l'Express*, July 1, 1968, and the more complete documentation published in *Esprit*, December 1968.

12. See *Le Monde* of August 21.

13. See *Le Monde* of September 26 and October 17. Details concerning what followed this affair may be found in *Esprit*, October 1968. Pierre Soulié died on September 9, 1970.

14. *Certificat d'aptitude à l'enseignement du second degré* (roughly equivalent to a Masters Degree in Education, authorizing teachers to teach in secondary schools).

15. They sometimes took place in July under almost clandestine conditions and with very reduced participation. Cf., for the case of the English CAPES, *Le Monde* of August 1, 1968.

16. Cf. the declaration by A. Kastler, *Le Monde*, May 16.

17. This was the result of intransigence on the part of both conservative professors and revolutionary students.

18. Cf. above, Chapter II, p. 192 and below pp. 518–521.

19. And yet, see J. Perret's opposition, *Inquiète Sorbonne*, pp. 112–120.

20. There exist several versions of this text. We have chosen the one that was voted at the *Institut d'Etudes Politiques* on May 31.

21. This is one of the points that was to be most discussed; cf. below, p. 503.

22. Another word that does not make for unanimity.

23. A typical sentence in that it is open to as many interpretations as one might want.

24. The critical University in this text does not mean anti-University, as in Berlin, but the University itself.

25. *Le Livre Blanc de la Réforme*, presented by the Paris medical students, together with the files of the *Faculté de Droit* on *l'Université critique*, and the plans of the *Institut d'Etudes Politiques* and the *Institut d'Anglais*, was the best formulated reform plan for the May–June crisis in Paris. Another text, summarizing in 33 points the demands of medical students, was published in *Esprit*, October 1968.

26. On the attack against the mandarinate, cf. above, pp. 469–475.

27. The CELU led a campaign with other moderate groups in the elections of student delegates (June 18). Its list was seriously beaten by the strike committee's slate. We give a text from the same group in Chapter IV, pp. 278–280.

28. CELU, *Université nouvelle régionalisée—Principes directeurs* (roneotype pamphlet).

29. Criticism of this document may be found above, pp. 514 ff.

30. A remunerated function attributed, after competitive examinations, to non-resident medical students, who work as assistants to resident interns.

31. This type of education being reserved, understandably, in the minds

of the reformers, for those who are not "inheritors." Cf. on this subject the remarks of J.-C. Passeron, in G. Antoine and J.-C. Passeron, *La Réforme de l'Université* pp. 202–295, and below, p. 498.

32. The co-equal commissions, consequently, only managed student problems. Later the CELU went so far as to use the word "co-management."

33. Excerpts were published in the *Le Monde* of May 21. During the crisis the Center of European Sociology published a series of documents of great value on the following problems: Fragmentary innovations and methodical innovations; The situation of academic instructors; Some suggestions for a policy of democratization; Technical instruction; Social and school background of the students at the *Grandes Ecoles;* Social functions of the dissertation; Over-selection and under-selection; The myth of democratization; The function of the educational system; Some aspects of the policy of cultural promotion in socialist countries; Caught up in the system; From the humanities to science and rational teaching of ancient cultures; Entry into first year of high school; Inequalities between the sexes; Docimology and Sociology; and Sociological prerequisites to all pedagogy.

34. Here we find again a theme which had been used against the student movement by G. Marchais as well as by the "Marxist-Leninists."

35. Sentence added after May 13.

36. *Collèges d'enseignements généraux* (formerly upper primary school), University institutes of technology.

37. Cf. reference to this text in Nanterre, below, p. 526.

38. Among others, H. Cartan, J. Monod, L. Schwartz, P. Vidal-Naquet. Responsibility for the secretariat of this commission and for the final text were assumed by Michel Alliot, professor at the *Faculté de Droit* and later M. Edgar Faure's Cabinet Director. First published in *Combat,* June 10 and 11.

39. This sentence, which did not figure in the original text, shows an anti-technocratic reflex.

40. In the initial project the order of principles was co-management, autonomy, contestation.

41. On the contrary, the original text referred to the government and society.

42. This is the only reference to a time factor.

43. On the crisis of the movement in Strasburg, a well-informed article by Charles Vanhecke, *Le Monde,* May 21. On the relationship between teachers and students inside the University Council, see G. Lanteri-Laura and M. Tardy, *Communications,* No. 12, 1968, pp. 134–147. A slogan familiar to the situationists, who were very numerous at the protestant *Faculté de Théologie,* was: "Profs-priests-cops"; near the office of the Dean of the *Faculté des Lettres* someone had written: "Don't say Dean any more, say: 'Up against the Wall . . . !' " (*crève salope!*) This insult had nothing personal about it. See P. Feuerstein, *Printemps de révolte à Strasbourg,* with a wealth of documentation on the action and the reaction.

44. Professor of English.

45. Respectively, professors of the physics of solids and of mathematics. R. Godement is a leftist militant known for his radicalism and for his anti-colonialist activity.

46. *Direction des recherches et des moyens d'essai,* a military organism. (Direction of research and means of testing.)

47. *Société d'études mathématiques appliquées,* a private group.

48. *Ecole Nationale Supérieure de Chimie de Paris.*

49. One might expect from this sentence that the anti-program proposed that

students should have 95 percent of the seats, but this is not true. The author of this document simply suggests—in a passage not given here—"at least 50 percent."

50. This is an attack on the theses of the *Mouvement du 22 mars*. The author implicitly refers to an article by L. Althusser, *"Problèmes étudiants,"* la *Nouvelle Critique,* January 1964, pp. 80–111, which takes position against the slogan: "The Sorbonne for the students," p. 90. It remains to be defined how from being a "student" one becomes a "teacher." By passing the *agrégation?* Or by being named instructor?

51. The "Centre théorique marxiste" in Besançon, in other words the action committee of the *Faculté des Lettres,* was badly defeated in the elections of the provisional management committee, having received in the teachers' college only 7 out of 79 votes.

52. The University was "autonomous" under the German regime.

53. The "preamble to a charter" for Nanterre was published in *Esprit,* August–September 1968, pp. 21–25.

54. Theme developed by P. Bourdieu, J.-C. Passeron, M. de Saint-Martin, *Rapport pédagogique et communication,* Mouton, Paris, 1965; see also the testimony of a worker in *Un ouvrier parle* by J. Minces, pp. 54–59.

55. In French, a concession to "worker-oriented" speech.

56. A similar organization is planned by the History Department of the Sorbonne.

57. An idea borrowed from the manifesto printed above, p. 498.

58. As defined by the Nanterre Charter, these co-equal commissions will be joint organisms elected on a single slate; see also the document that follows.

59. Cf. also the manifesto given above, p. 499.

IX

Beyond the "Facultés"

In an attempt to define a "faceless revolution," Edgar Morin wrote, "It is perhaps the word 'resonance' that can best allow us to imagine what happened. The occupation, desecration, desacralization, and de-sanctuarization of the Sorbonne set up a vibration that extended to the provincial universities, to entire sectors of the intelligentsia, to scientific research, the ORTF, the cinema, and to many writers; this same vibration shook the world of labor, and everything started to vibrate at the same time. . . ."[1] The word resonance projects an image; but of course an image explains nothing, and even has something dangerous about it. Morin is right, however, to underline that if authority was contested everywhere it was because it appeared everywhere homologous; and this fundamental fact explains the extension of the movement, whatever part may be attributed to contagion—You are all concerned!—or to imitation, which explains the rather ludicrous aspects it assumed at times, as when on May 21[2] a few writers occupied the quarters of the *Société des Gens de Lettres*. On the other hand one can only applaud those who brought out leaflets in Braille for the use of blind physiotherapists.

Whatever its aspect, whether that of *"grand patron"* in a hospital, factory boss, the ORTF board of directors, *lycée* principal, union bureaucrat, or the Central Committee of the French Communist Party, authority appeared to be fundamentally the same: hierarchical, authoritarian, monopolizing information for its sole benefit and allowing only what could serve its own ends to be circulated. The case of the General Secretary of the Ministry of Education, who insisted on having all mail addressed to the Ministry opened in his secretariat, is in itself a symbol. The same may be said of *l'Humanité,* which said nothing about the occupation on May 14 of the Nantes Sud-Aviation factory and then on May 16, without comment, announced in fifteen lines on p. 6 that the Cléon-Renault factory had been occupied the day before. There was also the ORTF which, on the evening of May 13, devoted only 90 seconds to the demonstration that had taken place that afternoon.

It is this phenomenon of homology that the texts grouped together in this chapter, admittedly in flagrantly insufficient number, will seek to show. We shall leave aside the problems, however vital, of the ORTF, to which other works have been devoted.[3] The most spectacular event of May '68—the partially uncontrolled explosion of the workers—is also represented by a very small number of documents: here too the phenomenon deserves individual consideration, which it will undoubtedly receive.[4] The movement of *lycée* pupils, on the contrary, appeared as a logical extension of the student movement, and it is in this context that we shall examine it more closely.

From the *Facultés* to the *Lycées*

A *lycée* principal, who made a liberal experiment in the Briançon mountain *lycée* that was rather like the one made by Dean Grappin in Nanterre, with "liberalism" that smacked strongly of boy-scouting, gave a perceptive analysis of the reasons for his failure:

> "Although its sphere of responsibilities in the matter was rather limited, the *lycée* administration appeared to have been delegated by this lot of technicians run amok, to play the role of *Ubu-Roi*. It was impossible and, moreover, of no interest, for the pupils to go and find out who was really responsible. Even the adults could not do it. Nobody was responsible, unless it was the unbelievable jamming of the entire administrative mechanism and the unbelievable lack of coordination. . . . For the pupils it was simpler and quicker to consider that *Ubu* was us."[5]

The CAL movement was the political response of the older *lycée* pupils to *Ubu*. We must underline this point, because at times it provoked genuine panic. Perfectly levelheaded people really believed that there existed a Chinese master-plan for conditioning the young people in the *lycées,* while others talked of a pre-Fascist or pre-Nazi atmosphere because the *lycée* pupils had no blueprint for reorganizing the world.

The exact contrary was true. The *"yé-yé"* movement that emerged on June 23, 1963, during the "mad night" on the Place de la Nation, or an ideology such as the review *Planète* stands for, can give rise to

Fascism; in any case, they indicate complete capitulation to mercantilism. The CAL movement was merely an attempt on the part of the *lycée* pupils to run their own affairs, and although it assumed enormous proportions as a result of the student movement, it appeared to be autonomous and, in a sense, preceded the latter. There had been a certain amount of politicization in the *lycées* during 1966–1967 in connection with the Vietnam war (activities of the *Comité Vietnam National* and the autonomous grass roots [Maoist] Vietnam committees), and even such innocent activities as those of the UNESCO clubs had helped this politicization.

Among the teachers, the problems of "selection" were posed all the more dramatically in that "democratization" on the first cycle level (11 to 14 years old) was at once real and ineffectual. On December 13, 1967, the pupils in 7 *lycées* voted to go on strike in opposition to the Fouchet Plan for reform. The principal of the *Lycée Rodin* told the pupils that the administration "did not recognize them, did not want to recognize them, that they had no rights other than to obey the rules, . . . that they were still minors, and that their only possible representatives were their families." On January 27, 1968, in front of the *Lycée Condorcet,* there was a demonstration of 500 *lycée* pupils in protest against the expelling of a member of the CVN. The CALS appeared at that time. On February 26, in several *lycées,* pupils took advantage of the professors' strike to shout: "No to selection!" and "Freedom of speech!" The "May days" found an already well-tilled field.[6]

On May 10 the movement outlined during the preceding days became very large. Thousands of *lycée* pupils in Paris and in the suburbs, after having demonstrated separately, joined the student procession at Denfert-Rochereau.

Document 206

We Lycée *Students Are in Solidarity*

With the University students for
> —immediate amnesty for those who are in jail,
> —waiving of legal action and withdrawal of sanctions,
> —democratic reform of education,
> —against repression.

With the workers for
    —defense of their just right to work.

LYCÉE AND UNIVERSITY STUDENTS, WORKERS, WE MUST
JOIN TOGETHER FOR THE SAME GOAL

—The Action Committee of the *Lycée Technique d'Aulnay,*
[May 10, 1968].

Most of the *lycées* were occupied in the same way that the
facultés were, and the same problems arose: demands for self-management, organization of joint committees, revolutionary references. The
Lycée Rodin text was put out by a joint committee; the Strasburg
one, on the contrary, expresses a hostile reaction to forms of teaching
that reveal a tension comparable to the tension in the University.[7]

Document 207

Declaration of the Professor-Pupil Committee
of the Lycée Rodin

The Professor-Pupil Committee of the *Lycée Rodin* (elected Tuesday,
May 21, 1968, by a ballot based on proportional representation) declares that it is in complete disagreement with the principles that now
govern National Education: authoritarian and bureaucratic administration, organization, and study content, which despite certain experiences make all general transformation of pedagogical methods
impossible. This heavy, anachronistic system is absolutely ineffectual
and shows little concern for the future of young people.

National Education cannot be considered as an isolated sector.
It is the product of a society founded on the inequality and exploitation
of workers, a situation which it perpetuates and encourages. Mere cog
in the wheels of a centralized and bureaucratic government, it cannot be democratically administered.

Only through the radical transformation of society and of the
government will it be possible for National Education to serve all the
workers: this is the goal set by our committee to guide its action.
For the immediate future, our demands are the following:

    1. When school starts in the autumn, elected councils, to be
composed for the most part of pupils of the second cycle and of teachers, should be set up in each institution and on all levels of National

Education. These councils are to be given power of decision in all domains: management of the budget, organization and control of studies, choice and application of pedagogical methods, disciplinary problems. Each council is to appoint one of its members, a professor elected by other professors, members of the council, and responsible to the entire council, to execute its decisions (modalities to be studied by the co-management commission).

    2. The number of pupils in each class to be limited to 25.

    3. A very substantial increase in the financing of National Education and autonomous management of each institution's budget, personnel salaries excepted.

    4. Fundamental revision of the present role of monitors.

    5. Free exercise of political and union activities inside the institutions under the responsibility of the elected council, which particularly entails recognition of the CALS.

In any case, the Professor-Pupil Committee has decided:

    1. to remain in office until the end of the present school year;

    2. to organize its renewal at the beginning of the next school year by means of an election based on proportional representation, with additional votes going to the party having the largest number of odd votes;

    3. to maintain its headquarters in the place allocated for this purpose (Room 407);

    4. to continue to assume responsibility for political information and meetings in the *lycée,* and for invitations to outside persons;

    5. to make the newspaper *La Source* its regular organ of information and liaison;

    6. to freely dispose of the technical means necessary for information;

    7. to continue the work of analysis undertaken in the commissions and to create new ones as needed;

    8. to call a general assembly of older pupils and professors at least once each trimester. Emergency assemblies may be called if needed at the request of the committee, or of a group constituted by at least 75 pupils and 10 professors;

    9. to further and organize an experiment in the new pedagogy in two groups of classes—for which the number of pupils will be obligatorily limited to 25—at the levels of the *sixième* (11–12 years old) and the *seconde* (15–16 years old). This experiment should be capable of being progressively applied in all classes. It will be based on the following principles:

—coordination between the different disciplines;

—a permanent dialogue between professors and pupils.

Each class becomes an autonomous group in which pupils and professors in a "class council" decide in common their program and their methods, as well as the means for checking their work. It maintains regular contacts with the other classes of the same level, whether or not they are affected by the experiment (modalities to be studied by the pedagogical commission, particularly the role of monitors).

—[May 22, 1968].

Document 208

What Do Lycée Pupils Want?

From the very first, *lycée* pupils joined the fight of the students, workers, and teachers:

—*because they opposed* the brutal and scandalous police repression against students, workers, and teachers;

—*because they opposed* a rigid, repressive educational system controlled by the conservative forces of a clerical and authoritarian administration, and a faculty composed of usually reactionary professors who are integrated into bourgeois society;

—*because they refuse* to become the docile, demoted, and over-exploited manpower that they are destined to become through the reforms set up by the government (Fouchet Plan);

—*because they refuse* to swallow the alleged "Culture"—militarized, clericalized, and commercialized—that they are being fed through archaic and aseptic courses and manuals;

—*because they reject* the traditional forms of discipline and order that confine them within a network of constraints and repression and, after having subjected them to the "joys" of a barracks-type schooling, make them partake of the "pleasures" of military life;

—*lastly, because the* lycée *crisis is only the individual expression of a general crisis in present-day society which is dominated by the exploitation of man by man.*

Today, after a month of fierce fighting during which students, *lycée* pupils, teachers, and workers have demonstrated their firm desire to transform the world, the administration and "right-thinking" institutions are seeking to completely re-establish their order.

THERE IS NO QUESTION OF CAPITULATING; THE FIGHT CONTINUES

We particularly call on teachers, students, and workers to support our fight:

—*against school orientation* under the control of hired pseudo-psychologists who claim the right to decide our future by means of a series of tests and prejudiced, self-interested evaluations (to eliminate waste);

—*against all forms of selection* on whatever level, particularly between the two cycles of secondary school and entrance to the University.

—*against para-police control* of knowledge (tests and traditional examinations) which are only an indirect form of pressure through control, selection, and blackmail;

—*against return to repressive and authoritarian methods of teaching;*

—*against military recruiting in school;*

—*against the clerical obscurantism* of chaplains in the *lycées;*

—*against repression of* lycée *pupils, both boys and girls,* whom the administration hastens to call, according to its humor, "leaders" and "agitators";

—*for the right* of free speech and free information inside the *lycées* (headquarters, newspapers, talks, etc.);

—*for the right* of control over, and criticism of, all administrative, school, and disciplinary decisions that concern our future;

—*for the right* to vote at 18 years of age;

—*for the right* to sexual information and free contraception, with no age limit, the latter ruling always justified in the name of hypocritical and repressive arguments.

—*Lycée* liaison committee for continuing the fight, Strasburg
[June 7, 1968].

A few small groups of teachers, not many, adopted for themselves all the demands made by the *lycée* pupils. Some pedagogical institutions joined the movement, nevertheless, and the *Institut Pédagogique National* took the name *Institut Pédagogique Populaire*. It became the center of an exhibit devoted to the May events.

Document 209

Faced with the events of the past few days, members of the graduating class feel that they are particularly concerned. At the very moment when repression has descended upon the students, they do not accept being kept in a hothouse atmosphere under a pretext of neutrality. In three months they will have to face problems which the government already tends to present as about to be solved. Actually, it is trying to head off the protesters by promoting reforms which the contradictory structure of society makes quite futile in advance.

At present teachers in the second degree are divided. Some are worried and self-questioning. Others are trying to dam the flood by seeking refuge in the alibi of curricula and the principle of authority. Others still, not wanting to be "had," are actively working in the context of recent events to formulate a theory, to transform themselves, and to transform the form and content of their teaching.

They have denounced (a) the myth of an apolitical school policy which sends out into the world uncertain, disturbed adolescents; and (b) the search for security and self-preservation of an intellectual mandarinate which, being primarily concerned with maintaining its prerogative of hegemony over people's minds, is taking refuge in the finicky formalism of administrative and union quibbling.

It is time to understand however that the fate of the pupils for whom we are responsible depends not only on problems of form, but also on *content*.

We do not hesitate to denounce the rigidity of certain "educators" who, safe in the sanctuary of their courses and schedules, would like to keep their pupils isolated from the din of outside events.

Today the situation is irreversible: new wine will not ferment in old bottles.

The vital forces must be encouraged; we must work in the thrust of the student movement, we must promote the new structures that are inseparable from a new concept of government.

To accomplish this, teachers, parents, students, and pupils, there will never be too many of us.

—The "groupuscule" of *"enragé" teachers* [about May 11, 1968].

The *lycée* movement tried almost desperately to enter into contact with the parents. The tone of the pupils from the two *lycées* in the Basses-Alpes has an element of pathos about it, while the strike committee at Michelet (Vanves, near Paris) seeks to inspire confidence. In some cases, as is evident in a text from Clermont, the parents' associations reacted favorably. This was often true in May. In June, however, relations between rebellious *lycée* pupils and parents frequently resembled the description given in a text from the *Lycée Colbert*.

Document 210

Information for Parents

Dear Madame, Dear Sir,

Parallel with the student movement, which is seeking to recast University structures independently of all political movements, we, the *lycée* pupils of Château-Arnoux, Saint-Auban, in agreement with:

—members of the teaching body;

—the parents' council;

—the *lycée* pupils of the Basses-Alpes;

wish to inform you that our movement has as its goal to improve educational conditions for YOUR CHILDREN and to permit them to take a more active part in the life of the school.

In order that you may be further informed, this communiqué will be followed by a program of demands.

—The Saint-Auban *Lycée* Committee, May 24, 1968.

Document 211

Call to Students

Unanimously passed at the Departmental Congress, May 19, 1968

We have often felt the need of contacts with responsible student representatives, but these contacts have not been easy to arrange. Now an opportunity is offered us. We hope that these contacts may become regular.

We are asking students as well as professors, in the name of the many families of modest origin who constitute the majority of our members, to take into consideration the burden that would weigh on them if the chances of their young people's obtaining the diploma expected from a year's work were endangered.

This concern is not incompatible with a desire for renewal of the University. We are in agreement that students should participate in this renewal and in its management, and we favor its adaptation to the world of today.

But we demand the honor and the right to make our contribution to the discussions because the University is not only the place where professors and the present generation of students work; it must also be a place for receiving the future students that our young children of today will become.

We condemn selection for admission to higher education founded on the immediate needs of the economy, and hope that structures will be set up that will permit students to receive a progressively specialized general education that will help their integration into professional and social life.

But we do not want to see the University subordinated to the needs of a rigid society; within its necessary adaptation it must be able to make it possible for the cadres of tomorrow to accomplish the necessary mutations toward a juster, more humane society.

In the overall reform of education, we cannot separate the fate of the students from that of other young people who, without valid professional training or even a diploma, are jobless even before they've started to work, and we call on all academics to help us better their lot.

—Departmental Council of Parents of Pupils in the Public Schools of the Puy-de-Dôme, Clermont-Ferrand.

Document 212

What the Parents Said Last Monday

Parents took the floor (three times, alas!!!) during the June 10 session.

From the very first words we understood their position; the first man to speak accused us of having kept his children from going back into the *lycée* at the beginning of the strike; we who had had such difficulty checking the people who came in because our security system was not well set up then!!?? . . . ?? Was he so eager to get rid of his children as to reproach us on this point!!??!!

One father proposed abolishing the possibility of our deciding what we wanted: "Soon they'll be asking kindergarten children to decide for themselves," said this worthy man. We booed him in proportion to his reactionary stupidity. You can imagine the uproar; a shudder of horror ran through the audience of pupils when he shouted: "I could be your father!!! . . . !!!"

Generally, the other parents were opposed to our action, for absurd reasons: loss of authority over their own children . . . (I will not quote the other remarks of these parents, which would simply make the pupils laugh, and cause these same parents to blush).

This meeting proved that there is deep disagreement between pupils and their parents.

—Excerpt from CAL Colbert, R. M. [Paris] *le Pavé,* No. 4, June 17, 1968.

During the days that followed de Gaulle's May 30 speech, reaction became more perceptible. A professorial reaction made curious references at the *Lycée Henri-Bergson* to secularism, and promised the moon in exchange for abandon of political activity, intervention by outside commandos, or by parents. At times the incidents were very violent, as at the *Lycée Henri-IV*. *Lycée* pupils in Villeneuve-le-Roi (a suburb south of Paris) reacted to official disbanding of revolutionary student groups by superbly quoting Rimbaud. Shortly afterwards, on June 15 and 16, the movement held its preparatory congress, at which a slight majority founded the *Union Nationale des* CAL, under Communist leadership. As for the government, it finally preferred to advance the summer holiday date, which made those who had talked of time wasted look ridiculous. Meanwhile, CAL members had a much more bitter surprise, which is discussed in the *Lycée Colbert* newspaper: the surprise of finding that they had become a minority.

Document 213

Although professors were not consulted, they want genuine educational reform; that is to say, one that is

1. discussed by everybody, unionized or not;
2. thought out, conceived, and executed calmly;
3. which, far from politicizing school life, would depoliticize it completely through elimination of all political or religious activity inside the institution;
4. which would ensure real pupil representation;
5. which would ensure, as well, a complete recasting of curriculum, methods, teaching personnel, schedules, and enrolment: (less homework, lessons, abolition of quarterly tests).

In short, the professors, who have not been consulted, want a genuine dialogue and not a one-way politicized discussion in which they cannot participate.

They are for real freedom of speech and freedom of work which at present no longer exists in the *lycée*.

—Co-Ed State *Lycée Henri-Bergson*, Paris, June 5, 1968.

Document 214

Since Wednesday, May 21, occupation of the ex-*Lycée Thiers,* decided in a general assembly at the Marseilles *Faculté des Sciences,* has made it possible for us, in close relationship with the professors, to give concrete form to our occasionally idealistic views on education and the present structures of society.

All these motions were clarified as a result of political and pedagogical commissions, of individual statements, and of film showings followed by discussions.

Little by little the general excitement of the first days gave way to better organized work, divided among the following different groups:

—an occupation committee composed of six pupils from the preparatory classes to the *grandes écoles,* six *lycée* pupils, and one professor;

—a security guard composed of a day team and a night team;

—a press committee in charge of distributing radio bulletins and gathering all news, inside or outside the *lycée;*

—a service for distributing food supplied by means of collections, and providing meals for the occupiers;

—a headquarters manned by *lycée* action committees, where all *lycée* pupils in Marseilles and from the region would be welcome.

Not only has the occupation never been challenged, it has even been strengthened by certain provocations to direct confrontation. This was the case on Tuesday, June 4, when a commando of fake garbage collectors, armed with real firearms, tried to force open the *lycée* doors and to influence the real *lycée* students present, as a result of false information. One professor was hit on the head.

But what is most striking—most superficial too, we must say—is the presence of a certain folklore, like a new way of life: the *law of May 13, 1968.*

It is forbidden to forbid, explains the expression of all the political, poetic, or purely imaginative tendencies inside the *lycée:* the red flag of the *Commune* and the *Internationale* are the two symbols—revolt and hope—that unite us.

What positive goals has the occupation attained?

For the participants, to have become aware of our potential for action in society. This we must share with all *lycée* pupils.

The experience of freedom must become a general and lasting reality.

> —Editorial from CAL, *Lycée* of the *Commune de Paris* (ex-*Lycée Thiers*), Marseilles, No. 7, June.

Document 215

"J'accuse"

The Villeneuve-le-Roi CAL vehemently protests against the government's decision to disband certain leftist student organizations which through their action have aroused the conscience of the general public. In this way the government lays the blame for the violence that its repression has provoked on the student movement.

Moreover, this measure seems to us to be arbitrary and anti-democratic. The government's claim to allow freedom of speech is therefore violated. The aim of this interdiction is to crush political con-testation, which should be a right under any non-dictatorial regime. We note that the government is allied with organizations having a fascist and rightist tendency (*Occident*), and that by liberating Salan it has encouraged revival of such groups as the OAS. By imposing "its order" the present government is attacking individual freedoms and is showing its determination to sacrifice the general interest to indi-vidual interests, which are those of the ruling class. The CAL is fearful of the consequences of decisions such as these.

Clearance Sale . . .
The Voices reconstituted; the fraternal awakening of all choral and orchestral energies and their immediate application; the oppor-tunity, unique, of freeing our senses! . . .

For sale—anarchy for the masses; irrepressible satisfaction for connoisseurs; frightful death for the faithful and for lovers!

While the public funds are poured out in feasts of brotherhood, a bell of rose-colored fire tolls in the clouds.

Enough! Here is the punishment—*March!*
Ah! My lungs are burning, my temples are throbbing! Night revolves in my eyes, under this sun! My heart . . . my limbs. . . .

Where are we going? To battle? I am so weak! The others are advancing. Equipment, weapons . . . the weather! . . .

Fire! Fire at me! Here! or I'll give myself up.—Cowards!—I shall kill myself!

Ah! . . .

—I shall get used to it.
That would be the French way to live, the path of honor!

—RIMBAUD [Olivier Bernard, tr., Penguin edition, 1962],
the Villeneuve-le-Roi CAL [June 16, 1968].

Document 216

Watch Out: Danger!

We had hoped that many among you would join our movement and
would take useful part in it. Unfortunately, for the most part you have
not lifted a finger. We have not been able to count on you because you
have remained apathetic: this is why we have not been able to do anything really positive. Our little group is not big enough to organize
everything. Those who do not help us slow up our movement and
almost go against it. Do not forget that the CAL defends your interests.
Unfortunately, we must be more and more on the alert because people
are trying to do us harm. They are trying to destroy the CAL in the
lycée; I am speaking of members of the administration of our *lycée.*

We thought that they were with us, but we have to recognize
that under the appearance of friendship they are "knifing us in the
back." Until Saturday evening we were defending our *lycée* at the request of the principal. We even prevented a fire from spreading alarm-
ingly. And yet the principal withdrew his "confidence" in us, suspecting
that there was probably a "pyromaniac" among us. He actually asked
some of us to spy on the others. We will not stand for being treated
like fools by the administration. We have also learned that they counted
on closing the *lycée* before the date set in order to prevent us from
continuing our action. We must not let them do this to us! Our movement must become much more independent as regards the administration. We must not let anybody sabotage our movement.

R.M.

—Excerpt from CAL Colbert, *le Pavé,* No. 5, June 22, 1968.

Student Speech in the Workers' World

The influence of the student movement on the worker movement is
probably the most complex feature of the entire May revolution. It is

pretty well known that the last thing the students expected was to play an inspirational role for the workers, from whom on the contrary they were expecting to learn. And yet more or less well-intentioned warnings had not been lacking, as for instance the following, written in April by Daniel Mothé (a worker at the Renault factory and a former *Socialisme ou Barbarie* militant) which appeared early in May 1968 in *Esprit*.

"Students who are in search of political leadership among the working class will find a traditional-minded working class that would rather be under the authority of others than assume it themselves." He did add, however, "But it would be a good thing if, in their endeavors, they were not able to make contact with the proletariat they are looking for, they would be content to meet with militant workers who, like them, are in the minority and are trying to express in the language of union demands, ideas that are very close to their own."

Such men did exist, and not only among the militants. In the Sorbonne student-worker action committee those who were present will not soon forget the spectacle of workers from every category (although small businesses seemed better represented than large ones), who had come to get ideas, and the language to express them in, from the students.

It is impossible here to give more than an idea of the impact of these scenes. At the most all we can do in this context is to pose the problem. The role of the younger workers in starting the movement was evident, particularly in Cléon. Young men from the government-owned Renault factory explained their problems to the students, especially the problem of the low grading given their work in comparison with their elders, even though the young workers were technically more competent. The CGT was violently opposed to all direct contact and all gestures of solidarity, other than verbal, between the two struggles. At Flins its attitude was characteristic: the "luxurious car" driven by Alain Geismar (an updated version of Léon Blum's "silver service" and Maurice Thorez's "villas") was inveighed against as much by the CGT-Renault cell as by M. Alain Peyrefitte in his election campaign.

It would be a mistake to believe that this campaign had no effect. Many workers had the same reaction to the students that most people had: they were shocked by the car burnings. Besides, the great force of the CGT—and of the PC—in the factories was its very political inaction, as was noted by L. Magri, then a member of the Italian Communist Party: "the facts speak for themselves: no meetings or political discussions in the occupied factories, no resolutions of a political nature, and few organisms and unitary political committees on the enterprise or branch level, no meetings outside the factories, no large worker demonstrations, at least not until May 13."[8]

The CEDT was, in fact, the only union organization to declare, on May 16, that "the students' struggle for democratization of the University is the same as the workers' struggle for democracy in enterprise. The restraints and unbearable structures against which the students have revolted exist to the same extent, and often even more intolerably, in factories, in construction yards, in the different services, and in administrations." A leaflet put out by its Paris local union asserted, *as of May 11,* that the workers' struggle and the students' struggle were the same.

But the minority position that permitted this audacity also permitted it to justify its retreat in the face of the CGT's ultimatums. A Renault text signed "Young auto-workers in a government-owned factory" (the *Régie*) proposed setting up committees of unionized and non-unionized workers in every workshop or service, that would continue to function after the end of the strike. Members of certain "leftist 'groupuscules'" (among them, *Tribune Ouvrière*[9]) had made similar proposals much earlier. That they should have reappeared in May, and apparently been carried out, was proof of the influence of the action committees. The problems of self-management were posed with especial clarity in the most modern enterprises, which included a large proportion of cadres.[10] Here is an example of this from the Alsthom electricity plant.[11] And a Citroën leaflet, after slipping into the usual union language, pays extraordinary tribute to the student movement. When they did find a common language, it was not devoid of mystification. The self-management movement was far from general among the workers.

Document 217

One and the Same Combat

The extremely violent confrontations, the blind and bloody governmental repression, the fierce combat of the students who held out against a siege of several hours, are expressions of a profound malaise: a malaise of students as well as of all our society.

THE IMMEDIATE CAUSES
The attitude of the government
        —by arresting several hundred students at a meeting in the

Sorbonne courtyard on Friday, May 3, whereas many other meetings of this kind had already been held there without harm to anyone;

—by instigating police attacks with a brutality that the press has widely publicized;

—by refusing all "advances," rejecting all measures of appeasement such as liberation of the imprisoned students;

—by sentencing several students under inadmissible conditions, with no proof. These arrests and these sentences, which took place within an unprecedentedly short time, constitute a new tactic that was inaugurated in Caen against the striking workers, of which the workers will be the next victims.

Whereas the peacefulness of the large demonstration organized by the UNEF on Tuesday the 7th proved that the students are perfectly capable of assuring their own security system if only the police do not intervene.

THE PROFOUND CAUSES
Student anxiety about the future.

The University, which is an enormous machine for manufacturing diplomas, has now become industrialized and is producing without concern for job opportunities for its trainees. For instance, students who have been working for several years in the social sciences learn with bitterness today that employment possibilities for them are extremely rare. And nobody told them of this situation. Unfortunately, examples of this sort are very numerous. The question they ask, therefore, and which we workers are in a good position to understand, given our own employment problems, is the following:

TOMORROW, WILL WE BE EMPLOYED
OR UNDER-EMPLOYED?

Rejection of governmental authoritarianism.

There exists an important problem: the increasing number of students, which poses the problem of professional job opportunities.

The government seeks to make a unilateral decision by refusing discussion both with the student unions and with the teaching unions of its authoritarian selection measures for admission to the *faculté*.

It uses this method, moreover, in exactly the same way to exclude every year an increasing number of our children from admission to long term education.

When were the parents' organizations consulted?

Capitalist society incriminated.

On this subject we would like to return to an assertion made by workers and, alas, picked up in certain leaflets: "Students are the sons of the bourgeois. Tomorrow they will be the PDGS of our companies. We have nothing in common with them."

About that, we have two observations:

1. If the number of workers' sons is so low in the universities, the responsibility does not lie with the students themselves, but with a system that the government wants to make even worse, and which excludes the children of lower income families from higher education.

2. Whatever their social origin, students are contesting, as we are, a society that does not satisfy them because, dominated as it is by oppressive capitalism, this society is incapable of satisfying men's deepest aspirations.

The following excerpt from a UNEF leaflet (students' union organization) is eloquent in this respect:

". . . the workers are rejecting the society that exploits them; the students are rejecting a University which tends to make them the docile cadres of a system founded on exploitation, at times even the direct accomplices of this exploitation."

This rejection of an automobile-, T.V.-, publicity-conditioned society in which men are sick from no longer knowing why they are alive is extremely salutary.

If we so desire this can be the point of departure for a positive action for effectively building our society, not on anarchic production and waste, nor the wealth founded on the misery of others, but on justice, solidarity, freedom, responsibility, and the respect for every man, whoever he is.

THE CFDT POSITION

We workers must not let ourselves be drawn into unjustified reactions that would cut us off from our age-old allies, the students.

On the contrary, with them we demand:

—liberation of prisoners and annulment of the sentences unjustly pronounced;

—withdrawal of police forces from the Latin Quarter;

—re-opening of University premises;

—a solution to basic University problems, a solution that interests us all the more since it will be our children who will benefit from it.

This is why we are calling on workers, men and women,

—to join the 24-hour general strike set for Monday, May 13;

—to participate massively in the demonstration decided upon by the union organizations.

—CFDT Paris Local, May 11, 1968.

Document 218

For Mass Unity

We want to recall what started the unlimited strike we have been pursuing now for eleven days: although it was started by all the workers, both men and women, the unions later took over responsibility for this movement with the precise demands everybody already knows.

We want to recall too that out of this mass of striking workers only a small percentage is unionized. About 20 percent of the workers in the state-owned factory are represented by the unions.

And the others, the 80% who are non-unionized, who represents them?

This is what leads us to propose, to both unionized and non-unionized workers, to organize a meeting in each shop or department in order to discuss all together how we can fight the people who exploit us, by forcing them to take our demands into consideration and obliging them to accept these demands, even if we have to continue the strike until we receive total satisfaction.

Once our demands are satisfied we must keep the organizational forms we have set up with the aim, not of competing with existing union organizations, but, on the contrary, of achieving union unity and giving it a democratic form that will reflect the opinions of everybody.

We hope to speak at the meeting this morning, to explain what this affair, which concerns us all, consists of.

EVERYBODY COME TO THE MEETING ON THE ISLAND AT 9 A.M.

—The Young Workers in the State Factory [Renault], May 27, 1968.

Document 219

The workers at Alsthom-RSC-SIG, without meaning to neglect immediate demands, hope that the advantages they won as a result of their struggle will not quickly become deceptive. Consequently, they consider that the real problem posed in business is the problem of *power,* and therefore of *management.*

In fact the power of the workers, which implies participation of each one of them in management of the company and organization of the work, is the *only* thing that will permit development of the company and economic expansion in the best interests of the workers.

For these reasons the workers claim responsibilities in management that they will only really be able to assume if they own the tools of production; the latter, which are very often the property of distant stockholders, are in fact the property of the workers because they are the ones who use them.

It is therefore necessary, in order for workers' power to be expressed on all levels, to set up *management committees whose duty it will be to check the hierarchy's application of the objectives defined by the workers' general assembly.*

The workers will freely determine how the proceeds of the business shall be used, especially:

—remuneration of capital, which is a means of production placed at the disposal of the company;

—investments;

—remuneration of personnel.

These objectives can be completely attained only through the solidarity and action of all the workers in businesses having economic contacts with the business under consideration, that is to say, essentially: banks, customers, and suppliers.

The workers of Alsthom-RSC-SIG have decided to give maximum publicity to their position, among other workers, and ask for support of this priority objective by all the union organizations.

—Alsthom–RSC–SIG [rectifiers, semiconductors, signalling devices],
[about May 25, 1968].

Document 220

Comrades . . .

We are continuing and reinforcing this strike more than ever! The strike of the century! OUR STRIKE!

However, rumors are circulating, and radios are announcing: "Such and such a company, such and such a sector has gone back to work. . . ."

WATCH OUT!

This is part of the government campaign and of action by the capitalists who are dismayed in the face of such a movement. As for the Gaullist majority, in return for money, gas, and protection they are issuing a call to the civic action committees which should be neutralized at all cost, without delay, and insofar as possible without too many clashes. This neutralization is necessary in order not to lead very quickly to a civil war, which would bring only *misery, unhappiness,* and *shame* to the French people!

WE MUST BE VERY VIGILANT, VERY FIRM! First of all, in order to obtain *complete* satisfaction of our demands.

Don't forget! Our strike is above all for specific demands! In fact our union leaders keep reminding us of this; we must listen to them.

Naturally, in the context of the events that have followed in rapid succession, and particularly in thinking about the monumental errors committed by the government, we can say that our strike is becoming more and more political.

In fact the spark, the signal for this historical spring in which youth, thanks to its power, can finally speak up, is undoubtedly the student movement.

When the working class movement also came out into the open, a certain distrust and certain divergencies then became evident. This was the consequence of a serious lag, politically speaking, in the worker world.

Thirteen days of strikes, thirteen days of discussions, thirteen days of increased understanding, and thirteen days of solidarity have ironed out these differences.

TOGETHER WE WILL BUILD THE NEW SOCIETY

Because the ridiculous, desperate maneuver of diversion and intimidation represented by "His Majesty" de Gaulle's May 30 speech, when all is said and done, is the cement of *unity*

UNIVERSITY-FACTORY

—Striking comrades at Citroën[12] [June 11, 1968].

Communist Intellectuals

"In May the Communist Party was the only institution in which the officials were not explicitly contesting the hierarchy."[13] Implicit contestation did exist, however. After Georges Marchais's outbursts the "politbureau's" May 12 resolution,[14] introduced by Roger Garaudy, noted that the "revolutionary demands" of the students were the same as those of the workers and declared that they supported "unreservedly" the student-teacher movement. But even after the PC had taken this turning, traces of infighting remained very evident. In opposition to the unscathed assurance in defeat evinced by Waldeck-Rochet, René Andrieu,[15] and L. Salini, or to the denunciations by J. Duclos of police infiltration in anarchist circles,[16] there was the infinitely more flexible attitude of *Démocratie Nouvelle* which, notwithstanding, used perfectly transparent dodges to reproduce the May[17] posters before disappearing.

On the contrary, contestation was quite open in intellectual circles, where many such earlier opponents of all tendencies, both "rightist" and "leftist" united in their mutual hatred of Stalinism saw their ranks increase. The sharp PC condemnation of the May 24 student demonstration brought forth a letter signed by 36 intellectuals on May 26. Quite exceptionally its signers,[18] despite the eminently fractional nature of their action, were invited to meet with a delegation composed of R. Garaudy and R. Leroy for the "politbureau," and G. Besse, J. Chambaz, and P. Juquin for the Central Committee[19] on the afternoon of June 1 and the day of June 3.

The demands put forward by the protesters included publication of a joint statement in the Party paper *l'Humanité* which would also inaugurate a free discussion column; two-way talks with the students, to be made easier by certain symbolical gestures such as the hoisting of a red flag over the Sorbonne by workers from the Renault factory; and retirement of G. Marchais and P. Juquin. With the exception of R. Garaudy, the leaders claimed that they had anticipated everything that had happened, and P. Juquin attempted to say to his comrades what he had not been allowed to say on April 25 in Nanterre, which provoked something of a hue and cry.[20] On June 5, *l'Humanité* published a communiqué which, while not acrimonious, was of exclusive editorial origin.

There follow, in addition to the "letter from the 36," two characteristic declarations, summarized in their own words, by J. Vernant, a high-ranking professor at the *Ecole Pratique des Hautes Etudes* and former leader of the Toulouse armed resistance, and by J. Durand, an upper-echelon official in the Ministry of Urban Development.

Document 221

Letter from the 36

The Communists who have signed this document assert their political solidarity with the movement which, having started with the students, has brought out millions of workers, young people in the factories, those in the *lycées,* and the great majority of intellectuals. Beyond the Gaullist regime their common contestation challenges the very foundations of the present social system.

By attempting at the very start to restrain this exceptional impetus, the leadership has separated the Party from a great force for socialist renewal.

Fifty thousand demonstrators at the Gare de Lyon shouted their anger against the government decision which by forbidding Cohn-Bendit to remain on French territory violated the amnesty. Many Communists were present. The Party was not.

In this way provocation by the government, which sought to isolate, even to crush, the student movement, was made easier.

And yet without this movement, which catalyzed the determination of the masses to fight, the factories would not have been occupied, the barriers of the SMIG [minimum wage law] would not already have crumbled, and the future would not henceforth hold out other prospects to the combat of the workers, whose role is a decisive one.

A break between the Communists and the mass of students and intellectuals would have tragic consequences. Two-way talks should start as soon as possible.

The discussion, which has been made imperative by events, on the subject of orientation and the structure and future of the revolutionary movement, can no longer be evaded. A frank analysis of reality and bold political initiative must at all costs allow for the establishment of ties with the new forces that have come to light in the fight for socialism and freedom.

—May 26, 1968.

Document 222

Party Strategy

What strikes me in the twin speeches of Juquin and Besse is that they have not heard what has been said here. A lot of precise and significant facts have been given on the physiognomy of the movement, its breadth and its importance, and the possibilities it has opened up for a revolutionary party. They remained deaf to what we were saying, just as they were blind in the face of events. And for the same reasons. They do not try to understand the facts, with all that is new and unforeseen that these facts imply. They have got into the habit of always referring to texts and to outdated resolutions. Their intellectual approach consists in starting with these texts, then commenting on them in order to make events fit into them, at the same time that they fail to mention the ones they cannot fit in.

To hear Juquin, we are in the same situation today that we were in before the events: it is still important to prepare the elections as best we can. You have the impression that in reality, for him, nothing has happened. The May crisis is not explained and not analyzed: it is erased. And yet for Marxist dialectics the most interesting part of history is always the part that cannot be foreseen: things that are new, sudden changes, mutations, breaking points, crises because of which a situation must be reconsidered, to which we must adapt ourselves and from which we must learn for the future.

For several years now the Party has been trying to bring together and mobilize the masses on the bases of a common program, to be negotiated with the FGDS in the hope of winning an election. This plan could have been valid and the strategy worth while in a relatively stable social and political situation. But the May explosion has shattered both. A breach in the equilibrium of political forces took place where it was least expected, and the whole political scene was changed by it. The action of the students, *lycée* pupils, and other young people which caused a split in French society, and then the onset of the big worker strikes, constituted a blow to the Gaullist regime that took the form of direct contestation of the government.

Young people questioned the entire system of the exercise of authority in present-day French society; within this contestation, which interfered with the worker struggles for satisfaction of demands, Gaullism, with its system of authority conferred from above, appeared as the symbol of what had to be destroyed. An important phenomenon is the fact that a wide section of what are called the middle classes (a term that covers many varied realities), in any case a large number of intellectuals and artists from middle and upper echelons, lawyers, doctors, and technicians of every kind, participated in the movement with an enthusiasm and an inventiveness that nobody knew they possessed.

The Gaullist government was surprised by this explosion, no less than the Party. There were a few days, perhaps a week, when there was no authority. It was there for the taking. If the regime did not fall it was because nobody wanted or dared to make it fall. But that moment was a brief one. Politics is the art of opportunity. After the start of the strikes, with occupation of the factories, while the movement was spreading every day without having yet reached its crest, it was then that we should have understood that entirely new prospects existed for overthrowing Gaullism. The situation was certainly not revolutionary. But neither is Gaullism a regime like any other: having started in an atmosphere of popular uprising, it has abolished or weakened all the institutions representative of parliamentary democracy that can play a role of intermediary or buffer in periods of great crises between the government and the people.

It is hard to see how we could overthrow this regime through purely electoral procedures as long as Gaullism kept the upper hand. And yet during the critical days the government stood alone and bewildered, faced with events in the streets, at the *facultés,* and in the occupied factories. The police were uncertain; and the army, whose power the General had broken and which no longer constituted an autonomous political force, remained reserved (to say the least) and on the "wait-and-see."

That was the moment to link the workers' demands with the fall of the regime by clearly declaring that there could be no valid dialogue with a government responsible for the reactionary decrees of 1967. The working masses, for the most part, felt this way instinctively. And the petty bourgeoisie—that portion of the middle classes which was already extremely worried—had but one desire when they saw the movement spreading day after day: that the Old Man would leave as quickly as possible in order to avoid the worst and that the ship should not risk sinking with the captain.

There would perhaps have been a transitional government without a common platform with the FGDS. But the youth movement, nine million strikers, and a victory over Gaullism are worth a lot more than a signature at the bottom of a work plan. Elections held under these conditions would have been won. Many of those who demonstrated on the Champs-Elysées would not have been the last to climb on the bandwagon and see in the Party the only disciplined, coherent force for promoting a new policy that would emerge on something else besides disorder and anarchy.

Instead the Party chose another strategy; or rather, it continued on its own momentum as though nothing had happened. It saw in the events a means of pressure in order to bring the FGDS to conclude the pact for the coalition government that would result from the coming elections. And at the start it oriented the strikes toward the direction of a new Matignon Agreement with the existing government. This meant giving the government clear notice that they were not trying to overthrow it, nor was its existence or its legitimacy being questioned. In this way it was allowed to last, to catch its breath, and to wait and see what would happen. This strategy would have paid off if it had led to rapid agreements, to their ratification by the workers, and to an orderly return to work. In that case the Party would still have appeared to be the only organized political force having a hold over the movement and capable of controlling it in order to lead it in the direction of positive, reasonable solutions.

It would have come out of this test strengthened, its prestige reinforced, and in a favorable position for continuing the fight within the framework of the present regime. But this strategy was condemned to failure for two reasons—which the Party failed to recognize or the importance of which it had underestimated. On the one hand there was the frame of mind of the working masses, which was evidenced by rejection of the protocol of agreements negotiated with the government; on the other was the government's ability to launch a vigorous counterattack as soon as things had begun to change.

It may be said that from the day when the workers chose to reject the agreement project, the game was up. The government knew then that we did not really have the determination to commit ourselves entirely, and that it would suffice to let things "rot" until the moment when it would be possible to retake the initiative it had lost. The petty bourgeoisie, seeing the strikes continue after negotiations that had been presented as bound to reach a solution, concluded that either the Party itself was submerged and controlled nothing at all, or that the Party was playing a double game and that behind the so-called grievances it was preparing to seize power—two explanations which, although contradictory, nevertheless pointed in the same direction: the direction of fear, distrust, and hostility.

De Gaulle, who is not a general for nothing, did not let pass the opportunity this offered him. When the time came he imposed his own strategy by questioning the mass movement on the very terrain on which it had developed against him, the terrain of the streets; and by setting up elections under conditions and on the date he had decided upon and chosen. Earlier, his "tour of the mess halls"[21] had made his opponents, friends, and those who hesitated clearly understand that there could be no mistake: the government was present and would remain so.

Perhaps it was already too late to refuse this poker deal, in spite of the bluff it might have involved. But to accept it right away, within the hour that followed, was to go along with the game of the opponent and to fight under the worst conditions. One doesn't need to be a historian to understand that a movement which, for one month, had caused all the French social structures to tremble, but had not achieved its aims, not ended in a great political success, such as the fall of the government would have been, can only arouse in those who participated the resentments, divisions, and anarchic reactions of high hopes betrayed, even though it should lead to important material advantages. Among those who remain uninvolved it provokes the reactions of hatred and violence left by intense fear, when the feeling of danger has passed and the enemy ceases to appear really as frightening as had been believed.

During the May events the Party wanted to be reassuring and patriotic. It remained aloof from the extremists. It reassured the authorities and the government, which were able to survive and to prepare their counter-attack. It disappointed and offended many of those who were on the front line, fighting. But nobody among the petty bourgeoisie and among all those whom the movement disturbed will be grateful to the Party for having put a brake on the movement and for not having led it to its full term. They are all the more resentful towards us because of the fear they had felt now that it is no longer so dangerous to attack us. We have lost on every count.

We are assured that the Party has won a great success by obtaining the elections that had not been foreseen, and that it had hoped for. No one is a prophet. But we believe that the Party is sadly mistaken if it thinks it is going toward fair elections.

—Jean-Pierre Vernant.

Document 223

The Strike at the Ministry of Urban Development

I have been a member of the Party since 1949. I belong to the cell at the Ministry of Urban Development and Housing (16th *arrondissement* of Paris, Passy section). I do not occupy any position of responsibility at any level, neither in the Party nor in any mass organization. I am what is called a grass roots militant.

I am forty-five years old and I am a government employee, belonging to the category that is sufficiently highly placed in the administrative hierarchy to participate in drafting governmental decisions in the domains in which I am competent to do so: I am what is called a bureaucrat or, sometimes, a technocrat. . . .

I would like to call the attention of the Party leadershp to two points and make known my opinions concerning them; these are: the state of mind in the Party, as far as my personal experience is concerned, and the political strategy adopted and followed during the recent period.

For the first time since the Liberation the personnel of the Ministry of Urban Development decided on May 20, 1968, to call an unlimited sit-in strike.[22] During this strike, the general assembly decided to constitute work commissions (a list of grievances, administrative reform . . .), which met every day including Ascension and Whitmonday, in spite of transport difficulties. With a few others, non-Communists, I was put in charge of this movement. Here are the facts.

During this period the 16th *arrondissement,* Passy section, of our Party (which includes our cell) behaved as follows:

On May 17 and 18 a section conference was held to prepare the federal conference. During the course of the very open discussions that took place on May 18 I proposed the following resolution.

> *The present situation is rapidly evolving under pressure of the popular masses. Conditions now exist for rapidly putting an end to monopoly power and Gaullist power. . . .*

The discussion was centered on the point of knowing whether these conditions actually did exist or whether they were rapidly ripening, as the communiqué of the "politbureau" had declared the night before. It goes without saying that this was not just a quarrel of words, but a basic question with particular bearing on the evaluation of the student movement, its representative force and fundamental orientation, and the prospects offered by entry into the fight of the working class and other entire sectors of the population. In brief, of the conditions under which there might be new prospects of overthrowing the Gaullist government: no longer simply elections, but also launching of the mass movement in the streets and in places of work.

The following objection was raised:

> *There are only 300,000 workers on strike. Perhaps conditions will exist in a few days but, for the moment, they do not.*

Was this not a passive and objectivist attitude toward events? We will not try to bring about these conditions but will wait until they are created. Isn't this behavior opportunist? You confine yourself to taking note of the situation at a given moment without analyzing either the dynamics of the movement or the conditions under which it is developing.

Here, comrades, I shall open a parenthesis.

During the section conference I furnished some highly important information. "Did you bring that to the attention of the Party leaders?" I was asked.

"No, but the comrade from the federal committee can take care of it."

I should like to ask our comrades in the central committee if this information was transmitted to them. I myself think it was not. In the Party there exists a succession of filters between the base and the summit, and all you know about what is happening on the bottom is what they want to tell you and how they want to tell it.

The comrades who lead us should know that many cells and sections of the Party have only a formal existence. The section conference of the 16th *arrondissement,* about which I spoke earlier, includes 29 comrades; half of the cells were not represented; practically none of the comrades present had been elected, and mandates had been given to those who could take part in the conference. This, then, is the illusory state of the Party in the 16th *arrondissement,* and it has been like that for several years. Also, I doubt if things are very different in many other sections. Were you told that? Did you know that? My questions are put to our comrades at the top.

In addition I must earnestly call your attention to the cumbersomeness of all the intermediaries between the base and the summit, to the rigidity instituted by the captains, lieutenants, first lieutenants, sergeant-majors, and corporals of the Party; to the filters and screens they set up between the summit and the base, between the base and the summit.

Now I shall return to my original story. So, on May 18, the conditions were not yet ripe but they were rapidly ripening. This is what the comrades in the section leadership thought.

On May 29 I met one of the important members of this leadership. By then there were ten million workers on strike, the demonstration we were marching in at the call of the CGT alone had brought out 600,000 people, and the government was practically non-existent. I said to him, "So, comrade, are conditions ripe today for rapidly overthrowing the Gaullist regime, or are they still ripening?"

"They are still ripening," he replied.

"At this rate," I answered him, "they will never be ripe and, in the end, they will even rot."[23]

This being the case, how are we to interpret the total lack of initiative on the part of the section committee with respect to our Ministry? (But if it was not demonstrated here, why should it be elsewhere?)

Not once in two weeks did any of the leaders come to see us, to take part in one of our general assemblies, to discuss with us, or propose their possible support or how to coordinate our section with those of the other groups in the *arrondissement,* as for instance the ORTF (quai Kennedy). Not once, comrades, in two weeks! I expressed surprise at this absence to the section head, a member of the federal committee of our Party, whom I also met on May 29 at the CGT march. What do you think he replied? "We tried to phone you four or five times and we couldn't get hold of you." During that same time, comrades, we received dozens of telephone calls from Paris and the provinces at the headquarters of the strike committee. You had only to ask the switchboard to get us! After all, the section is less than a quarter of an hour's walk from the Ministry!

What can the leaders who ignored us like that know and understand about our movement? How can they analyze and evaluate the situation? Besides, do you believe that the section head took advantage of our meeting to ask how things were going in our place of work? Not at all! He confined himself to informing me that there were section meetings every evening at 9 P.M.!

Another anecdote. On the morning of May 20 I went to call for a comrade in the suburbs, a paid worker in our CGT union at the Ministry. On the way I asked her, "Tell me, what's going on in Asnières?" The big strike was gaining in impetus and I thought she was going to tell me about the morale of the workers, their fighting spirit, the nature and breadth of the movement in a suburb she knew well.

"Yesterday," she told me, "we went with my husband to visit the places that are on strike, to talk to various comrades. Well, you know, it's going well; it's even going much better: the boys are more aware than they were of the leftist [*gauchiste*] danger." This is the degree of caricatural deformation that three weeks of denunciation of leftists has finally led to—just when one of the most powerful movements in our history is starting!

The facts I wanted to point out to the CGT leaders are no less significant. On Sunday, May 19, I tried to reach the people at the head of the Ministry union to find out what they planned to do Monday morning at our place of work. Not having their address, I thought of going to the UGFF office [*Union générale des fédérations de fonctionnaires*] where I expected to find a lot going on. Actually I walked through empty rooms for a quarter of an hour, entered unguarded, deserted offices without being stopped, calling, "Is anyone here?" In fact there was no one, except one comrade on duty. He could tell me nothing except to come back on Monday morning at 8 o'clock to get some leaflets for distribution. It was after four in the afternoon and the UGFF of CGT employees did not seem to be oriented toward general organization of the strike in the public sector.

I went twice to the UGFF, on May 20 and 27, where I met one official (if I am not mistaken, a member of the Party's federal committee). Our interview was interrupted constantly by phone calls: "Well,

well! It's going well; so much the better! Fine!" Then, like Marshal MacMahon,* "So you are *le nègre!* Bravo! Keep it up!" But when, by chance, someone seemed to be asking for advice, he took refuge in the pretext of democracy: "That's up to you; you'll have to examine the situation. I can't decide for you." Democracy, or irresponsibility?

I should add that we never saw the comrade in question, or any other member of the CGT committee of government employees, during the entire strike. Not a single bit of information was furnished us voluntarily about the administrations on strike.

Better still, comrades! The day after de Gaulle's speech, on May 31, the general assembly of our strike having decided to call on the personnel of other ministries to strengthen the movement and follow our example, we distributed leaflets at the doors of the Ministry of Industry and the Ministry of Agriculture, which the UGFF told us had not been affected by the movement. Imagine our surprise when we learned that Agriculture had been on strike ever since the preceding Friday!

One last fact. As you know, comrades, important things happened on May 27. In the morning the union national headquarters ended negotiations with Pompidou, while Renault and Citroën decided, in spite of everything, to continue the strike. Now I would like to read you the paper we picked up at the main office of the CGT government workers. It is dated May 28 and entitled "Report on the events of May 27." You heard, comrades: "report on the events." And here is how it starts:

The most essential feature of this day was the meeting of the Confederal Administrative Commission, which was open to General Secretaries of the Federation.

The "most *essential* feature," you understand, was that! We are reminded of Louis XVI: "July 14th—Nothing."

I shall hold this document at the disposal of the Party leaders.

A last point on the subject of the state of mind in the Party. As regards comrade Besse's declaration, addressed a little while ago to comrade Leclerc,[24] who was speaking to us about the movement of the Nanterre students and the influence of the "groupuscules": "How many students were backing them? How many people did they represent?" And while comrade Besse was saying this, I suddenly recalled

* *Translator's note: Versaillais* commander during the 1871 Paris Commune. Reviewing the cadets at St. Cyr, where the star pupil was dubbed *le nègre* (or drudge), the Marshal greeted the first in line with, "So you're *le nègre.* Bravo! Keep it up." In the telling the star pupil became a black man and the Marshal a butt of ridicule.

those identical words being spoken three days earlier by the personnel director speaking to a delegation of strikers at the Ministry. He, too, had asked us, "How many people do you represent?"

Without consulting each other, we had answered him about as follows: "The important thing is not to know how many of us are on strike, nor in the name of how many people we speak. The important thing is to understand *what* we represent and *the meaning* of our movement." The way comrade Besse reasons seems to me to be characteristic of a narrowness of mind and thought that is extremely harmful to our Party. To me it is distressing to hear the same words from a comrade at the head office, and from the personnel director of a place that's on strike.

These few facts, among many others, seem to me to be symptomatic: the state of mind that they denote is in effect included in the Party's strategy. They are isolated facts, separated from their context and in some ways distorted, but they correspond to the Party line and to its general attitude during the events: they are the anecdotal and individualized expression of the political line.[25]

—J. Durand.

The Cadres

Another amazing phenomenon was the use of student terminology by the cadres, those in the most modern types of enterprises as well as those in the *Institut National de Statistique* and in the Ministries.[26] Their language was all the more remarkable in that it contrasted sharply with the demand for a graduated salary increase that the CGC succeeded in getting accepted. A stand at the Sorbonne was manned by "contesting cadres," one of whose leaflets follows. The one put out by the CFDT cadres from the chemical industries is very characteristic of the strong current set in motion by the students.[27]

Document 224

Manifesto!

For a good number of cadres the student movement has given rise to a new analysis of their mission in enterprise and of the final goal of the consumer society which, whether consciously or unconsciously, they are helping to build.

For these cadres the student movement represents a fundamental questioning of the nature of our society, and the verbal excesses this contestation may have given rise to only express the magnitude of the problem posed.

The cadres believe that they have an important role to play in order to contribute to formulating the bases and structures of a society which would make men into something else besides mere consumers.

Such a revolution involves:

1. Organization of an original industrial society, that will transcend those that are generally proposed, whether of the American or the Soviet type. It will have as its fundamental characteristic the fact of having been built for and by the wage earners who constitute its driving force.

2. Organization of concrete solutions for democratization of the government, of enterprise, and of general economic orientations. Development of the personality, both in work and in leisure, should be added to the usual objectives of profitability and expansion—the material fruits of which are real.

For a short term period—to the same degree as in society—questioning of union and political organizations, traditionally in charge of defending and expressing the aspirations of the wage earners, is essential.

Aware that the battle being waged at the University cannot be ended without extending the movement to all economic sectors, the "C. 4" proposes:

—to participate with the students in recasting both methods and structures for training;

—to introduce analysis and action inside professional circles.

—The Committee for Coordination of the Contesting Cadres "C. 4,"
May 20, 1968 (printed leaflet).

Document 225

At Last, Fresh Air!

The movement launched by the students permits us all to fill our lungs with a breath of freedom to which we were no longer accustomed.

The impossibility of obtaining satisfaction for grievances oriented toward the future, the repeated refusal on the part of the employers in reply to requests for negotiations, and the scornful attitude of the political authorities toward union organizations had created an increasingly heavy atmosphere, accompanied by mounting pressure.

Under these conditions it is not surprising that there should be a strong wind blowing; but this should not upset us; we should even be glad of it.

The student movement is above all an extraordinary demonstration of good health that people had ceased to believe in, but which everybody senses.

Engineers and junior executives are particularly sensitive to this because they have a rather natural solidarity with the students, but also because democratization of the University awakens in them not only memories but also a deep feeling of envy as regards their present situation.

Over and above satisfaction of immediate needs, complete dissatisfaction is spontaneously or progressively surfacing, however deeply buried it may have been. This dissatisfaction concerns advancement, participation in collective creation, a sense of team work, awareness of a situation that is common to all workers, the desire to be informed, and to participate in decisions. . . .

CFDT engineers and junior executives propose the following lines for analysis and action.

UNION FREEDOM IN ENTERPRISE

Engineers and junior executives must be able to unionize without having to fear measures of intimidation.

This implies that the unions must be recognized in enterprise and that they should be able to organize practically in such a way as to fulfill their tasks of information, representation, and defense of the workers.

This organization includes the right of assembly, the right to distribute union information and publications, the right to collect dues, free exercise of duties for elected representatives, and free exercise of the right to strike.

Collective action and worker solidarity must have these rights recognized and respected.

DEMOCRATIZATION IN ENTERPRISE

All legislative, executive, and judiciary powers are in the hands of Administrative Councils and of their representatives who, within the framework of present structures, are not required to give an accounting to anyone.

We do not confuse enterprise management and policy making.

But we do assert that if decisions are the domain of the executives, the right of wage earners to participate in their making and supervision must be recognized.

For this purpose the rights of worker councils and of elected representatives must be broadened.

All workers, engineers, and junior executives know better than anyone else that the information now given to the worker councils does not allow them to act effectively.

We refuse to lead rear-guard combats with disappointing results; we want to control our future.

Like the students in their *facultés,* and the students at *Polytechnique,* who are not afraid to violate military orders, engineers and junior executives must discuss the problems both inside and outside their enterprises, and develop, in liaison with other categories of workers and with union organizations, the exact demands that can satisfy the need for liberation that people feel today.

—UNICIC (*Union Nationale des Ingénieurs et Cadres des Industries Chimiques* CFDT [about May 20, 1968].

From Posters to Analysis of City Planning:
The Beaux-Arts

During the night of May 20–21, contesting architects occupied the premises of the *Ordre des Architectes.* The only thing that made such a move possible was the fact that since May 8 the *Ecole Nationale des Beaux-Arts* had been on strike. In Paris, Lyons, and Marseilles the strike had assumed a dual aspect. It was first marked by the creation of people's workshops, mentioned in a document put out in Paris five days before the *Ecole* was closed by the police; at the same time, it was characterized by thoughtful analysis of the role of architects and city planners in contemporary society ("No, to city slums. No, to slum cities," declared one leaflet that was circulated at the Sorbonne[28]), and by what should be its action in a different type of society. This is evident both in the manifesto put out by the Paris strike committee, and in the project proposed by architectural students in Lyons, who also occupied the premises of their Order and took over the terms of a text from Paris.

Document 226

Origin, Development, Structures, and Prospects

*of the strike at the ex-*Ecole Nationale
Supérieure des Beaux-Arts *in Paris*

ORIGIN

The strike was started by the section unions of the UNEF and of the
SNESup., of the ENSBA following the events of May 3, 4, 5, and 6 in
answer to the call sent out by the UNEF and the SNESup. for the satisfaction of the three UNEF points:

Free our comrades!

Withdraw the cops from the Latin Quarter!

Open the Sorbonne!

It was at the same time a manifestation of the profound malaise
that existed at the school. For a long time it had been evident that both
content and structures of teaching were completely outmoded. The
school had to be adjusted and integrated into a precise social-economic
circuit. Reform was imperative. They proposed that we participate in
its drafting and open a "fruitful and constructive" dialogue. So-called
co-equal commissions (students, teachers, professionals, and administrators) were set up, but we soon saw that this was actually a measure
of caution, not participation.

There is no participation without unity.

There is no unity around contradictory interests.

There was a rapid split between

—those who were defending existing interests and authorities;

—the administrators and employers, who refused to go beyond
the framework of a mini-reform that would increase their class
privileges;

—and those who, in the context of the teaching problem, posed
the problem of completely reconsidering all concepts which, directly or indirectly, could concern construction in general.

*On the one hand there is the intention of strengthening the pres-
ent socio-economic system*

—by adjusting the number of architects to the needs of big capital, as defined in the Fifth Plan;

—by keeping the present hierarchy of architects: a few "geniuses"
(*prix de Rome,* public buildings, etc.) and an army of obedient
hacks and technicians carrying out the designs of their teachers;

—by increasing social segregation in teaching (hierarchization of diplomas);

—by increasing centralization—division into national and regional schools.

On the other hand there is radical questioning of the objective role of the architect in a capitalist society, and even of the concept of architecture.

We think that the objective role of the architect in a capitalist society is to decide the architectonic setting for an oppressive structure. For us the expression "watchdog of the bourgeoisie" is not an empty phrase. Architects who have worked on so-called "low income" housing, who have awarded contracts to the lowest bidders, who reduce the habitable surface in order to lower the ceiling price; or the urbanists who, by zoning, have increased social segregation, know this is true. In the same way that *lycée* pupils in their barrack-*lycées* and patients in prison-hospitals know it.

We are asking ourselves questions
What is architecture?

Is it an abstract idea, an eternal, timeless value? Or is it the definite expression of a given period which corresponds to a social-economic reality?

Who will carry it out?

A small number of specialists invested with enormous powers, or all those who are concerned: the technicians and the people who use it?

Whom does it work for?

Does it work for private interests to ensure the maximum yield, or for the largest number of users?

We want to pose the problem of architecture in terms of class struggle. Architecture is not of itself revolutionary (whatever some people may say to clear their consciences). On the contrary, it is a factor for alienation and oppression. All attempts to solve social problems through regulation of the height of buildings and skillful distribution of green space are merely superficial and ineffectual remedies since they do not attack the causes but try to enhance the effects.

Adoption of these principles has given our action and our strike a clearly political character, if by "political" we understand a determination to change the structures established by the society in which we live.

DEVELOPMENT

One of our first decisions has been to close the *Ecole des Beaux-Arts* in order to extend discussions to everybody who is, or may be, concerned with construction, builders as well as users.

Action has taken place on two levels
  —on the level of teaching and of the profession;
  —on the level of the class struggle.

At the University, in order to achieve a real liaison at the grass roots with all those who participate in construction planning (sociologists, economists, engineers, students, and teachers).

In the architectural profession, for a profound transformation:
  —by demanding the abolition of such feudal structures as the Order of Architects;
  —by denouncing all forms of corporatism and all attempts to present the movement as such. We are consequently opposed to the action of unions and special interest architectural groups who follow this policy for defense of privileges, most often to the detriment of the general interest, and, in particular, we oppose the *Syndicat des Architectes de la Seine* (SAS), which is trying to pursue this corporate policy, even inside the strike;
  —by denouncing the economic structures based on forced speculation and the search for maximum profit, that define the framework of present-day urbanism, in which the organisms for national planning and urbanization are totally, or in part, financed by commercial banks. At present an architect has the choice between being a thief (i.e., becoming the head of an agency—that is, a financial shark in search of new business), or being robbed (being a good "nigger," meaning draftsman in an agency—that is, letting himself be exploited by the big shots).

We have wanted our movement to participate in the reality of the class struggle and, with this aim in view, have created "action committees" whose role it is to set up genuine contacts with the combatant workers, in all forms of this struggle. Just now this action is developing among the strikers, the workers, the immigrants in the shanty towns, and among neighborhood action committees, in the form of strengthening liaison, financial aid, and contributions to self-defense. . . .

One of the forms of this action that ties in with possibilities for art school students is the creation of a people's atelier in which, with slogans furnished by the workers, we make and distribute posters. These posters, made collectively with no "big names," try to show what a popular art can be—that is, an art that is at the service of the people.

STRUCTURES

We refuse the old structures, as well as traditional parties and parliamentarianism, because they are based on the principle of delegation of power and abandonment of responsibilities for the benefit of a few they call leaders.

We are trying to evolve structures in which it would be possible for everybody to express himself and feel responsible for the movement as a whole; in which, too, the division of work would be reduced to a strict minimum, being neither hierarchized nor rigid. This means creating an *awareness* of all the problems we have enumerated. Awareness is the only guarantee of the development of our movement. But this awareness appears progressively, in stages, and can only be affirmed and developed through personal commitment in the concrete political actions that correspond to these different stages.

The structures that we have set up are not institutionalized and seem for the moment to best correspond to the objectives we have set ourselves.

The general assembly alone possesses the power of decision. It ratifies the results of the work of the commissions. Political orientation is discussed in the general assemblies.

The commissions meet to discuss a precise problem. There is no set division, so that each person can participate in the commissions that interest him.

These commissions have considered the following themes, among others:

—de-feudalization of the profession;
—economic structures of the construction sphere;
—student struggles and worker struggles;
—the objective role of the ENSBA.

The committee for action and information is responsible for liaison with the outside and it publicizes the strike in all the building trades.

The coordination committee supervises the entire strike and takes no decisions except those concerning the security of the strikers. It tries to instigate discussion, to prolong the movement, and also to define the political line as it emerges from the general assemblies and from the work commissions.

PROSPECTS

We are only a supplementary force, the principal front being that of the workers. They alone can radically change the balance of power,

which is determinant if our movement is to succeed. On our own terrain we will pursue the struggle as far as possible.

  Our immediate objectives are:
      —repeal of the 1962 prescriptive decree, which defines reform of
          architectural studies and is the equivalent of the Fouchet Plan;
      —attachment to the University.

But we do not expect to stop there. We must create an irreversible situation both inside the school and in the profession. We shall do
all in our power to destroy the old structures. The Order must disappear,
and the big shots who run the school as well as the profession must
resign. We will not permit introduction of reforms that would try to
adapt teaching to the needs of a society which we reject. We refuse all
reforms that would leave intact the fundamental structures of capitalist
society, i.e., relationships between production and ideological lines (su-
periority of intellectual work over manual work; theories about Art,
Taste, and Beauty).

  Our movement will develop in two directions:
      —it will be strengthened at school and in the University through
          abolition of archaic structures as well as of reformist attempts.
          We can only construct if the existent edifices are demolished
          and the ground is cleared;
      —there will be outward-oriented expansion through efforts to
          achieve a real grass roots junction with all the workers, whether
          in the building sector or in others.

                                          —Strike Committee, June 10, 1968.

Document 227

Architecture and City Planning

First of all, the objectives:
According to the provisions of the National Planning Commission
(*Commission Nationale d'Aménagement du Territoire,* CNAT) in 1985
the urban population of France will constitute 73 percent of the total
population which, at the same date, is foreseen as being 80 million inhabitants. It is the conclusion of the commission members that in order
to cope with this growth, if we do not want to see the population of
the Paris region more than doubled before the end of the century
(which would bring national planning to a critical threshold) all the
other French cities should be more than doubled—even tripled—in or-

der to achieve an urban "balance." This gives an idea of the dimensions of the problems that will arise during the years ahead.

We should immediately start to consider by what means we can attain these goals. And the government will not contradict us, even though we do question its methods for dealing with the problem that its own figures pose, if we use these same figures, even to claim that we have reached a dramatic situation in the organization of urban centers.

"City planning should no longer be conceived as planning for private interests, but as overall organization of the activity of the entire population."

"City planning is not planning for roads and systems constructed at community expense for the use of a few private housing projects having a potential of profit from the homes to be built and sold."

"The aim of city planning is to provide dwellings and the necessary installations for their inhabitants, under the best conditions for occupation of a site. In addition it organizes relationships between their different activities through means of good communications." City planning must constitute the framework, the driving and directing force behind all construction plans.

In point of fact, at the end of the last war when the problem of reconstruction was posed, the capitalist government turned over almost this entire field of activity to private enterprise, only assuming its own responsibilities through ineffectual regulations, since by virtue of its very principle it had to recognize its powerlessness in this matter. Regarding the portion of the building obligations that devolved upon it, it could therefore do nothing beyond continuing the game it had inaugurated, and act like any other promoter.

Seeing a free field for its speculations, private enterprise began to organize. In order to cover up its intrigues it established contact with, among others, a corporative organism that had sprung up under the Vichy regime (Law of December 31, 1940): *l'Ordre des Architectes.*

The latter, in order to attain the goals that were set for it, had first of all to establish its authority. It therefore had itself recognized by law: the Decree of October 18, 1945. And Article 2 of the professional regulations states that "any person who is not registered as a member of the Order, if he is of French nationality or, if of foreign nationality, who uses the title or practices the profession of architect in France without having been authorized to do so under the conditions prescribed by law, is subject to legal action, including the penal sanctions laid down in existing legislation, for illegal appropriation and use of a state-regulated professional title." Moreover, Article 54 declares that:

"The Order is responsible for the honor, morale, and interests of the Order, and is the only spokesman for architects in meetings with government authorities."

Having thus taken over the profession it provided its own moral guarantee by defining itself as follows:

"The Supreme Council of the Order maintains discipline within the Order and generally sees to it that the laws and regulations that govern it are respected. For this purpose it gives all necessary instructions to the regional Councils. In order for it to be able to exercise these prerogatives it has the right of permanent and direct control over all the activities and functioning of regional Councils, as well as over all the organisms created in application of Articles 29 and 30 which interest the entire Order."

It then completed its apparatus by infiltrating the administrative mechanism through a series of commissions that would carry out its projects by means of opinions calling for good taste and an artistic sense.

Finally, by holding exclusive rights to professional activity, it put constraints on all architects to defer to its view through application of ten-year contracts and mutual insurance policies.

With these structures as point of departure the architects' offices, which were do-it-yourself type private drafting rooms, became the only practicable form to be given legal recognition for exercising this so-called liberal profession. Being subsidized by private capital as well, they ended by dominating city planning and guaranteeing its tutelage through financially ridiculous government contracts on the model set up by the Order with government representatives.

Due to this fact, projects for city planning had become the prerogative of big agencies, serving them as a means for prospecting land and creating good "sells" that they later put into the hands of their investment promoters.

For anyone who was not otherwise subsidized, city planning had become financial suicide. But with the ever increasing needs and the impossibility for promoters to face them, the scandal became too evident. So for these people there were substituted banking and monopoly trusts, who thus far had operated through intermediaries in an attempt to make people believe in the existence of a more powerful and coherent organization.

And yet the methods remain the same; and real estate remains sacred, hampering any sort of coherent organization of urban centers.

A plan for land occupation has just completed the series of plans concerning building density that are trying to control the reaction of private enterprise to the lack of government investment in general construction promotion. So the problem stands just as it was before.

As a consequence, research in the realm of urban organization remains doomed to failure.

The practice of architecture and of city planning has become the privilege of an increasingly restricted number of architects; while at the same time schools of architecture are flooding the labor market with an increasing number of young graduates, an increasing number of architects are finding themselves relegated to the position of what they call "nigger."

As usual in the traditionally and scientifically disorganized wage earning class, it's the ones who do the work who pay—draftsmen, technical contractors, etc. Faced with the evolution of these problems, architects' unions were created and have been trying to organize our profession, but they have come up against the Order-dictated code of ethics and have not yet succeeded in obtaining satisfaction of their grievances.

We consequently note that the Order of Architects is an obstacle to the organization of our activities in the field of construction, and we contest the claim to represent all architects that the Order has arrogated to itself.

We urge the government to set up valid conditions for analysis and discussion in order to create new structures in the framework of which we will be able to pursue our training and carry on our activities.

With this as point of departure it will perhaps be possible to suggest forms of organization that synthesize the disciplines concerned by the problems of planning and construction, and to pose the problems as they should be posed and find valid solutions to them. In this way the context in which a method of architectural training might be found will be defined.

Lastly, we encourage all employees in architectural offices and drafting rooms to organize inside the unions.

We declare the Order dissolved and demand occupation of its premises,

[Paris, May 20].

PLATFORM OF AGREEMENT

The undersigned architects and students, being determined to make a thorough examination of the situation, declare that they are in agreement on the following points.

1. They will undertake to examine objectively and without an

employer-dictated a priori viewpoint the exact position of the function of architect in the present process of planning and producing built-up areas.

2. Considering that architecture, which is a public service, must satisfy the needs of society, the fundamental objective will be to find a way of limiting, then of abolishing, the all but absolute control that financial power through its economic system now exerts over the planning and producing of built-up areas.

3. They look forward to concrete and concerted action, effectively aimed at destroying the control that "monopoly" power exerts over architects with the sole aim of satisfying its own interests. This determination must not take the form of maintaining or creating corporative bodies whose formal ethics would only result in hiding reality. It will therefore be necessary to join together within organisms that have given up defense of a badly defined title in order to formulate precise objectives and grievances.

4. Lastly, considering the fact that their role in the process of planning and producing built-up areas and the weakness of their numbers does not allow architects to look forward realistically to an isolated action, it would be advisable, without excluding anyone, to depend upon the social and professional categories that, because of their contesting position, are the only ones who are able effectively to combat the monopolies.

> *In solidarity with the movement of general contestation, the students of architecture in the Lyons region, calling into question the value of their professional organization, have occupied the premises of the Order of Architects, asked for its dissolution, and signed the above platform of agreement of May 27* AS A BASIS FOR ANALYSIS AND ACTION.

—Lyons, May 27, 1968.

Everywhere

Managers of popular-priced theaters and Cultural Centers seriously reflecting on the "non-public," the old and disabled reminding us that they too are human beings, Paris priests finding in the Gospels a criticism of the consumer society, and even a consumer group inviting its members to become more aware, doctors analyzing the repressive role of medicine, with allowances for imitation, for habitual cranks (anti-vaccination fanatics, or the psychiatrists who wanted to liberate the inmates of the Sainte-Anne Asylum, and who only backed down when they were reminded that their patients risked not having a roof over their heads), everywhere, or almost everywhere,[29] one and the same form of discourse, the discourse of the student revolution.

Document 228

Directors of People's Theaters and Cultural Centers

meeting in a permanent committee at Villeurbanne, May 25, 1968, declare:
Until recently, culture in France was hardly questioned by the non-cultivated except in the form of an indifference as regards which the cultivated themselves felt little concerned. Here and there however a certain disquiet did appear; certain efforts were made with the desire to get out of the rut, to break with the reassuring belief in a more equitable distribution of the cultural heritage. Because simple "circulation" of works of art, even embellished with a little life, already seemed more and more incapable of bringing about an actual encounter between these works and the large numbers of men and women who persisted in surviving inside our society, but who in many respects remained excluded from it, forced to participate in it by producing material goods but deprived of the means of contributing to the very orientation of its general development. In fact, the break continually worsened between the one side and the other, between the ones who were excluded and those of us who, whether willingly or not, were daily becoming more and more the accomplices of their exclusion.

All at once the student revolt and the workers' strike came to throw a particularly harsh light on this familiar and more or less accepted situation. What some of us had glimpsed without wanting really to dwell on has now become evident to everybody; the rape of events has put an end to the uncertainties of our fragile considerations. We know it now and no one cannot know it any longer: the cultural gap is deep; it covers at the same time an economic-social gap and a gap between generations. In both cases, on the level that concerns us, it is our own attitude toward culture which is being challenged in the most radical way. Whatever the purity of our intentions, this attitude appears to a considerable number of our fellow citizens as an option

made by the privileged in favor of a hereditary, separatist culture—
that is, quite simply, bourgeois.

On the one side is the "public"—our public—and little does it
matter if, according to the case, it is real or potential (that is, capable
of being made real at the cost of supplementary efforts concerning the
price of seats or the size of the publicity budget); and then there is, on
the other side, a "non-public": a vast human expanse composed of all
those who have not yet had any access—or any chance of access in the
near future—to the cultural phenomenon in the forms it persists in
assuming in almost all cases.

On parallel lines there is a more and more rigid official teaching,
which no longer opens any prospects of culture in any direction whatsoever; and there is a growing number of young people who refuse to
integrate into a society that is so little apt to furnish them within its
confines the slightest chance of becoming real adults.

The very function assigned to us forces us to consider ourselves
responsible on these two levels with regard to a situation we certainly
did not want, which we have often denounced, but which it behooves
us in any case to undertake rapidly to transform by using every means
compatible with our mission.

But even the first of these means, the one from which the use of
all the others derives, depends only on us: only a radical attitude can
oppose with any chance for success this radical dead end in which culture finds itself today. We must frankly and clearly substitute for the
traditional conceptions (of which we had been until now more or less
victims, at least at first) an entirely different conception, one that
does not a priori refer to a given pre-existent content but which expects, merely from contacts between men, a progressive definition of
content that they could *recognize*.

Because it is now entirely clear that no definition of culture will
be valid or have meaning other than at the price of seeming useful to
the interested parties themselves—that is to say, to the exact degree in
which the "non-public" will be able to find in it the tool it needs. And
what we can already consider sure is that culture should consequently
furnish this "non-public" with—among other things—the means of
breaking down its present isolation, of escaping from its ghetto, by
becoming more and more consciously a part of the social and historical
context, and continuing to free itself from the mystifications of every
kind that tend to make it an unwitting accomplice of the real situations that are inflicted upon it.

This is why any effort of a cultural nature will seem vain to us as long as it does not specifically propose to be an undertaking for *politicization:* that is to say, it must keep inventing for this non-public opportunities for politicizing *itself,* for freely choosing itself, over and above the feeling of powerlessness and absurdity that is being constantly aroused in it by a social system in which men are practically never in a position to invent *together* their own humanity.

This is why we deliberately refuse any concept of culture that makes it into an object of mere transmission. Not that we consider as nil or in itself questionable this heritage without which today we would perhaps not be able to bring ourselves to the point of radical contestation; but because we can no longer ignore the fact that for the very great majority of our contemporaries, access to this heritage entails a re-examination which must above all enable them to confront and more and more effectively live in a world that in any case has not the slightest chance of becoming humanized without them.

Beyond the people we have already reached, it is with this majority that our various undertakings must allow us to establish contact, and this urgency must decisively influence our overall action. If the word "culture" can still be taken seriously, it is to the extent that it implies a demand for an effective intercession that would tend to change existing relationships between men and, consequently, for an active, step-by-step investigation that would reach everybody; in other words, an authentic *cultural action.*

We are neither students nor workers, and we have no power of numerical pressure. The only conceivable justification of our public existence, and of our demands, resides in the very specificity of this function of bringing people together, and in the present light to be shed on the social context in which we must perform it. But such a function would be immediately doomed to remain unperformable if it were refused the means to assert its creativity in all the domains that are within its scope. To speak of an active culture is to speak of a permanent culture; it is recalling the actual resources of an art in continuous creation. And the theater, in this respect, immediately appears as a particularly effective form of expression, among all possible forms of expression, in that it is a collective human endeavor proposed to the community of men.

This is why we wish to assert, in the name of the very principle of our various undertakings, the necessity for a close correlation between theatrical creation and cultural action. Because without doubt the former needs the latter in order to be able to make an increasingly genuine appeal to this human community it has in view. Yet the latter also needs the former insofar as a certain dramatization, or non-mystifying "theatricalization" of the contradictions that haunt mankind, can further considerably an awareness of them within a given society.

We therefore undertake to conserve under all circumstances this dialectical tie between theatrical (or more generally artistic) action and cultural action in order that their respective needs should continue to enrich each other mutually, even to the very contradictions that will not fail to arise between them.

From now on this is the sole basis upon which we can look forward to pursuit of our efforts. There remains however the fact that the modalities for application of this fundamental orientation will have to be defined in close liaison with the interested parties themselves; that is to say, on the one hand with the members of our respective companies, and on the other with different sectors of the public: the "nonpublic" (through relays of all kinds which by degrees would give us access to it), the students, and the already existing public.

At this degree of discernment to which we are now forced, under pressure from the most dynamic sectors of the community, it would be scandalous if on the very level of our so-called "cultural" activities, culture itself should be unable to recover the power of positive contestation that has always been the sign of its vitality.

In the name of all of us we must now demand the means to wield this power if we do not want to be forced to betray or abandon the very cause that has been officially entrusted to us.

—Excerpt from *Art et Révolution*, a *roneotype* pamphlet
published in Lyons.

Document 229

There are many priests who would like to share with other men their daily preoccupations and express in their midst all the ties that they discover between life and the Gospel. This was true before Vatican II, but since then the urge has become still greater. Present events have led the undersigned priests (who speak only for themselves) to make known publicly the essential features of their thinking. They believe that by so doing they concur with what was expressed by Father Marty [Archbishop of Paris] in his letter to the clergy on May 22.

In solidarity with the people in our neighborhoods, and by accepting to be challenged by them as priests, we believe that at a time when a fresh wind is blowing across our country we cannot remain silent.

An entire paternalistic and authoritarian concept of politics, the economy, and the University is now being questioned. We know that the Church does not escape this criticism. We contest today, in every domain, the way our thoughts and decisions are made for us.

Being in contact with working class families, students, militants from many horizons, believers or non-believers, who appear to us to represent the world's conscience, the profound conviction that we could not be the priests of a people otherwise than by really sharing their hopes, their failures, their hunger for justice, and their desire for freedom and responsibility, has little by little taken form in us.

We can no longer speak a language that at once spares all and sundry and yet allows all and sundry to recognize and justify themselves in it.

Consequently, in the present crisis and whatever the provisional political issues that will be invested tomorrow, we state without ambiguity that we wish to stand in complete solidarity with the contestation of a world in which man is sacrificed to profit and money in a capitalist system. This contestation is not a request for a few appeasing reforms but the radical questioning of a way of life among men.

We declare:

—that a society in which man is considered to be merely a force for production or consumption, and in which he himself can be spoken of in such terms as "waste," "manpower supply," or "acceptable percentage" is in absolute contradiction to the message of Jesus Christ;

—that we do not feel bound to any established power and that we want to retain our freedom with respect to such power;

—that there can be no solution that is not "political," and on this point we recognize that our way of life has often kept us from justly appraising reality;

—that we do not have to defend any institution or position of force or power;

—that we intend to defend the dignity of each human being and therefore take a stand on concrete situations.

In short, at the very moment when our country is disturbed we approve of this vast movement of solidarity that is getting under way and that seems to us to be more in conformity with the Gospel than an individualistic consumer world.

We strongly hope that this stand may be a call for dialogue and for participation.

—Some Priests in the Paris Area [end of May].

Document 230

The Old and Disabled Also Contest

Will the new society forget no one?
The academics, cadres, office employees, and workers have ceased their activities; they have gone down into the streets, they are occupying the factories, and they are demanding

—improvement of their living standard;

—real participation in the life of the nation, of the locality, and of the place of work;

—respect for their human dignity.

The millions of old and disabled persons represented by the undersigned associations are joining this struggle because they have the same motives for doing so, and they especially want

—the right to education, which is not at this time respected for the disabled;

—the right to work, which only exists in a caricatured form;

—the right to good health, which would imply prevention of disability and would limit its consequences as well as those of old age;

—the right to live, which can only be realized in terms of an income at least equal to the inter-professional guaranteed minimum wage for each disabled person and for each old person.

The young, able person of today will perhaps be the disabled and very probably the old person of tomorrow.

MAKE OUR PROGRAM YOURS

It is humanly and economically in the interest of a well-constituted society.

—General Union of the Blind and Completely Disabled; General Confederation of the Blind, Deaf, Completely Disabled, and Old People,* [May] (printed leaflet).

* *Union générale des aveugles et grands infirmes; Confédération générale des aveugles, sourds, grands infirmes et personnes âgées.*

Document 231

Communiqué
from the Federal Consumers' Union[30]

Faced with the serious criticism being raised here and there against the dangers of a "consumer society," the *Union Fédérale de la Consommation* (UFC) would like to recall the action it has pursued for the last 15 years, to make consumers aware of the part they should play in the economic life of our country.

More than ever the Consumers' Unions have a role to play in order to create a new spirit which alone will permit the serious, long term changes we all desire. The goal sought should be complete development of the individual from both the material and spiritual standpoints.

It would be well, therefore, to elevate the whole population and in particular all the "under-consumers" (jobless, agricultural workers, very large families, the aged, widows, foreign workers, etc.) to a sufficient level of consumption, rather than tend to increase artificially the needs of those who have the means to pay. Thus it is necessary—and this is becoming extremely urgent for the future of our civilization—to begin now to create collective institutions capable of satisfying and even stimulating social and cultural needs that are too often neglected.

All of us should participate in this new spirit: producers, merchants, the government, and consumers. By organizing, consumers will become aware of their rights and their duties and will be able to influence the economic decisions that concern them. The Federal Consumers' Union calls upon all consumers desirous of cooperating in this matter and proposes to examine with them the concrete actions to be carried out on these bases.

—May 27, 1968.

Document 232

Medicine and Repression

It is not an "accident" that has awakened for a time the de-politicized consumer, an accident the cause of which would be police brutality. Police repression cannot be reduced to the "sadism of cops" and the "stupidity" of their chiefs, any more than the student revolt can be reduced to the fanaticism of a few *"enragés"*; and no more in the one case than in the other is it an isolated event, a momentary, inconsequential anomaly of our harmonious civilization.

On the contrary, this civilization is the disguise that permament repression assumes in order to conceal and perpetuate itself; because as a rule this repression has not the obvious shiny appearance of a helmeted gendarme, but of less shocking, more acceptable uniforms, ones that are often even desired, such as a doctor's gown or a professor's cap and gown.

Instead of shedding tears over the wounded (because wounds for us must be the lesson of courage that they provide) we would do better to concern ourselves with Rector Roche's blunders, for instance, which have allowed us to live so intensely that police and University have the same function: to maintain and produce bourgeois order.

The health structure shares with the two preceding structures and a few others (the judiciary, for instance) the role of cementing and filling in the cracks that could appear in our social edifice. This repressive and adapting function of the health structure that we wish to reveal here can be shown at the following three levels.

1. *The sociological distribution of health services.*
A doctor thinks he is the boss when actually he is only the foreman. Permission to "touch" the patient, which he parsimoniously hands out to other health workers, like so many scraps of his "power," is the good mark he confers in payment for the good relations he has with his "subordinates." The limits of these permissions are the interdictions that the doctor issues like so many *diktats,* justification for which he bases on knowledge that is supposed to be deposited in him and solely in him.

Why, for instance, draw the line that limits the competence of the nurses between intramuscular and intravenous injections? Because the doctor owes it to himself to conceal the absence of scientific bases for his "art" and this makes him set up arbitrary distinctions; otherwise this absence of scientific bases would reveal the ideological nature of medical knowledge, and its submission to the ruling—bourgeois—ideology.

As a result of this restraint, which makes it impossible for doctors to radically criticize their methods and aims (that is to say, quite simply, which deprives them of freedom of thought), the ideological system compensates them, contrary to other health workers, by attaching them to the bourgeois class and giving them the illusion of being the only ones to possess therapeutic powers, consequently forcing them to be the guardians of this ideology.

Medical studies bring only fragmentary knowledge: study of the sick body and of the healthy body, amputating men from two essential dimensions which are social man and man subject to desires (excluding the social sciences and partially excluding psychiatry): analyses made in the form not of a critical apprenticeship but of acquisition through memory of a pseudo-science which only finds its substance by means of disordered recourse to concepts taken over from other sciences that lose all coherency in transit.

The importance attached to presence at the hospital, and especially the manner of student integration, are revealing: the student immediately assumes the status of doctor and is even called "Doctor" the first day. From then on he cannot do otherwise than tend towards this mythical image; he is deprived of all possibility of criticism and contestation; nor may he question the kind of relationship he will have with his future "subordinates."

The basic institution of medical studies remains, in any case, *le concours* [a competitive and eliminatory examination], the function of which is to syncretize this acquisition of pseudo-knowledge and mythical status.

3. The modalities by which society assumes responsibility for illness, and the position these modalities confer upon doctors.
Apparently one of the roles of the *Faculté de Médecine* is to prepare students for their real task. With an exclusively biological conception as point of departure, it trains doctors to serve capitalist oppression inasmuch as it forbids them to question illness as such in its social-economic dimensions.

Capitalist society, underneath an apparent neutrality (liberalism, the medical calling, non-militant humanism, etc.), ranks doctors among the repressive forces: they are responsible for keeping people in condition to work and consume (e.g., industrial medicine); they are also responsible for getting people to accept a society that makes them ill (e.g., psychiatrists).

Although the independence of doctors is proclaimed and defended by the *Ordre des Médecins* (which does not say a word when the police oppose giving first aid to the wounded), this independence is extremely reduced because of the fact that doctors are responsible not so much for combatting illness as for taking charge of it by excluding it from social life. Genuine contestation of illness, implying consider-able extension of the idea of prevention, would rapidly become political and revolutionary because it would be contesting an inhibiting, repres-sive society.

—National Center of Young Doctors [*Centre national des jeunes médecins*], about May 12, 1968.

Notes

1. La Brèche, p. 71.
2. For documents on this affair, cf. *Les Lettres Nouvelles*, Sept.–Oct. 1968, pp. 149–158.
3. *Libérez l'*ORTF, 1968, J. P. Manel and A. Planel, *La crise de l'*ORTF; R. Louis, *l'*ORTF *un combat.*
4. It is also intentionally that we have left untouched the complex problem of the peasants during the May Revolution. Not having collected the necessary docu-mentation, the action of elementary school teachers has also been almost entirely neglected; see below, however, pp. 541 ff.; on the occupation of a public nursery school, see *Au joli mai*, No. 1, p. 33.
5. A Rouède, *le Lycée impossible*, le Seuil, 1967; see discussion by the same author in *Esprit*, June–July 1968, pp. 1003–1014, and the reply of a woman col-league, *Esprit*, Oct. 1968, pp. 360–364.
6. The CAL movement is the subject of the book *les Lycéens gardent la parole*, le Seuil, collection *"Politique"*; see also discussions and documents published in *Esprit*, Oct. 1968, pp. 346–359, and in *Partisans*, May–June 1968, pp. 219–236; *l'Homme et la Société*, April–May–June 1968, pp. 123–132 (on the *Lycée Pasteur*, in Neuilly); *Projet*, July–August 1968, pp. 780–799; *les Cahiers Pédagogiques*, No. 76, Sept. 1968. The most complete documentation concerning the CALs was published by four of their own moving spirits in *Partisans*, No. 52, Sept.–Oct. 1969. Raymond Aron's assertion (*La Révolution introuvable*, p. 98), which attributes creation of the CALs to the PSU, is unfounded. M. Winock's article in *Esprit*, Nov. 1968, gives a fair account of what happened in an average *lycée*.
7. Cf. above, Chapter VIII, pp. 518–521.
8. *"Considerazioni sui fatti di maggio,"* taken from *les Temps Modernes*, Aug.–Sept. 1969, p. 29. Daniel Singer notes: "Mobilization of the workers was limited to the necessary minimum, to the numbers needed for such indispensable duties as picketing. Workers were allowed to drift home, while those who stayed in the factory were encouraged to play games rather than to indulge in dangerous debates," *Prelude to Revolution*, p. 162.
9. See Daniel Mothé, *Journal d'un ouvrier*, Editions de Minuit, 1958; *Mili-tant chez Renault*, le Seuil, 1965.
10. Apparently the repercussions of the management-type demands were in inverse proportion to the small number of skilled workers. See, for example, the collection of eye-witness accounts in *Des Soviets à Saclay?*, Maspero. But other factors must naturally be considered: the proportion of young workers with respect to older workers, educated workers with respect to illiterate ones, etc.; cf. the case of Renault-Cléon in *Notre arme c'est la grève*.
11. See also Michel Bosquet's report on the Thomson electronic factory in

Bagneux, *Le Nouvel Observateur,* June 7, 1968; a leaflet put out at this factory in J. P. Simon's *La Révolution par elle-même,* pp. 75–76. In pointing out these facts I do not expect to settle the discussion now taking place between sociologists; between those (Serge Mallet or Alain Touraine) who are aware of the existence of a "new working class" capable of applying itself to the problems of management, and those who are struck by the fact that the strike was relatively tougher and longer among the metal workers—that is to say, at the very heart of the "traditional" working class (cf. Gérard Adam, *Revue française de science politique,* February 1970, pp. 105–119).

12. We cannot completely exclude the possibility that this leaflet may have been written by the students, but this seems hardly probable. It is hard to believe, in the atmosphere of working class lyricism that prevailed among the militant students, that the latter would describe the difficulties between the worker and student movements as being the result of a "serious lag" in the worker movement. Could it be a JCR text?

13. A. Glucksmann, *Stratégie et révolution en France 1968;* M. Goldstein's article, "Le parti communiste du 3 mai au 6 juin", *les Temps Modernes,* Nov. 1968, pp. 827–894, is confined to an analysis of *l'Humanité.*

14. *L'Humanité* of May 13. On this evolution cf. J. Ferniot's remarks in *Mort d'une révolution,* pp. 33–46.

15. Waldeck-Rochet, *les Enseignements de mai-juin 1968;* R. Andrieu, *les Communistes et la Révolution;* L. Salini, *Mai des prolétaires,* Editions sociales, 1968.

16. *Anarchistes d'hier et d'aujourd'hui,* Editions sociales, 1968. J. Duclos forgets in fact that Marcel Gitton, who was controlled by the police, was still general secretary of the PC in 1939; or the role of André Baranès, journalist employed by *Libération* [defunct post-war Paris daily] and an agent for Préfet Baylot, until he was shown up in 1954.

17. Cf. the note on p. 24 in the very lavish special number of June–July 1968: "The Paris walls cried out loudly! Sometimes a little too loudly, sometimes beside the point. What the following pages show is not what *Démocratie Nouvelle* thought, but what the walls in Paris said in May." The special number of *La Pensée* (Aug.–Oct.) contained, side by side, a Stalinist article by P. Bourtayre, the lyrical memoirs of R. Jean, and an intelligent analysis of the concept of contestation by J. Colombel.

18. Among whom were E. Bottigelli, J. Bouvier, J. Chesneaux, J. Durand, Doctor Klotz, G. Leclerc, Architect A. Kopp, Maître Matarasso, I. Meyerson, Hélène Parmelin, E. Pignon, J. Pronteau, Madeleine Rebérioux, A. Soboul, Marc Saint-Saëns, and Charles Tillon. One signer of the letter, A. Cullioli, left the Party shortly after, and many more left or were excluded in 1969 and 1970.

19. Cf. the account by Katia D. Kaupp, *le Nouvel Observateur,* June 12–18. These discussions are also mentioned in a somewhat veiled form by Paul Rozenberg in *Vivere in Maggio,* pp. 120–122.

20. P. Juquin later stated his position in an article in *la Nouvelle Critique,* Sept. 1968, pp. 10–14. In it he defends such frankly incoherent ideas as, for instance, that the organization of elections is a victory over de Gaulle (the Party position *before* June 23), but their acceptance is comparable to Brest-Litovsk (a position which is comprehensible only after the defeat). The threat of a working class general strike prevented the government from having tanks go into action during the night of the 10th to 11th! But the best was the following: why did the Nanterre movement "become a mass movement? Isn't this proof that it had been

well oriented?" On the other hand: "the leftist contagion won because it was not well oriented." The University is, undoubtedly, a class University.

21. The meeting in Germany with the generals on May 29.

22. See on this subject *les Cahiers de Mai,* No. 2, July 1–15, 1968.

23. In fact, as J.-P. Vernant shows above, at this date they were already rotting.

24. Guy Leclerc, instructor at Nanterre.

25. J. Durand then gives an analysis of the PCFS strategy which, being very similar to that of J.-P. Vernant, we have omitted.

26. On the "sit-in" strike at the Ministry of Urban Development (May 20–June 8), see the documentation published in *les Cahiers de Mai,* No. 2, July 1–15, 1968, and above pp. 561–566, J. Durand's account.

27. A parallel reaction is to be found in the article by G. Desseigne, national secretary of the *Union des Ingénieurs et Cadres,* CGT, published "independently" in *Le Monde* of May 17. Naturally it would be a mistake to believe that this reaction was unanimous. There is nothing more ambiguous, in fact, than the term "cadre," and Robert Cottave, the General Secretary of the *Fédération Force Ouvrière des cadres* pointed out with justification (*Combat,* January 17, 1968) that "It looks as if, in France, there were now left only three categories of buyers, whether of cars, cosmetics, or any other consumer products that lend themselves to advertising, and they are: young people, women, and cadres." Concerning the activity in May of the "contesting" cadres, faced with the employers and traditional syndicalism, cf. Alfred Willener, Catherine Gajdos, and Georges Benguigui, *Les Cadres en mouvement,* Epi, Paris 1969, pp. 115–194.

28. See also above, Chapter VII, pp. 433–434. Analysis of city planning was one of the premonitory symptoms of the May Revolution. H. Lefebvre devoted a book to these problems: *Le Droit à la ville,* Editions Anthropos, 1968; see also *L'Irruption de Nanterre au sommet,* pp. 106–110, and especially Anatole Kopp, *Ville et Révolution, Architectes et Urbanistes soviétiques des années 20,* Ed. Anthropos, 1967, in which he analyzes revolutionary city planning before Stalinist decadence set in. On the strike at the *Ecole des Beaux-Arts,* see also A. Brocard, *Projet,* July–August 1968, pp. 782–785; Fanny Vallon, *Partisans,* No. 43, July–September 1968, pp. 156–181; and especially M. and R. Fichelet and J. M. Fourcade, *Esprit,* Oct. 1968, pp. 378–389.

The essential points of the motions adopted during the strike, and rather comprehensive documentation concerning the architects, appeared in the supplement to No. 167 (July 1968) of *Architecture-Mouvement-Continuité,* bulletin of the Society of Architects Holders of Government Diplomas.

29. The text by the young doctors is used in the account by R. Viénet, *Enragés et situationnistes,* pp. 295–297. The same collection published, among other documents, a remarkable leaflet, *"Le football aux footballeurs!"* pp. 301–303. The leaflets of the "action committee for revolution in the Church," which demonstrated at St.-Séverin, are published in *Mai 68. La rue dans l'Eglise,* presentation by R. Davezies, drawings by A. Scob, *l'Epi,* pp. 13–14, 36, and 71–72.

30. Association for consumer education, set up on the model of the American Consumers' Leagues.

Postface

This book was started in the early summer of 1968, the elements that compose it having been collected in the heat of the fray. Whatever revisions, changes, or additions made since for the French edition and now for the American edition, whatever the shortcomings[1] noted, it has seemed preferable to leave the essential parts untouched; in particular, the general interpretation given in the introduction remains. Certain of these shortcomings, too, were contained in the very wording of the title: by giving priority to the student movement this was bound to separate it from the worker movement, with which it so ardently desired solidarity and which, alone, gave to the revolt begun in Nanterre the proportions of a world event.[2]

To tell the truth, this ambiguity is at the very heart of all that has been written about May 1968. To be convinced of this one has only to read two recent works of analysis based on these events by Alfred Willener and by Daniel Singer.[3] In the first case, the historical "precedents" for May '68 are identified as Dada, Surrealism, and Free Jazz; while in the second—the author is very conscious, however, of the fact that May '68 did not have, properly speaking, a "model"—the student revolt and the workers' strike belong, nonetheless, in the cycle of bourgeois, then proletarian, revolutions. It is easy to say that these contradictions are not real ones and that it is possible to resolve them "dialectically"; with the facts in hand, this is not so easy. There is no doubt, however, that the May movement really did "embrace all that lies between" (Pascal), and that the themes of "We're on our way" that proclaim "May painters invent a thousand flags for us, flags that will symbolize research, effort, inner revolution, enthusiasm, invention! May musicians and poets compose new songs for us! May people invent new kinds of vacations for this summer, in order not to interrupt the movement"[4] are as representative of the May movement, however aristocratic they may seem, as the call for revolt directed to the factories and the shanty towns.

The dialectics of fight and feast did not oppose students and

591

workers to each other, it traversed the student movement itself. We can even go further. The originality of May '68 lay precisely in the fact that it aroused at the same time the marginal "square pegs," the sub-proletarians etc., as well as the group that is in direct contact with the most modern production apparatus, i.e., workers from the electronic industries, engineers, technicians, and scholars, all seeking a new rationality.

Inside the University one might say that the movement was revolutionary precisely because it succeeded in winning the reformers to its side. For several weeks it seemed that there was no real contradiction between the activity of those who believed in reform and that of the action committees organizing solidarity with the strikers. The revolutionaries readily believed that to carry on a revolution, meant acting as though it had already taken place. Time itself had entirely changed its rhythm and nature,[5] to the very extent that the processes of production and expanded reproduction of capital were interrupted. "May," then, was experienced in the form of the apocalypse, of immediate realization of the phrase "everything is possible," and the transition from feast to resumed production, from revolution to reform (soon followed by reaction), from the spirit of the apocalypse to the spirit of eschatology, could not be otherwise than difficult.

It was all the more so precisely because "May" had taken place, and it served as a more or less mythical reference, as a saga with its heroes and its traitors; because to "start May over again" was to become a permanent endeavor. As the summer of 1970 advanced there was no longer any question of "inventing new kinds of vacations." Alain Geismar, former general secretary of the snesup. and since become the leader of the *Gauche Prolétarienne,* predicted a "hot summer for the rich"; but this "hot summer" only succeeded in having arrested for "willful arson" of a forest in the Var a professor whose only crime was to have a slightly bewildered look.[6] Hundreds of thousands of students took to the streets to shouts of "Free our comrades," when no more than a dozen had been sentenced. Today there are more than a hundred student and worker militants in prison, many of whom have been given heavy sentences by "ordinary" or "extraordinary" tribunals [the latter judge cases involving State security], which at times have included being deprived *for life* of all civil and family rights.

On October 22, 1970, Alain Geismar was given a prison sentence of 18 months that was followed in November by an additional sentence of two years. Despite these facts, however, "events" in the Latin Quarter, beginning with those that took place in late May 1970 after the disbanding of the *Gauche Prolétarienne* and the trial of the first two editors of *La Cause du Peuple* (before J.-P. Sartre assumed editorship) were nothing but a rather pale caricature.

As for solidarity between students and workers, on the organizational level it has never seemed so remote. On March 11, 1969, during a union demonstration in Paris that took place after salary negotiations had broken down, massed CGT security services isolated the demonstrators from the students, whom they turned over to the police for blackjacking. On May 1, 1970, these same security services went a stage further, shouting in rhythm *"les casseurs sont derrière"* [the wreckers are behind us], thereby justifying the law covering "new forms of delinquency" called the "anti-wrecker" law, which the entire Left had voted against in Parliament.

There can be no question here of giving a historical account of the disintegration of the May movement. At the very most, a few essential points of reference may be indicated.[7] At the height of the Nanterre crisis Daniel Cohn-Bendit announced, "From now on, there are no more 'groupuscules'!" In point of fact, as could already be sensed in May, "the sects had been swallowed by the movement. They had not been digested."[8] At the beginning of the 1968 academic year the "microbolchevisms" had re-formed and even the anti-repression fight was unsuccessful in organizing any kind of common action. Certain of these "groupuscules" are purely and simply the same ones that had been disbanded on June 12, 1968. *L'Alliance des jeunes pour le socialisme* (AJS), for instance, is a prolongation of the FER, or the "Communist league," which has become an integral part of one of the "Fourth Internationals" and which succeeded the JCR. Alain Krivine, who was the candidate of this organization in the June 1, 1969, presidential elections, debated very little with any but members of his own party's political board. On this terrain he was bound to be badly beaten by Jacques Duclos. *L'Humanité Rouge* took over from the Stalinist PCMLF, with but momentary success.

The situation is not much brighter on the level of the union organizations. In the SNESUP. leftism lost the majority to the PC as a result of an emergency conference (March 14–16, 1969), which its inner dissensions had made inevitable. Until late 1970, the UNEF was still controlled by the PSU, allied with *l'Humanité Rouge,* in opposition to the AJS and the UNEF *Renouveau* (a front for the UEC), but it had become little more than a rapidly disintegrating ghost organization. On January 10, 1971, the PSU leadership withdrew, after having recognized the vanity of their efforts to make a revolutionary instrument out of a student union. The result is two inimical UNEF's, one controlled by the AJS, and the other by the PCF.

In reality, the only "groupuscule" that stands out at all against the grayness of the neo-Leninists is certainly the *Gauche Prolétarienne* (GP),[9] composed of former members of the UJC(m-l) (which was disbanded and broke up), of militants from the *22 mars,* and even of a few members of the JCR who did not accept membership in the "Fourth International." The GP, known at first under the name of "Mao-Spontex," has kept student radicalism alive at the cost of absurd violence, particularly in the universities, and also at the cost of such confusion as is rarely seen and that would need to be analyzed if it is true, to quote Barrington Moore Jr., that ". . . whatever else academic intellectuals do, they should not spread myths."[10]

The GP militants have the following rather unusual peculiarity: since they believe what they say (one should perhaps say that they are *believers* in the sense that this word has for the Russian *Raskolniki*), they really do put it into practice. Some of them being from "upper bourgeois" families, to a point that would delight the Communist leader Georges Marchais (it is true, however, that the sons and daughters of militant Communists are as numerous in the GP as those of upper bourgeois families), they have actually broken with their own milieux and have frequently taken factory jobs. They have inherited from the *Mouvement du 22 mars* their loose structures—in reality not Leninist—and a preference for spectacular, symbolic actions, the most typical of which were distribution in the spring of 1970 of free subway rides to workers in protest against a price increase, or "pillaging" the luxury grocery, Fauchon, for the benefit of immigrant workers in the shanty towns.

Whereas the UJC(m-l) marched in May '68 to shouts of "support class struggle; long live the CGT" and formed groups of "proletarian unionists," the GP, in the name of anti-authoritarianism, made sharp criticism of "the little bosses," of everything in the factories that represents a fraction of employer power, including occasionally representatives of the union apparatus, who are considered to be undercover agents of this power. What is perhaps most characteristic of the GP is its language, at least as it appears in *La Cause du Peuple;* a language that is intended to be entirely plain and concrete, at the same time that it is "ideologized," and which by straining its effects the way Hébert's *Père Duchesne* did during the French Revolution actually does reproduce proletarian and sub-proletarian speech. It would not be hard to find in *La Cause du Peuple* the equivalent of the language of the Black Panthers, which is the same as that of the students at Columbia with its "porkmobiles," "pigs," and "motherfuckers."

This language gives evidence of actual presence in the factories and is a very concrete, practical condemnation of the most violent forms of exploitation and humiliation, among them the "fiendish work rhythms" that are forced upon the workers. There remains the fact that whenever it is a question of political action, the language of the GP becomes entirely metaphorical. Mentally identifying themselves with the working people to the point of headlining quite seriously one day: "Toulouse: the Maoists are the masses,"[11] members of the GP define themselves as "new partisans," or "new resistants"[12] combatting a new occupation—employer and bourgeois authority being likened to that of the Nazi "occupant." The "Maoism" of the GP militants (the "Maos," as they call themselves) poses a difficult question, for it is very different from the frankly neo-Stalinist Maoism of *l'Humanité Rouge*. *La Cause du peuple* prints few Peking communiqués, hardly mentions "Mao Tse-tung's thought," and Stalin is a "controversial question" among GP militants. Their Maoism is naturally not that of the old Chinese Communist party, but of the "great proletarian cultural revolution."

To the extent that this has brought the ideology to a chemically pure state, and that there exists in Mao Tse-tung's thought a "tendency to define subjectively the class nature of individuals and organizations," which is evident in the very name, Great Proletarian Cultural Revolution, because this revolution is only proletarian in the sense that all who support Chairman Mao and apply his thought are considered to be ipso facto proletarians;[13] to this extent, the heritage could be legitimate.

Over and above the special case of the GP, a general observation should be made with regard to the irrationalism shown by a large part of the student movement.

Irrationalism carried to this point bears witness to a social crisis that is in reality very serious, even though its representatives are only a small minority. And to the same extent that rationality is identified and identifiable with the forces of oppression,[14] those who want to be free are led to become in reality the bearers of myth and the irrational, to consider themselves as being the new barbarians. It was like that in the Eighteenth Century when Rousseau set nature *against* civilization. The risks that this attitude involves are only too evident,[15] but the really guilty ones are those who mistake reason for reality, and reality for the existing social order.

Needless to say, in the situation to which the French student movement has been reduced, collective actions other than in the "group-uscule" context, have been very rare, the only example that can be cited being the resistance of the Nanterre students, in early March 1970, to "banalization" of the campuses; that is, to allowing the police to have access to University grounds, if not to the buildings.[16]

One is struck by the fact that the war in Vietnam, which before 1968 had been an essential rallying point, has been almost entirely neglected since. Even the American aggression in Cambodia and the huge student demonstrations that followed provoked no violent reactions in France, and the Communist Party, with its peaceful demonstrations, has practically regained leadership of opposition to the war in Vietnam.[17] Of course to some extent the official policy of repression is responsible for this inaction, and those who have tried to do something have often ended in the detention center at the former Beaujon Hospital. But however well organized the repression practiced by the services of the Minister of the Interior, M. Marcellin, this does not explain everything.

In the University, the 1968–1969 academic year was the year of the Edgar Faure reforms, and the next, the year of pure and simple reaction. The law for "orientation in higher education,"[18] which received unanimous parliamentary approval in November 1968 (the Communists having abstained from voting) and was sponsored by a minister of exceptional acumen and intelligence, proclaimed autonomy for the universities and introduced assistants, assistant professors, and students into the University councils, which until then had been limited to titular professors. It also accepted responsibility for many of the May demands, with the understanding, however, that contestation was to be replaced by what was very explicitly stated to be its opposite—that is, by participation. The students only "participated"—that is to say, only voted in University elections—in rather small numbers,[19] the *facultés* of pharmacy, medicine, and law, however great their reformist ardor in May '68, giving proof nevertheless of greater compliancy than the *faculté des Sciences* and, especially, than *Lettres*.

Having been broken up into teaching and research units (UER), there was not much left to manage in the *facultés,* all the more so since the monetary crisis of November had ushered in a period of short rations for the University. The orientation law, moreover, was not even applied at the *faculté des Sciences* of Paris, whose Dean, Marc Zamansky, simply maintained the old regime. Similar tendencies appeared much more clearly even, in 1969-1970; the big scare was a thing of the past, and in the Chaban-Delmas ministry, formed on June 22, 1969, M. Olivier Guichard had replaced M. Edgar Faure.

In the different disciplines, elections in the *"Comité Consultatif des universités,"* which plays a key role in matters of promotion to the more advanced grades of higher education, resulted in a triumph for the most conservative professors. In the institution to which the author of the present article belongs, at the start of the 1968–1969 academic year, nobody any longer even mentioned the texts that had been set up in June 1968 by a duly elected commission.

If we except Nanterre, and to a certain extent Nantes and Strasburg, the May movement had supervened so rapidly that the professors —many of whom backed the students during the repression—had not had an opportunity to observe a change in the attitude of the students toward themselves. The frequently callous, brutal forms that student contestation assumed traumatized them and often inclined them to serene acceptance of repression.[20] The more discerning, however, felt that a new biological species had entered the University and that they would have to try to adapt themselves to it.

But the major fact of the 1968–1969 school year was perhaps not so much the orientation law as the creation of an experimental University center in the Paris suburb of Vincennes. With a faculty composed of professors who represented everything at one time: ambition, reform, leftism, and communism, all of which made for an interesting tilting ground; a student body that brought together especially leftists from Nanterre or the Sorbonne and students without the *baccalauréat* from the professions,[21] Vincennes, which is an interdisciplinary university oriented toward study of the modern world, witnessed the inauguration of an absolutely unheard-of freedom of relationships between teachers and students who together planned the university courses and set up a system for checking the knowledge acquired.

Vincennes functioned somewhat like a bomb inside the French university system.[22] Nor can it be said that this bomb (or, in the eyes of the government, this induced abscess) has been rendered entirely harmless. Vincennes still exists, but the Minister, M. Guichard, has declared devoid of "national" validity the diplomas conferred in certain departments (essentially in the department of Philosophy), while other departments have felt obliged to integrate with the system by agreeing to prepare students for the competitive examinations required for secondary teaching.

The two pillars upon which French higher education rests—the "doctorate" thesis and the *"agrégation"*—remain, moreover, practically untouched.[23] It would be far from true, however, to assert that the University of today is identical with the University of yesterday. The consequences of the May movement, of the reform and of the reaction, have been twofold and, in certain respects, ironic. The most obvious

fact is certainly politicization which, although it varies considerably
from one university to another,[24] is generally speaking very real; it is
hard to see how it could possibly be reversed other than by setting up
a totalitarian regime.

The other fact is more ironic. When the huge Paris University
broke up into thirteen universities, it was almost bound to introduce,
at least in those places where the new universities are not purely and
simply a continuation of earlier institutions, the not only differentiated
but also the competitive character that had been the dream of the
technocratic reformers before May '68. And what's more, the only one
of these universities that is really multi-disciplinary, Paris VII (which
through the makeup of both its teaching and student bodies may well
become a new Vincennes), may also, by virtue of the very high level
of its teaching, be the most selective of all the French universities.[25]

It may legitimately be considered that in the economic and social
regime of contemporary France, the May movement will have had as
one consequence the adaptation of the former liberal, marginal University to the laws of competition and expanded reproduction of
capital.

Should we stop there? This would be to suppose that history will
stand still. The French events belong in an international context,
which is that of "creeping May" in Italy, and the generalized campus
revolt in the United States. From now on, "student unrest" is a
characteristic of all developed countries with a "liberal economy,"[26]
and none can say what will be the future repercussions of the student
"discourse"[27]—itself a repercussion of so many sounds to which one
might have thought they were deaf.

Many people, even in the most conformist circles, have condemned the Ministry of Education's strange idea of situating a campus
alongside a shanty town. But when all is said and done, the idea may
turn out to be more symbolic than appears. Even if the world it
borders on is a nightmarish one, that does not in itself summarize our
civilization, the University, by coming closer to it, has lost its innocence. The students' firm refusal to become the keepers of that world
is in itself cause for hope.

"May," of course, will not happen again, and it is vain to dream
of an impossible recommencement. But at a time when conformity is
overwhelmingly triumphant, when society has reinstated the minor
hierarchies that conceal the major ones, the student movement, which
is both foreign to this society and inserted in a vital sector of it,
still allows us to imagine another world.[28]

Notes

1. In this connection I have been reproached, and justifiably so, with having relatively underestimated the impact of the Chinese cultural revolution among the students. On this subject, see Edoarda Masi, "Le Marxisme de Mao et la gauche européenne," *Les Temps Modernes*, March 1970, pp. 1367–1387. This article appeared originally in Italian in the *Quaderni Piacentini*, No. 39. For a critical view of French Maoism see Robert Pagès, "Lignes de force (et de faiblesse) du gauchisme en mai 1970," *L'Homme et la Société*, April–May–June 1970, pp. 137–149, and the *enquête* mentioned in Note 7 below by M. A. Burnier and B. Kouchner.

2. In a review of this book published in the April 3, 1969, issue of the Times Literary Supplement the writer stated, "What is needed now is a similar collection on the workers' movement, which nearly turned a revolt into a revolution." A collection, certainly, but in no case similar. A volume containing the leaflets that were distributed in the factories, which in the large majority of cases were put out by the union organizations would only give the latter's very centralized point of view. The films and tapes that were made would be much more revealing, but in any case it is vastly more difficult for workers to "take the floor" than it is for students.

3. Alfred Willener, *L'Image-action de la société et la politisation culturelle*, Paris, Seuil, 1970; Daniel Singer, *Prelude to Revolution, France in May 1968*, New York, Hill and Wang, 1970. For a rather brief analysis of the different interpretations that have been proposed, see Ph. Bénéton and J. Touchard, "Les Interprétations de la crise de mai–juin, 1968," *Revue française de Science Politique* 20, 3 (June 1970), pp. 503–544. Their eight models of interpretation are the following: 1) organized subversion; 2) a University-centered crisis; 3) a feverish, youthful revolt; 4) a spiritual revolt, a crisis of civilization; 5) a social conflict, expressed in a new kind of social movement; 6) a traditional type of social conflict; 7) a political crisis; 8) a chain of circumstances. To these could be added a ninth, or rather a variation of the third. According to the pediatrician Robert Debré (member of the *Académie de Médecine*), student revolts are a consequence of more precocious physical maturity in the developed countries of the young people from well-to-do families, to which he adds the contradiction of their late social integration. ("La biologie aide-t-elle à comprendre la jeunesse révoltée?" *Revue de Paris*, December 1969, pp. 25–32, and an interview in *Le Figaro*, Sept. 21, 1970). Other "biological" interpretations compare youthful aggressiveness to that of animals. (Roger Masters, *Preuves*, Feb.–March 1969, pp. 74–81).

4. Cf. above, p. 458.

5. C. R. Linbaum, in A. Willener, *op. cit.*, p. 93. "The rhythm and very sense of time were different. For instance, the line to be followed was worked out in the morning for the same evening . . . 'where shall we go?' Nobody said it, and it was not written down; it had to be decided together and carried out immediately afterward. . . . Before, society advanced in a nascent, gradual rhythm. Then, suddenly, there was a break, and instead of living according to the rhythm they normally followed—morning, evening, vacation—people discover that they are in a rhythm that obliges them to decide what they will do one minute later. . . .'"

6. Ernest Bolo, who translated Isaac Deutscher's biography of Trotsky, was arrested at St. Maxime (Var) on July 16, 1970, then released on July 22. The local papers announced that he was a professor at Nanterre, which was inaccurate.

7. The best account of the contestation movement in France after May '68 appears to me to have been given in the *enquête* carried out by Michel Antoine Burnier and B. Kouchner, *La France sauvage,* Paris, 1970, which includes an excellent description of the new "groupuscules."

8. Daniel Singer, *op. cit.,* p. 274. The only ones who entirely escaped this "regroupusculization" process were the editors of the *Cahiers de mai,* who have continued to publish a great deal of important material from essentially working class sources. On the contrary, *Action,* which appeared as a daily during the 1969 presidential campaign, had completely deteriorated before it disappeared. A good critical analysis of the different "groupuscules" was published anonymously in *Les Cahiers révolutionnaires* (supplement of *La Voie,* 1970).

9. In some ways the *Gauche Prolétarienne* may be compared to the American "Weathermen." Another closely related group, but with a humorously anarchistic tint, was *"Vive la Révolution!"* which scuttled ship in April 1971. We might say that if the Trotskyites of the *Ligue communiste* are the Jesuits of the far left, the Maoists are its mendicant order—it being understood, of course, that the reference is to sects, not religions.

10. "On Rational Inquiry in Universities Today"; *The New York Review of Books,* April 23, 1970, p. 30.

11. *La Cause du Peuple,* May 15, 1970.

12. This line of thinking is not absolutely new, having appeared during the Algerian war. In 1960 the advocates of non-compliance and help to the FLN were called *Jeune Résistance,* and they described themselves as "new resistants." Shortly afterwards their adversaries imitated them; that is, the group that succeeded the OAS called itself the CNR (*Conseil National de la Résistance*). We note that the GP even adds to the mythology created by the PCF, which, at the Liberation (1945), claimed to be the party, 75,000 of whose members had been shot (whereas the real figure was considerably lower). *La Cause du Peuple* for July 10, 1970, speaks of the "party of 100,000 shot."

13. H. Carrère d'Encausse and S. R. Schramm, *L'URSS et la Chine devant les révolutions d'une société pré-industrielle,* Paris, Armand Colin, 1970, p. 28. Here it might be noted that in the case of the Chinese Maoists, this "substitutism" is a direct heritage from Bolshevism.

14. This remark is intended especially for psychoanalysts, for whom obedience to the principle of reality is identified with acceptance of the rules of existing society. We recall one of the May slogans: "I take my desires for reality, because I believe in the reality of my desires."

15. One example, among countless others, of the veritable delirium to which the neo-naturalism of certain leftists can lead: on September 4, 1970, at the International Congress of Mathematicians in Nice, Laurent Schwartz suggested to certain of his colleagues that they organize a movement of solidarity with Vietnamese mathematicians. He received the following reply from certain American and French mathematicians: is it really necessary for us to export our mathematics, which is the supreme expression of our occidental alienation, to Vietnam?

16. We might also mention, as a symbolic action, the hunger strike of professors and students in the department of Ethnology at Nanterre that in February 1969 succeeded in obtaining withdrawal of the rector's marshals, also called *"appariteurs musclés"* (which, translated as "strong-arm men," is descriptive of their function, they having distinguished themselves by their brutality). Another spectacular action—not a "groupuscule" one—was simultaneous occupation, on January 10, 1970, of the CNPF (National Employers' Association) headquarters and of a "home"

for African workers in Ivry that had neither water nor electricity. These actions followed the tragic death of five African workers in a death-trap "home" in the Aubervilliers slum district of Paris. See, on this subject, A. Gorz and Ph. Gavi, *"La Bataille d'Ivry,"* *Les Temps Modernes,* March 1970, pp. 1388–1416.

17. The Palestinian cause provoked much greater action, the motivation for which was not always absolutely pure, with violent clashes between "Zionists" and "anti-Zionists" (quite often Jews themselves).

18. Certain of its technical measures conform quite closely to the conclusions of the "National Interdisciplinary Commission" (see above, Document 199), the moving spirit of which had been Michel Alliot, who became head of Edgar Faure's cabinet.

19. Officially, participation in the vote was placed at 52 percent, but this proportion only took into consideration the students who were registered on the voting lists.

20. There were a great many more scenes of brutality and acts of destruction after than during May '68. It should be noted, however, that the people who expressed the greatest indignation at the squandering of public funds and destruction of public property (to a point where students and faculty were imprisoned for writing slogans on walls), remained generally indifferent to the unpunished speculations that brought on the November 1968 monetary crisis, or to the unbelievable waste (110 billion old francs, more than $200,000,000) resulting from the useless construction and abandonment in July 1970 of the new Villette slaughter house.

21. To recruit these students, certain "moderate" professors called on the CGT, hoping in this way to submerge the contestors.

22. At the Sorbonne, attempts to introduce a Vincennes type of teaching were rapidly nipped in the bud. See, for instance, Robert Jaulin's account of endeavors to set up a "pirate" ethnological course, in *La Paix blanche,* Seuil, Paris, 1970, pp. 266–277.

23. The orientation law had provided for defense of the doctor's thesis on presentation of a dossier, or by participation in some form of collective research; but the teaching body set up a resolute barrier against its application in most "literary" disciplines. As for the *agrégation,* Edgar Faure had been planning to reform it on the eve of his removal from office, but it could be no more than a shot in the air.

24. When the June 1970 Paris *baccalauréat* examinations took place, a rightist university organization distributed among the candidates (presumably future students) a pamphlet classifying the different Paris universities according to their degree of "leftism."

25. The nucleus of Paris VII was a section of the former English Institute of the Sorbonne, which leftist students had helped to run longer than anywhere else after May 1968. In June 1970, the President of Paris VII was M. Michel Alliot (see above, Note 18).

26. This is now true even in Israel, which until now had been characterized by the nationalistic conformity of its students. Today certain groups, particularly American and French-speaking, have begun to sow the seeds of restlessness.

27. Traveling in northern Italy during the summer of 1969, I noticed two posters that dated from the May events in France. The first, a clenched Maoist fist, illustrated, in Turin, a call to strike and for worker solidarity, which was hardly to be wondered at. The second, in the Val d'Aoste, and which in the Paris version had attacked, in the form of a horrible rat, the "fascist vermin" of the "civil action" groups, was aimed this time at everybody who was opposed to use of the French

language by the peasants in this part of Italy. The caption was: "Against French. Fascist vermin."

28. "Hypocrisy is a tribute that vice pays to virtue." This maxim of La Rochefoucauld has frequently been quoted in connection with the Gaullist plans for "participation" as a substitute for self-management. The same might be said of the sudden decision taken in October 1970 by the French Communist Party to organize "open" meetings, at which, as in May, the microphone would circulate among the audience; the party leaders would be presented somewhat the way big business presents its public relations men: "A question to M. Marchais . . . ."

Bibliography

BIBLIOGRAPHICAL ESSAY

The bibliography that follows offers in many respects a limited and incomplete choice. For everything concerning the period before May, as well as for the student movement outside France, the only titles mentioned will be those we have found to be directly useful or that appear to be most significant. Consequently, this is a partial bibliography, chosen with partiality. With regard to the months of May and June 1968, we had at first considered giving a complete bibliography, but were dissuaded from this task by other similar undertakings. We therefore confined ourselves to a rather limited choice, keeping only the works that were the most significant, either in quality or for quite other reasons. For example, Jean Cau's pamphlet, *le Pape est Mort* (La Table Ronde de Combat), actually interests no one but specialists of his work. The same may be said of the little work by Jean-Jacques Servan-Schreiber, *Le Réveil de la France* (Collection e Défi, Denoël, Paris, 1968), in spite of the importance its author has recently assumed in French politics. A really complete bibliography, in fact, would also have to assemble and classify a large number of journals of the movement throughout France, but this would require an entire book.

Certain books and articles that we found useful for this or that point of detail are not mentioned here, but may be found in the notes of the book proper. Classification is inevitably arbitrary, and names of the works cited could slip from under one heading to another.* Final listing of French publications in this essay was, generally speaking, terminated in November 1970.

* Three important bibliographical works have already been published:
  1. In *Communications,* No. 12 (1968).
  2. Michel de Certeau, *La Prise de parole* (see below, Section III, 8), pp. 137–152 and pp. 160–163, and *Une Littérature inquiète: mai 1968. Pour une mode d'emploi, Etudes,* May 1969, pp. 751–763.
  3. In the catalogue of an exhibit organized in Amsterdam (February 7–March 7, 1969) by the International Institute of Social History, *Parijs mei juni '68.* To this might be added the selective bibliography published in February 1969 by R. Gombin, *op. cit.* (see below, Section III, 8).

I. THE STUDENT MOVEMENT IN THE WORLD

1. *Books and Collections of General Interest*

J. J. BROCHIER and B. OELGARD, *L'Internationale étudiante*, Julliard, Paris, 1968. Cursory.

ALEXANDER COCKBURN and ROBIN BLACKBURN (edited by), *Student Power, Problems, Diagnosis, Action*, Penguin Books, Harmondsworth, 1969. This collection, published in collaboration with *The New Left Review*, is based for the most part on Anglo-American examples.

Combats étudiants dans le monde, Berkeley-Berlin-Rome-Madrid-Tokyo-Ankara-Belgrade-Prague-Rio-Varsovie-Mexico, Collection "Combats," le Seuil, Paris, 1968. Documents and chronology.

Daedalus, Journal of the American Academy of Arts and Sciences, Winter 1968, "Students and Politics" (Proceedings of the American Academy of Arts and Sciences, 97, No. 1). Covers an extremely wide field in the line of American political science. The article on the American student left by R. E. Peterson (pp. 293-317) is excellent.

FR. DUPRAT, *L'Internationale étudiante révolutionnaire*, Collection "Points de Vue," Nouvelles Editions Latines, Paris, 1968. The imaginative viewpoint of a young fascist.

Esprit, Paris, May 1969, *"La Révolte des étudiants dans le monde."*

L'Homme et la société, April–May–June, 1970. Articles on the U.S.A., Canada, Italy, Germany, Spain, France, Czechoslovakia, Japan.

J. JOUSSELLIN, *Les Révoltes de jeunes*, Editions Ouvrières, Paris, 1968. Goes beyond the student world and, above all, furnishes a useful index.

Kursbuch, 13, 1968. "Die Studenten und die Macht, Spanien, Italien, Frankreich, Polen, Tschechoslowakei, Latein-amerika, U.S.A.," edited by B. Nirumand, O. Negt, H. M. Enzensberger, Suhrkamp Verlag, Frankfort-on-the-Main. Viewpoint of the revolutionary student left; very useful collection. The study on France by Walter Kreipe, finished on May 11, 1968, pp. 154–178, is excellent.

Partisans, 44, October–November 1968, "Le Complot international."

STEPHEN SPENDER, *The Year of the Young Rebels*, Random House, New York, 1969. Written after a visit to Columbia, the Sorbonne, Prague, and West Berlin. Claims to be "comprehensive."

We were not able to consult the collection edited by S. K. Lipset, *Students and Politics,* New York, 1967, nor the bibliography listed by Ph. G. Altbach, *Select Bibliography on Students, Politics and Higher Education,* Cambridge, Mass., 1967.
On education as a business in the entire world, see Lê-Thanh-Khôi, *L'Industrie de l'enseignement,* Collection "Grands Documents," Editions de Minuit, Paris, 1967.

2. Germany

IDA BERGER, *Werden sie Durchhalten?* Hartmut-Lüdke Verlag, Hamburg, 1970. French translation by Odile Meuvret, *Tiendront-ils? Etude sociologique sur les étudiants des deux bords du Rhin.* Anthropos, Paris, 1970. Comparative study of student activities in Marburg, Germany (1967), and in Nancy, France (early 1968).

S. BOSC and J.-M. BOUGUEREAU, "Le Mouvement des étudiants berlinois," followed by "Documents sur l'Université critique," *Les Temps Modernes,* July 1968, pp. 1–79, with bibliography. The most important collection that has appeared in French.

R. DUTSCHKE, *Ecrits politiques,* Christian Bourgois, Paris, 1968, preface by G. Sandoz, postface by Claus Menzel.

Februar 1968, Tage die Berlin eschütterten, Collection "res novae, provokativ," Europäische Verlaganstalt, Frankfort-on-the-Main, 1968. Good general documentation.

F. MAYER and U. SPINNARKE, *Was Wollen die Studenten?* Fischer Bücherei, Frankfort-on-the-Main and Hamburg, 1968.

Partisans, No. 41, March–April 1968, "L'Allemagne fédérale après le miracle." Study and documentation on the opposition of the left by R. Reiche and P. Gäng.

Quaderni Piacentini, No. 34, May 1968. Interviews and articles by G. Backhauer, R. Dutschke, and documents.

3. United States

A. BERKELEY

HAL DRAPER, *Berkeley: The New Student Revolt,* introduction by Mario Savio, Grove Press, New York, 1965.

S. M. LIPSET and S. S. WOLIN, *The Berkeley Student Revolt, Facts and Interpretations,* Anchor Books, New York, 1965.

M. V. MILLER and S. GILMORE, with an introduction by I. Howe, *Revolution at Berkeley,* Laurel, New York, 1965.

These three collections concur on more than one point, but the volume by H. Draper expresses the position of the "Free Speech Movement," whereas the other two give more contrasting reactions.

B. AFTER BERKELEY

Crisis at Columbia, An Inside Report on the Rebellion at Columbia, from the Pages of the Columbia Daily Spectator, New York, 1968. The chronicle of the revolt in a student paper.

On Columbia, see also *Columbia Liberated,* published by "The Columbia Strike Coordinating Committee," September 1968, the charter of the university in revolt, *The Columbia Statement,* New York, September 1968; and the report of the Cox Commission, paternalistic but very critical with respect to the administration, *Crisis at Columbia, Report of the Fact Finding Commission Appointed to Investigate the Disturbances at Columbia University in April and May 1968,* Vintage Books, New York, 1968.

It was only after publication of the present volume that we learned of the collection signed by Jerry L. Avorn and members of the staff of the *Columbia Daily Spectator,* entitled "Up Against the Ivy Wall, a History of the Columbia Crisis," Atheneum, New York, 1969.

H. and J. JACOBS and J. PETRAS, "U.S.A.: la Génération inquiète," *Revue internationale du socialisme,* February 19, 1967, pp. 145–165.

K. KENISTON, *Young Radicals, Notes on Committed Youth,* Harcourt, Brace and World, New York, 1968. The psychology of the organizers of the Vietnam summer, 1967.

On Europe in general, some useful information may be found in the book by J.-L. Brau, *Cours camarade, le vieux monde est derrière toi,* Albin Michel, Paris, 1968, the title of which is taken from a wall writing at the Odéon and at the Sorbonne.

4. *Italy**

Documenti della rivolta universitaria, Laterza, Bari, 1968. *Lettre à une maîtresse d'école par les écoliers de Barbiana* (Lettera a una professoressa). French translation by M. Thurlotte, collection "En Direct," Mercure de France, Paris, 1968. Against student selection; in favor of celibacy for professors.

---

* The Italian review *Il Manifesto* brought out, at the beginning of 1970, a *"Bibliografia Sistematica sul movimento studentesco"* (s.l., s.d.), essentially useful for the Italian movement.

Libro Bianco sul movimento Studentesco, edited by Massimo Barone, with a statement by Oreste Scalzone, Edizioni Galileo, Rome, 1968.

ROSSANA ROSSANDA, *l'Anno degli Studenti,* de Donato, Collection "Dissensi," 11, Bari, 1968. A brilliant analysis by a left-wing leader, member until November 1969 of the Italian Communist Party; not limited to the Italian scene. The last part of the book was translated in *Les Temps Modernes,* August–September 1968.

Università: l'ipotesi rivoluzionaria, documenti delle lotte studentesche, Trento, Torino, Napoli, Pisa, Milano, Roma, libri contro no. 1, Marsilio Editori, Padua, 1968.

The review *Quaderni Piacentini* published a very large number of articles and documents on the Italian movement and its relationship to the world student movement. See especially Nos. 28 (September 1966), principally about the German movement, and 35 (July 1968), with articles by G. Bakaus on Berlin and S. Bologna and G. Daghini on France.

On the new features of the working class struggles which, as in France, have influenced the student movement, see "Quaderni Rossi," *Luttes ouvrières et capitalisme d'aujourd'hui,* "Cahiers libres" No. 118–119, Maspero, Paris, 1968.

Les Temps Modernes of May–June 1968 translated two interesting articles by O. Scalzone on the occupation of the School of Literature at the University of Rome and especially by Cl. Petruccioli, "L'Assemblée et la Délégation," in which are to be found themes that were well known in the French movement.

5. Poland

In addition to the documentation published in *Kursbuch,* 13 (see above, Section I, 1) and *Combats étudiants dans le monde,* see André Martin, "La Révolte des jeunes en Pologne," *Etudes,* June–July 1968, pp. 60–79, and in *Esprit,* May 1969, pp. 859–870; and "La Résistance des jeunes en Pologne," *Etudes,* June 1970, pp. 864–889.

6. Czechoslovakia

Here again, see *Kursbuch,* 13, *Combats étudiants dans le monde,* and the account by Pavel Tigrid, *Le Printemps de Prague,* le Seuil, Paris, 1968.

The special issue of *L'Homme et la société,* dated April–May–June 1970, contains an interesting article by Antonin Matejovsky.

II. FRANCE BEFORE MAY 1968

1. *Youth Problems*

EMILE COPFERMANN, *La Génération des blousons noirs,* "Cahiers libres" 30, Maspero, 1962; *Problèmes de la jeunesse,* Petite Collection Maspero, Paris, 1967.

Enquête sur la jeunesse, carried out by M. Davranche, with commentary by G. Fouchard, Collection "Idées," Gallimard, Paris, 1968.

JEAN MONOD, *Les Barjots, Essai d'ethnologie des bandes de jeunes,* Julliard, Paris, 1968.

EDGAR MORIN, *Commune en France, la métamorphose de Plodemet,* Fayard, Paris, 1967.

Socialisme ou Barbarie, Nos. 33 (December 1961–February 1962), and 34 (March–May 1963), published an important documentation on both student and working class youth.

2. *Pedagogy and Repression*

C. FREINET, *Naissance d'une pédagogie populaire,* Collection "Textes à l'appui," Maspero, Paris, 1967.

F. OURY and A. VASQUEZ, *Vers une pédagogie institutionelle,* Collection "Textes à l'appui," Maspero, Paris, 1967.

Partisans, no. 39 (October–December 1967), "Pédagogie: éducation ou mise en condition."

Partisans, No. 50 (December 1969–January 1970), "L'alibi pédagogique."

Since 1966 the review *Recherches,* publication of the Fédération des Groupes et Recherches Institutionnels, has published a great deal of documentation on these questions, influenced, like the above works, by the methods of C. Freinet and the idea of self-government for children. For the pedagogy of secondary school teaching, see also the review *Les Cahiers Pédagogiques.*

A. ROUÈDE, *Le Lycée impossible,* le Seuil, Paris, 1967, is the testimony of a principal on why he failed.

3. *Student unionism up to the end of the Algerian War.*

F. BORELLA and M. DE LA FOURNIÈRE, *le Syndicalisme étudiant,* le Seuil, Paris, 1957. Testimony and study by two leaders of the "minority" boards in the UNEF.

P. GAUDEZ, *Les Etudiants,* preface by D. Wallon, Julliard, Paris, 1961. *Les sources du syndicalisme depuis 1945,* 463 *roneotype* pages, numerous graphs (Paris, 1964). A work of excellent quality, unfortunately almost unknown; brings the history of the UNEF up to 1964.

UNEF, *Le Syndicalisme étudiant et la guerre d'Algérie,* AGEL, Lille, 1960.

4. *Youth and the Algerian War*

ROBERT BONNAUD, *Itinéraire,* preface by P. Vidal-Naquet, Collection "Documents," Editions de Minuit, Paris, 1962.

JANINE CAHEN and MICHELINE POUTEAU, *Una resistenza incompiuta. La guerra d'Algeria e gli anticolonialisti francesi 1954–1962,* 2 vols., Il Saggiatore, Milan, 1964. This is by far the most complete collection of documents.

XAVIER GRALL, *La Génération du djebel,* Desclée de Brouwer, Paris, 1962.

F. MASPERO, *Le Droit à l'insoumission, dossier des 121,* Cahiers libres 14, Maspero, Paris, 1960.

Partisans, No. 1, September–October 1961, published a document on "Une génération algérienne."

5. *Student Unionism After the Algerian War*

The most important documentation by far is that published by *Les Temps Modernes;* it also touches upon the problems of pedagogical relationships; articles by Marc Nacht, Marc Kravetz, J.-B. Pontalis, February 1964; J. G. Cluzel, J. Colombel, April 1964; M. and J.-P. Briand, R. Misrahi, May 1964; A. Griset, M. Kravetz, April 1965; F. Josse, A. Griset, M. Kravetz, May 1965.

See also L. Althusser, "Problèmes étudiants," *la Nouvelle Critique,* January 1964, pp. 80–111; and in the book by A. Gorz, *Le Socialisme difficile,* le Seuil, Paris, 1967, the chapter entitled "Etudiants et ouvriers," pp. 47–67.

6. The Intellectuals

F. BON and M.-A. BURNIER, *Les Nouveaux Intellectuels,* preface by J.-P. Vigier, Cujas, Paris, 1967. The consequences of the scientific revolution, with a bibliography; new edition, Seuil, Paris, 1971.

F. BON, *Les Existentialistes et la Politique,* Collection "Idées," Gallimard, Paris, 1967.

Les Lettres Nouvelles, published in February 1961 during the Algerian War, documentation entitled "Vers un parti intellectuel." See also on the intellectuals and the Algerian War, the repentant article by Michel Crouzet, *La Nef,* October 1962–January 1963.

7. Students, Teachers, and Problems of the University

G. ANTOINE and J.-C. PASSERON, *La Réforme de l'Université,* Collection "Questions d'actualité," Calmann-Lévy, Paris, 1966, preface by R. Aron. The two authors in reality express very different views.

"Avant-projet, Propositions pour une réforme démocratique de l'enseignement," *L'Ecole et la Nation,* September 1966. This is the Communist Party plan.

IDA BERGER and ROGER BENJAMIN, *L'Univers des instituteurs. Etude sociologique sur les instituteurs et institutrices du département de la Seine,* Collection "Grands Documents," Editions de Minuit, Paris, 1964.

P. BOURDIEU and J.-C. PASSERON, *Les Héritiers,* second edition, Collection "Le sens commun," Editions de Minuit, Paris, 1966. The continuation of this work is given in *La Reproduction. Eléments pour une théorie du système d'enseignement,* Collection "Le sens commun," Editions de Minuit, Paris, 1970.

Esprit, "Faire l'Université," No. 5-6, May–June 1964. The most complete general documentation.

B. KAYSER and P. DE GAUDEMAR, with the collaboration of R. BAGES, A. LOZE GACHY, and J.-M. DE GAUDEMAR. *Dix années d'une génération d'étudiants de la Faculté des Lettres et Sciences Humaines de Toulouse, recherches sur les étudiants inscrits en propédeutique en 1956–57,* preface by J. Godechot (publication of the Toulouse Faculté des Lettres et Sciences Humaines, 1967). A study of elimination procedures.

A. PROST, *L'Enseignement en France, 1800–1967,* Collection "U," Armand Colin, Paris, April 1968. This book makes it possible to situate students and professors historically.

Regards sur une révolte. Que faisaient-ils en avril?, Revue Montalembert, Desclée de Brouwer, Paris, 1969. Replies to a questionnaire distributed in the *facultés* March–April 1968, and which later was used for an article entitled "Le Scepticisme de demain? Regards sur le monde étudiant." The replies were followed by commentaries of little general interest by nineteen *"personnalités."*

The *Revue Française de Sociologie* devoted two special numbers (1967 and 1968) under the editorship of Pierre Bourdieu and Viviane Isambert-Jamati to the sociology of education.

C. VALABRÈGUE, *La Condition Etudiante,* Petite Bibliothèque Payot, Paris, 1970.

GÉRARD VINCENT, with the collaboration of Janine Mossuz, Jean-Pierre, and H. Thomas, *Les Professeurs du second degré,* Cahiers de la Fondation Nationale des Sciences Politiques, No. 160, Armand Colin, Paris, 1967. A sociological study.

8. *Daily Life, Consumer Society, and Situationist Themes*

JEAN BAUDRILLARD, *Le Système des objets,* Gallimard, Collection "Les Essais," Paris, 1968. The author of this remarkable analysis is instructor of Sociology at Nanterre. One of the slogans that appeared on the Sorbonne walls in May was "Cache-toi, objet" (Object, hide yourself). By the same author, see now *La Société de consommation,* Collection "Le Point de la question," SGPP, Paris, 1970.

GUY DEBORD, *La Société du spectacle,* Buchet-Chastel, Paris, 1967.

GEORGES PÉREC, "Les Choses," Collection *Lettres nouvelles,* Paris, 1965. A novel about the world of objects.

HUBERT TONKA, *Fiction de la contestation aliénée,* Pauvert, Paris, June 1968. Comics illustrating the situationist themes.

RAOUL VANEIGEM, *Traité du savoir-vivre à l'usage des jeunes générations,* Gallimard, Paris, 1967.

Hermès, critique politique de la vie quotidienne, first issue, March 1968.

L'Internationale situationniste (12 issues had appeared by September 1970); *De la misère en milieu étudiant considérée sous ses aspects économique, politique, psychologique, sexuel, et notamment intellectuel et de quelques moyens pour y remédier,* by members of the Situationist International and Strasburg students, Second Edition, Paris, 1967. The first edition was published as a supplement to *L'Etudiant de France,* publication of the UNEF under the auspices of the *Association Fédérative Générale des*

Etudiants de Strasbourg, in 1966. The text was published again
in the book by R. Viénet, *Enragés et situationnistes dans le
mouvement des occupations* (see below, Section III, 6). About
this group, see the article by R. Estivals, *Communications,* 12
(1968) and *le Situationnisme ou la nouvelle Internationale* by
E. Brau, Collection "Révoltes," Debresse, Paris, 1968.
Themes close to those of the situationists appear again in numerous
works in the surrealist tradition; for instance, R. Borde, *L'Extricable,*
Losfeld, Paris, 1964. Lastly, the situationists owe much to Henri
Lefebvre, who recently summarized his works on these problems in
La Vie quotidienne dans le Monde moderne, Collection "Idées," Galli-
mard, Paris, 1968.

It should be pointed out that among the works by Herbert Marcuse
that deal with these questions, the only one that had been translated
into French before May 1968 was *Eros et Civilisation* (Collection
"Arguments," Editions de Minuit, Paris, 1963). *One Dimensional
Man* did not appear until the May crisis was under way, in the same
collection. Wm. Reich's books were known because they had appeared in *Partisans,* 32–33, Oct.–Nov. 1966, in the special number entitled "Sexualité et Répression."

9. *Anarchism, Leftism, Self-Management, and Communism*

Principally since the end of the Algerian war, the decomposition of
Stalinism, and the Soviet-Chinese conflict, works giving an anarchistic
or anarchist-oriented criticism of Leninism and of the Communist
Party line have increased in number. Pierre Juquin expressed regret
(*La Nouvelle Critique,* September 1968, p. 12) that during the preceding two or three years the PC had not devoted more attention to
publishing, in pocket books, excerpts from the writings of Bakunin
(brought out by Jean-Jacques Pauvert, publisher since May 1968 of
L'Enragé); of Proudhon, *Idées,* etc.; not forgetting the works of Trotsky,
or the numerous publications of the Editions Maspero, or of the
Editions du Seuil: all that Lenin called "the phrase," and that is typical
of the "vacillating by nature and sometimes angered through necessity" petty bourgeois.

Despite their importance, we shall omit here the Luxemburgist,
Trotskyist, or Maoist critiques, which are the subjects of well-known
works, as well as the Castrist and Guevarist literature—also targets for
Juquin—the importance and influence of which have been consider-

able; and that of Black Power, which would require an independent study. We shall merely mention several less known works.

YVON BOURDET, *Communisme et Marxisme, notes critiques de sociologie politique,* Michel Brient, Paris, 1963. See now, by the same author, *La Délivrance de Prométhée, Pour une théorie politique de l'autogestion.* Anthropos, Paris, 1970.

DANIEL GUÉRIN, *L'Anarchisme, de la doctrine à l'anarchie,* Collection "Idées," Gallimard, Paris, 1965. *Jeunesse du socialisme libertaire,* Marcel Rivière, Paris, 1959, the essential elements of which appear in *Problèmes du Marxisme libertaire,* Collection "Libertés," Robert Laffont, Paris, 1969.

Ni Dieu ni Maître, Histoire et Anthologie de l'Anarchie, preface by D. Guérin, Editions de Delphes, Paris, 1965. Second Edition, La Cité, Lausanne, 1969. New Edition in 4 vols. Petite Bibliothèque Maspero, Paris, 1970.

GEORGES LAPASSADE, in 1963, by developing the themes of non-directivity and popularizing group dynamics, influenced the leaders of the FGEL: *L'Entrée dans la vie, Essai sur l'inachèvement de l'homme,* Collection "Arguments," Editions de Minuit, Paris, 1963. *Groupes, Organisations et Institutions,* Collection "Hommes et Organisations," Gauthier-Villars, Paris 1967. By the same author, but after the revolt, *Procès de l'Université, institution de classe,* Collection "J'accuse," Pierre Belfond.

For a description of French Communism on the eve of the crisis, see *Le Communisme en France,* Cahiers de la Fondation Nationale des Sciences Politiques, No. 175, A. Colin, Paris, 1969. Also contains an "Etat des Travaux" (report of work stage) by Nicole Racine.

Lastly, we recall the reviews, *Arguments* (1957–1963), *Autogestion* (since December 1966), *Noir et Rouge* (since 1959), and *Socialisme ou Barbarie* (1949–1965).

III. FRANCE IN MAY–JUNE 1968.

The archives of the student movement are being constituted and are now accessible at the Bibliothèque Nationale,* at the Sorbonne Institut d'Histoire du Syndicalisme, directed by Jean Maitron, at the

---

* The originals of the leaflets that compose this collection have been deposited in the Bibliothèque Nationale, which has had them bound and will make them available to research workers, who should apply to the *réserve.*

Bibliothèque de Documentation Internationale Contemporaine (BDIC), Paris, at the International Institute of Social History in Amsterdam, and in various university libraries (for instance, in Nancy); not to mention, of course, official organisms. As for the literature already published, it is immense. The first book published, by A. Ayache, *Les Citations de la révolution de mai,* Pauvert, Paris, 1968, defied description. In fact, for the most part the literature on the May Revolution is a good example of the "consumer society" it wanted to bring into question. For a useful guide to the details of daily events, see "Chronologie des événements de mai-juin 1968," *Notes et études documentaires* Nos. 3722–3723 (September 28, 1970), published by "La Documentation française."

1. *Photographs*

France Soir Magazine, les journées de mai, special issue, *Connaissance de l'histoire,* 56 bis (sensation seeking). Similar collections were published in June by *Noir et Blanc* and by *Paris-Match;* Philippe Labro, *Barricades 68,* photographs from the Gamma agency, Solar, Monaco; *Paris, mai-juin 1968,* 94 documents by E. Dejay, P. Johnson, and C. Moliterni, printed by Berg, Paris, 1968. The bulletin No. 151, issued by the Préfecture de Police in September 1968, published documentation giving, among other types of information, details of matériel found on the demonstrators.

ANDRÉ ROSSEL (presented by), *Mai 68,* Collection "Encyclopédie de l'Image," Edition Les Yeux Ouverts, Paris, 1968. Seven excellent photographs; *in folio.*

2. *Films and Recordings*

A first list of films is given in *Le Cinéma s'insurge,* Nos. 1, 2, and 3, Losfeld, Paris, 1968. See now especially *Parijs mei juni '68,* pp. 28–29. The same collection gives a list of recordings, p. 30.

3. *Wall Writings*

JULIEN BESANÇON (preface by), *Les Murs ont la parole, Sorbonne, mai 68,* Tchou, Paris, 1968. The texts are sometimes badly chosen.

W. LEWINO, *L'Imagination au pouvoir,* photographs by Jo Schnapp, Losfeld, Paris, 1968.

The wall writings at the Odéon are quoted in the above-mentioned book by Ch. Bouyer; those in Strasburg in the book by P. Feuerstein (see below Section III, 7).

4. Poems

Only one collection, but excellent: *Poèmes de la révolution mai 1968,* Caractères, Paris, 1968.

5. Posters and Drawings

Atelier populaire présenté par lui-même, 87 posters from May-June 1968, Collection "Bibliothèque de mai," Usines Université Union, Paris, 1968. The same publisher has published, in London, a collection of 90 posters in color, printed by Dobson.

v. h. BRANDES and h. SYLVESTER, *Merde, Karikaturen der Mai-revolte. Frankreich 1968.* Collection "Trikont-Aktuell" 6, Trikont Verlag, München, 1968. Drawings taken principally from *Action* and *L'Enragé.*

JEAN CASSOU (preface by), *Mai 68, Affiches,* Tchou, Paris, 1968. This collection, which is, like the preceding one, very incomplete, was published under questionable conditions. A "pirated" collection was published by an unknown publisher under the title *Paris mai 1968;* it is composed of a certain number of spurious documents.

LOUIS F. PETERS, *Kunst und Revolte, Das politische plakat und der aufstand der französischen Studenten.* Verlag M. Dumont Schauberg, Cologne, 1968. 220 black and white photographs, and 34 posters in color.

It is strange that none of the collections published mentions the posters brought out in the provincial ateliers (especially in Lyons, Montpellier, and Marseilles), a magnificent collection of which exists in the engravings department of the Bibliothèque Nationale. It should also be pointed out that the collection by Claude Dejacques, *A toi l'angoisse, à moi la rage,* Les Fresques de Nanterre, Collection "Le Document du mois," Nalis, Paris, 1968, would appear to be very indebted to the imagination.

For an analysis of the meaning of these posters and a comparison with the posters of the Russian Revolution, cf. D. Avron, B. Lemenuel, and J. F. Lyotard, "Espace plastique et espace politique," *Revue d'Esthéthique,* Nos. 3-4 (1970), pp. 255-273.

6. Evidence and Documentation, classified and unclassified

Analyses et documents, No. 154, "De la lutte étudiante à la lutte ouvrière"; No. 155, "De l'occupation des usines à la campagne électorale"; No. 156, "De l'étranglement à la répression." These documentation "card files," which contain numerous valuable texts, were processed immediately after the event and form a remarkable working tool.

Architecture-Mouvement-Continuité, Bulletin of the Society of Architects holding government diplomas, "Spécial mai 68," supplement to No. 167 (July 1968). Contains practically all of the texts and manifestos adopted at the Ecole des Beaux-Arts, Paris. A good choice of posters.

BERNARD AUDREY and LOUIS MILLET, *La Révolution universitaire. L'expérience de l'Institut de Psychologie de Grenoble,* Collection "Etudes supérieures," Bordas, Paris, 1968.

MICHEL ANTOINE BURNIER, BERNARD KOUCHNER, and the group of *Edition Spéciale, La France Sauvage,* Editions et Publications Premières, Paris, 1970. Extremely interesting interviews with the "inheritors" of May.

JEAN-LOUIS BRAU, JEAN-JACQUES LEBEL, and PHILIPPE MERLHES, *Sois jeune et tais-toi,* Feltrinelli, Milan, 1968. Italian translations of leaflets, several of which antedate May 1968. The same collection was published in German, with a few variations, under the title *Le Chienlit, Dokumente zur fransösischer Mai-Revolution,* Josef Melzer Verlag, Darmstadt, 1968.

J. CAPDEVIELLE and R. MOURIAUX, *Les Syndicats ouvriers en France,* Collection "U²," Armand Colin, Paris, 1970. A small handbook containing, at the end, documents on the attitude of the unions during the strikes.

JACQUES CHALENDAR, *Une loi pour l'Université,* Desclée de Brouwer, Paris, 1970. Contains documents on the *orientation* law.

MADELEINE CHAPSAL and MICHÈLE MANCEAUX, *Les Professeurs, pour quoi faire?* Collection "L'Histoire Immédiate," le Seuil, 1970. Interviews with teachers and professors, from the extreme right to Maoism. Reactions to what followed May in the University.

M. CLAVEL, *Combat de franc-tireur pour une libération,* Collection "Libertés Nouvelles," Pauvert, Paris, 1968. A highly personal viewpoint.

MAURICE COHEN, editor of a joint report, *Le Bilan social de l'année 1968* preface by Henri Krasuki, Secretary of the CGT. *Revue pratique de droit social,* Paris, 1969. A bulky volume (574 pages) of documents on the negotiations between the employers' association and the unions. Contains the text of the Grenelle "protocol" (May 25) and of all subsequent agreements.

Comité d'action lycéens, *Les Lycéens gardent la parole,* Collection "Politique," le Seuil, Paris, 1968.

A. DUCLENT, M. FICHELET, R. FICHELET, M. JOURDAN-LAFORTE, NICOLE MAY, FRANÇOISE PICQ: *Les Représentations sociales et les sentiments associés au mouvement de mai chez les jeunes de la région parisienne,* Association européenne pour les études d'opinion et du marketing, Somar, Paris, 1970. Concerning this *roneotype* analysis see Pierre Souyri, *Annales E.S.C.,* January–February 1970, pp. 183–184.

J. DURANDEAUX, *Les Journées de mai 68, rencontres et dialogues,* Desclée de Brouwer, Paris, 1968. Interviews with students, for the most part Catholic.

CL. ESTIER, *Journal d'un fédéré,* Fayard, Paris, 1970. Contains information about the role of the FGDS in May–June 1968.

MICHÈLE FIRK, *Ecrits réunis par ses camarades,* Eric Losfeld, Paris, 1969. Letters and articles by a militant "Guevarist" who killed herself in Ciudad Guatemala, September 8, 1968. A letter dated May 14 gives a vivid picture of the Sorbonne after it was "liberated."

CHRISTIAN FOUCHET, *Mémoires d'hier et d'aujourd'hui, Au Service du Général de Gaulle.* Plon, Paris, 1971. Contains an account of May '68 as recalled by the then Minister of the Interior.

ROGER GARAUDY, *Toute la Vérité,* Grasset, Paris, 1970. Contains documents on the attitude of the author and of the leaders of the PCF during and after the crisis. Certain of the documents were questioned by the politbureau of the PCF (see *Le Monde* of March 22, 1970), which spoke of "falsification."

PHILIPPE GAVI, *Les Ouvriers,* Collection "En Direct," Mercure de France, Paris, 1970. Interviews important for their presentation of working class reactions to the May events.

La grève à Flins, documents and evidence assembled by J.-Ph. Talbo, "Cahiers libres," 121, Maspero, Paris, 1968.

"La Grève générale de mai 68," *Le peuple,* Nos. 799, 800, 801, May 15–June 30, 1968. This collection summarizes the official positions taken by the CGT. It skims rather rapidly over embarrassing facts; for instance, rejection of the Grenelle Agreements of May 27 is given six lines, on p. 61, in a very questionable way.

YVES GUÉNA, *Sauvegarde de l'Etat,* Fayard, Paris, 1970. Blow-by-blow account of the events as seen from the Ministry of Information during the ORTF crisis.

L'Insurrection étudiante, 2–13 mai, 1968, a critical and documentary ensemble collected by M. Kravetz with the collaboration of R. Bellour and A. Karsenty, Collection "Le Cours nouveau," 10/18, Union Générale d'Editions, Paris, 1968. Excellent collection of leaflets and excerpts from the Paris press.

PHILIPPE LABRO and the team of "Edition spéciale," *Ce n'est qu'un début,* Editions et Publications Premières, No. 2. Some outstanding evidence.

BERNARD LERIVRAY, *La mer aussi se meurt. Bloc-notes d'un aumônier d'étudiants. Mai–juin 1968,* Editions Ocep—Editions de la mission étudiante, Coutances, 1968.

JEAN-MARIE LEUWERS, *Un Peuple se dresse. Luttes ouvrières mai 1968,* Editions Ouvrières, Paris, 1969. Contains principally statements of Catholic workers.

Mai 68, la rue dans l'Eglise, presented by R. Davezies, drawings by A. Scob, Epi, Paris, 1968. Interviews and a few documents.

JACQUES MARNY, *L'Eglise contestée. Jeunes chrétiens révolutionnaires,* le Centurion, Paris, 1968. Interviews and documents from Franciscanism to Maoism.

J. MINCES (investigation by), *Un Ouvrier parle,* Collection "Combats," le Seuil, Paris, 1969. First class.

Un Mois de mai orageux, 113 étudiants parisiens expliquent les raisons du soulèvement universitaire, introduction by A. Délédiq, Privat, Paris, 1968.

"Le Mouvement des lycéens," *Partisans,* No. 49, October–November 1969.

Mouvement du 22 mars, *Ce n'est qu'un début, continuons le combat,* presented by E. Copfermann, "Cahiers libres," 124, Maspero, Paris, 1968. Important.

Notre arme c'est la grève, "Cahiers libres," 137, Maspero, Paris, 1968. The strike at Renault-Cléon.

"Ouvriers-Etudiants, un seul combat!", *Partisans,* No. 42, May–June 1968. Very important collection of leaflets, listed chronologically, in a slightly unorganized way, but published from the very beginning of July.

Ouvriers face aux appareils une expérience de militantisme chez Hispano-Suiza, "Cahiers libres," 183–184, Maspero, Paris, 1970. Essential information about a left-wing worker minority in an automobile factory, from the Algerian war until after May 1968.

MICHELLE PERROT, JEAN-CLAUDE PERROT, MADELEINE REBÉRIOUX, and JEAN MAITRON (documents assembled and presented by), Mai-Juin 1968, *La Sorbonne par elle-même*, "Le Mouvement social," No. 64, Editions Ouvrières. Contains the essential texts of the Paris *Faculté des Lettres;* very well classified.

Quelle université? Quelle société? Texts assembled by Le Centre de Regroupement des Informations Universitaires, Collection "Combats," le Seuil, Paris, 1968. Contains a few essential texts, especially the themes of the "Nous sommes en marche" committee at Censier; also published as a separate pamphlet, but very badly classified (*Nous sommes en marche*, Seuil, 1968).

PIOTR RAWICZ, *Bloc-notes d'un contre révolutionnaire ou la gueule de bois*, Gallimard, Paris, 1969. Bitter and ironic, although occasionally tender, viewpoint of a Jew who had been deported. Cruel to the adults who attempted to become identified with the cause.

Recherche et Contestation, Editions Anthropos, Paris, 1969. Minutes of a discussion among CNRS researchers, which took place in July 1968.

"La Remise en question de l'Université, mai–juin 1968," special issue, July 1968, of *La Revue Internationale, les sciences de l'éducation pour l'ère nouvelle*. Loose documentation.

La Révolution par elle-même, tracts révolutionnaires rassemblés et présentés par J.-P. Simon, Albin Michel, Paris, 1968. 160 leaflets from May to August, especially from Censier.

J. SAUVAGEOT, A. GEISMAR, D. COHN-BENDIT, J.-P. DUTEUIL, *La Révolte étudiante, les animateurs parlent*, Collection "L'Histoire Immédiate," le Seuil, Paris, 1968. Short interviews. English translation entitled: *The Student Revolt, The Activists Speak*, Panther Books, London, 1968.

R. SERROU, *Dieu n'est pas conservateur*, Collection "Contestation," R. Laffont, Paris, 1968. Documents assembled by *Paris-Match* specialists on religious questions.

Des Soviets à Saclay?, first account of an experiment in workers' councils at the Atomic Energy Commission, reported by J. Pesquet, "Cahiers libres," 127, Maspero, Paris, 1968.

UNEF-SNESup., *Le Livre noir des journées de mai*, Collection "Combats," le Seuil, Paris, 1968. The repression.

UNEF-SNESup., *Ils accusent*, Collection "Combats," le Seuil, Paris, 1968.

R. VIÉNET, *Enragés et situationnistes dans le mouvement des occupations*, Collection "Témoins," Gallimard, Paris, 1968. Analysis and documentation.

A. WILLENER, C. GADJOS, G. BENGUIGI, *Les Cadres en mouvement*, Fondation Royaumont, Epi, Paris, 1969. Contains especially transcriptions from tapes.

S. ZEGEL, *Les Idées de mai*, Collection "Idées actuelles," Gallimard, Paris, 1968. Rather varied documentation, loosely classified, with no mention of source.

We also cite two pamphlets: one published by the Sorbonne Revolutionary Action Committee, *Fascicule M, mai 68*, which contains a certain number of leaflets brought out especially by the worker-student action committee; and the other by the CFDT Union of the CSF in Brest, *Notre potion magique c'est l'unité, mai 1968*, CSF Brest.

7. *Features and Stories* (see also following section)

PHILIPPE ALEXANDRE, *L'Elysée en péril, 2–30 mai 1968*, Collection "Grands Documents Contemporains," Fayard, Paris, 1969. With the books by Claude Paillat and by J.-R. Tournoux mentioned below, this book forms a trilogy of sensational feature stories that are generally rather vapid.

PH. ANDRO, A. DAUVERGNE, L. M. LAGOUTTE, *Le Mai de la révolution*, Julliard, Paris, 1968.

PH. BAUCHARD and M. BRUZEK, *Le Syndicalisme à l'épreuve*, Collection "Le Monde qui se fait," R. Laffont, Paris, 1968. Interviews and accounts by union members.

L. BERTOLINO, *Les "Trublions,"* Stock, Paris, 1968. Excellent on Nanterre.

GEORGES CHAFFARD, *Les Orages de mai, histoire exemplaire d'une élection*, Collection "Questions d'actualité," Calmann-Lévy, Paris, 1968. The revolution in the Vendôme region: the only account having appeared thus far that gives information about how the peasants reacted.

CHRISTIAN CHARRIÈRE, *Le Printemps des Enragés*, Fayard, Paris. Story in the sensational style of *France-Dimanche* by a journalist from *Combat*.

EMIL MARIA CLAASEN and LOUIS FERDINAND PETERS, *Rebellion in Frankreich: Die Manifestation der Europäischen Kultur-revolution 1968*, Deutscher Taschenbuch Verlag, Munich, 1968. Cursory and sometimes inaccurate.

FRANÇOIS DUPRAT, *Les Journées de mai 68, les dessous d'une révolution*, introduction and postface by Maurice Bardèche, Nouvelles Editions Latines, Paris, 1968. An absolutely hysterical book in which facts and characters are often pure inventions; see also, by the same authors, the special issue (June) of *Défense de l'Occident*, mai 1968, "La Comédie de la révolution."

P. FEUERŞTEIN, *Printemps de révolte à Strasbourg, Mai–Juin 1968*, Saisons d'Alsace, Strasburg, 1968.

CLAUDE FRÉDÉRIC, *Libérez l'*ORTF, Collection "Combats," le Seuil, Paris, 1968.

R. GASCON, *La Nuit du pouvoir ou le 24 mai manqué*, Collection "Révoltes," Debresse, Paris, 1968. The rather suspicious testimony of a stooge.

YANNICK GUIN, *La Commune de Nantes*, "Cahiers libres," 154, Maspero, Paris, 1969. One of the rare good feature stories about the provinces.

JEAN-CLAUDE KERBOURC'H, *Le Piéton de mai*, Julliard, Paris, 1968 ("Chroniques d'un rêveur éveillé," published in *Combat*).

R. LOUIS, L'ORTF: *un combat*, Collection "L'Histoire Immédiate," le Seuil, Paris, 1968. Debunking of the ORTF inter-union committee.

MARIA-ANTONIETTA MACCIOCCHI, *Lettere dall' interno del* PCI *à Louis Althusser*, Feltrinelli, Milan, 1969. The student revolt seen from an election campaign among the Naples sub-proletariat. The French edition: *Lettres de l'intérieur du parti*, "Cahiers libres," 175–176, Maspero, Paris, omits the replies from L. Althusser, at his request.

F. DE MASSOT, *La Grève générale (mai–juin 68)*, supplement of No. 437 of *Information Ouvrière*. Gives the point of view of the OCI (Lambertist Trotskyites).

CLAUDE PAILLAT, *Archives secrètes, 67–68, La vérité sur une période tragique de notre histoire*, Denoël, Paris, 1969. Secrets that are often flat. The least bad book of the trilogy.

JACQUES-ARNAUD PENENT, *Un Printemps rouge et noir*, Collection "Contestation," R. Laffont, Paris, 1968. Articles from *Combat*, plus several observations about the "groupuscules" by someone who knew many of them.

P. PEUCHMAURD, *Plus vivant que jamais*, Collection "Contestation," R. Laffont, Paris, 1968. A student's story.

A. QUATTROCCHI and T. NAIRN, *The Beginning of the End, France, May 1968*, Panther Books, London, 1968. The authors belong respectively to the editorial board of *L'Avanti* (Milan) and the *New Left Review* (London). The former's contribution is a journalistic report, the latter's an analysis.

MALTE J. RAUCH and SAMUEL H. SCHIRMBECK, *Die Barrikaden von Paris*, Collection "Res Novae, provokativ" Europäische Verlagsanstalt,

Frankfurt, 1968. Rather romantic feature story illustrated with a good choice of posters from the Ecole des Beaux-Arts.

P. RAVIGNANT, *La Prise de l'Odéon,* Stock, Paris, 1968. A slightly mad Odéon.

L. RIOUX and R. BACKMAN, *11 mai 68, l'explosion de mai. Histoire complète des "événements,"* Collection "Ce jour-là," R. Laffont, Paris, 1968. By far the most complete account.

PATRICK SEALE and MAUREEN MAC CONVILLE, *French Revolution 1968,* Penguin Books, Harmondsworth, Middlesex (England), 1968. On the whole, a remarkably exact and well-informed account, in spite of its questionable viewpoint.

DANIEL SINGER, *Prelude to Revolution, France in May 1968,* Hill and Wang, New York, 1970. Combines reporting and history, in the great tradition of Isaac Deutscher and Harold Isaacs.

J.-R. TOURNOUX, *le Mois de mai du Général, Livre blanc des événements,* Plon, Paris, 1969. Rather insignificant.

PÂQUERETTE VILLENEUVE, *Une Canadienne dans les rues de Paris pendant la révolte étudiante, mai 1968,* "Cahiers de Cité libre," Editions du Jour, Montreal, 1968. Ingenuous.

8. *Analyses and Reflection*

RENÉ ANDRIEU, *Les Communistes et la révolution,* Julliard, Paris, 1968. Says little about the May Revolution.

RAYMOND ARON, *La Révolution introuvable, réflexions sur la révolution de mai,* Collection "En toute liberté," Fayard, Paris, 1968. The most intelligent of the books that were hostile to the movement; gives numerous explanatory elements, but speaks about the events only through hearsay.

A. BARJONET, *La Révolution trahie de 1968,* Collection "Controverses," John Didier, Paris, 1968. See also *Les Temps Modernes,* July 1968, and the passage devoted to May in the book by the same author, *La CGT,* Collection "Politique," le Seuil, Paris, 1968.

GÉNÉRAL BEAUFRE, *L'Enjeu du désordre. De la contagion révolutionnaire à la guerre atomique,* Grasset, Paris, 1969.

D. BEN SAÏD and H. WEBER, *Mai 1968. Une répétition générale,* "Cahiers libres," 133, Maspero, Paris, 1968. The JCR analysis; certainly the most significant study that has been published by representatives of a "groupuscule."

J. M. BENOIST, *Marx est mort,* Collection "Idées," Gallimard, Paris, 1969. Structuralist criticism of the May movement.

JEAN BLOCH-MICHEL, *Une Révolution du XX° siècle, les journées de mai 1968,* Collection "Contestation," R. Laffont, Paris, 1968. Short, intelligent statement.

F. BON and M.-A. BURNIER, *Si mai avait gagné,* Collection "Enragés," Pauvert, Paris, 1968. A little masterpiece of political fiction.

ROBERT BRÉCHON, *La Fin des lycées,* Grasset, Paris, 1970. The testimony of a *lycée* principal on the events and their consequences. "I am not on the side of the barbarians. But I haven't a sufficiently clear conscience myself to condemn them without a hearing." Compare with the account given by A. Rouède (Section II, 2) before May '68, and with the one given by Raymond Mallerin, principal of the *lycée* in Salon, Cahiers Pédagogiques, No. 85, November 1969, pp. 5–40.

A. BUHLER, *Petit Dictionnaire de la révolution étudiante,* preface by G. Conche, Collection "Controverses," John Didier, Paris, 1968. Remarkable for the Cabu drawings that illustrate it, and for the errors accumulated in 46 pages.

M. DE CERTEAU, *La Prise de parole,* Desclée de Brouwer, Paris, 1968. Very fine reflection on language.

JEAN CHARDONNET, *L'Université en question,* France-Empire, Paris, 1968. A reactionary viewpoint.

FRANÇOIS CHATELET, *La Philosophie des Professeurs,* Grasset, Paris, 1970. A violent pamphlet against members of the "PSU" (*Philosophie Scolaire et Universitaire*), whom the author ironically identifies with the same initials as those of the non-Communist leftist *Parti Socialiste Unifié.*

P. H. CHOMBART DE LAUWE, *Pour l'Université. Avant, pendant et après mai 1968.* Collection "Etudes et documents," Payot, Paris, 1968.

D. COHN-BENDIT, *Le Gauchisme, remède à la maladie sénile du communisme,* Collection "Combats," le Seuil, Paris, 1968. Narration and especially ideological anthology. English: *Obsolete Communism, the Left-Wing Alternative,* McGraw-Hill, New York, 1969.

JEAN COIN, *J'en appelle à 100,000 hommes,* Collection "Tribune libre," Plon, Paris, 1969. Criticism of the PC line by a former militant.

COMITÉ D'ACTION SANTÉ, *Médecine, Ce texte n'est qu'un début,* "Cahiers libres," 137, Maspero, Paris, 1968.

MICHEL CROZIER, *La Société bloquée,* le Seuil, Paris, 1970. Analyses and calls put out before, during, and after May '68, by one of the Nanterre sociology professors who was in direct confrontation with the *"enragés."* A vivid description of the author may be found in the book by L. Bertolino (cf. preceding subtitle).

ADRIEN DANSETTE, *Mai 1968*, Plon, Paris 1971. Claims to be *the* historical synthesis, but does not entirely achieve this aim; contains an important hitherto unpublished document (which could not be considered here) i.e., the official record of the proceedings of the University Council meeting that took place on Saturday, May 11, 1968.

MANUEL DE DIEGUEZ, *De l'Idolâtrie. Discours aux clercs et aux derviches.* "It is the intellectuals who will produce the contesting class in the world administrative caste."

MAURICE DRUON, *L'Avenir en désarroi*, Plon, Paris, 1968. By the author of *Les Mémoires de Zeus.*

EPISTÉMON, *Ces idées qui ont ébranlé la France, Nanterre novembre 1967–juin 1968*, Collection "Le Monde sans frontières," Fayard, Paris, 1968. Brilliant analysis of the ideological preconceptions of the movement, insisting upon the importance of Sartre's *Critique de la raison dialectique* in order to understand certain aspects of it; a rather restricted witness to Nanterre.

EDGAR FAURE, *L'Education nationale et la participation*, Collection "Tribune libre," Plon, Paris, 1968. The July 24 speech followed by several declarations; the text was directed to the entire French teaching body. By the same author, *Philosophie d'une réforme*, Collection "Tribune libre," Plon, Paris, 1969: interviews and speeches given in October 1968; *L'Ame du Combat, Pour un nouveau contrat social*, Collection "En toute liberté," Fayard, Paris, 1970.

J. FERNIOT, *Mort d'une révolution, la gauche de mai*, Collection "Ré flexions," Denoël, Paris, 1968.

ANDRÉ FONTAINE, *La Guerre civile froide*, Collection "Les Grandes Etudes contemporaines," Fayard, Paris, 1969. By the head of *Le Monde*'s foreign policy section.

F. FONVIEILLE-ALQUIER, *Les Illusionnaires*, Collection "Contestation," R. Laffont, Paris, 1968.

MAX GALLO, *Gauchisme, réformisme et révolution*, Collection "Contestation," R. Laffont, Paris, 1968. Defense of a reformist action supported by the impact of the leftist movement.

ALAIN GEISMAR, SERGE JULY, EVELYNE MORANE, *Vers la guerre civile*, Publications premières, Paris, 1969. Oscillates between extreme clear thinking and a certain hysterical confusion. In the appendix there are a certain number of important documents. As regards facts, insists upon the little known role of the Permanent Mobilization Commission with headquarters at the Ecole des Beaux-Arts.

A. GLUCKSMANN, *Stratégie et Révolution en France 1968.* Christian Bourgois, Paris, 1968. The movement, since Marx and Lenin.

RICHARD GOMBIN, *Le Projet révolutionnaire, Eléments d'une sociologie des événements de mai–juin 1968,* Mouton Paris—The Hague, 1969. Presentation of "groupuscule" literature.

JOHN GRETTON, *Students and Workers, an Analytical Account of Dissent in France, May–June 1968,* MacDonald, London, 1969. Combines felicitously analysis, narrative, and translated documents. Occasional errors. The appendix contains information on Dijon, Grenoble, and Avranches.

M. J. LE GUILLOU, O. CLÉMENT, J. BOSC, *Evangile et révolution, au coeur de notre crise spirituelle,* le Centurion, Paris, 1968. Three theologians: Catholic, Protestant, and Orthodox.

HENRI GUNSBERG, *Le Lycée unidimensionnel,* Collection "En Direct," Mercure de France, Paris, 1970. A scathing and in certain respects salutary criticism of the illusions of present-day pedagogy.

JACQUES JURQUET, *Le Printemps révolutionnaire de 1968. Essai d'analyse marxiste-léniniste,* Editions Gît-le-Coeur, Paris, 1969. Very far from the facts; a Stalinist description. In the appendix are the documents published during the crisis by the PCMLF, the principal leader of which was the author.

A. KRIEGEL, *Les Communistes français,* Collection "Politique," le Seuil, Paris, 1968. Includes a conclusion on the PC and the May crisis.

M. LABI, *La Société en révolution,* Editions syndicalistes, Paris, 1968. By one of the speakers (FO) at Charléty.

HENRI LEFEBVRE, *L'Irruption de Nanterre au sommet, Sociologie et révolution,* Editions Anthropos, Paris, 1968. Published also in *L'Homme et la Société* (see below, Section III, 9). It should be noted that this book is translated under the title *The Explosion, Marxism and the French Upheaval* (on the cover), and *Revolution* on the inside. Monthly Review Press, New York, 1969.

GEORGES LEFRANC, *Le Mouvement syndical, de la libération aux événements de mai–juin 1968,* Bibliothèque Historique, Payot, 1969. Makes it possible to situate historically the attitude of the unions, but the chapter devoted to May (pp. 224–256) contains some material errors.

RENÉ LOURAU, *L'Instituant contre l'institué, Essais d'analyse institutionnelle,* Editions Anthropos, Paris, 1969. Collection of essays by a sociology instructor at Nanterre. By the same author, *L'Illusion pédagogique,* Epi, Paris, 1969.

LUCIEN MAGRI, *Considerazioni sui fatti di maggio,* De Donato, Bari, 1968. By a leader of the group, *"Il Manifesto,"* who was expelled

from the PCI in November 1969. Essential fragments were translated in *Les Temps Modernes,* August–September, October, and
November 1969.

SERGE MALLET, *Le Pouvoir ouvrier, Bureaucratie ou démocratie ouvrière,*
Anthropos, Paris, 1971. A collection of surveys written before,
during, and since May '68.

RAYMOND MARCELLIN, *L'Ordre public et les groupes révolutionnaires,*
Collection "Tribune libre," Plon, Paris, 1969. Plea by the Minister of the Interior in favor of an international police organization. Contains, in the appendix, a certain number of documents
of which one at least is spurious.

GILLES MARTINET, *La Conquête des pouvoirs,* Collection "L'Histoire
Immédiate," le Seuil, Paris, 1968. Severe criticism of the movement's ideology and a strategic analysis: what should have been
done in order to win.

GÉRARD MENDEL, *La Crise des générations, études socio-psychanalytiques,*
Payot, Paris, 1969. Completes *La Révolte contre le père* by the
same author (Payot, Paris, 1968). A much more liberal study of
youthful contestation than the one mentioned below by André
Stéphane. Good presentation of the problem of a "generation
with no inheritance."

PIERRE MENDÈS-FRANCE, *Pour préparer l'avenir, Propositions pour une
action,* Denoël, Paris, 1968.

GUY MICHAUD, *Révolution dans l'Université,* Classiques Hachette, Paris,
1968. Several pages on Nanterre.

EDGAR MORIN, CLAUDE LEFORT, JEAN-MARC COUDRAY, *Mai 1968: la Brèche,
premières réflexions sur les événements,* Collection "Le Monde
sans frontières," Fayard, Paris, 1968. Analysis made at the moment; remains one of the most remarkable published to date.

GILBERT MURY, *La Société de répression,* Collection "Citoyens," Editions Universitaires, Paris, 1969. Essay by a pro-Chinese not
involved, at the time, with the "groupuscules."

JACQUES PERRET, *Inquiète Sorbonne,* Classiques Hachette, Paris, 1968.
Testimony and analysis by a conservative academic, who was
present.

A. PHILIP, *Mai 68 et la foi démocratique,* Collection "Histoire du travail
et de la vie économique," Aubier, Paris, 1968. Socialism, Gaullism,
Protestantism.

ANDRÉ PIETTRE, *La Culture en question: Sens et non-sens d'une révolte.*
Desclée de Brouwer, Paris, 1969. Humanism vs. contestation.

JEAN POPEREN, *Une Stratégie pour la gauche,* Collection "Le Monde
sans frontières," Fayard, Paris, 1969. Rather close to G. Martinet,

but insists more on the role of the traditional working class organizations.

POURQUOI DES EXAMENS?, texts collected and presented by Lucien Brunelle. Editions rationalistes, Paris, 1968. A collection of analyses, certain of which antedate May considerably.

CLAUDE PRÉVOST, *Les Etudiants et le gauchisme,* Collection "Notre Temps," Editions Sociales, Paris, 1969. Serenely orthodox Communist analysis.

FERNAND ROBERT, *Un Mandarin prend la parole,* PUF, Paris. The belated unbosoming of a classicist. Almost too good to be true.

J. ROBERT, *Un Plan pour l'Université,* Collection "Tribune libre," Plon, Paris, 1968.

MICHEL ROCARD, *Le PSU et l'avenir socialiste de la France,* Collection Politique, le Seuil, Paris, 1969.

JACQUELINE DE ROMILLY, *Nous autres professeurs. Ces maîtres que l'on conteste,* Fayard, Paris, 1969. Revives the "quarrel between the ancients and the moderns" (second half of the 17th century); for Euripides' *Hippolytus,* against Racine's *Phèdre.*

PAUL ROZENBERG, *Vivere in Maggio,* preface by Jean Chesneaux, Coll. Sagg. No. 449, Einaudi, Turin, 1969. By a Communist anglicist who has since been dropped from the party. Proposes a new political way of life.

L. SALINI, *Mai des prolétaires,* Collection "Notre Temps," Editions Sociales, Paris, 1968. Against student action in May.

JEAN-PAUL SARTRE, *Les Communistes ont peur de la révolution,* Collection "Controverses," John Didier, Paris, 1969. Interview given to *der Spiegel.*

ALFRED SAUVY, *La Révolte des jeunes,* Collection "Questions d'Actualité," Calmann-Lévy, Paris, 1970. Against the illusions of neo-naturalism in favor of a technocracy "in broad daylight."

ANDRÉ STÉPHANE [Pseudonym], *L'Univers contestationnaire, Etude psychanalytique,* Petite Bibliothèque, Payot, Paris, 1969. The principle of reality used like a police tool; concerning this book, see the commentaries by Michel de Certeau and by the psychoanalyst Anne-Lise Stern in *Le Nouvel Observateur,* June 3, 1969.

J. SURET-CANALE (Ed.), *Lutte de classes ou conflit de générations,* Editions du Pavois, Brussels, 1969. Record of the Semaine de la pensée marxiste, Brussels, October 24–29, 1968.

A. TOURAINE, *Le Mouvement de mai ou le communisme utopique,* Collection "L'Histoire immédiate," le Seuil, Paris, 1968. Attempts to define the conditions of a new class struggle, between the "technocrats," including those who administer the University, and the "professionals," on whose margin are situated the students. François Bourricaud, from the Nanterre Sociological Center, makes a harsh criticism: "Alain Touraine à la recherche d'un sujet historique," *Preuves,* 220 (July–September 1969).

    Actually, the reviewer explains the student revolt by "under-administration" (see his article "Le Grand dérapage," *Preuves,* June–July 1968, in which he follows exactly the line taken by Jacques Soustelle in connection with the Algerian revolt of 1954). For another violent criticism of Touraine, see Raymond Boudon, "Mai 68; crise ou conflit, aliénation ou anomie?" *L'Année sociologique,* 1968 (published in 1970), pp. 223–242.

J. VUILLEMIN, *Rebâtir l'Université,* Collection "Le Monde sans frontières," Fayard, Paris, 1968.

WALDECK-ROCHET, *Les Enseignements de mai–juin 1968,* Collection "Notre Temps," Editions Sociales, Paris, 1968. The author was not present.

ALFRED WILLENER, *L'Image-action de la société ou la politisation culturelle,* le Seuil, Paris, 1970. Psycho-sociological investigation.

MARC ZAMANSKY, *Mort ou résurrection de l'Université,* Collection "Tribune libre," Plon, 1969. By the former fiery dean of the Paris *Faculté des Sciences.*

As readers of these books will soon see, for a number of them the two words "Analysis" and "Reflection" are perhaps over-serious. We have attached greater importance to the intention than to its realization. In any case, all the works mentioned are of interest, if only secondary.

9. Reviews*

It is impossible to list here even the more outstanding articles that appeared in reviews. A number of special issues will be found under earlier headings. We shall merely mention the following.

Annales, Economie-Sociétés-Civilisations, May–June 1969. Contrasting articles by Raymond Boudon and Edgar Morin.

L'Année sociologique, 1968 (appeared in 1970), published, in addition

---

* Special issues of periodicals devoted to the May 1968 events were alphabetically listed by Françoise Rougier for the Diploma of the *Institut National de Documentation* in June 1969. This list includes both the periodicals brought out by the movement and those that spoke of it. Although it cannot claim to be entirely complete, it can be extremely useful. A copy exists in the *Histoire de France* department of the Bibliothèque Nationale. Unless otherwise indicated, all reviews were published in Paris.

to the above-mentioned analysis by R. Boudon, an article by M. Rubel entitled "Sociologie et Utopie," pp. 243–252.

L'Archibras, No. 4, Surrealism on June 18, 1968.

Autogestion, Nos. 5–6 (March–June). Self-management and the "May Revolution," with a round-table discussion.

Communications, 12 (1968). Thanks especially to the articles by R. Barthes, Noëlle Bisseret, J. Dubois, and J. Sumpf, also to G. Lanteri-Laura and M. Tardy, it certainly presents the best analysis of the language of the student movement; also articles containing evidence by J.-P. Aron and E. Morin, and an important study by R. Estivals on the artistic avant-garde and situationism. No. 13 (1969), *Les objets,* also contains much useful analysis. The article by Jean Baudrillard, "Le monde des objets," completes his book, *Le Système des objets,* mentioned above, Section II, 8.

Démocratie nouvelle, June–July 1968, "Pour servir à l'histoire de mai 68." Recalcitrant communism.

2000, No. 9, special issue, "Partage des pouvoirs, Essai sur la participation, autonomie et solidarité, partage des décisions." Especially concerns the problems of decentralization.

Esprit, Nos. 6–7 (June–July 1968), "Mai 68"; Nos. 8–9 (August–September 1968), "La Révolution suspendue"; No. 10 (October 1968), "Le Partage du savoir." Three essential issues, as much because of the documents published in Nos. 8–9 as of the round-table discussion on the workers' strike in No. 9, and in Nos. 6–7, the articles on the repression by Casamayor, J.-M. Domenach, and Paul Ricoeur, and "Rebâtir l'Université," by R. Stith and P. Thibaud. Of particular interest in the May 1969 issue (mentioned above in Section I, 1) is an important study by Paul Thibaud on the crisis at the Paris *Faculté de Droit.*

Etudes, 329 (June–July 1968). Already mentioned above, in Section I, 5, for its documentation on Poland, as well as important articles by D. Julia and by M. de Certeau.

L'Evénement, No. 29 (June 1968), "Première histoire de la révolution de mai."

France-Forum, Nos. 90–91 (1968). From the student barricades to the workers' strikes.

Frères du Monde, Nos. 52 and 53 (1968). Review published by the Franciscan order. A certain amount of information on the movement in Toulouse.

Information et Correspondance ouvrières, "La Grève généralisée en France," Supplement No. 72. Anarchist analyses based on precise facts.

L'Homme et la Société, 8 (April–May–June 1968). In addition to Henri Lefebvre's book, this issue contains documentation on the *Lycée Pasteur* as well as an important round-table discussion.

Les Lettres Françaises, special issue, "Etudiants," May 15, 1968.

The New Left Review, No. 52 (November–December 1968) takes over from *Les Temps Modernes* the greater part of its special issue and translates completely the above-mentioned book by André Glucksmann (Section III, 8).

Noir et Rouge, supplement to No. 41, May 1968, "L'Autogestion, l'état et la révolution."

La Nouvelle Critique, N.S., No. 15 (June 1968) and No. 16 (September 1968). Orthodox Communist articles by R. Leroy, P. Juquin, Cl. Prévost, and M. Simon.

Paysans, Nos. 71 (April–May) and 72 (June–July) 1968. Brief notes on the crisis as seen by the rural population.

La Pensée, Special No. 140–141, August, October 1968. "L'Université en mouvement." An astonishingly composite general picture. Among the evidence of diverse tendencies, a structural analysis of contestation by J. Colombel, who corrects Epistémon somewhat on this point. No. 143 (February 1969) contains a skilful and brilliant polemic by Michel Verret, "Mai étudiant ou les substitutions," to which Louis Althusser and Roger Garaudy, for once in agreement, reply in issue No. 145 (June 1969).

Positif, Revue de Cinéma, No. 97, Summer 1968, "Un Cinéma pour la révolution."

Politique Aujourd'hui, successor since 1969 to *Démocratie Nouvelle*, a Communist review that was scuttled by the French Communist Party. A number of articles on the May movement, particularly in the August–September and October 1969 issues, "Pour une histoire de mai," "Nantes et son 'second pouvoir,'" and in the February 1970 issue "Usinor à Dunkerque, la CFDT à Lyon."

Projet, July–August 1968. Documents on the *lycées* and on the worker movement.

Sciences, special issue, No. 54–55, "L'Université et la Recherche." Documentation on the *Ecole Polytechnique*, the Orsay *Faculté des Sciences*, and the CNRS.

Sociologie du Travail, special issue, No. 3, July–September 1970, *Le Mouvement ouvrier en mai 68*. First important roundup of sociological analyses.

La Table Ronde, No. 251 (December 1968–January 1969), "Analyse d'un vertige." Contains, among other information, an article by R. Boudon that is a résumé of the one in *Les Annales*.

Les Temps Modernes, July 1968. Interviews with workers and considerations by J.-M. Vincent; August–September 1968, articles by Michel Johan on the CGT, by A. Gorz, "Limites et potentialités du mouvement de mai," and by E. Mandel, "Leçons du mouvement de mai." The June–July 1969 issue contains a new collection on "impatient revolutionaries."

Among the newspapers and reviews that appeared during the events and were inspired by them, *Action* and *L'Enragé* brought out by J. J. Pauvert, outlived the movement for a certain time, while J.-J. Lebel's *Le Pavé* had only one issue, in May. *Les Cahiers de mai,* the only May newspaper still in existence, contains a very large number of documents on the student movement as well as on the reactions of cadres and on the working class strike.

"Au joli mai," No. 1, with a foreword by J. Sauvageot, May–June 1968, with directives for action, a pamphlet "for workers and students," contains several interesting documents on the *lycées,* on the activity of action committees, on the art schools, on the occupation of a nursery school, and on an attempt at cultural occupation of a small city square.

List of Abbreviations*

ACGIS   *Association pour la construction et la gestion immobilière de Sannois* (Association for Construction and Management of the Sannois Housing Complex).

AF   *Anciens Francs* (Old francs).

AFGEN   *Association fédérative générale des étudiants de Nanterre* [UNEF] (General Federating Association of Nanterre Students [UNEF]).

AFGES   *Association fédérative générale des étudiants de Strasbourg* [UNEF] (General Federating Association of Strasburg Students [UNEF]).

AG   *Assemblée Générale* (General Assembly).

AGE   *Association générale d'étudiants* (General Student Association).

AGEB   *Association générale des étudiants de Besançon* [UNEF] (General Association of Besançon Students [UNEF]).

AGEC   *Association générale des étudiants de Clermont* [UNEF] (General Association of Clermont Students [UNEF]).

AGEL   *Association générale des étudiants de Lille* [UNEF] (General Association of Lille Students [UNEF]).

AGEL a   *Association générale des étudiants de Lyon* [UNEF] (General Association of Lyons Students [UNEF]).

AGEM   *Association générale des étudiants de Marseille* [UNEF] General Association of Marseilles Students [UNEF]).

AGEN   *Association générale des étudiants de Nantes* [UNEF] (General Association of Nantes Students [UNEF]).

AGES   *Association générale des étudiants en maison de santé* (General Association of Students in Health Institutions).

AGET   *Association générale des étudiants de Tours* (General Association of Tours Students).

AGTAG   *Association générale des travailleurs antillo-guyanais* (General Association of Antillean-Guinean Workers).

* With English equivalents or, occasionally, definitions. *Translator's note.*

633

ALN   *Armée de libération nationale* [*Algérie*] (National Liberation Army [Algeria]).

AP   *Année préparatoire* [*à l'Institut d'études politiques*] (Preparatory Year at the Institute of Political Studies).

AP *a*   *Assistance Publique* (Health and Welfare Administration).

ARCUN   *Association des résidents de la cité universitaire de Nanterre* (Association of Student Boarders in Nanterre).

BCG   [*Vaccin*] *bilié de Calmette et Guérin* ([Vaccination] Bacillus Calmette and Guérin Against Tuberculosis).

BN   *Bureau national* (National Board).

BO   *Bulletin officiel* (Official Bulletin).

BP   *Bureau politique* (Policy-making Committee).

C   *Certificat* (Certificate).

CA   *Comité d'action* (Action Committee).

CAC   *Comité d'action civique* (Committee for Civic Action).

CAET   *Comité d'action de l'enseignement technique* (Technical Training Action Committee).

CAL   *Comités d'action lycéens* (*Lycée* Action Committees).

CAP   *Certificat d'aptitude professionnelle* (Certificate of Professional Competence).

CAPES   *Certificat d'aptitude professionnelle à l'enseignement du second degré* (Certificate of Professional Competence to Teach in Secondary Schools).

CAPET   *Certificat d'aptitude professionnelle à l'enseignement technique* (Certificate of Professional Competence to Teach in Technical Schools).

CAR   *Comité d'action révolutionnaire* (Revolutionary Action Committee).

CB   *Gaz orthochlorobenzalmalononitrile* (Type of gas used by the police as a riot-control agent).

CC   *Comité central* (Committee usually composed of the officers and other policy-makers of an organization).

CCN   *Comité confédéral national* [*de la* CGT] (National Confederating Committee [of the CGT]).

CDR   *Comité de défense de la République* (Committee for Defense of the Republic).

CDJA   *Centre départemental des jeunes agriculteurs* (Departmental Center for Young Farm Workers).

CE   *Conseil étudiant* (Student Council).

CEI   *Collège d'enseignement industriel* (Industrial Training School).

CELU   *Comité étudiant pour les libertés universitaires* (Student Committee for Academic Freedoms).

CES   *Certificat d'études supérieures* (Certificate of Higher Studies).

CES *a*   *Collège d'enseignement secondaire* (Secondary School).

CET   *Collège d'enseignement technique* (Technical Highschool).

CEUD   *Comité étudiant pour une université démocratique [Besançon]* (Student Committee for a Democratic University [Besançon]).

CFDT   *Confédération française démocratique du travail* (Democratic French Confederation of Labor).

CFTC   *Confédération française des travailleurs chrétiens* (French Confederation of Christian Workers).

CGC   *Confédération générale des cadres* (General Confederation of Cadres).

CGT   *Confédération générale du travail* (General Confederation of Labor).

CHU   *Confédération hospitalo-universitaire* (Confederation of University College Hospitals).

CIA   Central Intelligence Agency.

CIR   *Commando d'intervention rapide [Katangais]* (Commando for Instant Action [Katangans]).

CLEO (or CLEOP)   *Comité de liaison étudiants-ouvriers [paysans]* (Student-Worker [Peasant] Liaison Committee).

CLER   *Comité de liaison des étudiants révolutionnaires* (Liaison Committee of Revolutionary Students).

CLIF   *Comité de liaison interfacultés* (Interdepartmental Liaison Committee).

CLU   *Collège littéraire universitaire* (University School of Literature).

CMLF   *Centre marxiste-léniniste de France* (Marxist-Leninist Center in France).

CN   *Chloroacétophénone* (Chloroacetophenetidin [tear gas]).

CNA   *Comité national d'action* (National Action Committee).

CNID   *Commission nationale interdisciplinaire* (National Interdisciplinary Commission).

CNJA   *Centre national des jeunes agriculteurs* (National Center of Young Farmers).

CNPF   *Conseil national du patronat français* (National Council of French Employers).

CNRS   *Centre national de la recherche scientifique* (National Center for Scientific Research).

CPME   *Confédération des petites et moyennes entreprises* (Confederation of Small and Medium Business Enterprises).

CPREA   *Centre pour la réforme de l'enseignement artistique* (Center for Reform of Teaching the Arts).

CRAC   *Comité révolutionnaire d'action culturelle* (Revolutionary Committee for Cultural Action).

CRAP   *Centre de recherches et d'action pédagogiques* (Center for Pedagogical Research and Action).

CRIR   *Centre révolutionnaire d'information et de réflexion* (Revolutionary Center for Information and Analysis).

CRIU   *Centre de regroupement des informations universitaires* (Office for Centralization of University Information).

CRS   *Compagnies républicaines de sécurité* (Armed Security Police).

CS   See CB

CSF   *Compagnie de télégraphie sans-fils* (Wireless Telegraphy Company).

CSU   *Collège scientifique universitaire* (University School of Science).

CVB   *Comités Vietnam de base* (Grass-roots [Maoist] Vietnam Committees).

CVN   *Comité Vietnam national* (National Vietnam Committee).

DST   *Direction de la sureté du territoire* (National Security Headquarters).

DUEJ   *Diplôme universitaire d'études juridiques* (University Law School Diploma).

DUEL   *Diplôme universitaire d'études littéraires* (University School of Letters Diploma).

DUES   *Diplôme universitaire d'études scientifiques* (University School of Science Diploma).

ED   *Enseignement dirigé* (Guided Teaching).

EDF   *Electricité de France* (Government-owned Electric Company).

EN   *Education nationale* (Ministry of National Education).

ENS   *Ecole normale supérieure* (Normal School for Higher Education).

ENSBA   *Ecole nationale supérieure des Beaux-Arts* (National School of Advanced Fine Arts).

ENSCP   *Ecole nationale supérieure de chimie de Paris* (Paris National School of Advanced Chemistry).

ENSEP   *Ecole normale supérieure d'éducation physique* (Normal School for Advanced Physical Education).

EPHE   *Ecole pratique des hautes études* (No exact equivalent. High university-level seminars on many subjects).

ESU   *Etudiants socialistes unifiés* (Students affiliated with the PSU political party).

FA   *Fédération anarchiste* (Anarchist Federation).

FAPL   *Forces armées patriotiques de la libération [Sud Vietnam]* (National Liberation Army of South Vietnam).

FDSEA *Fédération départemèntale des syndicats d'exploitants agricoles* (Departmental Federation of Farm Unions).

FEANF *Fédération des étudiants d'Afrique noire en France* (Federation of Students in France from Black Africa).

FEN   *Fédération de l'éducation nationale* (National Education Federation).

FER   *Federation des étudiants révolutionnaires* (Federation of Revolutionary Students).

FGDS   *Fédération de la gauche démocratique et socialiste* (Federation of the Democratic, Socialist Left).

FGEL   *Fédération des groupes d'études de lettres [UNEF, Sorbonne]* (Federation of Literary Study Groups [UNEF, Sorbonne]).

FGERI *Fédération des groupes d'étude et de recherche institutionnelles* (Federation of Groups for Institutional Study and Research).

FLN   *Front de libération nationale [Algérie]* (Algerian National Liberation Front).

FNEF   *Fédération nationale des étudiants de France* (National Federation of Students in France).

FNL   *Front national de libération [Sud Vietnam]* (South Vietnamese National Liberation Front).

FNSEA *Fédération nationale des syndicats d'exploitants agricoles* (National Federation of Farm Unions).

FO   *[Confédération générale du travail] Force-Ouvrière* (Independent Unions of the CGT).

FSM   *Fédération syndicale mondiale* (World Federation of Labor Unions).

FUAM   *Front universitaire anti-marxiste* (Anti-Marxist University Front).

GDF   *Gaz de France* (Government-owned Gas Company).

GEH   *Groupe des étudiants d'histoire* (Group of History Students).

GP   *Gauche Prolétarienne* (Proletarian Left).

IBM   International Business Machines.

IEP   *Institut d'études politiques* [*Sciences-Po*] (Institute of Political Studies).

IFOP   *Institut français d'opinion publique* (French Institute of Public Opinion Polls).

INOP   *Institut national d'orientation professionnelle* (National Institute for Professional Orientation).

INSA   *Institut national de sciences appliquées* (National Institute for Applied Science).

INSEE   *Institut national de statistique et d'études économiques* (National Institute of Statistics and Economic Analysis).

INSERM   *Institut national de santé et de recherche médicale* (National Institute for Health and Medical Research).

IPES   *Institut préparatoire à l'enseignement secondaire* (Training Institute for Secondary Teaching).

IPN   *Institut pédagogique national* (National Pedagogical Institute).

IPRES   *Institut préparatoire à la recherche et à l'enseignement supérieur* (Training Institute for Research and University Teaching).

IS   *Internationale situationniste* (Situationist International).

IUT   *Institut universitaire de technologie* (University Technological Institute).

JC   *Jeunesses communistes* (Young Communists).

JCR   *Jeunesses communistes révolutionnaires* (Young Revolutionary Communists).

JSU   *Jeunesses socialistes unifiées* (Young people affiliated with the PSU political party).

LSD   The hallucinatory drug.

M   *Maîtrise* (Masters Degree).

MAU   *Mouvement d'action universitaire* (then, after the opening trimester, 1968, *Mouvement action et unité*) (Movement for University Action: Movement for United Action).

MJC   *Mouvement de la jeunesse communiste* [UEC, JC, UJFF] (Communist Youth Movement).

MR   *Mouvement révolutionnaire* (Revolutionary Movement).

MSLP   *Mouvement de soutien aux luttes du peuple* (Movement for Support of the People's Struggle).

NMPP   *Nouvelles messageries parisiennes de presse* (New Paris Press Distribution Service).

NPD   *National demokratische Partei Deutschlands* (Neo-Nazi German Party).

OAS *Organisation armée secrète* (Secret Army Organization, responsible for the attempted Algerian putsch, 1958).

OCI *Organisation communiste internationaliste* [*Trotskyste*] (Internationalist Communist Trotskyist Organization; not belonging to the IVth International).

ORA *Organisation révolutionnaire anarchiste* (Revolutionary Anarchist Organization).

ORTF *Office de radio et de télévision françaises* (Office of French Radio and Television, government-owned).

OS *Ouvrier spécialisé* (Skilled worker).

P,1,2,3 *Ouvrier professionnel, les chiffres 1,2,3, désignant la qualification* (Specialized worker, the figures 1,2,3, designate degree of competence).

PC or

PCF *Parti communiste français* (French Communist Party).

PCI *Partito communista italiano* (Italian Communist Party).

PCI *a* *Parti communiste internationaliste* [*Trotskyste*] (Internationalist Communist Party [Trotskyist]).

PCMLF *Parti communiste marxiste-léniniste de France* (Marxist-Leninist French Communist Party).

PDG *Président directeur-général* (Corporation Board President).

P et T *Postes et Télécommunications* (Post and Telecommunications Service).

PO *Pouvoir ouvrier* (Worker power).

PSIUP *Partito socialista italiano d'unità proletaria* (Italian Socialist Party of Proletarian Unity).

PSU *Parti socialiste unifié* (Unified Socialist Party).

RATP *Régie autonome des transports parisiens* (Paris Transport Administration).

RDA *République démocratique allemande* (Democratic German Republic).

RDV *République démocratique du Vietnam* (Democratic Republic of Vietnam).

RFA *République fédérale allemande* (Federal German Republic).

RNUR *Régie nationale des usines Renault* (Government Administration of the Renault Factories).

RTL *Radio télévision Luxembourg* (Luxemburg Radio and Television Station).

SAVIEM *Société automobile de véhicules industriels et d'équipement mécanique* (Industrial Motor and Mechanical Equipment Company).

SDS   *Sozialistischer Deutscher Studentenbund* (Federation of German Socialist Students).

SDS*a*   Students for a Democratic Society (U.S.A.).

SEMA   *Société d'études mathématiques appliquées* (Society for the Study of Applied Mathematics).

SFIO   *Section française de l'internationale ouvrière* (French Section of the Workers' International: the original French Socialist Party).

SGEN   *Syndicat général de l'éducation nationale* [CFDT] (General National Education Union [CFDT]).

SM   *Sa Majesté* (His [Her] Majesty).

SMIG   *Salaire minimum interprofessionnel garanti* (Interprofessional Guaranteed Minimum Wage).

SNALC   *Syndicat national autonome des lycées et collèges* (Independent National Union of *Lycées* and other Secondary Schools).

SNCC   Students' Nonviolent Coordinating Committee.

SNCS   *Syndicat national des chercheurs scientifiques* (National Union of Scientific Research Workers).

SNES   *Syndicat national des enseignements du second degré* [FEN] (National Union of Second Degree Teaching Personnel [FEN]).

SNESup   *Syndicat national de l'enseignement supérieur* [FEN] (National Union of University Teaching Personnel [FEN]).

SNI   *Syndicat national des instituteurs* [FEN] (National Union of Primary School Teachers [FEN]).

SS   *Schutzstaffeln* (World War II German military detachment).

SS *a*   *Sécurité Sociale* (Social Security, or French National Welfare Administration).

TP   *Travaux pratiques* (Work in small study groups).

UAS   *Université autonome de Strasbourg* (Autonomous University of Strasburg).

UD   *Union départementale* [*d'une confédération syndicale*] (Departmental Union [of a confederation of unions]).

UEC, or UECF   *Union des étudiants communistes de France* (Union of Communist Students in France).

UJCF   *Union de la jeunesse communiste de France* [*voir* MJC] (Union of Communist Young People in France [see MJC]).

UGE   *Union des grandes écoles* (Union of *Grandes Ecoles*).

UGEA   *Union générale des étudiants d'Aix-en-Provence* [UNEF] (General Student Union of Aix-en-Provence [UNEF]).

UEG   *Union des étudiants guyanais* (Union of Guinean Students).

UJC(m-l)   *Union des jeunesses communistes* [*marxiste-léniniste*] (Union of Communist Young People [Marxist-Leninist]).

UJFF   *Union des jeunes filles de France* (*section jeunes filles du* MJC (Union of Young French Girls [young girls' section of the MJC]).

UL   *Union locale* [*d'une confédération syndicale*] (Local Union [of a Union Confederation]).

UNEF   *Union nationale des étudiants de France* (National Union of French Students).

URP   *Union de la région parisienne* [*de la* CFDT] (Union of the Paris Area [of the CFDT]).

VO   Voix Ouvrière (Voice of the Worker).

Index

Propaganda: 94, 154, 171, 270, 289,
    361, 377
Protective measures, students': 165,
    326–331
Proudhon, Pierre: 276
Prouvost's: 98
Provocators: 248–249, 290, 329, 330
PSF: 26
PSIUP: 17, 26, 78
PSU: 9, 26, 36, 149, 155, 167, 213,
    231, 233, 241, 273, 355, 362, 418,
    436, 593
Psychologists: 96; criticized, 173, 275
Public opinion: 1, 25, 41, 42
Pure speech: 2

Racism: 453; Algeria, 4
Radio: 42, 90, 154, 157, 190, 219,
    308, 354, 388, 395–396. *See also*
    ORTF; RTL
Raptis, Michel ("Pablo"): 322
RATP: 208, 382
Raymond, Henri: 107
Reaction: 22–25, 157, 328, 375–377,
    440, 465
Realism: 6
Redon, workers demonstration: 3, 80,
    85, 93, 160, 161, 166, 194, 206,
    207, 261, 272, 274, 367
"Red pioneers" (Poland): 81
"Reflections on Violence": 327–328
Reforms: proposed, 8, 29, 139–140,
    170; educational, 11–12, 28, 125,
    170, 466–467, 521–530; university,
    2, 11–12, 15, 35, 334–335, 454–456,
    487–493, 496–509, 521–530. *See
    also* Fouchet Plan; Orientation law
Régie Renault. See Renault factory
Regionalism: 435–437
"Regulative centers": 2
Rémond, René: 137
Renault factory, demonstrations: 40–
    41, 85–92, 202, 206, 209–210, 231,
    249, 263, 339, 364, 383, 384
Rennes: 80, 91, 168, 379–380
Repression: 25–26, 37, 163, 167, 210,
    213, 214, 217, 219, 222–223, 227,
    259, 272, 305, 311, 374–375, 380,
    384, 392, 476, 523, 541, 586, 596;
    police, 149, 155, 162, 164, 178,
    182–185, 194–195, 199, 222, 249,
    325–326, 359, 366, 385–391, 470,
    476, 585
"Republican Front": 4
Researchers: 33, 44
Reservists: 7; "Africans," 7; move-
    ment, 4; Pacification medals, 7
Revisionism: 176, 265, 267

Revisionists: 167
Révoltes: 179, 253–254
Revolution: 31, 43, 47, 378, 382,
    408, 592; China, 269–270; Latin
    America, 292; Poland, 83–84. *See
    also* May revolution
Revolutionary movement. *See* Student
    movement
Rhodiaceta factory: 85, 160–161, 166,
    194, 198, 200, 209, 274
Riesel, René: 162
Riesman, David: 117
Rightists: 278–280
Rimbaud, Arthur: 485, 545
Rimini student conference: 31
Rio de Janeiro: 19
Rivarol: 280
Roche, Jean: 23, 38, 153, 157, 181,
    187, 586
Rogers, Carl: 96
Rome: 19, 21, 23, 24, 32, 441
Rossi, Paolo: 24
Rossman, Michael: 18, 27
Rostagno, Mauro: 20
Rousseau, Jean-Jacques: 595
Rousseauism: 46
Rozenberg, Paul: 241
RTL: 395, 397
Rude Pravo: 21
Rumania: 25
Rumor spreading: 45
"Russell Tribunal": 2, 8, 69
Russia: 30, 55, 245, 316, 355–356,
    376; "groupuscles," 245; intellec-
    tuals in, 22

St. Nazaire: 92, 160
Salan, Raoul: 397, 547
Salini, L.: 556
Salvatore: 77–78
Sartre, Jean-Paul: 593
Sauvageot, Jacques: 9, 41, 206, 325
SAVIEM: 85–92
Savio, Mario: 2, 19, 34
Schnapp, Alain: 49
Scholastic explosion: 33, 291
Schwartz, Laurent: 133, 187, 204
Scienlit: 365
SDS: 17, 18, 29, 74–79, 130, 174–175,
    326, 355, 367
SDSA: 17, 20, 441
Secondary education: 13–14
Second degree. *See Agrégation;* CAPES
Segni, Antonio: 51
Séguy, Georges: 40–41, 176, 230, 232–
    233, 234, 284, 376, 378, 393, 425
Selection: 94–95, 106, 208, 255, 296,